ECONOMICS
for GCE A Level

THE COMPLETE GUIDE
Second Edition

ECONOMICS
for GCE A Level

THE COMPLETE GUIDE
Second Edition

Benjamin Thong

World Scientific

NEW JERSEY • LONDON • SINGAPORE • BEIJING • SHANGHAI • HONG KONG • TAIPEI • CHENNAI • TOKYO

Published by

World Scientific Publishing Co. Pte. Ltd.

5 Toh Tuck Link, Singapore 596224

USA office: 27 Warren Street, Suite 401-402, Hackensack, NJ 07601

UK office: 57 Shelton Street, Covent Garden, London WC2H 9HE

National Library Board, Singapore Cataloguing in Publication Data
Name(s): Thong, Benjamin.
Title: Economics for GCE A level : the complete guide / Benjamin Thong.
Description: Second edition. | Singapore : World Scientific Publishing Co. Pte. Ltd., [2023]
Identifier(s): ISBN 978-981-12-7540-1 (hardcover) | 978-981-12-7590-6 (paperback) |
978-981-12-7541-8 (ebook for institutions) | 978-981-12-7542-5 (ebook for individuals)
Subject(s): LCSH: Economics--Examinations--Study guides. | Economics--Examinations, questions, etc.
Classification: DDC 330.076--dc23

British Library Cataloguing-in-Publication Data
A catalogue record for this book is available from the British Library.

For any available supplementary material, please visit
https://www.worldscientific.com/worldscibooks/10.1142/13384#t=suppl

Desk Editor: Nicole Ong

Typeset by Diacritech Technologies Pvt. Ltd.
Chennai - 600106, India

Printed in Singapore

ABOUT THE AUTHOR

Benjamin Thong

Bachelor of Arts (BA) in Economics, National University of Singapore, Singapore;
Postgraduate Diploma in Education (PGDE), National Institute of Education, Singapore;
Master of Education (MEd), National Institute of Education, Singapore.
Email: ghthong@gmail.com

For over 10 years, Benjamin Thong has been teaching and helping students better understand the study of Economics. He is a former Economics teacher and lecturer at St. Andrew's Junior College, Singapore. His interactions with the students have allowed him to understand their challenges and needs which inspired him to develop effective learning materials, specifically for pre-university Economics education. He also served as the Assistant Year Head for Student Development in the school.

Before entering the teaching service, Benjamin completed his Bachelor of Arts (BA) majored in Economics and minored in Southeast Asian Studies, at the National University of Singapore. After graduation, he received the MOE Teaching Award from the Ministry of Education, Singapore, to pursue the Postgraduate Diploma in Education (PGDE), specialised in Economics in Junior College, at the National Institute of Education, Nanyang Technological University, Singapore.

In 2020, he was conferred the Master of Education (MEd) in Developmental Psychology by the National Institute of Education, Nanyang Technological University, Singapore. He focused on the cognitive, social, and emotional development of children and adolescence.

CONTENTS

INTRODUCTION

Economics at the A Level is divided into two broad areas of study: microeconomics and macroeconomics. They differ in terms of the units being analysed.

In Microeconomics, the units of analysis are the individuals and firms, which make up the players in the markets for various goods and services. Examples of what is studied includes the market price and quantity of a good and the efficiency of markets in terms of the allocation of resources.

For Macroeconomics, the unit of analysis is the study of the economy as a whole. An example of what is studied would include the performance of the Singapore economy in terms of growth, inflation, unemployment, and the balance of payments.

Definition(s):

Microeconomics is the study of economic behaviour of individuals and firms.

Macroeconomics is the study of the economy as a whole.

Positive Economics and Normative Economics

All economic issues, regardless of whether they are microeconomics or macroeconomic issues, have two aspects to be analysed—the positive aspect and the normative aspect.

The positive aspect is concerned with facts and cause-and-effect relationships. This includes the development and testing of theories. This is the aspect of Economics that we term "value-free" economics. The idea of "value-free" economics will be better understood in contrast to "values-based" normative economics which is described in the following paragraph. Positive economic statements are distinguished by whether they can be tested to be true or false. For example, "an increase in the goods and services tax (GST) from 5% to 7% would reduce consumption expenditure by 3%" is a positive economic statement. One could collect data and prove whether the statement is true. In other words, positive economics is objective.

In contrast, the normative aspect of economics involves making value judgements about what "should be". This could be in relation to what economic outcomes are desirable for society or what policy measure(s) ought to be adopted. Normative economic statements cannot be judged to be objectively true or false. Instead, whether one agrees with a normative economic statement is subject to one's value system. For example, "the government should prioritise the welfare of the low-income households above the middle-income households" is a normative economic statement. Whether one agrees with the statement depends on one's view of what economic fairness is.

Positive and normative economics are complementary. For example, in deciding whether to raise taxes on the middle-income households, to provide more subsidies to the low-income households, the government needs to analyse the effects of raising the tax rates on the welfare of the middle-income households and the effects of subsidies on the welfare of the low-income households. Both of these involve positive economic analysis. At the same time, the government must also answer the normative economic question of the extent to which the welfare of the low-income households should be prioritised over that of middle-income households. The two types of economics complement each other because normative economics guides the government in determining the ideal extent of transferring welfare from one group to another, and positive economics informs them of how effective their policy would be in doing so. Similarly, for the General Certificate of Education (GCE) A Level, candidates are expected to apply positive economic analysis to complement normative economic judgements.

Definition(s):

Positive economics is the branch of economics that studies facts and cause-and-effect relationships. It includes the development and testing of economic theories.

Normative economics is the branch of economics that expresses value judgements about economic fairness or what the outcome of the economy and policy measure(s) should be.

CHAPTER 1

THE CENTRAL ECONOMIC PROBLEM

1.1 Scarcity, Choice, and Opportunity Cost

1.1.1 Scarcity - the central economic problem

The central problem of economics is scarcity. Scarcity is the situation of humans having unlimited wants but limited resources to satisfy these wants. Scarcity is faced at both the individual and societal level. At the individual level, every person has unlimited wants and limited resources to satisfy these wants. Human wants consist of either goods or services. Goods are tangible and visible, whereas services are intangible and invisible.

Because society is made up of individuals, scarcity at the societal level is simply the sum of individuals' unlimited wants but society's limited resources to satisfy these wants.

Definition(s):

Scarcity is the situation of humans having unlimited wants but limited resources to satisfy these wants.

The resources that can be used to satisfy wants are also termed factors of production. As the name suggests, factors of production are used to produce goods and services. The four factors of production are land, labour, capital, and entrepreneurship/enterprise.

- **Land** refers to all natural resources. Examples include crude oil under the ground, the trees in forests, fishes in the sea, and land.
- **Labour** refers to all human effort, both mental and physical. Examples include the effort of those who design oil rigs as well as those who work on oil rigs, the effort that a programmer puts in to code an application, and the effort a waiter puts in to take and deliver orders.
- **Capital** refers to all man-made resources. Examples include crude oil that has been extracted from the ground, petrol, and machines such as computers and engines.
- **Entrepreneurship** refers to the specialised type of human resource that makes the decision to and assumes the risk of combining the other three factors of production to produce goods and services. This typically refers to business owners who hire people and obtain the other necessary factors of production to produce the goods and services for sale.

The four factors of production are illustrated in the following picture to show how they come together to produce extracted crude oil (Figure 1.1). For any society, at any point in time, these resources are clearly finite/limited.

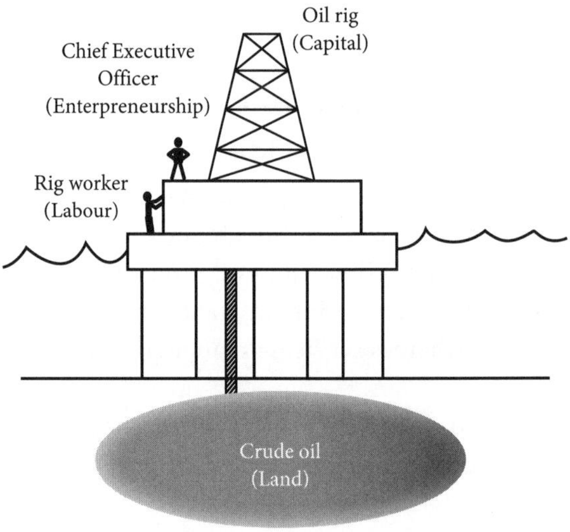

Figure 1.1: Four factors of production in producing oil.

1.1.2 Choice

Because limited resources can only produce limited goods and services, the unlimited human wants cannot all be fulfilled or satisfied. Therefore, it becomes necessary to make choices based on which wants should be met and which should be foregone. Since scarcity is experienced at both the individual and societal level, choices have to be made at both levels too.

In economics, individuals can be classified according to which type of economic agent they are—consumers, producers, or the government. Therefore, choices at the individual level would refer to consumers making choices about what goods and services to purchase; producers making choices about what goods and services to produce; and government making choices about which markets to intervene in and how to do so.

Similarly, at the societal level, choices have to be made about what combination of goods and services a society is to produce, how this combination of goods and services is to be produced, and whom these goods and services are to be produced for. These three choices can be summarised in the following three questions: "What to produce?", "How to produce?", and "For whom to produce?".

For example, in terms of what to produce, Singapore needs to decide whether to produce 10 million units of financial services and 2 million units of construction; or to produce 3 million units of financial services and 5 million units of construction; or some other combination of the two. Also, whichever combination is chosen, Singapore would need to answer the question of how the chosen combination of financial services and construction are to be produced. Financial services could be produced with a greater proportion of capital compared to labour, and construction could be produced with a greater proportion of labour compared to capital. Finally, Singapore would also need to decide whom to allocate the financial services and construction to. Should every individual be allocated the same units of financial services and construction? Or, should the units of goods and services be allocated according to who values them the most?

1.1.3 Opportunity cost

For every choice made, an opportunity cost is incurred. The opportunity cost is the value of the next best alternative foregone when a choice is made. This again can be seen at the individual and societal level. At the individual level, when consumers choose to consume one good rather than another, the opportunity cost of the choice is the enjoyment of the good that they chose to forego. Similarly, for producers, choosing to produce one good rather than another incurs opportunity cost in the form of the profit they could have received from producing the other good. For governments choosing to intervene in one market rather than another, the opportunity cost is the benefits society would have reaped from the intervention in the other market. At the societal level, when resources are used to produce one good, they cannot be used to produce other goods and the opportunity cost of producing the good is the quantity of the other goods that had to be foregone.

Definition(s):

Opportunity cost is the value of the next best alternative foregone when a choice is made.

1.2 Scarcity, Choice, Opportunity Cost, and the Production Possibility Curve (PPC)

1.2.1 The production possibility curve (PPC)

The production possibility curve (PPC) shows the maximum possible combinations of two goods that an economy can produce, with all its resources fully and efficiently employed, within a specified period of time, with technology being constant. Figure 1.2 shows a typical PPC for a society[1]. Capital goods (on the vertical axis) refers to goods that are used to produce other goods (e.g., machines)[2] and consumer goods (on the horizontal axis) refers to goods and services meant for final consumption (e.g., candy and clothes). Combinations on the PPC (e.g., point B) or within the PPC (e.g., point A) are attainable whereas combinations outside the PPC (e.g., point C) are not attainable. When the society is operating on the PPC (e.g., point B), all resources are fully and efficiently utilised. This also implies that every output (every consumer good and every capital good) is being produced at the lowest average cost. We say that such an economy is productively efficient.

Definition(s):

Productive efficiency is the production of every output at the lowest average cost.

1 Refer to Annex 1.1 for more details about the possible shapes of the PPC.

2 Recall the four factors of production. Capital as a factor of production refers to capital goods.

1.2.2 Illustrating scarcity, choice, and opportunity cost on a given PPC

The concepts of scarcity, choice, and opportunity cost at the societal level can be illustrated with a PPC.

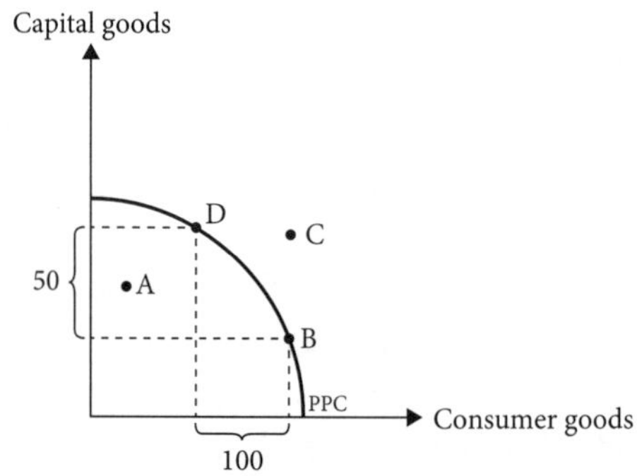

Figure 1.2: Illustrating scarcity, choice, and opportunity cost on the PPC.

We first illustrate scarcity. The situation of having unlimited wants but limited resources to satisfy those wants can be seen from the existence of points that lie outside the PPC (e.g., point C). This illustrates that some of the unlimited wants, such as the specific combination of goods that point C represents, cannot be met by society's limited resources even when these resources are fully and efficiently utilised.

Choice can also be illustrated on the PPC through the different combinations of goods that society can choose to produce. For example, using the PPC in Figure 1.2, society can choose between producing a combination with more consumer goods and less capital goods (point B) or producing a combination with more capital goods and less consumer goods (point D). That illustrates choices regarding what goods to produce. Society would also need to make choices regarding what combination of resources or factors of production will be used to produce these goods (choosing how to produce the goods) and how the combination of goods would be allocated to the individuals in the society (choosing who the goods would be produced for). However, the latter two choices of how to produce the goods and for whom to produce the goods cannot be illustrated on the PPC.

Finally, the PPC can also be used to illustrate the concept of opportunity cost. Recall that opportunity cost is the value of the next best alternative forgone when a choice is made. Referring to Figure 1.2, in choosing combination D over combination B, society is choosing to produce 50 units more of capital goods and 100 units less of consumer goods. The opportunity cost of producing 50 more units of capital goods is the 100 units of consumer goods that could have been produced instead. The opportunity cost of choosing combination D over combination B is hence, illustrated.

1.2.3 Shifts in the PPC affecting scarcity

Thus far, we have only studied how scarcity, choice, and opportunity cost can be illustrated on a given PPC. However, the PPC can actually shift over time. Since the PPC shows the maximum possible combinations of two goods that an economy can produce, with all its resources fully and efficiently employed within a specified period of time, and with technology being constant, it is possible for the PPC to shift either inwards or outwards[3] when the quantity or quality of resources changes, or when technology changes. An increase in the quantity and/or an improvement in the quality of resources would cause the PPC to shift outwards from PPC_0 to PPC_1 in Figure 1.3. For example, through land reclamation, Singapore's total land area has increased over the years which will contribute to the outward shift of Singapore's PPC, because Singapore now has more land (which is a factor of production).

An improvement in technology would have a similar effect. An outward shift of the PPC is also known as either potential growth or an increase in the economy's productive capacity.

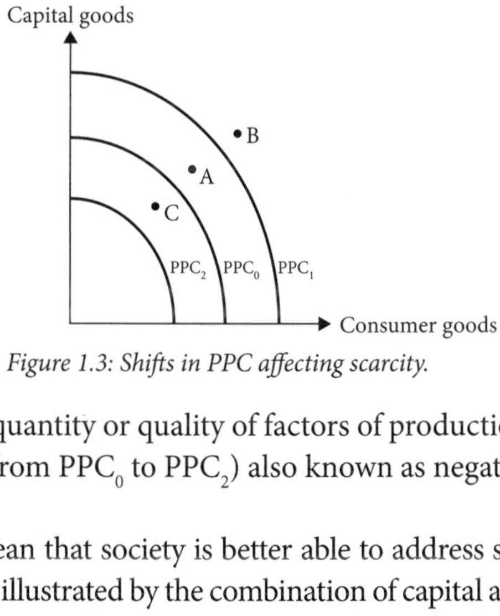

Figure 1.3: Shifts in PPC affecting scarcity.

Conversely, reductions in quantity or quality of factors of production (resources) would cause the PPC to shift inwards (from PPC_0 to PPC_2) also known as negative potential growth.

An outward shift would mean that society is better able to address scarcity because more wants can now be satisfied. This is illustrated by the combination of capital and consumer goods at point A, which was previously unattainable under PPC_0 and is now attainable under PPC_1. However, the central economic problem of scarcity will still exist because human wants are unlimited which is illustrated by any point or the area outside PPC_1 (e.g., point B). It shows that there are combinations of capital and consumer goods (wants) that cannot be met by the limited resources.

An inward shift of the PPC (from PPC_0 to PPC_2) would mean that society is less able to address scarcity as even fewer wants can be met. This is illustrated by the combination of capital and consumer goods at point C, which was previously attainable under PPC_0 but is now unattainable under PPC_2. Inward shifts of a country's PPC are usually caused by disasters that result in significant loss of factors of production, such as earthquakes and volcanic eruptions that destroy factories (capital) and lives (labour).

3 We have only illustrated an even outward shift of PPC here. However, it is possible for the shifts of the PPC to be skewed. Those are explained and illustrated in Annex 1.2.

1.2.4 Choices on the current PPC affecting future PPC: The opportunity cost of consumption over time

Capital goods are one of the four factors of production (resources) for an economy. In theory, when capital goods are produced, there will be an outward shift of the PPC in the next period.

However, in the real world, existing capital goods such as machines will experience wear and tear and break down. The wearing down of existing capital goods is called capital depreciation. Capital depreciation will cause the PPC to shift inwards in the next period because there will be fewer capital goods in the next period.

So, if the current production of capital goods is more than capital depreciation, the PPC will shift outwards in the next period. Conversely, if the current production of capital goods is less than capital depreciation, the PPC will shift inwards in the next period.

For example, if two machines (capital goods) broke down and three machines (capital goods) were produced in 2017, the PPC will shift outwards in 2018. The breakdown of the two machines is the capital depreciation and the production of the three machines is the current production of capital goods.

Definition(s):
Capital depreciation is the wearing down of capital goods.

So, if capital production exceeds capital depreciation, the PPC will shift out in the next time period. Conversely, if capital production is less than capital depreciation, the PPC will shift inwards in the next time period.

An economy that devotes less of its current resources to producing capital goods as compared to consumer goods would have lesser resources in the next time period and hence, a smaller outward shift[4] of the PPC (point A now and PPC_A in the future in Figure 1.4). An economy that produces more capital goods than consumer goods now would experience a larger outward shift of its PPC in the next time period (point B now and PPC_B in the future in Figure 1.4).

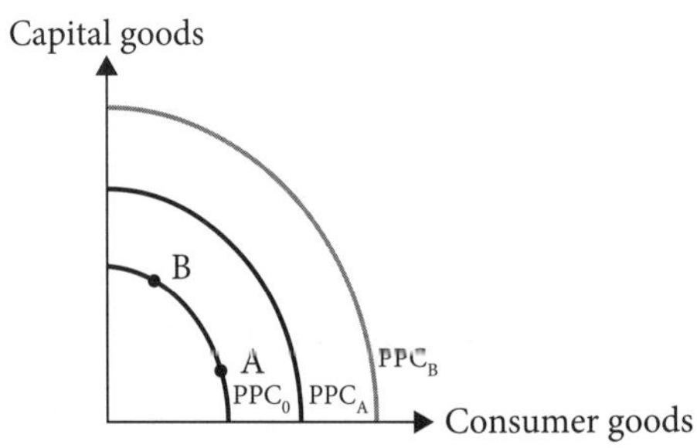

Figure 1.4: Current choices affecting shifts of PPC.

As such, the opportunity cost of producing more consumer goods (choosing point A rather than point B) would not only be the units of capital goods given up in this period, but also the reduced outward shift of the PPC in the next period.

4 Assuming the production of capital goods is still more than capital depreciation.

For all societies, there will always be a trade-off between present consumption and production of capital goods for future consumption.

1.3 Rational Decision-Making Process by Economic Agents

In the earlier section, the central economic problem and how to illustrate it on the PPC was presented. The study of economics is basically a study in how to best address the central economic problem, and this will be revisited in the subsequent chapters. For this section, the focus is tuned away momentarily to study how economists believe people behave (i.e., how people make decisions). We assume that all economic agents are rational in their decision-making process. What rationality means is explained in the sections that follow.

1.3.1 Understanding the objectives of economic agents

As mentioned, in economics, individuals can be classified according to three types of economic agents—consumers, producers, and the government. The objective of each of the three economic agents is as follows.

- Consumers aim to maximise utility. Utility refers to the satisfaction that consumers enjoy from consuming goods and services.
- Producers aim to maximise profits. Profit refers to the difference between total revenue and total costs.
- Governments aim to maximise social welfare. Social welfare can be thought of as the amount of social satisfaction. The concept social welfare will be revisited in more detail in Chapter 4: Market Failure.

1.3.2 Recognising constraints

In trying to achieve their objectives, economic agents recognise their constraints. Constraints are imposed by the maximum amount of resources that economic agents are willing and able to utilise to achieve their objectives.

- A common constraint consumers face is their budgets or their incomes. The combinations of goods and services (e.g., three bowls of noodles and two cans of drinks; or one bowl of noodles and seven cans of drinks) they can consume are constrained by the amount of money they are willing and able to spend.
- A common constraint producers face is the resources they can utilise in a given period of time. In theory, producers are not constrained in terms of the quantity they can produce, as what they produce can be sold to cover the cost of producing it. Therefore, producers do not face any constraints when deciding what quantity of a good to produce. In reality, however, even if a firm knows that the amount to produce, that would maximise profits, is 100,000 units in a particular year, it may not be able to produce that quantity as it may not have the resources to produce that amount in that year. Additionally, producers may also face constraints when deciding whether they can undertake other activities such as advertising or conducting research and development.

- A common constraint the governments face is the government budget. The amount that the government is able to spend a year is dependent on how much tax revenue is collected that year, the existing amount of reserves, and how much the government is able to borrow.

1.3.3 Gathering information and considering perspectives

Economic agents may also gather information and consider perspectives when making their decisions. The information gathered is usually related to the benefits and costs of the alternatives being considered. Perspective taking is relevant to economic agents when their objectives being achieved depends on the reaction of other economic agents.

- When making consumption decisions, consumers may gather information about the usefulness of the products and their prices. As consumers' utility from consumption typically does not depend on the behaviour of other economic agents, the extent to which they consider different perspectives is limited.
- When making production decisions, producers may gather information about the revenue that can be earned from selling the product and the cost of producing it. In gathering the information about the revenue that can be earned, producers may also consider the perspective of the prospective consumers. Producers may also need to consider the perspectives of other producers as how they react (e.g., start a price war) would have an effect on the expected profits.
- When making policy decisions, governments may gather information about how effective the policy would be and how much it would cost. In gathering information about how effective a policy may be, governments may need to consider the perspectives of consumers and producers as policies are often meant to influence consumers and/or producers to behave differently.

1.3.4 The marginalist principle

Economic agents weigh costs and benefits in making a decision. The costs and benefits weighed are the marginal costs and benefits. Marginal costs and benefits are the additional costs and benefits of your next decision. For example, if you have already bought a movie ticket for $12 but have yet to go for it, the next decision is whether to turn up and watch it. The marginal benefit would be the enjoyment from turning up and watching the movie, and the marginal costs would be the value of the time spent in the theatre and the cost of travelling to the theatre. The $12 that you already paid for the movie is not part of the marginal costs[5]. If you have not bought the movie ticket, however, the next decision would be whether to buy the ticket. In that case, the ticket price of $12 would be part of the marginal costs.

5 We say that this $12 is sunk cost because it cannot be recovered (i.e., whether you turn up for the movie or not, the $12 has already been spent).

Economic agents weigh the marginal costs of their next decision against the marginal benefits, to determine if they should go with the decision. If the marginal costs exceed the marginal benefits, they would not go forward with the decision. If the marginal costs are lower than the marginal benefits, they would. If the two are equal, they would be indifferent.

- For consumers, in making consumption decisions, the marginal utility (satisfaction of consuming the good minus the non-monetary costs such as the inconvenience of purchasing the good) they derive from consuming a particular good is the marginal benefit of consumption. The price represents the marginal costs. If the marginal utility exceeds the price, then marginal benefit exceeds marginal cost and the consumer should consume more of the good, because the additional consumption would add to his total utility. If the price exceeds the marginal utility, then marginal cost exceeds marginal benefit and the consumer should consume less of the good, because the additional consumption would subtract from his total utility. To maximise utility, consumers would consume units of the good up to the point where marginal utility equals the price.

  For example, after a marathon, a runner is thirsty and the benefits or satisfaction of consuming the first bottle of water would likely be the highest (i.e., the marginal utility of the first bottle of water is high). If a bottle of water is priced at a dollar, the runner will buy and consume it if the satisfaction from drinking the first bottle is more than a dollar. After the first bottle, the runner is now less thirsty. So, the marginal utility from the second bottle will be less than the first. However, the runner will still buy and drink this second bottle if the marginal utility is more than a dollar. As the runner consumes more and more bottles of water, the runner will become less thirsty and the marginal utility of a bottle of water will decrease after every bottle. Once the benefits from consuming the next bottle of water becomes less than a dollar, the runner will not buy and consume anymore. For the last bottle of water that the runner consumes, the marginal utility should be just equal to the price. Note that the runner made a decision of how many bottles of water to consume based on the marginal utility and price of the next unit that he is deciding to consume.
- For producers, in making production decisions, the marginal revenue (the addition to their total revenue) they derive from producing a particular good is the marginal benefit of production. The marginal cost of production (the addition to their total production cost) represents the marginal costs. If the marginal revenue exceeds the marginal cost of production, then marginal benefit exceeds marginal cost and the producer should produce more of the good, because the additional production would add to his total profit. If the marginal cost of production exceeds the marginal revenue, then the marginal cost exceeds marginal benefit and the producer should produce less of the good, because the additional production would subtract from his total profit. To maximise profits, producers would produce up to the point where marginal revenue equals marginal costs of production.

  For example, for the seller of bottled water at the marathon, the marginal benefits (the marginal revenue) of selling one bottle of water would be a dollar (the price of a bottle of water). The marginal cost will be the cost incurred to produce the next bottle of water. The seller will continue to sell the bottled water as long as price of the next bottle is higher than the cost of producing the next bottle.

- For the government, in making policy decisions, the marginal benefit to society (marginal social benefit) that the policy brings about is the marginal benefit. The marginal cost to society (marginal social cost) represents the marginal costs. If the marginal social benefit exceeds the marginal social cost, then marginal benefit exceeds marginal cost and the government should go forward with the policy, because it would add to society's welfare. If the marginal social cost exceeds the marginal social benefit, then marginal cost exceeds marginal benefit and the government should not go forward with the policy, because it would subtract from social welfare. To maximise social welfare, governments would implement policies such that marginal social benefit equals marginal social cost.

1.3.5 Recognising trade-offs

For all economic agents, every decision carries a trade-off and this is termed opportunity cost. To recap, when consumers choose to consume one good rather than another, the opportunity cost of the choice (i.e., the trade-off) is the next highest level of enjoyment or satisfaction from the good(s) that they chose to forego. Similarly, for producers, choosing to produce one good rather than another incurs opportunity cost (i.e., the trade-off) in the form of the profit they could have received from producing the other good instead. For governments choosing to intervene in one market rather than another, the opportunity cost (i.e., the trade-off) is the benefits society could have reaped from the intervention in the other market instead.

1.3.6 Recognising intended and unintended consequences

The decisions of economic agents can have both intended and unintended consequences.

- For consumers, the intended consequences of consumption are the utility gained from consuming the good and the cost in terms of the price paid for the good. However, there may be unintended consequences on the environment in the form of pollution (e.g., single-use plastic straws and packaging) or if the good was less satisfying than the consumer thought (e.g., buying a dress online and then realising the cut of the dress is not flattering). These unintended consequences can become a source of information for the consumer for when they make consumption decisions next time (e.g., not buying dresses from the brand that produces styles that are not flattering for the consumer).
- For producers, the intended consequences of production are the profits to be made from producing and selling a good. However, again, there may be unintended consequences in the form of polluting the environment (e.g., when fertilisers applied to a field end up polluting rivers), or triggering an unexpected response from a rival producer, or legislation from the government. Again, the unintended consequences become a source of information for the producer and influence the next round of decision-making.
- For governments, the intended consequence of policies is to maximise social welfare. However, here too, there could be unintended consequences if other economic agents do not behave as predicted (e.g., if a tax on cigarettes does not discourage smokers at all). As before, the unintended consequences become a source of information for the government and influence the next round of decision-making.

Summary for Chapter 1

1. Scarcity is the situation of having unlimited wants and limited resources to satisfy those wants.
2. At the societal level, resources refer to factors of production which are land, labour, capital, and entrepreneurship.
3. Because of scarcity, society has to make choices about how resources are to be allocated to meet some wants. These choices to be made are what to produce, how to produce, and for whom to produce.
4. Every choice made incurs an opportunity cost, which is the value of the next best alternative foregone.
5. The PPC can be used to illustrate the concepts of scarcity, choice, and opportunity cost.
6. Economic agents refer to consumers, producers, and governments.
7. Rational economic agents make decisions to achieve their objectives by recognising constraints, gathering information, considering perspectives, weighing costs and benefits, and recognising trade-offs.
8. The costs and benefits to be weighed are the marginal costs and marginal benefits.
9. Maximisation of utility (consumers' objective) is achieved when marginal utility = price.
10. Maximisation of profit (producers' objective) is achieved when marginal revenue = marginal cost of production.
11. Maximisation of social welfare (governments' objective) is achieved when marginal social benefit = marginal social cost.
12. After the decision is made, intended and unintended consequences serve as information for future decision-making.

Putting it concretely

To concretely understand the problem that society faces, imagine a shipwreck causes you to get stranded on an island with 20 other people. The 21 of you now form a society. Although everybody has unlimited wants (e.g., food, warmth, and shelter), the resources the 21 of you have are clearly limited (i.e., your society faces scarcity). Together, the resources you have are the natural resources like coconut trees and animals living on the island (land), 21 people (labour), the tools the 21 of you happen to have such as pocket knives and swimming gear (capital), and the cleverness to put these resources together to produce certain goods such as getting agile people to climb the coconut trees and use the pocket knives to cut down the coconuts (entrepreneurship).

Since there are limited resources, the 21 of you need to decide how many coconuts are to be harvested and how many animals should be hunted for meat (what to produce?); who should be doing the gathering and hunting and which tools should be used for which tasks (how to produce?); and how should the coconuts and meat be divided eventually (for whom to produce?).

Not all answers to the previous questions are equally good. In terms of what to produce, if everyone stranded loves meat and always prefers meat to coconuts, then clearly it is better to use the resources to hunt and not waste any resources on harvesting coconuts. But, at the same time, hunting is clearly more dangerous than harvesting coconuts. So, even though everybody prefers meat to coconuts, it would still make sense to harvest some coconuts because the cost of harvesting coconuts is lower. In general, the stronger the preference towards meat, the more animals should be hunted and the less coconuts should be harvested. At the same time, the lower the cost of harvesting coconuts compared to hunting animals, the more coconuts should be harvested instead of getting meat.

In terms of how to produce, not everyone is equally good at harvesting coconuts and hunting and those who are relatively better at harvesting coconuts should be sent to do so whereas those who are relatively better at hunting should be sent to do so.

In terms of for whom to produce, if half the people strictly prefer coconuts to meat and the other half strictly prefer meat to coconuts, it would be silly to divide up the coconuts and meat amongst everyone such that everyone has both coconuts and meat. Everyone would be happier if those who prefer coconuts just received the coconuts and those who prefer meat just received meat.

In short, for the question of what to produce, depending on the people's preferences and the cost of obtaining each good, there is an answer that will maximise society's welfare (e.g., producing only coconuts if everybody strictly prefers coconuts to meat and if the cost of harvesting coconuts and hunting meat is equal). For the question of how to produce, there is an answer that allows the coconuts and meat to be produced most efficiently. For the question of for whom to produce, there is an answer that allows the coconuts and meat to be distributed such that the total satisfaction (sum of everybody's satisfaction) is the highest.

The next issue then, is how can we arrive at the abovementioned answers? One way would be for a very, very clever person in the group to coordinate all activities and dictate how many coconuts and how much meat is to be harvested each day, who should do what and with what tools, and who will receive what at the end of the day. This is the idea of a centrally planned economy where a central planner coordinates and answers the three questions. For this method to work well, this central person must indeed be very clever and have complete information about everyone's preferences and abilities (which is highly unlikely).

The other way is to not rely on one person to coordinate all activities but to allow people to act independently and trade with one another. This would be what we term the market economy, which we will study in our next chapter. In the market economy, although people are acting independently, we will eventually find ourselves producing just the right amounts of each type of good, using just the right resources to produce each type of good, and distributing the goods just the right way. This market mechanism that naturally allocates the resources to maximise society's welfare is what Adam Smith, an early economist, termed "the invisible hand." We will see how the market mechanism does so in Chapter 2.

Annex 1.1 Shape of the PPC

The PPC is usually concave to the origin because of the law of increasing opportunity cost as the factors of production are not homogeneous. The law of increasing opportunity cost states that as more of a particular good is produced, its opportunity cost per extra unit will increase. This is because resources are not equally well suited to the production of all goods. Therefore, as more and more of one good is produced, factors of productions that are less suitable have to be allocated causing more of the other good to be given up.

In the Figure 1.5, we start at point A where all resources are directed into producing capital goods. One hundred units of capital goods are produced and zero units of consumer goods are produced. The first unit of consumer goods requires one unit of capital goods to be given up (moving from point A to point B). The second unit of consumer goods requires two units of capital goods to be given up (moving from point B to point C). And, we can see that as we move along the PPC, each extra unit of consumer good requires more and more units of capital goods to be given up. Since the opportunity cost of producing the consumer goods is the capital goods given up, we can see that the more consumer goods are produced, the higher the opportunity cost of producing them. If the opportunity cost remained constant, we would have a straight line PPC, as in Figure 1.6, where each consumer good produced consistently requires two units of capital goods to be given up.

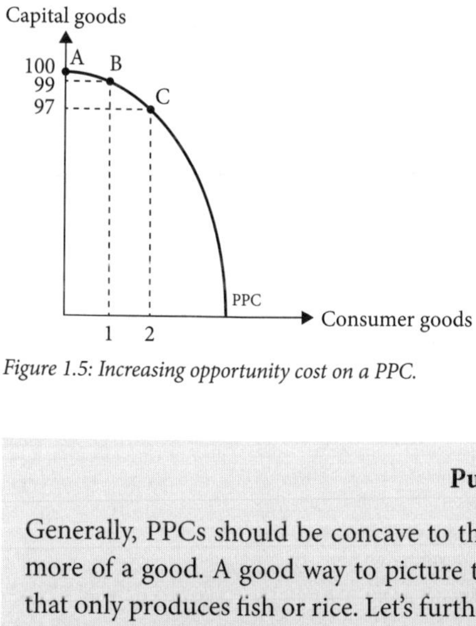

Figure 1.5: Increasing opportunity cost on a PPC.

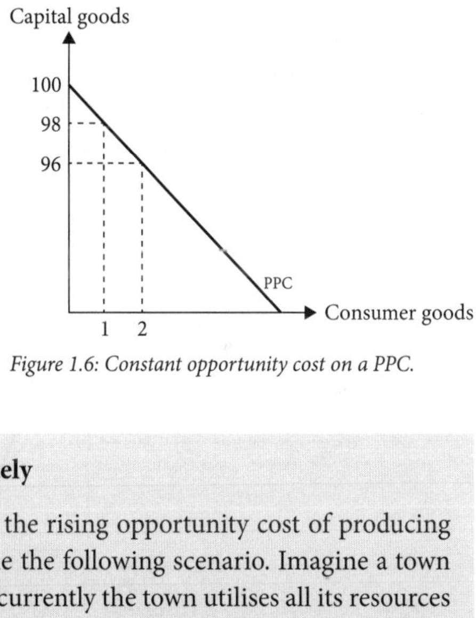

Figure 1.6: Constant opportunity cost on a PPC.

Putting it concretely

Generally, PPCs should be concave to the origin due to the rising opportunity cost of producing more of a good. A good way to picture this is to imagine the following scenario. Imagine a town that only produces fish or rice. Let's further imagine that currently the town utilises all its resources in the most efficient manner to only produce rice. Suppose the townspeople then decide to produce their first few units of fish (i.e., start catching fish). Who would they send away from the rice fields to be a fisherman instead? If they wish to maximise the amount of rice and fish that they can produce, the one that they would send away from the rice field would be the one who is the least efficient in farming (i.e., the worst farmer). This is because the amount of rice production forgone from this farmer leaving the rice fields would be little. If the town would like to produce more fish, the next worst farmer would be transferred from producing rice to catching fish and the amount of rice production forgone would be more than the first one. As the town produces more and more units of fish, the next worst farmer would be redeployed and the amount of rice production foregone would be more and more. This carries on until at last, to produce more fish, the town's best farmer has to go catch fish too and the rice production foregone would be the highest. It can be seen that as more and more fish is produced, the amount of rice that had to be given up increased. The opportunity cost of producing fish increased.

Annex 1.2 Skewed Shifts of the PPC

The shifts of the PPC can be skewed if the factor of production that experiences a change in the quantity or quality is better suited for producing only one of the two types of goods, or if the change in technology only affects the production of only one of the two types of goods.

For example, if there is an improvement in technology that only affects the production of capital goods, the shift in the PPC would be as shown below (PPC_0 to PPC_1) (Figure 1.7).

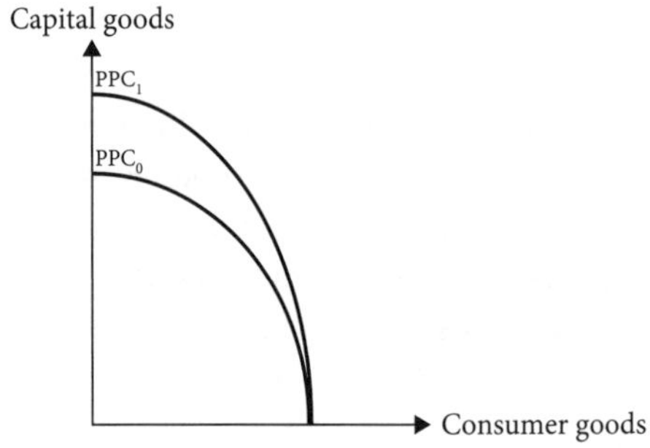

Figure 1.7: Skewed shift of PPC for capital goods.

Conversely, if the improvement in technology only affects the production of consumer goods, the shift in the PPC would be as shown below (PPC_0 to PPC_1) (Figure 1.8).

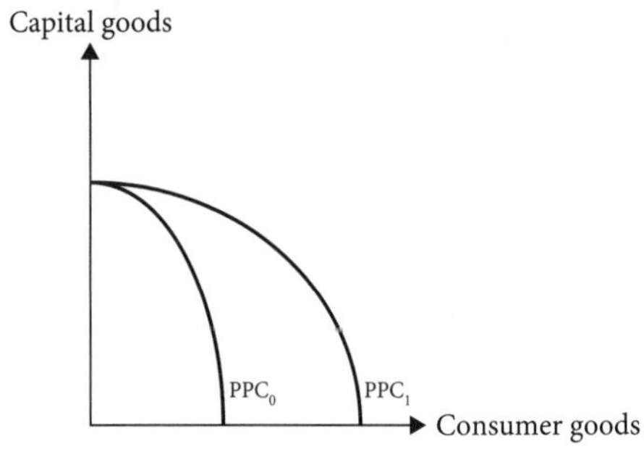

Figure 1.8: Skewed shift of PPC for consumer goods.

Putting it concretely

To try to picture how there can be changes in technology that only affect one good but not another, let us imagine a town that only produces fish or rice. Suppose someone in the town invents a better type of fish bait that attracts more fish per hour of fishing. This improvement will only increase the maximum number of fish that can be caught but not the maximum amount of rice that the town can produce. Thus, the PPC would experience a skewed shift.

PART I: MICROECONOMICS

CHAPTER 2

THE MARKET – DEMAND AND SUPPLY

2.1 Price Mechanism and its Functions

2.1.1 Resource allocation in a free market

In Chapter 1, we learned what scarcity is and were introduced to the term "market mechanism" to address the questions of what to produce, how to produce, and for whom to produce. Chapter 2 studies what this market mechanism is and how resources are allocated in the free market.

Market

Definition(s):

A **market** is where consumers and producers interact through their demand and supply, respectively, to determine the market equilibrium price and quantity at which goods and services are exchanged.

A market can be a physical place or a digital space where consumers and producers interact to buy and sell a good or service. For example, in a new car market, the buyers and sellers of new cars will interact to determine the price of the car. It could be at a physical car showroom or on a website online.

Examples of markets include:

For goods: car, clothing, books, medicine, and food

For services: tourism, education, and health care

For factors of production (i.e., factor markets): labour market

You will also learn more about other types of markets later in the book such as the Foreign Exchange Market (Forex).

Resource allocation in a free market

Definition(s):

A **free market** is where consumers and producers interact with each other **without any intervention** from the government.

All societies face the problem of scarcity as the limited resources are unable to satisfy the unlimited human wants for goods and services. Limited resources can only produce a limited amount of goods and services. Therefore, society needs to allocate these scarce resources by answering the three questions — "What to produce?", "How to produce?", and "For whom to produce?".

In a free market, scarce resources are allocated to produce different quantities of different goods (i.e., "What to produce?") through the interaction of demand and supply in the goods and services markets. "How to produce?" is answered by the interaction of demand and supply in the factor markets. "For whom to produce?" is answered jointly by the interaction of demand and supply in the factor markets and in the goods and services market. This process of demand and supply interacting to determine the allocation of resources is known as the price mechanism or the market mechanism. Hence, to understand how the price mechanism allocates resources, we need to first understand how demand and supply interact.

2.2 Interaction of Demand and Supply

To understand the interaction of demand and supply, we need to first understand what makes up demand and supply respectively.

Hence, we will now turn to the study of demand and supply in detail before returning to how they interact to determine the equilibrium price and quantity. We will then make the link back to how the price mechanism answers the questions of "What to produce?", "How to produce?", and "For whom to produce?".

2.2.1 Consumers and their demand

Definition(s):

Demand is the amount of a good or service consumers are willing and able to buy, at various prices, over a period of time, ceteris paribus.

Ceteris Paribus is a Latin phrase meaning "other things being constant". When economists analyse how a certain factor(s) affects an outcome, we always assume all other factors except for those being analysed remains constant.

The demand curve

Demand is the amount of goods and services consumers are willing and able to buy, at various prices, over a period of time, ceteris paribus. We now try to illustrate the concept of demand graphically by drawing a demand curve. The "amount of good and services" can be seen on the horizontal axis represented by quantity and "various prices" can be seen on the vertical axis represented by Price (Fig. 2.1).

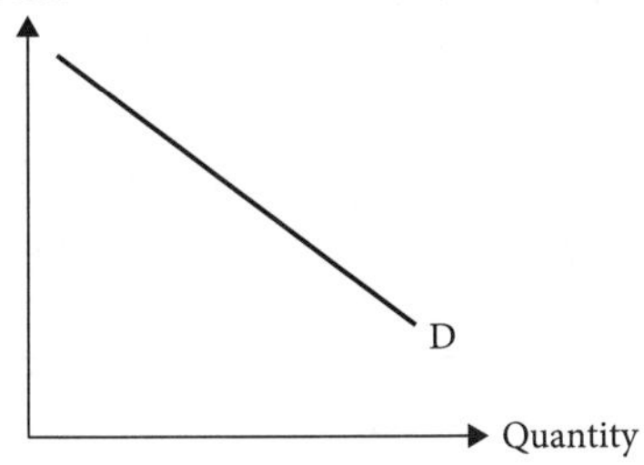

Figure 2.1: The demand curve.

Law of demand

For most cases in the real world, the demand curve is downward sloping as there is an inverse relationship between the price of the good and the quantity demanded. This means that when price changes, the quantity that consumers demand will experience the opposite change. For example, when the price of a good increases, the quantity demanded of that good will decrease. It is important to note that quantity demanded changes because of changes in price and not the other way round (i.e., changes in quantity demanded will not change price).

Therefore, the law of demand states that there is an inverse relationship between price of a good and the quantity demanded of that good. Why this is so can be understood from the derivation of the demand curve.

Derivation of the individual demand curve

An individual consumer's demand curve is derived from the marginal utility (MU) of the good to the consumer. The MU curve is downward sloping because of the law of diminishing marginal utility (LDMU).

> *Definition(s):*
>
> The law of diminishing marginal utility (LDMU) is the decrease in marginal utility (MU) for additional units of the same good consumed.

This law means that the satisfaction derived from each additional unit of a good consumed brings less satisfaction than the last. For example, the first ice cream one eats on a hot day brings a lot of satisfaction. However, after the first ice cream, the second ice cream eaten brings less satisfaction compared to the first, and the third ice cream will bring even less satisfaction.[1]

We show how the individual's demand curve is derived from the individual's MU curve with the use of an example. Let us imagine that the first unit of a good gives a consumer \$5 worth of utility (MU = \$5), the second unit of the good gives the consumer \$3 worth of additional utility (MU = \$3), and the third unit of the good gives the consumer \$1 worth of additional utility (MU = \$1). This is illustrated in Fig. 2.2.

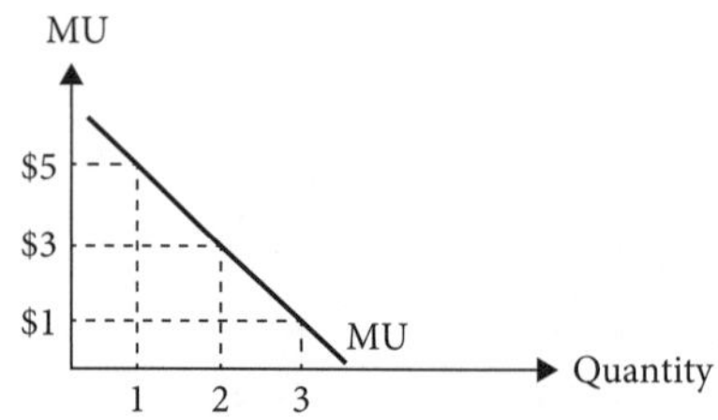

Figure 2.2: A MU curve.

Since the MU of the first unit of the good is \$5, the consumer would be willing to pay a price of up to \$5 for that first unit. By similar reasoning, the consumer would be willing to pay up to \$3 for the second unit, and up to \$1 for the third unit.

So, if the price of the good was \$5, the consumer would buy 1 unit of the good (recall that he was willing to pay \$5 for the first unit of the good but only \$3 for the second unit of the good and \$1 for the third unit of the good). If the price of the good was \$3, the consumer would buy 2 units of the good. And, if the price of the good was \$1, the consumer would buy 3 units of the good. What this shows is that for a given price, an individual consumer will be willing to purchase all the units of the good where the MU exceeds or is equal to the price. We say that for a given price, the consumer will consume a quantity of the good such that MU of the last unit will be equal to its price.[2] So, the individual demand curve will trace out the individual's MU curve. Since the MU curve is downward sloping, the individual demand curve would be downward sloping.

Market demand

The market demand for a good consists of all the individual demands added together.

For example, if there are only three consumers in the market, the summation of their three demands would be the market demand (Fig. 2.3).

Because the individual demands traced the MU curve of the individuals, the market demand, which is the sum of the individual demands, would trace the MU of the goods to all consumers

1 In fact, the third ice cream might even lead to dissatisfaction instead.

2 This was actually first introduced in Chapter 1 when we explained the decision making process of a rational consumer.

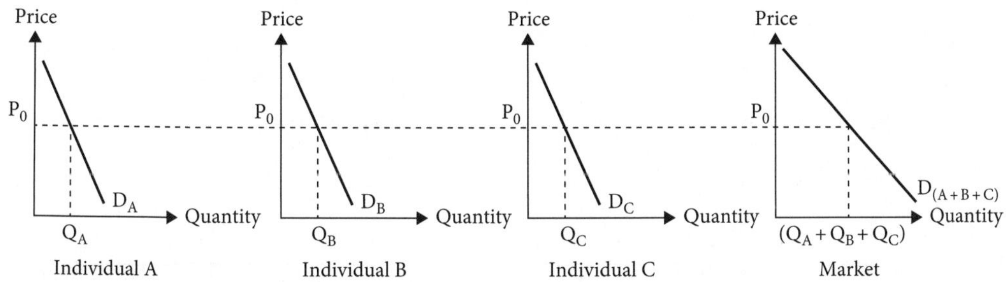

Figure 2.3: Market demand as the sum of three individuals' demands.

as a whole. This MU of the goods to all consumers as a whole is referred to as the marginal private benefit of the good to society.

> *Definition(s):*
> **Marginal private benefit (MPB)** is the benefit enjoyed by consumers from the consumption of an additional unit of a good or service.

Hence, the market demand curve is also the MPB curve.

Note that the term "demand" usually refers to the market demand. If we want to refer to the individual demand, we would use the term "individual demand".

Changes in price versus non-price determinants of demand

Thus far, we have established that changes in the price of the good will change the quantity demanded of the good. This is illustrated by a movement along the same demand curve, seen in Figure 2.4 below. A fall in price from P_0 to P_1 increases the quantity demanded from Q_0 to Q_1, and a rise in price from P_0 to P_2 reduces the quantity demanded from Q_0 to Q_2 (Fig. 2.4).

However, it is possible that the quantity demanded of the good changes even though the price has not changed (e.g., more umbrellas are demanded on a rainy day although the price of umbrellas remains the same). Factors that cause such changes are called non-price determinants and will affect the demand of the good by causing it to shift. In Figure 2.5 below, a change in a non-price determinant that increases the demand, will cause it to shift right from D_0 to D_1. We can see that at the same price of P_0, a larger quantity of the good is demanded (Q_0 increased to Q_1). Conversely, a change in a non-price determinant that decreases the demand will cause it to shift left from D_0 to D_2. We can see that at the same price of P_0, a smaller quantity of the good is demanded (Q_0 decreased to Q_2) (Fig 2.5).

Non-price determinants of demand

The non-price determinants of demand changes the demand and shifts the demand curve by affecting the total consumers' willingness and ability to buy the good. When these factors

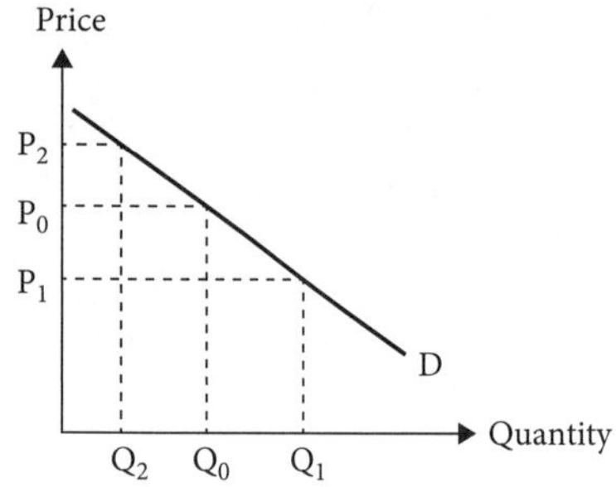

Figure 2.4: Changes in price causing movements along the demand curve.

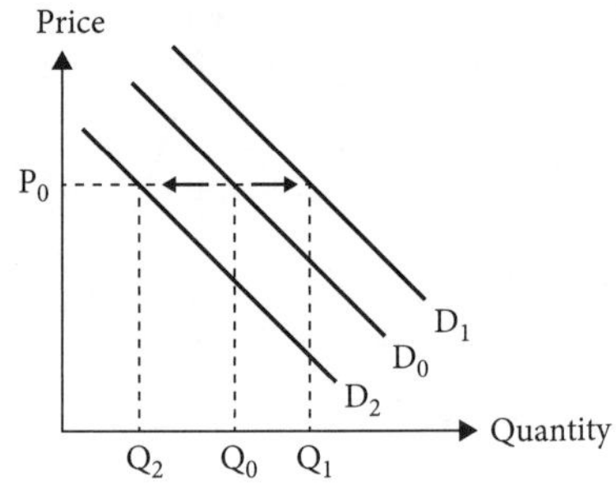

Figure 2.5: Changes in non-price determinants causing shifts of the demand curve.

change, the ceteris paribus assumption for the original demand curve no longer holds and the original demand will no longer exist. There will be a new demand curve instead.

Changes in the following non-price determinants will change the demand of the good and shift the demand curve:

- Income level (disposable income)
- Taste and preferences towards the good
- Prices of related goods—substitutes and complements
- Interest rate and the ease of getting loans
- Expected future prices
- Expectation of future economic conditions
- Governmental interventions
- Weather
- Population

As mentioned, each determinant will either affect the total consumers' willingness and/or ability to consume a good. Demand increases when consumers become more willing and/or able to consume a good and decreases when consumers become less willing and/or able to consume a good.

Income level—When consumers' incomes change, their willingness and ability to consume goods and services will also change. Income level will increase during a period of economic growth.[3] When incomes increase, consumers will consume more of some goods and less of others. The former and latter are known as normal goods and inferior goods, respectively.

3 Economic growth will be properly explained in Chapter 6. For now, it is sufficient to understand economic growth as an increase in consumers' incomes.

Definition(s):

Normal goods are goods that consumers demand more of when their incomes increase.
Inferior goods are goods that consumers demand less of when their incomes increase.

Putting it concretely: Normal goods in one context may be inferior in another context

The idea of inferior is relative.

For the very poor, almost all goods are normal. Nothing seems to be inferior to them—even instant noodles and canned food. In the context of a very poor region or country, when incomes increase, the demand for instant noodles and canned food would increase (i.e., instant noodles and canned food are normal goods).

For those with higher incomes, instant noodles and canned food may be inferior goods as consumers would choose to consume less of them in favour of 'better' food (e.g., fresh produce) when incomes increase. Hence, instant noodles and canned food may be inferior goods and fresh produce may be normal goods in regions or countries with higher incomes.

For those with even higher incomes, fresh produce sold in supermarkets might be considered inferior goods as they would choose to consume less generic fresh produce in favour of organic or genetically modified (GM) free produce. In this context, fresh produce becomes an inferior good instead.

In summary, whether a good is inferior or normal depends on the context. Goods that are considered normal goods in a market where consumers have low incomes could be inferior in a market where consumers have higher incomes.

Further details about normal and inferior goods are provided in the later section of this chapter under income elasticity.

Conversely, when incomes of consumers decrease (e.g., during a recession,[4]) the demand for normal goods would decrease and the demand for inferior goods would increase.

Taste and preferences towards the good—Consumers' tastes and preferences towards a good may change due to various reasons, such as fashion trends, news, and advertisements. Fashion trends are a common factor that change the tastes and preferences of consumers. For example, if the colour orange becomes fashionable and popular while the colour blue becomes unfashionable, consumers will be more willing to buy orange-coloured clothing and

4 Recessions will be properly explained in Chapter 6. For now, it is sufficient to understand recession as a decrease in consumers' incomes.

less willing to buy blue clothing. The demand for orange clothing will increase while demand for blue clothing will decrease.

Unpleasant news related to a good would result in a fall in demand for that good, while pleasant news related to a good would result in an increase in demand for that good. For example, when there was news that consumption of preserved canned food increased the chances of health problems, the demand for preserved canned food decreased. Conversely, when there was news of chia seed consumption increasing the likelihood of healthy weight loss, the demand for chia seeds increased.

Advertisements can also affect taste and preferences. Advertisements presenting a good in a positive light would cause consumers to prefer the good and be more willing to buy it. That increases the demand for the good. This is the reason why producers will hire celebrities to endorse their goods. Celebrities are able to influence consumers' taste and preferences and increase the demand for the good they endorse.

Prices of related goods: substitutes and complements—Changes in prices of related goods can also change the demand for a good. Two goods can be related; they can be substitutes of each other or complements to each other. Two goods are substitutes if they serve a similar purpose and can be used in place of one another. Two goods are complements if consumers' satisfaction and utility increase when the two goods are used together.

The demand for a good would increase if the price of its **substitute** increases. For example, fruit juice and milk are substitutes as they are both beverages and serve a similar purpose of quenching thirst. The demand for milk would increase when the price of fruit juice increases as milk would become relatively cheaper for consumers, causing consumers to switch from drinking fruit juice to milk. Conversely, the demand for milk would decrease when the price of fruit juice decreases as milk would now be relatively more expensive, causing consumers to switch from drinking milk to fruit juice.

Putting it concretely: Relatively cheaper (or more expensive) versus absolutely cheaper (or more expensive)

It is important to distinguish between a good becoming cheaper (or more expensive) in absolute terms and it becoming cheaper (or more expensive) in relative terms.

A good becoming cheaper (or more expensive) in absolute terms means that the actual numerical price of the good has become lower (or higher) than the actual numerical price of the other good.

A good becoming cheaper (or more expensive) in relative terms means that the actual numerical price of the good as a proportion of the actual numerical price of the other good has decreased (or increased).

A good can become relatively cheaper without becoming absolutely cheaper. This is shown in the example below.

Suppose the price of Coke is $1 and price of Pepsi is $0.80. Coke is more expensive than Pepsi in absolute terms.

Now suppose the price of Coke decreases from $1 to $0.90.

Coke is still more expensive than Pepsi in absolute terms but it has become relatively cheaper compared to Pepsi. The price of Coke as a proportion of the price of Pepsi fell from 125% ($1/$0.80 × 100%) to 112.5% ($0.90/$0.80 × 100%).

Since Coke became relatively cheaper than Pepsi, the demand for Pepsi will fall although Pepsi is still cheaper than Coke in absolute terms.

It is important to note that the original demand for Pepsi was based on the price of Coke being $1 while the new lower demand for Pepsi would be based on the price of Coke being $0.90.

It is also important to note that if the terms "cheaper" or "more expensive" are used without explicitly stating whether they are in relative or absolute terms, we assume that they are in absolute terms.

The demand for a good would increase if the price of its **complement** decreases. For example, movies and popcorn are complements as consuming them together would will increase consumers' satisfaction and utility. The demand for popcorn would increase when price of movie tickets decreases as consumers would go to the movies more and therefore also buy more popcorn. Conversely, the demand for popcorn would decrease when the price of movie tickets increases as fewer consumers would want to go to the movies and hence, fewer units of popcorn will be demanded.

Interest rate and ease of getting loans—The interest rate can be considered the cost of borrowing money from the banks or the return on savings in the bank. When the interest rate decreases, the cost of borrowing money from the banks is lower. Therefore, consumers will be more willing and able to borrow money from the bank to purchase goods and services, especially for big ticket items such as cars and properties. This increases the demand for goods and services. The same effect will be observed if we consider the interest rate to be the returns on savings in the bank. When the interest rate decreases, the opportunity cost of using the savings to buy goods and services is lower since the foregone returns are lower. Hence, consumers will increase their demand for goods and services.

Definition(s):
The **interest rate** is the cost of borrowing money as well as the returns earned from savings in financial institutions such as banks.

The ease of getting loans from banks would have a similar effect as the interest rate. If the banks reduce the requirements to borrow and make it easier to borrow money, demand for goods and services, especially those that require loans to purchase, would also increase.

Conversely, a rise in the interest rate or a reduction in the ease of getting loans would reduce the demand for goods and services.

Expectation of future prices—Consumers' demand for a good today is also affected by their expectation of the future price of the good. When consumers expect the future price of a good to be higher, they might bring forward their purchase which would result in an increase in present demand for the good. On the other hand, if consumers expect the future price of a good to be lower, they might delay their purchase, which would result in a decrease in present demand for the good.

For example, if the government announces that the goods and services tax (GST) would increase from 7% to 11% one month from now, the demand for many goods and services will increase as consumers would want to buy the goods and services now to avoid paying 4% more for the same good or service a month from now. It is important to note that the current price of the good has not actually changed yet.

Definition(s):
The **goods and services tax (GST)** is a broad-based consumption tax levied on goods and services in Singapore. In other countries, it is commonly known as the value-added tax (VAT).

Expectation of future economic conditions—When consumers become more optimistic about future economic conditions and expect future economic conditions to be positive (e.g., if they expect strong economic growth and increases in their incomes in the next period), they will be more willing to consume goods and services as there is less need to save for a rainy day, causing demand for goods and services to increase. On the other hand, if consumers expect future economic conditions to worsen (e.g., if they expect a recession and reductions in their incomes in the next period), their need to save increases and they will become less willing to consume today in order to save more for rainy days ahead. This will cause the current demand for goods and services to decrease.

For example, the announcement by the Singapore government to give out cash handouts to all Singapore citizens above the age of 21 in 2018 caused an increase in consumer spending and demand of goods and services, even when the handouts had not been paid out. On the other hand, the China and United States trade war in 2018 worsened predictions of economic conditions worldwide and caused a fall in the demand for goods and services.

Government intervention[5]—Government intervention will affect consumers directly through regulations, subsidies, and taxation. These measures can affect consumers' willingness and ability to consume goods and services. For example, if the government increases the personal income tax, consumers' disposable income (i.e., consumers' post-tax income) would decrease, causing the demand for normal goods and services to decrease and the demand for inferior goods and services to increase. On the other hand, if the government decreases the personal income tax, consumers' disposable income would increase. This would increase the demand for normal goods and services and decrease the demand for inferior goods and services.

Definition(s):

Disposable income is the income of consumers after the deduction of income taxes.

Weather conditions—Weather and climate conditions could affect consumers' willingness and ability to consume goods and services. For example, during the haze season, demand for N95 masks and health care services for the treatment of throat irritation and asthma will increase while demand for outdoor exercise equipment will decrease. During the rainy season, demand for rain coats and umbrellas will increase as well.

Population—The larger the population, the more consumers there are, the larger the market demand as there are more people willing and able to buy the good. This increase in population need not be about the population of the country as a whole. It could also refer to the population segment that buys a particular good. For example, an ageing society would mean that the population segment of elderly consumers is increasing even though the total population is decreasing. Nonetheless, because the absolute number of elderly people is increasing, the demand for goods that cater to the elderly (e.g., supplements to improve knee joint health) would increase. Conversely, since the absolute number of young people is declining, goods that cater to the young (e.g., skateboards) would experience a fall in demand.

End of Section Note:

It is important to note that the level of demand is determined by the level of these non-price determinants. A change in the demand (i.e., shift in the demand curve) must be due to change(s) in these non-price determinants.

2.2.2 Producers and their supply

Definition(s)

Supply is the amount of a good or service producers are willing and able to produce and sell at various prices over a given period of time, ceteris paribus.

The supply curve

Supply is the amount of goods and services producers are willing and able to produce and sell at various prices over a period of time, ceteris paribus. We now try to illustrate the concept of

5 More details on various forms of government intervention are provided later in this chapter.

supply graphically by drawing a supply curve. The "amount of good and services" can be seen on the horizontal axis represented by Quantity and "various prices" can be seen on the vertical axis represented by Price (Fig. 2.6).

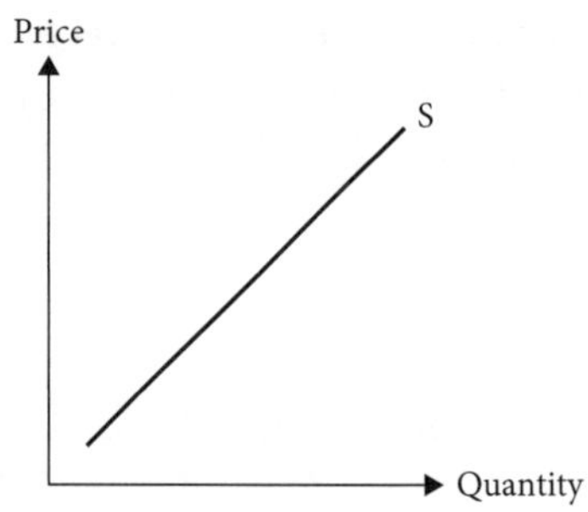

Figure 2.6: The supply curve.

Law of supply

For most cases in the real world, the supply curve is upward sloping as there is a direct relationship between the price of the good and the quantity supplied. This means that when the price changes, the quantity supplied will experience a similar change. For example, when price of a good increases, quantity supplied of that good will increase. Is it important to note that quantity supplied changes due to changes in price but changes in quantity supplied will not change the price.

The Law of Supply states that there is a positive relationship between the price of a good and the quantity supplied of that good. Why this is so can be understood from the derivation of the supply curve.

Derivation of the individual supply curve

An individual producer's supply curve is derived from the marginal cost (MC) of the good to the producer. The MC curve is upward sloping because it rises with additional units of the good produced.[6] The cost of each additional unit of a good produced is more than the last.

We show how the individual supply curve is derived from the individual firm's MC curve with the use of an example. Let us imagine that the first unit of a good cost a producer \$1 to produce (MC = \$1), the second unit costs \$3 to produce (MC = \$3), and the third unit costs \$5 to produce (MC = \$5). This is illustrated in Fig. 2.7.

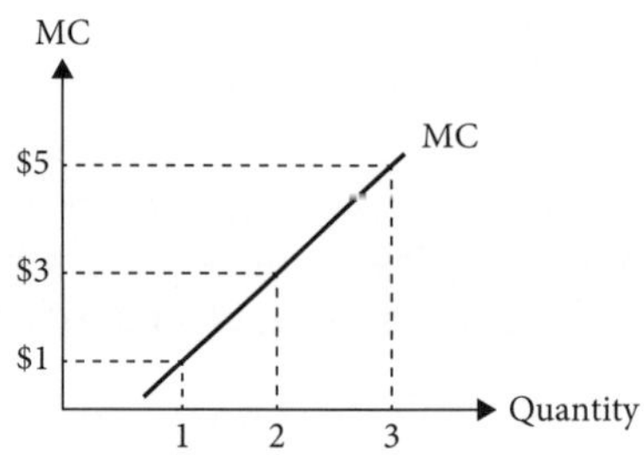

Figure 2.7: A MC curve.

6 Why this is so is explained later in Chapter 3.

Since the MC of the first unit of the good is \$1, the producer would be willing to accept a price of at least \$1 for that first unit. By a similar reasoning, the producer would be willing to accept at least \$3 for the second unit, and at least \$5 for the third unit.

So, if the price of the good was \$1, the producer would produce and sell 1 unit of the good (recall that he was willing to accept \$1 for the first unit of the good but needed at least \$3 for the second unit and \$5 for the third unit). If the price of the good was \$3, the producer would produce and sell 2 units of the good. And, if the price of the good was \$1, the producer would produce and sell 3 units of the good. What this shows is that for a given price, an individual producer will be willing to produce and sell all the units of the good where the MC is less than or equal to the price. We say that for a given price, the producer will produce and sell a quantity of the good such that the MC of the last unit will be equal to its price.[7] So, the individual supply curve will trace out the individual firm's MC curve. Since the MC curve is upward sloping, the individual supply curve would be downward sloping.

Market supply

The market supply would consist of all the individual supply curves added together.

For example, if there are only three producers in the market, the summation of their three supply curves would be the market supply (Fig 2.8).

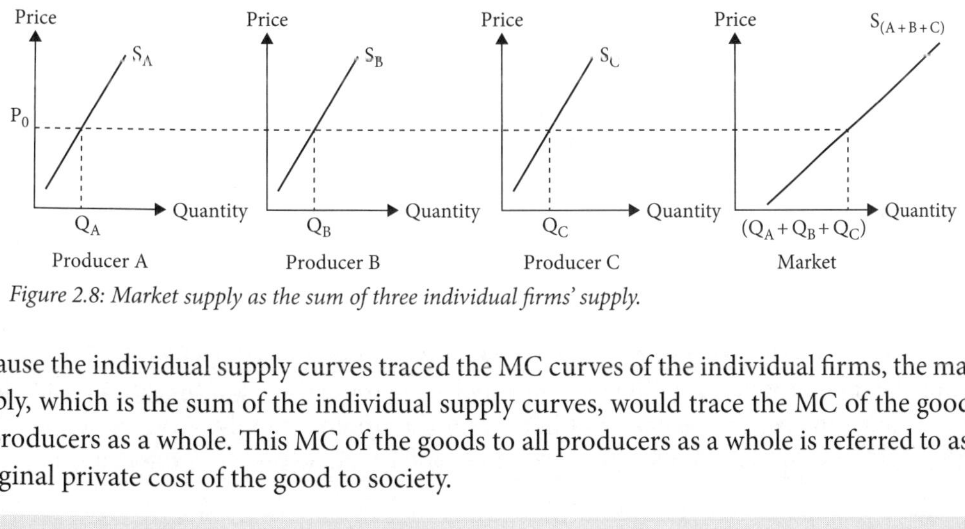

Figure 2.8: Market supply as the sum of three individual firms' supply.

Because the individual supply curves traced the MC curves of the individual firms, the market supply, which is the sum of the individual supply curves, would trace the MC of the goods to all producers as a whole. This MC of the goods to all producers as a whole is referred to as the marginal private cost of the good to society.

Definition(s):

Marginal private cost (MPC) is the cost incurred by producers from the production of an additional unit of a good or service.

Hence, the market supply curve is also the MPC curve.

7 This was actually first introduced in Chapter 1 when we explained the decision making process of a rational producer.

Note that the term "supply" usually refers to the market supply. If we want to refer to the individual supply, we would use the term "individual supply".

Changes in price versus changes in non-price determinants of supply

Thus far, we have established that changes in the price of a good will change the quantity supplied of the good. This is illustrated by a movement along the same supply curve seen in Figure 2.9 below. A fall in price from P_0 to P_1 decreases the quantity supplied from Q_0 to Q_1, and a rise in price from P_0 to P_2 increases the quantity supplied from Q_0 to Q_2 (Fig. 2.9).

However, it is possible that the quantity supplied of the good changes even though the price has not changed (e.g., when farmers produce and sell more crops simply because there was a good harvest). Factors that cause such changes are called non-price determinants and will affect the supply of the good by causing it to shift. In Figure 2.10, a change in a non-price determinant that increases the supply will cause it to shift right from S_0 to S_1. We can see that at the same price of P_0, a larger quantity of the good is supplied (Q_0 increased to Q_1). Conversely, a change in a non-price determinant that decreases the supply will cause it to shift left from S_0 to S_2. We can see that at the same price of P_0, a smaller quantity of the good is supplied (Q_0 decreased to Q_2) (Fig 2.10).

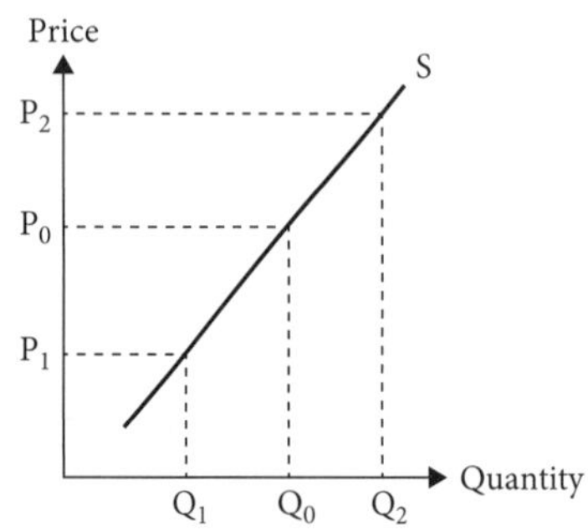

Figure 2.9: Changes in price causing movements along the supply curve.

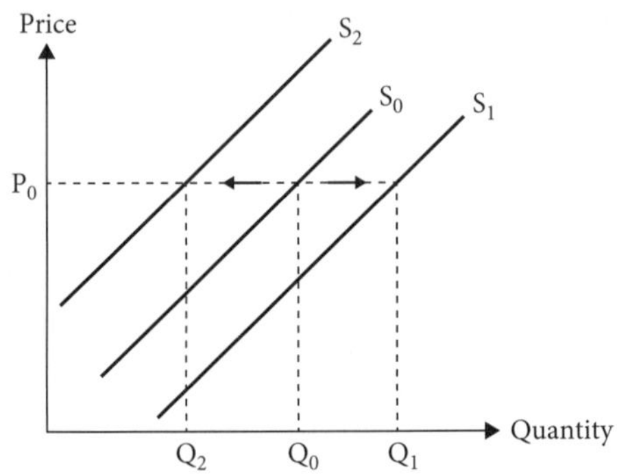

Figure 2.10: Changes in non-price determinants causing shifts of the supply curve.

Non-price determinants of supply

The non-price determinants of supply changes the supply and shifts the supply curve by affecting the total producers' willingness and ability to produce and sell the good. When these factors change, the ceteris paribus assumption for the original supply curve no longer holds and the original supply will no longer exist. There will be a new supply curve instead.

Changes in the following non-price determinants will change the supply of the good and shift the supply curve:

- Cost of production/prices of factors of production
- Technology
- Government policies
- Firms' objectives
- Price of goods in competitive supply

- Price of goods in joint supply
- Number of sellers
- Expectation of future prices

As mentioned, each determinant will affect either the total producers' willingness and/or ability to produce and sell a good. Supply increases when producers become more willing and able to produce and sell a good and decreases when producers become less willing and able to produce and sell a good.

Cost of production/prices of factors of production—When the cost of production increases, producers will become less willing and able to produce and sell a good. This is because, for a given price, there are now fewer of units of the good with a MC less than or equal to the price. One common reason for the increase in cost of production is the increase in prices of factors of production. For example, when the price of crude oil increases, the cost of producing electricity increases (crude oil is a factor of production in producing electricity as it is burnt to generate electricity).[8] Hence, the supply of electricity will decrease. Conversely, a reduction in cost of production (caused by a reduction in prices of factors of production or otherwise) would increase supply.

Technology—Technological improvement can lead to more efficient methods of producing goods and services. This increases the productivity of factors of production as each factor of production can now produce more output on average. This decreases the MC of production of each unit of output and hence, increases supply. Such technology improvements can be the result of research and development (R&D). R&D commonly leads to innovation in the form of new and better production techniques and methods.

Government policies—Governments can tax or subsidise producers. Taxes and subsidies will affect the supply through changing the cost of production. When a government imposes taxes on producers, the producers will need to pay a charge for every unit of the good produced. This increases the MC of production and hence, reduces the supply, as explained before. When the government subsidises producers, the producers will receive a payment for every unit of the good produced. This reduces the MC of production and hence, increases the supply.

> *Definition(s):*
> **Taxes** are monetary charges imposed by the government on producers or consumers.
> **Subsidies** are monetary grants given by the government to producers or consumers.

Other government policies such as rules and regulations would also affect how much producers are willing and able to produce.[9]

8 To be more precise, it is burnt to generate heat, to boil water to generate steam, to turn the turbines to generate electricity.

9 More details on various forms of government intervention are provided later in this chapter.

Firms' objectives—Thus far, we have assumed that firms are profit-maximising and will supply the quantity of goods up to where the MC equals the price. However, firms may have alternative objectives apart from profit-maximisation.[10] For example, if they are trying to establish themselves as the most dominant brand, they may try to flood the market with their goods. In that case, at the same market price, the quantity supplied would increase and the supply curve would shift rightwards.

Price of goods in competitive supply—Two goods are in competitive supply if they use similar factors of productions. This is because if more of one good is produced, less of the other must be produced since the factors of production have been used to produce the former good. The supply of a good will decrease when the price of the good it is in competitive supply with increases. This is because when price of the good in competitive supply increases, producers would be more willing to produce that good. Factors of production would be directed towards producing that good, causing a fall in supply of this good.

For example, corn and rice are in competitive supply because when a piece of land is used to grow rice, that same piece of land cannot be used to produce corn. When the price of rice increases, producers will be more willing to produce rice and less willing to produce corn. Therefore, the supply of corn will decrease.

Conversely, a fall in the price of a good in competitive supply with another, would cause the supply of the other good to increase.

Price of goods in joint supply—Two goods are in joint supply when the production of one good would lead to the production of the other. This would be the case when both goods are simultaneously produced, using the same factors of production. The supply of a good will increase when the price of the good it is in joint supply with increases. This is because when price of the good in joint supply increases, producers would be more willing to produce that good. In producing more of that good, more of this good would naturally be produced, causing an increase in supply of this good.

For example, beef and leather are in joint in supply because when producing beef, producers will produce leather as well, since obtaining beef would involve killing the cow, which would also make its hide available for leather production. When the price of beef increases, producers will be more willing to produce beef (i.e., kill more cows), which will also increase the supply of leather.

Conversely, a fall in the price of a good in joint supply with another, would cause the supply of the other good to decrease.

Number of sellers—The number of sellers will directly affect the market supply of a good. When there is an increase in the number of sellers or producers, the supply of the good will

10 The alternative objectives of firms will be more formally dealt with in Chapter 3.

increase. For example, the entry of low-cost or budget airlines have increased the supply of air travel. Conversely, a reduction in the number of sellers would reduce the supply of a good.

Expectation of future prices—When producers expect the price of the good to increase in the future, they might delay selling the goods now so that they can sell the same good in the future for a higher price. This causes the current supply to decrease. Conversely, when producers expect the price of the good to decrease in the future, they would want to bring forward the selling of the goods and sell the goods now, as they would earn less if they sold it in the future. This would increase the current supply. It is important to note that these changes in supply are due to producers' expectations. The current price of the good has not changed yet.

End of Section Note:

As with demand, it is important to note that the level of supply is determined by the level of these non-price determinants. A change in the supply (i.e., shift in the supply curve) must be due to a change(s) in these non-price determinants.

2.2.3 Equilibrium price and equilibrium quantity

Demand and supply interact to determine the equilibrium price and quantity of a good traded in a market. By equilibrium price and quantity traded, we mean a market price and quantity traded that has no further tendency to change unless external factors influence or change the demand or supply.

This equilibrium is reached when the market price is such that quantity demanded equals quantity supplied. When this is so, every unit of good that consumers are willing and able to buy at the market price is exactly matched by the number of units that producers are willing and able to sell at the market price. Since this is so, there is no reason for the price or quantity traded[11] to change since consumers are able to get every unit that they wish to buy and producers are able to sell every unit that they wish to sell. We say that the market is in equilibrium.

Market disequilibrium

In contrast, a market can be in disequilibrium when quantity demanded exceeds or is less than quantity supplied. If quantity demanded exceeds quantity supplied, we say that there is a shortage. If quantity demanded is less than quantity supplied, we say that there is a surplus.

Definition(s):

A **shortage** is when the quantity demanded of a good is more than the quantity supplied at the market price.

11 In this scenario, quantity traded equals quantity demanded equals quantity supplied. This is best explained through an example. Imagine that at the market price, 100 units of the good are demanded (quantity demanded = 100) and 100 units of the good are supplied (quantity supplied = 100). In this case, all 100 units that are produced would be sold. Therefore, the quantity that was traded would be 100.

A **surplus** is when the quantity supplied of a good is more than quantity demanded at the market price.

Price adjustment process

For a given demand and supply, the market equilibrium will be reached through the price adjustment process. (Fig. 2.11)

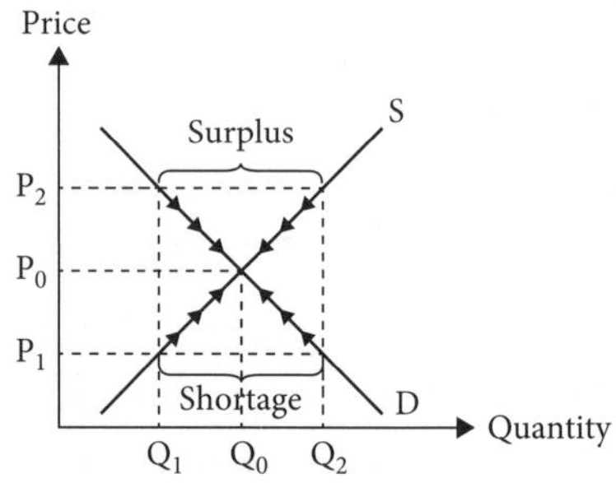

Figure 2.11: Adjustment towards the market equilibrium.

If the current price is below the equilibrium price (e.g., at P_1), then quantity demanded (Q_2) would exceed quantity supplied (Q_1). There would be a shortage. This shortage would create an upward pressure on price since more units of the good is being demanded than supplied, causing consumers to bid up the price of the good. As price increases, the quantity demanded would decrease, causing an upward movement along the demand curve. At the same time, quantity supplied would increase, causing an upward movement along the supply curve. This continues until the equilibrium price P_0 is reached where quantity demanded equals quantity supplied at Q_0.

Conversely, if the current price is above the equilibrium price (e.g., at P_2), then quantity demanded (Q_1) would be less than quantity supplied (Q_2). There would be a surplus. This surplus would create a downward pressure on price since more units of the good are supplied than demanded, causing producers to reduce the price of the good. As price decreases, the quantity demanded would increase, causing a downward movement along the demand curve. At the same time, quantity supplied would decrease, causing a downward movement along the supply curve. This continues until the equilibrium price P_0 is reached, where quantity demanded equals quantity supplied at Q_0.

Hence, we see that the price will always adjust such that the market reaches an equilibrium. Now that we understand demand, supply, and how they interact to reach an equilibrium, we return to the question of how the market addresses "what to produce?", "how to produce?", and "for whom to produce?".

Equilibrium price and quantity in the goods and services market determining "What to produce?"

In a free market, the demand and supply of every good and service would result in an equilibrium price and quantity traded for each good. This answers the question of "What to produce?" as the demand and supply in each market would determine how much of every good and service is produced. For example, the demand and supply of shoes in China may result in 10 million pairs of shoes being produced a year and the demand and supply of rice in China may result in 5 billion bags of rice being produced every year. In which case, the free market's answer to "What to produce?" for China would be 10 million pairs of shoes and 5 billion bags of rice.

We also note that since the demand for each good also represents the MPB of that good and the supply of each good represents the MPC of that good, the equilibrium quantity of each good, determined by demand being equal to supply, will also be the quantity where MPB = MPC. Thus, the "right" quantity of each good that maximises social welfare will be produced.[12]

Equilibrium price and quantity in the factor markets determining "How to produce?"

The bulk of this chapter dealt with demand and supply in the goods market. However, demand and supply forces could also be at work in the factor markets. For example, in the market for labour (a factor of production), there would be demand from firms, who are willing and able to pay, to hire labour, and supply of labour from people willing and able to work. The demand and supply of labour then interact to determine the price of labour, much like how the demand and supply of a good interact to determine the price of the good. This price of labour is termed wages.

> *Definition(s):*
>
> **Wages** are the price of labour in the labour market. They represent the income earned from the provision of labour.

Demand and supply in the other factor markets would also determine the price of these factors of production.

These factor prices then determine the free market's answer to "How to produce?". The firms will use these factor prices to find the method with the lowest cost of production (e.g., produce the goods using more labour if the price of labour (wages) is low).

Equilibrium price and quantity in the goods and services market, and the factor markets jointly determining "For whom to produce?"

In the market for goods and services, goods and services are allocated to people with the ability and willingness to pay the market price. For example, if the market equilibrium price of shoes is $100 and the equilibrium quantity traded was 500 pairs of shoes, those 500 pairs of shoes would have been bought by the people who were willing and able to pay $100 for a pair of shoes. The people who bought the shoes are the ones "for whom" the shoes were produced.

The ability to pay would be determined in the factor markets. The higher the price of the factor of production owned by the individual, the greater his ability to pay. Since a factor of production will only be able to fetch a high price if it is greatly valued by the firms

12 How the quantity at which MPB=MPC maximises social welfare will be fully developed in Chapter 4.

(i.e., there is a high demand from firms), the more valuable the factor of production the individual owns, the higher his ability to pay. And since, the higher his ability to pay, the more likely he will get the good he is willing to pay for, the more likely he will receive the good.

So, in terms of "For whom to produce?", the free market's answer is to produce the good for the owners of factors of production that are most valuable to firms, and amongst those with the same ability to pay, to those who are most willing to pay for it (i.e., to those who value it the most).

In summary, we have seen how demand and supply interact to determine the equilibrium price and quantity, and how the determination of equilibrium price and quantity in every market (both goods and services markets and factor markets) answers the questions of "What to produce?", "How to produce?", and "For whom to produce?". The process through which demand and supply allocate resources to answer these questions, through determining the prices of goods and services and factors of production, is called the price mechanism.

2.2.4 Changes in demand and supply leading to changes in market equilibrium

We have seen how the price mechanism works for a given demand and supply. We now turn to study how changes in demand and supply will change the market equilibrium in the goods market and how it changes the allocation of resources in terms of "What to produce?"[13]

The market equilibrium will change when non-price determinants of demand and/or supply change. We will study the scenarios of an increase and decrease in demand, an increase and decrease in supply, and simultaneous changes in demand and supply.

Increase in demand

To recap, an increase in demand of a good can be due to the following factors:

- An increase in income (for normal goods)
- A decrease in income (for inferior goods)
- A change in taste and preferences towards a good
- An increase in the price of a good's substitutes
- A decrease in the price of a good's complement
- A decrease in the interest rate or an increase in the ease of getting loans
- An expectation of an increase in the future price of a good
- Increased optimism about future economic conditions
- Change in government legislation to make it easier to buy a good (e.g., decrease in the minimum age of buying a good)
- A change in the weather that requires more of a good to be bought (e.g., winter increasing the demand for coats and anti-freeze)
- An increase in the population

13 A broad understanding of how demand and supply affects resource allocation in terms of "How to produce?" and "For whom to produce?" is sufficient for the A Level syllabus and this has been already explained in the previous section. Hence, we will not go into the details of how changes in demand and supply will affect resources allocation in terms of "How to produce?" and "For whom to produce?"

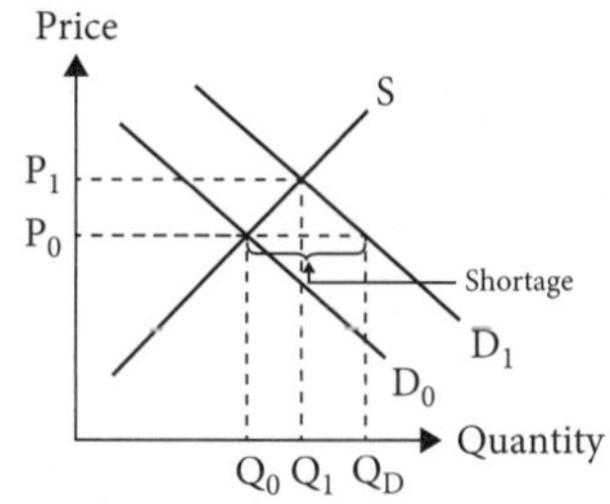

Figure 2.12: Change in equilibrium due to an increase in demand.

Refer to Fig. 2.12, due to the increase in demand, consumers will be more willing and able to buy the good, causing demand to decrease and the demand curve to shift right (D_0 to D_1), as seen in Figure 2.12 above. At the original price P_0, there will be a shortage as quantity demanded Q_D is more than quantity supplied Q_0. The shortage will lead to upwards pressure on the price as consumers bid up the price of the good. This will signal to the producers to channel or allocate more resources to producing this good. When the price of the good increases, consumers decrease the quantity demanded and producers increase the quantity supplied. This will result in a decrease in the shortage.

The price will stop increasing when the shortage is eliminated at P_1 where the new demand is equal to supply. Therefore, the increase in demand will cause both market equilibrium price and quantity to increase from P_0 and Q_0 to P_1 and Q_1, respectively. Society has also increased the allocation of resources to producing this good. In terms of "What to produce?", now more of this good is produced.

Decrease in demand

To recap, a decrease in demand of a good can be due to the following factors:

- A decrease in income (for normal goods)
- An increase in income (for inferior goods)
- A change in taste and preferences away from a good
- A decrease in the price of a good's substitutes
- An increase in the price of a good's complement
- An increase in the interest rate or a decrease in the ease of getting loans
- An expectation of a decrease in the future price of a good
- Reduced optimism about future economic conditions
- Change in government legislation to make it harder to buy a good (e.g., increase in the minimum age of buying a good)
- A change in the weather that requires less of a good to be bought (e.g., winter decreasing the demand for sunblock lotion)
- A decrease in the population

Refer to Fig. 2.13, due to the decrease in demand, consumers will be less willing and able to consume a good, causing demand to decrease and the demand curve to shift left (D_0 to D_1) , as seen in Figure 2.13 below. At the original price P_0, there will be a surplus as quantity demanded Q_D is less than quantity supplied Q_0. The surplus would lead to a downward pressure on price as producers reduce the price of the good. This will signal to the producers to channel or allocate

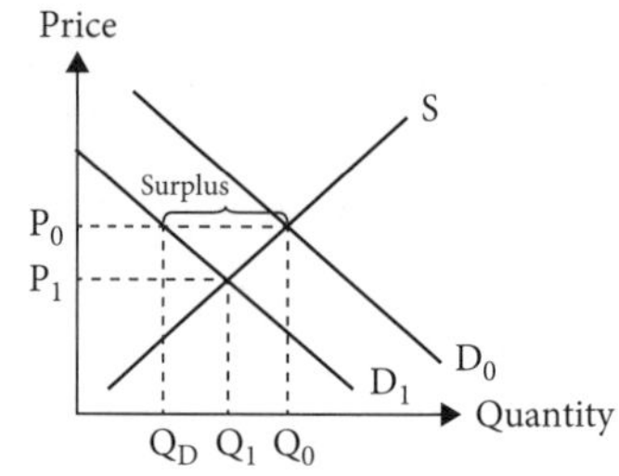

Figure 2.13: Change in equilibrium due to a decrease in demand.

less resources to producing this good. When the price of the good decreases, consumers increase the quantity demanded while producers decrease the quantity supplied. This will result in a decrease in the surplus.

The price will stop decreasing when the surplus is eliminated at P_1 where the new demand is equal to supply. Therefore, the decrease in demand will cause both market equilibrium price and quantity to decrease from P_0 and Q_0 to P_1 and Q_1, respectively. Society has also decreased the allocation of resources to producing this good. In terms of "What to produce?", now less of this good is produced.

Increase in supply

To recap, an increase in supply of a good can be due to the following factors:

- A decrease in prices of factors of production (e.g., wages and price of oil)
- An improvement in technology
- A subsidy given to producers

  (The above factors will cause a decrease in the cost of production)
- Firms changing their objectives such that they produce more at the same price of the good (e.g., to create brand recognition by simply flooding the market with their products)
- A decrease in the price of goods in competitive supply
- An increase in price of goods in joint supply
- An increase in the number of sellers
- Expectations of a decrease in the price of the good in the future

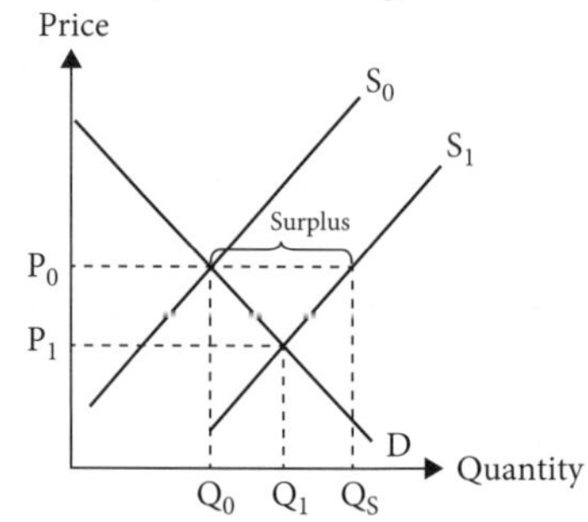

Figure 2.14: Change in equilibrium due to an increase in supply.

Refer to Fig. 2.14, due to an increase in supply, producers will be more willing and able to produce the good, causing supply to increase and the supply curve to shift right (S_0 to S_1), as seen in Figure 2.14 above. At the original price P_0, there will be a surplus as quantity demanded Q_0 is less than quantity supplied Q_S. The surplus would lead to a downward pressure on price as producers reduce the price of the good. This will signal to the producers to re-channel or re-allocate[14] less resources to producing this good. When the price of the good decreases, consumers increase the quantity demanded while producers decrease the quantity supplied. This will result in a decrease in the surplus.

The price will stop decreasing when the surplus is eliminated at P_1 where demand is equal to the new supply. Therefore, the increase in supply will cause the market equilibrium quantity to increase from Q_0 to Q_1 and the market equilibrium price to decrease from P_0 to P_1. Overall, society has increased the allocation of resources to producing this good. In terms of "What to produce?", now more of this good is produced.

Decrease in supply

To recap, a decrease in supply of a good can be due to the following factors:

- An increase in prices of factors of productions (e.g., wages and price of oil)
- A tax levied on producers
  (The above factors will increase the cost of production)
- Firms changing their objectives such that they produce less at the same price of the good (e.g., returning to profit-maximisation after they have successful created brand recognition by flooding the market with their products)
- An increase in the price of goods in competitive supply
- A decrease in price of goods in joint supply
- A decrease in the number of sellers
- Expectations of an increase in the price of the good in the future

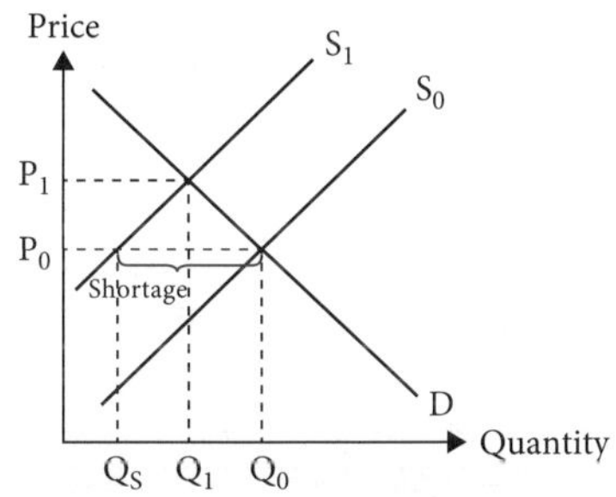

Figure 2.15: Change in equilibrium due to a decrease in supply.

Refer to Fig. 2.15, due to a decrease in supply, producers will be less willing and able to produce the good, causing supply to decrease and the supply curve to shift left (S_0 to S_1), as seen in Figure 2.15 above. At the original price P_0, there will be a shortage as quantity demanded Q_0 is more than quantity supplied Q_s. The shortage will lead to an upward pressure on price as consumers bid up the price of the good. This will signal to the producers to re-channel or re-allocate[15] more

14 We use the term "re-channel" or "re-allocate" as the original increase in supply already meant that producers had channeled more resources into producing the good. The resultant surplus and fall in price acts as feedback to the producers to not channel too much resources into producing the good.

15 We use the term "re-channel" or "re-allocate" as the original decrease in supply already meant that producers had channeled less resources into producing the good. The resultant shortage and rise in price acts as feedback to the producers to not reduce the resources channeled into producing the good by too much.

resources to producing this good. When the price of the good increases, consumers decrease the quantity demanded while producers increase the quantity supplied. This will result in a decrease in the shortage.

The price will stop increasing when the shortage is eliminated at P_1 where demand is equal to the new supply. Therefore, the decrease in supply will cause the market equilibrium quantity to decrease from Q_0 to Q_1 and the market equilibrium price to increase from P_0 to P_1. Overall, society has decreased the allocation of resources to producing this good. In terms of "What to produce?", now less of this good is produced.

Summary table of a singular change in demand or supply

	Market price will	Market quantity will
When demand increases	Increase	Increase
When demand decreases	Decrease	Decrease
When supply increases	Decrease	Increase
When supply decreases	Increase	Decrease

Simultaneous changes in both demand and supply

When there are simultaneous changes in both demand and supply for the good or service, one of the market outcomes (price or quantity) can be determined. However, the other market outcome (quantity or price) would depend on whether demand or supply changed by the greater extent. We will look at the four possible scenarios: increase in both demand and supply, decrease in both demand and supply, increase in demand and decrease in supply, and decrease in demand and increase in supply.

- **Scenario 1: Increase in both demand and supply**

  When both demand and supply increase, market quantity will increase while the change in the market price will depend on whether demand or supply increased to a larger extent.

<table>
<tr><th>If demand increases more than supply</th><th>If demand increases less than supply</th><th>If demand and supply increase to the same extent</th></tr>
<tr><td>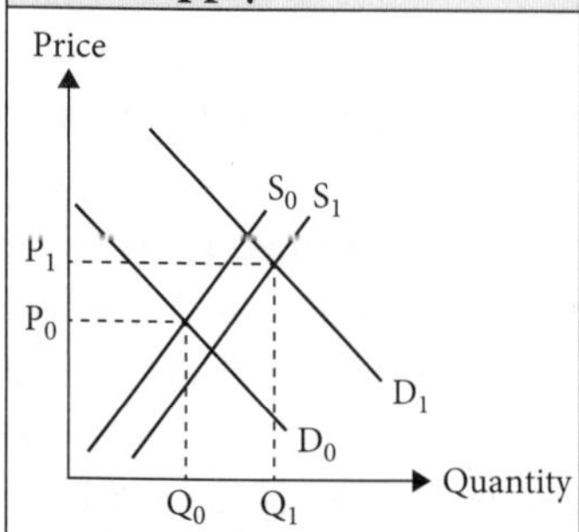
</td><td>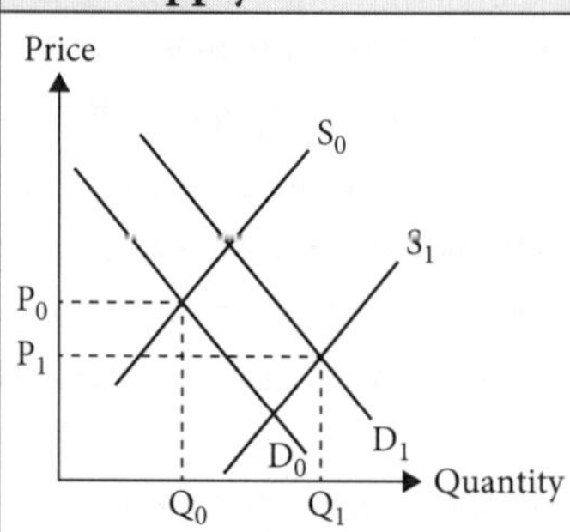
</td><td>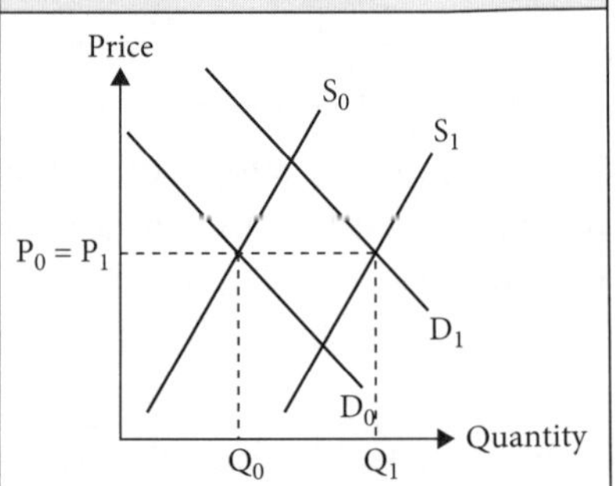
</td></tr>
<tr><td>Q increases (Q_0 to Q_1)
P increases (P_0 to P_1)</td><td>Q increases (Q_0 to Q_1)
P decreases (P_0 to P_1)</td><td>Q increases (Q_0 to Q_1)
P remains unchanged
($P_0 = P_1$)</td></tr>
</table>

- **Scenario 2: Decrease in both demand and supply**

  When both demand and supply decrease, market quantity will decrease while the change in the market price will depend on whether demand or supply decreased to a larger extent.

If demand decreases more than supply	If demand decreases less than supply	If demand and supply decrease to the same extent
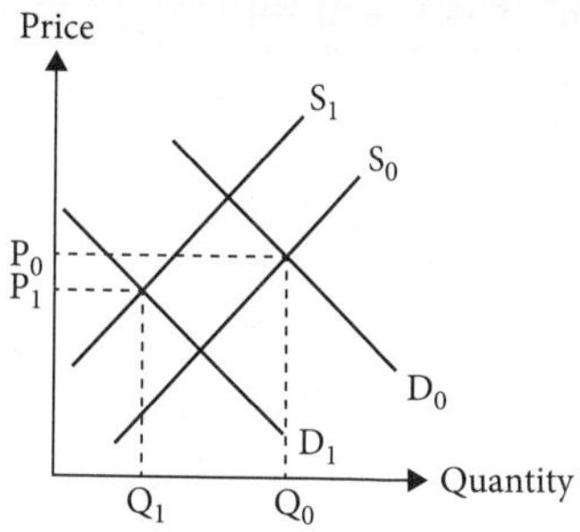	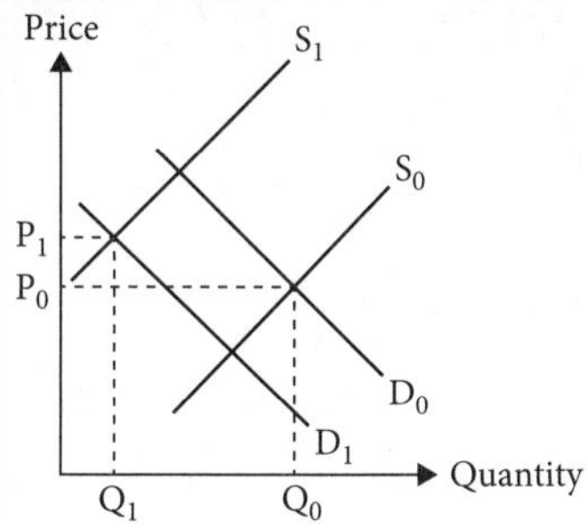	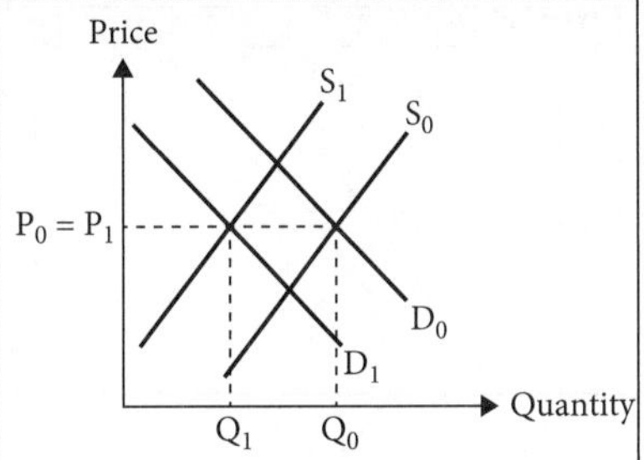
Q decreases (Q_0 to Q_1) P decreases (P_0 to P_1)	Q decreases (Q_0 to Q_1) P increases (P_0 to P_1)	Q decreases (Q_0 to Q_1) P remains unchanged (P_0 to P_1)

- **Scenario 3: Increase in demand and decrease in supply**

  When demand increases and supply decreases, the market price will increase while the change in the market quantity will depend on whether demand increased or supply decreased to a larger extent.[16]

If demand increases more than the decrease in supply	If demand increases less than the decrease in supply	If demand increases to the same extent as the decrease in supply
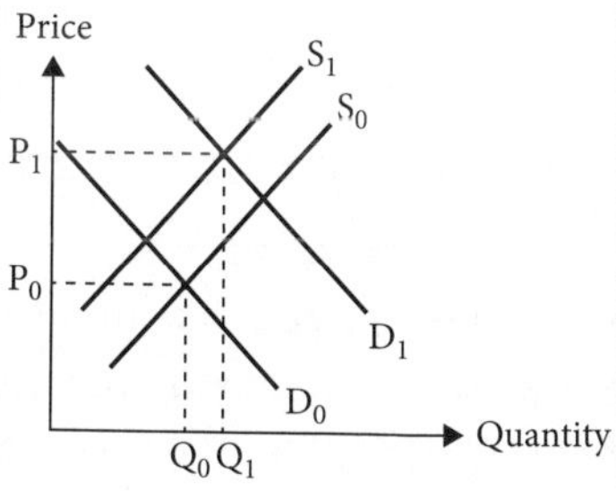	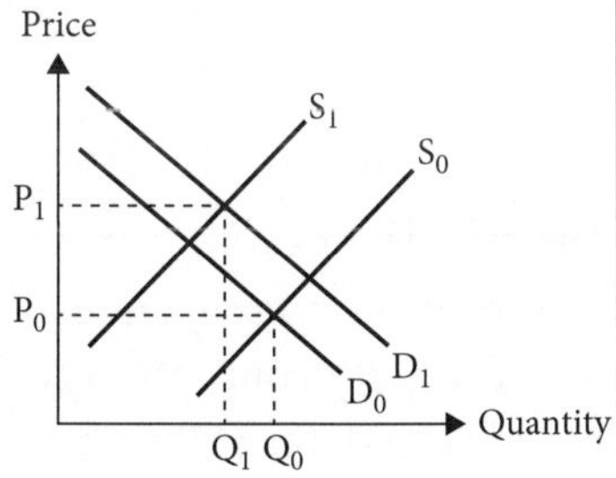	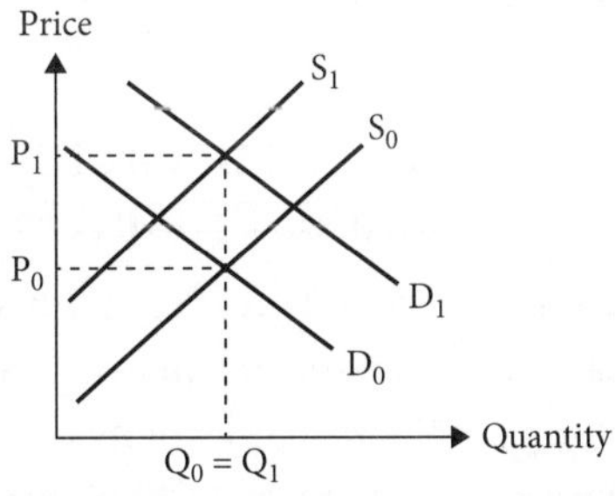
Q increases (Q_0 to Q_1) P increases (P_0 to P_1)	Q decreases (Q_0 to Q_1) P increases (P_0 to P_1)	Q remains unchanged ($Q_0 = Q_1$) P increases (P_0 to P_1)

16 Technically, it will also depend on the slope of the demand and supply curves. For example, a supply curve could shift left by a greater extent than the demand curve shifting right and still cause an increase in the equilibrium quantity if the supply curve was really flat and the demand curve was really steep. But that is beyond the scope of this book. Here we stick to simpler analyses.

- **Scenario 4: Decrease in demand and increase in supply**

  When demand decreases and supply increases, the market price will decrease while the change in the market quantity will depend on whether demand decreased or supply increased to a larger extent.

<table>
<tr><th>If demand decreases more than the increase in supply</th><th>If demand decreases less than the increase in supply</th><th>If demand decreases to the same extent as the increase in supply</th></tr>
<tr><td>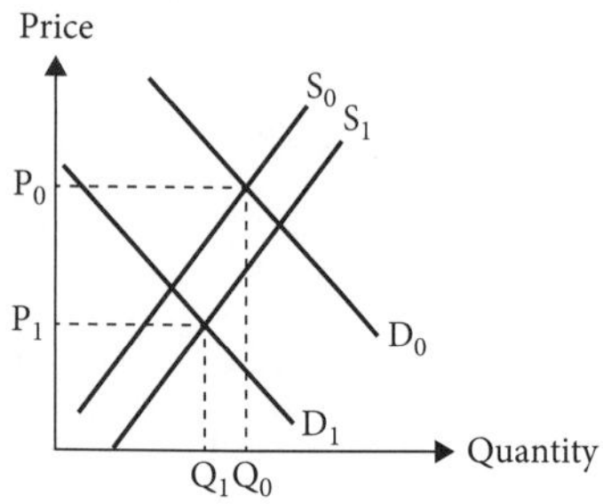
</td><td>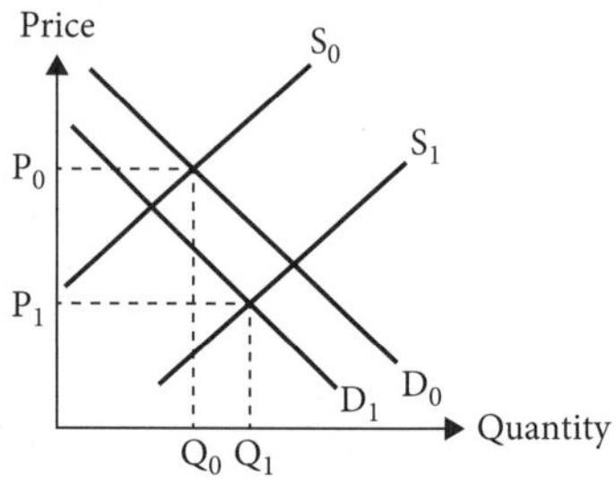
</td><td>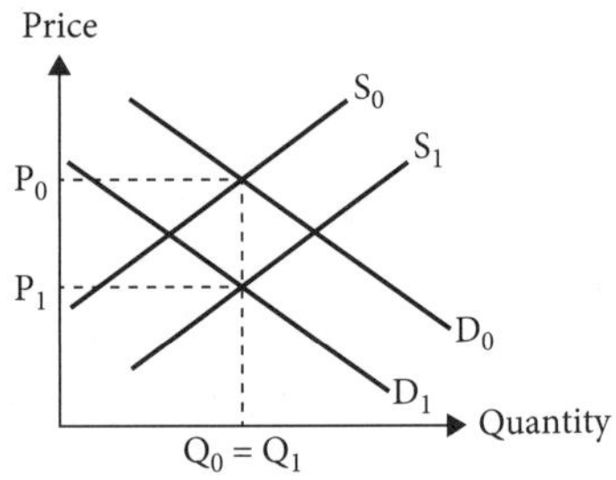
</td></tr>
<tr><td>Q decreases (Q_0 to Q_1)
P decreases (P_0 to P_1)</td><td>Q increases (Q_0 to Q_1)
P decreases (P_0 to P_1)</td><td>Q remains unchanged ($Q_0 = Q_1$)
P decreases (P_0 to P_1)</td></tr>
</table>

Summary table of simultaneous changes in demand and supply

	Change in demand	+	Change in supply	=	Effect on market price	Effect on market quantity
Scenario 1	Increase	+	Increase	=	Indeterminate	Increase
Scenario 2	Decrease	+	Decrease	=	Indeterminate	Decrease
Scenario 3	Increase	+	Decrease	=	Increase	Indeterminate
Scenario 4	Decrease	+	Increase	=	Decrease	Indeterminate

2.3 Applications of Demand and Supply: Responsiveness of Consumers and/or Producers (Elasticities)

The responsiveness of consumers and producers to a change in price and non-price determinants can be understood using the various elasticity concepts. The four elasticity concepts we will study are the price elasticity of demand (PED), the price elasticity of supply (PES), the income elasticity of demand (YED), and the cross elasticity of demand (XED).

PED, YED, and XED are collectively known as the elasticities of demand. PES is the only elasticity of supply we will study.

The various elasticity concepts help us analyse how much quantity demanded or supplied of a good will change in response to a change in the price of the good itself (PED and PES), a change in income (YED), and/or a change in the price of another good (XED). It is important to note that the study of elasticity concepts is an extension from the study of demand and supply.

Demand and supply analyses enables us to explain the direction (increase or decrease) of the changes in price and quantity. Elasticity concepts help us explain the extent of these changes.

Each elasticity concept will be studied in terms of its:

- Definition
- Formula
- Sign of its numerical value
- Magnitude of its numerical value
- Determinant(s)
- Application(s) from the perspective of firms, and/or governments

2.3.1 Price elasticity of demand

Definition(s):
Price elasticity of demand (PED) measures the responsiveness of quantity demanded of a good to a change in the price of the good itself, ceteris paribus.

In simpler terms, the PED measures how much quantity demanded will change when price of the good itself changes.

Formula

$$PED = \frac{\text{\% change in Qd of good A}}{\text{\% change in price of good A}}$$

Sign of the numerical value

PED always has a negative numerical value due to the law of demand which states that the price of a good and its quantity demanded must have an inverse relationship. As such, an increase in the price of a good (a positive % change) would cause a decrease in the quantity demanded of a good (negative % change). This would give rise to a negative PED value as a negative number divided by a positive number results in a negative number. If the price of the good decreases, the quantity demanded would increase, which would still result in a negative value of the PED.

Magnitude of the numerical value

The magnitude of the numerical value of PED (denoted by |PED|) can be classified into "between 0 and 1", "1", or "more than 1" as well as two extreme cases of |PED| = 0 and |PED| = infinity (denoted by the symbol "∞"). The way to interpret these values is shown in the table below:

PED value	Graph[17]	Description	Interpretation
|PED| = 0 OR PED = 0	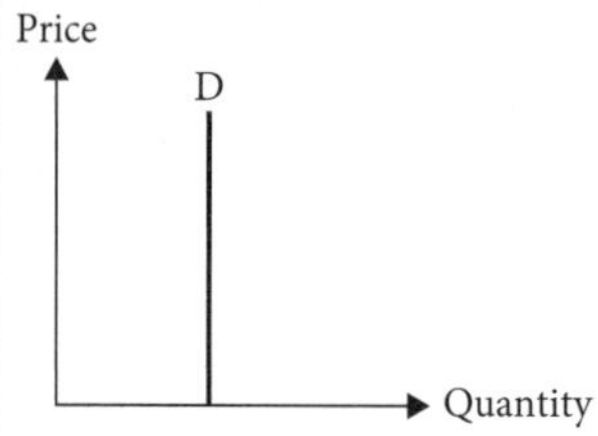	Demand is perfectly price inelastic	A change in price causes a no change in quantity demanded of the good. (e.g., a 10% increase in price causes a 0% decrease in quantity demanded of the good) Consumers are willing and able to purchase a fixed quantity of the good at any price.
0 < |PED| < 1 OR −1 < PED < 0	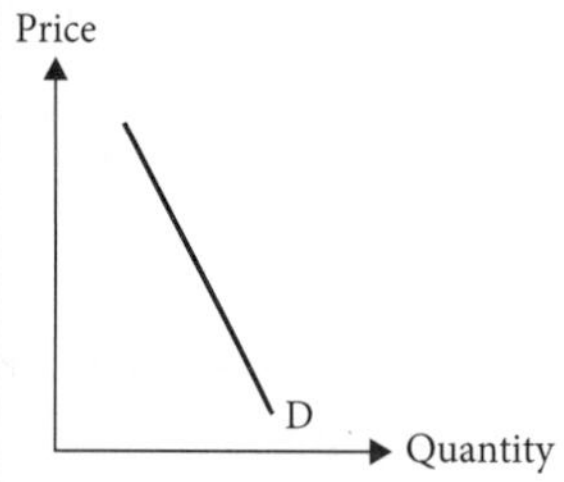	Demand is price inelastic	A change in price causes a less than proportionate change in quantity demanded of the good. (e.g., a 10% increase in price causes a 5% decrease in quantity demanded of the good)
|PED| = 1 OR PED = −1	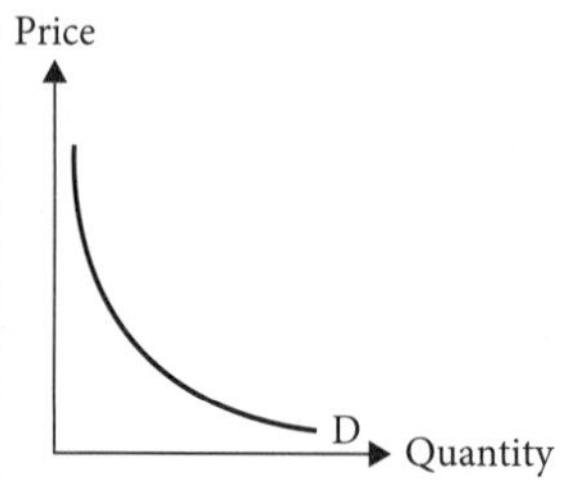	Demand is unitary price elastic[18]	A change in price causes an exactly proportionate change in quantity demanded of the good. (e.g., a 10% increase in price causes a 10% decrease in quantity demanded of the good)
|PED| > 1 OR PED < −1	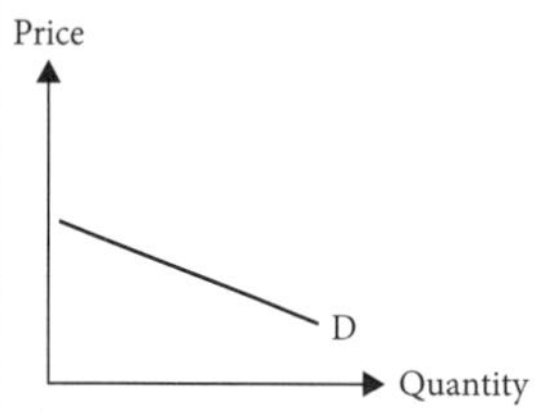	Demand is price elastic	A change in price causes a more than proportionate change in quantity demanded of the good. (e.g., a 10% increase in price causes a 15% decrease in quantity demanded of the good)
|PED| = ∞ OR PED = -∞	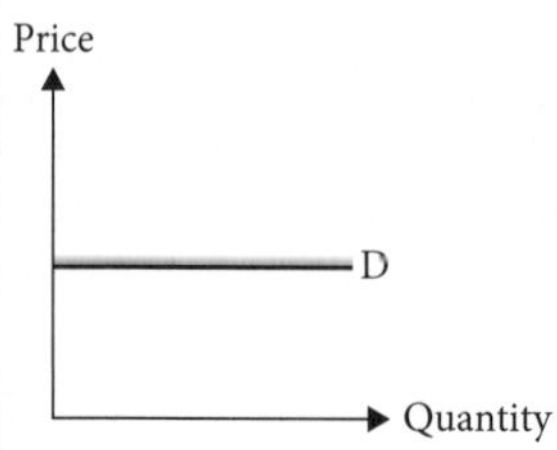	Demand is perfectly price elastic	A change in price causes an infinite change in quantity demanded of the good. (e.g., a 10% increase in price causes quantity demanded of the good to fall from infinity to zero) Consumers are willing and able to purchase any amount of good at a specific price.

17 Technically, the value of PED could vary along a straight line demand curve. Annex 2.1 addresses this issue.

18 The graph of the unitary price elastic demand curve is not in the syllabus.

Determinants of PED

Whether the demand of a good is price elastic or price inelastic is determined by the following determinants:

- Availability of substitutes
- Closeness of available substitutes
- Proportion of income spent on the good
- Degree of necessity
- Time period

Availability of substitutes—The greater the number of substitutes for a good available, the more price elastic the demand of the good will be. This is because when the price of the good increases, consumers will find that it is easier to switch to other substitutes, if there is a larger number of substitutes available. Hence, the quantity demanded will fall by a greater extent in response to the increase in price. Conversely, the fewer the number of substitutes for a good available, the more price inelastic the demand will be.

Closeness of available substitutes—The closer the available substitutes for a good, the more price elastic the demand of the good will be. This is because when the price of the good increases, consumers will find that it is easier to switch to the other substitutes, if the available substitutes are close substitutes for the good. Hence, the quantity demanded will fall by a greater extent in response to the increase in price. Conversely, the less close the available substitutes for a good are, the more price inelastic the demand will be.

Proportion of income spent on the good—The smaller the proportion of income spent on a good, the more price inelastic the demand of the good will be. This is because when the proportion of income spent on the good is low, a given percentage increase in price of the good would cause a small change in the proportion of the consumers' income spent on that good, even if they do not change the quantity demanded in response. Hence, consumers will not respond significantly to this change and quantity demanded would fall by a small extent, in response to the increase in price. Conversely, the larger the proportion of income spent on the good, the larger the change in the proportion of income they would spend on the good if they do not change the quantity demanded, and hence, the more price elastic the demand of the good would be.

For example, suppose household A has a monthly household income of $5000. Every month, household A spends $1000 on hotel staycation ($250 a night for 4 nights a month) and $100 on bus transport ($1 a trip for 100 trips a month). The price of one night of staycation is $250 and the price of one trip of bus transport is $1. Now suppose both staycation and bus transport prices increased by 10%. The absolute increase in price of staycation will be $25 while that of transport will be $0.10. If household A does not change the quantity of the staycation and bus transport consumed, the increase in spending on staycation would be $100 ($25 × 4) and the increase in spending on bus transport would be $10 ($0.10 × 100). $100 is 2% of household A's income while $10 is just 0.2% of household A's income. Household A would therefore likely to respond more to the change in the price of staycation since it would have a larger impact on the household income.

Degree of necessity—The more necessary a good is, the more price inelastic its demand will be, and the less necessary it is, the more price elastic its demand will be. Goods and services that are considered a necessity include food, transport, and health care. Such goods are more indispensable compared to leisure goods and services such as games and movies. Therefore, when prices of food and movies both increase by 10%, the percentage decreases in quantity demanded of food would be less than the percentage decrease in quantity demanded of movies since food is more of a necessity and required for survival compared to movies.

The degree of necessity can also be applied to goods that are addictive. For example, cigarettes can be considered necessary for those addicted to smoking. The more addictive a good is, the more indispensable it is for the consumers, the more price inelastic the demand would be.

Time period—Demand for all goods and services will become more price elastic as the time period increases. This is because consumers will have more time to find substitutes for the good and to make the good less necessary. For example, the demand for the Apple iPhone was price inelastic when it was first launched because there was no close substitute in the market. However, ten years later, the demand for the iPhone has become more price elastic with the development of similar smartphones by rival companies.

Application of PED

PED is applied by producers to guide their pricing and non-price decisions,[19] and by governments to guide their policy decisions.[20]

PED guiding producers' pricing decisions—PED is useful for producers in their pricing decision in maximising total revenue. Total revenue for a firm is the price that a firm charges multiplied by the quantity of the good the firm sells.

> *Definition(s):*
> **Total revenue (of a firm)** is the price charged by a firm multiplied by the quantity of the good it sells.

With the knowledge of the PED of their goods or services, producers can vary their prices to maximise their total revenue. The different PEDs and the decisions the firm should make to increase total revenue is presented in the table below.

19 The decisions of producers are explored in more detail in Chapter 3.
20 The decisions of governments are explored in more detail later in this chapter as well as in Chapter 4.

If demand for the firm's good is price inelastic (|PED| < 1)	If demand for the firm's good is price elastic (|PED| > 1)
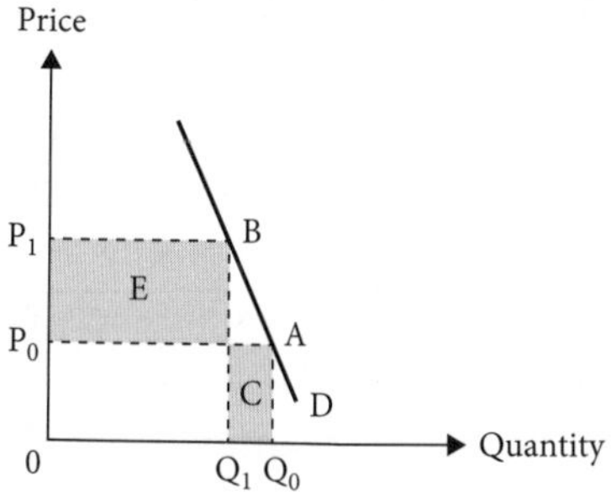	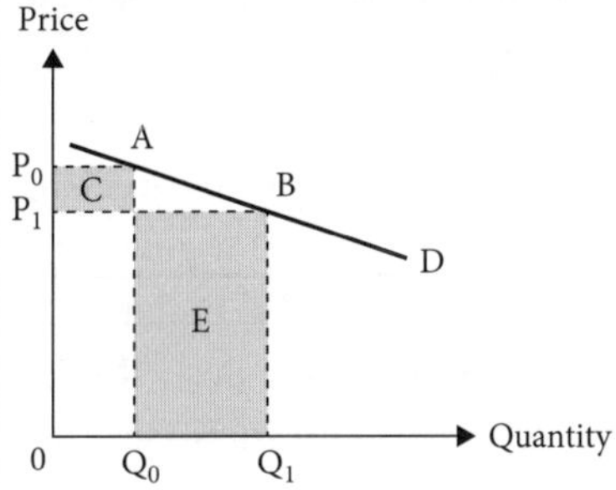
Firm should increase the price to increase total revenue. This is because an increase in the price will cause a less than proportionate decrease in quantity demanded. Thus, total revenue will increase. For example, assuming PED is −0.5, an increase in price of 10% will reduce quantity demanded by 5%. The increase in price is of a larger proportion compared to the fall in quantity demanded, resulting in an increase in total revenue.	Firm should decrease the price to increase total revenue. This is because a decrease in the price will cause a more than proportionate increase in quantity demanded. Thus, total revenue will increase. For example, assuming PED is −1.5, a decrease in price of 10% will increase quantity demanded by 15%. The increase in quantity demanded is of a larger proportion compared to the fall in price, resulting in an increase in total revenue.
Graphical description: Original TR = $P_0 \times Q_0$ = area $0P_0AQ_0$ With an increase in price from P_0 to P_1: New TR = $P_1 \times Q_1$ = area $0P_1BQ_1$ Loss in TR = area C Gain in TR = area E Since area E > area C, TR increases with the increase in price	Graphical description: Original TR = $P_0 \times Q_0$ = area $0P_0AQ_0$ With a decrease in price from P_0 to P_1: New TR = $P_1 \times Q_1$ = area $0P_1BQ_1$ Loss in TR = area C Gain in TR = area E Since area E > area C, TR increases with the decrease in price

PED guiding producer's non-price strategy—PED is useful for producers to measure the effectiveness of their non-price strategies. Non-price strategies such as advertising are meant to make a firm's product appear different from other firms' products so that it is less substitutable. If the producer's non-price strategies are effective, the demand of their good will become more price inelastic. Producers would want the demand of their goods and services to be as price inelastic as possible as it would allow them to be able to increase the price. Therefore, observing the change in PED post-advertising will allow the producer to determine if the strategy is effective. This allows the firm to decide whether to continue advertising or try other strategies instead.

PED guiding government's policy decisions—PED is useful for governments in making policy decisions. For example, if a government is trying to raise revenue by imposing a tax, knowledge of PED will be helpful in determining which goods to impose the tax on, such that the tax revenue generated is greatest. If the demand for a good is price inelastic, when a tax shifts the supply leftwards and increases the price of the good, the fall in quantity demanded would be less than proportionate. Hence, the quantity traded would remain fairly high. In that case, the tax revenue collected would be larger since it will be collected for a fairly high quantity of goods. This is illustrated in the following diagram.

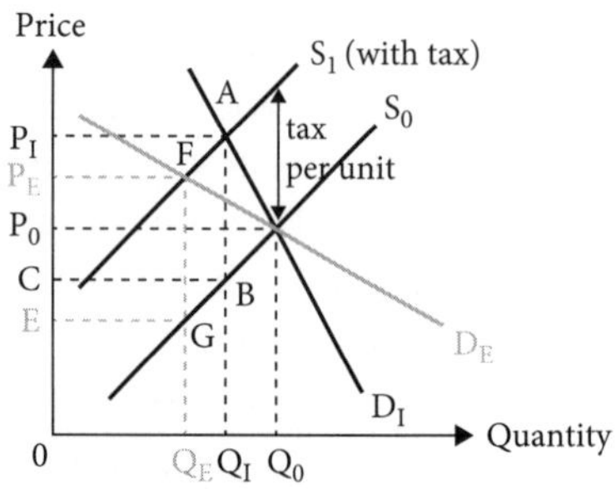

If demand for the good is price inelastic (D_I) Original equilibrium: P_0 and Q_0 Imposition of tax would reduce supply from S_0 to S_1 New equilibrium: P_I and Q_I Tax per unit = AB Tax revenue collected = tax per unit × quantity = AB × $0Q_I$ (or CB) = area CP_IAB	If demand for the good is price elastic (D_E) Original equilibrium: P_0 and Q_0 Imposition of tax would reduce supply from S_0 to S_1 New equilibrium: P_E and Q_E Tax per unit = FG Tax revenue collected = tax per unit × quantity = FG × $0Q_E$ (or EG) = area EP_EFG

Area CP_IAB is larger than area EP_EFG because CP_I and EP_E both represent the tax per unit and are therefore, equal in length, but CB is clearly longer than EG.

The government should levy the tax on goods with price inelastic demands if it wishes to collect more tax revenue.

2.3.2 Cross elasticity of demand (H2 ONLY)

Definition(s):

Cross elasticity of demand (XED) measures the responsiveness of demand (or quantity demanded) of the good to a change in the price of another good, ceteris paribus.

In the definition, both the terms "demand" and "quantity demanded" are allowed because a change in demand means a change in quantity demanded at all prices.

In actuality, since the price of another good is a non-price determinant that causes the demand to change (and the demand curve to shift), what XED measures is how much the demand of a good changes (how much the demand curve shifts) when the price of another good changes.

Formula

$$XED = \frac{\text{\% change in Qd of good A}}{\text{\% change in price of good B}}$$

Sign of the numerical value

XED can be either positive or negative.

A positive XED value would mean that the two goods (A and B) are substitutes. As we learnt in the section on non-price determinants of demand, when the price of a substitute (good B) decreases (a negative % change), the demand for good A will also decrease (also a negative % change). This will give rise to a positive XED since a negative number divided by a negative number gives us a positive value. If the price of good B increases, the demand for good A would increase, which would still result in a positive value of the XED. This is why we say that the demand for a good and the price of its substitute have a positive relationship.

A negative XED value would mean that the two goods (A and B) are complements. As we learnt in the section on non-price determinants of demand, when the price of a complement (good B) decreases (a negative % change), the demand for good A will increase (a positive % change). This will give rise to a negative XED since a positive number divided by a negative number gives us a negative value. If the price of good B increases, the demand for good A would decrease, which would still result in a negative value of XED. This is why we say that the demand for a good and the price of its substitute have a negative relationship.

Magnitude of the numerical value

The magnitude of the numerical value of XED (denoted by |XED|) shows the closeness in relationship of the two goods. The larger the value, the more the demand for a good changes in response to a change in the price of another good. The way to interpret the values is shown in the table below.

<table>
<tr><th>Sign and magnitude of XED</th><th>Description</th><th>Interpretation</th><th>Graph for increase in price of good B</th><th>Graph for decrease in price of good B</th></tr>
<tr><td>Positive and |XED| > 1

OR

XED > 1</td><td>Demand of good A is cross elastic with respect to the price of good B</td><td>Good A and B are close substitutes.

An increase (decrease) in the price of good B causes a more than proportionate increase (decrease) in the demand for good A.</td><td>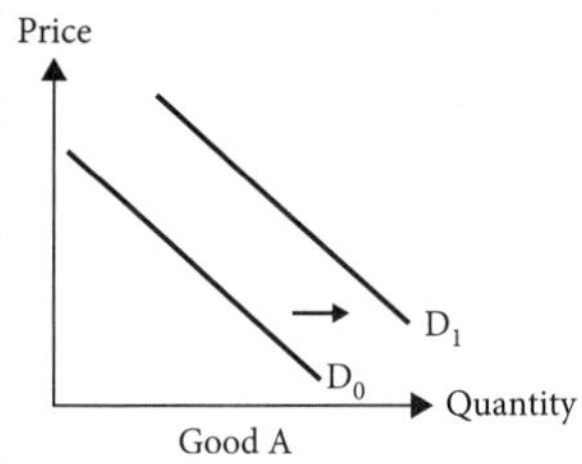
</td><td>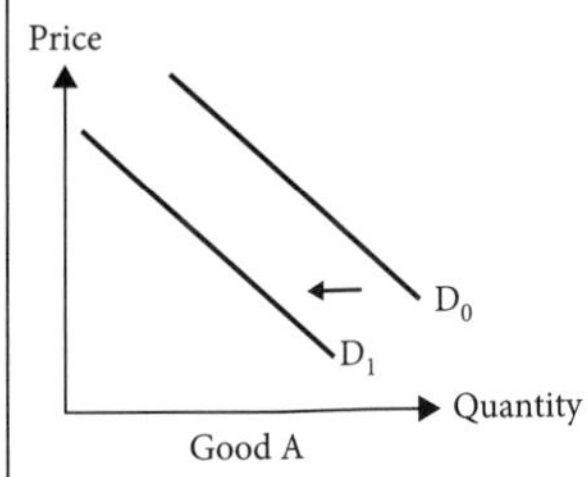
</td></tr>
<tr><td>Positive and |XED| < 1

OR

0 < XED < 1</td><td>Demand of good A is cross inelastic with respect to the price of good B</td><td>Good A and B are weak substitutes.

An increase (decrease) in the price of good B causes a less than proportionate increase (decrease) in the demand for good A.</td><td>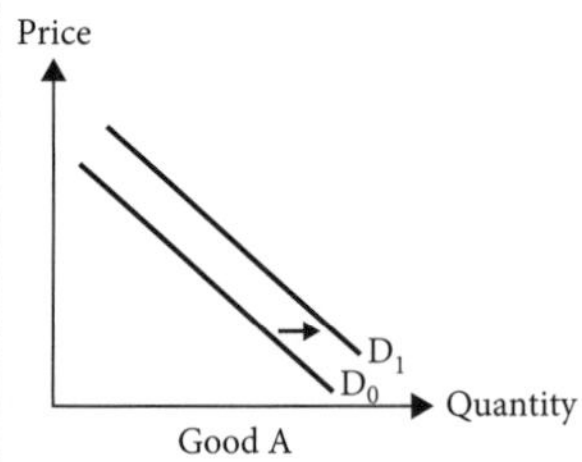
</td><td>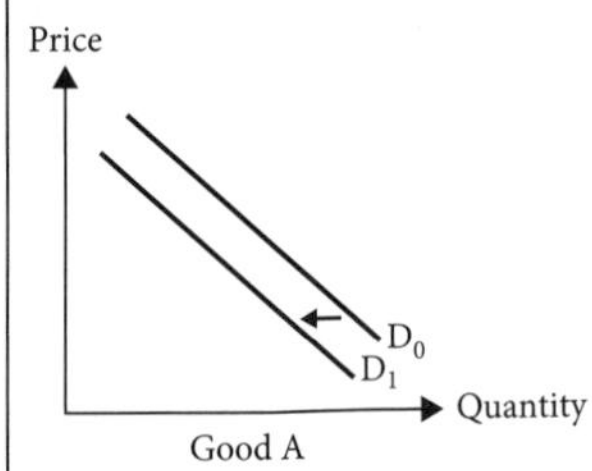
</td></tr>
<tr><td>|XED| = 0

OR

XED = 0</td><td>Demand of good A is perfectly cross inelastic with respect to the price of good B</td><td>Good A and B are unrelated.

A change in the price of good B does not cause any change in the demand for good A.</td><td>No change in demand of good A</td><td>No change in demand of good A</td></tr>
<tr><td>Negative and |XED| < 1

OR

−1 < XED < 0</td><td>Demand of good A is cross inelastic with respect to the price of good B</td><td>Good A and B are weak complements.

An increase (decrease) in the price of good B causes a less than proportionate decrease (increase) in the demand for good A.</td><td>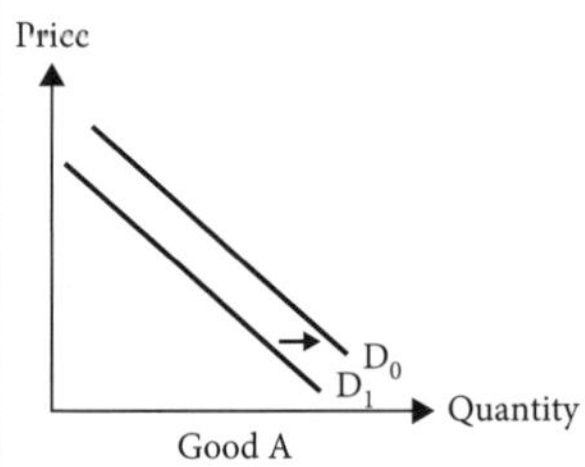
</td><td>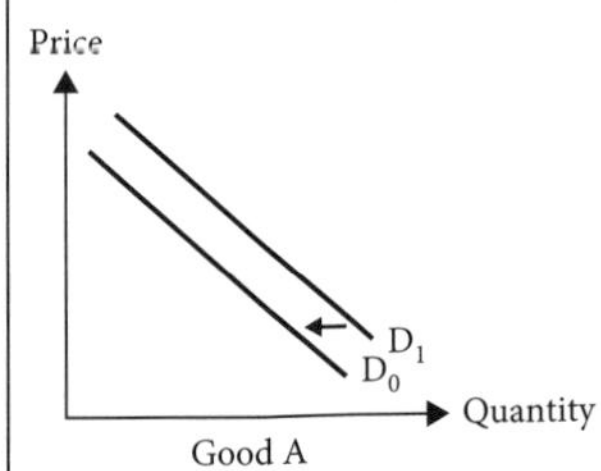
</td></tr>
<tr><td>Negative and |XED| > 1

OR

XED < −1</td><td>Demand of good A is cross elastic with respect to the price of good B</td><td>Good A and B are close complements.

An increase (decrease) in the price of good B causes a more than proportionate decrease (increase) in the demand for good A.</td><td>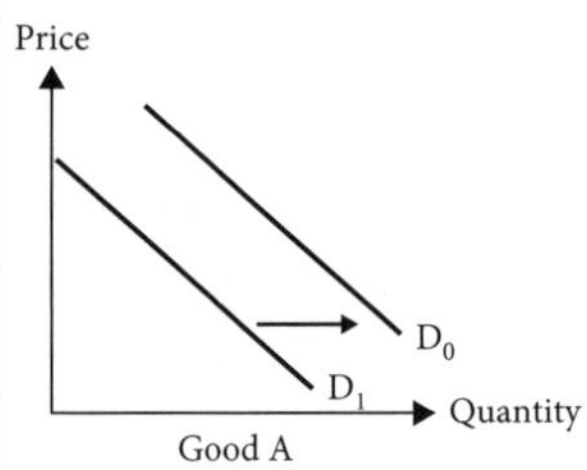
</td><td>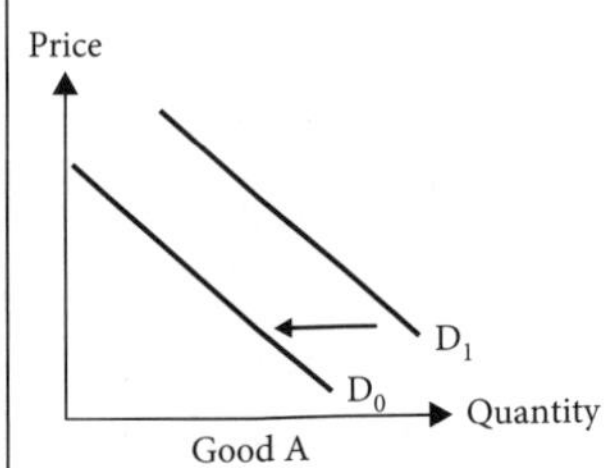
</td></tr>
</table>

Determinant of XED

There is only one determinant of XED—the closeness of the two goods (as substitutes or complements).

Closeness of the two goods as substitutes—How well the two goods can be used as substitutes for each other will determine the XED value. The closer the two goods are, the easier consumers can switch from one good to another, the larger the |XED| is.

For example, mineral water and Coca Cola are both substitutes for Pepsi. However, Coca Cola is a close substitute to Pepsi while mineral water is a poor substitute for Pepsi. Therefore, if the price of mineral water decreases by 10%, the demand for Pepsi will decrease less than proportionately (fall by less than 10%), whereas if the price of Coca Cola decreases by 10%, the demand for Pepsi would decrease more than proportionately (fall by more than 10%).

Closeness of the two goods as complements—How well the two goods complement each other will determine the XED value. The closer the two goods are as complements, the more consumers will consume them together, the larger the |XED| is.

For example, popcorn and sandwiches are both complements to movie tickets. However, popcorn is a close complement to movie tickets, whereas sandwiches are a weak complement to movie tickets. Therefore, if the price of sandwiches decreases by 10%, the demand for movie tickets will increase less than proportionately (rise by less than 10%) whereas if the price of popcorn decreases by 10%, the demand for movie tickets would increase more than proportionately (rise by more than 10%).

Application of XED

XED is applied by producers to guide their pricing and non-price decisions, and by governments to guide their policy decisions.

XED guiding producers' output decisions—XED is useful to producers for anticipating the change in demand of their good when prices of related goods change. Producers can then modify their production level and allocate their resources more efficiently. For example, when the price of a close substitute decreases, a producer would anticipate a large decrease in the demand of its good. The producer can then divert its factors of production to the production of other goods to prevent wastage of resources. On the other hand, when the price of a close complement decreases, the producer would anticipate a large increase in the demand of their good. Therefore, producers can divert their factors of production from other productions to the production of the good with the anticipated increase in demand.

XED guiding producers' non-price strategy (bundled deals)—XED is useful for producers for their non-pricing strategies in working with producers of complements. Producers can work together with producers of close complements to provide bundled goods and services at a lower price. For example, airlines usually collaborate with producers of complements such as travel insurance, hotels, and transports. The reduced price of the bundle can be analysed in two parts. Part of the reduced price of the bundle would be the reduction in the price of the good itself and the other part of the reduced price of the bundle is the reduction in price of the complement. For example, suppose the usual price of a return flight to Kuala Lumpur (KL) is $100 and the usual price of a hotel room in KL is $80 for two nights. A bundled deal might be one where a return flight to KL and two nights' stay in the hotel go for a price of $150. Of this $150, perhaps $90 goes to the airline and $60 goes to the hotel. Effectively, the airline reduced its price by $10 and the hotel reduced its price (for two nights' stay) by $20. From the airline's point of view, the reduction in price by the hotel has a positive effect on its demand and vice versa. This effect would be large if the complements are close. In that case, the bundled deal creates a win-win for both the airline and the hotel. XED is useful to the firm in identifying the close complements.

XED guiding producers' non-price strategy (selection of strategies)—XED is useful to producers for measuring the effectiveness of their non-pricing strategies such advertising to make their products seem different from other firms'. If the producers' non-pricing strategies are effective, the XED of their good with respect to the price of their substitutes should decrease (much like how the PED of the good should decrease). A lower XED means that the producer's good is deemed less substitutable and the producer will be less affected when producers of substitutes engage in price competition by decreasing their prices or offering discounts. Knowing the change in the XED after the producer has carried out its strategies enables the firm to determine if its strategy is working and if it isn't, to change it.

XED guiding governments' policy decisions—A government can use the concept of XED to formulate more policy options. Suppose the US government wants to discourage the purchase of guns. However, intervening directly in the gun market is too politically sensitive. Hence, it can try to discourage the purchase of guns by subsidising substitutes to guns (e.g., other thrill-seeking equipment) to reduce their price, or taxing complements to guns (e.g., bullets) to increase their price. These would then reduce the demand for guns. XED values are useful to the US government in determining which other markets to intervene in (these should be the closest substitutes and complements) to create the largest effect in the gun market.

2.3.3 Income elasticity of demand (H2 ONLY)

Definition(s):

Income elasticity of demand (YED) measures the responsiveness of demand (or quantity demanded) of the good to a change in income of consumers, ceteris paribus.

In the definition, both the terms "demand" and "quantity demanded" are allowed because a change in demand means a change in quantity demanded at all prices.

In actuality, since the income of consumers is a non-price determinant that causes the demand to change (and the demand curve to shift), what YED measures is how much the demand of a good changes (how much the demand curve shifts) when income changes.

Formula

$$YED = \frac{\%\ \text{change in } Qd \text{ of good A}}{\%\ \text{change in Y}}$$

Sign of the numerical value

YED can be either positive or negative.

A positive YED value would mean that the good is a normal good. As we learnt in the section on non-price determinants of demand, when income increases (a positive % change), the demand for normal goods would also increase (also a positive % change). This will give rise to a positive YED since a positive number divided by a positive number gives us a positive value. If income decreases, the demand for normal goods would also decrease, which would still result in a positive value of the YED.

A negative YED value would mean that the good is an inferior good. As we learnt in the section on non-price determinants of demand, when income increases (a positive % change), the demand for inferior goods would decrease (a negative % change). This will give rise to a negative YED since a negative number divided by a positive number gives us a negative value. If income decreases, the demand for inferior goods would increase, which would still result in a negative value of the YED.

Magnitude of the numerical value

The magnitude of the numerical value of YED shows how much the demand of the good would change in response to a change in income. The way to interpret the values is shown in the table below.

Definition(s):

Inferior goods are goods that will experience a decrease in demand when consumers' income increases and vice versa.

Normal good are goods that will experience an increase in demand when consumers' income increases and vice versa.

Necessities are goods that will experience a less than proportionate increase in demand when consumers' income increases and vice versa.

Luxury good: Luxury goods are goods that will experience a more than proportionate increase in demand when consumers' income increases and vice versa.

Sign and magnitude of YED	Description	Interpretation	Graph for increase in income	Graph for decrease in income
Positive and |YED| > 1 OR YED > 1	Demand of good A is income elastic	Good A is a luxury good. An increase (decrease) in income causes a more than proportionate increase (decrease) in the demand for good A.	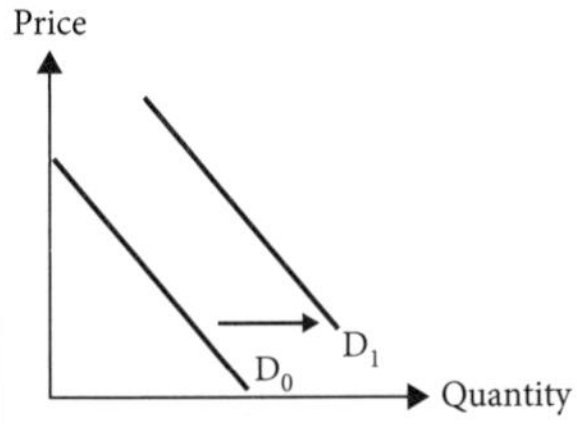	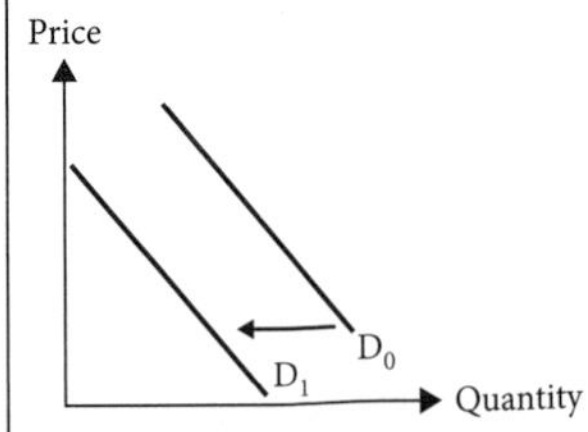
Positive and |YED| < 1 OR 0 < YED < 1	Demand of good A is income inelastic	Good A is a necessity. An increase (decrease) in income causes a less than proportionate increase (decrease) in the demand for good A.	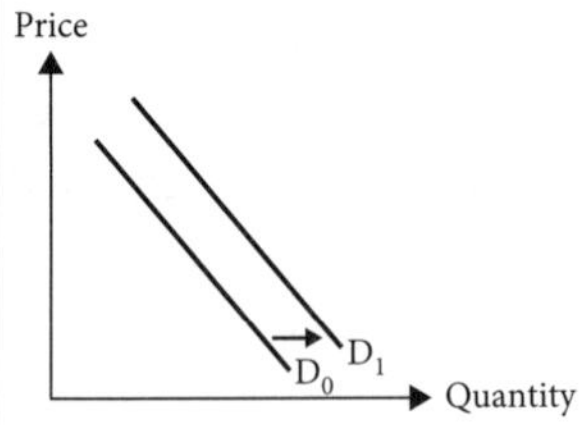	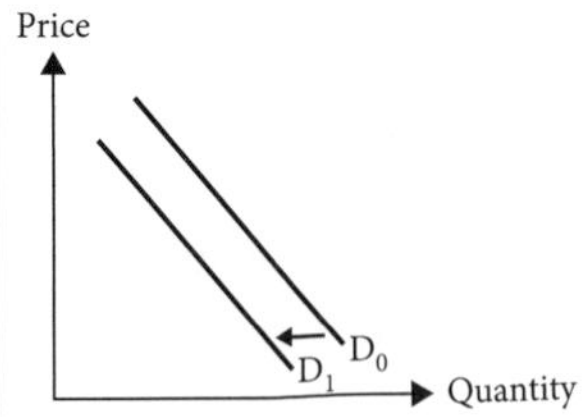
Negative and |YED| < 1 OR −1 < YED < 0	Demand of good A is income inelastic	Good A is a slightly inferior good.[21] An increase (decrease) in income causes a less than proportionate decrease (increase) in the demand for good A.	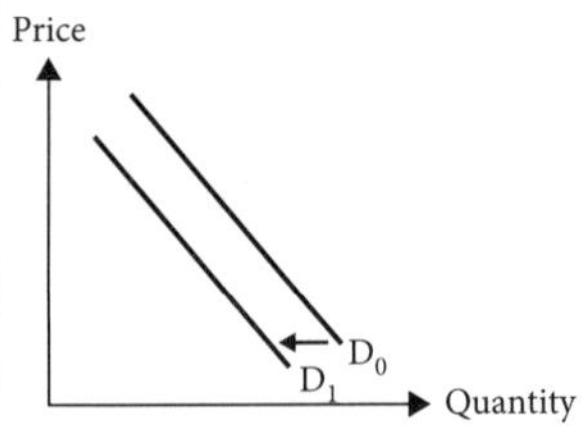	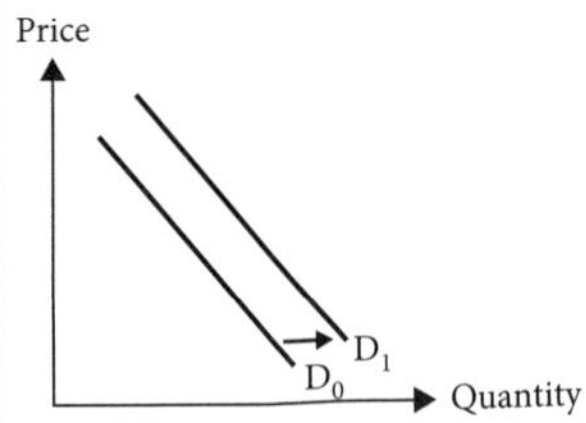
Negative and |YED| > 1 OR YED < −1	Demand of good A is income elastic	Good A is a very inferior good.[21] An increase (decrease) in income causes a more than proportionate decrease (increase) in the demand for good A.	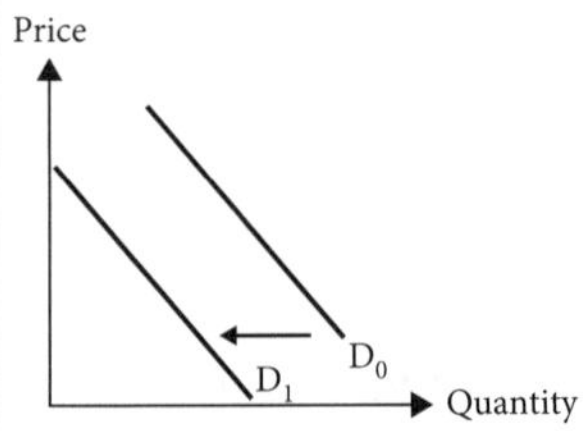	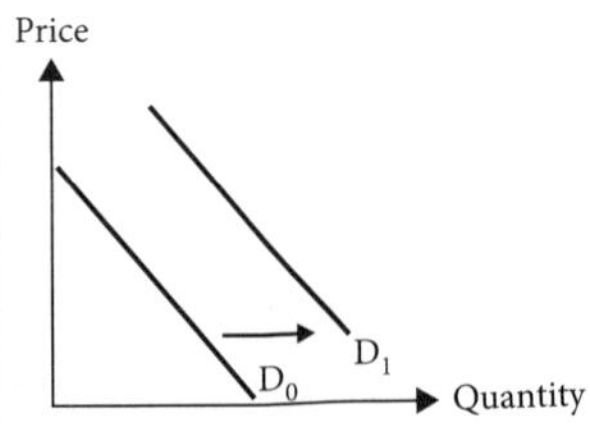

21 In the A Level syllabus, we do not distinguish between slightly inferior (1 < YED < 0) and very inferior (YED < 1) goods. The difference is just drawn here for deeper understanding. In the syllabus, it is sufficient to know that inferior goods have negative YED.

Determinants of YED

The determinants of YED are:

- Consumers' income level
- Nature of goods

Consumers' income level—Whether a good is an inferior, normal, or luxurious good is usually determined by the level of income of consumers. For most goods and services, as consumers' income level increases, the same good will change from being a luxury good to a necessity and eventually, an inferior good.

For example, in the context of Singapore, feature phones (i.e., "non-smart" phones) were a luxury good when incomes were low, became a necessity when incomes increased, and then became inferior goods when incomes increased even further.

Thus, the context of the market determines whether the good is a luxury good, necessity, or inferior good. In the context of a market for the good in which the consumers have high incomes, the good is more likely to be an inferior good and the demand would fall with an increase in income (YED < 0). In the context where the consumers have low incomes, the good is more likely to be a luxury good and the demand would rise more than proportionately when there is an increase in income (YED > 1).

Nature of goods—Some goods are necessities by nature. Examples include staple food items like rice and pasta. For such items, the nature of the good is such that they are priorities that have to be purchased first and so when incomes fall, the demand for them will not fall by much (i.e., demand falls less than proportionately when income falls). Additionally, their nature is also one where, beyond a certain amount needed for survival, consumers do not want to buy much more of them. So, when incomes increase, their demand increases just by a little (i.e., when incomes increase, their demand rises less than proportionately). This is in contrast to movies and private cars which are non-necessities by nature. When income decreases, spending on these goods would be cut first (i.e., demand falls more than proportionately to a fall in income) and when income increases, most of the increase in income would be spent on these goods (i.e., demand rises more than proportionately to an increase in income).

Application of income elasticity of demand (YED)

YED guiding producers' output decisions—YED is useful for producers to anticipate the change in demand of their good when consumers' incomes change. Producers can then modify their production levels and allocate their resources more efficiently. For example, when consumers' incomes decrease, a producer of luxury goods would anticipate a large decrease in the demand of their good. The producer can divert its factors of production to the production of other goods to prevent wastage of resources. On the other hand, a producer of inferior goods would anticipate an increase in the demand of its good. Therefore, the producer of inferior goods could divert its factors of production from the production of other goods to the production of inferior goods.

YED guiding producers' non-price strategy (diversification)—YED is useful for producers for their non-pricing strategy of diversification. To reduce the risk of changing economic conditions in the form of changes in consumers' income affecting the demand for a producer's goods, producers can diversify their product offerings to offer a wider range of goods that include inferior goods, necessities, and luxury goods with different YED values. For example, a shampoo firm could produce a line of luxury shampoos (luxury goods), a line of "everyday use" shampoos (necessities), and a line of "no-frills" basic shampoos (inferior goods). This is so that producers can spread or reduce their risks associated with changes in economic condition affecting consumers' income. With this diversification, whether the economy is experiencing economic growth (increase in incomes) or a recession (decrease in income), at least one of their goods will enjoy an increase in demand to offset the decrease in demand for the other two. The producer could also allocate their resources between the various types of goods during the different economic condition.

YED guiding producers' non-price strategy (marketing)—YED is also useful to producers in terms of planning their non-pricing strategy in the form of marketing their goods and services. If producers are expecting the economic conditions to improve and consumers' income to increase, they could launch a marketing campaign to make their goods and services appear more luxurious. If they are successful and consumers perceive their goods and services as luxury goods, the demand for their goods and services would increase more than proportionately with the increase in consumers' income. On the other hand, if a recession is expected where consumers' incomes are likely to decrease, producers could do the opposite and plan a marketing campaign to make their goods and services less luxurious (and more for everyday use) to reduce the decrease in demand for their goods and services. Changes in YED due to the marketing campaigns can be used to measure the success of these strategies.

2.3.4 Price elasticity of supply

> *Definition(s):*
>
> ***Price elasticity of supply (PES)*** *measures the responsiveness of the quantity supplied of a good to a change in the price of the good itself, ceteris paribus.*

In simpler terms, the PES measures how much quantity supplied will change when price of the good itself changes.

Formula

$$PES = \frac{\%\text{ change in } Qs \text{ of good } A}{\%\text{ change in price of good } A}$$

Sign of the numerical value

PES always has a positive numerical value due to the law of supply which states that the price of a good and its quantity supplied must have a direct relationship. As such, an increase in the price of a good (a positive % change) would cause an increase in the quantity supplied of a good (also a positive % change). This would give rise to a positive PES value as a positive number divided by a positive number results in a positive number. If the price of the good decreases, the quantity supplied would decrease, which would still result in a positive value of the PES.

Magnitude of the numerical value

The magnitude of the numerical value of PES (denoted by |PES|) can be classified into "between 0 and 1", "1", or "more than 1" as well as two extreme cases of |PES| = 0 and |PES| = infinity (denoted by the symbol "∞"). The way to interpret these values is shown in the table below:

PES value	Graph[22]	Description	Interpretation
|PES| = 0 OR PES = 0	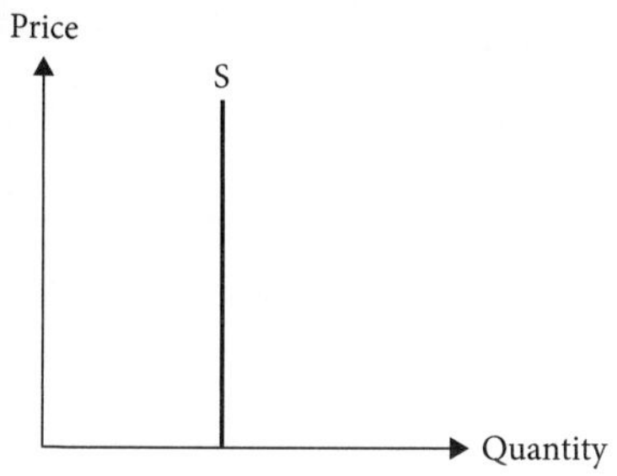	Supply is perfectly price inelastic	A change in price causes no change in quantity supplied of the good. (e.g., a 10% increase in price causes a 0% increase in quantity supplied of the good) Producers are willing and able to produce a fixed quantity of the good at any price.
0 < |PES| < 1 OR 0 < PES < 1	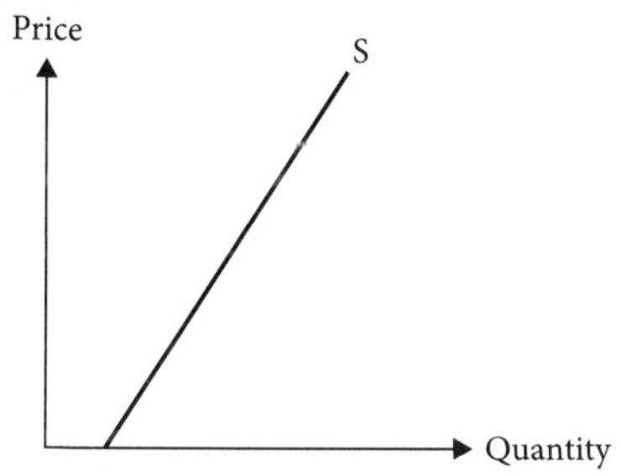 Note that the supply curve will intersect the horizontal axis (quantity) of the market diagram.[23]	Supply is price inelastic	A change in price causes a less than proportionate change in quantity supplied of the good. (e.g., a 10% increase in price causes a 5% increase in quantity supplied of the good)
|PES| = 1 OR PES = 1	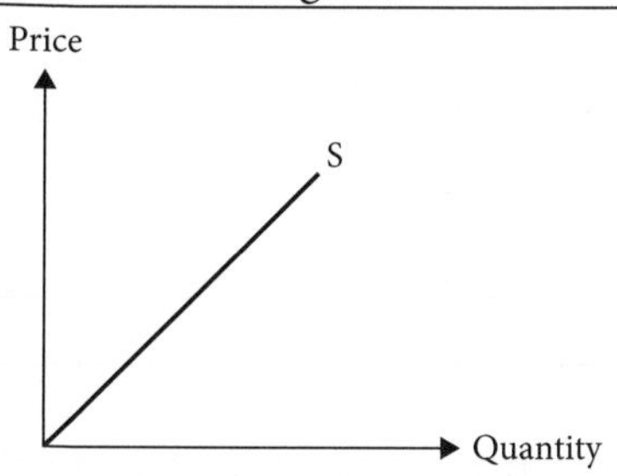 Note that the supply curve will pass through the origin of the market diagram.	Supply is unitary price elastic	A change in price causes an exactly proportionate change in quantity supplied of the good. (e.g., a 10% increase in price causes a 10% increase in quantity supplied of the good)

22 Technically, the value of PES could vary along a straight line supply curve. Annex 2.2 addresses this issue.

23 It's a mathematical result. Refer to Annex 2.3 for details of how supply curves of different PES will intersect the horizontal and vertical axes differently.

PES value	Graph[22]	Description	Interpretation
|PES| > 1 OR PES > 1	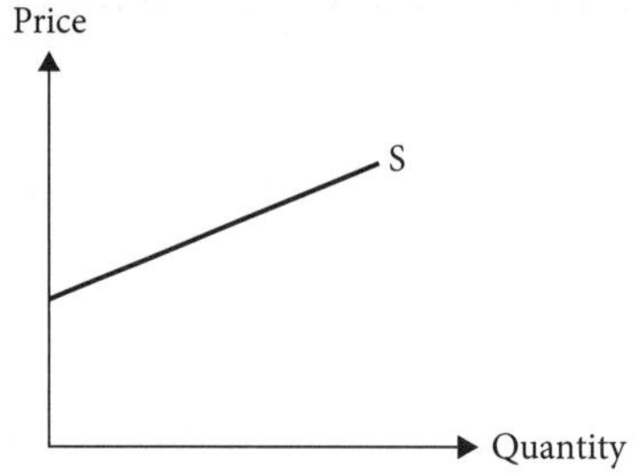 Note that the supply curve will intersect the vertical axis (price) of the market diagram	Supply is price elastic	A change in price causes a more than proportionate change in quantity supplied of the good. (e.g., a 10% increase in price causes a 15% increase in quantity supplied of the good)
|PES| = ∞ OR PES = ∞	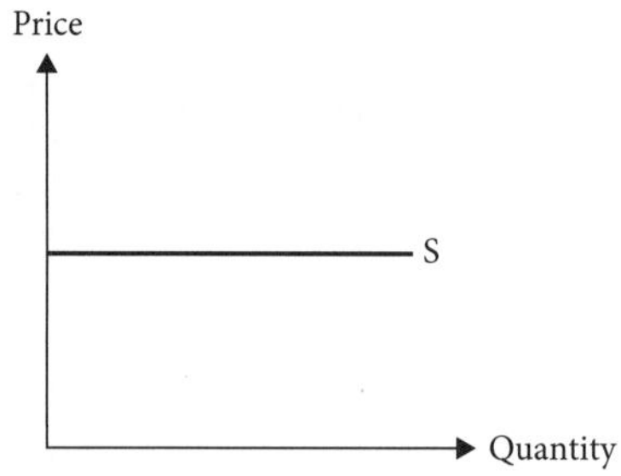 	Supply is perfectly price elastic	A change in price causes an infinite change in quantity supplied of the good. (e.g., a 10% increase in price causes quantity supplied of the good to rise from zero to infinity) Producers are willing and able to produce any amount of good at the specific price.

Determinants of PES

Whether the supply of a good is price elastic or price inelastic is determined by the following determinants:

- Level of stocks or inventories
- Availability and mobility of factors of production
- Length and complexity of the production process
- Nature of the good
- Time period

Level of stocks or inventories—Stocks or inventories refer to the unsold products that producers have that are waiting to be sold. For example, the shoes that are kept in the storeroom of a shoe shop are its stocks. The higher the level of stocks and inventories the producers have, the more price elastic the supply will be as producers can easily increase quantity supplied by bringing out unsold stock when the price of the good increases. Conversely, the lower the level of stocks and inventories, the more price inelastic the supply.

Availability and mobility of factors of production—The greater the availability of factors of production, the more price elastic the supply will be as producers find it easier to employ factors of production to increase output when the price of the good increases. For example, if farmers can easily employ more farmhands, they can harvest their crops more quickly to bring to the market when the price of their crops increases. Thus, the quantity supplied in the market would be more responsive to an increase in price.

Additionally, the more mobile the factors of production, the more price elastic the supply will be. Mobility of factors of production refers to the ease with which factors of production can be switched to producing other goods. So, the higher the mobility, the easier factors of production that were used to produced other goods can be switched to producing the good whose price increased, the more price elastic the supply would be. Conversely, the lower the availability and mobility of factors of production, the more price inelastic the supply would be.

Length and complexity of the production process—The shorter the length of the production process, the more price elastic the supply will be as producers will find it easier to increase output when the price of the good increases. For example, rice has a longer production process (months) compared to manufacturing of t-shirts (minutes). Thus, if both the prices of rice and t-shirts increase, producers of t-shirts can almost immediately increase the quantity supplied while rice farmers would need to wait for months before they can increase the quantity supplied. Hence, the supply of t-shirts would be more price elastic compared to the supply of rice.

Related to the length of production process, the less complex the production process is, the more price elastic the supply will be. This is because less complex production processes tend to take shorter time. For example, t-shirts can be manufactured in minutes because the production process is not complex but aeroplanes take months to manufacture because the production process is more complex. Hence, the lower the complexity, the shorter the length of the production process, the more price elastic the supply. Conversely, the longer and more complex the production process, the more price inelastic the supply.

Nature of the good—The nature of a good also affects the PES through affecting the previous factors. For example, the nature of the good can affect the level of stocks. The easier a good can be stored or the longer a good can be stored, the more producers are able to stockpile them in anticipation of future increase in price or store them if price decreases, the more price elastic the supply. For example, cloth and bricks can be easily stored for long periods of time while fresh produce cannot be. Hence, the level of stocks of cloth and bricks will be higher than that of fresh produce. When prices of cloth and bricks increase, producers can easily increase the quantity supplied using their existing stocks. However, for fresh produce, when the price increases, producers cannot easily increase the quantity supplied as there are no/very little existing stocks.

Time period—Similar to PED, supply for all goods and services will become more price elastic as the time period increases. This is because producers will have more time to build up stocks and inventories and shorten the production process.

Application of PES

PES guiding producers' decisions—PES is useful for producers as it allows the producers to anticipate the extent to which prices will change in the market.[24] This will then help them make decisions regarding whether they should enter contracts to fix the prices of their goods in the next period to reduce the variability in the prices they receive.

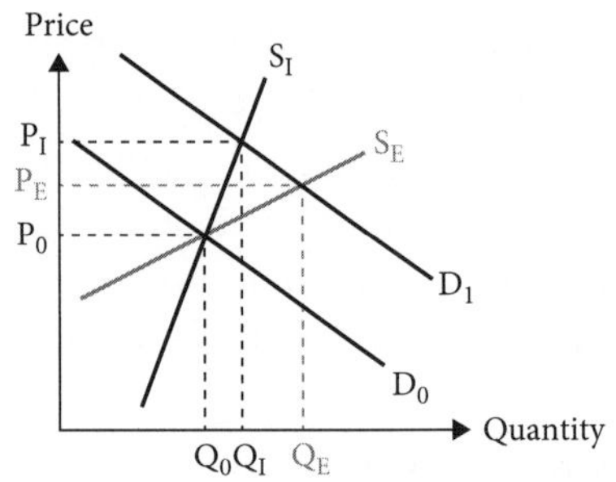

If market supply of the good is price inelastic (S_I) Original equilibrium: P_0 and Q_0 With increase in demand from D_0 to D_1 New equilibrium: P_I and Q_I Increase in price = P_0P_I	If market supply of the good is price elastic (S_E) Original equilibrium: P_0 and Q_0 With increase in demand from D_0 to D_1 New equilibrium: P_E and Q_E Increase in price = P_0P_E
Increase in price is larger when the market supply is price inelastic. If producers know that the market supply is price inelastic (e.g., for agricultural products), they should enter contracts to fix the prices that they receive in the future.	

PES guiding government's policy decision—PES is useful for governments in making policy decisions. For example, if a government is trying to raise revenue by imposing a tax, knowledge of PES will be helpful in determining which goods to impose the tax on, such that the tax revenue generated is greatest. If the supply of a good is price inelastic, when a tax is imposed, the eventual reduction in the equilibrium quantity would be limited, leaving a fairly high equilibrium quantity. In that case, the tax revenue collected would be larger since it will be collected for a fairly high quantity of goods. This is illustrated in the diagram in the following table.

24 This will be revisited later in this chapter too.

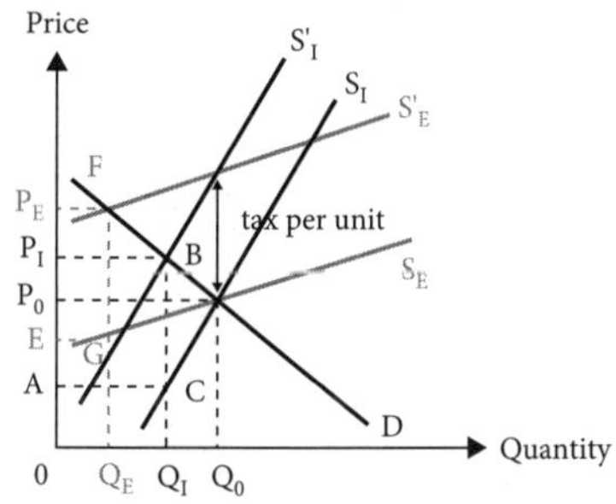

If supply for the good is price inelastic (S_I)	If supply for the good is price elastic (S_E)
Original equilibrium: P_0 and Q_0	Original equilibrium: P_0 and Q_0
Imposition of tax would reduce supply from S_I to S_I'	Imposition of tax would reduce supply from S_E to S_E'
New equilibrium: P_I and Q_I	New equilibrium: P_E and Q_E
Tax per unit = BC	Tax per unit = FG
Tax revenue collected = tax per unit × quantity = BC × $0Q_I$ (or AC) = area AP_IBC	Tax revenue collected = tax per unit × quantity = FG × $0Q_E$ (or EG) = area EP_EFG

Area AP_IBC is larger than area EP_EFG because AP_I and EP_E both represent the tax per unit and are therefore, equal in length, but AC is clearly longer than EG.

The government should levy the tax on goods with price inelastic supplies if it wishes to collect more tax revenue.

2.4 Application of Demand and Supply: Impact of Market Outcomes on Consumers and Producers

Having learnt how demand and supply determine price and quantity, how changes in demand and supply change price and quantity, and how elasticity concepts explain the extent of the changes, we now link them all back to the effects on consumers and producers.

2.4.1 Consumer expenditure and producer revenue

Using the elasticity concepts, we can study how changes in the market that change the market price and quantity can affect consumer expenditure and producer revenue. Consumer expenditure on a good is the total amount that all consumers in the market spend on the good. It will be numerically equal to producer revenue, which is the total amount that all producers in the market receive for the good. The other term for producer revenue is total revenue, which is equal to the market price multiplied by the market quantity. We will look at four scenarios where the elasticity concepts can be used to analyse the change in consumer expenditure/producer revenue in the market, and then look at the limitations of using elasticity concepts in general.

Scenario where PED can be used to analyse the change in consumer expenditure/producer revenue (change in supply)

PED can be used to analyse the change in consumer expenditure/producer revenue through analysing the extent of changes in price and quantity when the supply of the good changes.

- If supply of the good increases (S_0 to S_1 below):

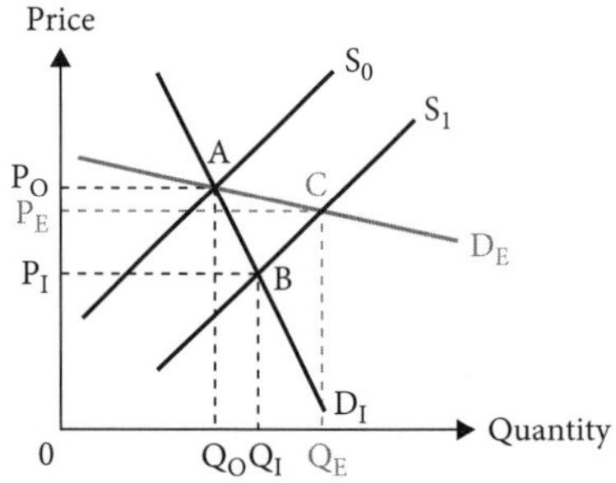

If demand is price inelastic (D_I), equilibrium shifts from P_0 and Q_0 to P_I and Q_I.	If demand is price elastic (D_E), equilibrium shifts from P_0 and Q_0 to P_E and Q_E.
Price falls from P_0 to P_I	Price falls from P_0 to P_E
Quantity rises from Q_0 to Q_I	Quantity rises from Q_0 to Q_E
Rise in quantity is less than proportionate to fall in price.	Rise in quantity is more than proportionate to fall in price.
Consumer expenditure/producer revenue falls from $0P_0AQ_0$ to $0P_IBQ_I$.	Consumer expenditure/producer revenue rises from $0P_0AQ_0$ to $0P_ECQ_E$.
Note also that the change in price will be large while the change in quantity will be small.	Note also that the change in price will be small while the change in quantity will be large.

- If supply of the good decreases (S_0 to S_1 below):

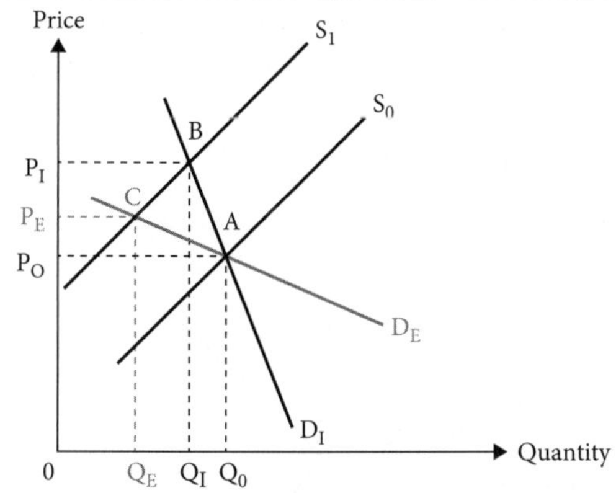

If demand is price inelastic (D_I), equilibrium shifts from P_0 and Q_0 to P_I and Q_I.	If demand is price elastic (D_E), equilibrium shifts from P_0 and Q_0 to P_E and Q_E.
Price rises from P_0 to P_I	Price rises from P_0 to P_E
Quantity falls from Q_0 to Q_I	Quantity falls from Q_0 to Q_E
Fall in quantity is less than proportionate to rise in price.	Fall in quantity is more than proportionate to rise in price.
Consumer expenditure/producer revenue rises from $0P_0AQ_0$ to $0P_IBQ_I$.	Consumer expenditure/producer revenue falls from $0P_0AQ_0$ to $0P_ECQ_E$.
Note also that the change in price will be large while the change in quantity will be small.	Note also that the change in price will be small while the change in quantity will be large.

Scenario where XED can be used to analyse the change in consumer expenditure/producer revenue (change in price of related good)

XED can be used to analyse the change in consumer expenditure/producer revenue through analysing the extent of changes in price and quantity when the price of a related good changes.

- If price of related good (good B) increases:

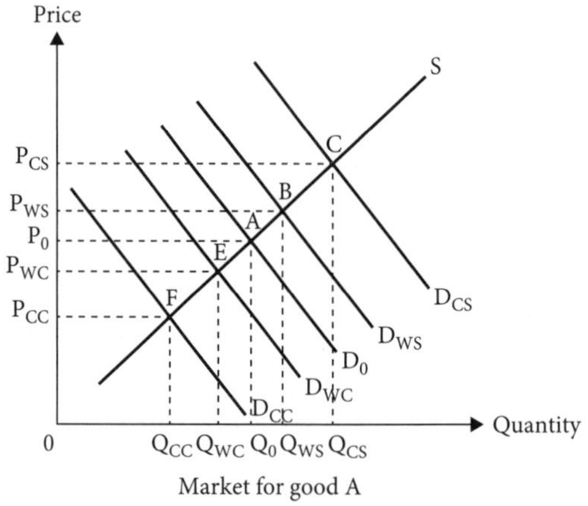

If goods A and B are close substitutes (XED > 1), demand for good A increases more than proportionately from D_0 to D_{CS}. Price rises from P_0 to P_{CS} Quantity rises from Q_0 to Q_{CS} Both price and quantity rise by a large extent due to the large increase in demand. Consumer expenditure/ Producer revenue rises by a large extent from $0P_0AQ_0$ to $0P_{CS}CQ_{CS}$.	If goods A and B are weak substitutes (0 < XED < 1), demand for good A increases less than proportionately from D_0 to D_{WS}. Price rises from P_0 to P_{WS} Quantity rises from Q_0 to Q_{WS} Both price and quantity rise by a small extent due to the small increase in demand. Consumer expenditure/ Producer revenue rises by a small extent from $0P_0AQ_0$ to $0P_{WS}BQ_{WS}$.	If goods A and B are weak complements (−1 < XED < 0), demand for good A decreases less than proportionately from D_0 to D_{WC}. Price falls from P_0 to P_{WC} Quantity falls from Q_0 to Q_{WC} Both price and quantity fall by a small extent due to the small decrease in demand. Consumer expenditure/ Producer revenue falls by a small extent from $0P_0AQ_0$ to $0P_{WC}EQ_{WC}$.	If goods A and B are strong complements (XED < −1), demand for good A decreases more than proportionately from D_0 to D_{CC}. Price falls from P_0 to P_{CC} Quantity falls from Q_0 to Q_{CC} Both price and quantity fall by a large extent due to the large decrease in demand. Consumer expenditure/ Producer revenue falls by a large extent from $0P_0AQ_0$ to $0P_{CC}FQ_{CC}$.

- If price of a related good (good B) decreases:

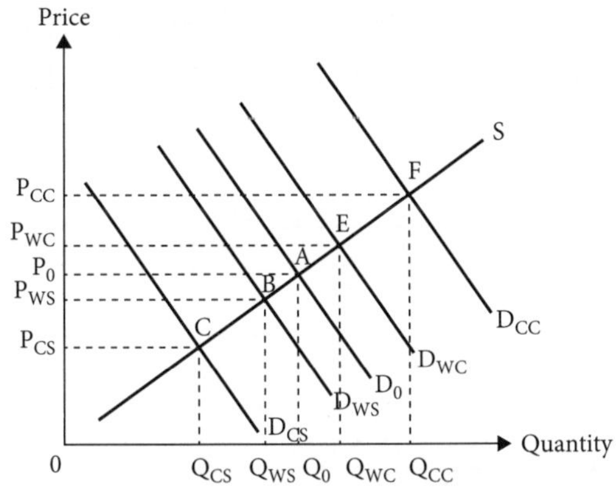

If goods A and B are close substitutes (XED > 1), demand for good A decreases more than proportionately from D_0 to D_{CS}.	If goods A and B are weak substitutes (0 < XED < 1), demand for good A decreases less than proportionately from D_0 to D_{WS}.	If goods A and B are weak complements (−1 < XED < 0), demand for good A increases less than proportionately from D_0 to D_{WC}.	If goods A and B are strong complements (XED < −1), demand for good A increases more than proportionately from D_0 to D_{CC}.
Price falls from P_0 to P_{CS}	Price falls from P_0 to P_{WS}	Price rises from P_0 to P_{WC}	Price rises from P_0 to P_{CC}
Quantity falls from Q_0 to Q_{CS}	Quantity falls from Q_0 to Q_{WS}	Quantity rises from Q_0 to Q_{WC}	Quantity rises from Q_0 to Q_{CC}
Both price and quantity fall by a large extent due to the large decrease in demand.	Both price and quantity fall by a small extent due to the small decrease in demand.	Both price and quantity rise by a small extent due to the small increase in demand.	Both price and quantity rise by a large extent due to the large increase in demand.
Consumer expenditure/ producer revenue falls by a large extent from $0P_0AQ_0$ to $0P_{CS}CQ_{CS}$.	Consumer expenditure/ producer revenue falls by a small extent from $0P_0AQ_0$ to $0P_{WS}BQ_{WS}$.	Consumer expenditure/ producer revenue rises by a small extent from $0P_0AQ_0$ to $0P_{WC}EQ_{WC}$.	Consumer expenditure/ producer revenue rises by a large extent from $0P_0AQ_0$ to $0P_{CC}FQ_{CC}$.

Scenario where YED can be used to analyse the change in consumer expenditure/producer revenue (change in income)

YED can be used to analyse the change in consumer expenditure/producer revenue through analysing the extent of changes in price and quantity when income changes.

- If income increases:

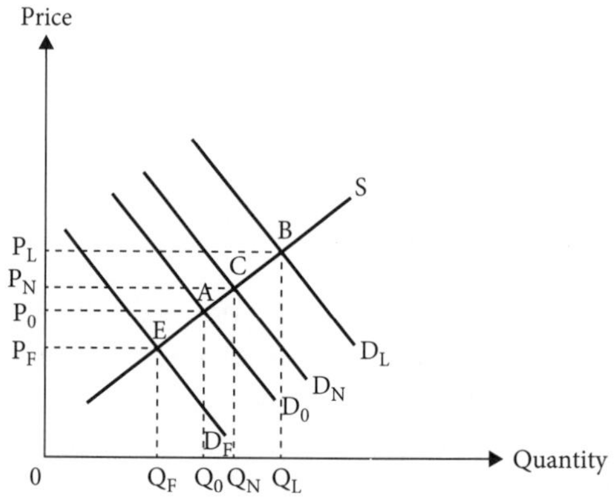

If the good is a luxury good (YED > 1), demand for the good increases more than proportionately from D_0 to D_L.	If the good is a necessity (0< YED < 1), demand for the good increases less than proportionately from D_0 to D_N.	If the good is an inferior good (YED < 0), demand for the good decreases from D_0 to D_F.
Price rises from P_0 to P_L	Price rises from P_0 to P_N	Price falls from P_0 to P_F
Quantity rises from Q_0 to Q_L	Quantity rises from Q_0 to Q_N	Quantity falls from Q_0 to Q_F
Both price and quantity rise by a large extent due to the large increase in demand.	Both price and quantity rise by a small extent due to the small increase in demand.	Both price and quantity fall due to the decrease in demand.
Consumer expenditure/ producer revenue rises by a large extent from $0P_0AQ_0$ to $0P_LBQ_L$.	Consumer expenditure/ producer revenue rises by a small extent from $0P_0AQ_0$ to $0P_NCQ_N$.	Consumer expenditure/ producer revenue falls from $0P_0AQ_0$ to $0P_FEQ_F$.

- If income decreases:

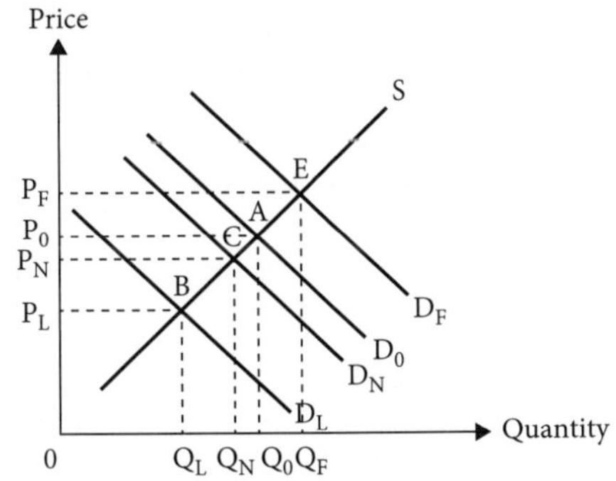

If the good is a luxury good (YED > 1), demand for the good decreases more than proportionately from D_0 to D_L.	If the good is a necessity (0< YED < 1), demand for the good decreases less than proportionately from D_0 to D_N.	If the good is an inferior good (YED < 0), demand for the good increases from D_0 to D_F.
Price falls from P_0 to P_L	Price falls from P_0 to P_N	Price rises from P_0 to P_F
Quantity falls from Q_0 to Q_L	Quantity falls from Q_0 to Q_N	Quantity rises from Q_0 to Q_F
Both price and quantity fall by a large extent due to the large decrease in demand.	Both price and quantity fall by a small extent due to the small decrease in demand.	Both price and quantity rise due to the increase in demand.
Consumer expenditure/ producer revenue falls by a large extent from $0P_0AQ_0$ to $0P_LBQ_L$.	Consumer expenditure/ producer revenue falls by a small extent from $0P_0AQ_0$ to $0P_NCQ_N$.	Consumer expenditure/ producer revenue rises from $0P_0AQ_0$ to $0P_FEQ_F$.

Scenario where PES can be used to analyse the change in consumer expenditure/producer revenue (change in demand)

PES can be used to analyse the change in consumer expenditure/producer revenue through analysing the extent of changes in price and quantity when the demand for the good changes.

- If demand for the good increases (D_0 to D_1 below):

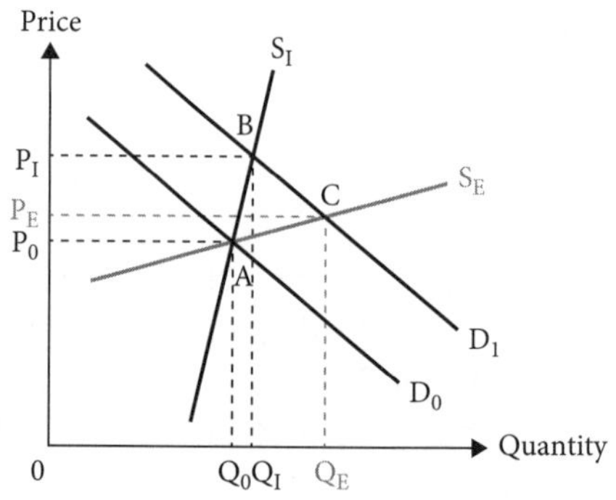

If supply is price inelastic (S_I), equilibrium shifts from P_0 and Q_0 to P_I and Q_I.	If supply is price elastic (S_E), equilibrium shifts from P_0 and Q_0 to P_E and Q_E.
Price rises from P_0 to P_I	Price rises from P_0 to P_E
Quantity rises from Q_0 to Q_I	Quantity rises from Q_0 to Q_E
Rise in quantity is less than proportionate to rise in price.	Rise in quantity is more than proportionate to rise in price.
Consumer expenditure/Producer revenue rises from $0P_0AQ_0$ to $0P_IBQ_I$.	Consumer expenditure/Producer revenue rises from $0P_0AQ_0$ to $0P_ECQ_E$.
Note also that the change in price will be large while the change in quantity will be small.	Note also that the change in price will be small while the change in quantity will be large.

Since consumer expenditure/producer revenue rises for both an inelastic and elastic supply, PES is not useful for analysing whether the consumer expenditure/producer revenue will increase (it will definitely increase when demand increases). Instead, PES is more useful for analysing the extent of the changes in price (large when supply is inelastic and small when supply is elastic) and quantity (small when supply is inelastic and large when supply is elastic) individually.

- If demand for the good decreases (D_0 to D_1 below):

<table>
<tr><td colspan="2">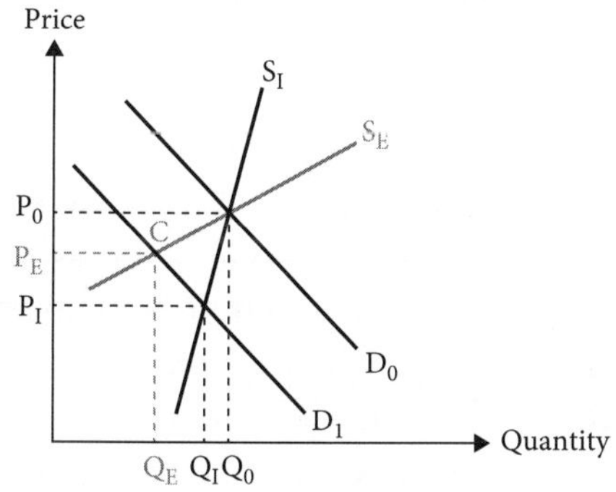
</td></tr>
<tr><td>If supply is price inelastic (S_I), equilibrium shifts from P_0 and Q_0 to P_I and Q_I.

Price falls from P_0 to P_I

Quantity falls from Q_0 to Q_I

Fall in quantity is less than proportionate to fall in price.

Consumer expenditure/producer revenue falls from $0P_0AQ_0$ to $0P_IBQ_I$.

Note also that the change in price will be large while the change in quantity will be small.</td><td>If supply is price elastic (S_E), equilibrium shifts from P_0 and Q_0 to P_E and Q_E.

Price falls from P_0 to P_E

Quantity falls from Q_0 to Q_E

Fall in quantity is more than proportionate to fall in price.

Consumer expenditure/producer revenue falls from $0P_0AQ_0$ to $0P_ECQ_{E.}$

Note also that the change in price will be small while the change in quantity will be large.</td></tr>
<tr><td colspan="2">Since consumer expenditure/producer revenue falls for both an inelastic and elastic supply, PES is not useful for analysing whether the consumer expenditure/producer revenue will increase (it will definitely decrease when demand decreases). Instead, PES is more useful for analysing the extent of the changes in price (large when supply is inelastic and small when supply is elastic) and quantity (small when supply is inelastic and large when supply is elastic) individually.</td></tr>
</table>

Limitations of using elasticity concepts

There are major limitations of using elasticity concepts to make decisions or analyse real-world changes.

First, the elasticity values for any good or service are difficult to compute. In the real world, what we can observe are the prices and quantities traded (and even such data may be hard to come by some times). However, we can never be really sure whether the changes we observe in the prices and quantities are purely due to a shift in demand or supply or a combination of the two. For example, if we observe that the price of chicken breast meat was $5 per kg in 2016 when 10,000 kg of it was traded, and that the price was $4 per kg in 2017 when 9,000 kg was traded, we can't tell whether only demand decreased, or both demand and supply decreased with supply decreasing to a smaller extent, or demand decreased and supply increased but to a smaller extent. As such, it is difficult to find out the demand and supply of goods and services and hence, obtain the elasticity values.

Second, even if we manage to obtain the elasticity values, these values are only applicable ceteris paribus. For example, if we obtain an accurate PED value of 1.3 for chicken breast meat in 2016, all we can say is that if the conditions of the chicken breast meat market are exactly the same as in 2016, then a 1% increase in the price of chicken breast meat would reduce its quantity demanded by 1.3%. However, it is unlikely that conditions in 2017 are exactly the same as 2016. Incomes may have changed across the year. Expectations of future incomes may have changed too. So could the cost of chicken feed. Hence, we see that because conditions are changing, we cannot easily apply the elasticity concepts.

The usefulness of elasticity concepts is very limited for exact analysis. However, they are still useful for broad understanding. For example, we may not know the exact PED and PES of agricultural products. But, we know that the big swings in the price of agricultural products is due to the PED and PES having low values.

2.4.2 Consumer and producer surplus

Thus far, we have studied the effects of changes in the market on consumers and producers in terms of changes in consumer expenditure/producer revenue. However, effects on consumers and producers can also be analysed in terms of changes in the consumer and producer surplus.

Consumer surplus

> *Definition(s):*
>
> **Consumer surplus** is the difference between how much consumers are willing and able to pay for a quantity of good or service and how much they actually pay.

For an individual consumer, the consumer surplus for a specific unit of good is the difference between how much that consumer is willing and able to pay for that unit of good or service and how much that consumer actually pays. It is the measure of the welfare of the consumer who paid a lower price for a good compared to the maximum amount he/she was willing and able to pay. For example, if John is willing and able to pay $10 for a notebook but buys the notebook at a price of $6, John's consumer surplus from buying that notebook is $4.

For the market, the total consumer surplus for a given quantity is the difference between the total amount that consumers were willing and able to pay for that quantity and the amount they actually pay for that quantity. It is a measure of the total welfare of consumers in the market. Since the total amount consumers are willing and able to pay is reflected in the demand curve, the consumer surplus is illustrated by the area below the demand curve and above the market price which shows how much they actually pay.

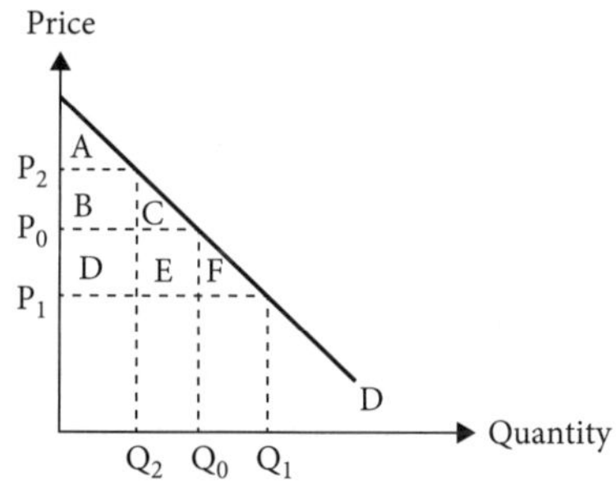

Figure 2.16: Consumer surplus at different prices.

With reference to Fig. 2.16, at price P_0, consumers buy a quantity of Q_0 and the consumer surplus is area (A + B + C). If the price decreases to P_1, consumers would buy a larger quantity of the good (Q_1) and the consumer surplus would increase to area (A + B + C + D + E + F). If the price increases to P_2, consumers would buy a smaller quantity of the good (Q_2) and the consumer surplus would decrease to area A instead.

Producer surplus

Definition(s):

Producer surplus is the difference between how much producers actually receive compared to how much they are willing and able to accept to produce a quantity of a good or service.

For an individual producer, the producer surplus from producing and selling a specific unit of a good is the difference between how much that producer actually received from selling the good compared to how much that producer was willing and able to accept to produce that good. It is a measure of the welfare of a producer who received a higher price for a good or service compared to the minimum amount he/she was willing and able to accept to produce the good or service. For example, if Firm A was willing and able to produce a notebook at $3 but sold the notebook at a price of $6, Firm A's producer surplus from producing and selling that notebook is $3.

For the market, the total producer surplus for a given quantity is the difference between the total amount that producers actually receive and how much producers were willing and able to accept to produce that quantity of goods. Since the total amount producers are willing and able to accept is reflected in the supply curve, the producer surplus is illustrated by the area above the supply curve and below the market price which shows how much they receive.

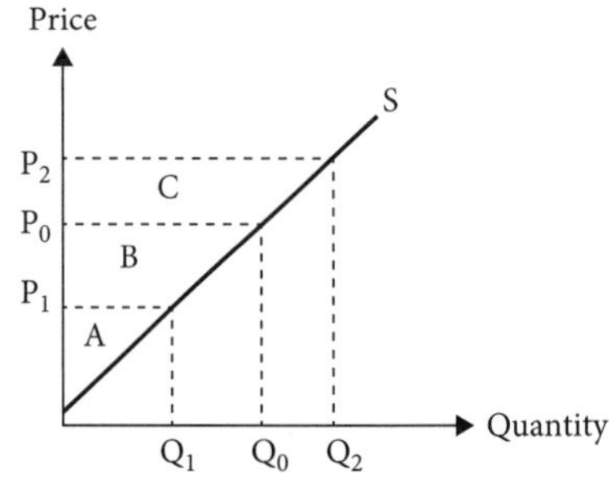

Figure 2.17: Producer surplus at different prices.

With reference to Fig. 2.17, at price P_0, producers produce a quantity of Q_0 and the producer surplus is area (A+B). If the price decreases to P_1, producers would produce a smaller quantity of the good (Q_1) and the producer surplus would decrease to area A. If the price increases to P_2, producers would produce a larger quantity of the good (Q_2) and the producer surplus would increase to area (A + B + C) instead.

Consumer and producer surplus at market equilibrium

At market equilibrium, the consumer surplus and producer surplus are illustrated by the areas CS and PS respectively on Fig. 2.18.

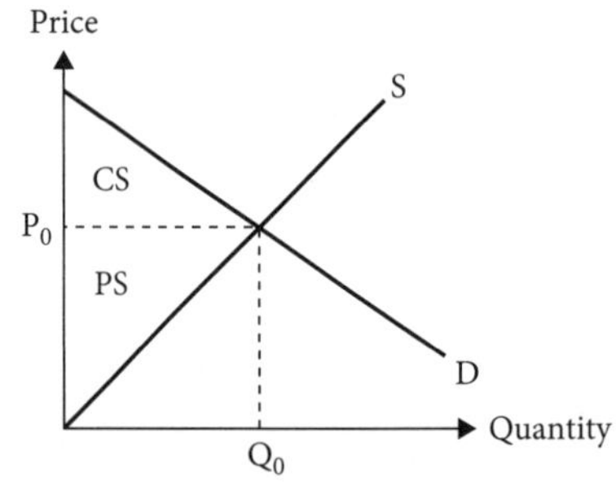

Figure 2.18: Consumer and producer surplus at market equilibrium.

The changes in consumer and producer surplus, when the market equilibrium changes due to a change in demand or supply, are presented below.

Social welfare can be measured by the sum of consumer and producer surplus. Note that when the quantity of the good increases (from an increase in demand or supply), social welfare increases. Conversely, when the quantity of a good decreases (from a decrease in demand or supply), social welfare decreases. This is intuitive. When the equilibrium quantity of a good decreases, the social welfare contributed by that good should also decrease.

<table>
<tr><th>Increase in demand</th><th>Decrease in demand</th></tr>
<tr><td>
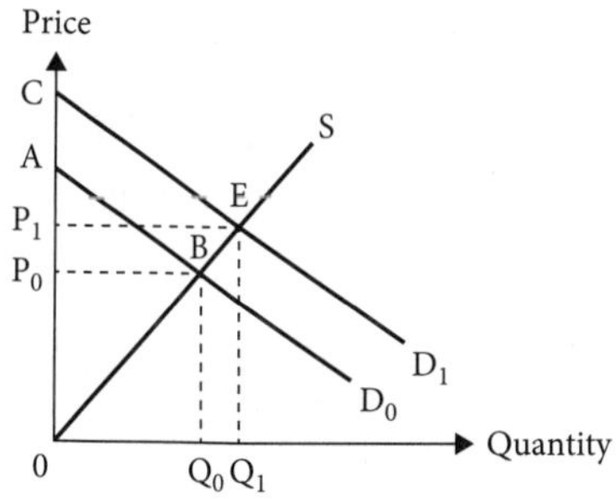

Consumer surplus increases from are AP_0B to are CP_1E

Producer surplus increases from area $0P_0B$ to area $0P_1E$
</td><td>
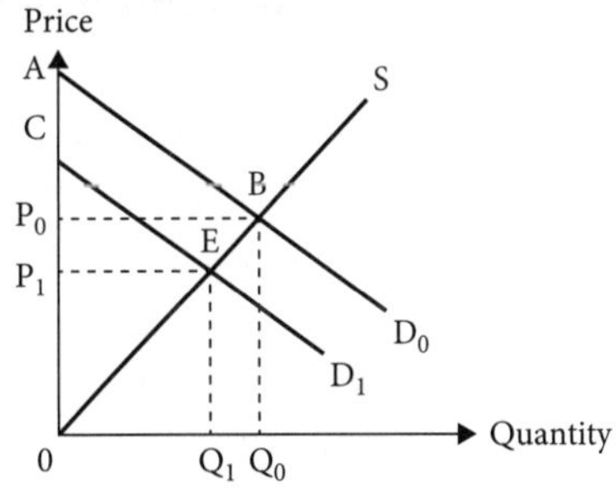

Consumer surplus decreases from area AP_0B to area CP_1E

Producer surplus decreases from area $0P_0B$ to area $0P_1E$
</td></tr>
<tr><th>Increase in supply</th><th>Decrease in supply</th></tr>
<tr><td>
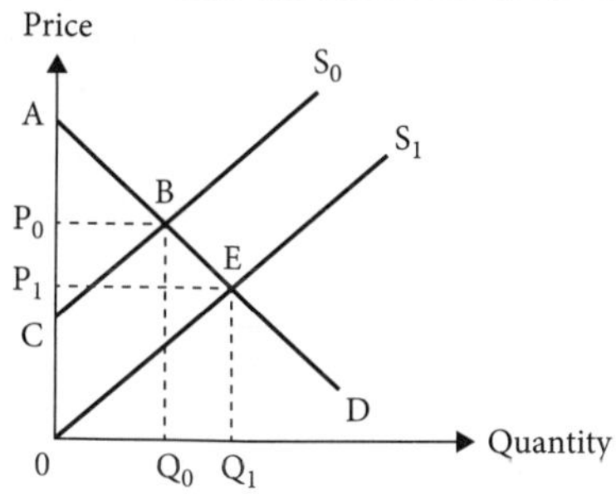

Consumer surplus increases from area AP_0B to area AP_1E

Producer surplus increases from area CP_0B to area $0P_1E$
</td><td>
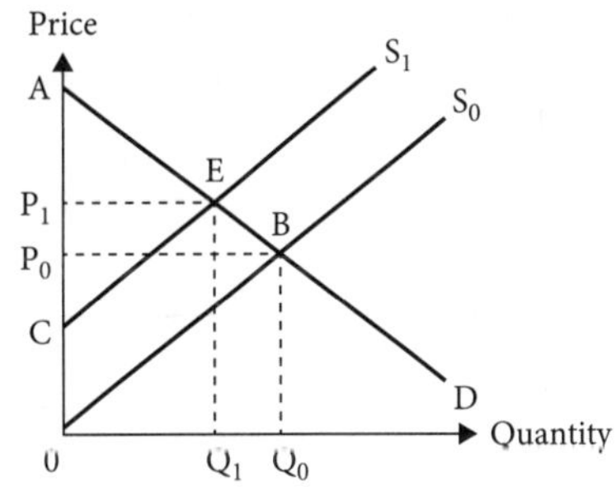

Consumer surplus decreases from area AP_0B to area AP_1E

Producer surplus decreases from area $0P_0B$ to area CP_1E
</td></tr>
</table>

2.5 Application of Demand and Supply: Rationale and Impact of Government Intervention on Consumers and Producers

As we learnt in the section on non-price determinants of demand and supply, a government's actions can affect the consumers and producers and hence, demand and supply, respectively. In this section, we will study the different forms of government intervention in terms of their rationale and their impact on consumers, producers, and society as a whole.

2.5.1 Taxes

Definition(s):

A **tax** is a charge or fee imposed by the government on a taxpayer

Taxpayers could be individuals, consumers, producers, households, and firms depending on the type of tax and how it is implemented.

Types of taxes: Direct and indirect taxes

There are two types of taxes—direct and indirect taxes.

Direct taxes are taxes imposed directly on taxpayers such as income tax for labourers and corporate tax for firms. Direct taxes will be further discussed in Chapter 6: Macroeconomic Aims, Problems, and Policies.

Indirect taxes are taxes imposed on the manufacturing or sale of goods and services. The taxes are paid to the government via an intermediary such as firms.

In microeconomics, indirect taxes are more commonly used by government as they influence a specific market instead of the whole economy and that is the focus here.

Rationale

The main purpose of indirect taxes is to increase the market equilibrium price and decrease the market equilibrium quantity of a good or service. Governments may want to do so if they think that too much of the good is being produced or consumed for some reason. Formal economic reasons will be explained in detail in Chapter 4 Market Failure but for now, intuitively, it makes sense that governments may want to discourage excessive production of some goods because they cause pollution (e.g., coal mining) or the consumption of some goods because they are not good for consumers (e.g., cigarette smoking).

The other purpose of taxation is for the government to collect tax revenue to fund government spending. However, this purpose is usually served more through the collection of more broad-based taxes like direct taxes (which is collected from every labourer or every firm).[25]

Impact of an indirect tax on consumers and producers

To recap, when an indirect tax is imposed on producers, it increases the cost of production and the supply of the good will decrease. Thus, the supply curve will shift upwards from S_0 to S_1 (in Figure 2.19 below). The upward shift of the supply curve is the value of the per unit tax. This is because a per unit tax of $2 would increase the MC of production of all units of goods by $2. Since the market supply is the sum of the individual firms' supplies, and the individual firms' supply curves trace their MC curves, the market supply curve would naturally shift up by $2.

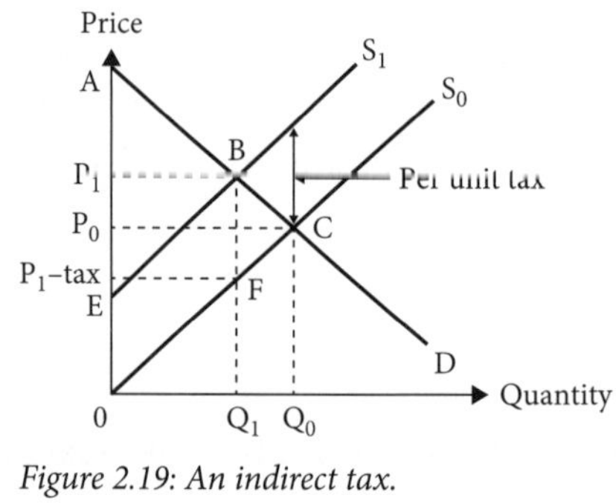

Figure 2.19: An indirect tax.

25 Having said that, there is a trend in developed countries to shift away from raising government revenue from direct taxes (e.g. income and corporate taxes) to consumption taxes, which are indirect taxes levied on a wide range of goods.

In short, the per unit tax would cause the entire supply curve to shift upwards by the amount of the per unit tax.[26]

Through the price adjustment process, the indirect tax will lead to a higher market equilibrium price P_1 and lower market equilibrium quantity Q_1. Note that while the market price is now P_1, the price received by the producer is only P_1-tax. This is because the price that the producers actually receive is the price they receive in the market (P_1) minus the tax per unit that they have to pay. The vertical gap between P_1 and P_1-tax is the per unit tax.

The impact on **consumers** can be understood in terms of the change in consumer expenditure and the change in consumer surplus. For the former, whether the total consumers' expenditure on the goods would increase or decrease would depend on the PED. If the demand is price elastic, the increase in price would lead to a more than proportionate decrease in quantity demanded and the consumers' expenditure would fall. If the demand is price inelastic, the increase in price would lead to a less than proportionate decrease in quantity demanded and the consumers' expenditure would rise. For the latter, consumer surplus would clearly decrease (from P_0AC to P_1AB) due to the higher price of the good.

The impact on **producers** can also be understood in terms of the change in producer revenue and the change in producer surplus. In terms of producer revenue, while the pre-tax revenue would be equal to consumer expenditure and thus, increase or decrease depending on the PED, the post-tax revenue will definitely decrease (from $0P_0CQ_0$ to $0P_1$-taxFQ_1). Intuitively, this should make sense. An indirect tax reduces the actual price received by the producer as well as the output sold by the producer. Naturally, the producer revenue post-tax should decrease. Producer surplus would also decrease from $0P_0C$ to $0P_1$-taxF/EP_1B (the two are equivalent in area).

The impact on **society** as a whole can be understood in two ways—

(i) the sum of the changes in consumer welfare (measured by the consumer surplus), producer welfare (measured by the consumer surplus), and government revenue (we have to include the government as taxes generate revenue for the government and that has to be accounted for) or

(ii) the change in the net benefit to society, which is the change in the total benefit to society (measured by the area under the MPB) minus the change in the total cost to society (measured by the area under the MPC).

The two ways will actually give the same result and the second way will be explained in more detail in Chapter 4. Using the first way, we see that the loss of consumer surplus is the area P_0P_1BC and the loss of producer surplus is the area P_1-taxP_0CF. The tax revenue gained by the government is the area P_1-taxP_1BF (tax revenue = per unit tax (P_1-taxP_1) × quantity traded ($0Q_1$, which is equal to P_1-taxF)). Summing up the benefits (gain in tax revenue by the government) and the costs (the losses in consumer and producer surpluses), we see a net loss of area FBC. This loss is named the deadweight loss to society and it shows that a tax imposes a net cost to society.

26 The assumption we have made is that the tax per unit is a fixed amount (e.g., \$2). This is what we call a specific tax. However, the indirect tax could be in the form of a percentage tax (e.g., 7% of the good's price). That is what we call an ad valorem tax and is explained in Annex 2.4.

Incidence of an indirect tax

The tax incidence tells us who actually pays the tax. Imagine a per unit tax of $2 has been imposed. So, for every unit of a good that is produced, the producer has to pay $2 to the government. Some part of this $2 may be "passed on" to consumers in the form of a higher price of the good. Let us say that the price of the good increases by $1.20 because of the tax so consumers pay $1.20 more for each unit of the good bought. In that case, of the $2 tax for each unit of the good, consumers effectively pay $1.20 of it and producers pay $0.80. We say that the tax incidence[27] falls more on the consumers than the producers. Specifically, the tax burden on the consumers per unit of the good is $1.20 and the tax burden on the producers is $0.80 per unit of the good. Just as we can calculate the tax burden on consumers and on producers for each unit of the good, we can also calculate the total tax burden on consumers and on producers for all the units of the good traded.

With reference to Figure 2.20 below, the indirect tax causes the supply curve to shift up from S_0 to S_1 by the amount of the per unit tax (i.e., the $2). This causes the market price to increase from P_0 to P_1 and the quantity traded to decrease from Q_0 to Q_1. The total tax revenue collected by the government would be area (A + B). Of this tax revenue, area A is the tax burden on the consumers while area B is the tax burden on the producers. Area A is obtained from taking the increase in market price P_0P_1 (i.e., the $1.20) and multiplying it by the quantity traded after the tax is imposed Q_1. Area B is obtained from taking the share of the tax paid by the producers P_1-taxP_1 (i.e., the $0.80) and multiplying it by the post-tax quantity traded Q_1.

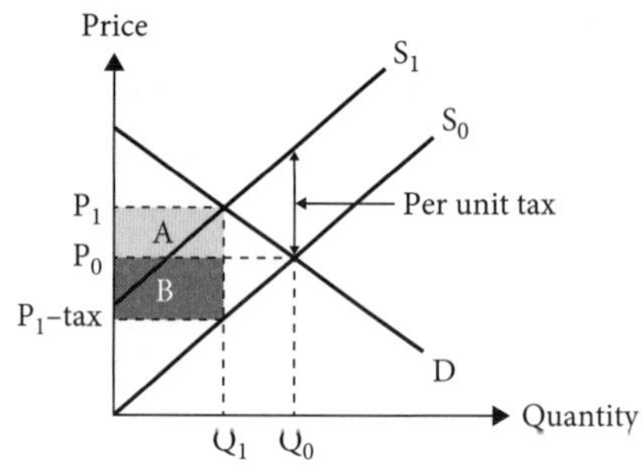

Figure 2.20: Incidence of an indirect tax.

Whether consumers or producers will bear a greater burden of the tax would depend on the relative values of PED and PES. Intuitively, the lower the PED, the more price inelastic the demand, the more producers can pass on the tax as a higher price since consumers are not responsive to price changes, the greater the tax burden on consumers. Conversely, the higher the PED, the lower the tax burden on consumers. For producers, the explanation is more technical and less intuitive. The lower the PES, the more price inelastic the supply, the less producers themselves can respond to the effective fall in the price that they receive post-tax, and the smaller the leftward shift in supply.[28] The smaller the leftward shift in supply, the

27 Tax incidence differs from tax impact. The tax impact is on whoever pays the actual tax to the government. In this case, the tax impact is on the producers since they are the ones who pay the $2 per unit of tax to the government. The consumers pay for the tax by paying a higher price to the producers. They do not pay the tax to the government directly so there is no tax impact on the consumers.

28 The extent of the leftward shift in supply when an indirect tax is imposed is dependent on the PES. This is illustrated in Annex 2.5.

smaller the degree to which the price increases, and the less they can pass on the tax as an increase in price. Hence, the lower the PES, the larger the tax burden on the producers and vice versa. Below, we look at three cases of relative PED to PES values to illustrate the differences in the tax incidence.

<table>
<tr>
<td>Case 1: |PED| > |PES|
(demand for the good is more price elastic than the supply of the good)</td>
<td>Case 2: |PED| < |PES|
(demand for the good is more price inelastic than the supply of the good)</td>
<td>Case 3: |PED| = |PES|
(demand and supply of the good have the same price elasticity)</td>
</tr>
<tr>
<td>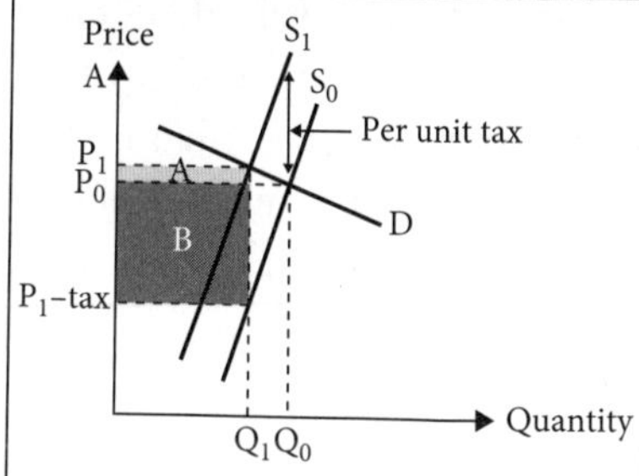
</td>
<td>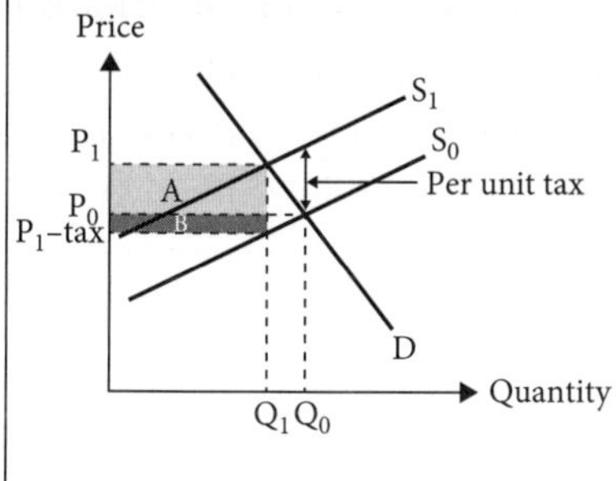
</td>
<td>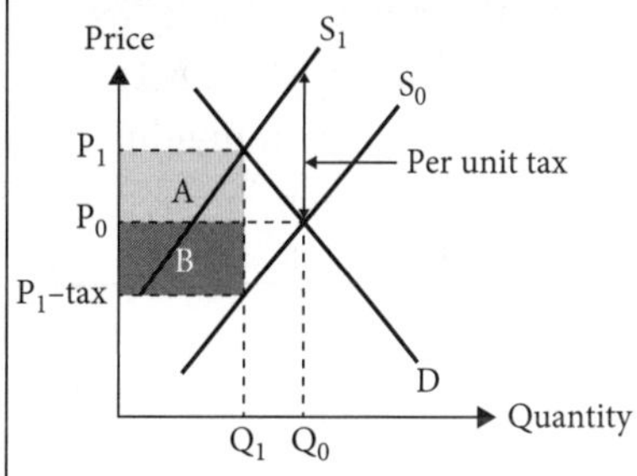
</td>
</tr>
<tr>
<td>Consumers bear a smaller burden of the tax (area A) and producers bear a larger burden of the tax (area B).</td>
<td>Consumers bear a larger burden of the tax (area A) and producers bear a smaller burden of the tax (area B).</td>
<td>Consumers and producers bear equal burden of the tax (area A for consumers and area B for producers).</td>
</tr>
</table>

2.5.2 Subsidy

Definition(s):

A **subsidy** is a form of spending by the government provided to different economic agents

Types of subsidies: Direct and indirect subsidies

Similar to taxes, there are two types of subsidies—direct and indirect subsidies.

Direct subsidies are subsidies provided directly to an economic agent, such as unemployment benefits. These will be further discussed in Chapter 6: Macroeconomic Aims, Problems, and Policies.

Indirect subsidies are indirectly provided for the manufacturing or sales of goods and services. They are paid by the government to an intermediary such as firms.

In microeconomics, indirect subsidies are more commonly used by the government as it influences a specific market instead of the whole economy and that is the focus here.

Rationale

The main purpose of indirect subsidies is to decrease the market equilibrium price and increase the market equilibrium quantity of a good or service. Governments may want to do so if they think that too little of the good is being produced or consumed for some reason. Formal economic reasons will be explained in detail in Chapter 4: Market Failure but for now, intuitively, it makes sense that governments may want to lower the price of some goods because they think everyone should be able to afford such goods (e.g., food) or encourage the consumption of some goods because they are good for consumers (e.g., health check-ups and vaccinations).

Impact of a subsidy on consumers and producers

To recap, when an indirect subsidy (henceforth, we will just refer to this as a subsidy) is given to producers, it decreases the cost of production and the supply of the good will increase. Thus, the supply curve will shift downwards from S_0 to S_1 (in Figure 2.21 below). The downward shift of the supply curve is the value of the per unit subsidy. This is because a per unit subsidy of $2 would decrease the MC of production of all units of the goods by $2. Since the market supply is the sum of the individual firms' supplies, and the individual firms' supply curves trace their MC curves, the market supply curve would naturally shift down by $2. In short, the per unit subsidy would cause the entire supply curve to shift downwards by the amount of the per unit subsidy.

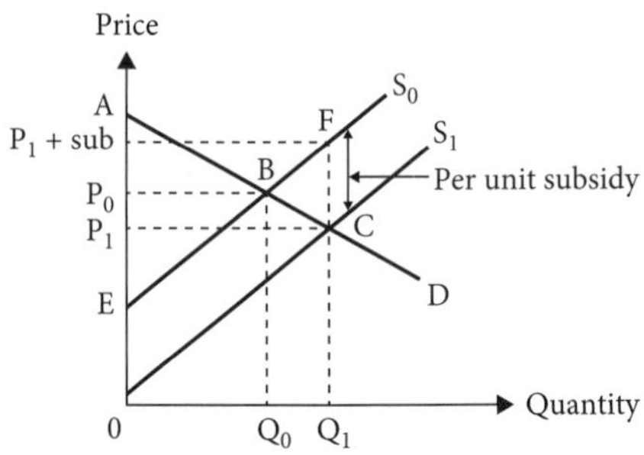

Figure 2.21: An indirect subsidy.

Through the price adjustment process, the subsidy will lead to a lower market equilibrium price P_1 and higher market equilibrium quantity Q_1. Note that while the market price is now P_1, the price received by the producer is actually P_1+sub. This is because the price that the producers actually receive is the price they receive in the market (P_1) plus the subsidy per unit that they receive from the government. The vertical gap between P_1 and P_1+sub is the per unit subsidy.

The impact on **consumers** can be understood in terms of the change in consumer expenditure and the change in consumer surplus. For the former, whether the total consumers' expenditure on the goods would increase or decrease would depend on the PED. If the demand is price elastic, the decrease in price would lead to a more than proportionate increase in quantity demanded and the consumers' expenditure would rise. If the demand is price inelastic, the decrease in price would lead to a less than proportionate increase in quantity demanded and the consumers' expenditure would fall. For the latter, consumer surplus would clearly increase (from P_0AB to P_1AC) due to the lower price of the good.

The impact on **producers** can also be understood in terms of the change in producer revenue and the change in producer surplus. In terms of producer revenue, while the pre-subsidy revenue would be equal to consumer expenditure and thus, increase or decrease in depending on the PED, the post-subsidy revenue will definitely decrease (from $0P_0BQ_0$ to $0P_1$+subFQ_1).

Intuitively, this should make sense. A subsidy increases the actual price received by the producer as well as the output sold by the producer. Naturally, the producer revenue post-subsidy should increase. Producers surplus would also increase from EP_0B to EP_1+subF / $0P_1C$ (the two are equivalent in area).

Like indirect taxes, the impact of a subsidy on **society** as a whole can be understood in two ways—

(i) the sum of the changes in consumer welfare (measured by the consumer surplus), producer welfare (measured by the consumer surplus), and government spending (we have to include the government as subsidies are government spending that has to be accounted for) or

(ii) the change in the net benefit to society, which is the change in the total benefit to society (measured by the area under the MPB) minus the change in the total cost to society (measured by the area under the MPC), which will be explained in more detail in Chapter 4.

Using the first way, we see that the gain in consumer surplus is the area P_1P_0BC and the loss of producer surplus is the area P_0P1+subFB. The government spending on the subsidy is the area P_1P_1+subFC (subsidy spending = per unit subsidy (P_1P_1+sub) × quantity traded ($0Q_1$, which is equal to P_1C)). Summing up the benefits (gain in consumer and producer surpluses) and the costs (the subsidy spending by the government), we see a net loss of area BFC. This loss is named the deadweight loss to society and it shows that a subsidy imposes a net cost to society.

Incidence of a subsidy

The incidence of a subsidy tells us who actually benefits from the subsidy. Imagine a per subsidy of \$2 has been given. So, for every unit of a good that is produced, the producer receives \$2 from the government. Some part of this \$2 may be "passed on" to consumers in the form of a lower price of the good. Let us say that the price of the good decreases by \$1.20 because of the subsidy, so consumers pay \$1.20 less for each unit of the good bought. In that case, of the \$2 subsidy for each unit of the good, consumers effectively enjoy \$1.20 of it and producers enjoy \$0.80. The subsidy benefits the consumers more than the producers. Specifically, the benefit to the consumers per unit of the good is \$1.20 and the benefit to the producers is \$0.80 per unit of the good. Just as we can calculate the benefit to consumers and to producers for each unit of the good, we can also calculate the total benefit to consumers and to producers for all the units of the good traded.

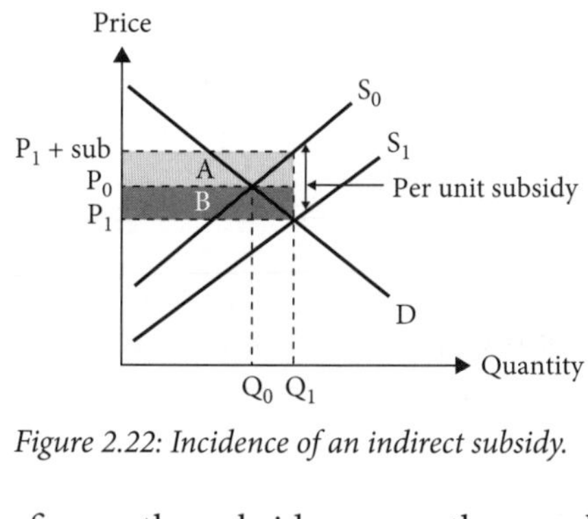

Figure 2.22: Incidence of an indirect subsidy.

With reference to the above figure, the subsidy causes the supply curve to shift down from S_0 to S_1 by the amount of the per unit subsidy (i.e., the \$2). This causes the market price to decrease from P_0 to P_1 and the quantity traded to increase from Q_0 to Q_1. The subsidy spending by the government would be area (A + B). Of subsidy spending, area B is the benefit to the consumers while area A is the benefit to the producers. Area B is obtained from taking the decrease in market price P_0P_1 (i.e., the \$1.20) and multiplying it by the quantity traded after the tax is imposed Q_1. Area A is obtained from taking the share of the subsidy received, paid by the producers P_0P_1+sub (i.e., the \$0.80), and multiplying it by the post-tax quantity traded Q_1.

Whether consumers or producers benefit more from the subsidy would depend on the relative values of PED and PES. For PED, the lower the PED, the more price inelastic the demand, the greater the extent of the fall in the market price, the greater the benefit to consumers. Conversely, the higher the PED, the lower the benefit to consumers. For producers, the explanation is more technical. The lower the PES, the more price inelastic the supply, the less producers themselves can respond to the effective rise in the price that they receive post-subsidy, and the smaller the rightward shift in supply.[29] The smaller the rightward shift in supply, the smaller the degree to which price decreases, and the less they pass on the subsidy as a decrease in price. Hence, the lower the PES, the larger the benefit of the subsidy to the producers and vice versa. Below, we look at three cases of relative PED to PES values to illustrate the differences in the benefits of the subsidy.

<table>
<tr>
<th>Case 1: |PED| > |PES|
(demand for the good is more price elastic than the supply of the good)</th>
<th>Case 2: |PED| < |PES|
(demand for the good is more price inelastic than the supply of the good)</th>
<th>Case 3: |PED| = |PES|
(demand and supply of the good have the same price elasticity)</th>
</tr>
<tr>
<td>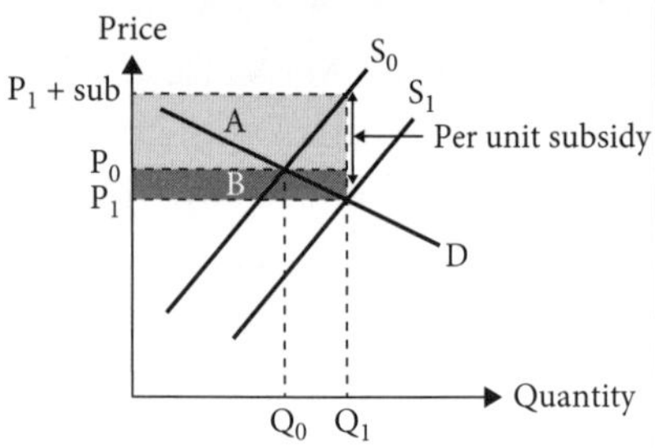
</td>
<td>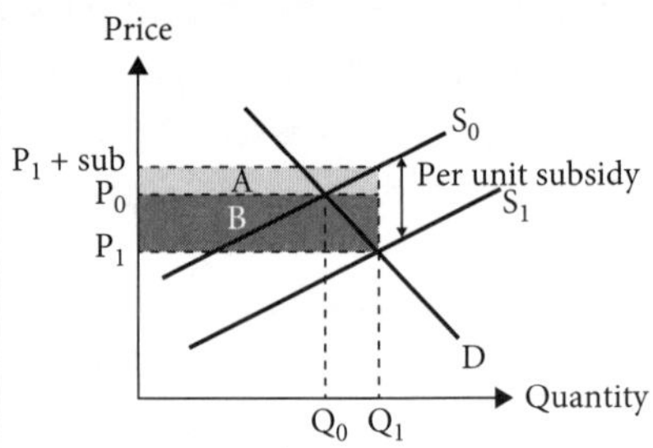
</td>
<td>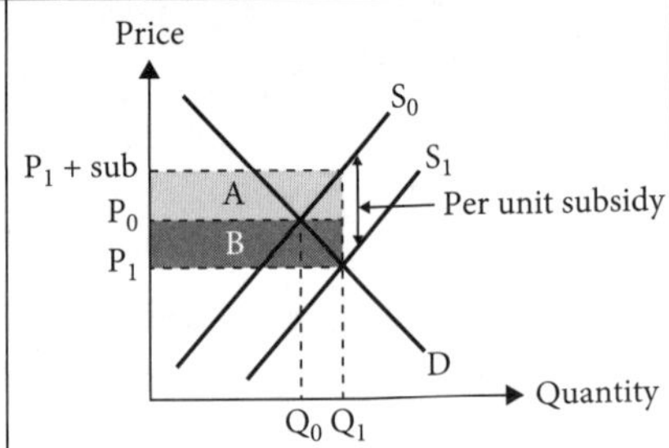
</td>
</tr>
<tr>
<td>Consumers enjoy a smaller share of the subsidy (area B) and producers enjoy a larger share (area A).</td>
<td>Consumers enjoy a larger share of the subsidy (area B) and producers enjoy a smaller share (area A).</td>
<td>Consumers and producers enjoy equal shares of the subsidy (area B for consumers and area A for producers).</td>
</tr>
</table>

2.5.3 Price control—Maximum price (Price Ceiling)

Definition(s):

A **maximum price (price ceiling)** is the highest price producers are legally allowed to charge for a good or service.

29 The extent of the rightward shift in supply when an indirect tax is imposed is dependent on the PES. The reasoning is the same as how PES affects the extent of the rightward shift in supply when an indirect tax is imposed in Annex 2.5.

Rationale

Governments may decide to impose a maximum price or a price ceiling to prevent prices of certain goods or services from rising above a certain level. It primarily aims to protect the welfare of consumers.

Impact of a price ceiling on consumers and producers

For the policy of price ceiling to be meaningful, it has to be set below the equilibrium price of the good or service.[30]

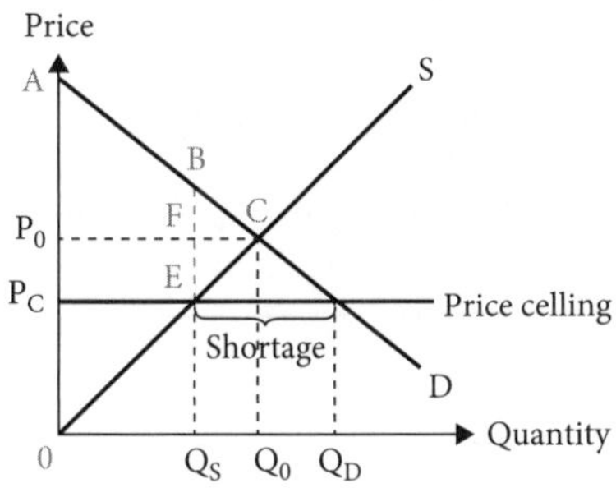

Figure 2.23: A price ceiling.

A price ceiling can be illustrated by Figure 2.23 above. The price ceiling is imposed at price P_C, which is below the original equilibrium price P_0. Such a ceiling would result in a shortage as a fall in price from P_0 to P_C would result in an increase in quantity demanded (from Q_0 to Q_D) and a fall in quantity supplied (from Q_0 to Q_S). In a free market, at price P_C, the price adjustment process would kick in to clear the market through increasing the price of the good. However, due to the price ceiling, the price will remain at P_C and the shortage (of Q_SQ_D) will persist. The actual quantity traded in the market is now Q_S as the actual goods that change hands will be constrained by the quantity that producers are willing and able to sell. The price at which this quantity of goods is sold is P_C.

The impact on **consumers** can be understood in terms of the change in consumer expenditure and the change in consumer surplus. For the former, total consumers' expenditure on the goods would decrease from $0P_0CQ_0$ to $0P_CEQ_S$. This is because consumers now buy less of the good (Q_0 to Q_S) at a lower price (P_0 to P_C). For the latter, consumer surplus would change from P_0AC to P_CABE. There is a gain of P_CP_0FE but a loss of FBC. The gain of P_CP_0FE comes from the quantity of goods from 0 to Q_S now being sold at a lower price to the consumers while the loss of FBC comes from the quantity of goods from Q_S to Q_0 no longer being sold due to the price ceiling. So, consumers who still manage to buy the good under the price ceiling will benefit while those who find that they can no longer buy the good will lose out. For example, if the government decides to impose a maximum price on home rentals, fewer people would be willing to rent out their homes at the lower price. Hence, the consumers who manage to rent the remaining homes cheaply gain while those that are no longer able to rent homes lose out. The overall effect on consumers as a whole would depend on whether the gain (P_CP_0FE) outweighs the loss (FBC).

30 If it is set above the market price, it is not meaningful as the market price would just settle at the market equilibrium. We call such a price ceiling a non-binding price ceiling.

The impact on **producers** can also be understood in terms of the change in producer revenue and the change in producer surplus. Since producer revenue is the consumer expenditure, producer revenue would also decrease from $0P_0CQ_0$ to $0P_CEQ_S$. Producer surplus would also decrease from $0P_0C$ to $0P_CE$.

For **society** as a whole, we sum up the changes in consumer and producer surplus. There was a gain in consumer surplus of P_CP_0FE. There was also a loss in consumer surplus of FBC and a loss in producer surplus of P_CP_0CE. Summing them up, we see a net loss of EBC. This loss is the deadweight loss to society and shows that a price ceiling imposes a net cost to society.

Putting it concretely: Price ceilings and black markets

Although we did not include this in our analysis, a price ceiling may result in a black market. This is because price ceilings create shortages. Such shortages may cause black markets (i.e., underground, illegal markets) to form, where the goods would be sold at prices above the price ceiling and likely above the original price too. For example, certain home owners would rent out their homes illegally and not register their tenants. This way, they stay out of the reach of the regulation and can charge higher rents. However, this also means that both the home owner and tenant would be without legal protection from each other (i.e., the home owner could evict the tenant without minimum notice and if the tenant escapes with the home owner's valuables, the home owner cannot make a proper police report).

Over time, if the black market is not regulated, producers will find it more profitable to sell their goods on the black market instead and move their goods from the formal market to the black market. The formal market would eventually collapse when there is no longer any supply in the formal market and the original equilibrium would be established in the black market instead.

2.5.4 Price control—Minimum price (Price Floor)

Definition(s):

A **minimum price (price floor)** is the lowest price producers are legally allowed to charge for a good or service

Rationale

Governments may decide to impose a minimum price or a price floor to prevent prices of certain goods or services from falling below a certain level. It primarily aims to protect the welfare of producers by protecting their revenue and hence, incomes.

Impact of a price floor on consumers and producers

For the policy of price floor to be meaningful, it has to be set above the equilibrium price of the good or service.[31]

31 If it is set below the market price, it is not meaningful as the market price would just settle at the market equilibrium. We call such a price floor a non-binding price floor.

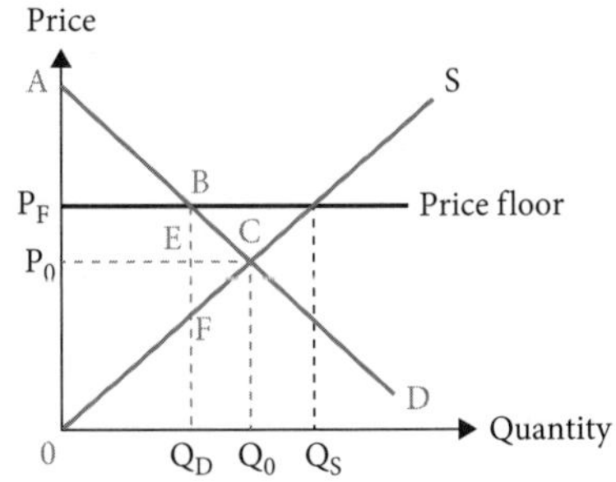

Figure 2.24: A price floor.

A price floor can be illustrated by Figure 2.24 above. The price floor is imposed at price P_F, which is above the original equilibrium price P_0. Such a floor would result in a surplus as the rise in price from P_0 to P_F would result in a decrease in quantity demanded (from Q_0 to Q_D) and a rise in quantity supplied (from Q_0 to Q_S). In a free market, at price P_F, the price adjustment process would kick in to clear the market through decreasing the price of the good. However, due to the price floor, the price will remain at P_F and the surplus (of Q_DQ_S) will persist. The actual quantity traded in the market is now Q_D as the actual goods that change hands will be constrained by the quantity that consumers are willing and able to buy. The price at which this quantity of goods is sold is P_F.

The impact on **consumers** can be understood in terms of the change in consumer expenditure and the change in consumer surplus. For the former, total consumers' expenditure on the goods would change depending on the PED. If the demand for the good is price elastic, the increase in price would cause a more than proportionate fall in quantity demanded and consumer expenditure would fall. If the demand for the good is price inelastic, the increase in price would cause a less than proportionate decrease in the quantity demanded of the good and consumer expenditure would rise. For the latter, consumer surplus would fall from P_0AC to P_FAB.

The impact on **producers** can also be understood in terms of the change in producer revenue and the change in producer surplus. Since producer revenue is the consumer expenditure, producer revenue would also decrease if the demand for the good is price elastic and increase if the demand for the good is price inelastic. Producer surplus would change from $0P_0C$ to $0P_FBF$. There is a gain of P_0P_FBE but a loss of FEC. The gain of P_0P_FBE comes from the producers receiving a higher price for the quantity of goods from 0 to Q_D while the loss of FEC comes from the quantity of goods from Q_D to Q_0 no longer being sold due to the price floor. So, producers who still manage to sell the good with the imposition of the price floor will benefit while those who find that they can no longer sell the good will lose out. For example, if the government decides to impose a minimum price on rice, fewer people would be willing to buy rice at the higher price. Hence, the rice farmers who still manage to sell their rice to the remaining consumers at the higher prices gain while those that are no longer able to sell their rice lose out. The overall effect on producers as a whole would depend on whether the gain (P_0P_FBE) outweighs the loss (FEC).

For **society** as a whole, we sum up the changes in consumer and producer surplus. There was a gain in producer surplus of P_0P_FBE. There was also a loss in consumer surplus of P_0P_FBC and a loss in producer surplus of FEC. Summing them up, we see a net loss of FBC. This loss is the deadweight loss to society and shows that a price floor imposes a net cost to society.

Putting it concretely: Price floor as minimum wage

Since labour is a form of service, the government can also introduce price floor in the labour market in the form minimum wage. The aim is to protect the welfare of producers, in this case the labourers or workers, by increasing their wages and hence, incomes. As seen in Figure 2.24, the price of labour would be in terms of wages, while the quantity will be in terms of quantity of labour employed.

With the minimum wage introduced, labourers who are the producers now are legally allowed to charge a minimum of P_F for their services while the employers, now the consumers of labour will have to pay a minimum of P_F.

Labourers ($0Q_D$) who still manage to be employed with the imposition of the price floor will be better off with higher wages and producer surpluses. While those labourers (Q_DQ_0) who lost their employment and labourers (Q_0Q_S) who are attracted by the higher wages and joined the labour market but could not find employment will be worse off.

For the consumers of labour (the employers), whether their total expenditure on wages will affect their total cost would depend on PED.

For the labour market, there will also be a deadweight loss of FBC incurred by society and as the minimum wage imposes a net cost to society.

2.5.5 Quantity controls—Quotas

Definition(s):

A **quota** is the maximum quantity[32] of a good or service that producers are legally allowed to produce or sell.

A quota is used to directly control the quantity of goods and services exchanged in a market.

Rationale

Governments may decide to impose a quota to prevent sales of certain goods or services from rising above a certain level. As with taxes, governments may want to impose quotas so if they think that too much of the good is being produced or consumed for some reason. Formal economic reasons will be explained in detail in Chapter 4: Market Failure but for now, examples of goods that governments may want to reduce production or consumption of could include steel (because steel production creates pollution) and soft drinks (because consumption of soft drinks is bad for health).

32 A quota can also refer to the minimum quantity that must be met (e.g., production quotas in communist China used to refer to the minimum quantity that had to be produced). However, in the context of the A Level syllabus, a quota usually refers to the maximum quantity that can be produced.

Impact of a quota on consumers and producers

For the policy of a quota to be effective, it has to be set below the equilibrium quantity of the good or service.[33]

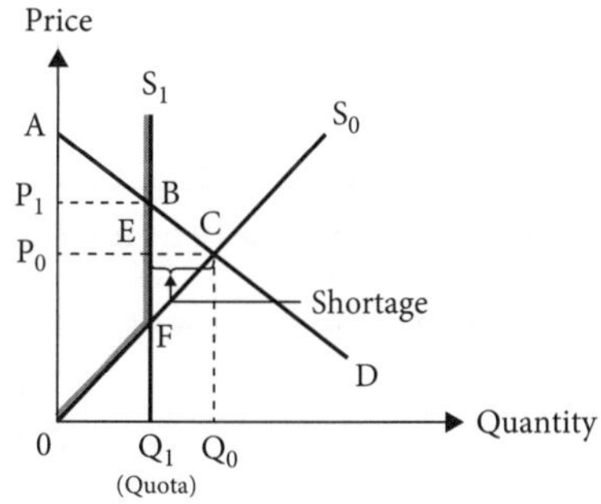

Figure 2.25: A quota.

A quota can be illustrated by Figure 2.25 above. The original equilibrium is at P_0 and Q_0.When a quota (of Q_1) is imposed on a good, it changes the supply curve of the good from S_0 to S_1. This is because when the quantity supplied reaches the quota at Q_1, producers are not allowed to produce any more even if the price of the good increases. Hence, the supply curve becomes a vertical line once it reaches Q_1. At the original price P_0, there will be a shortage as quantity demanded (Q_0) is now more than quantity supplied (Q_1). The price adjusts to eliminate the shortage until the new equilibrium is reached at P_1 and Q_1 where demand (D) equals to the new supply (S_1). Therefore, the quota will lead to a higher market equilibrium price P_1 and lower market equilibrium quantity Q_1.

The impact on **consumers** can be understood in terms of the change in consumer expenditure and the change in consumer surplus. For the former, total consumers' expenditure on the goods would change depending on the PED. If the demand for the good is price elastic, the increase in price would cause a more than proportionate fall in quantity demanded and consumer expenditure would fall. If the demand for the good is price inelastic, the increase in price would cause a less than proportionate decrease in the quantity demanded of the good consumer expenditure would rise. For the latter, consumer surplus would fall from P_0AC to P_1AB.

The impact on **producers** can also be understood in terms of the change in producer revenue and the change in producer surplus. Since producer revenue is the consumer expenditure, producer revenue would also decrease if the demand for the good is price elastic and increase if the demand for the good is price inelastic. Producer surplus would change from $0P_0C$ to $0P_1BF$. There is a gain of P_0P_1BE but a loss of FEC. The gain of P_0P_1BE comes from the producers receiving a higher price for the quantity of goods from 0 to Q_1 while the loss of FEC comes from the quantity of goods from Q_1 to Q_0 no longer being sold due to the quota. So, producers will benefit from selling the goods they are allowed to produce and sell under the quota at a higher price, but lose out from being made to produce and sell fewer of their goods. The overall effect on producers as a whole would depend on whether the gain (P_0P_1BE) outweighs the loss (FEC).

33 If it is set beyond the market quantity, it is not meaningful as the market quantity would just settle at the market equilibrium. We call such a quota a non-binding quota.

For **society** as a whole, we sum up the changes in consumer and producer surplus. There was a gain in producer surplus of P_0P_1BE. There was also a loss in consumer surplus of P_0P_1BC and a loss in producer surplus of FEC. Summing them up, we see a net loss of FBC. This loss is the deadweight loss to society and shows that a quota imposes a net cost to society.

2.5.6 Summary table for the effects of the various forms of government intervention on consumers, producers, and the society as a whole

Intervention	Effect on consumer expenditure	Effect on producer revenue	Effect on consumer surplus	Effect on producer surplus	Effect on social welfare
Tax	Depends on PED	Pre-tax: Depends on PED Post-tax: Decreases	Decreases	Decreases	Decreases
Subsidy	Depends on PED	Pre-subsidy: Depends on PED Post-subsidy: Increases	Increases	Increases	Decreases
Price ceiling	Depends on PED	Depends on PED	Depends	Decreases	Decreases
Price floor	Depends on PED	Depends on PED	Decreases	Depends	Decreases
Quota	Depends on PED	Depends on PED	Decreases	Depends	Decreases

Summary for Chapter 2

1. Demand and supply interact to determine the free market's answers to "What to produce?", "How to produce?", and "For whom to produce?" through the price mechanism.
2. The price mechanism refers to demand and supply jointly determining the price and quantity traded of goods and services as well as factors of production.
3. Shifts in demand and/or supply are a result of changes in non-price determinants. These shifts result in changes in the equilibrium price and quantity traded in a market.
4. Elasticity concepts are used to explain the extent of the changes in price and quantity when the non-price determinants change and cause demand and/or supply to shift.
5. The elasticity concepts related to demand are price elasticity of demand, cross elasticity of demand, and income elasticity of demand. The elasticity concept related to supply is the price elasticity of supply.
6. Effects of changes in demand and/or supply on consumers can be analysed in terms of their effect on consumer expenditure and consumer surplus. Consumer expenditure is the total amount of money that consumers spend on a good (it is equal to producer revenue) and consumer surplus is the difference between the amount that consumers were willing and able to pay for a good and the amount that they actually pay. Consumer welfare is measured by the consumer surplus.
7. Effects of changes in demand and/or supply on producers can be analysed in terms of their effect on producer revenue and producer surplus. Producer revenue is the total amount of money that producers receive for a good (it is equal to consumer expenditure) and producer surplus is the difference between the amount that producers actually receive for a good and the amount they were willing and able to accept for it. Producer welfare is measured by the producer surplus.
8. Effects of changes in demand and/or supply on society as a whole can be analysed in terms of the sum of the effects on consumers (in terms of consumer surplus), producers (in terms of producer surplus), and the government (in terms of tax revenue or subsidy spending).
9. Government intervention can affect the market. Their effects on producers, consumers, and society as a whole can be analysed.
10. The common forms of government intervention are taxes, subsidies, price ceilings, price floors, and quotas.

Annex 2.1 Varying price elasticity of demand (PED) along a straight line demand curve

Although we normally represent a price inelastic demand curve with a steep demand curve and a price elastic one with a gentle demand curve, technically, the PED along every point of the straight line demand curve differs such that every straight line demand curve would have an inelastic and elastic portion. We can see this from the formula for PED.

$$PED = \frac{\text{\% change in Qd of good A}}{\text{\% change in price of good A}}$$

$$PED = \frac{\frac{\text{change in } Qd}{Qd} \times 100\%}{\frac{\text{change in price}}{\text{price}} \times 100\%}$$

$$PED = \frac{\text{change in Qd}}{\text{change in price}} \times \frac{\text{price}}{\text{Qd}}$$

The $\left(\frac{\text{change in Qd}}{\text{change in price}}\right)$ is the inverse of the gradient of the demand curve, which will remain constant on a straight line demand curve but $\left(\frac{\text{price}}{\text{Qd}}\right)$ will not. In fact, while we move from left to right along the demand curve, price will decrease and quantity demanded will increase, causing $\left(\frac{\text{price}}{\text{Qd}}\right)$ to decrease. So, PED will decrease along the demand curve as we move from left to right.

For example, along the same demand curve, when there is an equal decrease in price of $1 from $10 to $9 (point A to A') compared to $5 to $4 (point B to B'), and an equal increase in quantity demanded from 10 to 11 (point A to A') compared to 15 to 16 (point B to B'), the percentage change in price for moving from point A to A' would be 10% while the percentage change in price for moving from point B to B' would be 20%; and the percentage change in quantity demanded for moving from point A to A' would be 10% while the percentage change in quantity demanded for moving from point B to B' would be 6.67%. Therefore the PEDs will differ. This is illustrated in the Fig. 2.26 below.

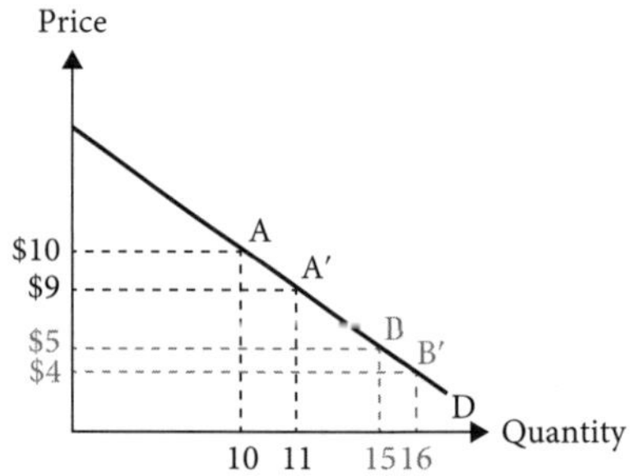

Figure 2.26: Differing PED along the same straight line demand curve.

In fact, the demand is price elastic at high prices and low quantities, then becomes increasingly more price inelastic until it becomes unitary price elastic at its mid-point (point A), then becomes price

PED at point A	PED at point B
PED = 10% / 10% = 1	PED = 6.67% / 20% = 0.33

inelastic and increasingly so. An example of the full range of PED values along a sample straight line demand curve is presented in the next table.

Table representation of varying PED values along a straight line demand curve (equation of demand curve: $P = 41 - 0.2Qd$).[34]

Price	Absolute Change in Price	Change in Price (%)	Quantity	Absolute Change in Quantity	Change in Quantity (%)	PED
40	−1	2.50	5	5	NA	NA
39	−1	2.56	10	5	50.00	0.1
38	−1	2.63	15	5	33.33	0.1
37	−1	2.70	20	5	25.00	0.1
36	−1	2.78	25	5	20.00	0.1
35	−1	2.86	30	5	16.67	0.2
34	−1	2.94	35	5	14.29	0.2
33	−1	3.03	40	5	12.50	0.2
32	−1	3.13	45	5	11.11	0.3
31	−1	3.23	50	5	10.00	0.3
30	−1	3.33	55	5	9.09	0.4
29	−1	3.45	60	5	8.33	0.4
28	−1	3.57	65	5	7.69	0.5
27	−1	3.70	70	5	7.14	0.5
26	−1	3.85	75	5	6.67	0.6
25	−1	4.00	80	5	6.25	0.6
24	−1	4.17	85	5	5.88	0.7
23	−1	4.35	90	5	5.56	0.8
22	−1	4.55	95	5	5.26	0.9
21	−1	4.76	100	5	5.00	1.0
20	−1	5.00	105	5	4.76	1.1
19	−1	5.26	110	5	4.55	1.2
18	−1	5.56	115	5	4.35	1.3
17	−1	5.88	120	5	4.17	1.4
16	−1	6.25	125	5	4.00	1.6
15	−1	6.67	130	5	3.85	1.7
14	−1	7.14	135	5	3.70	1.9

34 Note that the values of the PED would differ slightly depending on whether we use the new P and Q in the formula or the original P and Q. However, that level of technicality is beyond the scope of this book.

Price	Absolute Change in Price	Change in Price (%)	Quantity	Absolute Change in Quantity	Change in Quantity (%)	PED
13	−1	7.69	140	5	3.57	2.2
12	−1	8.33	145	5	3.45	2.4
11	−1	9.09	150	5	3.33	2.7
10	−1	10.00	155	5	3.23	3.1
9	−1	11.11	160	5	3.13	3.6
8	−1	12.50	165	5	3.03	4.1
7	−1	14.29	170	5	2.94	4.9
6	−1	16.67	175	5	2.86	5.8
5	−1	20.00	180	5	2.78	7.2
4	−1	25.00	185	5	2.70	9.3
3	−1	33.33	190	5	2.63	12.7
2	−1	50.00	195	5	2.56	19.5
1	−1	100.00	200	5	2.50	40.0

Annex 2.2 Varying PES along a straight line supply curve

While we normally represent a price inelastic supply curve with a steep supply curve and a price elastic one with a gentle supply curve, technically, the PES along every point of the straight line demand curve differs. We can see this from the formula for PED.

$$\text{PES} = \frac{\text{\% change in Qs of good A}}{\text{\% change in price of good A}}$$

$$\text{PES} = \frac{\frac{\text{change in Qs}}{\text{Qs}} \times 100\%}{\frac{\text{change in price}}{\text{price}} \times 100\%}$$

$$\text{PES} = \frac{\text{change in Qs}}{\text{change in price}} \times \frac{\text{price}}{\text{Qs}}$$

The $\left(\frac{\text{change in Qs}}{\text{change in price}}\right)$ is the inverse of the gradient of the supply curve, which will remain constant on a straight line supply curve but $\left(\frac{\text{price}}{\text{Qs}}\right)$ will not. In fact, while we move from left to right along the supply curve, price and quantity supplied will both increase but the ratio between them will change, causing $\left(\frac{\text{price}}{\text{Qs}}\right)$ to change. So, PES will change along the supply curve as we move from left to right.

For example, along the same supply curve, when there is an equal increase in price of $1 from $11 to $12 (point A to A') compared to $15 to $16 (point B to B'), and an equal increase in quantity supplied from 1 to 2 (point A to A') compared to 5 to 6 (point B to B'), the percentage change in price for moving from point A to A' would be 9.09% while the percentage change in price for moving from point B to B' would be 6.67%; and the percentage change in quantity supplied for moving from point A to A' would be 50% while the percentage change in quantity supplied for moving from point B to B' would be 20%. Therefore the PESs will differ. This is illustrated in the Fig. 2.27 below.

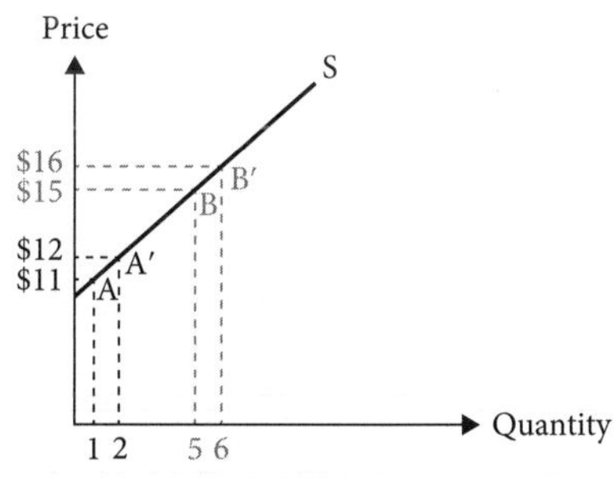

Figure 2.27: Differing PES along the same straight line supply curve.

PES at point A	PES at point B
PED = 50% / 9.09% = 5.5	PES = 20% / 6.67% = 3

However, unlike the differing PED along a straight line demand curve (Annex 2.1), the PES of a price elastic supply curve will always be more than 1, even as it varies along the supply curve, and that of a price inelastic supply curve will always be less than 1, even as it varies along the supply curve. The reason for that is found in Annex 2.3.

Annex 2.3 Why a price inelastic (elastic) supply curve must cut the horizontal (vertical) axis

This is just a mathematical proof.

Let us return to the formula for the PES.

$$PES = \frac{\%\text{ change in Qs of good A}}{\%\text{ change in price of good A}}$$

$$PES = \frac{\frac{\text{change in Qs}}{\text{Qs}} \times 100\%}{\frac{\text{change in price}}{\text{price}} \times 100\%}$$

$$PES = \frac{\text{change in Qs}}{\text{change in price}} \times \frac{\text{price}}{\text{Qs}}$$

When the supply curve cuts the horizontal axis (Fig. 2.28):

For any point on this supply curve:

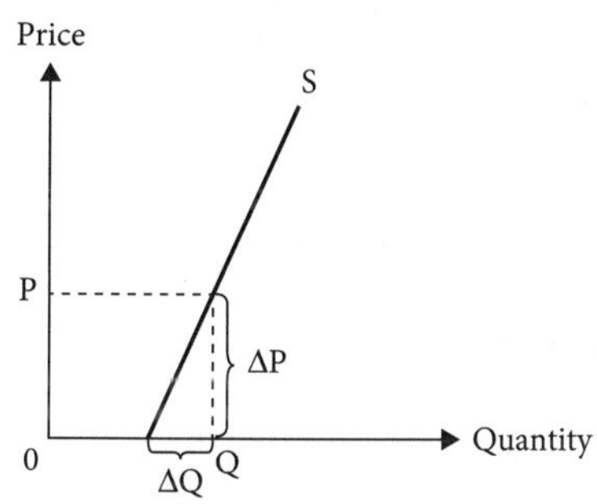

Figure 2.28: Geometric proof of an inelastic supply curve having to cut the horizontal axis.

Change in Qs = ΔQ

Change in price = ΔP

Price = 0P

Qs = 0Q

So,

PES = $(\Delta Q/\Delta P) \times (0P/0Q)$

PES = $(\Delta Q) \times (0Q)$ since $\Delta P = 0P$

PES = $(\Delta Q/0Q) < 1$ since clearly $\Delta Q < 0Q$

Working backwards, for PES to be less than 1, the graph must cut the horizontal axis. Also, this result is true for any point on this supply curve so even though the PES may vary along the supply curve, it will always be less than 1.

When the supply curve cuts the vertical axis (Fig. 2.29):

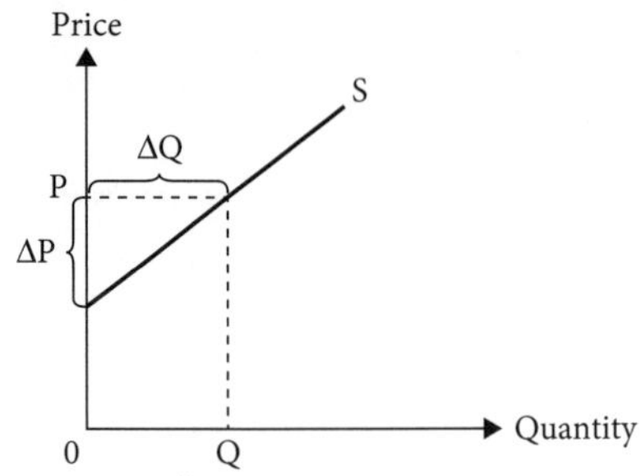

Figure 2.29: Geometric proof of an elastic supply curve having to cut the horizontal axis.

For any point on this supply curve:

Change in Qs = ΔQ

Change in price = ΔP

Price = 0P

Qs = 0Q

So,

PES = $(\Delta Q/\Delta P) \times (0P/0Q)$

PES = $(\Delta P) \times (0P)$ since $\Delta Q = 0Q$

PES = $(0P/\Delta P) > 1$ since clearly $0P > \Delta P$

Working backwards, for PES to be more than 1, the graph must cut the vertical axis. Also, this result is true for any point on this supply curve, so even though the PES may vary along the supply curve, it will always be more than 1.

Using the same steps, it should be clear that a unitary price elastic supply curve must pass through the origin.

Annex 2.4 Specific and ad valorem taxes

A specific tax is a fixed amount of tax imposed on each unit of good or service sold regardless of the price of the good or service. On the other hand, an ad valorem tax is a tax imposed on each unit of good or service sold based on a percentage of the original price of the good or service.

A specific tax imposed on producers will result in a parallel shift of the supply curve while an ad valorem tax imposed on producers will result in a diverging shift of the supply curve (or a pivotal shift of the supply curve). The parallel shift of a specific tax is explained in the main text. The pivotal shift caused by the ad valorem tax is due to the varying amount of the tax per unit. When the price of a good is low (e.g., \$10 in Fig. 2.30 below), the absolute value of the tax would also be low (e.g., 10% × \$10 = \$1). However, if the price of the good is high (e.g., \$20 in Fig. 2.30 below), the absolute value of the tax would also be high (e.g., 10% × \$20 = \$2). Hence, we see a pivotal shift of the supply curve when an ad valorem tax is imposed.

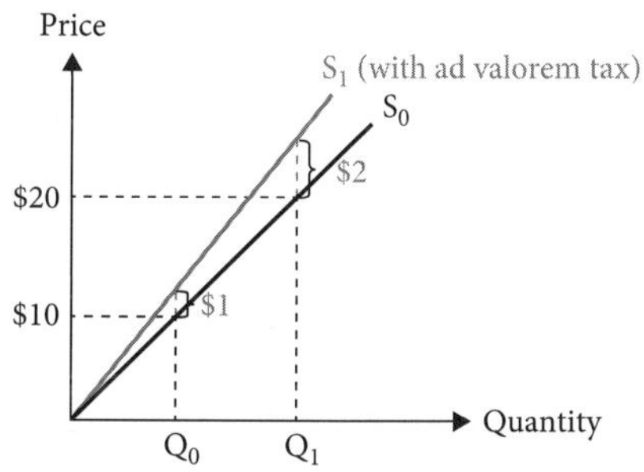

Figure 2.30: Pivotal shift of a supply curve under an ad valorem tax.

Annex 2.5 Extent of leftward shifts in the supply curve when an indirect tax is imposed

An indirect tax shifts the supply curve upwards by the same amount as the tax. However, the extent of the leftward shift depends on the PES. We illustrate this in the figure below.

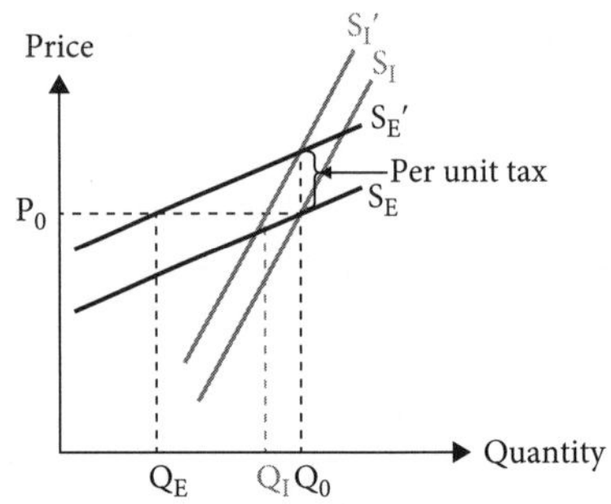

<table>
<tr><td>For a price elastic supply, the per unit tax shifts the supply from S_E to S_E'. The extent of the leftward shift is from Q_0 to Q_E (obtained from holding price constant at P_0 to see how much quantity supplied fell by).</td><td>For a price inelastic supply, the per unit tax shifts the supply from S_I to S_I'. The extent of the leftward shift is from Q_0 to Q_I (obtained from holding price constant at P_0 to see how much quantity supplied fell by).</td></tr>
<tr><td colspan="2">Since Q_EQ_0 is clearly more than Q_IQ_0, the same per unit tax causes a larger leftward shift for the price elastic supply than the price inelastic supply.</td></tr>
</table>

The intuition for this is as follows. The per unit tax effectively reduces the price the producers will receive for their goods. If the supply is price elastic, producers will be very responsive and reduce quantity supplied to a large extent (hence, the large leftward shift in supply). Conversely, if the supply is price inelastic, producers will be unresponsive and reduce quantity supplied to a small extent (hence, the small leftward shift in supply).

CHAPTER 3

FIRMS AND DECISION (H2 only)

The previous chapter dealt with analysing the markets where equilibrium price and quantity were determined by demand and supply. The economic agents involved were consumers that provide the demand, and producers that provide the supply. This chapter focuses on the individual producers, which are known as firms. A firm contributes to the supply of goods and services in the market. If there are many firms in the market, the market supply would be contributed by many firms. If there is only one firm in the market, the market supply would be contributed by the only firm.

3.1 Objectives of Firms

Firms need to make two types of decisions, price and output decisions and non-price decisions. The price and output decisions refer to the price that firms should set to achieve its objectives as well as the output to produce and sell in the market. Non-price decisions refer to other decisions that firms have to make, such as whether or not to engage in non-price activities of research and development (R&D) or advertising. Such decisions depend on the objectives of the firm.

3.1.1 The profit-maximising objective

Profit is the difference between total revenue (TR) and total cost (TC). Conventionally, we assume that all rational firms want to maximise profits. As explained in Chapter 1, to maximise profit, firms will make price and output decisions such that marginal revenue (MR) equals to marginal cost (MC). How price and output affect MR and MC will be explained in the subsequent sections.

It must be noted that in the real world, firms that want to maximise profits may have difficulty doing so, due to the lack of accurate data. For example, firms do not know for sure the MR for the different levels of output as that depends on the quantity demanded by consumers at each different price. As such, firms will have to make their decisions based on estimations of their demand.

3.1.2 Alternative objectives of firms[1]

Although profit maximisation is the conventional objective, in the short run, firms may have other objectives. This is especially so when there are different groups of decision-makers within the firm. These alternative objectives include the following:

- Revenue maximisation
- Profit satisficing
- Entry deterrence
- Market share dominance

1 Illustration of the alternative objectives of the firms can be found in Annex 3.1. They will only be understood after completing the section on cost and revenue concepts.

Each of the alternative objectives is explained in the subsequent paragraphs. It must be noted that although firms may have the abovementioned alternative objectives in the short run, in the long run, the primary objective of firms is usually profit maximising. Some of the short-run alternative objectives are to prepare for firms' long-run objective of profit maximising, for example, entry deterrence and market share dominance protect a firm's position in the market so that the firm can continue to make profits in the long run.

Revenue maximisation

A firm could pursue the objective of revenue maximisation rather than profit maximisation. In this case, instead of making price and output decisions such that MR equals MC (profit-maximising condition), the firm would make price and output decisions such that MR equals zero (MR = 0). This is because so long as the MR of producing one more unit of output is positive, production and sale of that unit would add to TR and increase TR. Total revenue is only maximised at the point where producing and selling the additional unit of output does not add to total revenue (MR = 0). This could be the case when the firm's decisions are heavily influenced by the sales manager or commission-based employees whose incomes are dependent on the firm's revenue instead of the firm's profit. This is because the output and TR of the firm when the firm is profit maximising is lesser compared to when the firm is revenue maximising. Therefore, if the managers' and employee's performance and bonuses are based on their revenue, the managers and employees might strive to revenue maximise instead.

Profit satisficing

Firms could also aim to be profit satisficing. In this case, instead of trying to maximise profit, firms aim to just enjoy some level of profit. If a firm's aim is profit satisfaction, so long as the TR exceeds total cost, the firm is currently earning some profits and they will not change their price or output. This is in comparison to profit-maximising firms where price and output decisions are continually adjusted to achieve the point where MR equals MC. The rationale behind this objective is that the effort and cost of obtaining information to achieve profit maximisation might be too high. Otherwise, it may also come about if the entrepreneur and managers of the firm are willing to accept lower profits for their own benefits, in the form of shorter working hours and lower stress.

Entry deterrence

Instead of profit maximising and making price and output decisions such that MR equals MC, a firm may decide to make price and output decisions to deter new firms from entering the market. This is usually done by producing a larger output at a price lower to the extent that potential entrants would be unwilling or unable to enter the market as they cannot compete against the lower price that the current firms are offering. Such a pricing strategy is known as limit pricing. Limit pricing involves the incumbent firm pricing at or just slightly above its average cost to prevent new firms from entering the market.

Market share dominance

Another possible objective could be that of a firm trying to compete with other firms for market share by poaching as many of the competitors' customers as possible. The decision is similar to entry deterrence with firms lowering the prices of their goods. However, instead of trying to discourage new firms from entering, the objective is to increase the firm's market share at the expense of its rivals. To do so, firms might price their products at a level below the cost of production of the products. This strategy is also known as predatory pricing. By lowering the price of their products, firms might end up incurring a loss; however, these losses are usually short term in nature and could eventually help a firm achieve other profits maximisations in the long run bcause it increases the firm's market share.

Social and environmental objectives

Other than maximising profits, firms may also consider the impact of their goods and production processes on society and the environment. Instead of using the lowest cost inputs and processes that might be harmful to society or the environment, firms might instead use less harmful inputs and processes but are of higher cost.

For example, farmers might be using more expensive production methods instead of using pesticides while farming, while restaurants or food manufacturers might use more expensive but healthier ingredients such as organic meats and unsaturated oils to prepare their products. Firms might also use biodegradable packaging rather than non-biodegradable plastics to pack and store their products so as to reduce environmental damage.

Some might argue that firms' decision to be socially and environmentally conscious might be due to an increase in the demand of consumers who are more socially and environmentally conscious. It is rational for firms to cater to the changing needs and demand of consumers in order to increase and maximise profits.

3.2 Costs and Revenue Concepts

3.2.1 Difference between short run and long run

Since profit maximisation requires the comparison of MR against MC, we turn to the study of a firm's cost structure (i.e., how the various components of a firm's cost changes as the firm changes the level of output). As a firm increases its output, its cost structure changes depending on whether some of its factors of production are fixed (e.g., having a fixed factory floor space versus being able to negotiate a new lease and have a smaller/larger factory floor space). This is because if some factors of production are fixed, increasing output must involve only increasing other factors of production that are variable (i.e., not fixed) such as labour. For example, if there is limited factory floor space (a fixed factor) and therefore, limited space for machines (also a fixed factor), the only way to increase output is to employ more labour (a variable factor).

However, if all factors of production are variable (e.g., if the firm is in the midst of deciding on a new lease and can choose to rent a factory space of any size), then, to increase output, the firm could use a larger factory with more floor space to accommodate more machines, on top of hiring more labour. As such, increasing output under the two scenarios (having fixed factors of production versus having all factors of production being variable) would affect the cost structure of the firm differently. This gives rise to a need to differentiate the conditions under which we study the cost structure of the firm.

The condition in which there is at least one fixed factor of production is termed the short run. The condition in which all factors of production are variable is termed the long run.

Definition(s):

Short run is the period in which at least one factor of production is fixed.

Long run is when all factors of production are variable.

A **fixed factor of production** is one whose quantity cannot be changed. As such, it will not vary with the amount of output produced.

A **variable factor of production** is one whose quantity can be changed. It varies with the amount of output produced. An increase in output would require an increase in variable factors of production employed and a decrease in output would also mean a decrease in variable factors employed.

3.2.2 Costs in the short run

In the short run, because there are fixed and variable factors, the total costs of production are also split into fixed and variable costs. It must be noted that all these costs are the opportunity cost of production.

Total cost

Total cost (TC) is the sum of all the costs incurred from employing all the factors of production. TC is the sum of both the total fixed cost (TFC) and total variable cost (TVC).

Total fixed cost

TFC is the sum of all the costs incurred from employing fixed factors of production. TFC is the total cost of all fixed factors. TFC does not change with the level of output.

Total variable cost

TVC is the sum of all the costs incurred from employing variable factors of production. TVC is the total cost of all variable factors. As variable factors are employed to increase output, TVC must also vary with output.

Average total cost

Average total cost (ATC) is the total cost divided by the amount of output. It is also the sum of average fixed cost (AFC) and average variable cost (AVC).

Average fixed cost

AFC is the TFC divided by the amount of output. It will decrease when output increases.

Average variable cost (AVC)

AVC is the TVC divided by the amount of output. It decreases before increasing when output increases.

Marginal cost

MC is the cost of producing an additional unit of output. It decreases before increasing when output increases. It also cuts AVC and ATC at their minimum points.

The graphs of TC, TFC, and TVC, and ATC, AFC, AVC, and MC are shown in Fig. 3.1.

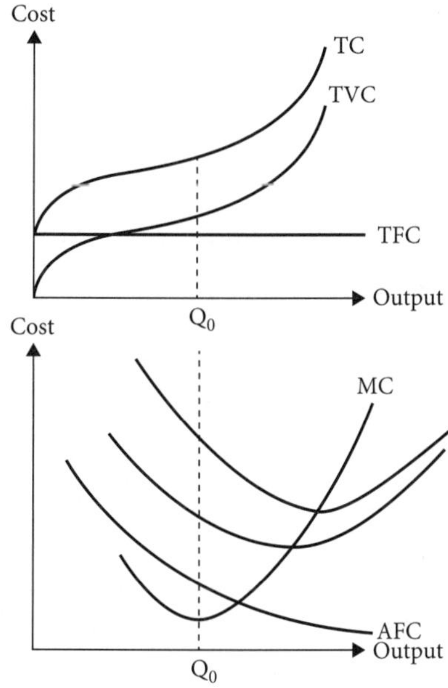

Figure 3.1: Illustration of costs in the short run.

In the short run, to increase output, more variable factors of production are added to the fixed factor(s). Since fixed factors do not vary with output, TFC does not vary with output. This explains why TFC is a horizontal straight line. AFC decreases with output as the TFC is spread over a larger output. This explains the downward sloping AFC.

To understand the shape of the TVC and AVC, we need to first study the shape of the MC.

Initially, as more variable factors of production are added to the fixed factor(s) of production, output will increase at an increasing rate. This is because with more variable factors of production (e.g., labour), each variable factor of production can play a more specialised role in production and each additional unit of variable factor of production will add more to the total output than the previous one. Each additional input adding more to the total output than the previous input also means that each additional output requires less input to produce than the previous output. As such, the MC (cost of each additional output) will decrease initially. This explains why the MC slopes downwards initially up to Q_0.

However, beyond Q_0, as more and more variable factors of production continue to be added to fixed factors to increase production, there starts to be overcrowding. Hence, each additional unit of variable factor of production will add less to the total output than the previous one. This phenomenon is known as the law of diminishing marginal returns. Each additional input adding less to the total output than the previous input also means that each additional unit of output requires more input to produce than the previous output. As such, the MC will increase. This explains why the MC slopes upwards again after Q_0.

We now turn back to the TVC curve. Since more variable factors of production are added to increase output, TVC increases with more output produced. However, up to Q_0, since MC is decreasing, the additional cost from each unit of output produced would decrease. Hence, TVC would increase at a decreasing rate. Beyond Q_0, since MC is increasing, the additional cost from each unit of output produced would increase. Hence, TVC would increase at an increasing rate.

AVC initially falls, reaches its minimum point at where it meets the MC, and then rises thereafter because of the mathematical relationship[b] between AVC and MC. If MC is less than AVC, the addition to the total cost is less than the current AVC and AVC will be "dragged" down. Numerically, if the current average cost (AC) is \$10, and the next unit of output costs \$8 to produce (i.e., MC = \$8), the AC once the new output is included would be less than \$10. Conversely, if MC exceeds AVC, AVC will be "dragged" up. This explains why AVC falls initially until it meets the MC, and then rises again when MC exceeds it.

The ATC also initially falls, reaches its minimum point where it meets the MC, and then rises thereafter because of a similar mathematical relationship.[2] Additionally, the gap between ATC and AVC decreases as the output increases. This is because the gap between the two represents the AFC because ATC = AFC + AVC, and AFC decreases with larger output.

3.2.3 Costs in the long run

In the long run, all factors of production are variable because even the previously fixed factors can now be changed, thus becoming variable too. As such, in the long run, to increase output, firms now increase output by increasing variable factors instead of adding variable factors to fixed factors like in the short run.

In the long run, since all the factors are variable, the AC is the same as AVC. To avoid confusion with short-run average cost (SRAC) and short-run AVC, the long-run AC is usually labelled as LRAC. LRAC is formed by tracing the lowest possible SRAC at each output. This is because since all factors are variable in the long run, rational profit-motivated firms would use the combination of factors to produce each level of output at the lowest possible AC. This is illustrated in Fig. 3.2 where a firm that wishes to produce Q' units of output would choose to operate on $SRAC_0$ instead of $SRAC_1$ as the AC of producing Q on $SRAC_0$ is AC_0' whereas that of producing on $SRAC_1$ is higher at AC_1'. If the firm wishes to produce Q'' units of output, it would choose to operate on $SRAC_1$ instead of $SRAC_0$ as the AC of producing Q'' on $SRAC_0$ is AC_0'' whereas that of producing on $SRAC_1$ is lower at AC_1''. So, the LRAC is derived by tracing out the lowest possible SRAC for every output level. It traces $SRAC_0$ for output levels below Q, and traces $SRAC_1$ for output levels above Q.

If we imagine there being very many SRAC curves, we will derive a smooth LRAC curve as shown in Fig. 3.3.

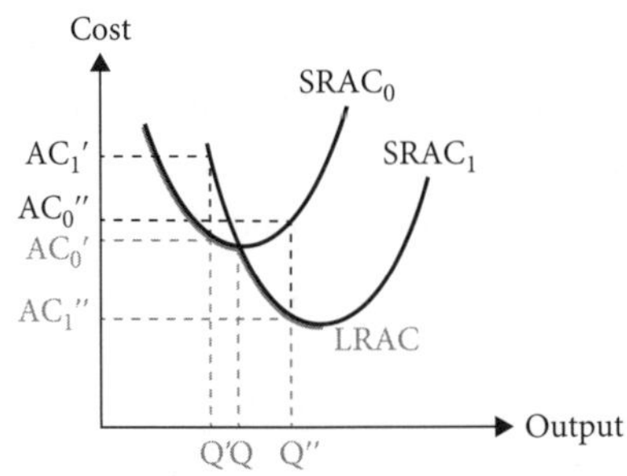

Figure 3.2: Deriving the LRAC.

2 The mathematical relationship is provided in Annex 3.2.

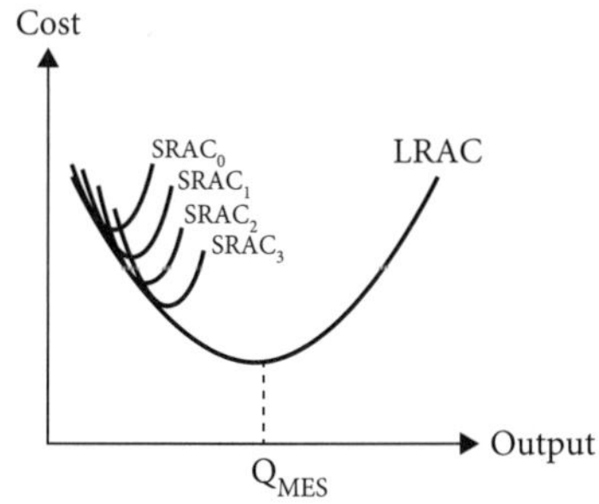

Figure 3.3: Deriving a smooth LRAC.

Changing the output in the long run is termed as changing the scale of production. Changing the scale of production could either cause the LRAC to increase or decrease. A firm's LRAC is a U-shaped curve with LRAC first decreasing before eventually increasing.[3] The output in which the lowest LRAC is first reached is known as the **minimum efficient scale (MES)**.

When increasing the scale of production results in a decrease in the LRAC, we say that the firm enjoys internal economies of scale (IEOS). Graphically, it is shown by the downward sloping portion of the LRAC curve as output increases from 0 towards the minimum efficient scale Q_{MES}.

When increasing the scale of production results in an increase in the LRAC, we say that the firm suffers internal diseconomies of scale (IDOS). Graphically, it is shown by the upward sloping portion of the LRAC curve as output increases beyond the minimum efficient scale Q_{MES}.

Definition(s):

Internal economies of scale (IEOS) are reductions in LRAC due to an increase in the scale of production.

Internal diseconomies of scale (IDOS) are increases in LRAC due to an increase in the scale of production.

The **minimum efficient scale (MES)** is the lowest output at which the lowest LRAC is reached.

3.2.4 Internal economies of scale (IEOS)

The main types of IEOS that a firm can enjoy or experience include the following:

- Technical economies of scale
- Financial economies of scale
- Risk-bearing economies of scale
- Managerial economies of scale
- Marketing economies of scale

Technical economies of scale

Technical economies of scale refer to the cost savings that a firm can enjoy from using more efficient methods of production, due to its larger scale of production.

3 Sometimes, it could decrease, remain constant, and then increase. However, such analysis is more rarely used.

Larger firms have the opportunity to utilise more efficient methods of productions which will lead to a lowered unit cost of production (fall in LRAC) when increasing the production of goods and services. Three common reasons are:

- Division and specialisation of labour
- Principle of increased dimensions
- Indivisibility of factors of production

Division and specialisation of labour—As a firm's scale of production or output increases to a large enough level, the firm could divide workers into groups to do more specific tasks and each worker will be able to specialise in the specific tasks assigned to them. As the workers specialise in doing the same tasks repeatedly, they will become better in those tasks and will be able to complete the tasks faster with fewer mistakes. By completing tasks faster, more goods can be produced in the same amount of time. With fewer mistakes, firms incur lesser cost due to wastage. Both will lead to lower AC of production and the LRAC will decrease due to increase in efficiency.

One example of division and specialisation of labour would be the Ford Motor Company, owned by Mr. Henry Ford, which introduced division and specialisation of labour by assigning each worker to one specific task during the manufacturing of the "Ford Model T" in the early 20th century. The manufacture of the car was divided into many stages and each worker only did one task (e.g., tightening of bolts and nuts, installation of engines, attachment of the car door, and polishing the car). The car would take shape as it moved down the production line and each worker carried out his task. Through division and specialisation of labour, cost savings were enjoyed as the man hours[4] required to produce each car was reduced and the AC decreases.

4 Man hours are the total number of hours all the labourers put in. For example, if 2 workers work 10 hours each to produce a car, the man hours used to produce a car would be 20 (2 workers × 10 hours each).

Principle of increased dimensions

As a firm's scale of production or output increases, due to the increased dimensions of factors utilised, the increase in output will require a less than proportionate increase in total cost. This idea of cost savings is especially relevant to the transportation and storage industries. Doubling the height and width of a storage space or building or transport vehicle leads to a more than proportionate increase in the cubic capacity. Even if the cost doubles, the unit cost of production will still decrease.

An example that is easy to visualise would be to imagine a freezer. When a freezer becomes twice as wide and twice as deep, its capacity increases by four times. So, four times as much of food can now be frozen. The electricity needed to power the freezer is unlikely to be four times what it was before. So, the AC of freezing one unit of food would now be lower.

This is one of the reasons why firms in freight (transport of goods) industries such as shipping firms and airlines continue to utilise larger container ships, tankers, and aircraft.

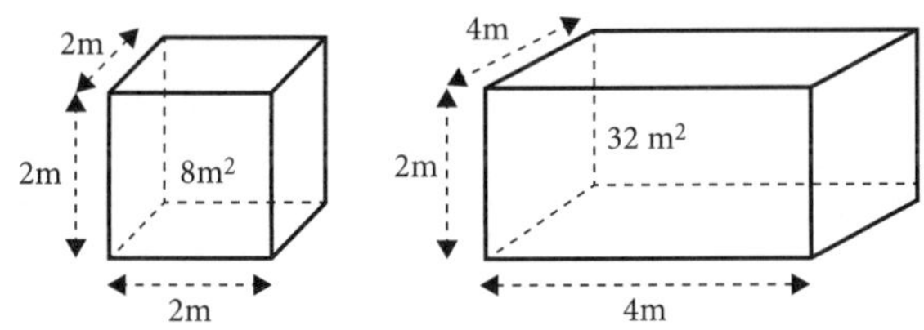

Indivisibility of factors of production—As a firm's scale of production or output increases to a large enough level, the firm can employ certain factors of production (e.g., machinery) designed for large-scale production. These factors are available only in large indivisible units. Smaller firms with their smaller scales of production are unable to utilise these machinery. Hence, the more efficient means of production only lowers the AC if the output produced is large enough. We say that factor indivisibility lowers AC only when the scale of production is large enough to utilise these indivisible factors.

One example would be the use of tractors in farming. If the farm is small and output is low, using a tractor would result in a higher AC as the cost of maintaining the tractors is spread over a small output. Hence, a shovel may be a cheaper way for farmers as the tractor would be underutilised. However, if the output is increased to a level that is large enough, it may then make sense for the farmer to use a tractor. Since the AC of using tractor is only lower than using a shovel when the output is large, when the firm produces a large enough scale of production, it can enjoy lower LRAC by switching to a tractor.

Financial economies of scale

Financial economies of scale refer to the cost savings that a firm can enjoy from having more favourable credit terms due to its larger scale of production.

Larger firms are deemed to be more "creditworthy" and enjoy more favourable credit terms such as lower interest rates compared to smaller firms. As larger forms tends to be less likely to fail and are safer debtors, banks and financial institutions would consider them more creditworthy and less risky to lend to. Larger firms are likely to have more assets that could be sold off to offset any debts, in the event that the firm defaults on its loans. Therefore, banks and financial institutions would then charge a lower interest rate on the loans that larger firms take. The lower interest rate that the firm pays contributes to the cost savings and the lowering of the LRAC.

For example, a large fast-food chain with 120 stores would most likely be charged a lower interest rate for the same amount of loan (e.g., one million dollars) compared to another small fast-food chain with 4 stores. If both fast-food chains close two stores due to poor business, the impact on the firms' ability to repay their loans will be smaller for the large fast-food chain with 120 stores.

Risk-bearing economies of scale

Rather similar to financial economies of scale, risk-bearing economies of scale refer to the cost savings that a firm can enjoy from being able to bear the risk of failure better than smaller firms, due to its larger scale of production. Larger firms with operations in various locations across various production plants experience lower location-specific risks and production plant–specific risks. Hence, they will also enjoy cost savings from paying lesser for insuring against risk. This reduces their AC of production.

Managerial economies of scale

Managerial economies of scale refer to the cost savings that a firm can enjoy from managers specialising in specific roles, due to its larger scale of production.

Similar to the division and specialisation of labour in technical economies of scale, larger firms with their larger scale of production can assign their managers to specialise in specific roles instead of one manager managing various departments. As the managers specialise in their specific tasks, they will become better in those tasks and will be able to complete the tasks faster and make fewer mistakes.

For example, large multi-national corporations (MNCs) typically have multiple departments (marketing, finance, audit, operations, and human resource) and specialised managers in each department, whereas small-and-medium enterprises (SMEs) typically have managers straddling various departments. The specialisation of managers in MNCs allows the firms to be more efficient and hence, enjoy a lower AC.

Marketing economies of scale

Marketing economies of scale refer to the cost savings that a firm can enjoy from purchasing factor inputs at a lower price due to its larger scale of production.

Larger firms with their larger scale of productions would require more factors of production such as raw materials and are more likely to buy these raw materials in bulk. Firms supplying those raw materials would be more interested to sell to larger firms buying in bulk and would hence, be more willing to offer bulk discounts to the large firms. Hence, the raw material cost per unit for a larger firm would be lower than that of a smaller firm buying raw materials in a smaller quantity. Lower raw material cost per unit would translate into lower AC for the firm.

For example, a large fast-food chain with 120 stores would most likely buy a larger quantity of burger buns from a bakery compared to a small fast-food chain with four stores. The bakery would be more willing to charge a lower price for each bun to the large fast-food chain compared to the small fast-food chain.

3.2.5 Internal diseconomies of scale (IDOS)

As a firm continues to expand its scale of production and increase its output, instead of enjoying IEOS and cost savings, the firm growing larger may suffer from IDOS instead and experience an increasing LRAC.

In another words, firms experience IDOS when an increase in their output or scale of production leads to an increase in their LRAC. The two main types of IDOS that a firm can experience are:

- High cost of monitoring and management
- Low morale of employees

High cost of monitoring and management

When a firm produces at a larger scale of production, the firm will have more departments and employ a greater number of workers, including hiring of people to monitor and manage employees to prevent shirking as well as to coordinate all the activities. More departments and employees would also lead to delays in decision-making processes and more miscommunication which would lead to an increase in wastage and cost. The higher cost of hiring additional labour for monitoring and managing purposes also adds to the unit cost and causes the LRAC to increase.

Low morale of employees

As a firm produces at a larger scale of production, due to the greater number of employees, each employee might feel less important or significant in the organisation and this may lead to employees feeling like they are "just another cog in the wheel." This would result in lower morale amongst employees and hence, a reduction in efficiency, causing LRAC to increase.

3.2.6 External economies and diseconomies of scale

Other than internal economies and diseconomies of scale which will affect the LRAC of firms, it is also possible for the firm's LRAC to change due to the expansion of the whole industry that the firm operates in.

In this case, the LRAC may increase or decrease, although the firm's output might remain constant.

A decrease in LRAC when the industry that a firm is in expands is known as external economies of scale (EEOS). This is illustrated in Fig. 3.4, where a decrease in LRAC due the expansion of the industry is represented by a downward shift of the LRAC ($LRAC_0$ to $LRAC_1$)

Increases in LRAC when the industry that a firm is in expands, are known as external diseconomies of scale (EDOS). This is illustrated in Fig. 3.4, where an increase in LRAC due to the expansion of the industry is represented by an upward shift of the LRAC ($LRAC_0$ to $LRAC_2$).

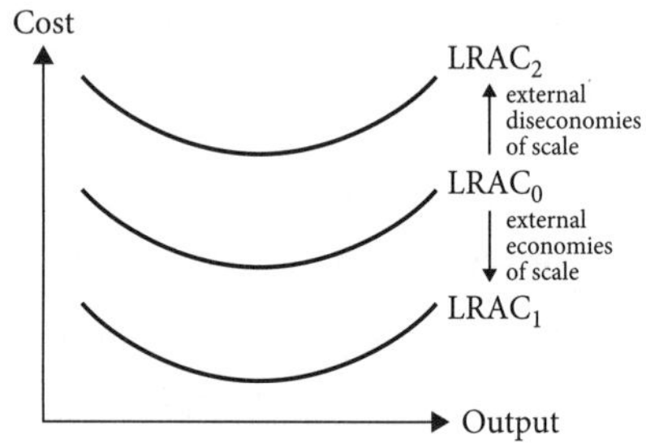

Figure 3.4: External economies and diseconomies of scale.

Definition(s):

External economies of scale (EEOS) are reductions in LRAC due to the expansion of the industry that the firm is in.

External diseconomies of scale (EDOS) are increases in LRAC due to the expansion of the industry that the firm is in.

For most industries, as the industry expands, firms will first experience EEOS and as the industry continues to expand, firms will then experience EDOS.

3.2.7 External economies of scale (EEOS)

Common reasons for EEOS include the following:

- Availability of shared resources
- Improvement in infrastructure
- Availability of industry-specific skilled labour

Availability of shared resources

A growing industry means that more firms must have joined the industry. As such, with more firms, there would be a greater pool of shared resources such as R&D facilities and knowledge, that every firm can tap on. This reduces the LRAC for every firm in the industry as they do not each have to bear the full cost of conducting all the R&D and knowledge generation. Thus, this shifts the LRAC for every firm in the industry downwards.

Improvement in infrastructure

When an industry grows, infrastructure may also be built to accommodate the growth. With improvement in infrastructure, production can take place with higher efficiency and lower unit cost of production, thus, reducing LRAC.

For example, the growth of the fishing industry by a river may prompt the government to build infrastructure like cold storage facilities, and proper piers or roads so that the fishes caught by the firms can reach their market faster without spoiling. This building of infrastructure by the government would reduce the LRAC of all firms in the industry.

Availability of industry-specific skilled labour

When an industry grows, relevant skilled labour or industry-specific skilled labour would naturally gravitate there to look for jobs. With the increased availability of industry-specific skilled labour, both quantity and quality of labour will increase, resulting in higher efficiency and lower unit cost of production, thus, reducing LRAC of all firms in the industry.

For example, the growth of the computer science industry in Singapore has attracted many more computer scientists to seek employment here. The increase in availability of skilled labour allows each firm in the industry to more easily employ skilled labour and hence, become more efficient. This gain in efficiency reduces LRAC for computer science firms in Singapore. Similarly, the best minds in the industries of computer programing and engineering might be attracted to Silicon Valley in San Francisco, California, where there are a large number of technology firms. This would also cause a reduction in LRAC of such firms in California.

3.2.8 External diseconomies of scale (EDOS)

Common reasons for EDOS include the following:

- Strain on physical infrastructure
- Shortage of industry-specific resources

Strain on physical infrastructure

As the industry keeps growing, it may cause a strain on the physical infrastructure if new infrastructure is not developed to keep up with the industry's growth. The strain on physical infrastructure such as road and utilities would lead to problems such as traffic jams developing on the roads leading to and from the industrial cluster, or power outages, and blackouts, causing firms to be less efficient, as it now takes more time and effort to produce each unit of good. This would cause an increase in LRAC and a higher unit cost of production for all the firms in the industry.

Shortage of industry-specific resources

Also, as the industry grows, there may be more firms competing for the limited industry-specific resources. As demand for these resources increases, there is a bidding up of the prices of these resources, causing an increase in LRAC and a higher unit cost of production for all the firms in the industry.

3.2.9 Revenue

Just as there are the concepts of total cost, AC, and MC, there are corresponding concepts of TR, average revenue (AR), and MR. However, unlike cost curves, there is no difference in the short-run and long-run revenue curves.

Total revenue (TR)

TR is the total sum a firm receives from selling certain units of output.

It is calculated by multiplying the quantity of the goods and services sold with the price of the goods and services sold. Just like how TR in a market is equal to $P_{\text{market}} \times Q_{\text{market}}$, the TR of a firm is equal to $P_{\text{firm}} \times Q_{\text{firm}}$.

Average revenue (AR)

AR is the revenue collected from each unit of output sold.

It is calculated by dividing TR by the quantity of the goods and services sold. Assuming all goods are sold at a single price, AR will be equal to the price of the good since $\text{AR} = \frac{\text{TR}}{\text{Q}} = \frac{P \times \text{Q}}{\text{Q}} = \frac{P \times \cancel{Q}}{\cancel{Q}} = P$

Marginal revenue (MR)

MR is the addition to the TR from producing an additional unit of output and selling it.[5] The MR of the nth unit of good sold is the difference between the TR from selling n number of units and selling $n-1$ number of units:

$\text{MR}_n = \text{TR}_n - \text{TR}_{n-1}$

> *Definition(s):*
>
> **Total Revenue (TR)** is the total sum a firm receives from selling certain units of output.
>
> **Average Revenue (AR)** is the revenue collected from each unit of good.
>
> **Marginal Revenue (MR)** is the addition to the total revenue from producing an additional unit of output and selling it.

5 MR was first introduced in Chapter 1. It is re-introduced here for the readers' convenience.

The shapes of these graphs depend on the features of the market structure that a firm operates in and will be revisited for each of the market structures.

3.3 Characteristics of Market Structures

To better understand firms' decisions, it is important to understand the types of market structure that a firm operates in. Different market structures with different characteristics will influence a firm's price and output decisions. The four main types of market structures include perfect competition (PC), monopolistic competition (MPC), oligopoly, and monopoly.

Characteristics that will determine the type of market structure a firm operates in and influence a firm's price and output decisions include the following:

- Level of the barriers to entry (BTE)
- Number and size of firms
- The degree of interdependence
- Type of product
- Degree of information

3.3.1 Level of barriers to entry (BTE)

BTEs refer to obstacles that prevent new firms from entering an industry. The level of BTE is one of the characteristics and is a key determinant of a market's structure. This determines how firms in the market behave.

The various types of BTEs include the following:

- Financial BTEs
- Cost BTEs
- Control of raw materials
- Legal barriers
- Strategic entry barriers by incumbent firms.

If none of these BTEs exist, the market is described as having no BTEs and firms are free to enter the market.

Financial BTEs refer to the difficulty faced by new firms entering the market, due to the difficulty in securing loans/obtaining credit.

Cost BTEs refer to the difficulty of new firms entering the market due to cost reasons such as high start-up cost or presence of significant IEOS in the industry. High start-up cost makes it difficult for new firms to enter as they may not have the funds to pay for the start-up cost. The presence of significant IEOS means that the incumbent firms which produce a larger scale of output would have lower LRAC than the potential entrant. This puts the potential entrant at a cost disadvantage should it enter the industry. Hence, this also acts as a BTE.

Control of raw materials acts as a BTE because if incumbent firms have control over raw materials, they could easily prevent new firms from entering the industry by withholding the raw materials. Potential firms without access to factors of production would not be able to enter the industry.

Legal BTEs refer to laws/regulations that prevent new firms from entering the industry. For example, a law requiring a firm to own a license to operate acts as a BTE as new firms must first obtain the license before they can enter the market. Similarly, patents and copyright laws also act as BTEs as they prevent new firms from entering the industry and selling the same product.

Strategic entry barriers by incumbent firms refer to actions taken by incumbent firms to specifically discourage new firms from entering the market. One such action where incumbent firms price at average cost to discourage potential entrants from entering the market is known as limit pricing.

3.3.2 Number and size of firms

Another characteristic is the number of firms as well as the size of firms.

- The number of firms refers to the total number of firms in the industry.
- The size of firms refers to the market share that each firm possesses.

The number of firms is inversely related to the size of firms. With a larger number of firms, the size of each individual firm will be smaller. On the other hand, with a smaller number of firms, the size of each individual firm will be larger.

In the real world, the size of each firm can be better understood using the concept of the market concentration ratio.

Market concentration ratio (n-firm concentration ratio)

In the real world, industries seldom fit perfectly into the characteristics of a market structure in terms of the number and size of firms. For example, in the fashion industry, there are a few large firms such as Uniqlo and H&M, but also many small firms such as clothing and apparel shops along Bugis street or at dry markets. Hence, economists measure the number and size of firms using the n-firm concentration ratio.

Definition(s):

The ***n*-firm concentration ratio** is the percentage of total sales or production accounted for by the largest *n* number of firms in an industry.

For example, the four-firm concentration ratio would be obtained by adding the percentage of total sales or production each of the four largest firms account for. A four-firm concentration ratio of 70% would mean that 70% of the sales in the industry belonged to the top four firms.

3.3.3 Degree of interdependence

Degree of interdependence refers to the degree to which one firm in the industry is affected by the actions of another firm in the industry. If the firm is affected to a large extent, we say that the degree of interdependence is high. The degree of interdependence is determined by the number of firms in the market structure. The lesser the number of firms, the higher the market share of each firm, and the more interdependent firms will be.

3.3.4 Type of good

Type of good refers to whether the output of the firms in the industry is homogenous or differentiated.

If the product sold by each firm is identical and exactly the same in every aspect (which means that the goods are perfect substitutes), we say that the products are homogenous.

On the other hand, if the goods that firms in the market produce are similar or serve similar purposes, but are not perfect substitutes, we say that the products are differentiated. If there are no substitutes, we say that the product is unique.

In the real world, most goods and services are differentiated in many ways. Two goods can serve a similar purpose but the differences can be either perceived (in terms of branding) or actual (in terms of quality).

3.3.5 Degree of information

The degree to which information is perfect refers to the extent to which economic agents have access to information. Perfect information would mean that consumers know the price that every single producer in the market is charging and that producers know their own cost and revenue conditions as well as every other firm's cost and revenue conditions. Any departure from this is imperfect information.

3.3.6 Overview of the characteristics of market structures

The following table presents a summary of the characteristics of each of the four market structures of PC, MPC, oligopoly, and monopoly.

	Perfect competition	**Monopolistic competition**	**Oligopoly**	**Monopoly**
Level of BTEs	None	Low	High	Very high
Number of firms	Many	Many	A few	One
Size of firms	Small	Small	Large	Large
Degree of interdependence	None	Low	High	None (no rivals)
Type of product	Homogenous	Differentiated	Homogenous/ differentiated	Unique
Degree of information	Perfect	Imperfect	Imperfect	Imperfect

In the subsequent sections, we study each market structure in detail to understand how the characteristics will affect the behaviour as well as performance of firms in each market structure.

3.4 Perfect Competition

3.4.1 Characteristics of PC

	Perfect competition
Level of barriers to entry	None
Number of firms	Many
Size of firms	Small
Degree of interdependence	None
Type of product	Homogenous
Degree of information	Perfect

The key characteristics of the market structure of PC are that there no BTEs, many small firms in the market, no interdependence, homogenous products sold by every firm, and perfect knowledge between consumers and producers.

Degree of BTEs

There are no BTEs for the PC market structure and new firms are free to enter the industry. Since whether a firm can easily exit an industry if things turn sour is also a consideration for firms deciding whether to enter in the first place (i.e., difficulty in exiting an industry is a barrier that prevents firms from entering an industry), having no BTEs also implies no barriers to exit.

Number and size of firms

In the PC market structure, there are many small firms to the extent that no individual seller has the ability to influence the market supply and the market price.[6] In terms of the market concentration ratio, the four-firm concentration ratio of the perfectly competitive market would be very small and insignificant.

Degree of interdependence

There is no interdependence between firms as firms neither engage in price nor non-price competition (to be explained in later sections) and hence, cannot affect one another through their actions.

Type of product

In the PC market structure, the product is a homogeneous product. The product sold by each firm is identical and exactly the same in every aspect. The product of any one producer is a perfect substitute for the products of other producers.

Degree of information

In the PC market structure, all the economic agents have perfect knowledge. Both the buyers and the sellers have perfect knowledge. Consumers are aware of all the prevailing market prices and product quality of every producer. Producers are aware of all the technology, cost conditions, production processes used by other firms, and the availability of substitutes.

6 Note that for all four market structures, we assume that there are many buyers, to the extent that no individual buyer has the ability to influence the market demand and the market price. The study of what happens if buyers have buying power (i.e., monopsony power) is not in the syllabus.

Note that in the real world, it is practically impossible for both consumers and producers to have perfect knowledge. PC is just a hypothetical market for us to benchmark other market structures against.

3.4.2 Price and output decision of firms in PC

The characteristics of PC will affect how firms in the PC market structure make price and non-price decisions. Given the characteristics of there being many firms producing a homogeneous product and perfect knowledge, each firm in a PC industry therefore, has no control over market price regardless of its output level. Every firm is a price-taker. This means that every firm sells its product at a market price that is determined by the interaction of the market demand and supply.

The PC firm's demand curve is perfectly price elastic (horizontal demand curve), at the market price which is determined by the market demand and supply. With reference to Fig. 3.5, given that the market demand curve is D_{market} and the market supply curve is S_{market}, the market price is P_{market}. So the PC firm's demand curve is perfectly price elastic at the market price of P_{market}.

Firms will not price their goods differently from the market price. This is because if a firm sets a price above the market price, then the quantity demanded of its goods would fall to zero because the product that it sells are perfect substitutes of the other firms' products (homogenous products). Consumers with their perfect knowledge will buy from other PC firms instead. On the other hand, it does not make sense for the firm to price below the market price. This is because since there are very many small firms, such that no single firm can influence the market supply, we can assume that a PC firm would be able to sell any amount of output the firms produces (i.e., no single firm would be able to increase the supply such that a surplus would be formed in the market). Since the PC firm is able to sell any output produced at the given market price, it does not make sense to reduce the price to increase the quantity demanded, as the firm can already sell as much at the given market price.

Therefore, a PC firm will only charge the good at the market price and is termed as a price-taker with the PC firm's demand curve being perfectly price elastic, as illustrated by the horizontal demand curve for the firm shown in Fig. 3.5.

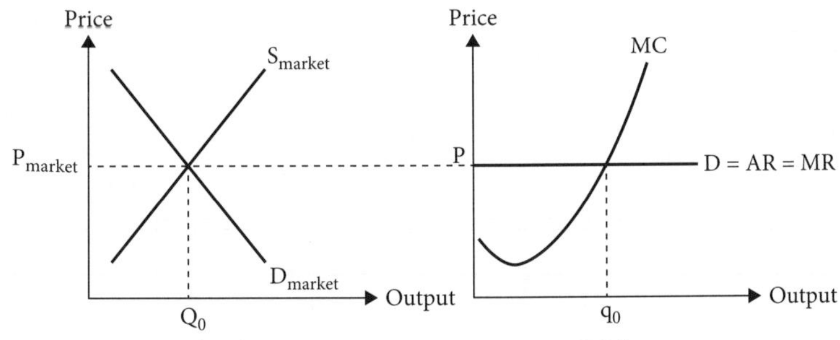

Figure 3.5: Price and output decision for PC.

Since the firm's price is taken from the market price, $P = P_{market}$. As established in the earlier paragraphs, the firm's demand is perfectly elastic at price P ($D = P$). Also, since each unit of good is sold at price P, the AR at any given level of output would be the price of the output ($P = \text{AR}$). Additionally, the MR each unit brings is also the market price ($P = \text{MR}$). In sum, $P = D = \text{AR} = \text{MR}$. To maximise profits, the firm will produce up to the output where MC = MR, where MC is rising. This is represented by q_0 in Fig. 3.5.

The profit maximising output is q_0 where MC = MR because at any output before q_0, the MC is lower than the MR (MC < MR), which means that the additional revenue the firm will collect from selling the next unit is more than the additional cost the firm will incur. If the firms increase output, the firm's profits will increase; therefore, the firms will increase production towards q_0 (where MC = MR).

At any output beyond q_0, the MC is higher than the MR (MC > MR), which means that the additional revenue the firm will collect from selling the next unit is less than the additional cost the firm will incur. If the firm increases output, the firm's profits will decrease, therefore, firms will not produce beyond q_0 (where MC = MR).

In sum, the PC firm will price the good at P and produce q_0 units of output by producing the output where MC = MR, where MC is rising.

3.4.3 Short-run profits for firms in PC

In the short run, when at least one of the factors of productions is fixed, firms in the PC market structure can earn either supernormal profits, normal profits, or subnormal profits. This could be determined by comparing the AC against AR (Price) at q_0 or TC against TR as shown in the following figures:

<table>
<tr><th>Type of profit</th><th>Description</th></tr>
<tr><td>Supernormal profit
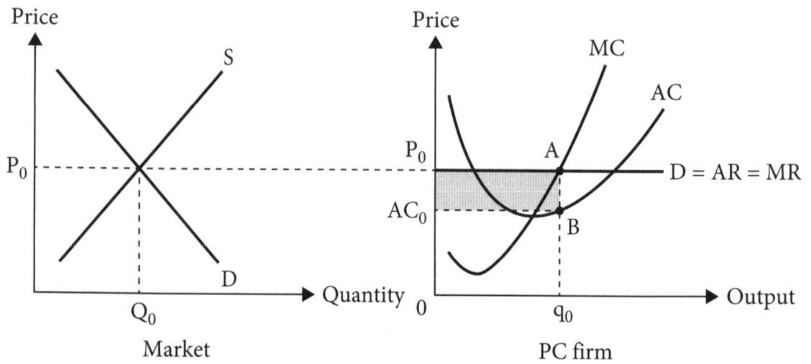
</td><td>$\text{TR} = P_0 \times q_0$
(area $0P_0Aq_0$)

$\text{TC} = \text{AC}_0 \times q_0$
(area 0AC_0Bq_0)

TR > TC as $P_0 > \text{AC}_0$

Supernormal profit is shaded</td></tr>
<tr><td>Normal profit
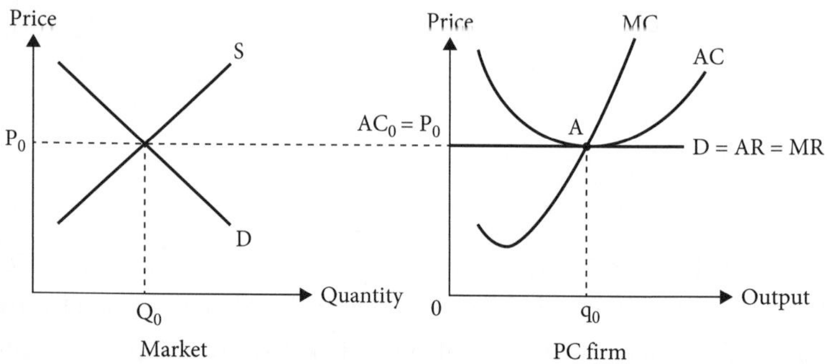
</td><td>$\text{TR} = P_0 \times q_0$
(area $0P_0Aq_0$)

$\text{TC} = \text{AC}_0 \times q_0$
(area 0AC_0Aq_0)

TR = TC as $P_0 = \text{AC}_0$</td></tr>
</table>

Subnormal profit

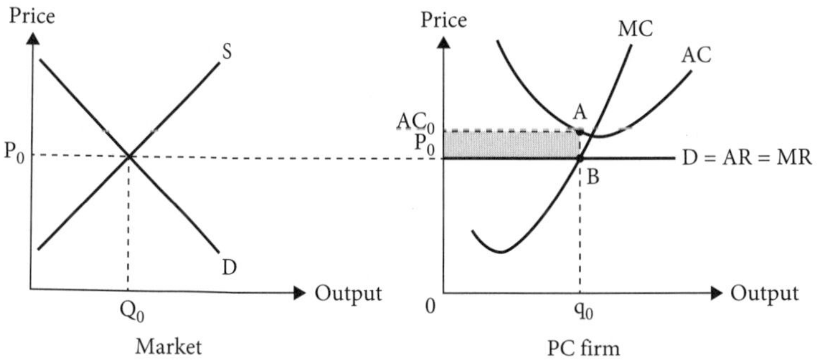

$TR = P_0 \times q_0$ (area $0P_0Bq_0$)

$TC = AC_0 \times q_0$ (area $0AC_0Aq_0$)

$TR < TC$ as $P_0 < AC_0$

Subnormal profit/loss is shaded

3.4.4 Short-run shut down condition for firms in PC

In event that a firm is earning subnormal profits (TR < TC), the firm would need to decide whether to continue production or shut down.

If a firm is earning subnormal profits in the long run, no profit-motivated firm will continue production. Firms will shut down. However, if they are making subnormal profits in the short run, firms have to decide whether to continue production depending on how much subnormal profits they are currently earning. Whether a firm earning subnormal profits would continue production or shut down is determined by whether their TR can cover their variable cost. This is because even if a firm chooses to shut down in the short run, it will incur fixed cost, which is cost incurred when the output is zero (e.g., rent still needs to be paid even if there is no production going on). So, it becomes necessary to consider whether the revenue is sufficient to offset some of the fixed cost. There are three possible scenarios in which the firm is making subnormal profits in the short run.

When TR is less than TVC (TR < TVC)

If a firm's TR is less than TVC, it means that the firm is unable to cover all their variable cost. If the firm chooses to continue production, the firm will incur all the fixed cost and some of the variable cost. On the other hand, if the firm chooses to shut down, the firm will only incur the fixed cost. Therefore, the firm should shut down.

Note that when TR < TVC, AR < AVC.

When TR is equal to TVC (TR = TVC)

If a firm's TR is equal to TVC, it means that the firm is able to cover all their variable cost only. If the firm shuts down, the firm will incur all the fixed cost. On the other hand, if the firm chooses to continue production, the firm will also incur all the fixed cost. Therefore, whether the firm chooses to shut down or stay in the market, the outcome would be the same. If the firm is optimistic of the future situation (e.g., expects higher revenue or lower cost), the firm should continue production. If the firm is not optimistic of the future situation or if there are other markets that might be more profitable for the firm, the firm should shut down. For simplicity's sake, we assume that such a firm will not shut down.

Note that when TR = TVC, AR = AVC.

When TR is more than TVC (TR > TVC)

If a firm's TR is more than its TVC, it means that the firm is able to cover all their variable cost and still be able to cover some of their fixed cost. If the firm shuts down, the firm will incur all the fixed cost. On the other hand, if the firm choose to continue production, the firm will only incur some of the fixed cost. Therefore, the firm should not shut down but continue production instead.

Note that when TR > TVC, AR > AVC.

The three scenarios above are illustrated as follows:

Decision of a firm earning subnormal profits in the short run

<table>
<tr><td>Shut down</td><td>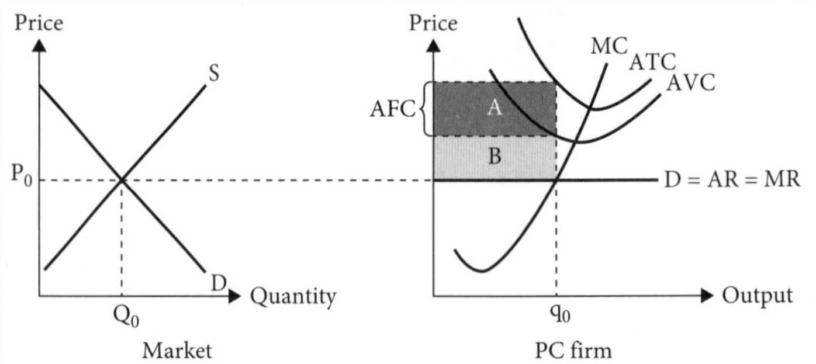
</td><td>AR < AVC
TR < TVC
Area A + B is the loss if it continues
Area A is the loss if it shuts down ($TFC = AFC \times q_0$)</td></tr>
<tr><td>Neutral (assumed not to shut down)</td><td>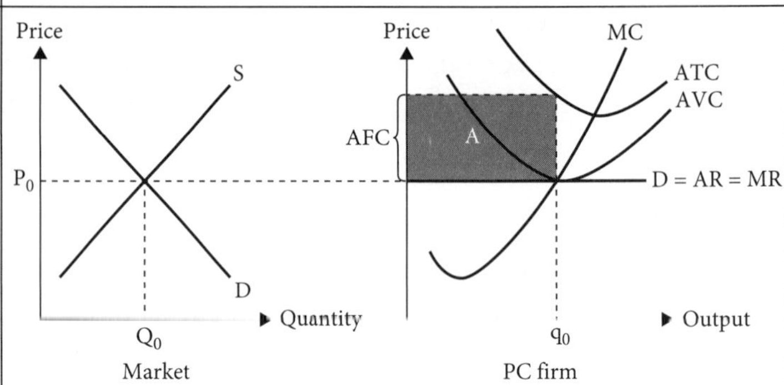
</td><td>AR = AVC
TR = TVC
Area A is the loss if it continues
Area A is the loss if it shuts down ($TFC = AFC \times q_0$)</td></tr>
<tr><td>Does not shut down</td><td>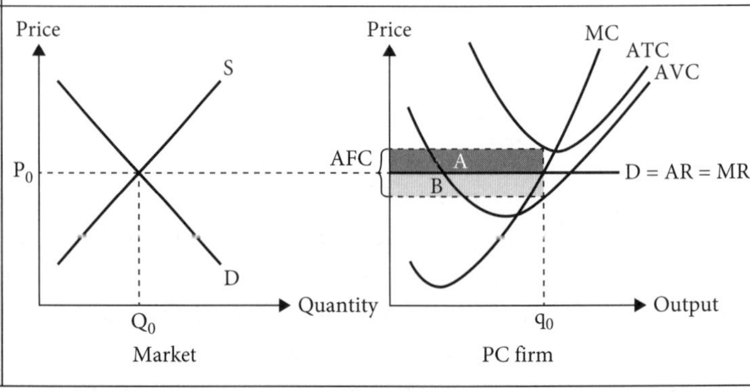
</td><td>AR > AVC
TR > TVC
Area A is the loss if it continues
Area A + B is the loss if it shuts down ($TFC = AFC \times q_0$)</td></tr>
</table>

Note: All firms will shut down when transiting into long run as long as firms are making subnormal profits.

3.4.5 Long-run price and output decision for firms in PC

As firms in the PC market structure move from the short run to the long run, the *P* and *Q* decisions may change.

When a firm moves from short run to long run, it will no longer incur any fixed cost as all factors are variable. As such, as a firm moves from short run to long run, it will continue production if it was making supernormal or normal profit in the short run, and shut down if it was making subnormal profit (i.e., the long-run shut down condition is TR < TC).

If a firm in the PC market structure is earning supernormal profits in the short run, as the firm transitions to the long run, the supernormal profits will make the market attractive to new potential firms. Since there are no BTEs in the PC market structure, new firms would be able to join the market, resulting in an increase in market supply, due to an increase in the number of producers. As the market supply increases (S_0 to S_1), the market price will fall (P_0 to P_1). As the market price decreases, as each firm is a price-taker, the price that it charges will also decrease and the demand of each PC firm will decrease and demand curve shifts down from being a horizontal line at P_0 to a horizontal line at P_1 and the firm will also reduce the output it sells from q_0 to q_1. This can be illustrated in the graph shown in Fig. 3.6.

So long as there are supernormal profits to be made, new firms will continue to enter the market and the supply will increase, causing the changes described earlier. In this manner, the price that the firm charges and the output produced will keep decreasing until there are only normal profits to be made. This is because when the firms are making normal profits, new firms will stop entering the industry.

The long-run price and output decision (P_1 and q_1) for the firm is hence, different from the short-run price and output decision (P_0 and q_0) when new firms enter the industry.

Figure 3.6: Long-run adjustment for short-run supernormal profits in PC.

If a firm in the PC market structure is earning normal profit in the short run, no new firms will be attracted to the market and the long-run price and output decision would be the same as the short-run price and output decision.

On the other hand, if a firm in the PC market structure is earning subnormal profits in the short run, as the firm transitions to the long run, some firms will shut down and leave the market, resulting in a decrease in market supply due to a decrease in the number of producers. As the market supply decreases (S_0 to S_1), the market price will increase (P_0 to P_1). As the market price increases, as each firm is a price-taker, the price that it charges will also increase and the demand of each PC firm will increase and the demand curve will shift up from being a horizontal line at P_0 to a horizontal line at P_1 and the firm will also increase the output it sells from q_0 to q_1. This can be illustrated in the graph shown in Fig. 3.7.

So long as there is subnormal profit, existing firms will leave the market and the supply will decrease, causing the changes described earlier. In this manner, the price that the remaining firms charge and the output produced will keep increasing until there is only normal profit to be made. This is because when the firms are making normal profit, existing firms will stop leaving the industry.

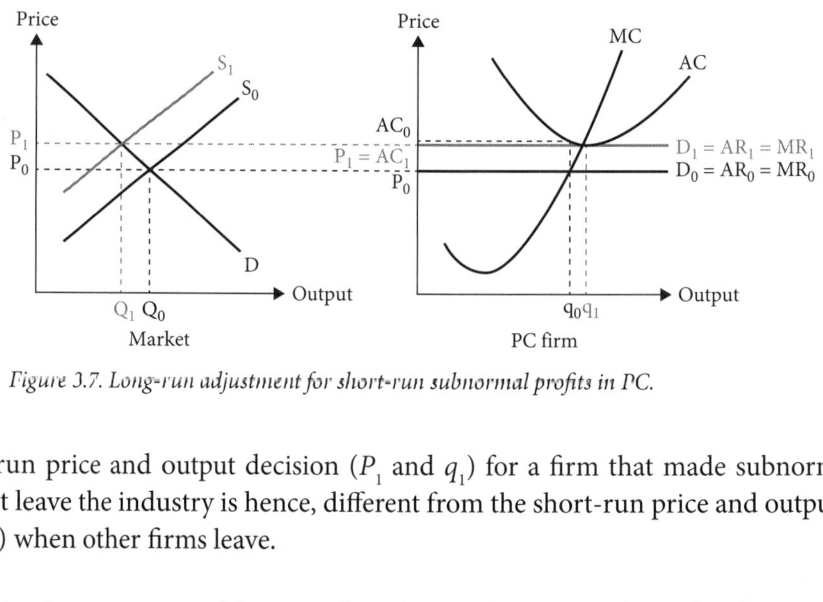

Figure 3.7. Long-run adjustment for short-run subnormal profits in PC.

The long-run price and output decision (P_1 and q_1) for a firm that made subnormal profits but did not leave the industry is hence, different from the short-run price and output decision (P_0 and Q_0) when other firms leave.

The following is a summary of the type of profit a PC firm can make in the short run, whether it will shut down in the short run, the adjustment from short run to long run, and the type of profit it will make in the long run.

<table>
<tr><th colspan="4">Short run</th></tr>
<tr><th>Supernormal profit</th><th>Normal profit</th><th colspan="2">Subnormal profit</th></tr>
<tr><td>$TR > TC$
$TR > (TFC + TVC)$</td><td>$TR = TC$
$TR = (TFC + TVC)$</td><td colspan="2">$TR < TC$
$TR < (TFC + TVC)$</td></tr>
<tr><td colspan="2" rowspan="3">Firms will continue production</td><td colspan="2">Firms will consider either continuing production or shut down</td></tr>
<tr><td>$TR \geq TVC$</td><td>$TR < TVC$</td></tr>
<tr><td>Short-run shut down condition is not met. Continue production in the short run.</td><td>Short-run shut down condition is met. Shut down in the short run.</td></tr>
<tr><th colspan="3">Transition to the long run</th><td>NA</td></tr>
<tr><td>New firms enter the industry, market supply increases, and market price will decrease.</td><td>No incentive for firms to enter or leave the market. Market supply remains constant. No changes to market.</td><td>Some firms will shut down and leave the industry. Market supply increases and market price will increase.</td><td>NA</td></tr>
<tr><th colspan="3">Long run</th><td>NA</td></tr>
<tr><td>Normal profit in the long run</td><td>Normal profit in the long run</td><td>Normal profit in the long run for firms that remained in the market</td><td>NA</td></tr>
</table>

In summary, in the short run, firms in the PC market structure can earn supernormal profits, normal profits, or subnormal profits. However, in the long run, firms in the PC market structure will only earn normal profits.

It should be noted that shutting down in the short run does not mean leaving the industry. It only means that the firm chooses not to produce any output (e.g., leave the factory idle). Shutting down in the long run means that the firm chooses to leave the industry. It will cease to exist. So, the short-run shut down condition is used by the firms to decide whether to produce any goods for that period, and the long-run shut down condition is used by the firm to decide whether to stay in the industry.

3.4.6 Non-price strategies of firms in PC

The characteristics of the PC market structure having homogenous products and perfect information, preclude the possibility of PC firms using non-price strategies. This is because non-price strategies involve differentiating a firm's product from other firms' in either perceived or actual differentiation. Regarding the former, because a feature of PC is that firms sell homogenous products, the possibility of non-price strategies is assumed away (i.e., if PC firms could carry out non-price strategies, their products would become differentiated and the market structure would no longer be a PC). Therefore, in a PC market structure, firms cannot carry out non-price strategies.

3.5 Monopoly

3.5.1 Characteristics of monopoly

	Monopoly
Level of BTEs	Very high
Number of firms	One
Size of firms	Large
Degree of interdependence	None (no rivals)
Type of product	Unique
Degree of information	Imperfect

The key characteristics of a monopoly are that there are high BTEs, only one firm in the market (no rivals), a unique product is sold by the firm, and there is imperfect knowledge between consumers and producer. The only firm (or the dominant firm) in the monopoly is known as monopolist. These characteristics will affect a monopolist's price and non-price decisions.

It is important to note that the idea of monopoly or whether a firm is a monopoly largely depends on the context. For example, the noodle stall in a school canteen is likely to be a monopoly for noodles if there is only one stall selling noodles. However, it is not a monopoly for food. The context in this case is the definition of the industry or the market. The drink stall is likely to be a monopoly in a shopping centre food court (if there is only one stall selling drinks). However, it is unlikely to be a monopoly for drinks in the whole shopping centre. Again, the context in this case is how we define the market.

Degree of BTEs

There are high levels of BTEs in the monopoly market structure and new firms have difficulties entering the industry. The BTEs refer to obstacles that prevent new firms from entering an industry. They include the following:[7]

- Financial BTEs
- Cost BTEs
- Control of raw materials
- Legal barriers
- Strategic BTEs by incumbent firms

In many countries, "Legal barriers" and "Control of raw materials" are the more likely reasons why a monopoly exists.

7 Refer to Section 3.3.1 for more details.

Number and size of firms

In theory, a monopoly has to be the sole producer in the entire market. In reality, if a single firm dominates most of the industry in terms of market share, we also consider it a monopoly even though there may be other small producers. In terms of the market concentration ratio, the four-firm concentration ratio of the monopoly would be very high and almost equal to the market share of the largest firm.

Degree of interdependence

There is no interdependence to speak of, as a monopoly is either the only firm in the market (and therefore has no competitors at all) or an overwhelmingly dominant firm in the market (in which case, it will be quite unaffected by the actions of the insignificant firms).

Type of product

A monopolist sells a unique product—a product with no close substitutes produced by other firms. Price elasticity of demand (PED) for the monopolist's product is likely to be the lowest (most inelastic) compared to other forms of market structure.

Degree of information

In the monopoly market structure, there is imperfect information between the various economic agents. The monopolist is in the position to keep information inaccessible to potential competitors and consumers.

3.5.2 Price and output decision of a monopoly

As the only firm in the industry, the entire market demand curve is the monopoly's demand curve. The demand curve for a monopoly is downward sloping as it has to lower its price to sell a greater quantity of output, unlike a PC firm where it can sell as much quantity of output as it desires, at the given market price. The demand curve for a monopolist is likely to be price inelastic due to the lack of substitutes available.

The downward sloping demand curve for a monopoly also means that if a monopolist wishes to charge a higher price, it must accept a lower quantity demanded, and if it wishes to sell a large quantity, it must charge a lower price. In other words, a monopolist cannot increase price and output at the same time.

The demand curve also maps out the AR curve from selling the different units of output. This is because the demand curve marks out the number of units that can be sold at each price and conversely, the price that a monopolist can charge for the different quantities that it wishes to sell (i.e., the demand curve shows us that when the price is \$5, 10 units of the good are demanded. Thus, if a monopolist wishes to sell 10 units of goods, it can do so by setting the selling price at \$5). If each unit of good is sold at the same price, then the AR contributed by each unit of the good must be equal to the price $\left(\text{AR} = \frac{\text{TR}}{\text{Q}} = \frac{P \times \text{Q}}{\text{Q}} = \frac{P \times \not{Q}}{\not{Q}} = P\right)$. Since the demand curve marks out the price for the different quantities of output, it must also be the AR curve.

The MR of a monopolist lies below the demand curve. The explanation for this is as follows. To sell an additional unit of a good, the monopolist needs to lower the price that it charges. This lowered price applies to the additional unit of the good, as well as the previous units of the good (e.g., a monopolist that was able to sell two units of the good at $10 each previously, must now sell three units of goods at $9 each now, if it wishes to sell one more unit of good). Thus, the MR from selling the additional unit of good would be the new price ($9) minus the loss in TR from selling the previous units at a lower price ($1 for each of the original two units of the good that now have to be sold for $9 instead of $10; the MR = $9 − 2 × $1 = $7). Since the demand curve maps out the price, and MR is the price minus the loss of revenue from lowering the price of the previous units of output, MR must lie below the demand curve. A downward sloping demand curve with the MR curve lying below the demand curve is illustrated in Fig. 3.8.[8]

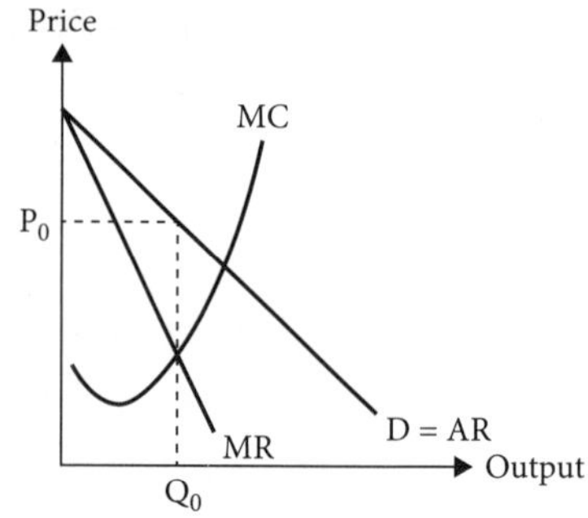

Figure 3.8: Price and output decision in a monopoly.

As with a PC firm, a monopoly that wishes to maximise profits will decide on a price and output level such that MC = MR, where MC is rising. This is achieved at P_0 and Q_0.

Similar to a PC firm, the profit maximising output is Q_0 where MC = MR because at any output before Q_0, the MC is lower than the MR (MC < MR), which means that the additional revenue the firm will collect from selling the next unit is more than the additional cost the firm will incur. If the firm increases output, the firm's profits will increase, therefore, firms will increase production towards Q_0 (where MC = MR).

At any output beyond Q_0, the MC is higher than the MR (MC > MR), which means that the additional revenue the firm will collect from selling the next unit is less than the additional cost the firm will incur. If the firm increases output, the firm's profits will decrease, therefore firms will not produce beyond Q_0 (where MC = MR).

In sum, the monopolist will price the good at P_0 and produce Q_0 units of output such that MC = MR.

8 For a straight-line demand curve, the MR curve will start at the same vertical intercept and be twice as steep. The mathematical proof is provided in Annex 3.3.

3.5.3 Short run profits for a monopoly

In the short run, when at least one of the factors of productions is fixed, a monopoly can earn either supernormal profits, normal profits, or subnormal profits. This could be determined by comparing the AC against AR (Price) at q_0 or TC against TR as shown in the following figures:

Type of profit	Description
Supernormal profit 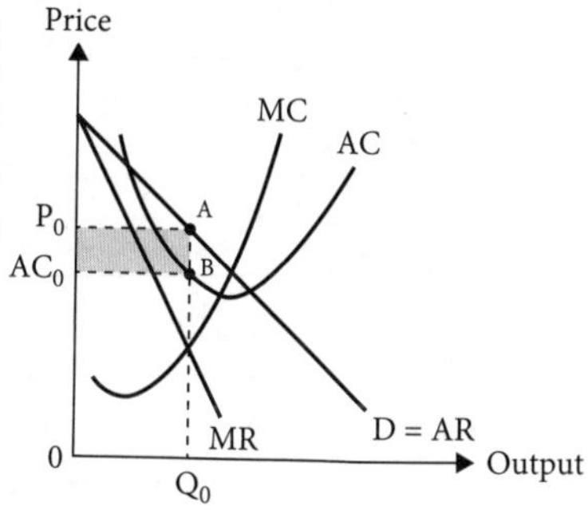	$TR = P_0 \times Q_0$ (area $0P_0AQ_0$) $TC = AC_0 \times Q_0$ (area $0AC_0BQ_0$) $TR > TC$ as $P_0 > AC_0$ Supernormal profit is shaded
Normal profit 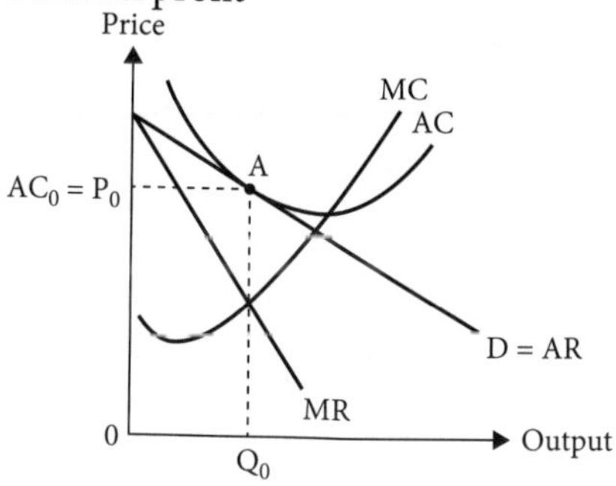	$TR = P_0 \times Q_0$ (area $0P_0AQ_0$) $TC = AC_0 \times Q_0$ (area $0AC_0AQ_0$) $TR = TC$ as $P_0 = AC_0$
Subnormal profit 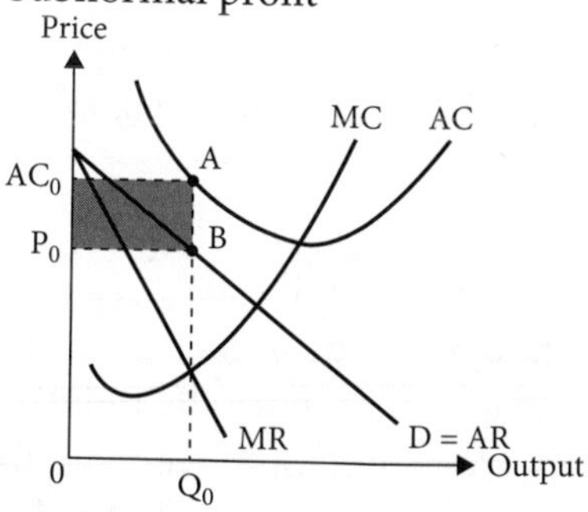	$TR = P_0 \times Q_0$ (area $0P_0BQ_0$) $TC = AC_0 \times Q_0$ (area $0AC_0AQ_0$) $TR < TC$ as $P_0 < AC_0$ Subnormal profit/loss is shaded

3.5.4 Short-run shut down condition for a monopoly

Just like a firm in a PC, in the event that a firm is earning subnormal profits (TR < TC), the monopolist would need to decide whether to continue production or shut down by comparing its TR and TVC.

The three scenarios of TR < TVC, TR = TVC, and TR > TVC are illustrated as follows:

Decision of a firm earning subnormal profits in the short run

Shut down	**Neutral (assumed not to shut down)**	**Does not shut down**
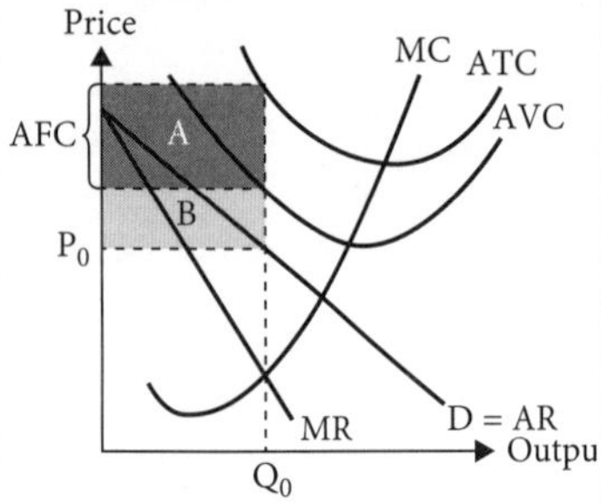	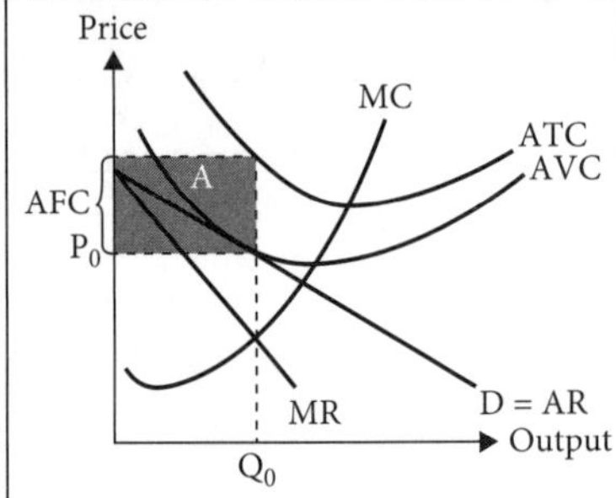	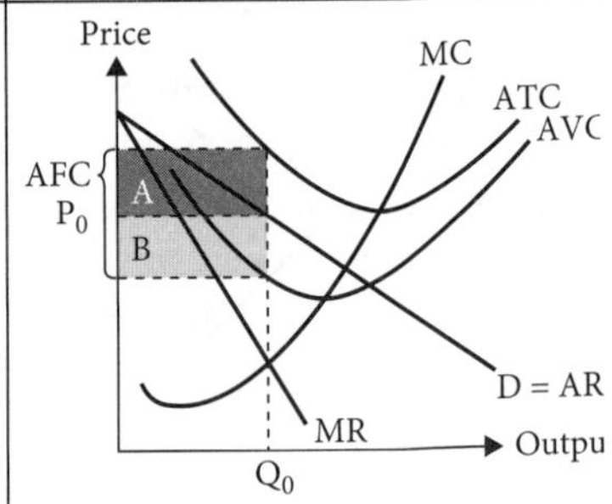
AR < AVC TR < TVC Area A + B is the loss if it continues Area A is the loss if it shuts down (TFC = AFC × Q_0)	AR = AVC TR = TVC Area A is the loss if it continues Area A is the loss if it shuts down (TFC = AFC × Q_0)	AR > AVC TR > TVC Area A is the loss if it continues Area A + B is the loss if it shuts down (TFC = AFC × Q_0)

Note: All firms will shut down when transitioning into the long run, as long as firms are making subnormal profits.

3.5.5 Long-run price and output behaviour for a monopoly

Just as with all the other market structures, a monopolist must make at least normal profits or supernormal profits to continue production in the long run. A monopolist that makes subnormal profit will shut down and leave the industry.

Different from firms in PC, a monopolist that earns supernormal profits in the short run will not have to adjust its price and output as it transitions to the long run, due to its high BTEs. Even if the monopolist is making supernormal profits, new firms cannot enter the industry. Since there is no change in the number of firms in the industry, the demand for the monopolist remains constant; therefore, the long-run price and output decision for a monopolist would be the same as the short-run price and output decision.

The following is a summary of the type of profit a monopolist can make in the short run, whether it will shut down in the short run, the adjustment from short run to long run, and the type of profit it will make in the long run.

Short run			
Supernormal profit	**Normal profit**	**Subnormal profit**	
TR > TC TR > (TFC + TVC)	TR = TC TR = (TFC + TVC)	TR < TC TR < (TFC + TVC)	
Firms will continue production		Firms will consider either to continue production or shut down	
		TR ≥ TVC	TR < TVC
		Short-run shut down condition is not met. Continue production in the short run.	Short-run shut down condition is met. Shut down in the short run.
Transition to the long run			NA
New firms unable to enter the industry. No changes in the market.	No incentive for new firms to enter the market or for monopoly to leave. No changes to market.	Long-run shut down condition is met. Shut down.	NA
Long run			NA
Continue to earn supernormal profit.	Continue to earn normal profit		NA

In summary, in the short run, a monopolist can earn supernormal profits, normal profits, or subnormal profits. However, in the long run, monopolist can earn supernormal or normal profits.

It should be noted that shutting down in the short run does not mean leaving the industry. It only means that the firm chooses not to produce any output (e.g., leave the factory idle). Shutting down in the long run means that the firm chooses to leave the industry. It will cease to be in existence. So, the short-run shut down condition is used by the firms to decide whether to produce any goods for that period, and the long-run shut down condition is used by the firm to decide whether to stay in the industry.

3.5.6 Non-price strategies of a monopoly

Although a monopoly does not face any actual competition, as it is the only firm in the market, it can still carry out non-price strategies in order to increase its profit. In this case, the purpose of the non-price strategies is not so much to differentiate its products (because there are no competitors whose products they can differentiate from) but to increase its demand and make it more price inelastic so that they can charge higher prices.

They can do so in many ways. For example, on the demand side, they could advertise, improve the quality of the product, improve the sales service, or create a loyalty programme for customers. All these strategies work the same way—they increase the demand for the firm's product and make it more price inelastic.

Figure 3.9 illustrates how non-price strategies can increase profit. Before adopting a non-price strategy(s), a monopolist was only making some supernormal profit of P_0ABAC_0. After adopting a non-price strategy(s), a monopolist now charges a higher price, produces a larger output, and earns a larger supernormal profit of P_1CEAC_1.

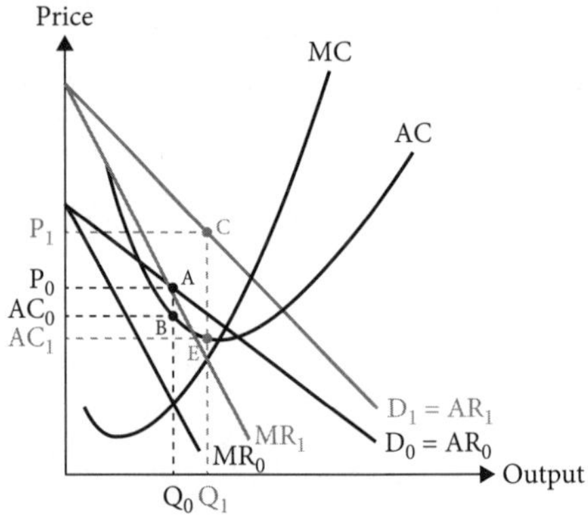

Figure 3.9: Non-price strategies increasing profit of a monopoly.

On the cost-side, if a monopolist discovers more efficient ways of production (possibly through R&D), then both the MC and AC of the firm will decrease. This would also increase the firm's profit, as illustrated in the following figure where the reduction in costs leads to an eventual increase in profits from $(P_0 - AC_0) \times Q_0$ to $(P_1 - AC_1) \times Q_1$.

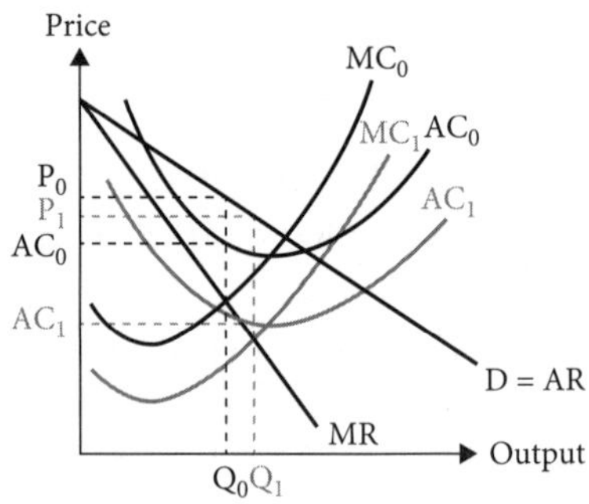

3.5.7 Consideration of cognitive biases in firm's decisions and strategies

Other than the typical pricing and non-pricing strategies, firms may also consider the cognitive biases of the consumers when deciding their strategies. A cognitive bias is a systematic deviation from rationality during the decision-making process. This applies

In this scenario, the consumer's decision-making process might be affected by one or more of the cognitive biases, and consumers will no longer make the most rational decision in maximising their satisfaction or utility. While consumers might still be thinking they are being rational and objective, these cognitive biases might actually lead to poor or bad decisions. Some of the cognitive biases include:

- Sunk cost fallacy
- Loss aversion
- Saliency bias

Sunk cost fallacy

Sunk cost refers to costs that have already been incurred and cannot be recovered. Sunk cost fallacy arises when the consumer's decision is affected by their sunk costs rather than MCs.

For example, certain hotel groups offer paid hotel memberships that allow members to enjoy discounts on hotel stays. Such members are more likely to stay in hotels belonging to the hotel group even though the discounted price of the stays might still be higher than the hotel stays offered by other hotels. Such behaviour may be explained by the sunk cost fallacy. In this case, the membership fee is the sunk cost, while the price of the hotel stay is the MC. Consumers may choose the more expensive hotel stays offered by the hotel group that they are a member of to "spread out" the membership fee to make the membership more worthwhile. However, this is not the most rational decision as the sunk cost cannot be recovered no matter what. So, regardless of whether they have paid for the membership fee, they should just choose hotel stays from the hotels offering them at the lowest price.

The example is summarised in the following table:

<table>
<tr><td colspan="2">Scenario:
• Membership fee for Hotel Group A (paid): $500
• Hotel stay in a hotel belonging to Hotel Group A: $200
(member's price discounted from usual price of $300)
• Hotel stay in a rival hotel of equivalent quality: $180</td></tr>
<tr><td>With sunk cost fallacy:
"I have paid $500 for the hotel membership. I will choose to stay in the hotel belonging to Hotel Group A to get some value out of this membership that I have paid for".</td><td>Without sunk cost fallacy:
"The $500 I have paid for the hotel membership is irretrievable. No matter which hotel I choose to stay in, this $500 is gone. So, what is within my control is to minimise my cost going forward. I will choose to stay in the rival hotel so that I pay $180 dollars instead of $200".</td></tr>
</table>

Another example would be paying $1,000 upfront for a one-year gym membership. Once payment has been made, even if the consumer does not use the gym at all for the entire year, he/she would not be able to get a refund. In contrast, the MC of consumption refers to the additional cost of consuming one more unit of the good. Using the example of a gym membership, after the $1,000 had been paid, the MC of visiting the gym is only the time and effort it takes to do so.

Firms may make use of sunk cost fallacies to gain repeat customers through convincing consumers to pay for memberships.

Loss aversion

Loss aversion arises when the consumers prefer a decision that would avoid making a loss over another decision with the potential of making an equivalent or greater gain.

For consumers, the compensation of breaking a contract, for example, telecommunications or television subscription plans, might actually be lower than the discounts that they will gain from starting another subscription plan with another firm that offers lower prices. The consumers might feel the loss from compensating the current firms is higher, while in reality, the potential gain from breaking the contract and switching is actually higher. Since switching would result in net savings for the consumer, switching is the rational decision. Hence, when loss aversion causes consumers to not switch, they are not making rational decisions. Firms may make use of loss aversion on the part of consumers to retain consumers through contracts that require consumers to compensate the firm when they terminate it early.

Saliency bias

Saliency bias arises when the consumers focus on factors or information that is more prominent and ignore others that are just as important but less prominent. Some of the salient factors include contrast, emotion, and placement.

- **Contrast**: Firms tend to use logos and designs that are differentiated or outstanding and contrast compared to rival firms. For example, firms tend to highlight their products with consistent branding style to ensure consumers will be able to recognise their varieties from the many other brands. Firms might also highlight one aspect of their product that is better compared to the rival firms and ignore other aspects that their product might be worse than their rivals. Consumers' decisions might be attracted to making the choice based on that one aspect and ignore the rest.
- **Emotion**: Firms tend to add images that would generate certain emotions in order to engage the consumers into buying them. Children's products tend to have pictures of smiling children, while fitness products tend to have pictures of healthy and fit individuals.
- **Placement**: Firms tend to place their products at the optimal location in a store to entice the consumers into buying them. For example, individual candies and chocolates tend to be located near cashier counters. At these locations, consumers while waiting to pay might be more willing to buy these individual items while their bigger bag options can be found in the sweet aisle. Firms also pay extra to have their products placed in the more attractive and strategic location of the store.

3.5.8 Impact of technological disruptions

Major technological disruptions in an industry can affect a firm's revenue, costs, and profits. Firms that are able to be the first mover or early adopters of technological changes can enjoy lower cost and higher demand. For example, firms like Uber in the United States and Grab in Southeast Asia have leveraged technological change in the private transport or ride-hailing industry to offer ride-hailing services without having to incur the cost of setting up a taxi fleet. Clothing firms that leverage on the expansion and popularization of online shopping through Amazon and Lazada will experience higher demand and sales.

Firms that are unable or slow in responding to such technological changes may eventually shut down and leave the industry, regardless of their current market share or size. For example, Nokia and Blackberry were dominant firms until they were not able to keep up with technological changes such as the popularisation of touch screen phones and WhatsApp.

3.5.9 The theory of contestable markets

A market is contestable if the barriers to entry and exit are low. Although the conventional analysis seems to suggest that monopolies would charge high prices in both the short- and long run, the theory of contestable markets suggests otherwise. Even if the market is currently monopolistic in that there is only one firm in the market, if there is a threat of competition (i.e., if the market is contestable), the monopolist might conduct price and non-pricing strategies to prevent the potential new entrant from entering the industry.

A contradiction seems to arise when we say that a monopoly is contestable. This contradiction comes from the fact that a feature of a monopoly is that BTEs are high. However, contestability means that BTEs are low.

This contradiction can be resolved quite simply by drawing a difference between the actual market structure and the theoretical features of a market structure. If there is only one firm in the industry, the actual market structure is that of a monopoly. And, this market can be contestable. The actual market structure need not fit all the features of the theoretical market structures (i.e., an actual monopoly could face low BTEs).

3.6 Monopolistic Competition

3.6.1 Characteristics of Monopolistic Competition (MPC)

	Monopolistic competition
Level of BTEs	Low
Number of firms	Many
Size of firms	Small
Degree of interdependence	Low
Type of product	Differentiated
Degree of information	Imperfect

The key characteristics of MPC are that BTEs are low, there are many small firms in the market, differentiated products are sold by each of the firms, there is very low interdependence between firms, and that there is imperfect knowledge between consumers and producers. These characteristics will affect the price and non-price decisions of firms in the MPC market structure.

Degree of BTEs

There are low BTEs for the MPC market structure and new firms are able to enter the industry without significant difficulty. Firms typically do not require high capital outlay or high start-up cost.

Number and size of firms

In the MPC market structure, there are a large number of small firms in the industry. Each firm has an insignificant share of the market. This means that none of the firms is large enough to dominate the industry. In terms of the market concentration ratio, the four-firm concentration ratio of the MPC would be small.

Degree of interdependence

In an MPC industry, because there are so many small firms, the effects of the actions of one firm on another given firm would be very limited as it would be spread across the many firms. Hence, there would be very little interdependence.

Type of product

In the MPC market structure, each firm's product is slightly differentiated from the others in the industry. Although the product of each firm is similar, they are not identical. This means that the firms' products are close but not perfect substitutes of one another. Product differentiation can be real or imagined.

Degree of information

Similar to a monopoly, in MPC, there is imperfect information between the various economic agents. An MPC firm is in the position to keep some information inaccessible to other firms and consumers. Firms are not fully aware of the production processes and costs of their rival firms. They are also not certain about the reactions of rival firms to their pricing decisions. Consumers are also not aware of all the prices charged by all the firms.

3.6.2 Price and output decision of a firm in MPC

Like a monopoly, because of the characteristics of the market structure, MPC firms are also price setters. As such, an MPC firm also has a downward-sloping demand and an MR that lies below the demand curve. However, while a monopoly has a unique product, an MPC firm's products are only slightly differentiated from the products of the many other firms in its industry. Hence, the demand curve for an MPC firm is likely to be price elastic due to the availability of many substitutes, causing its demand and MR curves to be flat as shown in Fig. 3.10.

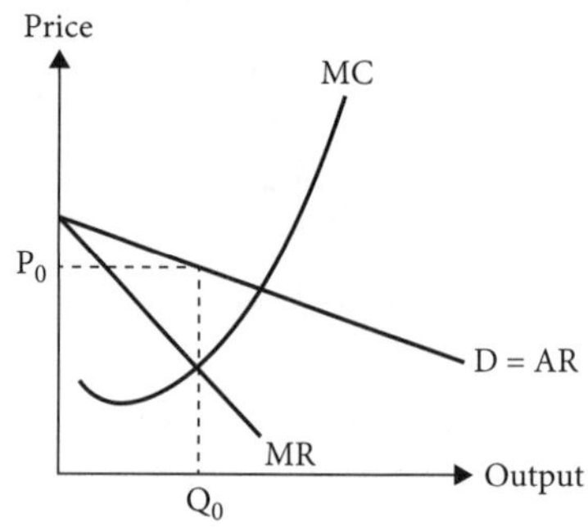

Figure 3.10: Price and output decision of an MPC firm.

As with a monopoly, an MPC firm that wishes to maximise profits will decide on a price and output level such that MC = MR, where MC is rising. This is achieved at P_0 and Q_0.

The profit maximising output is Q_0 where MC = MR because at any output before Q_0, the MC is lower than the MR (MC < MR), which means that the additional revenue the firm will collect from selling the next unit is more than the additional cost the firm will incur. If the firms increases output, the firm's profits will increase, therefore, firms will increase production towards Q_0 (where MC = MR).

At any output beyond Q_0, the MC is higher than the MR (MC > MR), which means that the additional revenue the firm will collect from selling the next unit is less than the additional cost the firm will incur. If the firm increases output, the firm's profits will decrease, therefore firms will not produce beyond Q_0 (where MC = MR).

In sum, the MPC firm will price the good at P_0 and produce Q_0 units of output such that MC = MR.

3.6.3 Short-run profits for a firm in MPC

Similar to PC firms and monopolists, in the short run, when at least one of the factors of productions is fixed, a firm in MPC can earn either supernormal profits, normal profits, or subnormal profits. This could be determined by comparing the AC against AR (Price) at q_0 or TC against TR as shown in the following figures:

Type of profit	Description
Supernormal profit 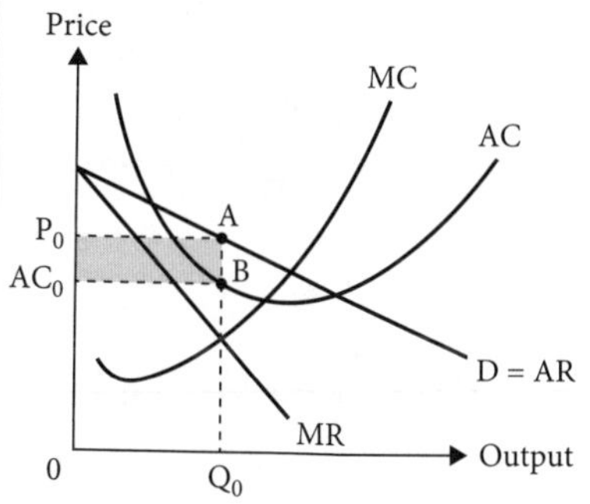	$TR = P_0 \times Q_0$ (area $0P_0AQ_0$) $TC = AC_0 \times Q_0$ (area $0AC_0BQ_0$) TR > TC as $P_0 > AC_0$ Supernormal profit is shaded
Normal profit 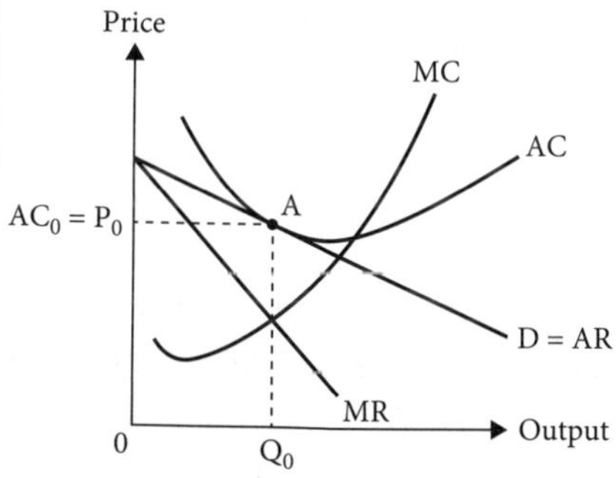	$TR = P_0 \times Q_0$ (area $0P_0AQ_0$) $TC = AC_0 \times Q_0$ (area $0AC_0AQ_0$) TR = TC as $P_0 = AC_0$
Subnormal profit 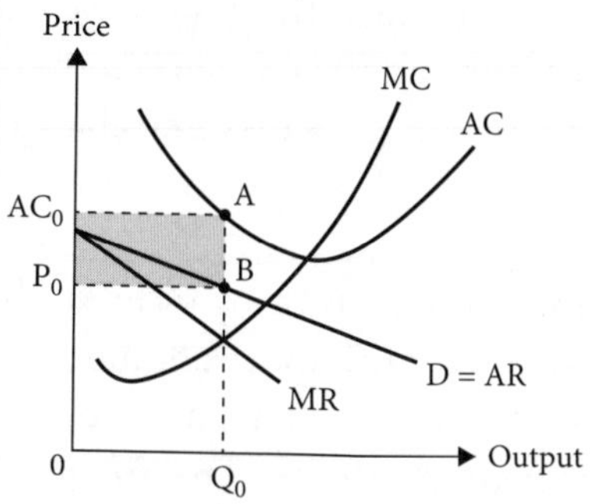	$TR = P_0 \times Q_0$ (area $0P_0BQ_0$) $TC = AC_0 \times Q_0$ (area $0AC_0AQ_0$) TR < TC as $P_0 < AC_0$ Subnormal profit/loss is shaded

3.6.4 Short-run shut down condition for an MPC firm

Just like a firm in a PC or a monopolist, in the event that an MPC firm is earning subnormal profits (TR < TC), the firm would need to decide whether to continue the production or shut down by comparing its TR and TVC.

The three scenarios of TR < TVC, TR = TVC, and TR > TVC are illustrated as follows:

Decision of a firm earning subnormal profits in the short run

Shut down	**Neutral (assumed not to shut down)**	**Does not shut down**
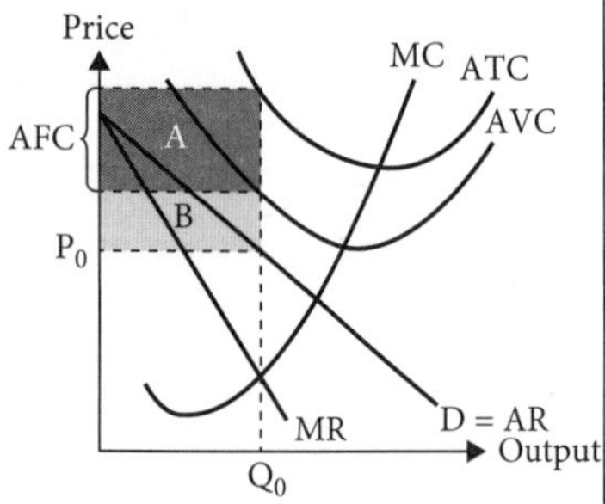	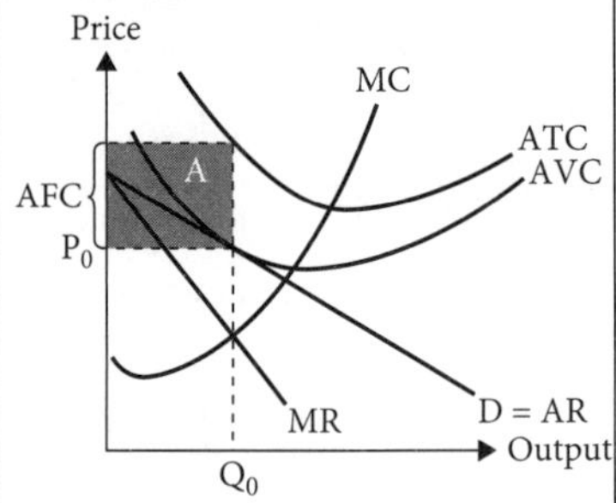	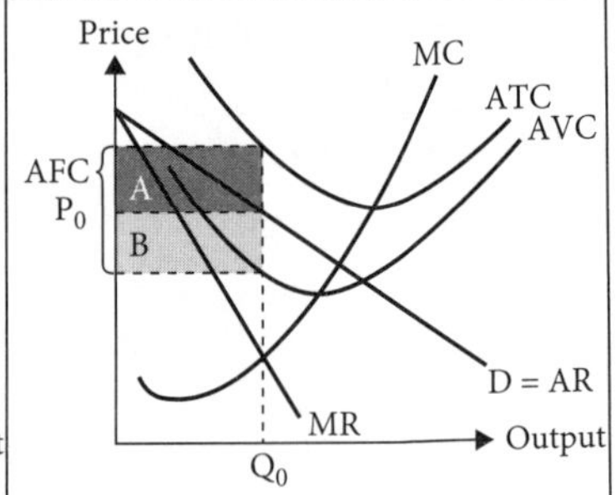
AR < AVC TR < TVC Area A + B is the loss if it continues Area A is the loss if it shuts down (TFC = AFC × Q_0)	AR = AVC TR = TVC Area A is the loss if it continues Area A is the loss if it shuts down (TFC = AFC × Q_0)	AR > AVC TR > TVC Area A is the loss if it continues Area A + B is the loss if it shuts down (TFC = AFC × Q_0)

Note: All firms will shut down when transitioning into the long run, as long as firms are making subnormal profits.

3.6.5 Long-run profits for a firm in MPC

Just as with all the other market structures, an MPC firm must make at least normal profits or supernormal profits to continue production in the long run. An MPC firm that makes subnormal profit will shut down and leave the industry.

However, unlike a monopolist, but similar to a PC firm, MPC firms' short-run price and output decisions can differ from their long-run price and output decisions. This is because like the PC market structure, the MPC market structure has low BTEs and the entrance and exit of firms in response to supernormal, normal, or subnormal profit would cause some changes to the firms' demands.

If an MPC firm made supernormal profits in the short run, as the firm transitions to the long run, new firms will be attracted to enter the industry. As such, with more competition in the market, the MPC firm's demand would decrease (shift left) and become more elastic (flatter) because there are now more substitutes for the firm's products. The firm will respond by reducing its price and output (profit maximising price and output will fall from P_0 and Q_0 to P_1 and Q_1 in the following diagram). So long as there is supernormal profit to be made, new firms will enter the market and the MPC firm's demands will keep decreasing and becoming more elastic, causing the changes described earlier. In this manner, the price that the firm charges and the output produced will keep decreasing until there is only normal profit to be made. This is because when the firms are making normal profit, new firms will stop entering the industry. This can be illustrated in the graph (Fig. 3.11).

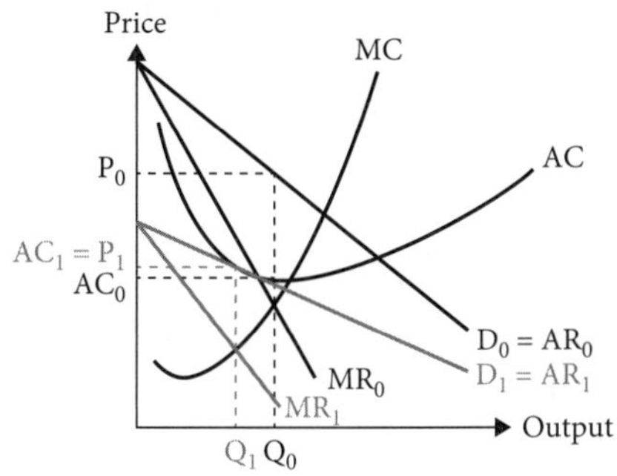

Figure 3.11: Long-run adjustment for an MPC firm making supernormal profits.

The long-run price and output decision (P_1 and Q_1) for the firm is hence, different from the short-run price and output decision (P_0 and Q_0).

If the MPC firms were making normal profit in the short run, no new firms will be attracted to the market and the long-run price and output decision would be the same as the short-run price and output decision.

If an MPC firm made subnormal profits in the short run, as the firm transitions to the long run, it will shut down and leave the industry. As such, with lesser competition in the market, the remaining MPC firms' demands would increase (shift right) and become more price inelastic (steeper) because there are now less substitutes for the firm's products. The remaining firms will respond by increasing its price and output (profit-maximising price and output will rise from P_0 and Q_0 to P_1 and Q_1 as shown in the following diagram). So long as there is subnormal profit, existing firms will exit the market and the remaining MPC firm's demands will keep increasing and becoming more price inelastic, causing the changes described previously. In this manner, the price that the firm charges and the output produced will keep increasing until there is normal profit to be made. This is because when the firms are making normal profits, existing firms will stop leaving the industry. This can be illustrated in the graph shown in Fig. 3.12.

The long-run price and output decision (P_1 and Q_1) for firms that made subnormal profits but did not leave the industry is hence, different from the short-run price and output decision (P_0 and Q_0).

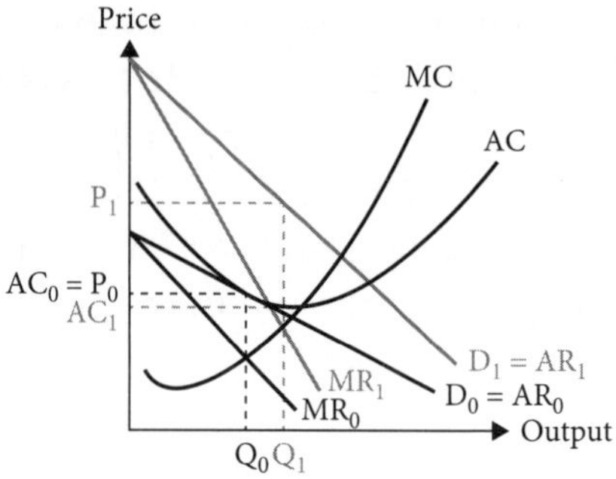

Figure 3.13: Non-price strategies increasing profit for an MPC firm.

Following is a summary of the type of profit an MPC firm can make in the short run, whether it will shut down in the short run, the adjustment from short run to long run, and the type of profit it will make in the long run.

Short run			
Supernormal profit	**Normal profit**	**Subnormal profit**	
TR > TC TR > (TFC + TVC)	TR = TC TR = (TFC + TVC)	TR < TC TR < (TFC + TVC)	
Firms will continue production		Firms will consider either to continue production or shut down	
		TR ≥ TVC	TR < TVC
		Short-run shut down condition is not met. Continue production in the short run.	Short-run shut down condition is met. Shut down in the short run.
Transition to the long run			NA
New firms enter the industry. Demand for each firm's product decreases and |PED| increases. *P* and *Q* both decrease.	No incentive for new firms to enter or for existing firms to leave the market. No changes to market.	Some firms will leave the industry. Demand for each remaining firm's products increases and |PED| decreases. *P* and *Q* of remaining firms increase.	NA
Long run			NA
Normal profit in the long run	Normal profit in the long run	Normal profit in the long run for firms that remained in the market	NA

In summary, in the short run, firms in the MPC market structure can earn supernormal profits, normal profits, or subnormal profits. However, in the long run, these firms will only earn normal profits.

It should be noted that shutting down in the short run does not mean leaving the industry. It only means that the firm chooses not to produce any output (e.g., leave the factory idle). Shutting down in the long run means that the firm chooses to leave the industry. It will cease to be in existence. So, the short-run shut down condition is used by the firms to decide whether to produce any goods for that period, and the long-run shut down condition is used by the firm to decide whether to stay in the industry.

3.6.6 Non-price strategies of a firm in MPC

Unlike a firm in a PC market structure that sells a homogenous product, an MPC firm sells differentiated products.

Unlike a monopolist that sells a unique product and faces little or no competition, an MPC firm faces competition from other firms.

The two differences observed earlier cause MPC firms to engage in both price and non-price competition. Price competition takes place when MPC firms decrease prices to compete with other firms.

MPC firms use non-price competition strategies such as branding and advertising to increase the demand of their products and reduce its substitutability with other firms' products. This reduces its PED. A larger and more price inelastic demand will enable the MPC firms to price higher and earn more profits in the short run (Fig. 3.13).

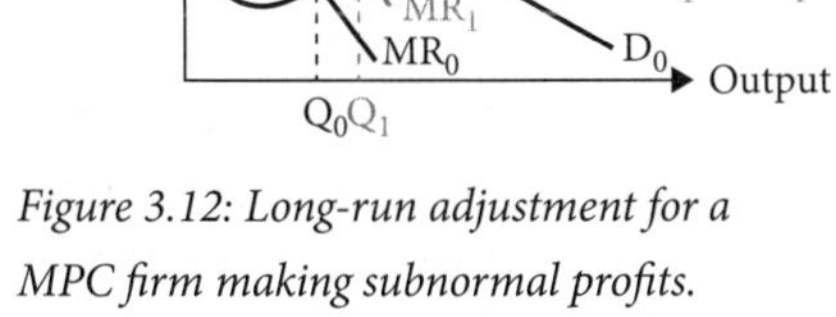

Figure 3.12: Long-run adjustment for a MPC firm making subnormal profits.

Let us assume that before branding and advertising, the MPC firm was only making normal profit. However, after branding and advertising, the MPC firm is now able to charge a higher price, produce a larger output, and earn supernormal profit. Although this profit will be eroded in the long run, the MPC firm still has an incentive to carry out non-price competition to earn supernormal profits in the short run.

However, it is important to note that these strategies tend to be small in scale as MPC firms can only make normal profit in the long run due to the low BTEs. The inability to earn supernormal profits in the long run reduces the MPC firm's ability to conduct large-scale strategies such as investment in R&D to develop new and innovative products, or products of much better quality.

3.7 Oligopoly

3.7.1 Characteristics of oligopoly

The key characteristics of an oligopoly market structure or an oligopolistic industry is that there are high BTEs, a few large firms that dominate the market with a high degree of interdependence, firms selling either homogenous or differentiated products, and imperfect information. The few large firms in the oligopoly are known as oligopolists.

	Oligopoly
Level of BTEs	High
Number of firms	Few
Size of firms	Large
Degree of interdependence	High
Type of product	Homogenous/differentiated
Degree of information	Imperfect

Degree of BTEs

Similar to a monopoly, there is high level of BTEs for the oligopoly market structure and new firms have difficulties entering the market. The BTEs is an oligopoly is lower than in a monopoly but higher than in an MPC market structure.

Types of BTEs include the following:[9]

- Financial BTEs
- Cost BTEs
- Control of raw materials
- Legal barriers
- Strategic entry barriers by incumbent firms

In many countries, "Legal barriers" and "Cost BTEs" are the more likely reasons why the oligopoly exists.

Number and size of firms

In the oligopoly market structure, there are a few large firms that dominate most of the industry in terms of industry's output or market share. There may be many other small firms; however, the combined total output of these small firms account only for a small proportion of the industry's output. As such, the four-firm concentration ratio of the oligopoly would be high.

Type of product

Oligopolists sell either homogeneous or differentiated products. In the real world, due to product differentiation, it is difficult for homogenous products to exist. However, there are products that are similar enough to be considered homogenous. For example, the services

9 Refer to Section 3.3.1 for more details.

provided by various telecommunication companies such as Singtel, Starhub, and M1 can be argued to be homogeneous.

Degree of information

Similar to a monopoly and MPC, in the oligopoly market structure, there is imperfect information between the various economic agents. An oligopolist is in the position to keep information inaccessible to potential competitors and consumers. Firms are not fully aware of the production processes and costs of their rival firms. They are also not certain about the reactions of rival firms to their pricing decisions.

3.7.2 Price and output decision of a firm in oligopoly

The key difference between an oligopolistic market structure and the other three market structures is the difference in terms of degree of interdependence. Due to the existence of only a few large firms, the actions of one oligopolist will have a large impact on the others, resulting in oligopoly being the only market structure in which there is a high degree of interdependence.

Due to the high degree of interdependence, the oligopolists can either decide to cooperate (collude) or compete during their price and output decisions. In the discussion of an oligopolist's behaviour, it is important to clarify whether the oligopoly is competitive or cooperative/collusive.

3.7.3 Price and output decision of a firm in competitive oligopoly

When the oligopolists compete, the price and output decision becomes more complicated. Similar to monopolies and MPC firms, oligopolists are price setters and will set the price and output accordingly to achieve profit maximisation. The price-setting ability is higher than that of MPC firms but lower than that of a monopoly, as each oligopolist will have a demand that is higher and more price inelastic than an MPC firm's but lower and more price elastic than a monopoly's.

Although oligopolists have the ability to set prices, due to firms being mutually interdependent, when a firm makes price and output decisions, the reactions of rival firms in the industry needs to be considered. Because of this, once the price and output of a firm have been established at some point, an oligopolist tends not to change its price and output decision. This is what we term price rigidity. This happens because if one of the firms increases its price, other firms will not follow. The firm that increased its price will then suffer a more than proportionate fall in the quantity demanded of its output as consumers switch to its rivals. Hence, TR will decrease. It is therefore not beneficial for the firm to increase its price.

On the other hand, if one of the oligopolists chooses to decrease its price, the rest of the rival firms will follow suit to maintain their market share as they do not wish to lose their customers. Hence, since every firm would reduce their price too, the increase in quantity demanded of the firm's output would only be less than proportionate and the TR will decrease.

As such, since increasing or decreasing the price would result in a loss of TR, the oligopolists will not change its price or output.

The abovementioned situation can be illustrated on the kinked demand curve in Fig. 3.14.

We start with a given P_0 and Q_0. At prices above P_0, the demand curve is elastic because an increase in price causes a more than proportionate fall in quantity demanded. At prices below P_0, the demand curve is price inelastic because a fall in price causes a less than proportionate increase in quantity demanded. The MR curve from quantity 0 to Q_0 would follow that of the elastic demand curve and the MR curve from quantity Q_0 onwards would follow that of the inelastic demand curve. It would naturally have a vertical portion.

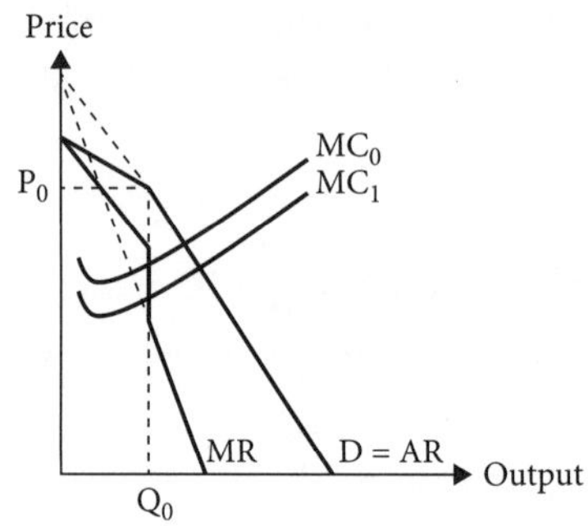

Figure 3.14: An oligopolist's kinked demand curve.

The price rigidity (also known as price stability) can be seen from how the MC can change over time (MC_0 to MC_1) without causing the profit maximising price (or quantity) to change. This can be seen from how the profit-maximising (MC = MR) output and price remain unchanged even when MC changes.

3.7.4 Price and output decision of a firm in cooperative/collusive oligopoly

Instead of competing with each other, oligopolists can also collude with each other. The market structure will then be known as a cooperative oligopoly or a collusive oligopoly. When the collusion is done formally and explicitly, a cartel is formed.

In a cartel, firms collectively behave like a monopoly and the price and output decision of the group of firms would be just like that of a monopoly. The only addition is that after deciding the collective profit-maximising price and output, they must then split the total output amongst the colluding firms. An example of this is shown in Fig. 3.15.

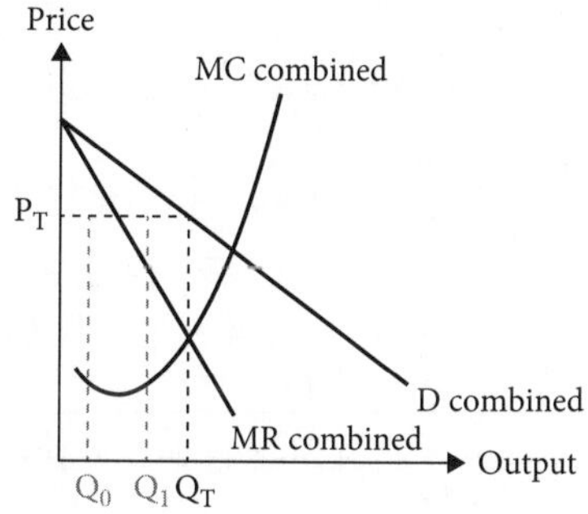

Figure 3.15: Price and output decision of collusive oligopolists.

The combined demand ($D_{combined}$) is the total demand in the market because the colluding oligopolistic firms are acting like a single monopoly. They then profit-maximise like a monopoly and jointly produce output Q_T and price it at P_T such that $MR_{combined} = MC_{combined}$. Since Q_T output is jointly produced, the production must be split amongst the colluding oligopolists. If there are just three firms, one firm would produce 0 to Q_0 units of output, another would produce Q_0 to Q_1 units of output, and the third would produce Q_1 to Q_T units of output.[10]

Although collusion can take place in a formal and explicit manner, it can also take place in a tacit and implicit manner. Without any formal agreement between the firms, the firms can decide to follow prices set by a price leader. The price leader usually is the largest firm among the few oligopoly. This is known as the price leadership theory.

3.7.5 Short-run profits for a firm in an oligopoly

Similar to all the firms in the other three market structures, in the short run, an oligopolist can earn either supernormal profits, normal profits, or subnormal profits. This could be determined by comparing the AC against AR (Price) at q_0 or TC against TR.

10 The split amongst the firms should be such that the MC of each firm is equal. If one firm has a higher MC than other, the collusion could reduce their total cost by reallocating the production from the firm with the higher MC to the firm with the lower MC.

For firms in a competitive oligopoly

The different profits of an oligopolist in a competitive oligopoly are illustrated as follows:

Type of profit	**Description**
Supernormal profit 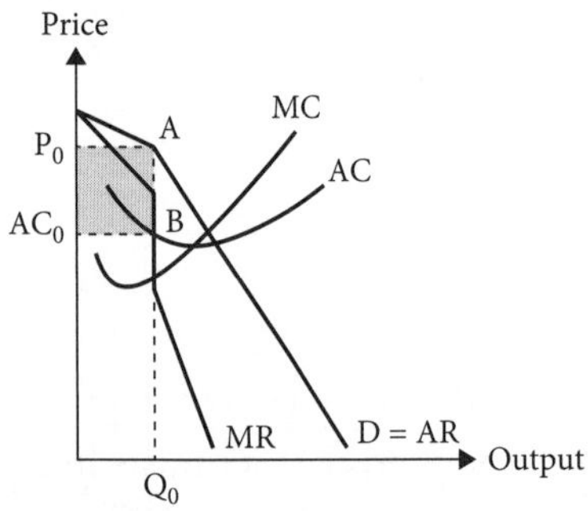	$TR = P_0 \times Q_0$ (area $0P_0AQ_0$) $TC = AC_0 \times Q_0$ (area $0AC_0BQ_0$) $TR > TC$ as $P_0 > AC_0$ Supernormal profit is shaded
Normal profit 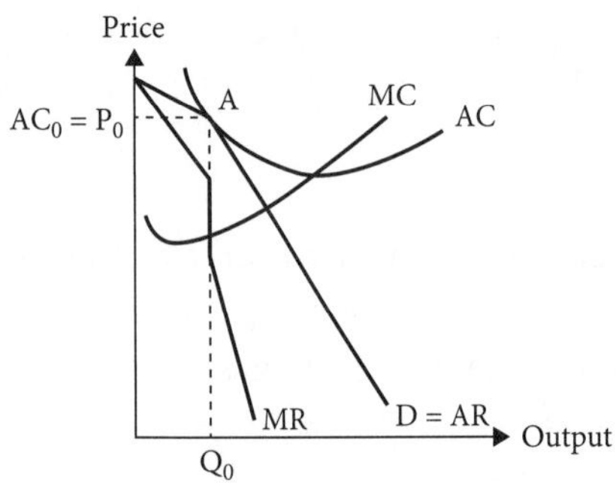	$TR = P_0 \times Q_0$ (area $0P_0AQ_0$) $TC = AC_0 \times Q_0$ (area $0AC_0AQ_0$) $TR = TC$ as $P_0 = AC_0$
Subnormal profit 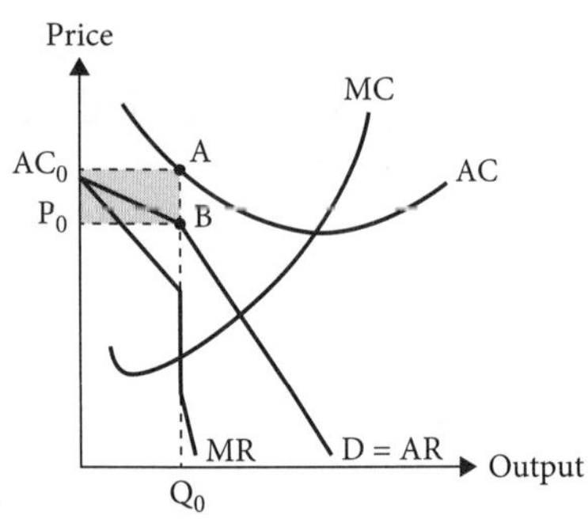	$TR = P_0 \times Q_0$ (area $0P_0BQ_0$) $TC = AC_0 \times Q_0$ (area $0AC_0AQ_0$) $TR < TC$ as $P_0 < AC_0$ Subnormal profit/loss is shaded

Note that although the kinked demand curve has been used in the illustration for the sake of accuracy, it is perfectly fine to illustrate the profits using a regular straight line demand instead.

For firms in a collusive oligopoly

The profits of an oligopolist in a collusive oligopoly cannot be illustrated directly. However, we can illustrate the type of profit made by the entire collusion, illustrated as follows:

Type of profit	Description
Supernormal profit 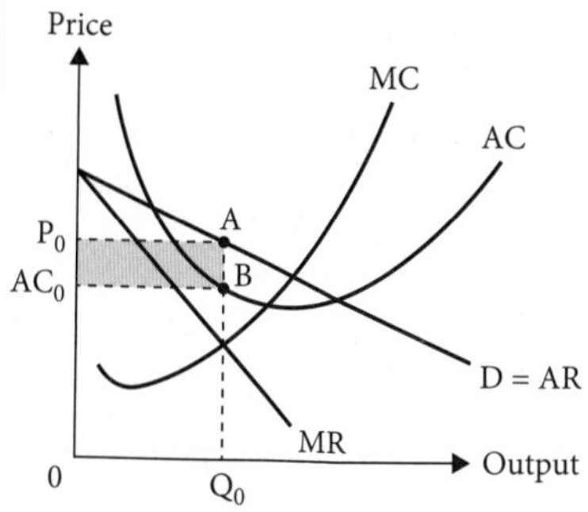	$TR = P_0 \times Q_0$ (area $0P_0AQ_0$) $TC = AC_0 \times Q_0$ (area $0AC_0BQ_0$) $TR > TC$ as $P_0 > AC_0$ Supernormal profit is shaded
Normal Profit 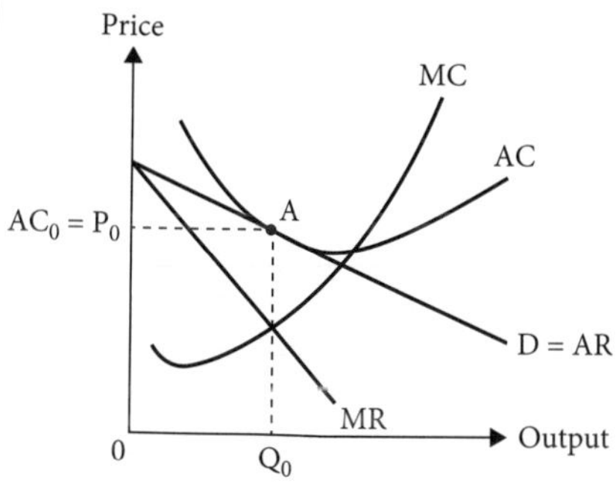	$TR = P_0 \times Q_0$ (area $0P_0AQ_0$) $TC = AC_0 \times Q_0$ (area $0AC_0AQ_0$) $TR = TC$ as $P_0 = AC_0$
Subnormal profit 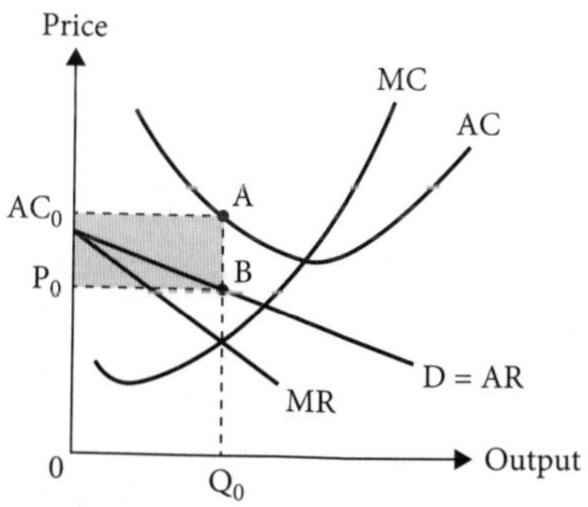	$TR = P_0 \times Q_0$ (area $0P_0BQ_0$) $TC = AC_0 \times Q_0$ (area $0AC_0AQ_0$) $TR < TC$ as $P_0 < AC_0$ Subnormal profit/loss is shaded

3.7.6 Short-run shut down condition for a firm in an oligopoly

Just like firms in the other three market structures, in the event that a firm is earning subnormal profits (TR < TC), the firm would need to decide whether to continue production or shut down by comparing its TR and TVC.

The three scenarios of TR < TVC, TR = TVC, and TR > TVC are illustrated as follows:

For firms in a competitive oligopoly

Decision of a firm earning subnormal profits in the short run

<table>
<tr><th>Shutdown</th><th>Neutral (assumed not to shut down)</th><th>Does not shut down</th></tr>
<tr>
<td>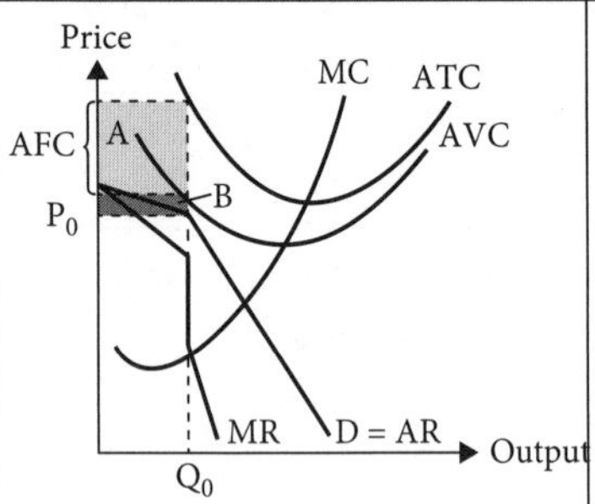
</td>
<td>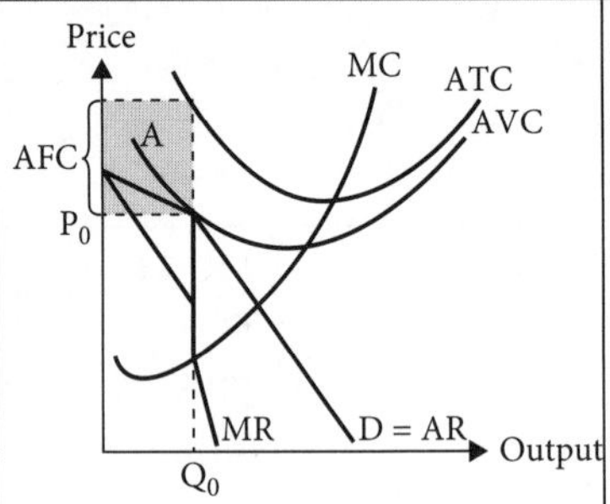
</td>
<td>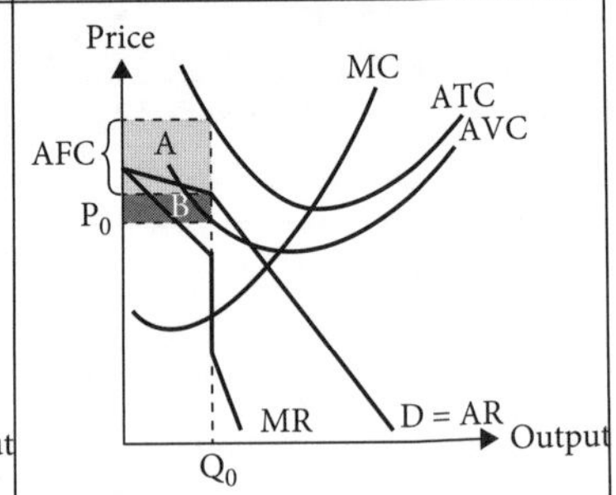
</td>
</tr>
<tr>
<td>AR < AVC
TR < TVC
Area A + B is the loss if it continues
Area A is the loss if it shuts down (TFC = AFC × Q_0)</td>
<td>AR = AVC
TR = TVC
Area A is the loss if it continues
Area A is the loss if it shuts down (TFC = AFC × Q_0)</td>
<td>AR > AVC
TR > TVC
Area A is the loss if it continues
Area A + B is the loss if it shuts down (TFC = AFC × Q_0)</td>
</tr>
</table>

Note: All firms will shut down when transitioning into the long run, as long as firms are making subnormal profits.

Note that although the kinked demand curve has been used in the illustration for the sake of accuracy, it is perfectly fine to illustrate the transitions of an oligopolistic firm from the short run to the long run using a regular straight line demand instead.

For firms in a collusive oligopoly

Whether an oligopolist in a collusive oligopoly ought to shut down cannot be illustrated directly. However, we can illustrate whether the entire collusion as a whole ought to shut down.

Decision of a firm earning subnormal profits in the short run

<table>
<tr><th>Shutdown</th><th>Neutral (assumed not to shut down)</th><th>Does not shut down</th></tr>
<tr><td>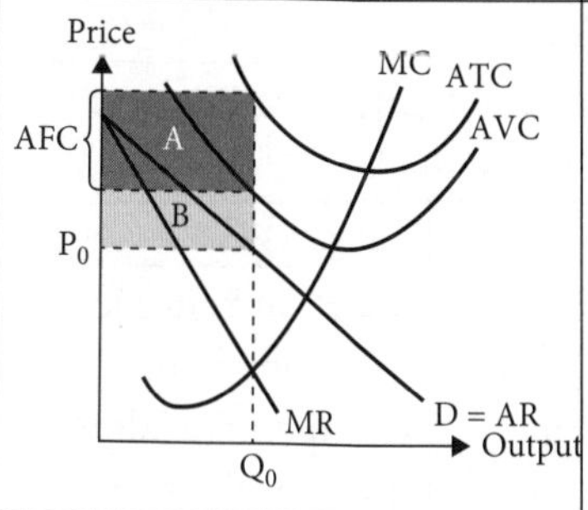
</td><td>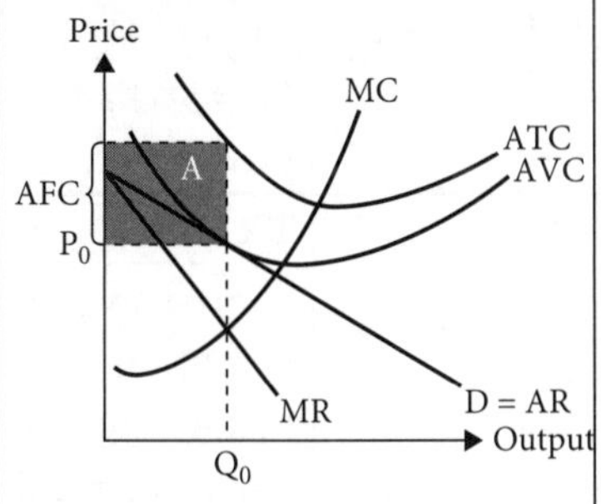
</td><td>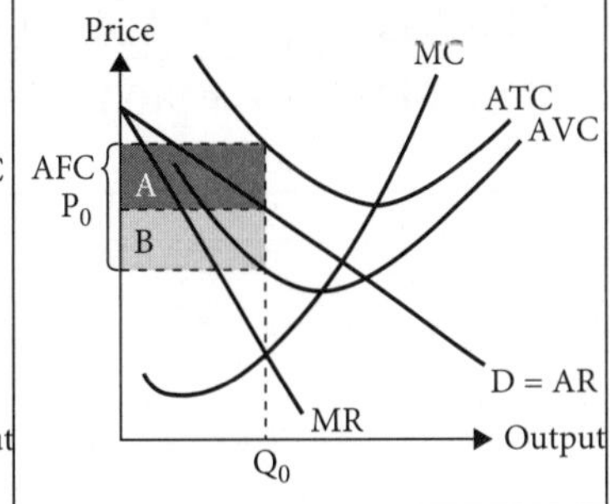
</td></tr>
<tr><td>AR < AVC
TR < TVC
Area A + B is the loss if it continues
Area A is the loss if it shuts down (TFC = AFC × Q_0)</td><td>AR = AVC
TR = TVC
Area A is the loss if it continues
Area A is the loss if it shuts down (TFC = AFC × Q_0)</td><td>AR > AVC
TR > TVC
Area A is the loss if it continues
Area A + B is the loss if it shuts down (TFC = AFC × Q_0)</td></tr>
</table>

Note: The implication of this is not necessarily that every firm in the collusion ought to shut down. The collusion may simply break up instead.

3.7.7 Long-run price and output decision for a firm in an oligopoly

Just as with all the other market structures, an oligopolist must make at least normal profits or supernormal profits to continue production in the long run. Any oligopolist that makes subnormal profit will shut down and leave the industry.

Different from firms in PC and MPC but similar to a monopoly, an oligopolist that earns supernormal profits in the short run will not have to adjust its price and output as it transitions to the long run due to its high BTEs. Even if all the oligopolistic firms are making supernormal profits, new firms cannot enter the industry. Since there are no changes in the number of firms in the industry, the demand for each oligopolist remains constant, therefore, the long-run price and output decision for an oligopolist would be the same as the short-run price and output decision.

Following is a summary of the type of profit an oligopolistic firm can make in the short run, whether it will shut down in the short run, the adjustment from short run to long run, and the type of profit it will make in the long run. This applies to both firms in competitive and collusive oligopolies.

In summary, in the short run, firms in the oligopolistic market structure can earn supernormal profits, normal profits or subnormal profits. However, in the long run, these firms will only earn supernormal or normal profits.

<table>
<tr><th colspan="4">Short run</th></tr>
<tr><th>Supernormal profit</th><th>Normal profit</th><th colspan="2">Subnormal profit</th></tr>
<tr><td>TR > TC
TR > (TFC + TVC)</td><td>TR = TC
TR = (TFC + TVC)</td><td colspan="2">TR < TC
TR < (TFC + TVC)</td></tr>
<tr><td colspan="2" rowspan="3">Firms will continue production</td><td colspan="2">Firms will consider either to continue production or shut down</td></tr>
<tr><td>TR > TVC</td><td>TR < TVC</td></tr>
<tr><td>Short-run shutdown condition is not met. Competitive: Continue production in the short run
Collusive: Consider breaking the collusion</td><td>Short-run shutdown condition is met. Competitive: Shut down in the short run
Collusive: Leave the collusion and consider other options</td></tr>
<tr><th colspan="3">Transition to the long run</th><td>NA</td></tr>
<tr><td>New firms unable to enter the industry. No change.</td><td>No incentive for new firms to enter the industry or for existing firms to leave. No change to the industry.</td><td>Long-run shutdown condition is met.
Competitive: Shut down
Collusive: Leave the collusion and consider other options</td><td>NA</td></tr>
<tr><th colspan="3">Long run</th><td>NA</td></tr>
<tr><td>Continue to earn supernormal profit.</td><td>Continue to earn normal profit</td><td></td><td>NA</td></tr>
</table>

It should be noted that shutting down in the short run does not mean leaving the industry. It only means that the firm chooses not to produce any output (e.g., leave the factory idle). Shutting down in the long run means that the firm chooses to leave the industry. It will cease to be in existence. So, the short-run shutdown condition is used by the firms to decide whether to produce any goods for that period, and the long run shutdown condition is used by the firm to decide whether to stay in the industry.

3.7.8 Non-price strategies of a firm in an oligopoly

For competitive oligopolies

Although oligopolists with their price-setting ability can embark on price competition by reducing prices, oligopolists tend to avoid price competition due to the reasons for price rigidity (Section 3.7.3).

Instead, oligopolists compete based on non-price competition such as branding and advertising, innovation, and product development to increase the demand of their products.

Even if they do not wish to change their prices, an increase in demand would mean a higher quantity demanded for their product, which increases their TR. Assuming the increase in total cost of producing more output is less than the increase in TR, profits will increase.

Another reason for firms in a competitive oligopoly to carry out non-price competition is that it can reduce the cross elasticity of demand (XED) of their products with respect to the price of their rivals' products. This makes the firms less vulnerable to possible predatory pricing strategies.

Additionally, because oligopolists tend to make supernormal profit in the long run, they have the ability to conduct large-scale non-price competition, such as R&D to develop new and innovative products, to differentiate themselves or fund more extensive advertising campaigns.

On the cost side, similar to monopolies, oligopolies will try to find more efficient means of production through R&D so that they can also enjoy higher profits through a reduction in total cost.

For competitive oligopolies

The same reasoning applies to collusive oligopolies. Collusive oligopolies often collude in terms of pricing. However, every firm still has a strong incentive to engage in non-price competition to increase its demand, or engage in R&D to find ways to reduce its cost, such that it can enjoy an increase in profits.

Putting it concretely: Effectiveness of non-price strategies

(branding, advertising, and product differentiation through innovation and product development)

Although non-price strategies may help a firm to increase profits, before firms decide whether to do so, they must also consider (i) whether the strategies will be effective, and (ii) whether the increase in revenue will outweigh the cost of advertising.

Non-price competition strategies may be ineffective if other firms are also doing the same such that every firm's effort cancels out each others. They may also be ineffective if the external conditions are unfavourable (e.g., during a recession).

Additionally, non-price competition strategies carry costs too. Even if the strategies are successful and the demand for the firm's products increases and becomes more price inelastic, if the increase in TR is less than the cost of carrying out the non-price strategies, profits will still decrease instead.

Putting it concretely: Business risks and uncertainty

One factor that we have not systemically considered in our study of firms' decisions in each of the market structures is business risk and uncertainty. A technical and theoretical analysis of business risk and uncertainty is not within the scope of the syllabus.

Nonetheless, in the real world, business risks and uncertainty will also be taken into account when a firm makes pricing and output decisions. For example, if a firm is unsure of whether there will be a recession and hence, a fall in demand for its goods (business risk), it may produce a smaller output just in case a recession does happen. Generally, when there is uncertainty, firms will try to take action to minimise risks. This could come in the form of producing lower quantities of output.

3.8 Impact of Decisions and Strategies on Consumers, Firms, and Governments

The impact of a firm's pricing and output decisions, as well as its non-price competition decisions can be analysed in terms of how it affects the following:

- Allocative efficiency
- Productive efficiency
- Dynamic efficiency
- Equity
- Consumer choice

We will compare the performance of firms in each market structure according to the abovementioned areas. Typically, PC firms are used as a benchmark when assessing the relative performance of firms as they are allocatively and productively efficient and promote equity even though they are dynamically inefficient and do not promote consumer choice. This will be explained in the next few sections.

3.8.1 Allocative efficiency

Definition(s):

Allocative efficiency is the allocation of resources to produce the goods most wanted by the society. It is achieved when P = MC.

PC firms are allocatively efficient because at the profit maximising output, P = MR = MC. The right amount of resources is allocated to produce the right amount of this good.

In contrast, firms in the other three market structures are allocatively inefficient. This is because in all the other market structures, at the profit-maximising output, MR = MC. However, for these market structures, MR always lies below the demand curve. This means that MR < *P*. Hence, at the profit-maximising output, *P* > MC. What this means is that consumers value the last unit of the good (*P*) more than it cost society to produce it (MC). As such, society's welfare can be increased if more of the good is produced. The current level of output represents underproduction and creates a deadweight loss. The allocative inefficiency is greatest under for a monopoly and least for an MPC.

Allocative inefficiency impacts the government as the government's objective is to maximise social welfare. It also affects consumers to some extent as part of the deadweight loss is due to a loss of consumer surplus from firms producing a lower output to charge higher prices. The comparisons of the four market structures in terms of allocative inefficiency is presented in the table on the next page.

3.8.2 Productive efficiency

Definition(s):

Productive efficiency is the production of goods and services at the lowest possible average cost.

PC firms are also productively efficient. They have to adopt production methods with the lowest possible ACs to survive, as they face a very high level of competition and will not be able to survive otherwise. If they do not adopt the least-cost method of production, other firms that do will be able to price lower and force them out of the market. This is also true of MC firms that face high competition from the many other firms in the industry. For oligopolists and monopolists, however, the high BTEs limit the amount of competition they face. Even if they do not produce their output at the minimum AC, they may still be able to survive. As such, they may not be productively efficient. This type of inefficiency is also termed x-inefficiency. x-inefficiency is likely to be larger under a monopoly than under an oligopoly, as a monopoly would likely have a larger buffer of supernormal profits and more room to slack.

It should be noted that while oligopolists and monopolists may not be productively efficient, they may have lower AC than PC and MC firms as they produce a larger scale of output and can reap IEOS.

Productive inefficiency could also have some impact on consumers. This is because the firm's wasted profits could have been directed into R&D to develop better products that increase consumers' welfare.

Comparison of market structures in terms of allocative efficiency

Long-run equilibrium of PC	Long-run equilibrium of MPC	Long-run equilibrium of oligopoly	Long-run equilibrium of monopoly
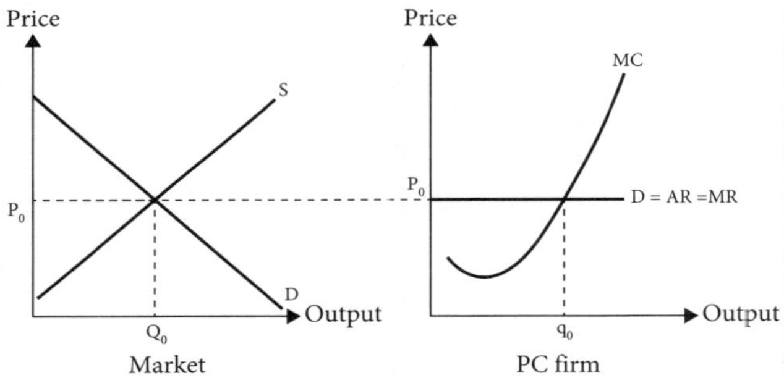	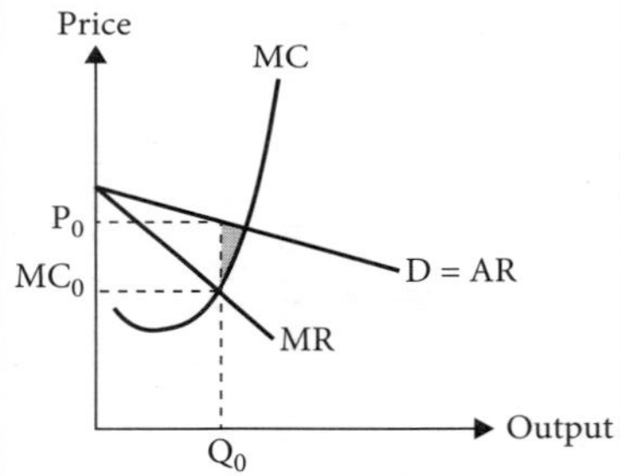	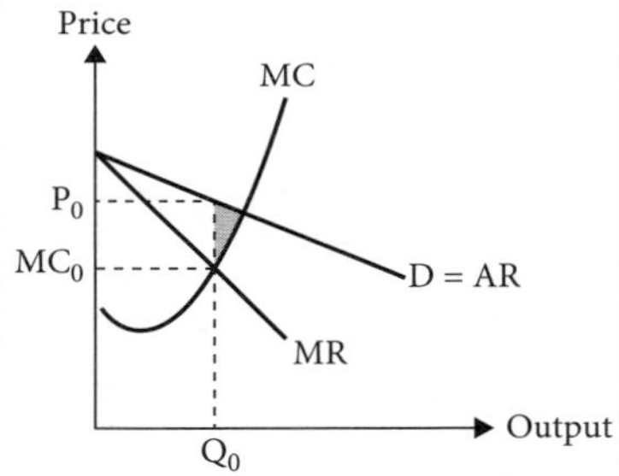	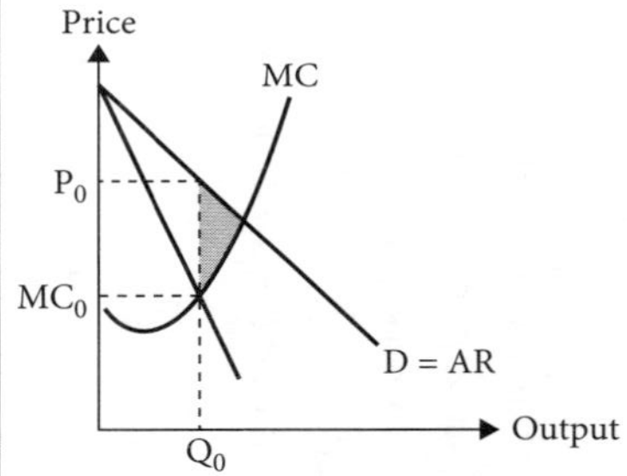
At equilibrium output q_0: Price = P_0 Marginal cost = MC_0 Price = Marginal cost ($P_0 = MC_0$) Allocatively efficient	At equilibrium output Q_0: Price = P_0 Marginal cost = MC_0 Price > Marginal cost ($P_0 > MC_0$) Allocatively inefficient (deadweight loss is shaded) Small gap between P and MC Small degree of allocative inefficiency	At equilibrium output Q_0: Price = P_0 Marginal cost = MC_0 Price > Marginal cost ($P_0 > MC_0$) Allocatively inefficient (deadweight loss is shaded) Large gap between P and MC Large degree of allocative inefficiency	At equilibrium output Q_0: Price = P_0 Marginal cost = MC_0 Price > Marginal cost ($P_0 > MC_0$) Allocatively inefficient (deadweight loss is shaded) Very large gap between P and MC Very large degree of allocative inefficiency

Comparison of market structures in terms of productive efficiency.

Long-run equilibrium of PC	Long-run equilibrium of MPC	Long-run equilibrium of oligopoly	Long-run equilibrium of monopoly
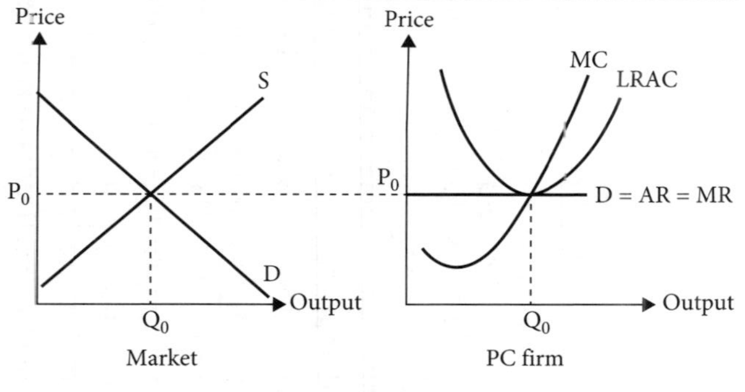	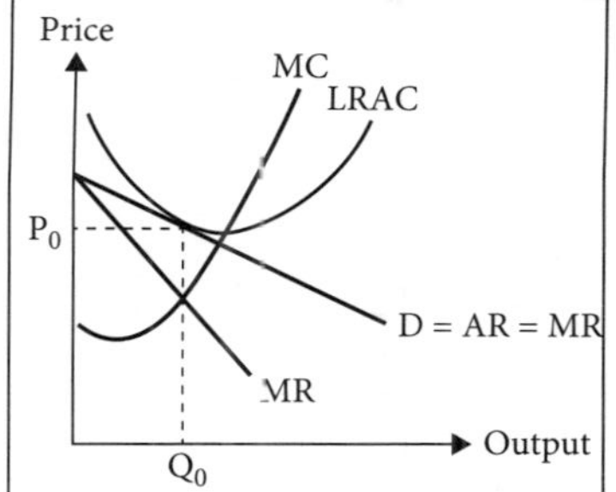	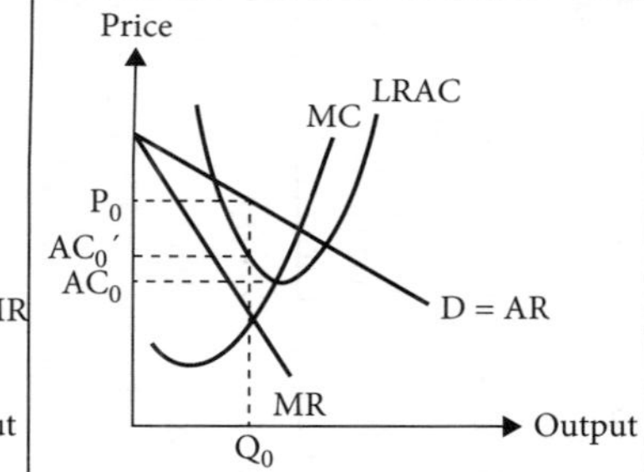	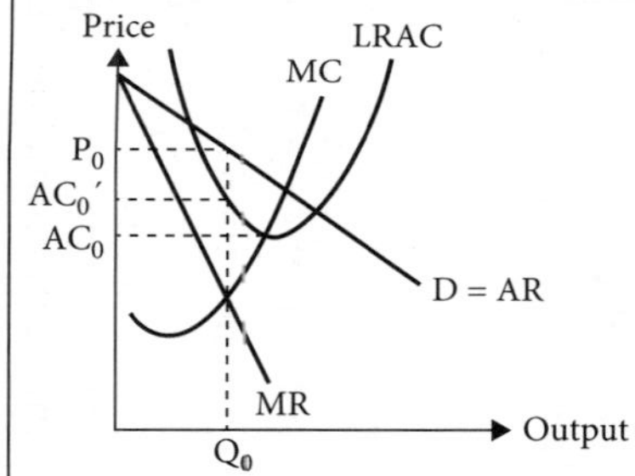
At equilibrium output q_0: Producing on the LRAC Productively efficient	At equilibrium output Q_0: Producing on the LRAC Productively efficient	At equilibrium output Q_0: May produce above the LRAC ($AC'_0 > AC_0$) Productively inefficient (smaller extent)	At equilibrium output Q_0: May produce above the LRAC ($AC'_0 > AC_0$) Productively inefficient (larger extent)

3.8.3 Dynamic efficiency

Definition(s):

Dynamic efficiency is the situation in which firms are technologically progressive (investing in R&D for product or process innovation) to meet the changing needs of consumers over time.

PC firms are not dynamically efficient. This is because they only earn normal profits in the long run and hence, do not have the ability to fund R&D. Additionally, they lack the incentive to do so for two reasons. Firstly, any gain in profit that R&D brings about will be eroded in the long run. Secondly, the assumption of perfect knowledge means that innovation brought about by R&D can be easily copied. The situation is similar for MPC firms which only make normal profit in the long run although MPC firms do not have perfect information. For oligopolists and monopolists, the situation is reversed. Firms in these two market structures have both the ability and incentive to conduct R&D and hence, achieve dynamic efficiency. The high BTEs allow them to retain supernormal profit in the long run. This gives them the ability to conduct R&D. Additionally, since any gains in profit from conducting R&D will be fully retained by the oligopolists and monopolists and not eroded by the entrance of new firms, they will have the incentive to carry out the R&D. The incentive is further strengthened by the fact that there is no perfect information, which means that the new innovation cannot be easily copied.

Dynamic efficiency could affect consumers' welfare as the development of new and innovative products would improve consumers' welfare. If the R&D efforts lead to better processes that reduce costs of production, consumers can also benefit if the reductions in costs are passed on as lower prices, increasing consumer surplus.

3.8.4 Equity

Definition(s):

Equity is defined as having fairness in the distribution of income and consequently, the distribution of goods and services.

The PC market structure promotes equity. This is because in the long run, PC firms only make normal profit. This means that shareholders' (owners of firms) incomes are similar to the incomes earned by owners of other factors of production. Since MC firms also only make normal profit in the long run, the MC market structure also promotes equity. For oligopolies and monopolies, however, the supernormal profits that are retained even over the long run mean that shareholders of these firms earn incomes that are higher than those earned by owners of other factors of production. The difference in incomes then causes differences in purchasing power and inequity as the rich will be able to gain access to more goods and services than the poor. The inequity is greater under a monopoly than under an oligopoly as a monopoly earns more supernormal profits compared to an oligopolist.

Equity impacts the government as one of the government's objectives is to achieve equity.

Comparison of market structures in terms of dynamic efficiency

Long-run equilibrium of PC	Long-run equilibrium of MPC	Long-run equilibrium of oligopoly	Long-run equilibrium of monopoly
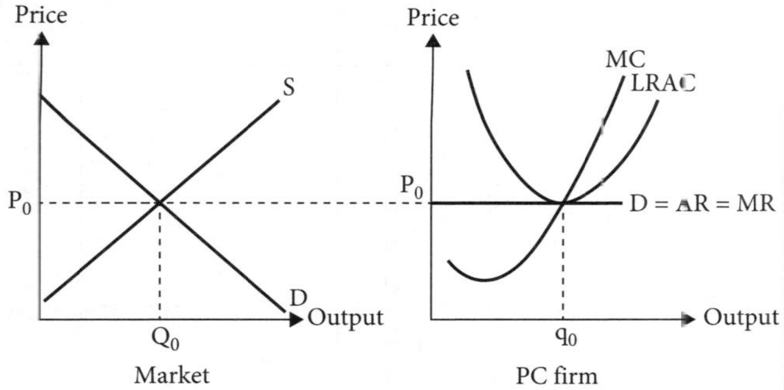	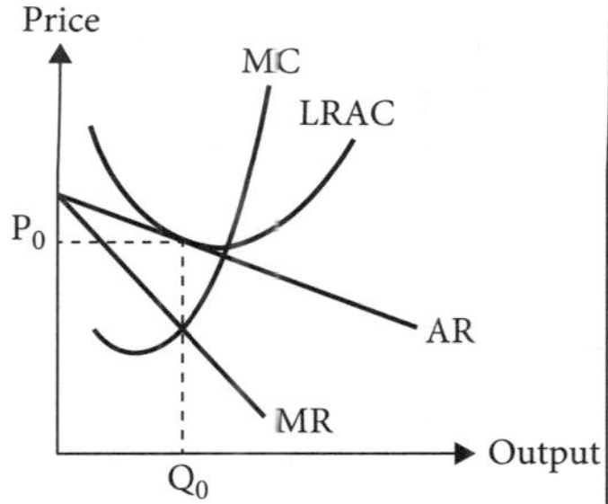	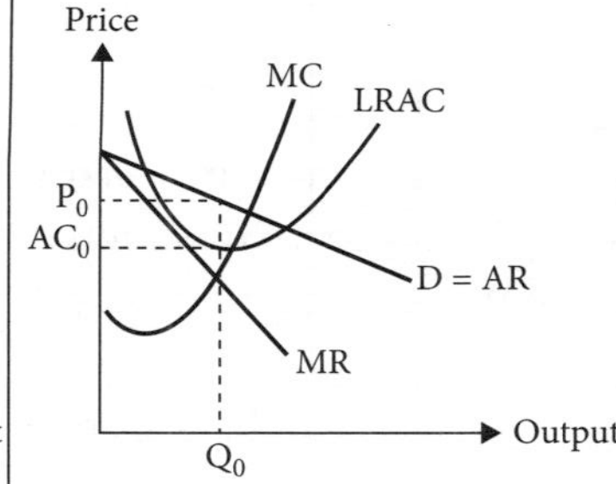	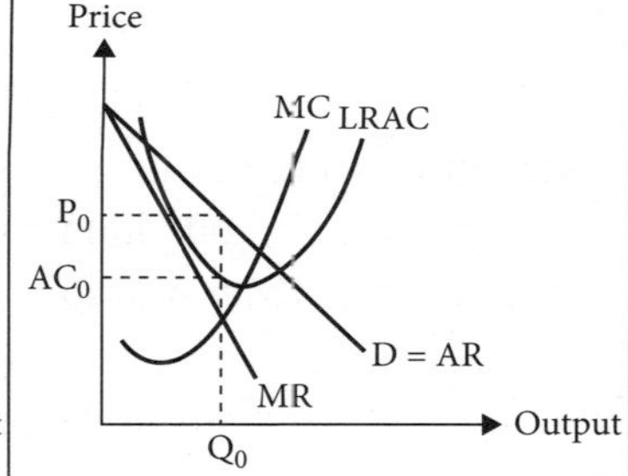
At equilibrium: No ability to innovate (only earns normal profits in the long run) No incentive to innovate Dynamically inefficient	At equilibrium: No ability to innovate (only earns normal profits in the long run) Limited incentive to innovate Dynamically inefficient	At equilibrium: Has ability to innovate (retains supernormal profits in the long run) Has incentive to innovate Dynamically efficient to a smaller extent due to lower supernormal profits (lower ability) compared to a monopolist	At equilibrium: Has ability to innovate (retains supernormal profits in the long run) Has incentive to innovate Dynamically efficient to a larger extent due to higher supernormal profits (greater ability) compared to an oligopolist

Comparison of market structures in terms of equity

Long-run equilibrium of PC	Long-run equilibrium of MPC	Long-run equilibrium of oligopoly	Long-run equilibrium of monopoly
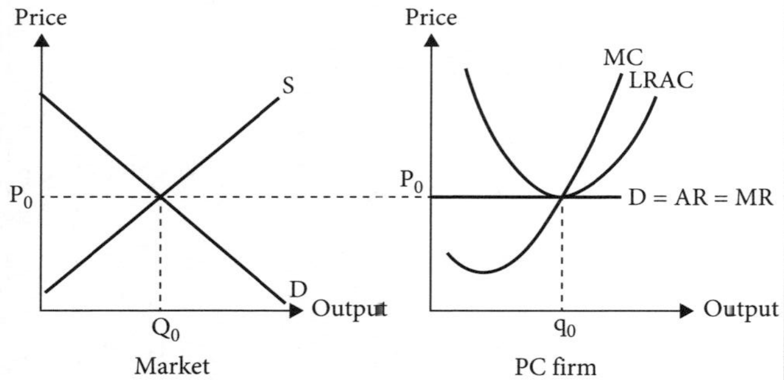	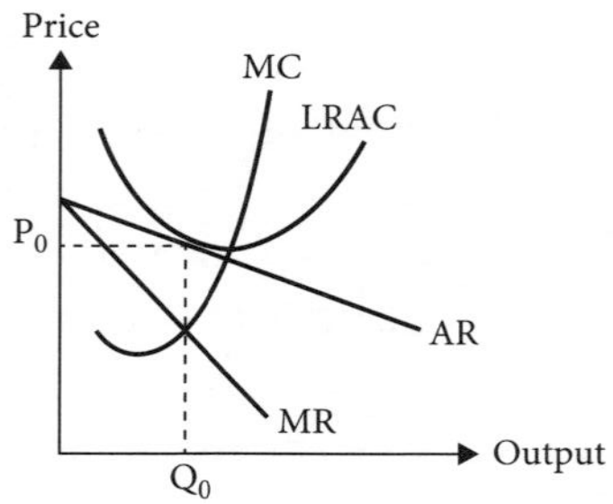	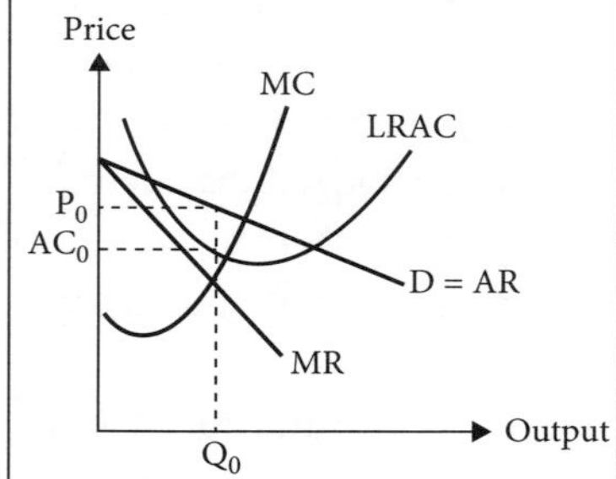	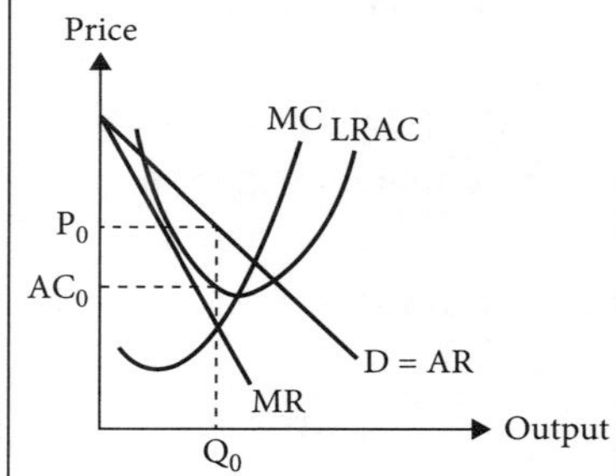
At equilibrium: Only earns normal profits Achieves equity	At equilibrium: Only earns normal profits Achieves equity	At equilibrium: Retains supernormal profits Causes inequity Extent is smaller than under a monopoly as amount of supernormal profit retained is lower	At equilibrium: Retains supernormal profits Causes inequity Extent is larger than under an oligopoly as amount of supernormal profit retained is higher

3.8.5 Choice

Definition(s):

Consumer choice is defined as the variety or range of goods and services that consumers can choose from.

Finally, the PC market structure does not promote consumer choice. Since all firms in the PC market structure sell homogenous goods, there is no variety of products for the consumers to choose from. This lack of choice would also apply to a monopoly (assuming the monopoly does not develop a whole line of products) or oligopolies that produce homogenous products. In contrast, MC, oligopolies that produce differentiated products, and monopolies that engage in product development would offer consumers choice.

Choice affects consumer welfare as consumers are better off with choices than without.

3.8.6 Summary of the performance of the four market structures

A summary of the performance of the four market structures is provided below. This table allows us to determine how the different aspects of performance are affected when changes in the level of competition moves a market from one structure towards another.

	PC	MPC	Oligopoly	Monopoly
Allocative efficiency	Yes	No (small degree of allocative inefficiency)	No (large degree of allocative inefficiency)	No (very large degree of allocative inefficiency)
Productive efficiency	Yes	Yes	No[11] (smaller degree of productive inefficiency)	No (larger degree of productive inefficiency)
Dynamic efficiency	No	No	Yes (smaller degree)	Yes (larger degree)[12]
Equity	Yes	Yes	No	No
Choice	No	Yes	Depends	Depends

11 A case can be made that the price rigidity of oligopolies gives them a very strong incentive to minimise costs since that is the only way they can increase profits. That incentive could be strong enough for them to be productively efficient (x-efficient).

12 It can also be argued that oligopolies could be more dynamically efficient than monopolies even though oligopolistic firms have a lower ability to conduct R&D. This is because oligopolists could have a stronger incentive to do so as they need to carry out non-price competition strategies to compete against their rivals whereas monopolists do not need to do so.

3.9 Price Discrimination

We have studied the pricing and output decisions of firms under the different market structures. However, the analysis had been based on the assumption that the firm just decides on one price for its products. In reality, firms may charge different prices for the different units of the product. When firms do so for reasons unrelated to differences in cost, we term that price discrimination.

> *Definition(s):*
>
> **Price discrimination** is the act of charging different prices for different units of output for reasons unrelated to cost differences.

For price discrimination to occur, these three conditions must be met:

1. The firm must be a price setter
2. The market segments that the firm hopes to charge different prices to must be separable and resale must be very unlikely
3. The PED of each segment must be different.

The first condition is necessary as a firm that cannot set its own price clearly cannot charge different prices. Thus, only firms operating in MPC, oligopolies, and monopolies can price discriminate.

The second condition is necessary if the markets cannot be separated, then it is impossible to charge a higher price in one market segment and a lower price in another. Note that a market segment could refer to a single consumer too.

The third condition is necessary because without a difference in PED, there would be no point in charging different prices. To increase revenue, the firm would charge a higher price in the market segment with the lower PED and a lower price in the market segment with the higher PED. If both markets have the same PED, naturally the price charged in both market segments should be the same.

Types of Price Discrimination

There are three types of price discrimination—first degree price discrimination, second degree price discrimination, and third degree price discrimination.

> *Definition(s):*
>
> **First degree price discrimination (also known as perfect price discrimination)** refers to the situation where the firm charges the maximum price for every unit of output.
>
> **Second degree price discrimination** refers to the situation where the firm charges a different price for different quantities of the output.
>
> **Third degree price discrimination** refers to the situation where the firm charges a different price for different consumer groups.

3.9.1 First degree price discrimination

First degree price discrimination also known as perfect price discrimination refers to the situation where the firm charges a (maximum) different price for every unit of output.

Effect of first degree price discrimination on profits

For each unit of output, the firm will charge the maximum price that the consumer is willing to pay. Hence, the price of each unit will be charged according to the demand curve (which marks out the maximum that consumers are willing to pay for the different units of output). The demand curve is hence, also the MR curve. When firms profit-maximise (produce output and price them such that MC = MR) under first degree price discrimination, they will produce Q_{PD} output.

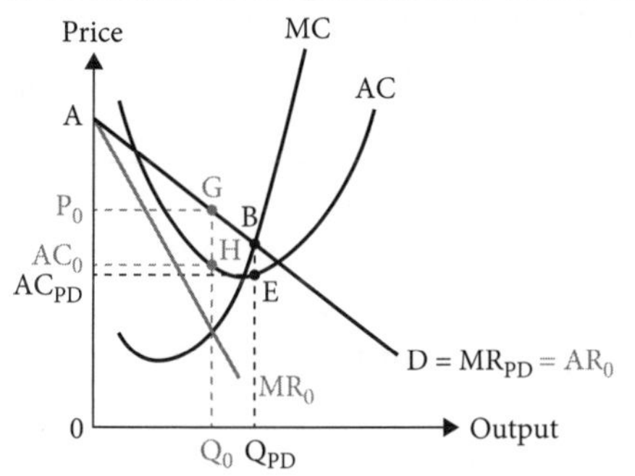

With first degree price discrimination:	Without price discrimination:
$TR = 0ABQ_{PD}$	$TR = 0P_0GQ_0$
$TC = 0AC_{PD}EQ_{PD}$	$TC = 0AC_0HQ_0$
$Profit = TR - TC = AC_{PD}ABE$	$Profit = TR - TC = AC_0P_0GH$

$AC_{PD}ABE > AC_0P_0GH$
Profit under first degree price discrimination > Profit without price discrimination

As illustrated above, first degree price discrimination increases profit.

Effect of first degree price discrimination on allocative efficiency

First degree price discrimination results in an **allocatively efficient** output being produced. Under first degree price discrimination, the level of output produced (Q_{PD} in Fig. 3.16) will be one where the price of the last unit of the good (P_{PD}) is equal to its MC (MC_{PD}). At this level of

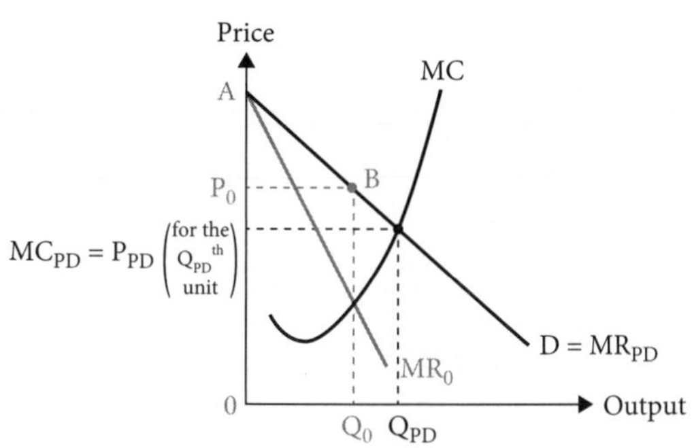

Figure 3.16: Allocative efficiency under first degree price discrimination.

output, society values the last unit of output the same as it costs to produce it. Social welfare is maximised.

Effect of first degree price discrimination on productive inefficiency

However, first degree price discrimination may result in **productive inefficiency** (if the firm was originally productively efficient) or an increase in productive inefficiency (if the firm was already productively inefficient). This is because first degree price discrimination will increase a firm's profits (as explained in the section 3.9.1). With an increase in profits, the firm now has some/more buffer to slack and may become x-inefficient (if it previously was not x-inefficient) or more x-inefficient (if it was already x-inefficient).

Effect of first degree price discrimination on dynamic efficiency

In terms of **dynamic efficiency**, since first degree price discrimination increases profits (from normal to supernormal; or from supernormal to even more supernormal), the firm's ability to carry out R&D increases. Assuming the incentive to do so remains unchanged (or increases), the greater ability to carry out R&D would translate into more R&D activities being carried out. More R&D activities being carried out would lead to a greater level of innovation being adopted over time, increasing the dynamic efficiency.

Effect of first degree price discrimination on equity

The effect of first degree price discrimination on **equity** can be studied in a number of ways. First, since first degree price discrimination results in more profits for the firm, it contributes to more income inequality and worsens inequity. Additionally, first degree price discrimination worsens inequity by transferring consumer surplus to firms in the form of increased TR. Referring to the Fig. 3.17 below, without first degree price discrimination, the firm would produce Q_0 units of output and price them at P_0 each. The consumer surplus is P_0AB. With first degree price discrimination, however, the consumer surplus falls to zero as every unit of output is priced at the maximum that consumers are willing and able to pay. This loss in consumer surplus that is gained by the firm represents worsened inequity. On the other hand, first degree price discrimination makes more units of the good available by lowering the price charged for some of them. Q_0 to Q_{PD} units of output would not be produced without first degree price discrimination. However, with first degree price discrimination, they are produced and priced between P_0 (the price that would be charged without first degree price discrimination) and P_{PD}. This could improve equity instead as some consumers who were previously unable to obtain the good can now obtain it.

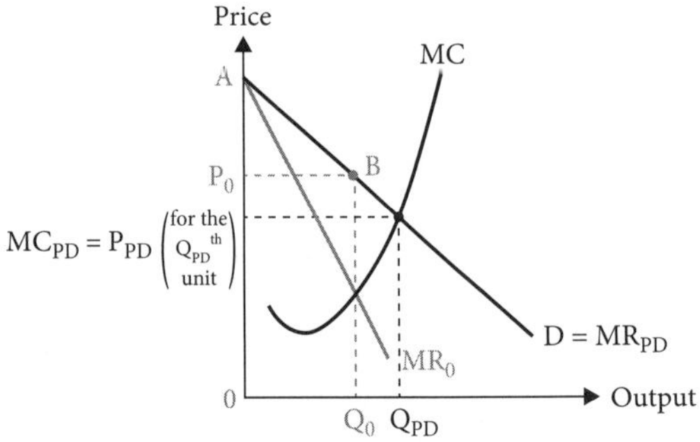

Figure 3.17

Effect of first degree price discrimination on choice(s)

First degree price discrimination could increase **choice** in two ways. Firstly, as explained in the preceding paragraph, first degree price discrimination makes some units of the good available to consumers who previously did not have access to them. This increases the choice of products available to some consumers. Secondly, price discrimination may make some goods, that were previously unprofitable to produce, now profitable (see Fig 3.18). The production of these goods increases the choice of products for consumers.

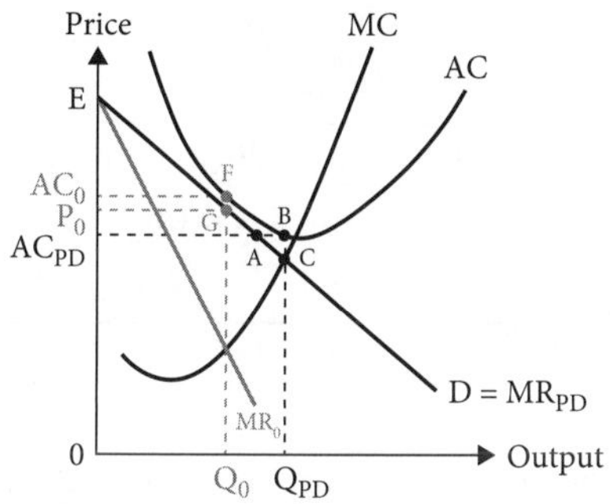

Figure 3.18: A good that is only profitable under first degree price discrimination.

With first degree price discrimination:	Without price discrimination:
$TR = 0ECQ_{PD}$ $TC = AC_{PD} \times Q_{PD} = 0AC_{PD}BQ_{PD}$ $Profit = TR - TC = 0ECQ_{PD} - 0AC_{PD}BQ_{PD} > 0$ as $AC_{PD}EA > ABC$	$TR = P_0 \times Q_0 = 0P_0GQ_0$ $TC = AC_0 \times Q_0 = 0AC_0FQ_0$ $Profit = TR - TC = 0P_0GQ_0 - 0AC_0FQ_0 < 0$

There is supernormal profit under first degree price discrimination but subnormal profit without price discrimination.

First degree price discrimination results in this good being produced

3.9.2 Second degree price discrimination

Second degree price discrimination refers to the situation where the firm charges a different price for different quantities of the output.

Effect of second degree price discrimination on profits

In second degree price discrimination, different prices are charged for different quantities of output. For simplicity's sake, let us assume in Fig. 3.19 that the output is only split into two blocks. P_{PD0} is charged for output 0 to Q_{PD0} and P_{PD1} is charged for output Q_{PD0} to Q_{PD1}. The MR will be equal to the price (P_{PD0}) charged for output 0 to Q_{PD0} and P_{PD1} for output Q_{PD0} to Q_{PD1}. To maximise profit (produce output and price them such that MC = MR), the firm will produce Q_{PD1} output in total.

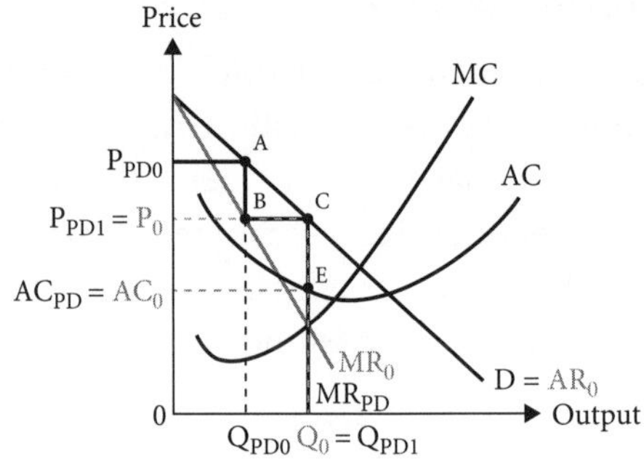

Figure 3.19

With second degree price discrimination:	Without price discrimination:
$TR = 0P_{PD0}ABCQ_{PD1}$ $TC = 0AC_{PD}EQ_{PD1}$ Profit = TR − TC = $AC_{PD}P_{PD0}ABCE$	$TR = 0P_0CQ_0$ $TC = 0AC_0EQ_0$ Profit = TR − TC = AC_0P_0CE
$AC_{PD}P_{PD0}ABCE > AC_0P_0FG$ Profit under second degree price discrimination > Profit without price discrimination	

Effect of second degree price discrimination on allocative efficiency

The effect of second degree price discrimination on **allocative efficiency** is indeterminate. Without any price discrimination, there would be underproduction of output by any price-setting firm as they would produce an output where price (P_0 in Fig. 3.20) exceeds the MC (MC_0 in Fig. 3.20). This was explained in Section 3.8. As such, if second degree price discrimination results in an increase in output, there would be less (or even zero) underproduction. This would mean that there would be less allocative inefficiency. A scenario where second degree price discrimination would result in allocative efficiency is illustrated in Fig. 3.20 where the output under second degree price discrimination (Q_{PD}) is more than without price discrimination (Q_0). At the Q_{PD}, the price (P_{PD1}) is equal to the MC (MC_{PD}).

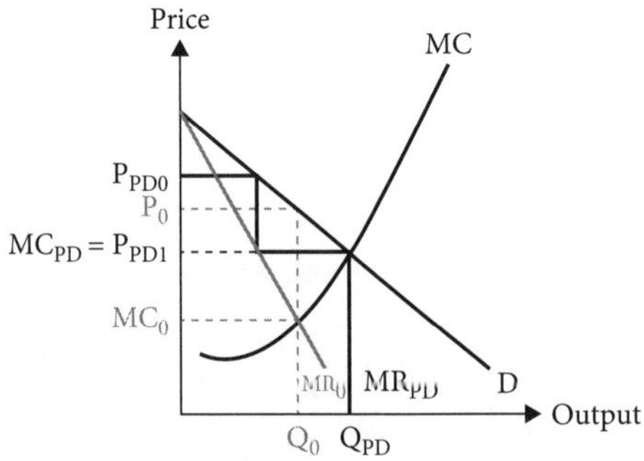

Figure 3.20: Allocative efficiency under second degree price discrimination.

However, second degree price discrimination does not guarantee that there would be an increase in output. If there is no increase in output, the level of allocative inefficiency would be the same as before. Such a scenario is illustrated in Fig. 3.21 where the output under second degree price discrimination (Q_{PD}) is the same as without price discrimination (Q_0). The gap between the price and MC is the same under second degree price discrimination (P_{PD1} – MC_{PD}) compared to without price discrimination (P_0 – MC_0).

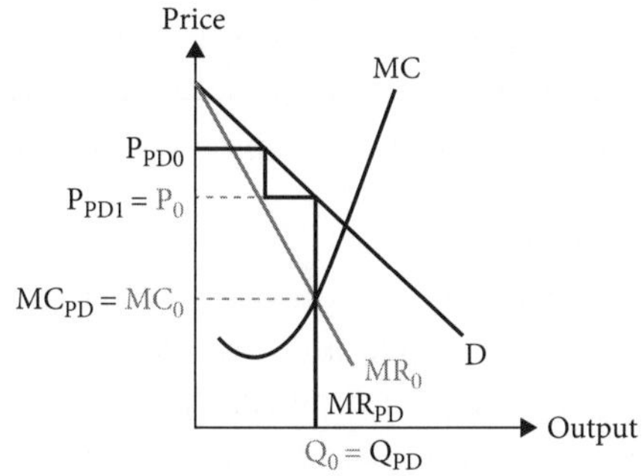

Figure 3.21: Allocative inefficiency under second degree price discrimination.

Effect of second degree price discrimination on productive inefficiency

Similar to first degree price discrimination, second degree price discrimination may result in **productive inefficiency** (if the firm was originally productively efficient) or an increase in productive inefficiency (if the firm was already productively inefficient). This is because just like first degree price discrimination, second degree price discrimination will increase a firm's profits. With an increase in profits, the firm now has some/more buffer to slack and may become x-inefficient (if it previously was not x-inefficient) or more x-inefficient (if it was already x-inefficient).

Effect of second degree price discrimination on dynamic efficiency

In terms of **dynamic efficiency**, since second degree price discrimination also increases profits like first degree price discrimination (from normal to supernormal or from supernormal to even more supernormal), the firm's ability to carry out R&D increases. Assuming the incentive to do so remains unchanged (or increases), the greater ability to carry out R&D would translate into more R&D activities being carried out. More R&D activities being carried out would lead to a greater level of innovation being adopted over time, increasing the dynamic efficiency.

Effect of second degree price discrimination on equity

The effect of second degree price discrimination on **equity** can be studied in a few ways. Firstly, since second degree price discrimination also results in more profits for the firm, it contributes to more income inequality and worsens inequity. And, similar to first degree price discrimination, second degree price discrimination worsens inequity by transferring consumer surplus to firms in the form of increased TR. On the other hand, if second degree price discrimination results in a more units of the good being available at a lowered price (e.g., $P_{PD1} < P_0$ in Fig. 3.18), this could improve equity instead, as some consumers who were previously unable to obtain the good can now obtain it.

Effect of second degree price discrimination on choice(s)

Second degree price discrimination could increase **choice** in two ways. Firstly, as explained in the preceding paragraph, second degree price discrimination may make some units of the good available to consumers who previously did not have access to them. This would increase the choice of products available to these consumers. Secondly, similar to first degree price discrimination, since second degree price discrimination also increases the profits of firms, it may make some goods that were previously unprofitable to produce now profitable. The production of these goods increases the choice of products for consumers.

3.9.3 Third degree price discrimination

Third degree price discrimination refers to the situation where the firm charges a different price for different consumer groups. For simplicity's sake, let us assume that the consumers only split into two groups—one with a lower |PED| (D_I and MR_I in Fig. 3.22) and one with a higher |PED| (D_E and MR_E in Fig. 3.22). The combination of the two submarkets forms the total market (D_T and MR_T in Fig. 3.22). D_T is the horizontal summation of D_I and D_E. MR_T is derived from D_T.[13] The firm first decides what the profit-maximising total output (Q_T) is by equating MR_T to MC. It then decides how much of the output to allocate to each submarket.

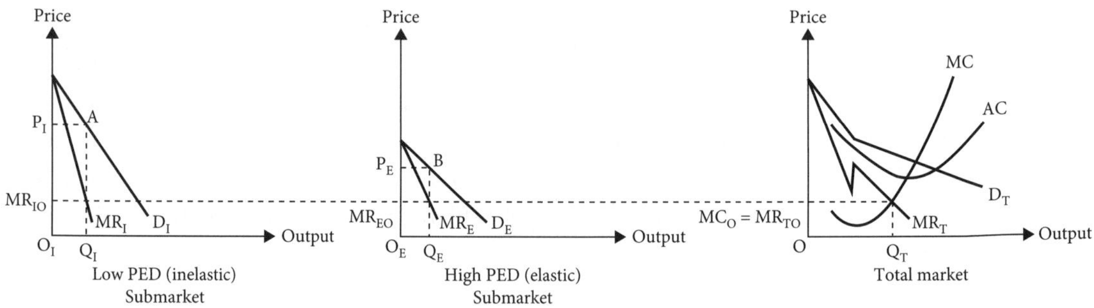

Figure 3.22: Price and output decision under third degree price discrimination.

The allocation of output between the two submarkets will be done such that the MR in both submarkets is equal. This is because, if the MR in one submarket is higher than the other, the firm can increase its TR by reallocating one unit of output from the submarket with the lower MR to the submarket with the higher MR. When it does so, it gives up a smaller amount of MR in return for a larger MR. For example, suppose the MR in submarket A is currently $10 and the MR in submarket B is currently $8. The firm can increase its TR by taking one unit of output from submarket B and selling it in submarket A. In this way, it loses $8 from not selling that output in submarket B, but gains $10 from selling that output in submarket A. It increases its TR by $2. So long as there are still differences in the MR of each submarket, reallocation of output can be done to increase TR. As such, to maximise TR, the eventual allocation of output will be the one where the MR in each submarket is equal ($MR_{TO} = MR_{EO} = MR_{IO}$ when output Q_I is allocated to the low PED submarket and output QE is allocated to the high PED submarket in the following figure, $Q_T = Q_I + Q_E$).

With the allocation of the output to each submarket, the price in each submarket can be determined. The price in the low |PED| submarket would be P_I and that in the high |PED| submarket would be P_E. The price in the low PED submarket would be higher ($P_I > P_E$).

13 Refer to Annex 3.4 for details of the derivation of D_T and MR_T.

Intuitively, this makes sense as in the low |PED| submarket, the firm would want to charge a higher price because quantity demanded is less responsive to price changes. Charging a higher price in the low PED submarket would allow the firm to increase TR. Conversely, in the high-|PED| submarket, the firm would want to charge a lower price because quantity demanded is more responsive to price changes. Charging a lower price in the high PED submarket would allow the firm to further increase TR.

Effect of third degree price discrimination on profits

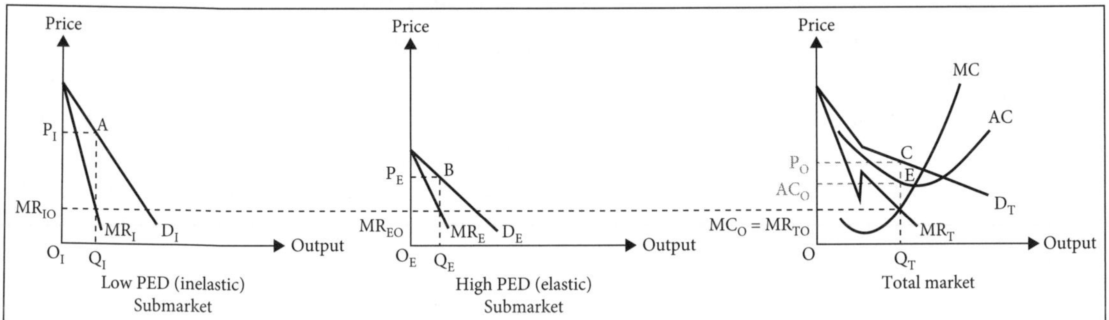

With third degree price discrimination:	Without price discrimination (from total market):
$TR = (P_I \times Q_I) + (P_E \times Q_E) = 0_IP_IAQ_I + 0_EP_EBQ_E$ TC (from total market) $= AC_0 \times Q_T = 0AC_0EQ_T$	$TR = P_0 \times Q_T = 0P_0CQ_T$ $TC = AC_0 \times Q_T = 0AC_0EQ_T$

The total cost under third degree price discrimination and without price discrimination are the same.

However, as reasoned in the paragraph before, TR is higher under third degree price discrimination ($0_IP_IAQ_I + 0_EP_EBQ_E > 0P_0AQ_T$) than without.

Therefore, profit under third degree price discrimination > Profit without price discrimination

Effect of third degree price discrimination on allocative efficiency

Third degree price discrimination would result in the same level of **allocative inefficiency** as no price discrimination. Without any price discrimination, there would be underproduction of output by any price-setting firm as they would produce an output where price (P_0 in Fig. 3.23) exceeds MC (MC_0 in Fig. 3.23). As illustrated in Fig. 3.23, third degree price discrimination does not result in any change of total output ($Q_T = Q_0$). It only allocates this total output into different submarkets and prices them differently in each submarket. Since there is no change in total output, the level of allocative inefficiency is the same as before.

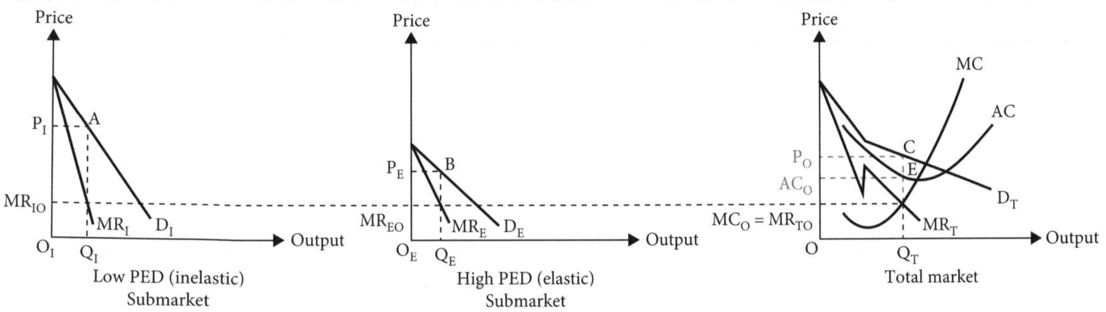

Figure 3.23: Allocative inefficiency under third degree price discrimination.

Effect of third degree price discrimination on productive inefficiency

Similar to first and second degree price discrimination, third degree price discrimination increases profits and creates (more) room for firms to slack and become (more) x-inefficient. This could result in **productive inefficiency** (if the firm was originally productively efficient) or an increase in productive inefficiency (if the firm was already productively inefficient).

Effect of third degree price discrimination on dynamic efficiency

In terms of **dynamic efficiency**, since third degree price discrimination also increases profits like first and second degree price discrimination (from normal to supernormal or from supernormal to even more supernormal), the firm's ability to carry out R&D increases. Assuming the incentive to do so remains unchanged (or increases), the greater ability to carry out R&D would translate into more R&D activities being carried out. More R&D activities being carried out would lead to a greater level of innovation being adopted over time, increasing the dynamic efficiency.

Effect of third degree price discrimination on equity

The effect of third degree price discrimination on **equity** can be studied in a few ways. First, since third degree price discrimination also results in more profits for the firm, it contributes to more income inequality and worsens inequity. And, similar to first and second degree price discrimination, third degree price discrimination worsens inequity by transferring consumer surplus to firms in the form of increased TR. On the other hand, third degree price discrimination involves charging a lower price in the submarket with a more price elastic demand and higher price in the submarket with the more price inelastic demand. The submarket with a more price elastic demand tends to be one with lower income consumers. This is because when the income is low, the proportion of income (a factor of PED) spent on a good would be high, causing the demand to be more price elastic. So, charging a lower price in the submarket with a more price elastic demand translates into charging low-income consumers a lower price. Conversely, higher income consumers would be charged a higher price. Higher income consumers effectively end up cross-subsidising low-income consumers, improving equity.

Effect of third degree price discrimination on choice(s)

Third degree price discrimination could increase **choice**. Similar to first and second degree price discrimination, since third degree price discrimination also increases the profits of firms, it may make some goods, that were previously unprofitable to produce, now profitable. The production of these goods increases the choice of products for consumers.

3.9.4 Summary of price discrimination

	First degree price discrimination	**Second degree price discrimination**	**Third degree price discrimination**
Discrimination criteria/via	Each individual consumer	Quantity purchased	Different groups of consumers
Impact on profits	All three types of price discrimination will increase a firm's profits. Intuitively, this makes sense as a firm would not carry out price discrimination if it did not increase profits		
Impact on allocative efficiency	Achieves	Depends	Does not achieve (same level of allocative inefficiency as without price discrimination)
Impact on productive efficiency	Creates/worsens x-inefficiency	Creates/worsens x-inefficiency	Creates/worsens x-inefficiency
Impact on Dynamic efficiency	Creates/improves dynamic efficiency	Creates/improves dynamic efficiency	Creates/improves dynamic efficiency
Impact on equity	Worsens in some aspects and improves in other(s)	Worsens in some aspects and improves in other(s)	Worsens in some aspects and improves in other(s)
Impact on choice	Increases	Increases	Increases

Summary for Chapter 3

1. Firms are usually assumed to want to maximise profits. However, there are possible alternative objectives.
2. To maximise profits, firms will decide on the level of output and the price such that marginal revenue equals marginal cost.
3. Costs need to be analysed in terms of the short run or the long run. In the short run, some factors of production are fixed while in the long run, all factors of production are variable.
4. Costs could be affected by internal and external economies and diseconomies of scale.
5. The behaviour of firms in terms of price and output, as well as in terms of non-price competition strategies depends on the market structure they operate in.
6. There are four market structures: perfect competition, monopolistic competition, oligopoly, and monopoly.
7. The four market structures are distinguished by their features in terms of the level of the BTEs, the number and size of firms in the industry, the degree of interdependence amongst firms in the industry, the type of product that is sold, and the degree of information available in the industry.
8. The behaviour of firms in the four market structures can be evaluated in terms of allocative efficiency, productive efficiency, dynamic efficiency, equity, and choice.
9. Perfect competition is a theoretical market structure that is very unlikely to exist in real life. However, it is studied to provide a benchmark as it achieves allocative efficiency, productive efficiency, and equity.
10. Price discrimination is a special pricing behaviour that firms can adopt if the necessary conditions are met. There are three type of price discrimination—first, second, and third degree price discrimination.
11. All three types of price discrimination will increase the profits of a firm.
12. The effects of the three types of price discrimination can also be evaluated in terms of allocative efficiency, productive efficiency, dynamic efficiency, equity, and choice.

Annex 3.1 Illustrating the alternative objectives of the firm

Alternative objective	Illustration
Entry deterrence: Adopt limit pricing (P = AC) Price = P_0 Output = Q_0	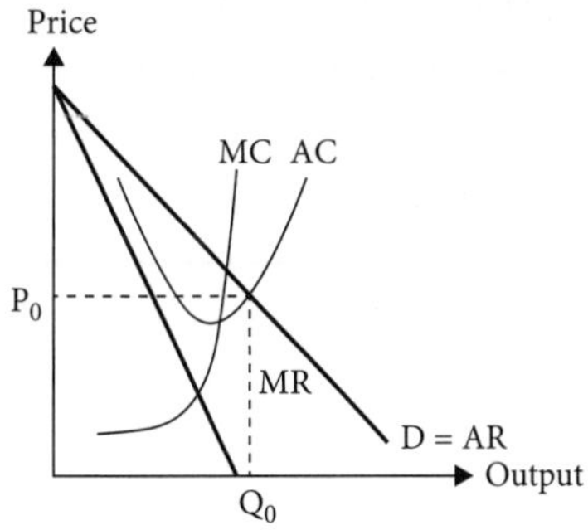
Revenue maximisation: Maximise TR (MR = 0) Price = P_0 Output = Q_0	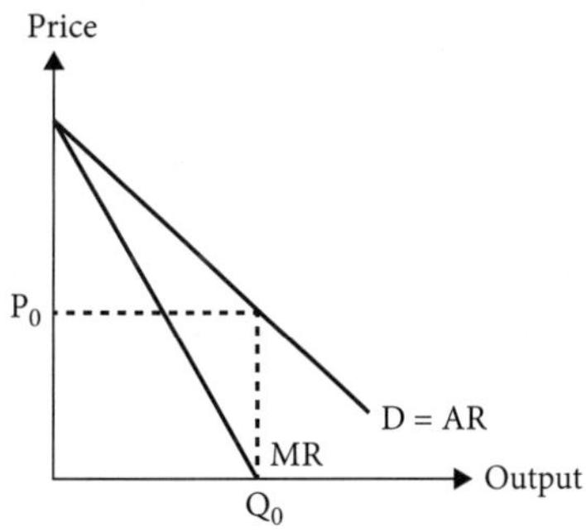
Profit satisficing: Accept any price and quantity so long as at least normal profit is made (i.e., so long as P ≥ AC) Price between P_0 and P_1 Output between Q_0 and Q_1	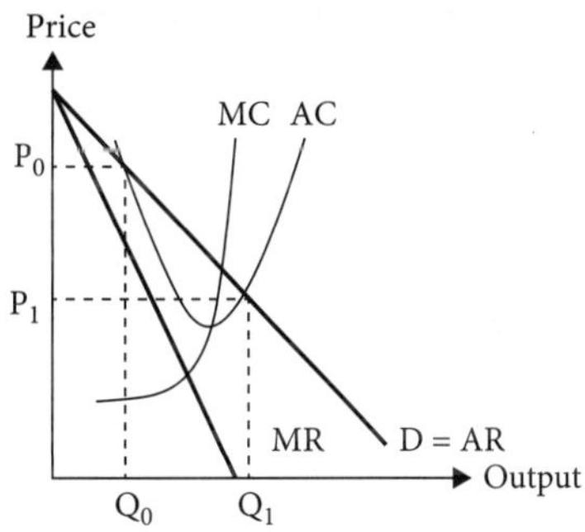
Market share dominance: Adopt predatory pricing (P < AC) Price < P_0 Output > Q_0	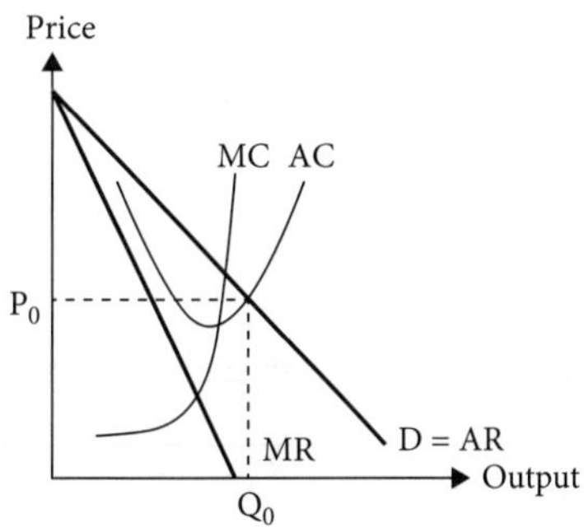

Annex 3.2 Mathematical proof of why marginal cost curve cuts average variable cost curve and average total cost curve at their minimum points

For this proof, knowledge of calculus (differentiation) is required.

Let total variable cost (TVC) be denoted by VC

Let output be denoted by q

Since VC is determined by q, we say VC is a function of q.

$$\text{VC} = f(q)$$

Let average cost be denoted by AVC.

$$\text{AVC} = \frac{\text{VC}}{q} = \frac{f(q)}{q}$$

Let marginal cost be denoted by MC

Since MC is the change in VC for an additional unit of q, MC is the rate of change in VC with respect to q. In other words, MC is the differential of VC with respect to q.

$$\text{MC} = \frac{d(\text{VC})}{d(q)} = f'(q)\lim_{x \to \infty}$$

At the minimum point of AVC, the differential of AVC should be equal to 0.

$$\frac{d(\text{AVC})}{d(q)} = 0$$

$$\frac{d\left(\frac{f(q)}{q}\right)}{d(q)} = 0$$

Applying the quotient rule,

$$\frac{q.f'(q) - f(q)}{q^2} = 0$$

Rearranging and cancelling the common factor in the numerator and denominator on the left-hand side

$$\frac{q.f'(q)}{q^2} = \frac{f(q)}{q^2}$$

$$\frac{f'(q)}{q} = \frac{f(q)}{q^2}$$

Multiplying both sides by q

$$f'(q) = \frac{f(q)}{q}$$

Since $f'(q)$ is MC and $\frac{f(q)}{q}$ is AVC

$$\text{MC} = \text{AVC}$$

Hence, at the minimum point of AVC, MC = AVC.

For the proof for MC cutting ATC at its minimum point, simply replace VC above with TC.

Annex 3.3 The marginal revenue curve for a straight line demand curve

This proof requires knowledge of calculus (differentiation) and equations of a straight line,

The demand curve is a straight line and can be expressed as:[14]

$$P = a - bQ$$

where a and b are both positive numbers; a is the vertical intercept and $-b$ is the gradient of the line. The gradient is negative as the line is downward sloping. P represents the price and Q represents the output.

Total revenue (TR) can then be expressed as:

$$\text{TR} = P \times Q = (a - bQ) \times Q = aQ - bQ^2$$

Marginal revenue (MR) is the change in TR for the additional output. In other words, it is the rate of change of TR with respect to a change in Q. This means that MR is the differential of TR with respect to Q and can be expressed as:

$$\text{MR} = d(\text{TR})/dQ = a - 2bQ$$

The vertical intercept of the MR curve is a and its gradient is $-2b$.

Comparing the expressions for the demand curve and the MR, we notice that both have a vertical intercept of a. Additionally, the gradient of MR ($-2b$) is twice that of the demand curve ($-b$).

14 Here, we have expressed P in terms of Q as P is on the vertical axis and this is a form that more students will be familiar with. However, in terms of derivation, Q is actually a function of P and not the other way round. In any case, even if we had expressed it at Q in terms of P, the MR would still end up having the same vertical intercept and be twice as steep as the demand curve.

Annex 3.4 Derivation of the total demand and marginal revenue of the total market under third degree price discrimination

Assume that the total market is made up of two submarkets—a low PED submarket with demand (D_I) and marginal revenue (MR_I) and a high PED submarket with demand (D_E) and marginal revenue (MR_E) as shown in Fig. 3.22

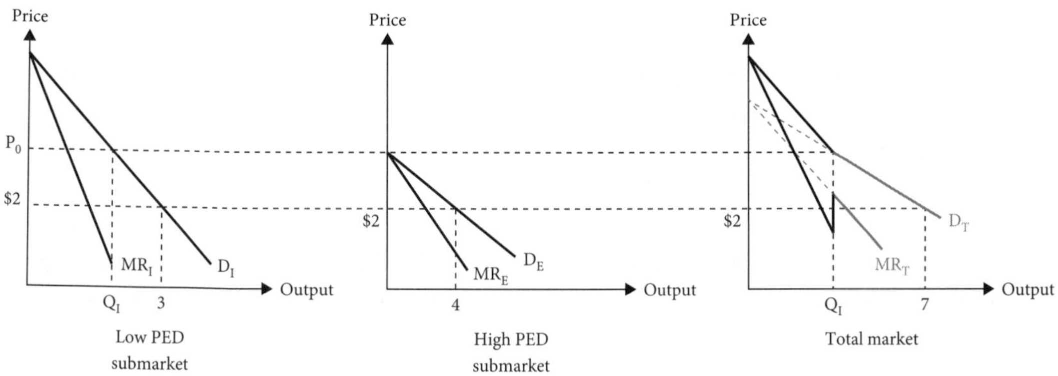

Figure 3.22: Derivation of D_T and MR_T under third degree price discrimination.

Deriving the Total Demand Curve (D_T)

The total market demand should be the horizontal summation of the two submarkets' demands. For example, if at a price of $2, three units of output are demanded in the low PED submarket and four units of output are demanded in the high PED submarket, then at $2, seven units (three units + four units) of output should be demanded in the total market.

When the price is above P_0, the only demand in the total market would come from the low PED submarket. Hence, above P_0, D_T is the same as D_I.

Below P_0, the demand in the total market would come from both the low PED submarket and the high PED submarket. Hence, below P_0, D_T is the horizontal summation of D_I and D_E and kinks outwards.

Deriving the MR Curve of the Total Market (MR_T)

Once D_T is derived, we notice that there are two parts to it. Before output Q_T, D_T is steep (in blue). After output Q_T, D_T is gentle. To derive MR_T, we simply derive the MR for D_T before output Q_T (in blue), then derive the MR for D_T after output Q_T (in red). For the latter, we imagine extending D_T back to the price axis and extending the MR from there (see red dotted lines). The MR_T will naturally have a double kink. MR was first introduced in Chapter 1. It is re-introduced here for the readers' convenience.

CHAPTER 4

MARKET FAILURE

In Chapter 1, we studied the central problem of Economics (scarcity) and realised that society has to answer questions of "What to produce?", "How to produce?", and "For whom to produce?" to address scarcity.

In Chapter 2, we looked at how the free market would allocate resources to answer the three questions through the market forces of demand and supply (the price mechanism), establishing an equilibrium price and quantity in every market for goods and services, as well as in every factor market.[1]

In this chapter, we pick up where Chapter 2 left off by examining how the free market equilibrium in the markets for goods and services would achieve allocative efficiency, and then examine how the free market fails by creating inefficiency and/or inequity. Due to these undesirable outcomes, there would be a need for government intervention.

The factors affecting the government's decision on whether to intervene in a market, how to intervene in a market, and the extent of the intervention will also be discussed.

4.1 Efficiency and Equity in Relation to Markets

4.1.1 Efficiency in relation to markets

The condition for achieving allocative efficiency in a market (marginal private benefit [MPB] = marginal private cost [MPC])

Allocative efficiency is achieved when the correct amount of every good or service is produced to maximize society's welfare.

> *Definition(s):*
>
> **Allocative efficiency** is the production of the correct amount of every good or service such that social welfare is maximised.

If society is only made up of consumers and producers, social welfare would be the sum of consumers' and producers' welfare, which would be the sum of consumer surplus (CS) and producer surplus (PS). So, allocative efficiency will be achieved when the sum of CS and PS is maximised in every market. The sum of CS and PS in a market will be maximised when the quantity in that market is such that MPB = MPC in that market. We illustrate this below.

1 Refer to Section 2.2.3 of Chapter 2 to refresh your memory.

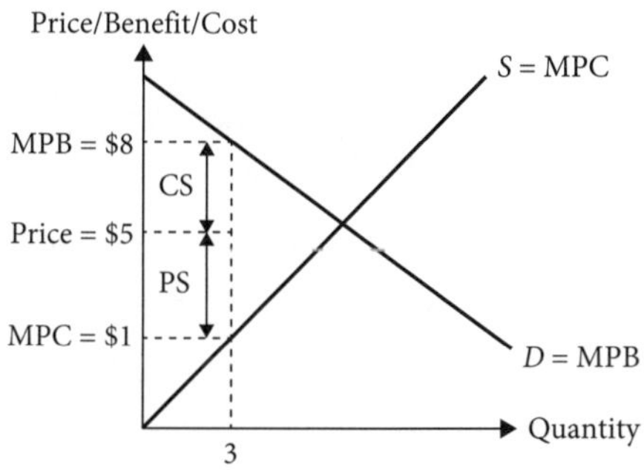

Let us look at the third unit of the good in the above figure to establish the relationship between CS, PS, MPB, and MPC. The consumer derives $8 of utility from the good (MPB = $8). The price of the good is $5, and it cost the producers $1 to produce it (MPC = $1). The marginal CS (i.e., the CS for this unit of the good) is $3 ($8 – $5) and the marginal PS (i.e., the PS for this unit of the good) is $4 ($5 – $1). The sum of the marginal CS and PS for this unit of the good would be $7 ($3 + $4). Since the sum of CS and PS is the social welfare, the marginal social welfare is $7. Notice that $7 is also the difference between MPB ($8) and MPC ($1). More generally, for a given unit of a good:

Marginal CS = MPB – Price
Marginal PS = Price – MPC
Marginal CS + Marginal PS = (MPB – Price) + (Price – MPC) = MPB – MPC
Marginal social welfare = MPB – MPC

So, if MPB exceeds MPC for the current quantity of goods, the marginal social welfare is positive for the last unit of the good and society can increase total social welfare by increasing the quantity of the good. For example, if the current quantity of a good is Q_1 as in the following figure, MPB exceeds MPC. An increase in the quantity from Q_1 to Q_0 would increase social welfare by area *A*. We say that at Q_1, there is underconsumption or underproduction of the good.

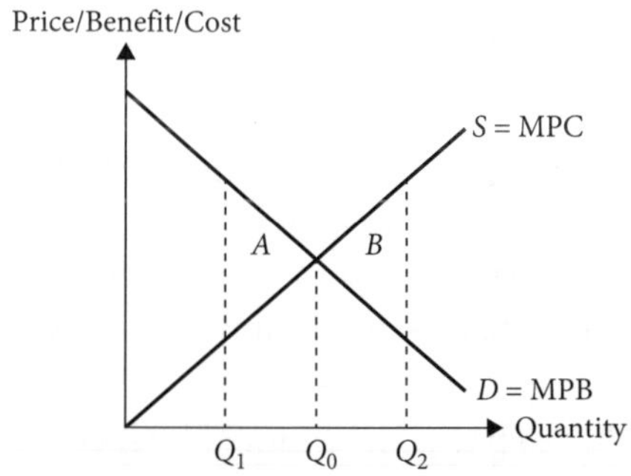

Conversely, if MPB is less than MPC for the current quantity of goods, the marginal social welfare is negative for the last unit of the good and society can increase the total social welfare by decreasing the quantity of the good. For example, if the current quantity of a good is Q_2 as in the above figure, MPB is less than MPC. A decrease in the quantity from Q_2 to Q_0 would increase social welfare by area *B*. We say that there is overconsumption or overproduction of the good in this scenario. Areas *A* and *B*, which are the loss of social welfare from not producing the socially optimal output Q_0, are both called the deadweight loss.

Definition(s):

Deadweight loss is the loss of social welfare from not producing the socially optimal output.

Since social welfare can be increased by increasing the quantity, if MPB exceeds MPC, and can also be increased by decreasing the quantity, if MPB is less than MPC, social welfare must be maximised when MPB = MPC. In other words, the sum of CS and PS is maximised when MPB = MPC.

Market forces of demand and supply achieving allocative efficiency

As established in Chapter 2, the demand curve is the MPB curve and the supply curve is the MPC curve. Hence, the equilibrium quantity in the market where demand intersects supply will naturally be the quantity where MPB = MPC. The equilibrium quantity naturally achieves allocative efficiency. In other words, the free market gives us the "correct" answer to the question of "What to produce?"

4.1.2 Equity in relation to markets

In Economics, the concept of equity is defined as fairness in the distribution of economic welfare. At this point, it is important to distinguish between equity and equality. Equity is about fairness. It is a moral concept. Equality, on the other hand, is a mathematical concept of things being equal. Giving everyone the exact same income would achieve equality. However, such a distribution could be inequitable (unfair) as people who work hard and people who do not both receive the same income. Conversely, rewarding hard workers with higher incomes would be treating everyone equitably but not equally. Hence, the terms "equity" and "equality" should not be used interchangeably.

The free market tends to achieve efficiency but not necessarily equity. One major criticism about the free market is that it creates inequity in the distribution of essential goods and services. Some goods and services such as health care and education may be considered essential and should be accessible to everyone, regardless of their income level. However, the market operates by distributing these goods and services only to those who are willing and able to pay the market price for them. Because low-income consumers may not have the ability to pay the market price, they would not have access to these goods and services. This is considered inequitable because society thinks that a fair distribution of such goods is one where everyone has access to them. So, for these goods, the free market results in an inequitable distribution of the goods. Because the ability to pay is determined by income, income inequality may lead to inequity as it creates differences in the ability to pay for essential goods and services that everyone should have access to.

However, it must be noted that there is no clear consensus on what these essential goods and services are. Every society would need to exercise value judgements on what is essential that everyone should have access to. For example, in developing countries, clean water may be considered essential while education may not be. In developed countries, however, education may also be considered an essential service.

4.2 Market Failure and Its Causes

In the first section, we studied how the market is supposed to achieve allocative efficiency and how it may not necessarily achieve equity. However, in reality, there could be the misallocation of resources in the market, which leads to allocative inefficiency. When this happens, there is deadweight loss and we say that the market has failed. The main sources of market failures are the following:

- Public goods
- Positive externalities in consumption and production
- Negative externalities in consumption and production
- Merit and demerit goods
- Information failure (imperfect information)
- Information failure (asymmetric information)
- Factor immobility
- Market dominance

We will study each source of market failure in turn.

4.2.1 Public goods

In our explanation of how demand and supply results in allocative efficiency, one assumption we made was that the goods and services being analysed were private goods and services. Private goods and services are goods and services that are excludable and rival in consumption. However, in real life, there are goods that are non-excludable and/or non-rival in consumption. We will examine how each of its characteristics causes the market to fail.

Definition(s):

Excludability is the situation in which consumption or use of a good or service can be limited to the consumers who have paid for it.

Non-excludability is the situation in which consumption or use of a good or service cannot be limited to the consumers who have paid for it.

Rivalry in consumption is the situation in which the consumption or use of a good or service by one consumer reduces the amount available to other consumers.

Non-rivalry in consumption is the situation in which the consumption or use of a good or service by one consumer does not reduce the amount available to other consumers.

Non-rejectability is the inability of the population or residents to refuse the benefits of the public good once it has been produced.

Goods can be categorised according to their characteristics

	Rivalrous in consumption	Non-rivalrous in consumption
Excludable	Private goods	Club goods[2]
Non-excludable	Common good[1]	Public goods

Non-excludability

Non-excludability is a situation where it is impossible or very costly to restrict the benefits of a good or service to only those who pay for them. Once the good is produced, the benefits are available to all. For example, when fireworks are released in the sky, it is almost impossible to prevent passers-by from enjoying the beautiful sight. Hence, fireworks can be considered non-excludable. The characteristic of non-excludability means that once a good is produced, anyone can enjoy the benefits even if they do not pay for it. This gives rise to the free-rider problem where consumers would rather not pay for the good in the hope that someone else would pay for it, so that they can get a free ride by enjoying the good without having to pay for it. Since demand is the ability and willingness to pay for a good, when there is no willingness to pay, there is no effective demand. Because there is no effective demand, there would be no production of the good. The market fails because production of the good would have created net benefits to society. In this case, since the good is completely not produced (underproduction where quantity traded equals zero), we say that there is complete market failure.

Flood defence presents a good example of non-excludability causing market failure. Once produced (i.e., once a flood barrier is erected), the benefits of the flood defence cannot be restricted to only those who paid for it. All homes in the area will be protected from flood whether they paid for the flood barriers or not. Hence, home owners in the area would rather not pay for the flood barriers in the hope that others would pay for it. However, when everyone thinks the same way, no flood barriers would be demanded, and the area would not enjoy any flood defences, even though it is in everyone's interest to have it. Therefore, non-excludability leads to non-provision of the public good.

Non-rivalry in consumption

It is easiest to understand non-rivalry in consumption through the use of an example. An online article has the characteristic of non-rivalry in consumption. When one reader reads the article, other readers still have equal access to the article. Words in the article do not disappear as one reader reads them. In contrast, there is rivalry in consuming a bowl of noodles. Each bite that a consumer enjoys is one bite less available for others. For public goods, since the consumption by one will not reduce the amount available to others, the marginal cost (MC)

2 Not within the scope of this book.

of providing the public good to an additional user of such a good is zero (MPC = 0) as there are no additional resources needed to satisfy the additional consumer once the good has been produced.[3] Again, we will use an example to illustrate this. Once a street lamp has been erected, there is no additional cost to provide visibility to another pedestrian who walks by. Even if five more pedestrians walk by, each of them enjoys the improved visibility without any additional cost. The MC of providing visibility to these additional pedestrians is zero.

In general, the problem with goods that have the characteristic of non-rivalry in consumption is that they will not be produced at the allocatively efficient level. This is because allocative efficiency would require the output of the good to be such that the price equals MPC (recall the allocative efficiency condition from Chapter 3). However, since MPC = 0, the allocatively efficient price would be zero, and the allocatively efficient output level will be one where the price is zero. However, firms will clearly not price a good at zero. Hence, the market will fail.

For public goods specifically, non-rivalry presents a different problem. Producing the wrong output level at the wrong price is a problem that is irrelevant to public goods because non-excludability already results in non-provision of the good. Instead, for public goods, non-rivalry in consumption presents a problem because the zero MPC means that the social welfare that is foregone is large when the good is not produced. This is illustrated below.

Market failure for public good

For public goods, market failure happens because non-excludability results in non-provision of the good, and non-rivalry in consumption results in the foregone social welfare to be large. Therefore, public goods will not be provided by the free market, or there will be non-provision of the public good in the free market and required government interventions to be provided.

Once the public goods are produced, it has an additional characteristic of non-rejectability. Non-rejectability is defined as the inability of the population or residents to refuse the benefits of the public good once it has been produced.

For example, the population or residents in the country or area will automatically enjoy the benefits of the provision of security by the police or national defence. They are unable to refuse these benefits, regardless of their keenness or willingness. Another example would be the light from the lighthouse; some residents in the area might find it disturbing and rather it not being there. However, they will still be protected as ships and vessels will be warned of dangerous shallows and rocky coasts.

4.2.2 Externalities in consumption and production

Even for the provision of private goods, the market can fail too. This is because in our explanation of how the free market achieves allocative efficiency, we made the assumption that the market was only made up of consumers and producers. Hence, when the sum of CS and PS is maximised, social welfare would be maximised. However, in reality, in the consumption or production of a good, third parties who are neither consumers nor producers of the good may be affected too.

3 Note that the MC for providing the public good to the first user would not be zero because the good needs to be produced. The MC is only zero for the second user onwards.

> *Definition(s):*
> **Third parties** are members of the society who are neither consumers nor producers of a good in a market.

Effects of consumption or production of a good on third parties are called externalities. Positive effects are called positive externalities (or external benefits) and negative effects are called negative externalities (or external costs). The external benefit of an additional unit of the good is the marginal external benefit (MEB) whereas the external cost of an additional unit of the good is the marginal external cost (MEC).

To take these externalities into account, instead of only considering MPB and MPC in determining allocative efficiency, we need to consider MEB and MEC too. To do so, we sum up MPB and MEB to get the marginal social benefit (MSB = MPB + MEB) to weigh against the marginal social cost (MSC) which is the sum of MPC and MEC (MSC = MPC + MEC).

> *Definition(s):*
> **Marginal external benefit (MEB)** is the additional external benefit enjoyed by third parties for an additional unit of that good or service produced or consumed.
> **Marginal external cost (MEC)** is the additional external cost incurred by third parties for an additional unit of that good or service produced or consumed.
> **Marginal social benefit (MSB)** is the additional benefits enjoyed by society for an additional unit of that good or service produced or consumed. It is the sum of MPB and MEC.
> **Marginal social cost (MSC)** is the additional cost incurred by society for an additional unit of that good or service produced or consumed. It is the sum of MPC and MEC.

Weighing MSB against MSC allows us to take the welfare of third parties into account because the external benefits and external costs are included in the MSB and MSC. Social welfare is then maximised when MSB = MSC instead of when MPB = MPC. Using this condition of MSB = MSC for allocative efficiency, we will now study exactly how the market fails when there are positive and negative externalities in consumption and production.

Positive externalities in consumption and production

Positive externalities in consumption would refer to benefits to third parties in the consumption of a good, whereas positive externalities in production would refer to benefits to third parties in the production of a good.

For the former, a good example would be the consumption of vaccinations. When a consumer consumes a flu vaccine he benefits the third parties around him because they would enjoy a lower risk of contracting the flu.[4] Hence, the consumption of vaccines creates positive externalities in the form of a lower risk of contracting diseases.

4 The formal name for this is called "herd immunity." For measles, for example, if 90%–95% of the population is vaccinated, the remaining 5%–10% of the population will effectively be immune to measles although they themselves are not vaccinated because they can't catch measles from the rest.

For the latter, a good example would be the production of honey. In the production of honey, bees would be released to collect nectar. In the process, they will also pollinate flowers. This creates positive externalities for the people who get to enjoy the view of flowers blooming and of nature in general, because the ecosystem can only be maintained when flowers are pollinated and plants reproduce.

When there are positive externalities (regardless of whether they are in consumption or production), for every additional unit of the good, there is now MEB on top of the MPB. Because of the MEB, the MSB would be greater than the MPB (MSB = MPB + MEB). We assume that there is no external cost and so MSC equals MPC. The illustration of this is shown in Fig. 4.1.

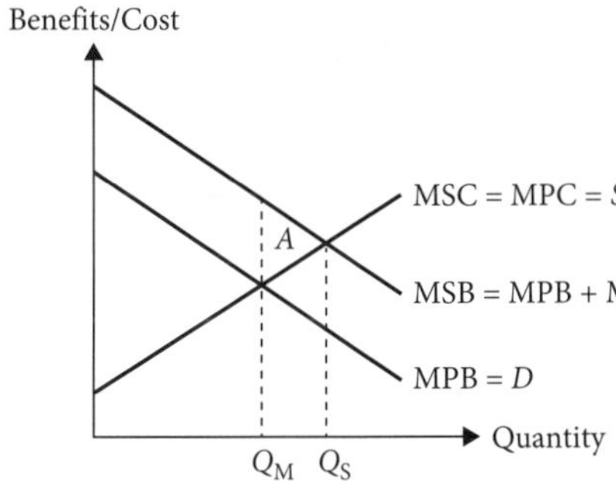

Figure 4.1: Illustration of the existence of positive externalities.

Because of the MEB, the market equilibrium of Q_M where MPB = MPC (D = S) no longer maximises social welfare (although it still maximises the sum of CS and PS). At Q_M, MSB exceeds MSC. Thus, social welfare can be increased by increasing the quantity. The quantity should be increased to Q_S where MSB = MSC as beyond this, MSC will be more than MSB instead. At Q_S, social welfare will be maximised. This is actually quite intuitive—because there are benefits to third parties as well, in order to maximise social welfare, more resources should be allocated to the production of this good. However, since the consumers and producers in the market only consider their self-interest and will ignore the external benefits to the third parties, the market equilibrium will remain at Q_M. Since Q_M is less than Q_S, we say that there is underconsumption (if the external benefits were in consumption) or underproduction (if the external benefits were in production). Area A represents the deadweight loss, which is the increase in social welfare that was not enjoyed due to the underconsumption/underproduction of Q_M to Q_S.

In summary, due to the existence of positive externalities generated during consumption or production, there will be underconsumption or underproduction resulting in a deadweight loss and market failure.

Negative externalities in consumption and production

Negative externalities in consumption would refer to costs to third parties in the consumption of a good whereas negative externalities in production would refer to costs to third parties in the production of a good.

For the former, a good example would be the consumption of cigarettes. When a consumer consumes a cigarette, he imposes costs on the third parties around him because they would suffer the negative effects of second-hand smoke such as lung damage. Hence, the consumption of cigarettes creates negative externalities in the form of lung damage.

For the latter, a good example would be the production of steel. In the production of steel, sulphur dioxide (a pollutant) is released into the air. The sulphur dioxide then dissolves in the rainclouds and causes acid rain. This creates negative externalities as acid rain causes damage to the environment and to health.

When there are negative externalities (regardless of whether they are in consumption or production), for every additional unit of the good, there is now MEC on top of the MPC. Because of the MEC, the MSC would be greater than the MPC (MSC = MPC + MEC). We assume that there is no external benefit and so MSB equals MPB. The illustration of this is shown in Fig. 4.2.

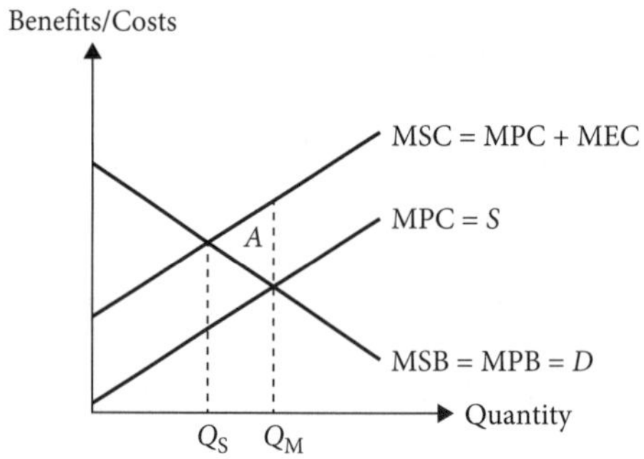

Figure 4.2: Illustration of the existence of negative externalities.

Because of the MEC, the market equilibrium of Q_M where MPB = MPC ($D = S$) no longer maximises social welfare (although it still maximises the sum of CS and PS). At Q_M, MSC exceeds MSB. Thus, social welfare can be increased by decreasing the quantity. The quantity should be decreased to Q_S where MSB = MSC, as any reduction beyond this would cause the MSB to exceed the MSC instead. At Q_S, social welfare will be maximised. This is actually quite intuitive because there are costs to third parties as well—in order to maximise social welfare, less resources should be allocated to the production of this good. However, since the consumers and producers in the market only consider their self-interest and will ignore the external benefits to the third parties, the market equilibrium will remain at Q_M. Since Q_M is more than Q_S, we say that there is overconsumption (if the external costs were in consumption) or overproduction (if the external costs were in production). Area *A* represents the deadweight loss, which is the decrease in social welfare that was incurred due to the overconsumption/overproduction of Q_S to Q_M.

In summary, due to the existence of negative externalities generated during consumption or production, there will be overconsumption or overproduction, resulting in a deadweight loss and market failure.

4.2.3 Information failure (Imperfect information)

In our analysis of how the free market results in allocative efficiency, an implicit assumption we made was that consumers had perfect information, in the sense that their estimations of the marginal utility (MU) of consuming a good was accurate. However, in reality, consumers may have inaccurate or incomplete information. Thus, they might overestimate/underestimate the benefits of a good to themselves or overestimate/underestimate the cost of good to themselves. When this happens, we say that consumers have imperfect information.

Definition(s):

Imperfect information refers to consumers misestimating the marginal utility of consuming a good.

The imperfect information could result in the perceived MU being higher than the actual MU, or the perceived MU being lower than the actual MU.

Perceived MU is greater than actual MU

At the individual level, if consumers overestimate the benefits of consuming a good (e.g., believing that consuming ground rhinoceros horn would improve their health) or underestimate the cost of consuming a good (e.g., underestimating their likelihood of developing liver failure from heavy drinking), the perceived MU would be higher than the actual MU. At the market level, when we sum up the individual demand curves (which are the individual MU curves) to obtain the market demand curve, the perceived MPB (the demand curve) would also be higher than the actual MPB. This is illustrated in Fig. 4.3.

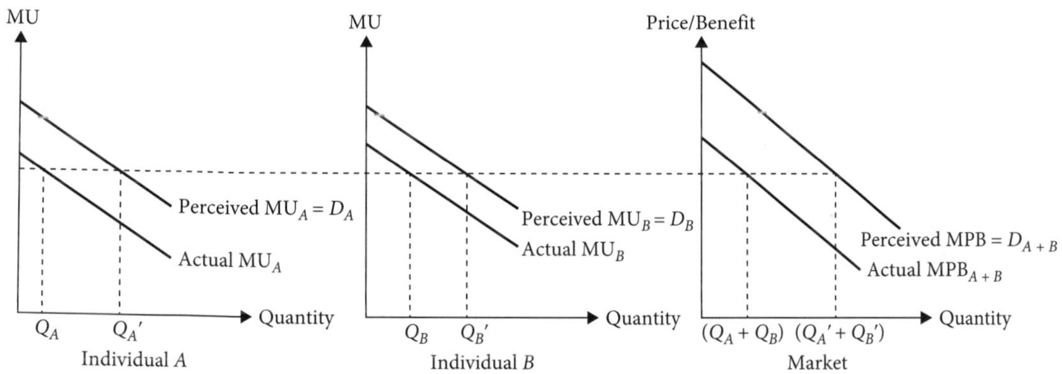

Figure 4.3: The perceived MPB being greater than the actual MPB causes market failure.

Referring to Fig. 4.4, the market equilibrium would be at Q_M where D intersects S. The demand curve is the perceived MPB curve because consumers act based on the imperfect information they have. However, at Q_M, the MPC exceeds the actual MPB. Thus, social welfare can be increased by decreasing the quantity. The quantity should be decreased to Q_S where actual MPB = MPC as any reduction beyond this would cause the actual MPB to be more than the MPC instead. At Q_S, social welfare will be maximised. This is actually quite intuitive—because consumers are overestimating the MU from consuming the good, less resources should be allocated to the production of this good. As Q_M is more than Q_S, we say that there is overconsumption. Area A represents the deadweight loss, which is the decrease in social welfare that was incurred due to the overconsumption of Q_S to Q_M.

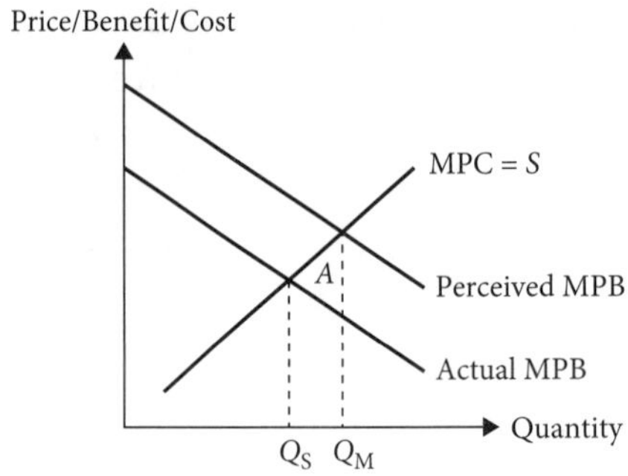

Figure 4.4

In summary, due to the imperfect information, the market will overallocate resources to the good, resulting in a deadweight loss and market failure.

Perceived MU is lesser than actual MU

The opposite scenario could also happen. At the individual level, if consumers underestimate the benefits of consuming a good (e.g., underestimating the importance of half-yearly dental check-ups in maintaining oral health) or overestimate the cost of consuming a good (e.g., thinking that even small amounts of red wine consumption will cause irreparable liver damage), the perceived MU would be lower than the actual MU. At the market level, when we sum up the individual demand curves (which are the individual MU curves) to obtain the market demand curve, the perceived MPB (the demand curve) would also be lower than the actual MPB. This is illustrated in Fig. 4.5.

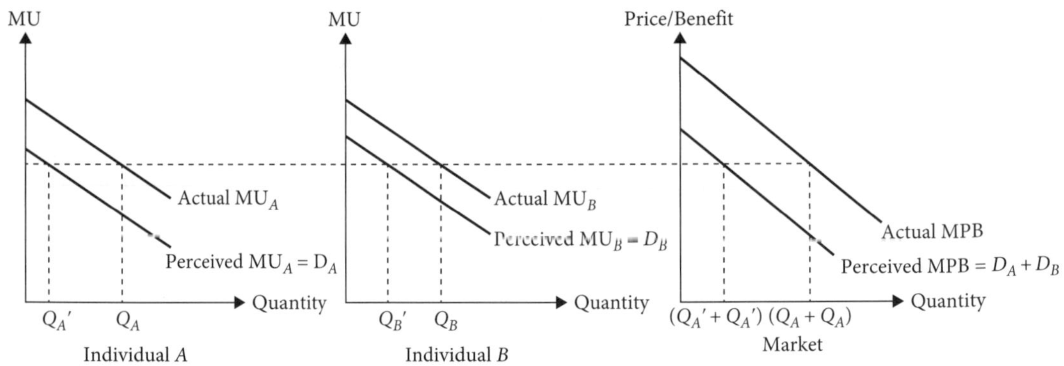

Figure 4.5: The perceived MPB being lower than the actual MPB causes market failure.

Referring to Fig. 4.6, the market equilibrium would be at Q_M where *D* intersects *S*. The demand curve is the perceived MPB curve because consumers act based on the imperfect information they have. However, at Q_M, the MPC is less than the actual MPB. Thus, social welfare can be increased by increasing the quantity. The quantity should be increased to Q_S where actual MPB = MPC as any increase beyond this would cause the actual MPC to be more than the MPB instead. At Q_S, social welfare will be maximised. This is actually quite intuitive—because consumers are underestimating the MU from consuming the good, more resources should be allocated to the production of this good. As Q_M is less than Q_S, we say that there is underconsumption. Area *A* represents the deadweight loss, which is the increase in social welfare that was not reaped due to the underconsumption of Q_M to Q_S.

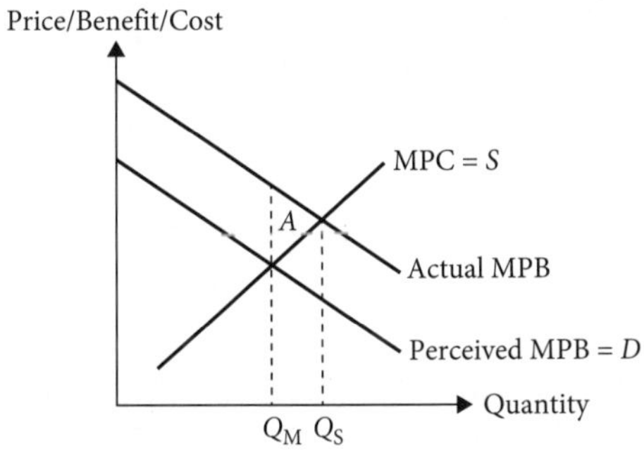

Figure 4.6

In summary, due to the imperfect information, the market will under allocate resources to the good, resulting in a deadweight loss and market failure.

4.2.4 Information failure (Asymmetric information)

Asymmetric information is the situation in which one economic agent involved in an economic transaction has more information than another economic agent. This information could be about the actions of the economic agents or the attributes of the good/service being traded in the market.

> *Definition(s):*
>
> **Asymmetric information** is the situation in which one economic agent involved in an economic transaction has more information than another economic agent.

Asymmetric information can give rise to two problems—moral hazard and adverse selection.

Moral hazard

Moral hazard arises when the asymmetric information is about the **actions** of the economic agents.

> *Definition(s):*
>
> **Moral hazard** is the tendency of economic agents who are imperfectly monitored to engage in undesirable behaviour when the resulting costs are not borne by them.

In this case, there is information asymmetry as the economic agent who is being monitored has more information about his/her own behaviour than the economic agent who is trying to monitor him or her.

Generally, for moral hazard, the economic agent who is imperfectly monitored (has more information about his behaviour) and does not bear the cost of his undesirable behaviour will carry out his undesirable behaviour. The behaviour then causes market failure as it will end up causing some wastage of resources.

We illustrate the abovementioned with two examples—moral hazard in the labour market and moral hazard in the insurance market. The first example shows information asymmetry about the actions of the seller where the seller has more information about his actions than the buyer. The second example shows information asymmetry about the actions of the buyer where the buyer has more information about his actions than the seller.

The labour market—If the owner of the firm cannot observe his workers' actions, there is information asymmetry, as the seller of labour (the worker) has more information about his actions compared to the buyer of labour (the firm's owner). The worker is more likely to shirk responsibility because his actions cannot be observed and the cost of his shirking (the loss of profits to the firm) is not borne by him.

The insurance market—If insurance firms are unable to observe how carefully travellers take care of their luggage, there is information asymmetry as the buyer of insurance (the traveller) has more information about his actions compared to the seller of insurance (the insurance firm). Travellers will be more careless with their luggage because the insurance firm cannot observe if they are negligent and the cost of the loss of luggage will be borne by the insurance firm.

The breakdown of the two examples showing how the elements of information symmetry cause moral hazard is provided in the following table.

Rows 1 and 2 show asymmetric information where one economic agent has more information than the other. The economic agent with more information is the one that is imperfectly monitored.[5] Rows 3 and 4 show how undesirable behaviour happens because the imperfectly monitored economic agent does not bear the cost of his actions.

		Labour market	**Insurance market**
1	Economic agent with more information	Worker	Traveller
2	Economic agent with less information	Owner of firm	Insurance firm
3	Economic agent who bears the cost of undesirable behaviour	Owner of firm	Insurance firm
4	Undesirable behaviour (which causes market failure)	Shirking responsibility	Being careless with luggage

The market failure due to the undesirable behaviour will depend on the specific undesirable behaviour. For example, the market failure due to shirking responsibility is the loss of productive efficiency because labour (the worker) is not being fully and efficiently utilised, causing the average cost of the output to be higher. For the undesirable behaviour of being careless with the luggage, the market failure is the wastage of resources in producing the items

5 If he were perfectly monitored, there would not be information asymmetry as both economic agents would have perfect information about his behaviour.

to replace those in the luggage that was lost. Nonetheless, a common result of this undesirable behaviour is that they will cause a wastage of resources.

Adverse selection

In contrast to moral hazard, adverse selection arises when there is asymmetric information regarding the **attributes** of the good/service being transacted in the market.[6]

> *Definition(s):*
>
> **Adverse selection** is the process in which the economic agent with more information (about the attribute of the good or service being traded in the market) decides whether to participate in the market, resulting in a negative impact on the other economic agents in the market.

Generally, for adverse selection, the economic agent who has less information about the attributes of the good/service in the market will act by offering or charging an average price based on the probability of encountering different types of the other economic agent. The economic agent with more information will then select whether to participate in the market, with one type choosing to participate and the other type choosing not to. The non-participation then causes a missing market and deadweight loss due to the loss of CS and PS in that market.

Like what we did with moral hazard, we illustrate the general process described in the paragraph above with two examples—adverse selection in the second-hand car industry and adverse selection in the insurance industry, respectively. The first example shows information asymmetry in terms of the seller having more information than the buyer. The second example shows information asymmetry about the attribute of the good/service being traded in terms of the buyer having more information than the seller.

The second-hand car industry—In the second-hand car industry, the sellers know the quality of the car that they are selling. For simplicity's sake, we classify the cars into high- and low-quality cars. The sellers know whether the car they are selling is a high- or low-quality car. The buyers are unable to differentiate the two. Hence, there is information asymmetry.

The sellers of high-quality cars would require a high price for their cars whereas, the sellers of low-quality cars are willing to accept a low price for their cars. Similarly, the buyers would be willing to pay a high price for a high-quality car and only a low price for a low-quality car. If the buyers can distinguish between the two, there would be a high-quality second-hand car market and a low-quality second-hand car market with the price in the former market higher

6 Moral hazard and adverse selection are sometimes differentiated by whether the information asymmetry applies before the economic transaction (adverse selection) or after the economic transaction (moral hazard), instead of whether the information asymmetry concerns the behaviour of agents (moral hazard) or the attribute of the good/service in the market (adverse selection), as explained in the main text. The two ways of differentiating them actually largely overlap. In the examples of moral hazard, the undesirable behaviour happens after the economic transaction (e.g., after the worker has been hired or after the traveller has bought insurance). Similarly, in the examples of adverse selection (explained later in the main text), the low-risk consumers of insurance and sellers of good second-hand cars choose to not participate in the market before the insurance is bought or the car is sold.

than that in the latter market. However, because the buyers of the cars cannot distinguish between the two, there is only one second-hand car market. And, in this market, since there is a mix of high- and low-quality cars, the buyers would only be willing to offer an average price that is in between the high price they are willing to pay for a high-quality car, and the low price they are willing to pay for a low-quality car.

However, when they do so, the sellers of high-quality cars would no longer be willing to sell their cars because the average price that the buyers are offering is lower than the price they are willing to accept. They will pull out of the market and the market would only be left with low-quality cars. A numerical example of this is provided in Annex 4.1.

In this case, we say that the car buyers are adversely selected against because the high-quality second-hand car sellers will pull out of the market, leaving only low-quality second-hand cars for the car buyers to buy.

There is market failure because the market for high-quality second-hand cars has disappeared since no transaction involving the sale of a high-quality second-hand car would take place. There is a deadweight loss because the CS and PS that would have been generated from the existence of this market is foregone. This is illustrated in the following figures.

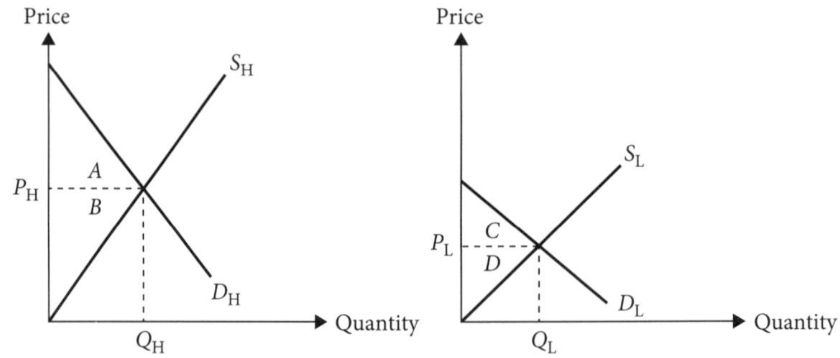

Market for high-quality second-hand cars

Market for low-quality second-hand cars

If there was no asymmetric information, there would be a market for high-quality second-hand cars with equilibrium price P_H and equilibrium quantity Q_H, and a market for low-quality second-hand cars with equilibrium price P_L and equilibrium quantity Q_L. The total surplus (CS and PS) from both markets would be area A + area B + area C + area D. However, because of the asymmetric information, there is no market for high-quality second-hand cars. Hence, the total surplus falls to just area C + area D. The loss of area A and area B is the deadweight loss.

The insurance industry—To understand the example of the insurance industry, we must understand what the market for insurance is. When a consumer buys an insurance policy, if he gets into some undesirable situation, he receives a payout. So part of the benefit to the consumer is the expected payout from the insurance[7] (expected payout is the amount of the payout multiplied by the probability that the policy holder gets into the undesirable situation and collects the payout). For example, an insurance policy might have a payout of $100,000 if the

7 The expected payout is only part of the benefit to the consumer because in getting the insurance, the consumer also enjoys the utility of having a peace of mind because he will be taken care of in case of undesirable circumstances.

policy holder (the buyer of the insurance) contracts cancer. If the policy holder has a 7% chance of contracting cancer, the expected payout from the policy would be \$7,000 (7% × \$100,000). The price that the consumer pays to buy the policy is called the policy premium.

For simplicity's sake, we divide the consumers in the insurance industry into two groups—high-risk consumers who have a high probability of getting into undesirable situations and low-risk consumers who have a low probability of getting into undesirable situations. Consumers know whether they are high- or low-risk consumers but the insurance firm is unable to differentiate between the two. Hence, there is information asymmetry.

The high-risk consumers would have a higher expected payout if they buy insurance as their probability of getting into an undesirable situation is high. Hence, they would be willing to pay a higher price for insurance. The low-risk consumers would have a lower expected payout if they buy insurance as their probability of getting into an undesirable situation is low. Hence, they would only be willing to pay a lower price for insurance. If the insurance firm can distinguish between the two, there would be an insurance market for high-risk consumers and a separate market for insurance for low-risk consumers. The premiums charged in the former market would be higher than that in the latter market. However, because the insurance firms cannot distinguish between the two, there is only one insurance market. And, in this market, since there is a mix of high- and low-risk consumers, the insurance firm would charge an average premium that is in between the high premium they would charge for a high-risk consumer, and the low premium they would charge for a low-risk consumer.

However, when they do so, the low-risk consumers would no longer be willing to buy insurance because the premium that the insurance firm is charging is higher than the premium that are willing to pay. They will pull out of the market and the market would only be left with high-risk consumers. A numerical example of this is provided in Annex 4.2.

In this case, we say that the insurance firm is adversely selected against because the low-risk consumers will pull out of the market, leaving only the high-risk consumers to buy the insurance. This is bad for the insurance firm as it would have to incur higher costs in the form of more payouts, because high-risk consumers are more likely to get into undesirable situations.

There is market failure because the insurance market for low-risk consumers disappeared since no transaction involving the sale of insurance to a low-risk consumer would take place. There is a deadweight loss because the CS and PS that would have been generated from the existence of this market is foregone. This is illustrated in the following figures.

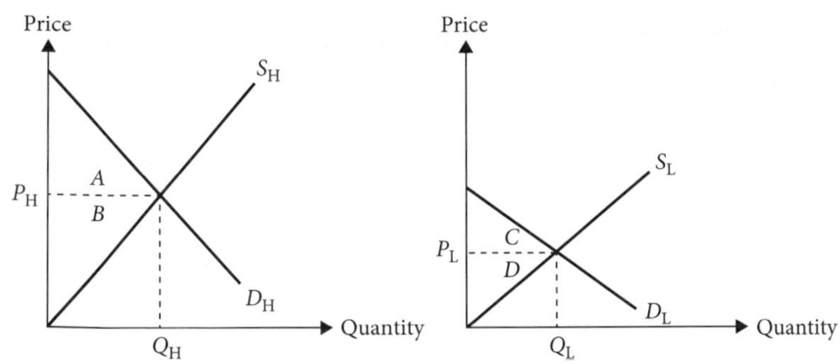

Insurance market for high-risk consumers

Insurance market for low-risk consumers

If there wasn't asymmetric information, there would be an insurance market for high-risk consumers with equilibrium price P_H and equilibrium quantity Q_H, and an insurance market for low-risk consumers with equilibrium price P_L and equilibrium quantity Q_L. The total surplus (CS and PS) from both markets would be area *A* + area *B* + area *C* + area *D*. However, because of the asymmetric information, there is no insurance market for low-risk consumers. Hence, the total surplus falls to just area *A* + area *B*. The loss of area *C* and area *D* is the deadweight loss.

The breakdown of the two examples showing how the elements of information symmetry cause adverse selection is provided in the following table.

		The second-hand car industry	**The insurance industry**
1	Economic agent with more information	Second-hand car sellers	Consumers of insurance (buyers)
2	Economic agent with less information	Buyers of second-hand cars	Insurance firms (sellers)
3	Action of the economic agent with less information, based on the probability of encountering different types of the other economic agent	Offer a price that is the average of what they are willing to pay for a high-quality car and what they are willing to pay for a low-quality car	Offer a premium that is the average of what they are willing to accept for high-risk consumers and what they are willing to accept for low-risk consumers
4	Adverse selection of economic agent with more information deciding whether to participate in the market	Sellers of high-quality cars pull out of the market Sellers of low-quality cars stay in the market	Low-risk consumers pull out of the market High-risk consumers stay in the market
5	Negative impact on economic agent with less information (the economic agent that is adversely selected against)	Only able to buy low-quality second-hand cars No market for high-quality cars	Only sells insurance policies to high-risk consumers No insurance market for low-risk consumers
6	Market failure	Loss of CS and PS from the high-quality second-hand car market	Loss of CS and PS from the insurance market for low-risk consumers

Rows 1 and 2 show asymmetric information since one economic agent has more information than the other. Example 1 shows sellers having more information than buyers, and example 2 shows buyers having more information than sellers. Rows 3–6 show how the market failure occurs. Note that the sequence of events is actually quite similar for both examples.

Putting it concretely: Complete dissolution of all markets due to adverse selection

In the two examples of adverse selection described, the final outcome was that we were left with one submarket. However, that is only true because we had simplified the analysis to have only two submarkets to begin with. In actuality, adverse selection would eventually lead to the dissolution of the market completely.

This is because the remaining submarket can be further divided into two submarkets, with adverse selection causing the elimination of one of the submarkets. This will go on until the market is entirely eliminated.

We return to the examples of the second-hand car market and the insurance market to see how this happens.

The second-hand car market—After the high-quality second-hand cars leave the market, there would only be low-quality second-hand cars left. However, amongst these low-quality second-hand cars, there could be some of slightly better quality than others. Buyers again cannot distinguish between them and offer a price between what they are willing to pay for the better quality ones and what they are willing to pay for the poorer quality ones. Again, the sellers of the better quality cars would find this average price too low and leave the market. Now there would be even lower quality second-hand cars left. But again, amongst these cars, some would be of better quality than others. Hence, the adverse selection process continues until in the end, no second-hand cars are sold at all.[8]

The insurance market—After the low-risk consumers leave the market, there would only be high-risk consumers left. However, amongst high-risk consumers, there could be some of slightly lower risk than others. Insurance firms again cannot distinguish between them and charge a premium between what they would charge for the consumers with the slightly lower risk and what they would charge for the consumers with the slightly higher risk. Again, the slightly lower risk consumers would find this premium too high and leave the market. Now there would be even higher risk consumers left. But again, amongst these, some would be of lower risk than the others. Hence, the adverse selection process continues until in the end, no insurance policies are sold at all.[9]

8 The assumption here, of course, is that there was a range in the quality of second-hand cars to begin with. If there were strictly only two types of car quality, the low-quality car submarket would persist because there is no longer any information asymmetry in that market. There would only be one type of second-hand car (low quality) and buyers would have that information.

9 The assumption here, of course, is that there was a range in riskiness of consumers to begin with. If there were strictly only two types of consumers, the high risk consumer submarket would persist since there is no longer any information asymmetry in that market. There would only be one type consumer (high risk) and insurance firms would have that information.

4.2.5 Merit and demerit goods

Externalities and information failure are the two main reasons why the price mechanism fails to achieve efficient resource allocation in the market for merit and demerit goods.

Merit goods

> *Definition(s):*
>
> **Merit goods** are goods or services deemed to be socially desirable by the government and would be underconsumed when left to the free market and the price mechanism.

The two main causes of the underconsumption of merit goods are the following:

- Consumers' imperfect information of their perceived MU to be lower than the actual MU (refer to Section 4.2.3).
- Consumers not taking the existence of positive externalities during consumption into account when making decisions of how much of the good is to be consumed (refer to Section 4.2.2).

Demerit goods

> *Definition(s):*
>
> **Demerit goods** are goods or services deemed to be socially undesirable by the government and would be overconsumed when left to the free market and the price mechanism.

The two main causes of the overconsumption of demerit goods are the following:

- Consumers' imperfect information of their perceived MC to be lower than the actual amount of MC (refer to Section 4.2.3).
- Consumers not taking the negative externalities during consumption into account when making decision of how much of the good to consumed (refer to Section 4.2.2).

4.2.6 Factor immobility (H2 ONLY)

Factor immobility refers to the inability to put factors of production to an alternative use. The alternative use could be in terms of being used in a different industry, or a different firm within the same industry. It is one of the causes of market failure, as the allocation of resources within a market system assumes that the resources can be reallocated from one use to another. When they cannot be, resources cannot be reallocated to where they are needed and the market fails. For example, if the demand for apples increases, the market forces of demand and supply would allocate more resources to producing apples (the equilibrium quantity of apples would increase). However, if factors of production are immobile (e.g., if workers in other industries cannot move into the apple industry), then they cannot be reallocated to the production of apples (equilibrium quantity of apples cannot increase).

Although all factors of production (land, labour, capital, and entrepreneurship) can be immobile, we usually focus on labour immobility when we discuss factor immobility. Two types of labour mobility are occupational immobility and geographical immobility.

Occupational immobility

Occupational immobility is due to the mismatch of skills between labourers and what is required by producers. As such, labourers are unable to change from one industry to another one.

An example of occupational immobility would be blue-collar workers in the car-producing regions of USA being unable to fill white collar job openings.

Geographical immobility

Geographical immobility is due to labourers being unable or unwilling to move from one place to other. Reasons could include the high cost of relocation, travelling time, and family ties.

An example of geographical immobility would be labourers from the rural parts of China facing difficulty in moving to the coastal cities to search for jobs. Geographical immobility is clearly almost (if not completely) non-existent in Singapore because of the small geographical size of the country. Unlike geographically large countries, it is unlikely that labourers in Singapore cannot take on a job because it would require relocation.

Putting it concretely: Barriers to rural-urban migration: Occupational or geographical immobility?

When rural labourers face difficulties in securing jobs in the cities, would we consider it occupational or geographically immobility?

The answer is quite likely both. This is because a rural labourer may lack the skills needed for jobs in the city (occupational immobility) and may also have difficulty in relocating because of the high cost of rental housing in the city or because of dependents that he/she cannot leave behind (geographical immobility).

This shows us that occupational and geographical immobility are not mutually exclusive and labour can be immobile because of both reasons.

4.2.7 Market dominance (H2 ONLY)

Market failure due to market dominance was explained in Chapter 3 when we saw how imperfectly competitive markets (monopolies, oligopolies, and monopolistically competitive markets) were allocatively inefficient.

To recap, such markets are allocatively inefficient because firms in these markets possessed market power (i.e., enjoy some degree of market dominance) and were price setters. Assuming that these firms aim to maximise their profits, the price set would be above the MC whereas the quantity produced would be below the socially optimal level. Therefore, the market fails due to underproduction of the good and society incurs a deadweight loss. Market failure would occur due to underallocation of resources.[10] Pricing above the MC ($P_M > MC_M$), underproduction ($Q_M < Q_S$), and the deadweight loss (shaded area) are illustrated in Fig. 4.7.

10 Read Chapter 3 for details.

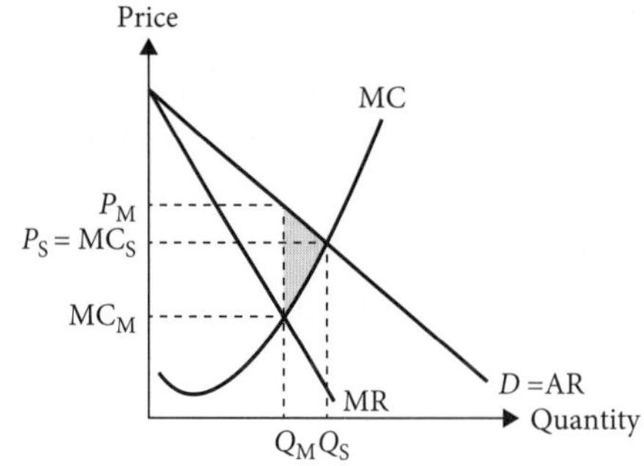

Figure 4.7

4.3 Government Intervention in Markets

Having studied the various ways in which the market can fail to achieve efficiency and equity, we now turn to the study of policy options that governments can use to correct the different sources of market failure.

4.3.1 Indirect taxes and their effectiveness

As we learnt in Chapter 2, indirect taxes will reduce the equilibrium quantity in the market. Hence, indirect taxes can be applied when there is a market failure due to overproduction or overconsumption. The sources of market failure that cause overproduction or overconsumption include the following:

- Negative externalities
- Imperfect information (perceived MPB being greater than actual MPB)
- Demerit goods (due to negative externalities and imperfect information)

The government can intervene in the market using indirect tax to reduce the production or consumption of a good or service.

Indirect tax in the case of negative externality

When an indirect tax is imposed on the producers by the government, it will increase the cost of production. Referring to Fig. 4.8, this causes the MPC to increase and the MPC curve shifts up from MPC to MPC + tax. Note that since the MPC is the supply curve, this analysis is the same as an indirect tax causing the supply to decrease and shift left (*S* to *S* with tax). The increase in the MPC forces firms to internalise the MEC. This means that through the indirect tax, the negative externality is now taken into account by profit-maximising firms, as

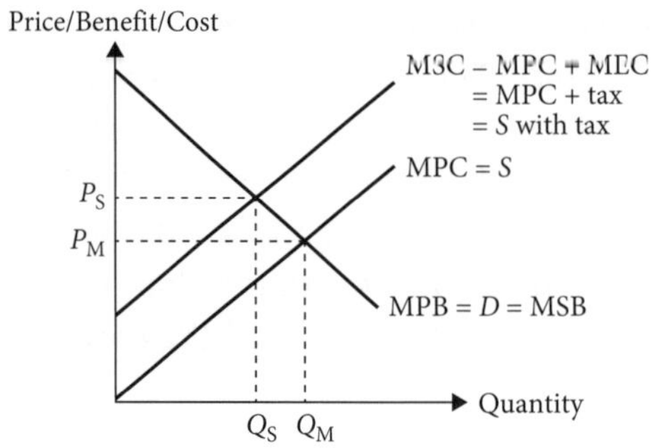

Figure 4.8

the producers now bear the external cost. With the tax, the market equilibrium would shift from price P_M and quantity Q_M to price P_S and quantity Q_S. The new equilibrium P_S and Q_S is where MPC + tax equals MPB (D equals S with tax).

As can be seen, to reduce the equilibrium quantity from Q_M to Q_S, the amount of tax per unit should be equal to the MEC at the socially optimum level of output Q_S (represented by the vertical distance between the MSC and the MPC at the socially optimum level of output Q_S). Therefore, if the correct amount of tax is introduced, the socially optimum level of output Q_S will be achieved and market failure is resolved.

Strengths of an indirect tax in correcting negative externalities

- Indirect taxes are relatively easy to implement and monitor. The government just needs to announce the tax per unit and collect the correct amount of taxes during tax collection (something every government already does).
- Indirect taxes are flexible in that the amount of tax imposed can be changed relatively easily. This is useful if the MEC changes over time and the tax per unit needs to be changed over time too.
- Market forces of demand and supply are not prevented from working to determine the equilibrium price and quantity. The market equilibrium can still change in line with changes in demand and/or supply. This results in the market equilibrium (with taxes imposed) always automatically adjusting to the socially optimal quantity. For example, with reference to Fig. 4.9, the original market equilibrium quantity is Q_M and the original socially optimal quantity (using MSB_0 and MSC) is Q_S. With the indirect tax imposed, the market equilibrium would fall to Q_S and the market failure is corrected. If the demand for the good falls from D_0 to D_1 (MSB_0 to MSB_1), the socially optimal quantity would also decrease from Q_S to Q_S'. Since the indirect tax causes the supply curve to be S with tax, the market equilibrium would also decrease to Q_S' (where D_1 equals S with tax). Hence, we can see that with an indirect tax, even if the market forces change and cause the socially optimal quantity to change, the post-tax market equilibrium quantity would automatically adjust to the new socially optimal quantity. This will be better appreciated when we study other policies that do not allow the market forces of demand and supply to work at all.
- Tax revenue collected can be used to compensate the third parties that suffered the negative externalities or finance other government spending such as public education and health care.

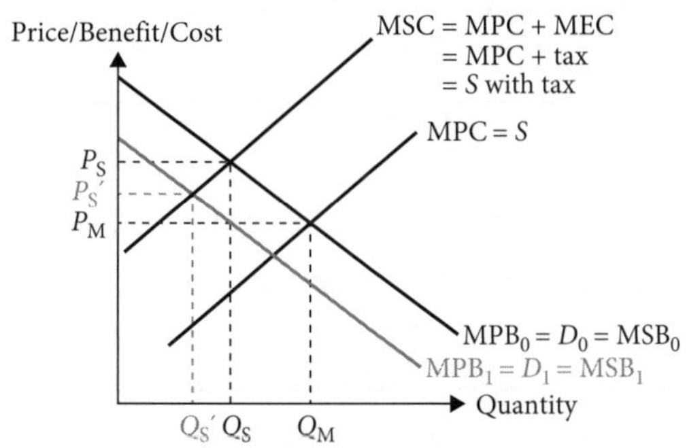

Figure 4.9

Limitations of indirect taxes in correcting negative externalities

- It is difficult to accurately measure or estimate both the MEC and the socially efficient level of output. Hence, there might be over- or undertaxation. Overtaxation might lead to underconsumption or underproduction of the good and might lead to government failure (Section 4.3.13). On the other hand, undertaxation would mean that there is still overconsumption or overproduction of the good, albeit less than before.
- Since the indirect tax is on the production of the good, producers will not be motivated to reduce the negative externalities in the production of the good (assuming the negative externalities is in production). For example, electricity production generates negative externalities in the form of carbon emissions that contribute to global warming. An indirect tax would be something like a $10 tax per unit of electricity produced. Such a tax does not incentivise electricity producers to find cleaner ways to produce electricity because whether or not a unit of electricity is produced in a carbon-intensive way, the tax levied is the same ($10). A similar argument can be made for negative externalities in consumption. A smoker does not have the incentive to smoke in a less crowded area (and generate less negative externalities) because he/she pays a tax for the number of cigarettes purchased and not the number of people who are affected by his/her smoking.
- Although the indirect tax is imposed on the producers, the incidence of the indirect tax is unclear. The incidence of the indirect tax depends on the relative values of PED and PES of the good concerned. If PES exceeds PED, the burden of the tax would fall more on consumers (especially the poor) and this would worsen inequity.

Putting it concretely: Pollutant taxes

The indirect tax is a tax that the producers have to pay per unit of good produced. A different type of tax is the pollutant tax. For example, Singapore taxes electricity producers for every tonne of CO_2 produced (the pollutant) and not make them pay a tax for every unit of electricity produced (the output).

In the short run, both an indirect tax and pollutant tax work the same way. Both increase the cost of production and cause the MPC to increase and cause the supply curve to shift leftwards, causing Q_M to decrease to Q_S.

However, in the long run, a pollutant tax will incentivise firms to find cleaner ways of producing their output that releases less pollutants so that they can avoid the tax. This will mean that the negative externalities will decrease in the long run. A tax on output will not create such an incentive and there would not be such an effect.

Indirect tax in the case of imperfect information (perceived MPB being greater than actual MPB)

When an indirect tax is imposed on the producers by the government, it increases the cost of production. Referring to Fig. 4.10, this causes the MPC to increase and the MPC curve to shift up from MPC to MPC + tax. Note that since the MPC is the supply curve, this analysis is the same as an indirect tax, causing the supply to decrease and shift left (*S* to *S* with tax). The market equilibrium would then shift from price P_M and quantity Q_M to price P_S and quantity Q_S. The new equilibrium P_S and Q_S is where MPC + tax equals perceived MPB (*D* equals *S* with tax).

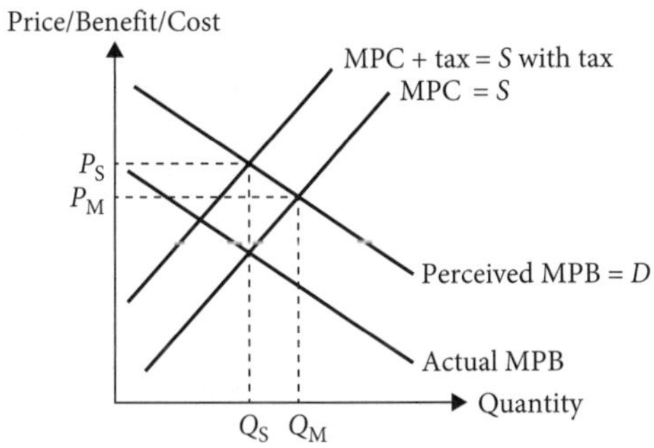

Figure 4.10

As can be seen, if the correct amount of tax is introduced, the socially optimum level of output Q_S will be achieved and market failure is resolved.

Strengths of an indirect tax in correcting imperfect information (perceived MPB being greater than actual MPB)

- Indirect taxes are relatively easy to implement and monitor. The government just needs to announce the tax per unit and collect the correct amount of taxes during tax collection (something every government already does).
- Indirect taxes are flexible in that the amount of tax imposed can be changed relatively easily. This is useful if the degree of imperfect information changes over time and the tax per unit needs to be changed over time too.
- Market forces of demand and supply are not prevented from working to determine the equilibrium price and quantity. The market equilibrium can still change in line with changes in demand and/or supply. This results in the market equilibrium (with taxes imposed) always automatically adjusting to the socially optimal quantity.
- Tax revenue collected can be used to finance complementary policies or other government spending such as public education and health care.

Limitations of indirect taxes in correcting imperfect information (perceived MPB being greater than actual MPB)

- The indirect taxes correct the behaviour of overconsumption but not the root problem of imperfect information. Consumers consume less of the good because taxes increase the price of the good and not because they actually know better.
- It is difficult to accurately estimate the amount of tax needed to achieve the socially efficient level of output. Hence, there might be over- or undertaxation. Overtaxation might lead to underconsumption or production of the good and might lead to government failure (Section 4.3.13). On the other hand, undertaxation would mean that there is still overconsumption or production of the good, albeit less than before.
- Although the indirect tax is imposed on the producers, the incidence of the indirect tax is unclear. The incidence of the indirect tax depends on the relative values of PED and PES of the good concerned. If PES exceeds PED, the burden of the tax would fall more on consumers (especially the poor) and this would worsen inequity.

Indirect tax in the case of demerit goods

Since demerit goods are goods with negative externalities and imperfect information, (perceived MPB higher than actual MPB), indirect tax can also be used to correct the market failure with the same explanation. The strengths and limitations are the same too.

4.3.2 Subsidies and their effectiveness

As we learnt in Chapter 2, subsidies will increase the equilibrium quantity in the market. Hence, subsidies can be applied when there is market failure due to underproduction or underconsumption. The sources of market failure that cause overproduction or overconsumption are the following:

- Positive externalities
- Imperfect information (perceived MPB being lesser than actual MPB)
- Merit goods (due to positive externalities and imperfect information)

Additionally, since subsidies reduce the price of a good, it also corrects market failure due to inequity.

The government can intervene in the market using subsidies to increase the production or consumption of a good or service.

Subsidies in the case of positive externality

When a subsidy is given to the producers by the government, it will reduce the cost of production. Referring to Fig. 4.11, this causes the MPC to decrease and the MPC curve to shift down from MPC to MPC with subsidy. Note that since the MPC is the supply curve, this analysis is the same as a subsidy causing the supply to increase and shift right (*S* to *S* with subsidy). The decrease in MPC causes firms to internalise the MEB. This means that through the subsidy, the positive externality is now taken into account by profit-maximising firms as the producers enjoy the external benefit. With the subsidy, the market equilibrium would shift from price P_M and quantity Q_M to price P_S and quantity Q_S. The new equilibrium P_S and Q_S is where MPC with subsidy equals MPB (*D* equals *S* with subsidy).

As can be seen, to increase the equilibrium quantity from Q_M to Q_S, the amount of subsidy per unit should be equal to the MEB at the socially optimum level of output Q_S (represented by the vertical distance between the MSB and the MPB at the socially optimum level of output Q_S). Therefore, if the correct amount of subsidy is introduced, the socially optimum level of output Q_S will be achieved and market failure is resolved.

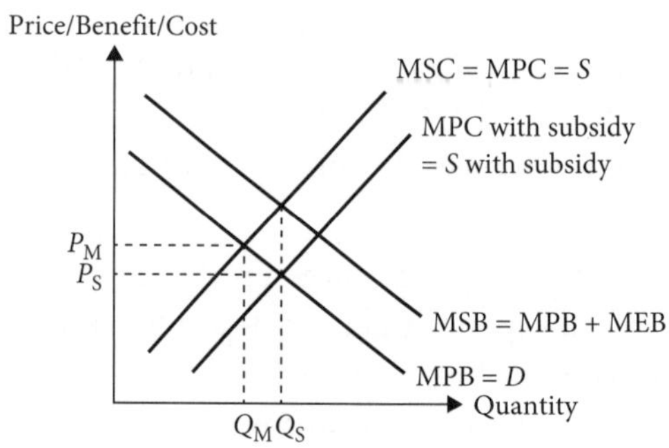

Figure 4.11

Strengths of subsidies in correcting positive externalities

- Like indirect taxes, subsidies are relatively easy to implement and monitor.
- Also, like indirect taxes, subsidies are flexible in that the amount of subsidy given can be changed relatively easily. This is useful if the MEB changes over time and the subsidy per unit needs to be changed over time too.
- Similar to imposing taxes, market forces of demand and supply are not prevented from working to determine the equilibrium price and quantity. The market equilibrium can still change in line with changes in demand and/or supply. This results in the market equilibrium (with subsidies) always automatically adjusting to the socially optimal quantity.

Limitations of subsidies in correcting positive externalities

- It is difficult to accurately measure or estimate the MEB and the socially efficient level of output. Hence, there could be over subsidy or undersubsidy. Oversubsidy would lead to overconsumption or overproduction of the good and might lead to government failure (Section 4.3.13). On the other hand, undersubsidy would mean that there would still be underconsumption or underproduction, albeit less than before.
- Subsidies given will cause the government to incur an opportunity cost as the subsidy could have been used to finance other government spending such as public education and health care.
- Subsidies will increase government spending and might lead to budget deficits and government debt.

Subsidies in the case of imperfect information (perceived MPB being greater than actual MPB)

When a subsidy is given to producers by the government, it will decrease the cost of production. Referring to Fig. 4.12, this causes the MPC to decrease and the MPC curve to shift down from MPC to MPC with subsidy. Note that since the MPC is the supply curve, this analysis is the same as a subsidy causing the supply to increase and shift right (*S* to *S* with subsidy). The market equilibrium would then shift from price P_M and quantity Q_M to price P_S and quantity Q_S. The new equilibrium P_S and Q_S is where the MPC with subsidy equals perceived MPB (*D* equals *S* with subsidy).

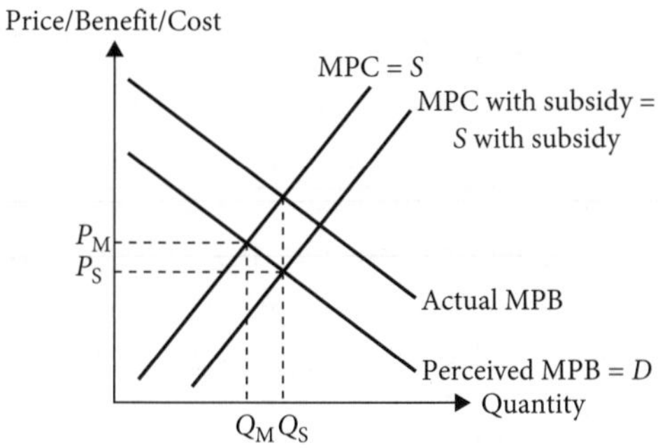

Figure 4.12

As can be seen, if the correct amount of subsidy is introduced, the socially optimum level of output Q_S will be achieved and market failure is resolved.

Strengths of a subsidy in correcting imperfect information (perceived MPB being lesser than actual MPB)

- Subsidies are relatively easy to implement and monitor.
- Subsidies are flexible in that the subsidy per unit given can be changed relatively easily. This is useful if the degree of imperfect information changes over time and the subsidy per unit needs to change over time too.
- Market forces of demand and supply are not prevented from working to determine the equilibrium price and quantity. The market equilibrium can still change in line with changes in demand and/or supply. This results in the market equilibrium (with subsidies) always automatically adjusting to the socially optimal quantity.

Limitations of subsidies in correcting imperfect information (perceived MPB being lesser than actual MPB)

- The subsidy corrects the behaviour of underconsumption but not the root problem of imperfect information. Consumers consume more of the good because subsidies decrease the price of the good and not because they actually know better.
- It is difficult to accurately determine the amount of subsidy per unit, to achieve the socially efficient level of output. Oversubsidy would lead to overconsumption of the good and might lead to government failure (Section 4.3.13) whereas undersubsidy would mean that underconsumption remains, albeit to a lesser degree.

Subsidy in the case of merit goods

Since merit goods are goods with positive externalities and imperfect information (perceived MPB lower than actual MPB), subsidy given to producers can also be used to correct the market failure with the same explanation. The strengths and limitations are the same too.

Subsidies to correct inequity

Since subsidies lower the price of the good, it makes the good more accessible to the poor. As such, it improves equity.

Putting it concretely: Means-tested subsidies

An indirect subsidy reduces inequity by reducing the cost of producing a good and hence, reducing its price, making the good affordable to the poor. However, it is a blunt instrument as the lower price also makes the good more affordable to the rich too. In contrast, means-tested subsidies are subsidies that are given only to people who meet the income criteria (i.e., only given to those with low incomes). Means-tested subsidies are hence, more targeted at reducing inequity. An example of means-tested subsidies in Singapore would be healthcare subsidies where the patients in lower-income brackets receive more subsidies.

4.3.3 Quotas and their effectiveness

Quotas refer to a maximum quantity that producers in a market are allowed to produce. Since it puts a limit to the quantity, it can be applied when there is market failure due to overproduction or overconsumption of a good or service. The sources of market failure that cause overproduction or overconsumption are the following:

- Negative externalities
- Imperfect information (perceived MPB being greater than actual MPB)
- Demerit goods (either due to negative externalities and imperfect information)

Quotas in the case of negative externalities

When a quota is imposed by the government, governments impose quotas by setting a legal maximum that producers can produce or sell. This is aimed at forcing firms to reduce the production of a good or service to the quota level, usually below the original private market output. A quota on the market is imposed by imposing quotas on individual firms' production (e.g., if there were 10 firms in an industry, an industry quota of 1000 units can be imposed by setting a quota of 100 units of output for each firm). The quota will not have any effect on the MPC or the MPBs. It restricts the quantity in the market directly such that the supply curve becomes vertical at Q_S where the quota is.

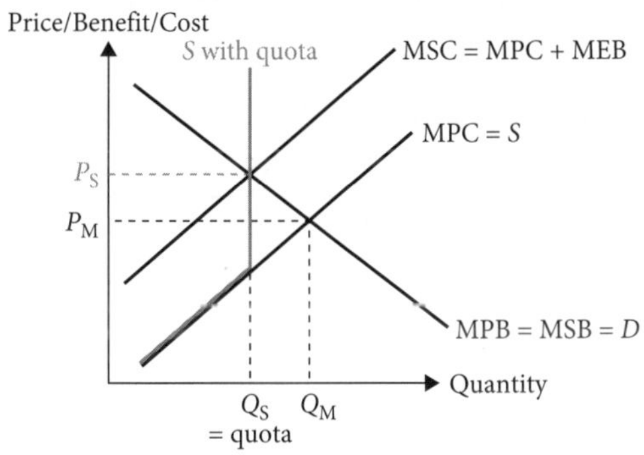

Referring to the above figure, with a quota imposed, the market equilibrium price and quantity changes from P_M and Q_M to P_S and Q_S. Therefore, if the correct amount of quota is set, at Q_S where MSB = MSC, the market failure will be resolved.

Strengths of quotas in correcting negative externalities

- If the correct amount of quota is imposed, the market failure will be resolved.
- Quotas are relatively easy to implement.
- Quotas are flexible as the amount of quota imposed can be changed relatively easily.

Limitations of quotas in correcting negative externalities

- Market forces are disrupted and demand and supply forces no longer automatically work to clear the market such that the socially optimal output is achieved. With reference to the following figure, if the demand of the good decreases from D_0 to D_1 (MPB and MSB also decrease from MPB_0 and MSB_0 to MPB_1 and MSB_1), the socially efficient output also decreases from Q_{S0} to Q_{S1}. However, if there was an existing quota at Q_{S0}, the market equilibrium quantity will remain at Q_{S0} where *S* with quota cuts the new demand curve D_1. This is different from taxes where the market equilibrium quantity would automatically adjust to the new socially efficient output.

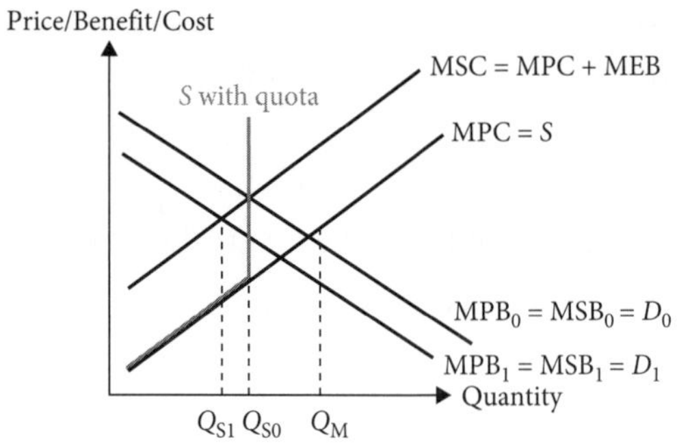

- It is difficult to accurately estimate the socially efficient level of output. Too tight a quota imposed might lead to underconsumption or underproduction of the good and might lead to government failure (Section 4.3.13) whereas too loose a quota would mean that overconsumption remains, albeit less than before.
- Quotas require governments to incur monitoring costs to ensure that firms stick to their quotas.
- Producers do not have incentives to reduce the negative externalities by finding less pollutive means of production. External costs will still be generated.

Quotas in the case of imperfect information (perceived MPB being greater than actual MPB)

Similar to the case when there are negative externalities, a quota aims to force firms to reduce the production of a good or service to the quota level, usually below the original private market output. The quota will not have any effect on the MPC or the MPBs. It restricts the quantity in the market directly such that the supply curve becomes vertical at Q_S where the quota is.

Referring to the following figure, with a quota imposed, the market equilibrium price and quantity change from P_M and Q_M to P_S and Q_S. Therefore, if the correct amount of quota is set, at Q_S where MSB = MSC, the market failure will be resolved.

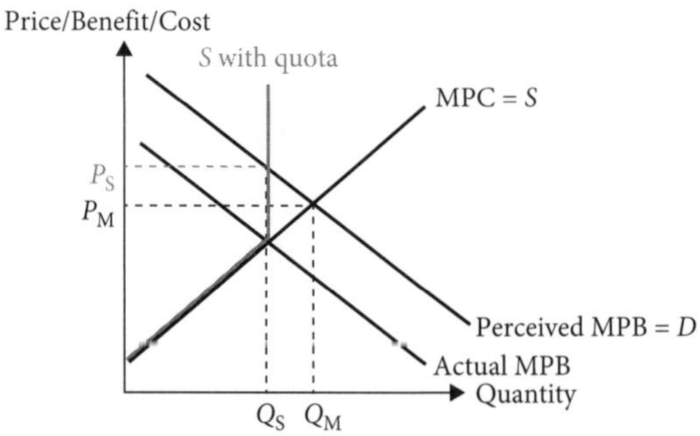

Strengths of quotas in correcting imperfect information (perceived MPB being greater than actual MPB)

- If the correct amount of quota is imposed, the market failure will be resolved.
- Quotas are relatively easy to implement.
- Quotas are flexible as the amount of quota imposed can be changed relatively easily.

Limitations of quotas in correcting imperfect information (perceived MPB being greater than actual MPB)

- Market forces are disrupted and demand and supply forces no longer automatically work to clear the market such that the socially optimal output is achieved.
- It is difficult to accurately estimate the socially efficient level of output. Too tight a quota imposed might lead to underconsumption or underproduction of the good and might lead to government failure (Section 4.3.13) whereas too loose a quota would mean that overconsumption remains, albeit less than before
- Quotas require governments to incur monitoring costs to ensure that firms stick to their quotas.
- Producers do not have incentives to reduce the negative externalities by finding less pollutive means of production. External costs will still be generated.

Quotas in the case of demerit goods

Since demerit goods are goods with negative externalities and imperfect information, in terms of perceived MPB being higher than actual MPB, the explanation for how quotas can correct the market failure for demerit goods is simply that quotas correct negative externalities and imperfect information, in terms of the perceived MPB being greater than the actual MPB. The strengths and limitations are the same too.

4.3.4 Tradable permits and their effectiveness

The government can intervene in the market using tradable permits to reduce the negative externalities during the production of goods and services (i.e., pollution).

Tradable permits in the case of negative externalities in production

It should first be noted that tradable permits are a policy that can only be used for correcting negative externalities in the form of pollution, and that the pollutant has to be a measurable one for it to work.

A tradable permit is a permit that allows producers to produce a certain amount of pollutants such as greenhouse gases. Without the permits, producers are not allowed to produce pollutants. Each permit allows the holder of the permit to release a certain amount of pollutants (e.g., 1000 m^3 of carbon dioxide per permit). These permits are tradable, which means that a holder of a permit can sell the permit to another firm if it finds that it is not releasing that much pollutants and therefore, has excess permits.

A government will first decide on the quantity of a particular pollutant (e.g., greenhouse gas) that may be emitted, usually on a yearly basis. This quantity of pollutant should be less than the current quantity of pollutant released for the policy to have any meaning. The government then divides this quantity up into a number of tradable emission entitlements and allocates or sells them to individual firms. If the government is the one that allocates the permits, the number of permits issued to each firm would normally be based on the size of the production. If the government sells these permits, the number of permits each firm gets depends on how much they were willing and able to pay for the permits. Whichever the case is, once the permits are all distributed, each firm would have a quota of the pollutant that it can emit in a year.

The permits can be traded within the industry. When a firm requires more permits in order to produce more goods and services, they could purchase permits from other producers, creating a demand for tradable permits, while producers with additional permits could sell off their permits for additional revenue, creating a supply for tradable permits. This creates a market for the permits where the market price of each permit is determined by the demand and supply for permits.

The trading of permits has two effects. One, it allows the reduction of pollution to be carried out most efficiently as the trading of permits will result in firms that find it cheapest to reduce pollution to reduce it the most, and firms that find it most expensive to reduce pollution to reduce it the least. This is because in the market for permits, producers who can reduce their emissions relatively cheaply will find it profitable to do so and to sell their emissions permits to other firms that find it harder to reduce pollution. With the sale of these permits, the firms that find it easier to reduce pollution would have to reduce their pollution more than the firms that find it harder to reduce pollution. The other effect is that the tradable permits create an incentive for producers to reduce their pollution level in order to sell the permits for revenue. Firms now have an incentive to implement more efficient methods of productions or engage in research and development to find less pollutive ways of production, to free up permits so that they can sell them. This reduces the negative externalities produced which increases the socially optimal output and moves it closer to the free market output, therefore, reducing the amount of deadweight loss and market failure.

In summary, the effect of tradable permits differs in the short run and long run. In the short run, before new methods of production are developed or implemented, a quota on the pollutant would translate into a quota on the good/service (i.e., if producing 1 unit of electricity requires 100 m^3 of carbon dioxide to be released, a permit that restricts carbon dioxide emissions to 200 m^3 would also effectively restrict the output of electricity to 2 units). In the long run, the permits create incentives for firms to find less pollutive ways of production. This means that the negative externalities generated per unit of output decreases (e.g., producing 1 unit of electricity now requires 50 m^3 of carbon dioxide to be released instead of 100 m^3). The illustration of how tradable permits work in the short run and long run is presented in Fig. 4.13.

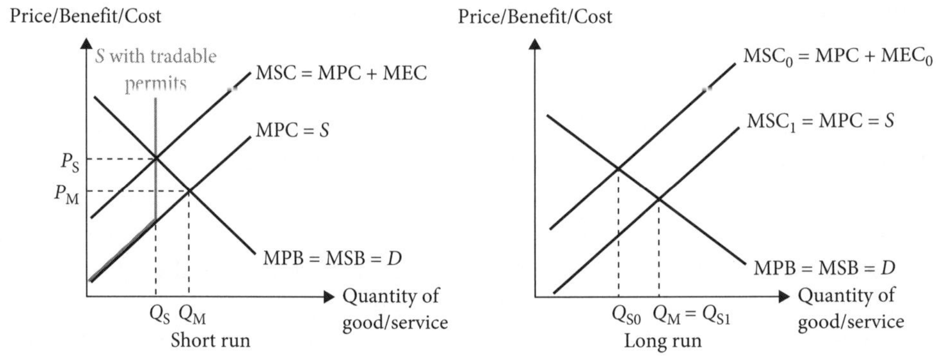

Figure 4.13: Effects of tradable permits in the short run and long run.

Strengths of tradable permits

- If the correct amount of permits is given, the market failure will be resolved.
- The reduction in pollution would naturally be done in the most cost-efficient way.
- This measure incentivises producers to reduce pollution levels to cut costs and also to reap revenue from selling their unused permits. This reduces the MEC in the long run.
- If governments sold the permits instead of allocating them, the sale of permits could raise government revenue.

Limitations of tradable permits

- It could be difficult for the government to accurately estimate the socially optimum level of pollution and hence, the number of permits to issue. If too many permits are allocated, it will not create enough of an incentive for firms to find less pollutive means of production.
- Letting demand and supply forces determine the price of the permit would mean that firms will suffer uncertainty in their business cost as the price of the permits they need to buy to produce their goods fluctuates.

4.3.5 Joint and direct provision and its effectiveness

The government can intervene in the market through joint or direct provision to produce a good or service.

Direct provision in the case of public goods

Public goods will not be produced by the free market due to their characteristics. Therefore, the government can intervene in the market by producing the good or service directly. In the case of direct provision, the government would be the sole producer of a public good such as flood defences or street lightings. The government would set up its own agency to oversee the production of these goods and pay for the cost incurred by collecting taxes. The government often provides public goods for free because of public goods' nature of non-rivalry in consumption. Non-rivalry in consumption means that the MC of providing the good to an additional person is zero. Since efficient pricing requires $P = \text{MC}$, when $\text{MC} = 0$, P should also be zero. Thus, the good is provided free.

Strengths of direct provision

- Public goods which otherwise would not be produced will be produced and market failure resolved.

Limitations of direct provision

- Direct provision might not be cost-efficient as government agencies are not profit driven, thus, resulting in wastage of resources.
- Direct provision would require government spending and might lead to budget deficits and government debt. Additionally, such spending will cause the government to incur an opportunity cost, as the subsidy could have been used to finance other government spending such as on public education and health care.

Putting it concretely: A better form of direct provision

The most severe limitation of direct provision is that government agencies are not profit motivated and have little incentive to produce public goods in the most cost-efficient manner. As such, a better form of direct provision is for the government to contract the work out to private firms to produce the goods without setting up its own agencies to oversee the production of these goods. Competition amongst firms to win the contract from the government ought to incentivise higher efficiency to reduce the cost of production so that a lower price can be quoted. However, a possible downside to this is a possible loss of quality when firms cut corners to try to quote lower prices.

Joint provision in the case of merit goods

Joint provision refers to governments and private sector firms both producing and supplying the goods in the market (e.g., public and private hospitals both providing healthcare services). The provision by the government increases the market supply, reducing prices and increasing quantity. This corrects the underconsumption of merit goods.

Strengths of joint provision

- Apart from increasing the supply of the merit good, the presence of the government acts as a form of competition for the private firms, incentivising improvements in efficiency and quality.

Limitations of joint provision

- Since joint provision involves the government's direct provision alongside private firms, the limitations of direct provision will also apply.

4.3.6 Rules and regulations and their effectiveness

The government can intervene in the market by using rules and regulations to influence the production or consumption of a good or service. Rules and regulations are set by the government through legislation and require the compliance of relevant individuals and economic agents. The analysis of rules and regulations is non-standard and requires an understanding of which source of market failure it is being targeted. We will illustrate the various ways to analyse rules and regulations through the use of examples.

Rules and regulations in the case of negative externalities in consumption of cigarettes and production of electricity

Rules and regulations reducing the area that smokers can smoke are meant to address negative externalities by reducing the amount of passive smoking third parties have to endure. By separating smokers from non-smokers, less negative externalities would be generated since there would be fewer passive smokers. This causes MSC to shift down to MPC, reducing the deadweight loss (Fig. 4.14).

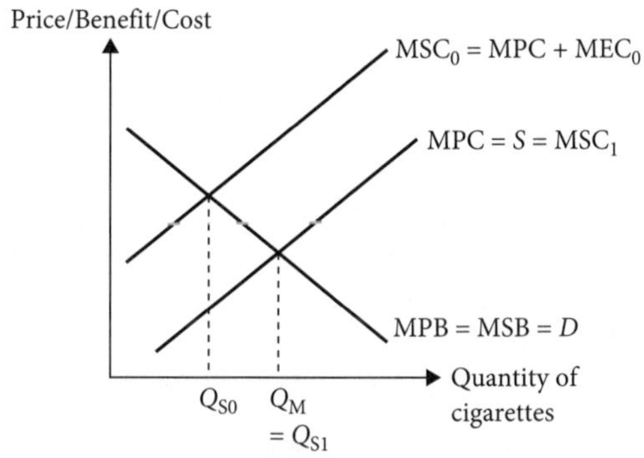

Figure 4.14: Effects of restricting the areas in which smokers can smoke cigarettes.

Rules and regulations requiring filters in the chimneys of electricity plants to trap toxic gaseous materials work similarly. These filters allow the production of electricity to take place with less pollution. This reduces the negative externalities and causes MSC to shift towards MPC too.

Rules and regulations in the case of imperfect information in consumption of cigarettes

A minimum age for smoking is meant to address imperfect information in the consumption of cigarettes as younger people are more likely to overestimate the MPB from smoking as they suffer the worst health effects from smoking (low actual MPB) and are the most misinformed (high perceived MPB). As such, the socially optimal quantity may be zero (or close to zero). The minimum age is effectively a ban on young people smoking, to achieve the socially efficient output of zero (Fig. 4.15).

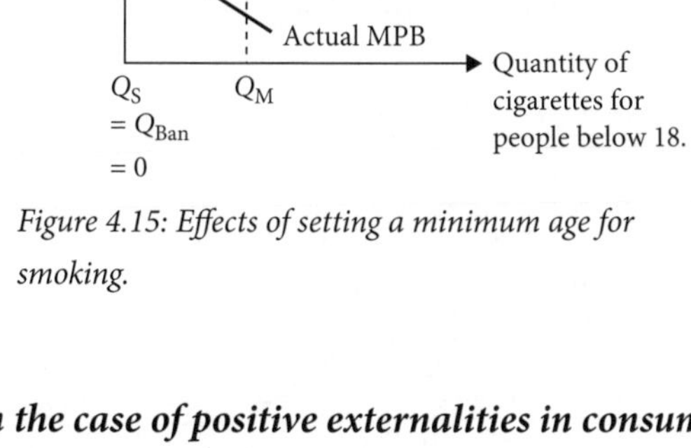

Figure 4.15: Effects of setting a minimum age for smoking.

Rules and regulations in the case of positive externalities in consumption of vaccinations

Compulsory vaccination is meant to correct the positive externalities in the consumption of vaccinations. It ensures that a certain quantity of vaccinations are consumed. This minimum quantity consumed should be Q_S (Fig. 4.16).

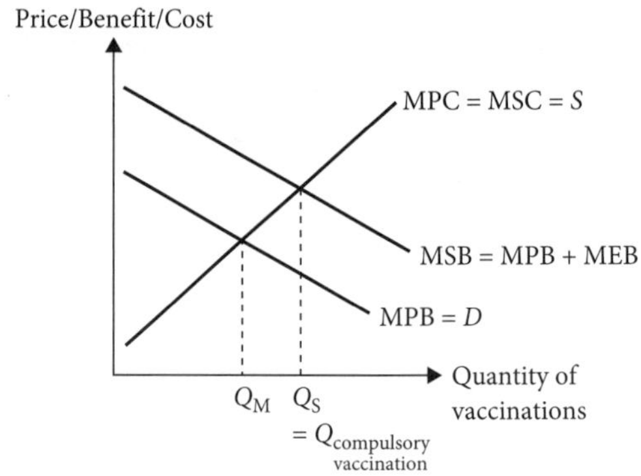

Figure 4.16: Effects of implementing compulsory vaccination.

Rules and regulations in the case of market dominance

The government can intervene in the market through rules and regulations.

The government can create laws that prevent the formation of monopolies, curb the collusive behaviour of firms, and reduce firms' market power. Examples of such rules and regulations include the following:

- Outlawing price-fixing practices
- Outlawing intra-industry arrangements between firms
- Prohibiting the formation of a monopoly in a market by preventing mergers or acquisitions that would lead to a firm gaining substantial market power
- Disallowing unfair competition practices

Real world examples include the Competition Act and the setting up of Competition Commission of Singapore (CCS) in Singapore as well as the Anti-Trust laws in the USA.

With the abovementioned rules and regulations, there will be more firms competing in the market, resulting in each firm having less market power. The demand for each individual firm will also be less and more price elastic. Referring to Fig. 4.17, the average revenue curve would decrease from AR to AR' and marginal revenue curve would also decrease from MR to MR'. Ceteris paribus, the new profit-maximising price and quantity would be *P'* and *Q'*. The difference between *P'* and MC' would be smaller than *P* and MC.

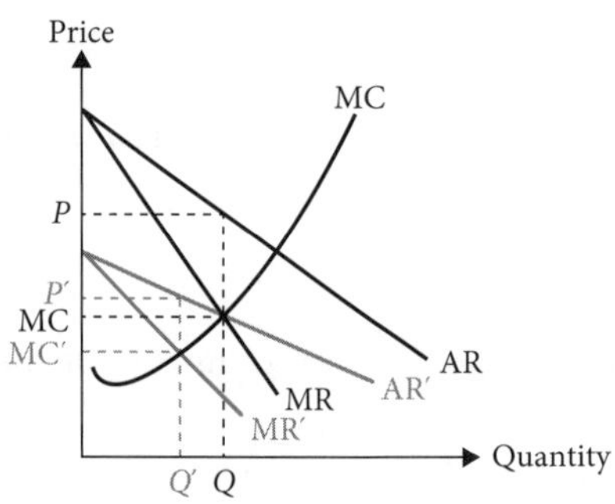

Figure 4.17: Reduction in market power.

Therefore, with lesser market power, the difference between the price of a good or service and its MC will be smaller, reducing the market failure.

Rules and regulations could also be in the form of regulations on prices. For example, a government could impose a price ceiling to prevent firms from abusing their monopoly power. This is illustrated in Fig. 4.18. The price ceiling transforms the MR curve from MR_0 to MR_1, causing the profit-maximising P and Q to change from P_M and Q_M to P_S and Q_S. At Q_S, the market failure is corrected.

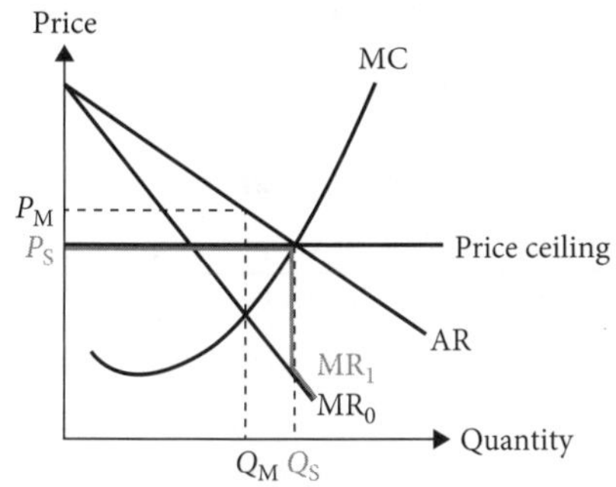

Figure 4.18: Price regulation to correct market dominance.

Strength and advantages of rules and regulations

- Rules and regulations are relatively easy to implement. The government simply needs to pass the law and notify the public. Assuming the law is easy to comprehend, firms are obligated to follow.
- Rules and regulations have a direct impact on firms which might make them more immediate or have a shorter time lag compared to other measures.

Limitations and disadvantages of rules and regulations

- For correcting market dominance: Rules and regulations to encourage competition prevent the formation of large firms or monopolies and thus, firms will be of smaller sizes and outputs. Smaller firms might not be able to achieve substantial internal economies of scale as compared to larger firms. Hence, the cost of production may increase. Firms may then pass on the higher cost to consumers in the form of higher prices, worsening consumer welfare.
- For correcting market dominance: Price ceilings that are set too low may cause firms to shut down instead. This would be worse for society as the market would completely not exist.
- In general: Rules and regulations require constant monitoring for it to be effective. Monitoring and enforcement will cause the government to incur additional costs due to manpower and administrative costs. These additional costs impose an opportunity cost as these funds could have been spent in other areas such as health care and education.

4.3.7 Public education and moral suasion and their effectiveness

The government can intervene when there is both under- and over-allocation of resources using public education and moral suasion.

Definition(s):

Public education is usually a campaign where the government aims to influence or change the behaviour of the public regarding certain issues by providing the public with more information.

Moral suasion is usually a campaign where the government aims to influence or change the behaviour of the public regarding certain issues by appealing to their morality.

Public education in the case of imperfect information

In the case of imperfect information where consumers' perceived MPB is higher than the actual MPB, the government can educate the public through providing more accurate information. With more accurate information, the perceived MPB will decrease and move closer to the actual MPB (a fall in demand). The new market quantity would decrease from Q_M to Q_S (Fig. 4.19).

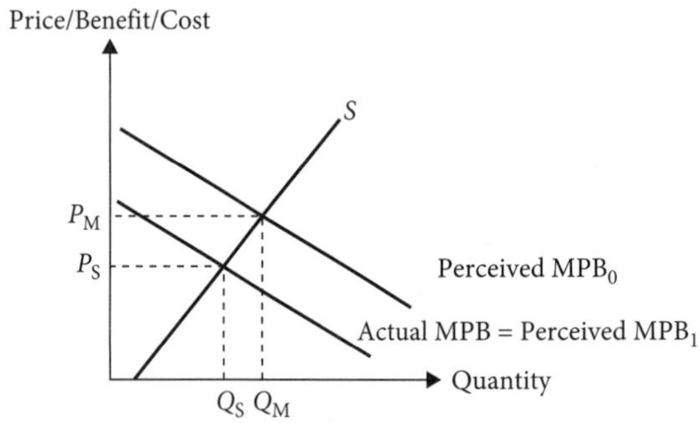

Figure 4.19: Effects of public education in correcting imperfect information.

Therefore, public education can help to bring consumption levels closer to the socially optimum level and deadweight loss is reduced or eliminated.

The explanation for public education correcting imperfect information, in terms of perceived MPB being lesser than actual MPB, is similar. With correct information, perceived MPB would increase to actual MPB (increase in demand). This then increases the market equilibrium quantity to the socially optimal quantity.

Moral suasion in the case of negative externalities in consumption

In the case of negative externalities in consumption where MPC is lower than the MSC, the government can employ moral suasion to appeal to the morality of consumers. In terms of economic analysis, the point is to make consumers internalise the external cost (i.e., feel bad for the external cost they impose on others). This will reduce the demand for the good (MPB decreases) and hence, reduce the market equilibrium quantity. Therefore, moral suasion can help to bring consumption levels closer to the socially optimum level and the deadweight loss is reduced or eliminated (Fig. 4.20).

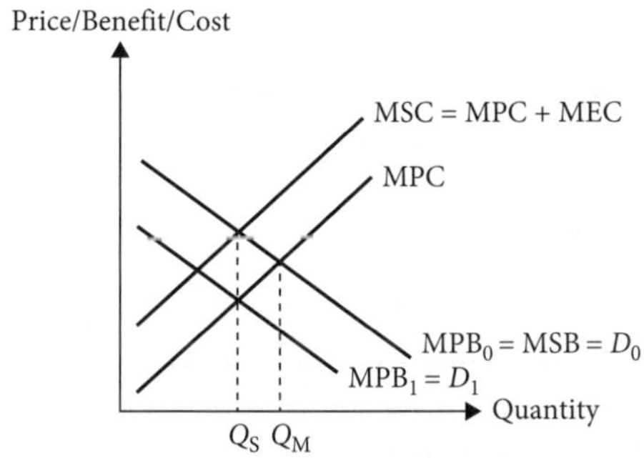

Figure 4.20: Moral suasion affecting MPC.

The explanation for moral suasion correcting positive externalities is similar. With moral suasion, consumers can be persuaded to feel good about the positive effects they bring to others. This increases the MPB (increase in demand). This then increases the market equilibrium quantity to the socially optimal quantity.

Strengths of public education and moral suasion

- These measures tackle the root causes of the problems (education targets imperfect information and moral suasion targets self-interested behaviour).
- The situations of the market failure can be improved or resolved if campaigns are successful.
- If the campaigns are successful, minimal government effort/funds will be needed in the future to solve the problem, making it a sustainable policy.

Limitations of public education and moral suasion

- These are long-term policies as results can only be seen after a considerable period. This is especially true should ingrained habits and mind-sets need to be changed.
- This policy does not guarantee results as consumers might not be influenced by public education or moral suasion campaigns.

4.3.8 Improving information flow

Improvement of information flow can reduce market failure due to asymmetric information. Since the problem lies with one economic agent having more information than another, government regulation that requires the economic agent to reveal information ought to correct the market failure. For example, the government allows insurance firms to insist that consumers go through a health check-up before they purchase an insurance policy. This reduces the asymmetric information as the insurance firm will now know the health status of the consumer. Similarly, consumers of resale homes can conduct an independent valuation of the house they are interested in.

One indirect way of improving information flow is to introduce a "lemon" law. This law would require sellers of defective products to exchange the products or refund the consumer. With this law in place, consumers would know the quality of the good they are purchasing as sellers of low-quality products would have no incentive to disguise their products as high quality products and charge a high price. Because they would end up having to refund consumers if they did so.

Strengths of improving information flow

- The measure targets the root cause of information asymmetry where one economic agent has more information than another.

Limitations improving information flow

- The government's role may sometimes be a limited as there is a limit on how much the government can mandate that information be shared.

4.3.9 Provision of training and relocation grants

Provision of training and relocation grants correct factor immobility due to occupational and geographical immobility, respectively. Provision of training or subsidies for training allows workers to pick up the skills they need to enter a new industry. Relocation grants reduce the cost of relocation and hence, reduce geographical immobility.

Strengths of provision of training and relocation grants

- The measures target the root causes of factor immobility.

Limitations of provision of training and relocation grants

- Provision of training may be ineffective if the take-up rate of workers is low. Occupationally immobile workers may not wish to attend training to pick up new skills for a variety of reasons. It is possible that the opportunity cost of time may be too high for them, or that their way of life and identity is too tied up with their old jobs.
- Relocation grants impose a burden on the government's budget. Such spending imposes opportunity cost in terms of the benefits of other government spending that has to be forgone.

4.3.10 Research & Development (R&D)

Governments can give grants to researchers to conduct R&D to reduce negative externalities. For example, the development of more energy efficient cars means that less petrol is burnt during driving and hence, fewer carbon pollutants are emitted. When this happens, the marginal external cost of driving is decreased. As such, there would be a smaller divergence between MSC and MPC (the MSC shifts towards the MPC). As such, the degree of market failure would also decrease. This is illustrated in Fig. 4.21 below.

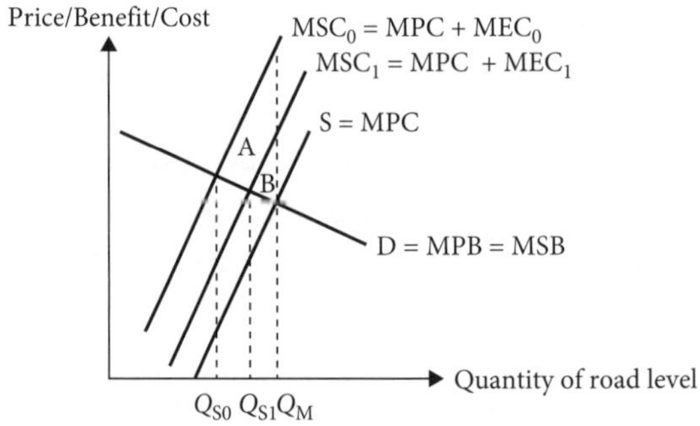

Figure 4.21

Referring to the diagram above, the original market equilibrium before R&D is at Q_M where MPB = MPC. The original social optimum is at Q_{S0} where MSB = MSC_0. The original deadweight loss is area A + B. As the R&D reduces the external cost, the MSC will decrease from MSC_0 ($MPC + MEC_0$) to MSC_1 ($MPC + MEC_1$). This causes the social optimum to shift from QS_0 to QS_1 where $MSB = MSC_1$. The deadweight loss is thus, decreased to the area B.

If the pollution can be completely eliminated (zero external costs), it would be the ideal solution as there would be no need to reduce production or consumption of the good.

Strengths of R&D

- R&D reduces the deadweight loss through targeting the root of the problem—removing the negative externality.

Limitations of R&D

- R&D only corrects the market failure in the long run as technology takes time to be developed.
- There is no guarantee of success. R&D grants can be costly but yield no returns.

4.3.11 Price floors

Price floors increase the price of a good and this reduces the quantity traded. Hence, price floors can be applied when there is market failure due to overproduction or overconsumption. The sources of market failure that cause overproduction or overconsumption are the following:

- Negative externalities
- Imperfect information (perceived MPB being greater than actual MPB)
- Demerit goods (due to negative externalities and imperfect information)

Strengths of price floors

- Easy to understand

Limitations of price floors

- Governments may have to incur high monitoring and enforcement costs to ensure that firms comply with the price floor.

Putting it concretely: Minimum wages; price floors in the labour market to reduce inequity

- In Chapter 2, we learnt that minimum wages were simply a price floor in the labour market. Such a policy would help to reduce inequity as minimum wages would increase the wages of the low income groups and increase their ability to pay for necessities.
- However, not all low income groups would enjoy the benefit as minimum wages would result in a surplus of labour. This means that while those who hold on to their jobs would enjoy an increase in income from the minimum wage law, some would lose their jobs and lose all income instead.

4.3.12 Price ceilings

- Price ceilings lower the price of a good and hence, can be used to reduce inequity by lowering the price of necessities (e.g., price ceilings on food items).

Strengths of price ceilings

- Easy to understand

Limitations of price ceilings

- Price ceilings result in shortages. This could result in the growth of black markets.
- Price ceilings are a blunt tool for reducing inequity as it lowers the price of the good to all consumers, which includes the rich.
- Assuming there is no other source of market failure, price ceilings reduce inequity at the expense of efficiency. This is because in the absence of other sources of market failure, price ceilings will result in deadweight loss.

4.3.13 Government failure

Government failure occurs when government intervention to resolve a market failure results in a deadweight loss larger than before governmental intervention. Instead of resolving or improving the allocative inefficiency, the government actually made things worse.

We discuss how government failure might take place in the cases of positive and negative externalities in consumption.

Government failure in the case of positive externalities in consumption

In the case of positive externalities in consumption (e.g., in education), one of the common methods of government intervention is to subsidise producers, which decreases the MPC. As MPC decreases, market quantity would increase from Q_M to a level where the new MPC intersects MPB. The optimal amount of subsidies that should be given is the amount of MEB at the socially optimal level Q_S. However, if the government estimates the MEB wrongly and oversubsidises the producer, it would lead to overconsumption of the good. If the subsidy results in overconsumption, where the deadweight loss is larger than before the subsidy was introduced, we have a situation of government failure as shown in Fig. 4.22 as area *A* (the deadweight loss before intervention) is smaller than area *B* (the deadweight loss after intervention).

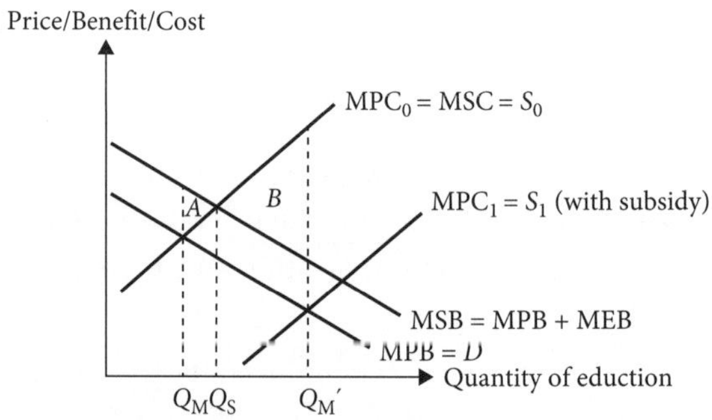

Figure 4.22

Similar applications can be made for cases when the government intervenes due to imperfect information, when the perceived MPB is lower than the actual MPB and for merit goods.

It is also important to note that it is not a case of government failure if the government undersubsidises. This is because while an undersubsidy is unable to resolve the market failure, the amount of deadweight loss after the intervention is reduced.

Free provision and government failure

Free provision can be thought of as providing such a large subsidy that the good becomes free. Since it involves providing a large subsidy, there is a risk that free provision is a form of oversubsidy. However, whether this is true depends on the extent of the market failure. If the market failure (underconsumption or underproduction) is severe enough, free provision may be appropriate. This is shown in Fig. 4.23 where Q_S is equal to Q_{free} at where $P = 0$.

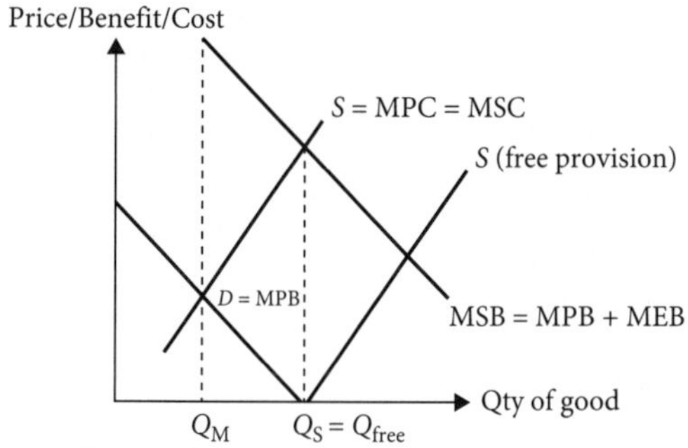

Figure 4.23

However, if the degree of underconsumption or underproduction is not large, free provision could lead to government failure as illustrated in Fig. 4.24 where the deadweight loss due to free provision at Q_{free} (area B) is larger than the original deadweight loss at Q_M (area A).

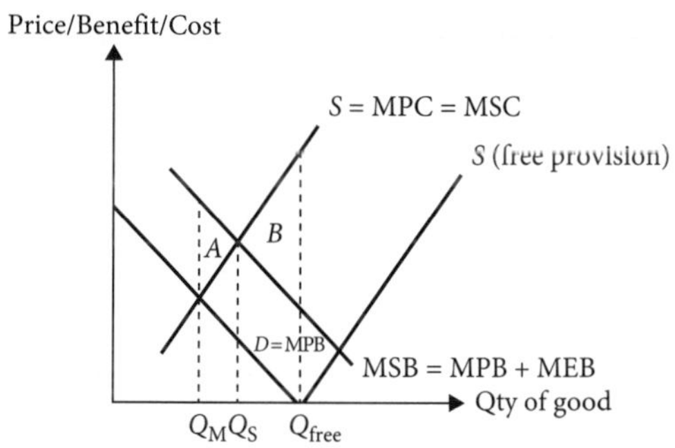

Figure 4.24

Government failure in the case of negative externalities in consumption

In the case of negative externalities in consumption (e.g., in smoking), one of the common methods government intervenes is to tax producers, which increases the MPC. As MPC increases, market quantity would decrease from Q_M to a level where the new MPC intersects MPB. The optimum amount of taxes that should be imposed is the amount of MEC at the socially optimum level Q_S. However, if a government estimates the MEC wrongly and overtaxes the producer, it would lead to underconsumption of the good. If the subsidy tax results in an underconsumption where the deadweight loss is larger than before the subsidy tax was introduced, we have a situation of government failure as shown in Fig. 4.25 as area *A* (the deadweight loss before intervention) is smaller than area *B* (the deadweight loss after intervention).

Similar applications can be made for cases when a government intervenes due to imperfect information, when the perceived MPB is higher than the actual MPB and for demerit goods.

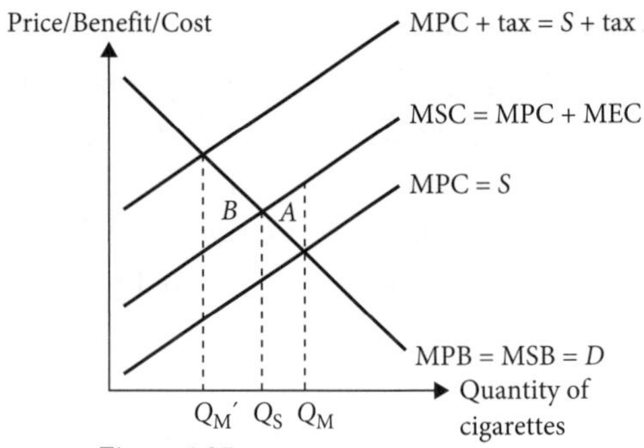

Figure 4.25

Once again, it is important to note that it is not a case of government failure if a government undertaxes. This is because although undertaxation is unable to resolve the market failure, the amount of deadweight loss after the intervention is reduced.

Bans and government failure

Complete bans can be thought of as an extreme form of quotas where the quota is set at zero. Since it is an extreme form of a quota, there is a risk that bans may cause overcorrections to the point of government failure. However, whether this is true depends on the extent of the market failure. If the market failure (overproduction or overconsumption) is severe enough, bans may be appropriate. This is shown in the Fig. 4.26 where Q_S is equal to 0.

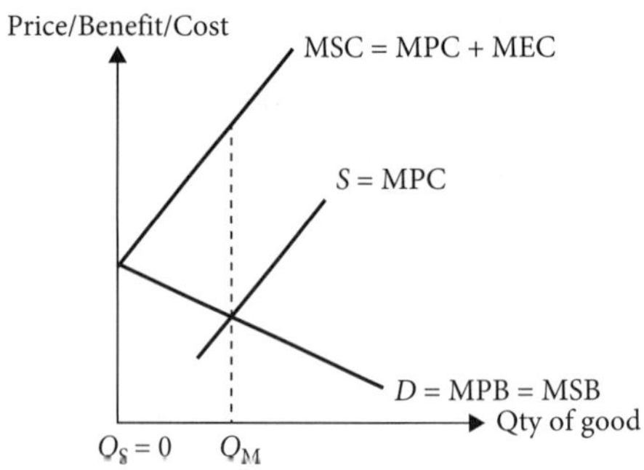

Figure 4.26

However, if the degree of overproduction or overconsumption is not large, bans could lead to government failure as illustrated in Fig. 4.27 where the deadweight loss due to the ban (area B) is larger than the original deadweight loss at Q_M (area A).

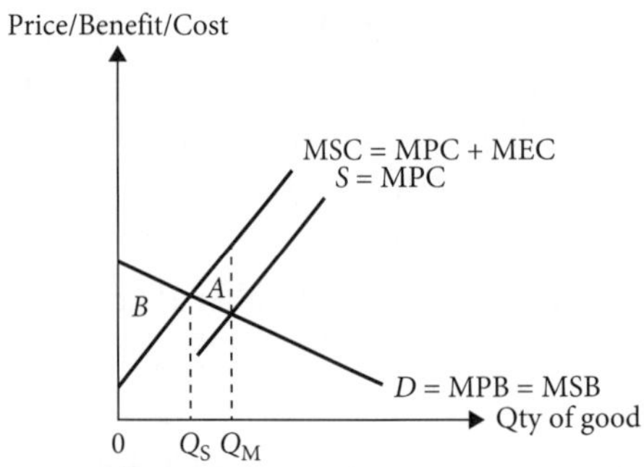

Figure 4.27

4.3.14 Overview of sources of market failure and the policies used to correct them

The following table provides a summary of the sources of market failure and the policies that can be used to correct them.

Source of market failure	Policy option(s) to correct it	Some examples
Public goods	Direct provision	Compulsory conscription by the Singapore Armed Forces to provide national defence (national defence is a public good)
Negative externalities	Taxes, quotas, tradable permits, moral suasion, and rules and regulations Price floors	Taxes on cigarettes, Certificate of Entitlement (COE) scheme (quota on cars), the European Union (EU) emissions trading scheme (carbon permit trading)
Positive externalities	Subsidies, moral suasion, and rules and regulations	Subsidised flu vaccinations at polyclinics, compulsory childhood immunisation
Imperfect information	Public education, subsidies, and taxes	Anti-gambling campaigns, posters that encourage people to take travel vaccinations
Asymmetric information	Improve information flow	Lemon laws
Merit goods	Subsidies, moral suasion, rules and regulations, public education, and joint provision	Posters to encourage annual health check-ups, education subsidies
Demerit goods	Taxes, quotas, tradable permits, moral suasion, rules and regulations, and public education	Tax on alcohol, rules and regulations concerning the consumption of alcohol
Factor immobility	Provision of training, relocation grants	SkillsFuture
Market dominance	Rules and regulation	Competition and Consumer Commission of Singapore's (CCCS) regulations
Inequity	Subsidies Minimum wages Price ceiling	Subsidised wards in hospitals

Summary for Chapter 4

1. Markets fail for a variety of reasons. When the market fails, it does not achieve allocative efficiency and/or equity.
2. Allocative efficiency is achieved when society's welfare is maximised.
3. Equity is achieved when there is fairness in the distribution of goods and services in an economy.
4. Allocative inefficiency may be a result of public goods, externalities, information failure, merit and demerit goods, or market dominance.
5. Governments intervene in markets to reduce market failure.
6. Each source of market failure may be resolved through a well-implemented policy.
7. Every policy has its strengths and limitations.
8. When a government's intervention results in a greater deadweight loss, government failure has occurred.

Annex 4.1 Numerical illustration of adverse selection in the used car market

1. 50% of all second-hand cars are high quality and 50% are low quality.
2. Sellers of high-quality second-hand cars are willing to accept \$17,000 for their cars.
3. Sellers of low-quality second-hand cars are willing to accept \$8,000 for their cars.
4. Buyers are willing to pay \$20,000 for high-quality second-hand cars.
5. Buyers are willing to pay \$10,000 for low-quality second-hand cars.

Without asymmetric information

There would be a high-quality second-hand car market where the price (P_H) is between \$17,000 and \$20,000. The total surplus generated per sale of each car would be \$3,000 (CS + PS = (\$20,000 − P_H) + (P_H − \$17,000) = \$3,000).

There would be a separate low-quality second-hand car market where the price (P_L) is between \$8,000 and \$10,000. The total surplus generated per sale of each car would be \$2,000 (CS + PS = (\$10,000 − P_L) + (P_L − \$8,000) = \$2,000).

With asymmetric information

Since buyers cannot distinguish between high- and low-quality second-hand cars, there would be only one second-hand car market.

For buyers, since there is a 50% chance of the car being high quality and 50% chance of the car being low quality, they will be willing to pay \$15,000 (50% × \$20,000 + 50% × \$10,000).

At this price, sellers of high-quality cars will not want to sell their cars because \$17,000 > \$15,000.

At this price, sellers of low-quality cars will be willing to sell their cars because \$8,000 < \$15,000.

The market supply would hence, only be made up of low-quality second-hand cars. The buyers have been adversely selected against.

Buyers will hence, lower the amount they are willing to pay to just \$10,000 (which is what they are willing to pay for low-quality cars).

Effectively, only the market for low-quality second-hand cars is left.

In this market, the equilibrium price (P_L) would be between \$8,000 and \$10,000. The total surplus generated per sale of each car would be \$2,000 (CS + PS = (\$10,000 − P_L) + (P_L − \$8,000) = \$2,000).

Conclusion

We can see that the total surplus decreases under adverse selection due to asymmetric information. The loss of surplus is due to the loss of the high-quality second-hand car market.

Annex 4.2 Numerical illustration of adverse selection in the insurance market

1. 50% of all consumers are high risk and 50% are low risk.
2. High-risk consumers are willing to pay premiums of $1000.
3. Low-risk consumers are willing to pay premiums of $500.
4. Insurance firms are willing to accept a premium of $800 for high-risk consumers.[11]
5. Insurance firms are willing to accept a premium of $400 for low-risk consumers.[12]

Without asymmetric information

There would be an insurance market for high-risk consumers where the premium (P_H) is between $800 and $1000. The total surplus generated per sale of each insurance policy would be $200 (CS + PS = ($1000 – P_H) + (P_H – $800) = $200).

There would be an insurance market for low-risk consumers where the premium (P_L) is between $400 and $500. The total surplus generated per sale of each insurance policy would be $100 (CS + PS = ($500 – P_H) + (P_H – $400) = $100).

With asymmetric information

Since sellers cannot distinguish between high- and low-risk consumers, there would be only one insurance market.

For insurance firms, since there is a 50% chance of consumer being high risk and 50% chance of the consumer being low risk, the premium they will be willing to accept (and hence, charge) would be $600 (50% × $800 + 50% × $400).

At this premium, low-risk consumers will not want to buy the insurance policy because $500 < $600.

At this premium, high-risk consumers will want to buy the insurance policy because $1000 > $600.

The market demand would hence, only be made up of high-risk consumers. The insurance firms have been adversely selected against.

The insurance firms will hence, increase the premium to $800 (which is what they are willing to accept for high-risk consumers).

Effectively, only the market for high-risk consumers is left.

In this market, the premium (P_H) would be between $800 and $1000. The total surplus generated per sale of each insurance policy would be $200 (CS + PS = ($1000 – P_H) + (P_H – $800) = $200).

Conclusion

We can see that the total surplus decreases under adverse selection due to asymmetric information. The loss of surplus is due to the loss of the insurance market for low-risk consumers.

---

11 This also means that the expected payout of a high-risk consumer is $800. The minimum that insurance firms will accept as a premium for a consumer is the expected payout they will make for that consumer.

12 This also means that the expected payout of a low-risk consumer is $400. The minimum that insurance firms will accept as a premium for a consumer is the expected payout they will make for that consumer.

PART II: MACROECONOMICS

CHAPTER 5

INTRODUCTION TO MACROECONOMICS

In Chapters 2 to 4, we studied microeconomics, which is the study of the economic behaviour of individuals and firms. In this chapter, we begin to study the economy as a whole (macroeconomics).

5.1 The Circular Flow of Income (H2 ONLY)

In order to study how an aeroplane flies, one could build a model plane to examine its properties. While the model is not exactly the same as the actual aeroplane, there are enough important similarities for one to infer how the actual aeroplane works. In the same way, in order to study the whole economy, we need to have a good enough model of how it works. This model is the circular flow of income.

5.1.1 The closed two-sector economy without savings and investments

The circular flow of income describes the flow of money in an economy. In the most basic form, an economy is only made up of two types of economic agents within the economy—firms (producers) and households (consumers).

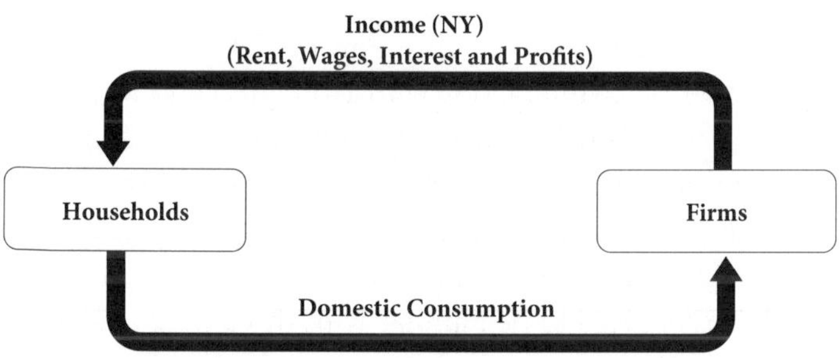

Figure 5.1: Closed two-sector economy without savings and investments.

Firms produce goods and services to be sold to households. In order to produce these goods and services, they need to employ factors of production (land, labour, capital, and enterprise) provided by households.[1]

1 It is probably easier to see how households provide labour compared to other factors of production. Nonetheless, households are also providers of the other factors of production. Households provide land (natural resources) when the households that are owners of these resources sell/rent them to firms (e.g., households who own the property rights of a plot of land lease it to firms to build a factory). They provide enterprise when people become entrepreneurs. The tricky one is the provision of capital. While there are some households that are the direct owners of machinery (capital) that is leased out, such occurrences are rare. Instead, most households provide capital indirectly through providing savings that banks lend to firms to purchase capital goods. This also explains why the payment to capital is known as interest. Firms pay interest to banks when they take loans to buy the capital goods. Banks pay this interest to households since the loans were made using the households' savings. A closed two-sector economy is clearly an overly simplistic model since it assumes that there are no banks, which would also mean that no loans can be made to purchase capital goods. Nonetheless, the model does provide a good starting point for understanding macroeconomic models.

Households buy the goods and services produced by the firms. This purchase of goods and services produced by firms within the economy is termed domestic consumption. In order to buy these goods, households need to obtain income. They do so by selling their factors of production to firms in return for income. Income paid to land (natural resources) is called rent, income paid to labour is called wages, income paid to capital is called interest, and income paid to enterprise is called profits.

Definition(s):

Domestic consumption (C_D) is households' spending on consumer goods produced by domestic firms (firms within the economy).

Income/Factor payment[2] (Y) is the payment from firms to households for employing factors of production owned by households.

Rent is the income payment for land (natural resources).

Wages is the income payment for labour.

Interest is the income payment for capital.

Profit is the income payment for enterprise.

The circular flow of income refers to the flow of money from households to firms in the form of domestic consumption and the flow of money from firms to households in the form of income. As illustrated in Fig. 5.1, such monetary flows are circular (which explains the name of the model).

This basic model is called a closed two-sector economy model without savings and investments. It is a closed economy as there is no interaction with a foreign economy (no exports or imports), and it is termed a two-sector model as there are only two agents in this model—firms and households. There are no savings and investments because we have omitted the existence of banks for now. These will be better appreciated later when the open four-sector economy with the presence of banks is introduced. We want to use this model to study how equilibrium is reached. In order to do so, we need to be familiar with three terms: national output, national income, and national expenditure.

Definition(s):

National output (NY) is the sum of the value of all the output produced in an economy within a certain time period, usually a year.

National income (NY) is the sum of all incomes earned in an economy within a certain time period, usually a year.

National expenditure (NE) is the total expenditure on goods and services produced in an economy within a certain time period, usually a year.

2 Income is denoted as "Y" because the letter "I" refers to investments, which will be explained later.

National output is always equal to the national income. This is best shown through an example. Suppose a firm produces a pen, and suppose the price of this pen is \$20. This means that the value of the pen (the value of the output) is \$20. Of this \$20, perhaps \$3 was the payment for the raw materials and rental of the factory space (land) to produce the pen (i.e., rent was \$3). Perhaps another \$10 was the payment for workers (labour) that made the pen (i.e., wages were \$10). Perhaps another \$2 was the interest payment for the loan the firm made to buy a machine (capital) to make the pen (i.e., interest was \$2). The remaining \$5 (\$20 – \$3 – \$10 – \$2 = \$5) would be profit, which is income for the entrepreneur. This is illustrated in Fig. 5.2.

Value of output (price)	=	Value of income generated
\$20		Rent – \$3 Wages – \$10 Interest – \$2 Profit – \$5
		Total income – \$20

Figure 5.2: Value of national output always equals value of national income.

Hence, we can see that the value of any unit of output (its price) will always generate an equal value of income. Since this is true for any unit of output, when we add up the value of all the output in an economy to get the national output, it should be equal to the sum of all the income in the economy (national income). Since national output is always equal to national income, we can use the two terms interchangeably. This also explains why both national output and national income share the same abbreviation (NY).

Referring back to Fig. 5.1, national income is the represented by the arrow pointing from the firms to the households. The value of this national income would be equal to the national output. National expenditure is represented by the arrow pointing from the households to the firms. In this case, national expenditure is only made up of domestic consumption.

Equilibrium in the closed two-sector economy without savings and investments

Equilibrium is reached when national expenditure equals national output.[3] If national expenditure exceeds national output, households are spending more on goods and services than firms are producing. This implies that firms must be running down their inventories (i.e., the stock of goods in the firms' warehouses would run low as the goods are brought out to be sold). In response, firms will increase their production. National output will hence, increase. So long as national expenditure exceeds national output, firms will respond by increasing production until national output equals national expenditure. At this stage, equilibrium would

3 See Annex 5.1 for the planned expenditure versus actual expenditure approach to determine the equilibrium national output. The thinking is similar although the terms used are different.

be reached as what is bought is exactly equal to what is produced. There is no more running down of inventories.

Conversely, if national expenditure is less than national output, households are spending less on goods and services than firms are producing. As a result, inventories will run up (i.e., the excess output will be stored in the warehouses). Firms will respond by decreasing production. National output would thus, decrease. This continues until national output falls to the same level as the national expenditure.

In summary, when the economy is not in equilibrium (NE > NY or NE < NY), national output will adjust (increase or decrease) until equilibrium is re-established. At equilibrium, national expenditure equals national output, which is also equal to national income. **The purpose of studying the circular flow of income model is to understand how national income is established**.

5.1.2 The closed two-sector economy with savings and investments

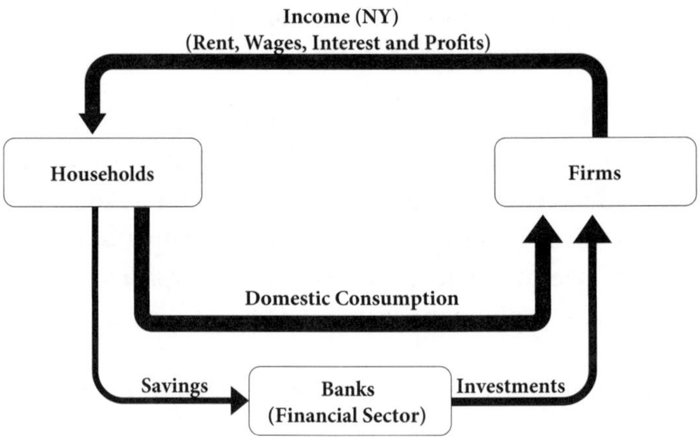

Figure 5.3: Closed two-sector economy with savings and investments.

We now make the model more realistic by introducing savings and investment. To do so, we need to add in banks (Fig. 5.3).[4] Banks play the role of matching savings to loans. In the model of a closed two-sector economy with savings and investments, instead of spending all their income on domestic consumption, households can save some of their income in banks. Since savings leave the circular flow of income, we call them withdrawals. Loans from banks are made by firms to purchase capital goods produced by other firms. The purchase of these capital goods is termed as investment. The money in the banks re-enters the circular flow when the firms use the borrowed funds to purchase capital goods from other firms (i.e., when firms invest). Therefore, investments are a form of injection because money is injected back into the circular flow.

4 More broadly, we need to add in financial institutions as it is not only banks that play the role of matching savings to investments. However, since the distinction between banks and other non-bank financial institutions is beyond the scope of this book, we shall keep things simple and just use the term "banks".

Definition(s):

Savings are the portion of household income that is deposited into banks.

Investments[5] are the purchase of capital goods.

Equilibrium in the closed two-sector economy with savings and investments

Equilibrium in this expanded model is still reached when national expenditure equals national output. The only difference is that national expenditure now comprises expenditure by households in the form of domestic consumption and expenditure by firms in the form of investments (when firms purchase capital goods). The reasoning is still the same as before. If national expenditure exceeds national output, firms' inventories will run down and they will respond by increasing production until national output equals national expenditure. Conversely, if national expenditure is less than national output, firms' inventories will run up and they will respond by decreasing production until national output equals national expenditure.

5.1.3 The open four-sector economy with savings and investments and the government (the four-sector economy)

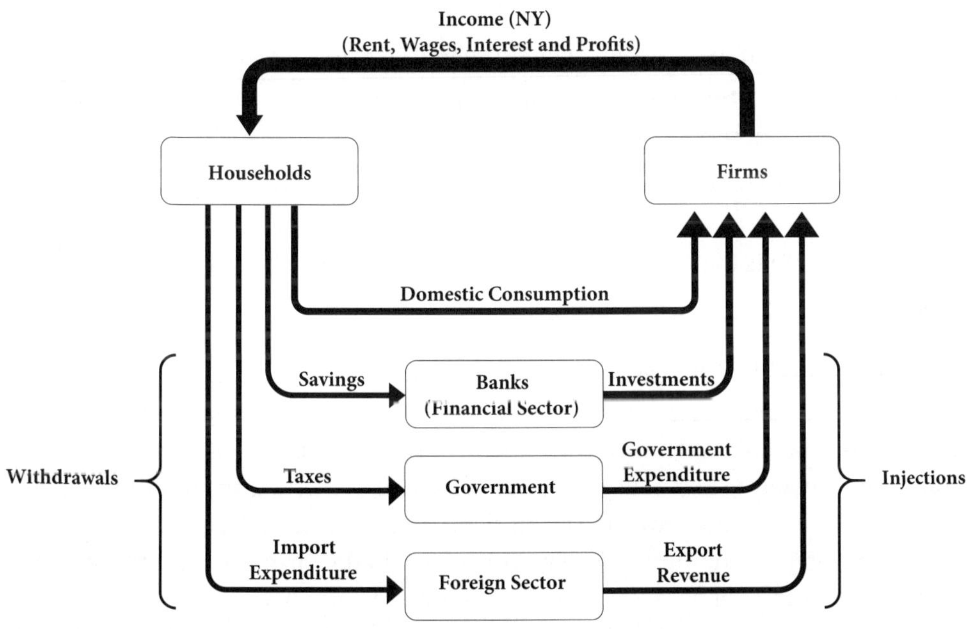

Figure 5.4: Open four-sector economy.

We now further expand the model by including the government sector and the foreign sector (Fig. 5.4). This model is called the "open four-sector economy with savings and investment and the government" or simply the "four-sector economy" for short. "Open" means that trade

5 Note that the definition of investments in economics is quite different from the layman's idea of investments. A layman would say that putting one's money in a bank to earn interest is a form of investment. However, to an economist, that is a form of savings. In economics, investment refers strictly to firms purchasing capital goods (e.g., machinery).

with foreign countries occurs and the four sectors are households, firms, the government, and foreign countries.[6]

Governments collect taxes from households[7] and purchase goods and services from firms. The government's purchase of goods and services from firms is termed government expenditure. Since taxes leave the circular flow of income, they are withdrawals. Also, since government expenditure causes money to enter the circular flow, they are injections.

The foreign sector trades with the domestic economy. When households buy goods and services from the foreign sector (i.e., when households purchase imports), money is leaked from the circular flow to the foreign countries. Hence, import expenditure is a withdrawal. When foreign consumers buy goods and services from the domestic firms (i.e., when foreigners purchase exports), money enters the circular flow from the foreign countries. Hence, export revenue is an injection.

In summary, in a four-sector model, withdrawals from the circular flow are savings, taxes, and import expenditure and injections into the circular flow are investments, government expenditure, and exports.

> *Definition(s):*
>
> **Taxes (*T*)** are the portion of income that households pay to the government.
>
> **Government expenditure (*G*)** is the amount of money that government spends on purchasing goods and services from domestic firms.
>
> **Import expenditure (*M*)**[8] is the portion of income that households spend on purchasing imports.
>
> **Export revenue (*X*)** is the amount of money that firms receive from selling exports.

Equilibrium in the four sector economy

Equilibrium in the four-sector model is still reached when national expenditure equals national output. The only difference from the previous models is that national expenditure now comprises expenditure by households in the form of domestic consumption, expenditure by firms in the form of investments (when firms purchase capital goods), expenditure by the government, and expenditure by foreign consumers in the form of export revenue. Same as before, if national expenditure exceeds national output, firms' inventories will run down and they will respond by increasing production until national output equals national expenditure.

6 Banks were not considered a sector as banks are not economic agents that decide how much savings there will be (that is determined by households) nor how much investments there will be (that is determined by firms). In contrast, governments are considered economic agents as they make decisions. They determine how much to tax and how much to spend. Similarly, the foreign country is considered a sector as consumers and firms in the foreign country make decisions about how much of the domestic country's exports they will buy.

7 In the real world, governments collect taxes from firms too. But to keep the model neat, we assume that the government only collects taxes from households for now. In any case, the analysis is not very much different when we include taxes on firms as such taxes are still withdrawals since they leave the circular flow of income.

8 The abbreviation for import expenditure is "*M*" because "*I*" already refers to investments.

Conversely, if national expenditure is less than national output, firms' inventories will run up and they will respond by decreasing production until national output equals national expenditure.

A summary of the equilibrium conditions of the three models presented is shown in the following table.

Equilibrium condition:	**National Expenditure (NE)**	=	**National Output (NY)**
In a closed two-sector economy without savings and investments	Domestic consumption (C_D)	=	National Output (NY)
In a closed two-sector economy with savings and investments	Domestic consumption (C_D) + Investments (I)	=	National Output (NY)
In a four-sector economy	Domestic consumption (C_D) + Investments (I) + Government expenditure (G) + Export revenue (X)	=	National Output (NY)

The closed two-sector economy without savings and investments and the closed two-sector economy with savings and investments were just introduced to show the development of the four-sector economy. For the purposes of actual economic analysis, we always use the four-sector economy.

Knowing the equilibrium condition and how the economy will move towards the equilibrium allows us to use the four-sector model of the circular flow of income to analyse what will happen to the national income when there are changes in the economy. For example, if there is an increase in government expenditure, national expenditure will increase and hence, exceed national output. Inventories will run low and firms will respond by producing more. Hence, national output will increase. Since national output must be equal to national income, as the production of output generates income, national income will increase. This mechanism still applies when we further develop the circular flow of income model into the aggregate demand (AD) and aggregate supply (AS) model.

5.2 Aggregate Demand and Aggregate Supply

The AD and AS model builds on the circular flow.

5.2.1 The AD curve

As was established in the four-sector circular flow of income model, the total demand for goods and services in an economy comes from the demand from consumers for consumer goods (domestic consumption), the demand from firms for capital goods (investments), the demand for goods and services by the government (government expenditure), and the demand for goods and services by foreign consumers (exports). In notation form:

$$AD = C_D + I + G + X$$

However, in reality, it is quite hard to estimate domestic consumption, as goods and services produced by domestic firms may have imported components in them. As such, the convention is to calculate the total consumption (C) in the economy (household spending on all consumer goods) and subtract the total value of import expenditure from it[9] to obtain an estimate of domestic consumption.

$$C_D = C - M$$

We replace C_D with $(C - M)$, $AD = (C - M) + I + G + X$, which can be reorganised as:

$$AD = C + I + G + (X - M).$$

We reorganise the AD this way because subtracting import expenditure (M) from export revenue (X) gives us net exports ($X - M$), which also allows us to study whether the domestic country is selling more to the rest of the world or buying more from the rest of the world.

The difference between national expenditure and AD is that national expenditure was simply the sum of the expenditure of the four sectors while AD tries to relate the sum of these expenditures to the general price level (GPL). The GPL refers to a hypothetical[10] average of the prices of all the goods and services produced in an economy.

What this means is that AD goes one step further by mapping out what the national expenditure is at different GPLs. In other words, the AD is the total value of goods and services demanded (i.e., the national expenditure) in an economy at a given price level (i.e., GPL).

---

9 In reality, it is not only consumer goods that have an imported component. There are also imported components in investments, government expenditure, and exports (e.g., if government expenditure is \$2 million, some part of that is likely spent on imports). However, to keep the explanation of the AD–AS model simple, we assume that the imported components are only in the consumer goods. In any case, when we extract the imported components from I and G and X, we will still end up with the expression $AD = C + I + G + (X - M)$.

10 Economists do try to estimate the general price level by using indicators like the consumer price index (CPI) which will be introduced in Chapter 6 as an indicator to measure inflation.

Definition(s):

The **general price level (GPL)** is an average price of all the goods and services produced in an economy.

The **aggregate demand (AD)** is the total value of goods and services demanded in an economy at various general price level, over a period of time, ceteris paribus.

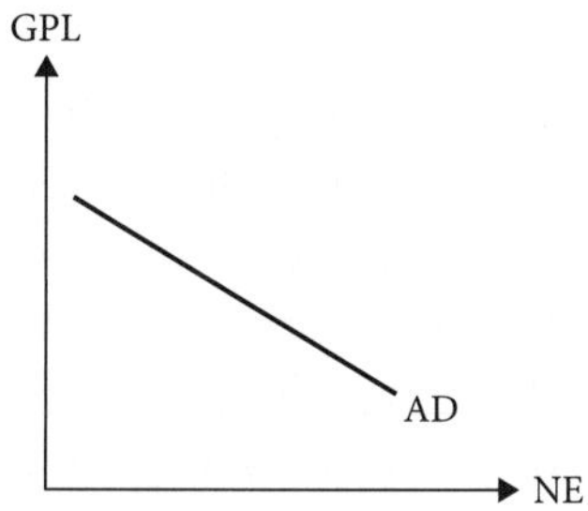

Figure 5.5: The aggregate demand (AD) curve.

The lower the GPL, the higher the amount of national expenditure. This is intuitively true.[11] Hence, the AD curve slopes downwards.

5.2.2 The AS curve

Just like how the AD curve relates national expenditure to the GPL, the AS relates national output to the GPL. The AS is the total value of goods and services produced in an economy (i.e., national output) at a given price level (i.e., GPL).

Definition(s):

The **aggregate supply (AS)** is the total value of goods and services produced in an economy at various general price level, over a period of time, ceteris paribus.

The AS curve is divided into three segments as national output can have three different relationships with the GPL (Fig. 5.6).[12]

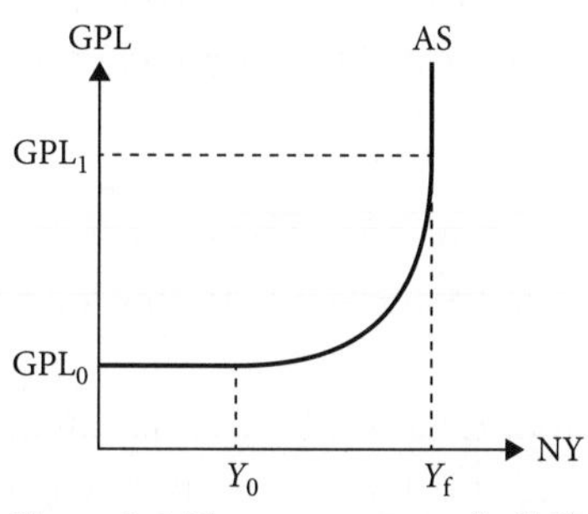

Figure 5.6: The aggregate supply (AS) curve

11 Refer to Annex 5.2 on the detailed explanation of why the AD curve slopes downwards.

12 An alternative way of deriving the AS curve is presented in Annex 5.3. While the approach presented in the main text is more commonly used, both approaches are equally valid for pre-university economics and yield similar results for the AD–AS analyses.

Between 0 and Y_0, the AS curve is perfectly horizontal. This means that in this range, national output has no relation to the GPL. This is because, at this low level of national output, the economy still has an abundance of unused factors of production. Hence, when national output is increased (movement along the AS curve from 0 to Y_0), there is no upward pressure on the prices of factors of production (e.g., there is no pressure on wage rates[13] to increase) as firms can easily employ more unused factors of production at the current factor prices. The average costs of production in the economy remains the same and so there is no pressure on firms to increase their prices. The GPL, thus, remains constant.

From Y_0 to right before Y_f, the AS curve slopes upwards. This means that in this range, national output has a positive/direct relation to the GPL. This is because at this higher level of national output, the economy starts to face some lack of unused factors of production. Hence, when firms produce more output and national output increases along the AS curve from Y_1 towards Y_f, they start to bid up the prices of the remaining unused factors of production (e.g., at this stage, to employ more labour, firms must pay higher wage rates). This causes the average costs of production in the economy to increase. In response, firms pass on some of the higher average costs of production as higher prices. Hence, the GPL increases.

At Y_f, the AS curve is vertical. This means that national output cannot increase anymore. Y_f is also known as the full-employment output. It represents the productive capacity of the economy, which is the maximum output that the economy can produce (i.e., it is the value of the output that the economy produces when all factors of production in the economy are efficiently employed).

Definition(s):

The **full-employment output/productive capacity** is the value of the maximum output that the economy can produce.

At Y_f, if a firm in the economy wishes to increase its output, it must offer higher prices for factors of production to attract them from other firms. This increases the average costs in the economy without increasing output in the economy, as the higher output by the firm which attracted the factors of production away from their previous employment will be matched by the lower output of the firm that lost its factors of production. The increased average costs will then be passed on as higher prices. Hence, we see an increase in the GPL but no increase in the national output.

The horizontal and upward sloping portions of the AS curve are called the short-run aggregate supply (SRAS) and the vertical part of the AS curve is called the long-run aggregate supply (LRAS).

The shape of the AS curve tells us that (i) at GPL_0, the national output could be at any level between 0 and Y_0, (ii) between GPL_0 and GPL_1, the national output would have a specific

13 Note that wages refer to the total amount of income paid to labour while wage rates are the wages paid per unit of labour (e.g., the wages for a delivery man may be \$2000 a month while his wage rate may be \$10 per hour).

relationship with the GPL (i.e., each GPL would correspond to one specific level of national output), and (iii) above GPL_1, national output would only be at Y_f.

5.2.3 Factors affecting AD

Since AD = $C + I + G + (X - M)$, the factors affecting AD are the factors determining C, I, G, and $(X - M)$, respectively. Factors that increase any component of AD would cause AD to increase and shift right. Naturally, factors that reduce any component of AD would then cause it to decrease and shift left.

Consumption

Consumption is affected by the following factors:

- Disposable incomes
- Expected future price changes
- Availability of credit
- Interest rates

Disposable income—Disposable income refers to households' income left after taxation. If income taxes increase, disposable incomes would decrease. Lower disposable incomes means that households have less purchasing power. Hence, consumption would fall. Conversely, a fall in income taxes would increase disposable income and hence, increase consumption.

> *Definition(s):*
>
> **Disposable income** is a household's income after taxation.

Expected future price changes—Expected future price changes affects households' behaviour and hence, changes consumption. If households expect the prices of consumer goods to increase in the future, they would try to bring forward their future spending. Hence, consumption (in the current period) would increase. Conversely, if they expect future prices to be lower, they would delay their spending on consumer goods and current consumption would decrease.

Availability of credit—Credit refers to loans. The greater the availability of credit, the easier it is for households to obtain loans (e.g., loans to buy cars), the higher the level of consumption will be. The opposite would also be true. The lower the availability of credit, the lower consumption will be.

Interest rates—Interest rates are both the returns to households' savings and the cost of borrowing[14] and it affects consumption in two ways. First, if interest rates increase, the returns on savings increase and households will hence reduce their consumption to save more instead.

14 In real life, the interest rate for deposits (savings) that banks pay out is clearly quite different from the interest rate that banks charge when they make loans (the cost of borrowing). However, the two are closely linked and often increase/decrease together. Thus, in economics, when we say 'interest rates' we refer to both the return on savings and the cost of borrowing at the same time. Read Annex 5.4 to understand why the two interest rates are closely linked and move together.

Second, if interest rates increase, the cost of borrowing increases and households would be less likely to borrow money for consumption (e.g., households will delay taking loans to purchase cars if interest rates are high). This also reduces consumption. Conversely, if interest rates fall, consumption would increase instead.

Investments

Firms undertake investments (purchase of capital goods) to be able to produce more output in the next period. They do so in the hope of being able to gain more profit by selling more output in the next period. For example, BreadTalk might choose to equip each of their stores with one new oven (investment) hoping that the ability to produce more bread when the ovens are installed would lead to more sales and hence, higher profits. However, to undertake investments, firms may need to borrow money from banks. As they need to pay back interest on these loans, firms will need to weigh the expected returns from their investments (expected increase in profits) against the cost of borrowing (the interest rate) to determine how much investments to undertake. However, interest rate is a percentage figure per year (e.g., interest rate could be 3% per year) while expected increase in profits is in dollars and cents (e.g., expected increase in profit of $2 m dollars a year). Hence, to compare them, the expected future profits needs to be converted to a percentage figure per year too.[15] This figure is called the Marginal Efficiency of Investment (MEI)[16] (e.g., the MEI of a unit of investment is 4% a year).

Definition(s):

The **marginal efficiency of investment (MEI)** is the expected return on additional units of investments. It is expressed as a percentage figure per year.

The MEI slopes downwards as successive units of investment tend to yield lower expected returns since the investments with the highest expected returns would be carried out first. The MEI curve is shown in Fig. 5.7.

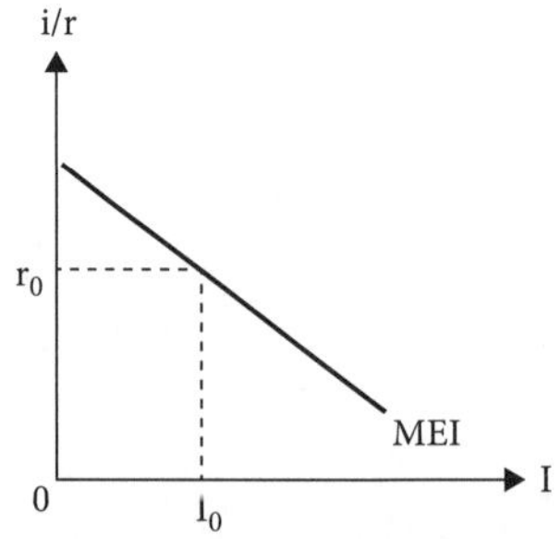

Figure 5.7: The marginal efficiency of investment (MEI) curve.

15 (Only for those interested to know more) The conversion involves estimating the future profits in each year and finding out the discount rate such that the present value of the future profits is equal to the immediate price of the investment. The discount rate would be in the form of a percentage figure per year.

16 Note that MEI is different from MEC (the marginal efficiency of capital). MEI is a flow concept and determines the optimal level of investments whereas MEC is a stock concept and determines the optimal level of capital stock. Using the two terms interchangeably is a common error.

The amount of investments carried out in an economy can be analysed by comparing the MEI against the interest rates. With reference to Fig. 5.7, at interest rate of r_0, investment projects from 0 to I_0 would be undertaken as their MEI exceeds the interest rate (i.e., the expected return exceeds the cost of borrowing). Hence, it is profitable for firms to borrow money at interest rate r_0 to undertake all these investments. Investments from I_0 onwards would not be undertaken as the MEI is less than the interest rate. Hence, at r_0, the level of investment would be I_0.

Using this model, we can see that the level of investments is determined by the following:

- The interest rate
- The level of technology (affects the MEI)
- The business outlook/expectations of future profits (affects the MEI)
- Taxes levied on firms (affects the MEI)

The interest rate—A fall in interest rates would increase investments. This is because with a fall in interest rates (from r_0 to r_1 in Fig. 5.8), more investment projects (those between I_0 to I_1) would become profitable as their MEI would now exceed the interest rate (which is the cost of borrowing). Hence, investments will increase (from I_0 to I_1). Conversely, a rise in interest rates (from r_0 to r_2) would increase the cost of borrowing and cause fewer investment projects to be profitable. Investment would thus, decrease (from I_0 to I_2).

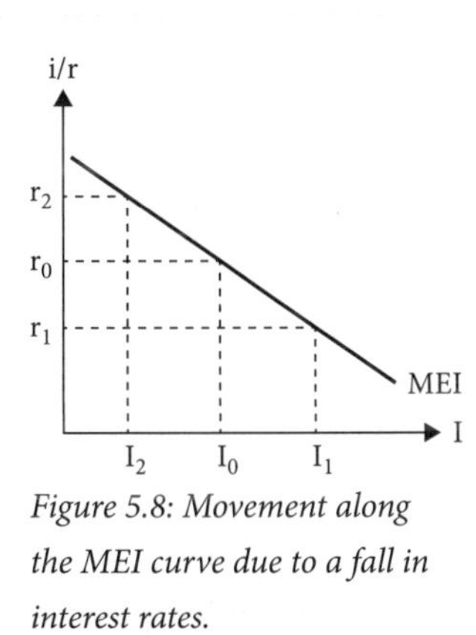

Figure 5.8: Movement along the MEI curve due to a fall in interest rates.

The level of technology—The level of technology could also affect investments. An improvement in the level of technology would increase the expected returns on investment (MEI). This would cause the MEI to shift up/right (MEI_0 to MEI_1 in Fig. 5.9). When the MEI increases, more investment projects (those between I_0 and I_1) would become profitable as their MEI would now exceed the current interest rate r_0 (which is the cost of borrowing). Hence, investments will increase (from I_0 to I_1). If the level of technology decreases,[17] then MEI would shift down/left (MEI_0 to MEI_2). Fewer investments would be profitable at the interest rate r_0 and investments would decrease from I_0 to I_2.

17 A reduction in technology is possible if there are natural or man-made disasters that wipe out knowledge in the economy. For example, the Cambodian genocide under Pol Pot resulted in the deaths of many intellectuals and a reduction of technology in Cambodia. Most civil wars have the same effect.

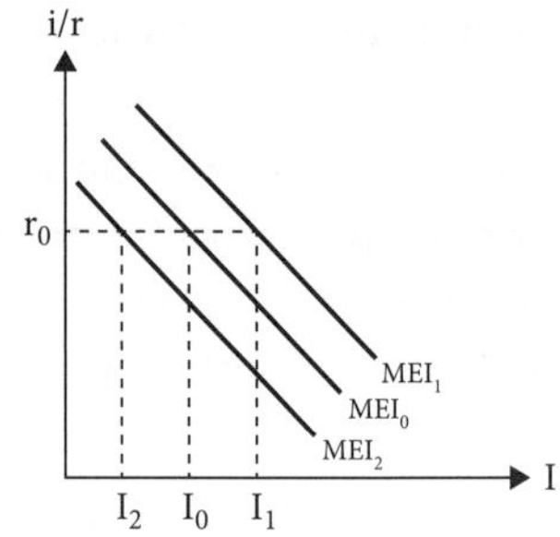

Figure 5.9: Shift of MEI due to non-interest rate factors.

Business outlook/expectations of future profit—Business outlook/expectations would directly affect the MEI because MEI is the expected return on investments. An improved business outlook such as expectations of higher profits would increase the MEI whereas a worsened business outlook would reduce the MEI. An increased MEI (MEI_0 to MEI_1 in Fig. 5.9) would mean that more investment projects become profitable at interest rate r_0 and investments will increase (I_0 to I_1). A reduced MEI (MEI_0 to MEI_2) would mean that fewer investment projects are profitable at interest rate r_0 and investments will decrease (I_0 to I_2).

Taxes levied on firms—Taxes on firms also affects the MEI. A decrease in corporate taxes (taxes levied on firms) increases the after-tax profits of investments and hence, increases the MEI. Conversely, an increase in corporate taxes decreases the after-tax profits of investments and hence, decreases the MEI. An increased MEI (MEI_0 to MEI_1) would mean that more investment projects become profitable at interest rate r_0 and investments will increase (I_0 to I_1). A decreased MEI (MEI_0 to MEI_2) would mean that fewer investment projects are profitable at interest rate r_0 and investments will decrease (I_0 to I_2).

Government expenditure

Government expenditure is affected by the government's objectives. If a government wishes to stimulate the economy by increasing AD, it would increase government expenditure. If it wishes to cool down the economy by decreasing AD, it would decrease government expenditure. Or, if it wishes to increase the productivity of the labour, it would increase government expenditure on subsidies for education and retraining. The objectives and policy options that a government undertakes will be discussed in Chapter 6 under macroeconomic policies.

Net exports

Net exports are affected by the following:

- Foreign income levels
- Domestic income levels
- Exchange rates
- Relative GPLs.

Foreign income levels—An increase in foreign income levels would increase foreign consumers' purchasing power. They would then buy more of the domestic country's exports. This increases export revenue (X) and hence, increases net exports ($X - M$). Conversely, a fall in foreign income levels would reduce their purchasing power and hence, the domestic country's export revenue (X). Net exports ($X - M$) would then decrease.

Domestic income levels—An increase in domestic income levels would increase domestic consumers' purchasing power. They would then import more goods and services from foreign producers. This increases import expenditure (M) and hence, decreases net exports ($X - M$). Conversely, a fall in domestic income levels would reduce households' purchasing power and hence, the domestic country's import expenditure (M). Net exports ($X - M$) would then increase.[18]

Exchange rates—The exchange rate is the rate at which foreign currency can be exchanged for domestic currency. It represents the price of the domestic currency as it shows how many units of foreign currency are needed to be exchanged for one unit of the domestic currency. For example, an exchange rate of 3MYR = 1SGD[19] means that the price of each Singapore dollar is 3 Malaysian ringgit. An appreciation is an increase in the value of the domestic currency in terms of the foreign currency (e.g., in the context of Singapore, a change in exchange rate from 3MYR = 1SGD to 4MYR = 1SGD). A depreciation is a decrease in the value of the domestic currency in terms of the foreign currency (e.g., in the context of Singapore, a change in exchange rate from 3MYR = 1SGD to 2MYR = 1SGD).

Definition(s):

The **exchange rate** is the rate at which foreign currency can be exchanged for domestic currency. It represents the price of the domestic currency.

An **appreciation** is an increase in the value of the domestic currency in terms of the foreign currency.

A **depreciation** is a decrease in the value of the domestic currency in terms of the foreign currency.

Changes in the exchange rate can affect net exports. An appreciation would make exports more expensive to foreign consumers and make imports cheaper to domestic consumers. Hence, foreign consumers would buy a smaller quantity of exports and domestic consumers would buy a larger quantity of imports. Hence, net exports would decrease. Conversely, a depreciation would make exports cheaper to foreign consumers and make imports more expensive to domestic consumers, causing net exports to increase.

Changes in the relative GPLs—Changes in the relative GPLs affect net exports. The domestic GPL may rise relative to the foreign GPL if (i) the domestic and foreign GPLs both increase but the increase in the domestic GPL is to a larger extent, (ii) the domestic and foreign GPLs both decrease but the decrease in the domestic GPL is to a smaller extent, and (iii) the domestic GPL increases while the foreign GPL decreases. For all the three cases,

18 We need to note that in this case, although $X - M$ changes, AD does not actually change. This is because the change in M would also change C ($C = C_D + M$) since there is no reason for C_D to decrease. Hence, since the change in C and M will cancel out each other, AD experiences no change since AD = $C + I + G + X - M$.

19 MYR is the abbreviation for the Malaysian ringgit. SGD is the abbreviation for the Singapore dollar.

domestically produced goods (exports) would become relatively more expensive to foreign consumers and imports would be become relatively cheaper to domestic households. Hence, foreigners will buy less exports and locals will buy more imports. Net exports would hence, decrease. If the domestic GPL falls relative to the foreign GPL, the opposite would happen and net exports would rise.

Changes in the abovementioned factors that affect *C, I, G*, and $X - M$ would also affect AD since AD $= C + I + G + (X - M)$. An increase in AD is represented by a rightward shift (from AD_0 to AD_1 as in Fig. 5.10) where national expenditure increases from NE_0 to NE_1 at the same GPL (GPL_0) and a decrease in AD is represented by a leftward shift (from AD_0 to AD_2 as in Fig. 5.10) where national expenditure decreases from NE_0 to NE_2 at the same GPL (GPL_0).

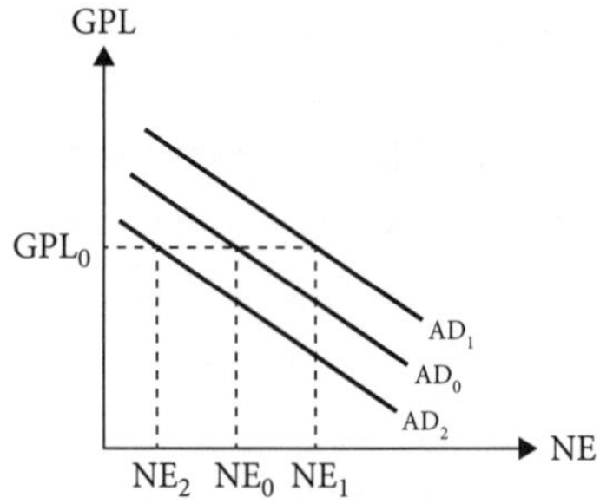

Figure 5.10: Shifts in the AD.

An upward shift of the AD is the same as a rightward shift (both show up as a shift from AD_0 to AD_1). Hence, for AD, upward and rightward shifts are the same thing. In the same manner, downward and leftward shifts are the same for AD (both show up as a shift from AD_0 to AD_2).

5.2.4 Factors affecting AS

For AS, however, leftward and rightward shifts are different from upward and downward shifts. Hence, before we go into the factors that affect AS, we need to understand the nature of upward and downward shifts of the AS, and leftward and rightward shifts of the AS.

The factors that affect the AS are the following:

- The costs of production
- The quality and quantity of resources (factors of production)
- The level of technology

Knowing the nature of how the AS shifts allows us to explain how these factors shift the AS.

The costs of production—Changes in the average cost of production would affect the SRAS and cause it to shift up or down. Such changes could be in the form of changes in prices of factors of production. For example, if a minimum wage policy is imposed, wages would increase. This would cause the average cost of production in the economy to increase and hence, shift SRAS up. Conversely, if the minimum wage is removed or lowered, wages would decrease and the SRAS would shift down instead.

The quality and quantity of resources (factors of production)—The quality of factors of production affects both the SRAS and LRAS whereas the quantity of factors of production affects the LRAS.

The quality of the factors of production affects their productivity where productivity refers to the units of output than can be produced per unit of factor of production.

> *Definition(s):*
>
> **Productivity** is the output per unit of factor of production.
>
> **Labour productivity** is the output per unit of labour.

Improved quality of factors of production (e.g., more educated and better-skilled labour) would increase the productivity of these factors of production. When productivity increases, the LRAS would shift right since maximum output that can be produced by the same quantity of factors of production would increase. This can be better understood using a numerical example. Suppose the economy has 100 units of labour and the productivity level is 5 units of output per unit of labour (i.e., each unit of labour can produce 5 units of output). The full-employment output would be 100 x 5 = 500 units of output. If the productivity increases to 7 units of output per unit of labour (i.e., each unit of labour can produce 7 units of output), with the same number of labourers, the full-employment output would increase to 100 x 7 = 700 units of output. This increase in the LRAS would cause it to shift right. The improvement in quality of the factors of production would also cause the SRAS to shift down. This is because a rise in productivity would reduce the average cost of production. A rise in productivity means that each factor of production can produce more output. This would also mean that the average cost of producing each output would decrease. This is also better illustrated with an example. Suppose the current wage rate for a factory worker is $10 per hour and the productivity of factory workers is 4 units of output per hour. The unit labour cost (the average labour cost of each unit of output) would be $10/4 = $2.50. If the productivity increases to 5 units of output per hour, the unit labour cost would decrease to $10/5 = $2. Since the unit labour cost decreases, the average cost of producing the output decreases.

> *Definition(s):*
>
> **Unit labour cost** is the cost of labour per unit of output.

Since improved quality of factors of production reduces the average cost of production, the SRAS would shift downwards. The combined increase in LRAS and SRAS is illustrated in Fig. 5.11 when AS_0 shifts outwards to AS_1. Conversely, a reduction in the quality of factors of production would cause SRAS and LRAS to both decrease and a shift inwards from AS_0 to AS_2.

Changes in the quantity of factors of production would affect the LRAS. An increase in the quantity of factors of production (e.g., when the population increases and more people enter the

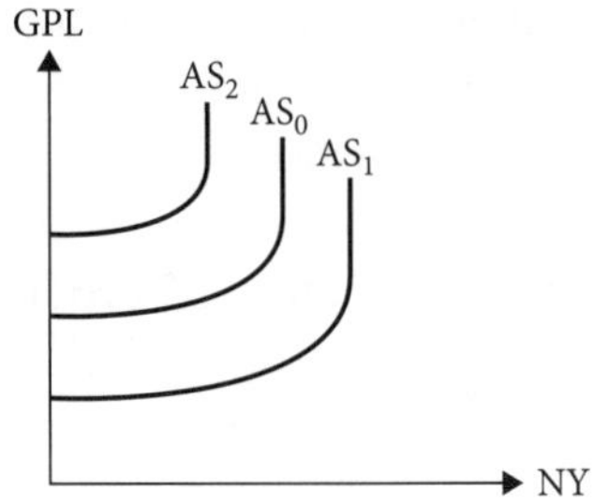

Figure 5.11: Outward and inward shifts of the AS curve.

labour force) would increase the full-employment output and shift the AS rightward. Conversely, a reduction in quantity of factors of production would decrease the LRAS and shift the AS leftward.

The level of technology—The level of technology affects the productivity of factors of production through affecting how efficiently factors of production can be combined to produce output.[20] For example, a courier (labour) uses a motorcycle (capital) to travel around to produce the service of parcel delivery. New computer programmes that help him plan out his route (technology) increase his productivity by helping him make better use of his motorcycle to take the shortest routes so that he can deliver more parcels per hour. Since improved technology increases productivity, it increases both LRAS and SRAS and shifts the AS outwards. A reduction in technology would reduce productivity and shift the AS inward.

Shifts of the AS curve	
Upward and downward shifts	Leftward and rightward shifts
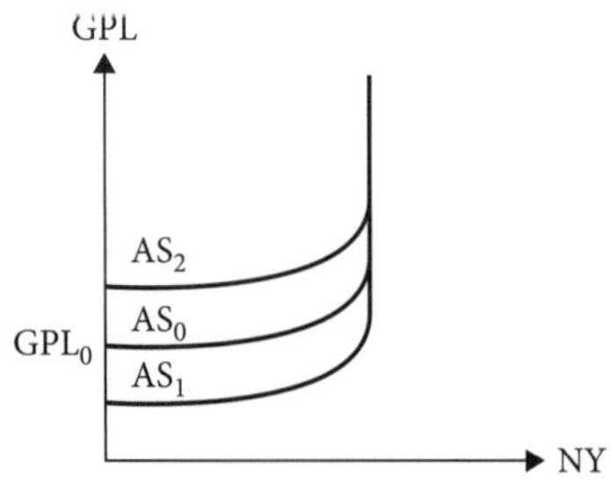	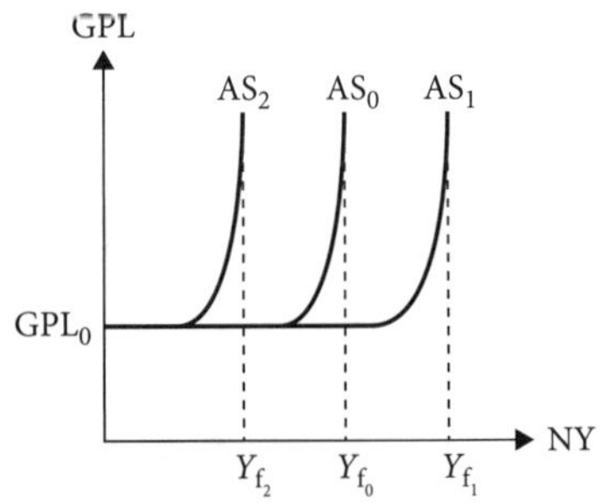

20 Instead of affecting how factors of production are combined to produce output, technology can also be embedded in the factor of production and increases the productivity of that factor of production directly (e.g., technology in machines that make them work faster).

Shifts of the AS curve	
The horizontal section of the AS shows the minimum GPL for national output to be produced. Using AS_0 as an example, we see that NY will only be produced at GPL_0 and above. If the GPL is below GPL_0, NY would be zero. The minimum GPL at which firms are willing to produce output must be the average cost of production in an economy. If a firm's average cost of producing a pair of shoes is $12, a minimum price of $12 must be reached before the firm will be willing to produce the shoes. This reasoning applies to all firms in the economy. Hence, the horizontal section of the AS is determined by the average cost of production in the economy. A decrease in average cost of production in the economy would shift the AS downwards (from AS_0 to AS_1) and an increase in average cost of production in the economy would shift the AS upwards (from AS_0 to AS_2). Since the section of AS that shifts up and down are the horizontal and upward sloping sections of the AS (i.e., the SRAS), we say that **changes in average costs of production shift the SRAS.**	The vertical section of the AS shows full employment output (also known as the productive capacity). Using AS_0 as an example, we see that maximum NY that can be produced is Y_{f_0} A rightward shift (AS_0 to AS_1) would mean that full employment output increases (Y_{f_0} to Y_{f_1}). A leftward shift (AS_0 to AS_2) would mean that full employment output decreases (Y_{f_0} to Y_{f_2}). Hence, factors that cause changes in the full employment output would shift the AS rightwards or leftwards. Since the section of AS that shifts right and left is the vertical section of the AS (i.e., the LRAS), we say that **changes in the full employment output shift the LRAS.**

5.2.5 The equilibrium level of national output and GPL

Equilibrium in the AD–AS is reached when AD = AS. Since AD is the national expenditure at a given GPL, and AS is the national output at a given GPL, when AD = AS, the equilibrium GPL is such that national expenditure equals national output. This is shown in Fig. 5.12.[21]

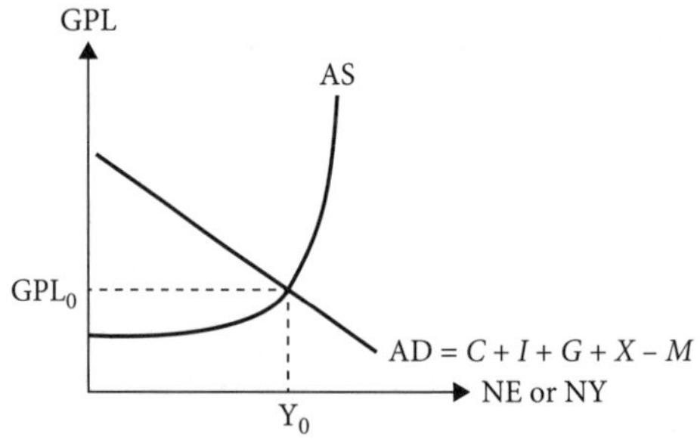

Figure 5.12: Equilibrium in the AD-AS model.

Disequilibrium between AD and AS can occur because of the changes in the factors of AD and AS, as explained before. If the economy was originally in equilibrium (AD = AS), when a factor of AD or AS changes, AD or AS would shift and that would cause a disequilibrium as AD would now be more than or less than AS (depending on what the shift in AD or AS was). For example, suppose the current equilibrium is a GPL of $5 and AD is equal to AS at $100 m each. If the government decides to increase its expenditure by $2 m, the AD would increase to $102 m while AS would still be $100 m. The AD now exceeds AS and this is a form of disequilibrium.

If there is a disequilibrium (AD > AS or AD < AS), the explanations of how the economy adjusts to reach the new equilibrium depends on which segment of the AS curve the disequilibrium is created in. The explanations for the possible scenarios are as follows.

For disequilibrium at the horizontal part of the AS curve

Possible scenarios for AD > AS	
Increase in AD	Downward shift of AS
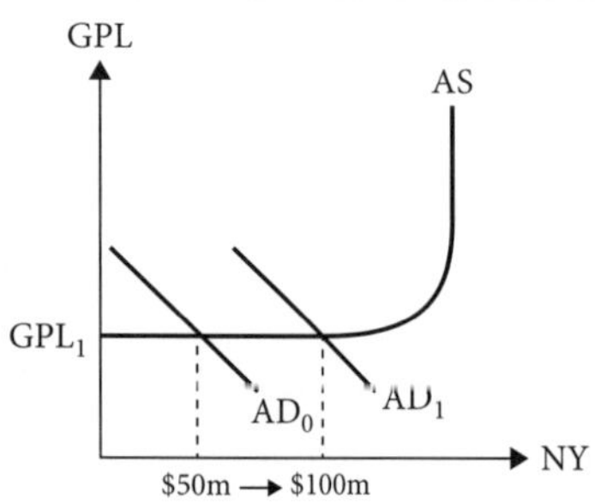	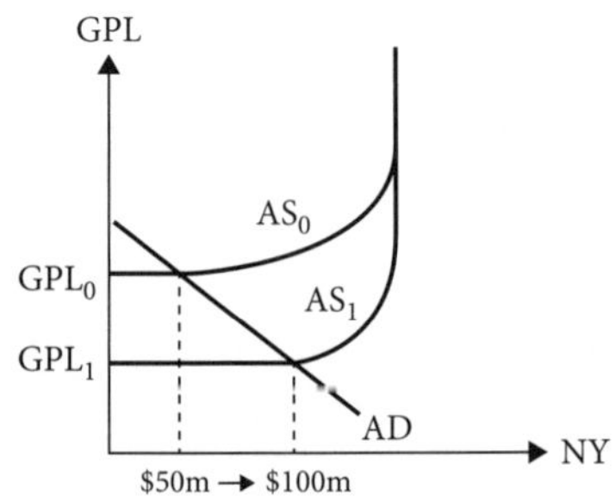

21 When the AD and AS are mapped on the same graph, the horizontal axis shows both the NE (from the AD) and the NY (from the AS). But the convention is to name the horizontal axis NY when both AD and AS are drawn on the same diagram. We will also follow this convention for all AD–AS diagrams henceforth.

Possible scenarios for AD > AS	
Original equilibrium: $GPL = GPL_1$ AD = AS = \$50 m With increase in AD from AD_0 to AD_1: At GPL_1, AD = \$100 m AS = \$50 m	Original equilibrium: $GPL = GPL_0$ AD = AS = \$50 m With downward shift of AS from AS_0 to AS_1: Now GPL is GPL_1, AD = \$100 m AS = \$50 m
(Explanation is the same for both scenarios) AD (\$100 m) exceeds AS (\$50 m). Inventories run down. Firms respond by increasing output. Since there are abundant unused factors of production, national output increases without causing an upward pressure on prices of factors of production. Average cost remains the same and national output simply increases (movement along AS) until AS equals to AD at \$100 m. Final equilibrium: GPL_1 and NY of \$100 m	

<table>
<tr><th colspan="2">Possible scenarios for AD < AS</th></tr>
<tr><td>Decrease in AD</td><td>Upward shift of AS</td></tr>
<tr><td>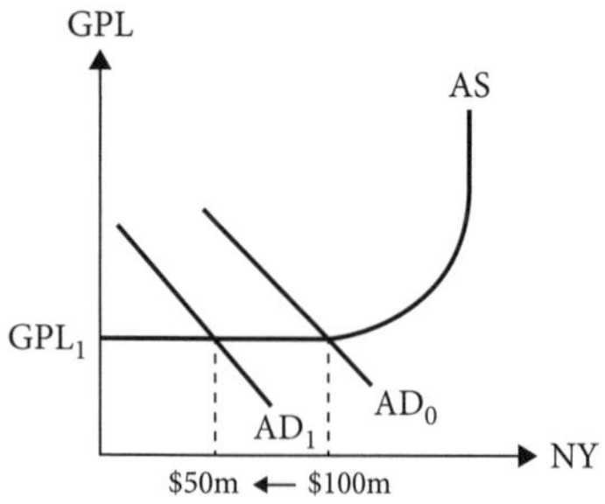
</td><td>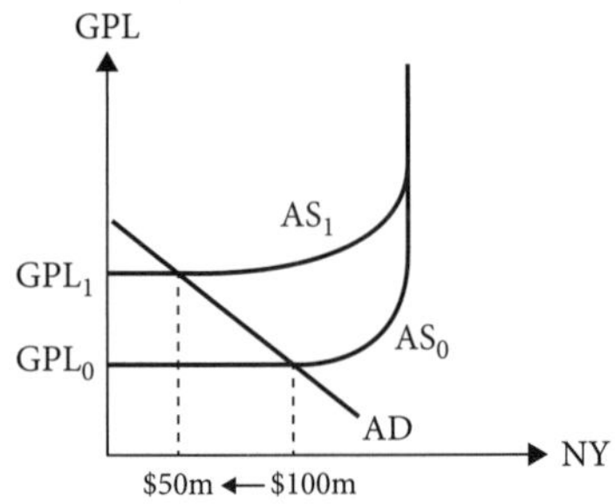
</td></tr>
<tr><td>Original equilibrium:

GPL = GPL_1

AD = AS = $100 m

With decrease in AD from AD_0 to AD_1:

At GPL_1,

AD = $50 m

AS = $100 m</td><td>Original equilibrium:

GPL = GPL_0

AD = AS = $100 m

With upward shift of AS from AS_0 to AS_1:

Now GPL is GPL_1,

AD = $50 m

AS = $100 m</td></tr>
<tr><td colspan="2">(Explanation is the same for both scenarios)

AD ($50 m) is less than AS ($100 m). Inventories run up. Firms respond by decreasing output. Since there were abundant unused factors of production, national output decreases without causing a downward pressure on prices of factors of production.[22] Average cost remains the same and national output simply decreases (movement along AS) until AS equals AD at $50 m.

Final equilibrium: GPL_1 and NY of $50 m</td></tr>
</table>

22 The current prices of factors of production were determined with the current abundance of unused factors of production. Reducing employment and adding to the abundance of unused factors of production would have no/insignificant additional effect on wages. In other words, the supply of factors of production in the factor markets is perfectly price elastic.

For disequilibrium at the upward-sloping part of the AS curve

<table>
<tr><th colspan="2">Possible scenarios for AD > AS</th></tr>
<tr><td>Increase in AD</td><td>Inward (leftward and/or upward) shift of AS</td></tr>
<tr><td>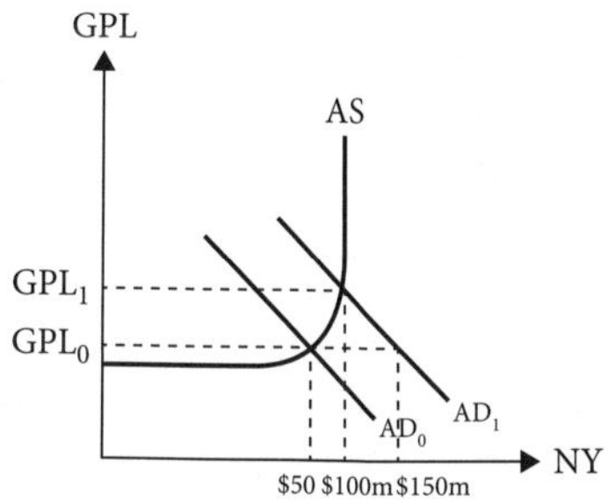
</td><td>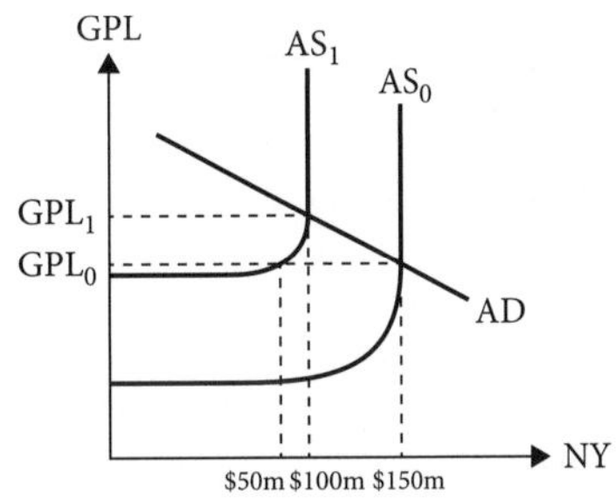
</td></tr>
<tr><td>Original equilibrium:

GPL = GPL_0

AD = AS = $50 m

With increase in AD from AD_0 to AD_1:

At GPL_0,

AD = $150 m

AS = $50 m</td><td>Original equilibrium:

GPL = GPL_0

AD = AS = $150 m

With inward shift of AS from AS_0 to AS_1:

At GPL_0,

AD = $150 m

AS = $50 m</td></tr>
<tr><td colspan="2">(Explanation is the same for both scenarios)

AD ($150 m) exceeds AS ($50 m). Inventories run down. Firms respond by increasing output. However, as there is some lack of unused factors of production, national output increases with an upward pressure on prices of factors of production. Average cost increases and national output increases with an increase in GPL (upward movement along AS). At the same time, because GPL increases, national expenditure decreases (upward movement along AD). This continues until equilibrium is reached when AD = AS.

Final equilibrium: GPL_1 and NY of $100 m</td></tr>
</table>

<table>
<tr><th colspan="2">Possible scenarios for AD < AS</th></tr>
<tr><td>Decrease in AD</td><td>Outward (rightward and/or downward shift of AS)</td></tr>
<tr><td>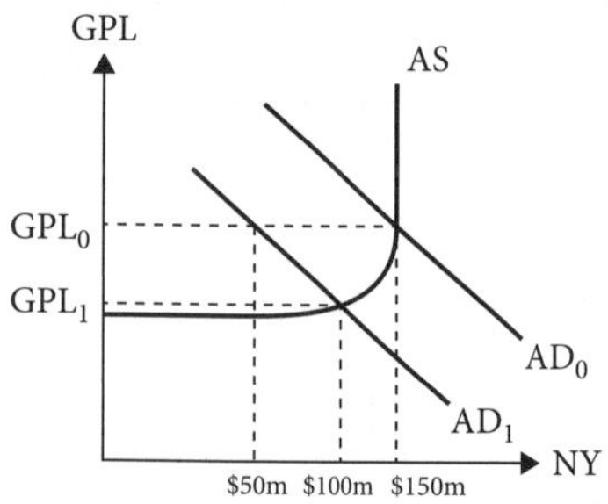
</td><td>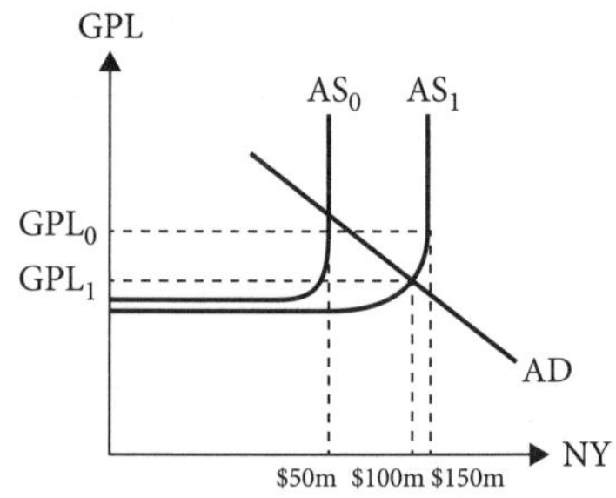
</td></tr>
<tr><td>Original equilibrium:

GPL = GPL_0

AD = AS = $150 m

With decrease in AD from AD_0 to AD_1:

At GPL_0,

AD = $50 m

AS = $150 m</td><td>Original equilibrium:

GPL = GPL_0

AD = AS = $50 m

With outward shift of AS from AS_0 to AS_1:

At GPL_0,

AD = $50 m

AS = $150 m</td></tr>
<tr><td colspan="2">(Explanation is the same for both scenarios)

AD ($50 m) is less than AS ($150 m). Inventories run up. Firms respond by decreasing output. However, as the factor market was quite tight (only a few unused factors of production in the economy), national output decreases with a downward pressure on prices of factors of production. Average cost decreases and national output decreases with a decrease in GPL (downward movement along AS). At the same time, because GPL decreases, national expenditure decreases (downward movement along AD). This continues until equilibrium is reached when AD = AS.

Final equilibrium: GPL_1 and NY of $100 m</td></tr>
</table>

For disequilibrium at the vertical part of the AS curve

<table>
<tr><th colspan="2">Possible scenarios for AD > AS</th></tr>
<tr><td>Increase in AD</td><td>Leftward shift of AS</td></tr>
<tr><td>

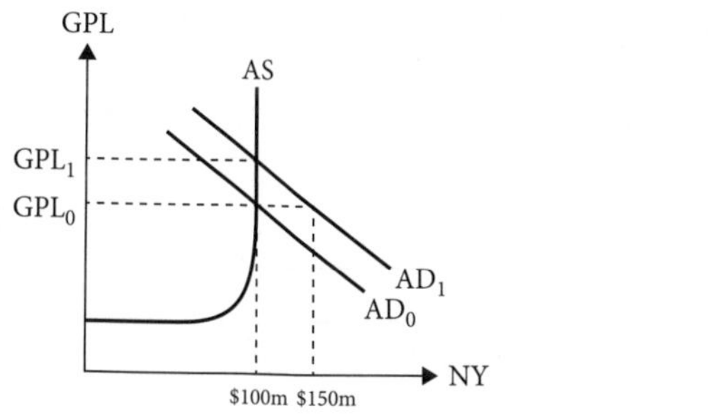

</td><td>

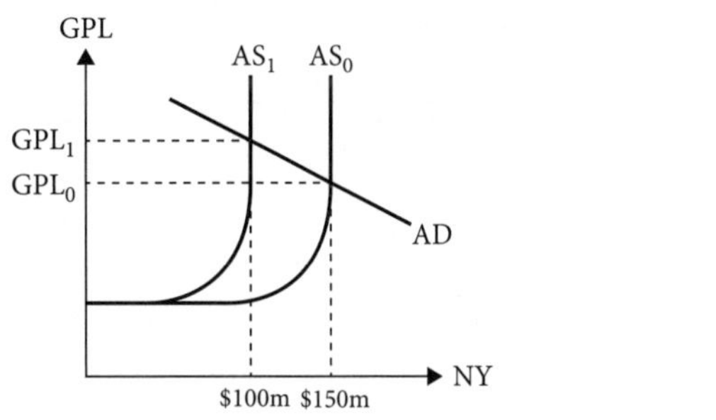

</td></tr>
<tr><td>Original equilibrium:

GPL = GPL_0

AD = AS = $100 m

With increase in AD from AD_0 to AD_1:

At GPL_0,

AD = $150 m

AS = $100 m</td><td>Original equilibrium:

GPL = GPL_0

AD = AS = $150 m

With leftward shift of AS from AS_0 to AS_1:

At GPL_0,

AD = $150 m

AS = $100 m</td></tr>
<tr><td colspan="2">(Explanation is the same for both scenarios)

AD ($150 m) exceeds AS ($100 m). Inventories run down. Firms respond by trying to increase output. However, as there are no unused factors of production, national output does not increase at all while prices of factors of production increase as firms bid higher and higher prices to attract factors of production from other firms. Average cost increases with no increase in national output, causing a pure increase in GPL (vertical movement up AS). At the same time, because GPL increases, national expenditure decreases (upward movement along AD). This continues until equilibrium is reached when AD = AS.

Final equilibrium: GPL_1 and NY of $100 m</td></tr>
</table>

<table>
<tr><th colspan="2">Possible scenarios for AD < AS</th></tr>
<tr><td>Decrease in AD</td><td>Rightward shift of AS</td></tr>
<tr><td>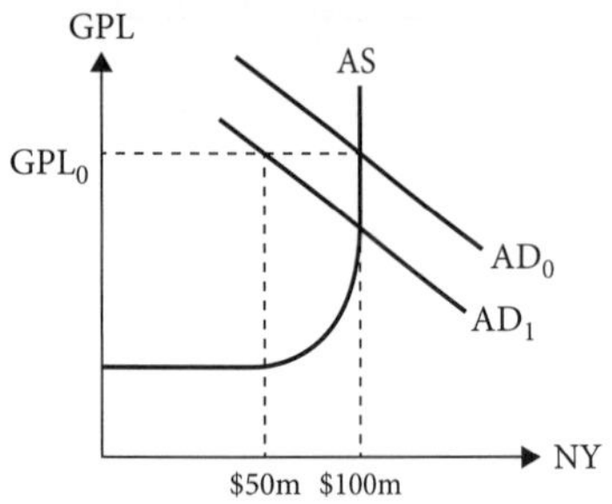
</td><td>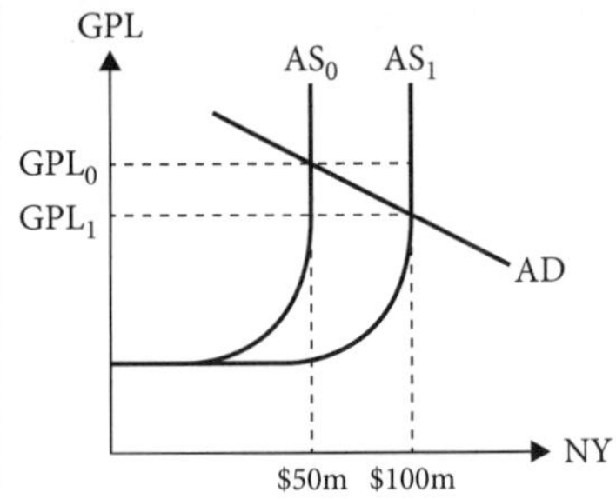
</td></tr>
<tr><td>Original equilibrium:

GPL = GPL$_0$

AD = AS = $100 m

With decrease in AD from AD_0 to AD_1:

At GPL$_0$,

AD = $50 m

AS = $100 m</td><td>Original equilibrium:

GPL = GPL$_0$

AD = AS = $50 m

With rightward shift of AS from AS_0 to AS_1:

At GPL$_0$,

AD = $50 m

AS = $100 m</td></tr>
<tr><td colspan="2">(Explanation is the same for both scenarios)

AD ($50 m) is less than AS ($100 m). Inventories run up. Firms respond by trying to decrease output. However, the situation is one where there is still sufficient demand for the factors of production to be fully employed, even when the demand for them decreases. Hence, national output does not decrease at all while prices of factors of production decrease. Hence, average cost decreases without a decrease in national output, causing a pure decrease in GPL (vertical movement down AS). At the same time, because GPL decreases, national expenditure increases (downward movement along AD). This continues until equilibrium is reached when AD = AS.

Final equilibrium: GPL$_1$ and NY of $100 m</td></tr>
</table>

Most economies seldom find themselves on the horizontal and vertical segments of the AS curve. So, for most part, only the explanations for when the disequilibrium occurs at the upward-sloping part of the AS curve (Page 240 to 241) would be relevant.

5.2.6 The multiplier effect of changes in AD

Thus far, we have analysed how changes in factors that affect AD and AS will affect the GPL and NY in terms of whether GPL and NY would increase or decrease. We now look at the extent to which NY will increase when there is a change in AD.[23]

23 The extent to which NY changes when there is a change in AS is outside the scope of this book. Nonetheless, interested students can look up factors determining the slope of the AD if they are interested.

The multiplier effect

The multiplier effect is the effect of a multiplied change in NY when there is a change in AD. For example, if AD increases by \$1 m, the eventual increase in NY will be a multiple of \$1 m (e.g., \$2 m or \$3 m). This relationship is expressed as:

$$\Delta \text{NY} = k(\Delta \text{AD})$$

The multiplier is represented by the letter *k*.

The explanation for the multiplier effect is as follows (Fig. 5.13). We will assume that the economy is operating at the horizontal part of the AS curve for simplicity's sake. This allows us to ignore changes in GPL for now.

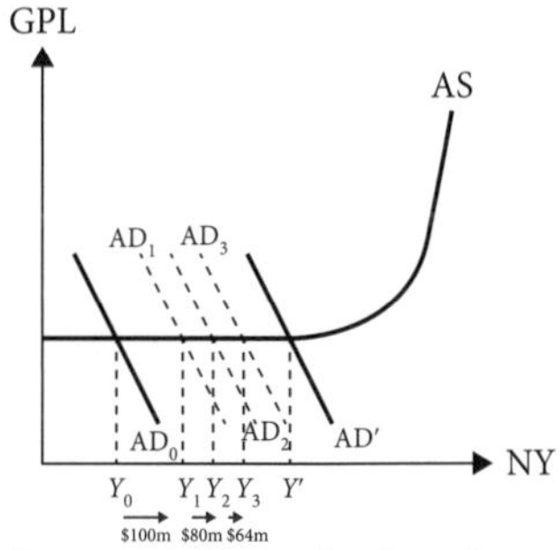

Figure 5.13: The multiplier effect.

Suppose the AD increases by \$100 m (due to an increase in *C* or *I* or *G* or (*X* – *M*)) and shifts from AD_0 to AD_1. This means that national expenditure increases by \$100 m. There will hence, be a running down of inventories of \$100 m. Firms will respond by increasing production by \$100 m. Hence, national output will increase by \$100 m from Y_0 to Y_1. National income would also increase by the same amount since the increased production of output will generate an equal increase in income (recall that national output is always equal to national income). The increased national income would cause consumers to consume more goods. For this illustration, let's take it that 80% of every increase in income will be consumed domestically. So, the increase in national income from Y_0 to Y_1 would cause *C* to increase by \$80 m through domestic consumption. This increase in *C* causes another shift from AD_1 to AD_2. However, the shift from AD_1 to AD_2 is smaller than the shift from AD_0 to AD_1. This is because only 80% of the increase in national income is consumed domestically as some of the increase in income would be saved, taxed by the government, or spent on imports (withdrawn from the circular flow of income). As AD shifts from AD_1 to AD_2, there will now be a running down of inventories of \$80 m. Again, firms will respond by producing \$80 m more output. This increase in national output will again mean an increase in national income of \$80 m from Y_1 to Y_2. This increase in income will again cause an increase in domestic consumption of \$64 m (80% of the increase in income of \$80 m). This will then cause another round of running down of inventories and increased production such that national output and national income increases by \$64 m from Y_2 to Y_3. The cycle of increased income, inducing increased domestic consumption, which causes more increase in income, will then continue. However, the cycle does not go on indefinitely as each round of increased domestic consumption is smaller than the last due to the leakages in the form of savings, taxes, and spending on imports. As such,

AD will eventually settle at AD′ when all of the original increase in AD has been leaked out. At the end of the process, we can see that national income decreases from Y_0 to Y′, which is a multiple of the original increase of AD of $100 m.

The multiplier works in reverse too (Fig. 5.14). A reduction in AD can cause a multiplied reduction in national income.[24]

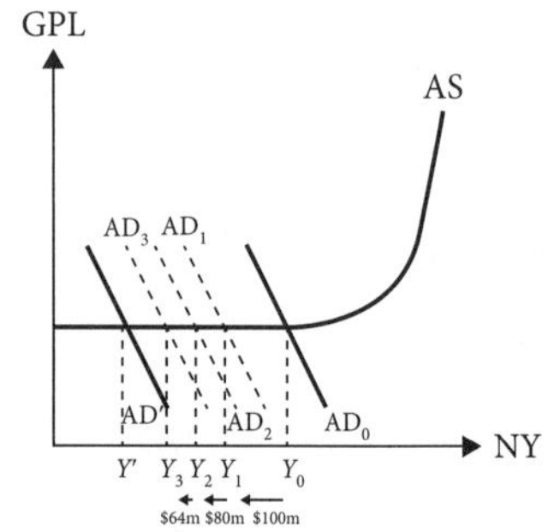

Figure 5.14: The multiplier in reverse

Suppose the AD decreases by $100 m (due to an increase in *C* or *I* or *G* or (*X* – *M*)) and shifts from AD_0 to AD_1. This means that national expenditure decreases by $100 m. There will hence, be a running up of inventories of $100 m. Firms will respond by decreasing production by $100 m. Hence, national output will decrease by $100 m from Y_0 to Y_1. National income would also decrease by the same amount since the decreased production of output will cause an equal decrease in income (recall that national output is always equal to national income). The decreased national income would cause consumers to consume less goods. For this illustration, let's take it that 80% of the decrease in income will be a reduction in domestic consumption. This is because when incomes fall, households would not only cut back on domestic consumption. They would also reduce their savings, pay less taxes, and spend less on imports. So, the decrease in national income from Y_0 to Y_1 would cause *C* to decrease by $80 m through reduction in domestic consumption (savings, taxes, and spending on imports decreased by $20 m to make up the $100 m decrease in national income). This decrease in *C* causes another shift from AD_1 to AD_2. However, the shift from AD_1 to AD_2 is smaller than the shift from AD_0 to AD_1. This is because only 80% of the decrease in national income is translated into a reduction in domestic consumption (20% of the fall in income is translated into lower savings, lower taxes, and lower spending on imports). As AD shifts from AD_1 to AD_2, there will now be a running up of inventories of $80 m. Again, firms will respond by producing $80 m less output. This decrease in national output will again mean a decrease in national income of $80 m from Y_1 to Y_2. This decrease in income will again cause a decrease in domestic consumption of $64 m (80% of the decrease in income of $80 m). This will then cause another round of running up of inventories and decreased production such that national output and national income decreases by $64 m from Y_2 to Y_3. The cycle of decreased income causing decreased domestic consumption, which causes more decrease in income, will then continue. However, the cycle does not go on indefinitely as each round of decreased domestic

24 Surprisingly, it seems much harder to explain the multiplier in reverse.

consumption is smaller than the last, due to some of the decreases in income translating into decreases in leakages, in the form of less savings, less taxes, and less spending on imports. As such, AD will eventually settle at AD′ when all of the original decrease in AD has been matched by the decrease in withdrawals. At the end of the process, we can see that national income decreased from Y_0 to Y', which is a multiple of the original decrease of AD of \$100 m.

The size of the multiplier

The larger the proportion of additional income that is consumed domestically (80% in our examples before), the larger the multiplier will be. The intuition is quite simple.

When income increases during the multiplier process, the larger the proportion of additional income that is consumed domestically, the larger the subsequent rightward shift of the AD, and the larger the next round of increase in income will be. Hence, the larger the proportion of additional income that is consumed domestically, the larger the eventual increase in national income.

The logic is the same when the multiplier works in reverse. When income decreases in the multiplier process, the larger the proportion of additional income that is consumed domestically, the larger the fall in domestic consumption when incomes decrease. Hence, the subsequent leftward shift of the AD would be larger, causing a larger fall in income in the next round. In summary, the larger the proportion of additional income that is consumed domestically, the larger the eventual increase in national income.

The proportion of additional income that is consumed domestically is known as the marginal propensity to consume (domestic) (MPC_D). The higher the MPC_D, the larger the multiplier. The direct relationship between the two can be expressed as the following.[25]

$$k = \frac{1}{1 - MPC_D}$$

Definition(s):

The **marginal propensity to consume (domestic) (MPC_D)** is the proportion of additional income that is consumed domestically.

The **marginal propensity to save (MPS)** is the proportion of additional income that is saved.

The **marginal propensity to tax (MPT)** is the proportion of additional income that is taxed.

The **marginal propensity to import (MPM)** is the proportion of additional income that is spent on imports.

The **marginal propensity to withdraw (MPW)** is the proportion of additional income that is withdrawn as savings, taxes, or spending on imports. MPW is the sum of MPS, MPT, and MPM. MPW = MPS + MPT + MPM

25 Refer to Annex 5.6 for the derivation of the formula for the multiplier.

When households receive additional income, all of it must either be spent on domestic consumption, saved, taxed, or spent on imports. Hence, $MPC_D + MPS + MPT + MPM = 1$. So, the formula for the multiplier can also be written as:

$$k = \frac{1}{1 - MPC_D} = \frac{1}{(MPS + MPT + MPM)}$$

And since $MPS + MPT + MPM = MPW$,

$$k = \frac{1}{1 - MPC_D} = \frac{1}{(MPS + MPT + MPM)} = \frac{1}{MPW}$$

This means that the multiplier (k) and MPW have an inverse relationship. The higher the MPW, the smaller the multiplier. Factors that cause MPW to be high will cause the multiplier to be small. This will be revisited in Chapter 6 when we study macroeconomic policies.

Dampened multiplier effect

In the explanation of the multiplier effect in the preceding paragraphs, we made a simplifying assumption that the economy was operating at the horizontal portion of the AS curve. As such, the full extent of the increase in AD translated into the increase in NY. However, if the economy was operating at/near the upward sloping portion of the AS curve, some of the increase in AD would have translated into a rise in GPL instead. The extent of increase in NY is reduced and we say that the multiplier effect is dampened. The difference in the extent of the increase in NY is shown in the following table.

<table>
<tr><th>Full multiplier effect</th><th>Dampened multiplier effect</th></tr>
<tr><td>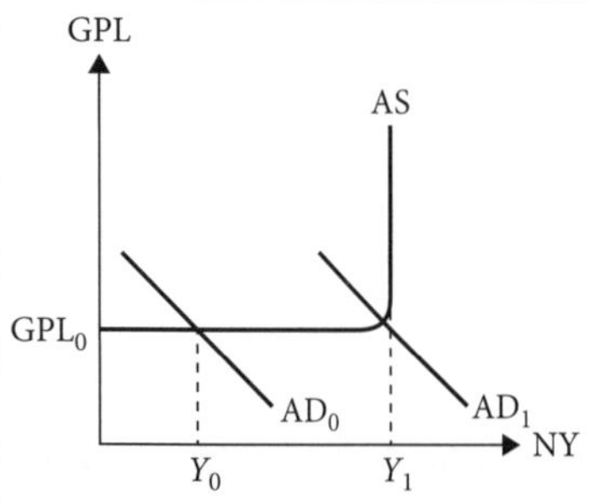
</td><td>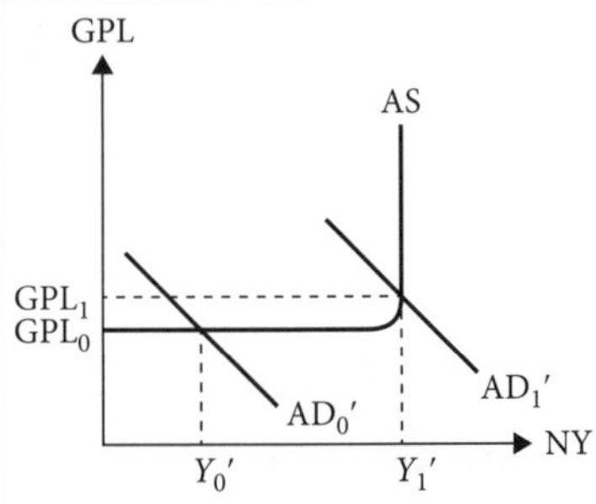
</td></tr>
<tr><td>When AD increases from AD_0 to AD_1, the full extent of the increase in AD is translated into an increase in NY from Y_0 to Y_1.</td><td>When AD increases from AD'_0 to AD'_1, only a part of the increase in AD is translated into an increase in NY from Y'_0 to Y'_1.

Some part of the increase in AD translates into a rise in GPL from GPL_0 to GPL_1 instead.</td></tr>
</table>

Summary for Chapter 5

1. The circular flow of income is a model for analysing the equilibrium in the economy.
2. In the circular flow of income, consumers pay money to firms for domestic consumption, and firms pay money to households as income payments for factors of production provided by households.
3. Withdrawals (W) from the circular flow are savings (*S*), taxes (*T*), and import expenditure (*M*). Injections (J) into the circular flow are investments (*I*), government expenditure (*G*), and export revenue (*X*).
4. Equilibrium is the circular flow of income reached when national expenditure (NE) equals national output (NY).
5. National output (NY) is always equal to national income (NY). So, at equilibrium, national expenditure (NE) equals national output (NY) equals national income (NY).
6. The AD–AS model is another model for analysing equilibrium in the economy. It differs from the circular flow of income as it takes the GPL into account.
7. As $AD = C + I + G + (X - M)$, factors affecting any of the components ($C, I, G, X - M$) would also affect AD, causing it to shift right when it increases or shift left when it decreases.
8. SRAS will shift up when the average cost of production in the economy increases, and shift down when it decreases. LRAS will shift left when the full-employment output decreases and right when it increases.
9. Equilibrium in the AD–AS model is reached when AD = AS. At this equilibrium, there is an equilibrium GPL as well as an equilibrium NY. Shifts in AD and/or AS will cause a new equilibrium to be established at a new GPL and NY.
10. The multiplier process explains how a change in AD will cause a multiplied increase in NY.
11. The extent to which NY changes when there is a change in AD is dependent on the size of the multiplier.
12. The size of the multiplier is directly related to the marginal propensity to consume (domestic) (MPC_D) and inversely related to the marginal propensity to withdraw (MPW).

Annex 5.1 Planned expenditure versus actual expenditure approach to determining equilibrium national output

The other approach to determining equilibrium in the circular flow of income is the planned expenditure versus actual expenditure approach. In this approach, planned expenditure refers to how much consumers, firms, governments, and foreign consumers plan to spend ("national expenditure" in the main text) and actual expenditure refers to how much consumers, firms, governments, and foreign consumers actually spend. For consumers, governments, and foreign consumers, the planned and actual expenditure are the same. For firms, however, planned investment and actual investment can differ. This is because a build-up of inventories is considered an investment too (i.e., inventory is considered capital). So, if inventories build up, planned investment is less than actual investment. Conversely, if inventories run down, we say that planned investment is more than actual investment.

This approach actually only involves a name change compared to the main text. The comparison between the two approaches is shown in the following table to show how the explanations for how equilibrium is reached in each approach do not differ.

	National expenditure versus National output approach (main text)	**Planned expenditure versus Actual expenditure approach (Annex 5.1)**
Equilibrium condition	National expenditure = National output	Planned expenditure = Actual expenditure
Inventories run down when . . .	National expenditure > National output	Planned expenditure > Actual expenditure
Firms respond by . . .	Increasing production	Increasing production
New equilibrium is reached when . . .	National output rises until it becomes equal to the national expenditure	Actual expenditure rises until it becomes equal to planned expenditure
Inventories run up when . . .	National expenditure < National output	Planned expenditure < Actual expenditure
Firms respond by . . .	Decreasing production	Decreasing production
New equilibrium is reached when . . .	National output falls until it becomes equal to the national expenditure	Actual expenditure falls until it becomes equal to planned expenditure

Annex 5.2 Explaining why the aggregate demand curve slopes downwards

The AD curve and the demand curve (for a single good) slope downwards for different reasons. For the demand curve, the downward slope is obtained by changing the price of the good while holding the prices of other goods constant. For the AD curve, a change in the general price level (GPL) means that the prices of all goods are changed.

The aggregate demand curve slopes downwards for three reasons—the wealth effect, the interest rate effect, and the exchange rate effect.

1. The wealth effect
   When the GPL decreases, all goods become cheaper. Thus, the real value of households' wealth increases (i.e., the wealth of households can be used to buy more goods and services). This increase in the real value of households' wealth increases consumption. Since consumption (*C*) is a part of national expenditure, national expenditure increases when GPL decreases, giving rise to a downward-sloping AD.
2. The interest rate effect
   When the GPL decreases, households do not need to hold on to as much cash as before for transaction purposes. Hence, they will save the excess cash to try to get some returns in the form of interest. The increase in savings means that banks have a greater supply of funds to loan out. The increase in supply of loans would reduce the price of loans, which is the interest rate. When interest rate decreases, the cost of borrowing decreases and stimulates *C* and investment (*I*). Since both *C* and *I* are components of national expenditure, national expenditure increases when GPL decreases, giving rise to a downward-sloping AD.
3. The exchange rate effect
   In response to the lower interest rates domestically (from the interest rate effect), domestic financial investors may decide to move their money abroad to earn better interest rates. To do so, the domestic financial investors need to convert the domestic currency to foreign currency. This will require them to sell the domestic currency in exchange for foreign currency. Selling the domestic currency increases the supply of the domestic currency in the foreign exchange market. This will reduce the price of the domestic currency in terms of foreign currency (i.e., the domestic currency will depreciate). A depreciation will make exports cheaper to foreign consumers and imports more expensive to locals. Foreigners will buy more exports while locals will buy less imports. Since $X - M$ is a component of national expenditure, national expenditure increases when GPL decreases, giving rise to a downward-sloping AD.

In summary, the AD slopes downwards because a fall in GPL would increase national expenditure by increasing real wealth, reducing interest rates, and causing a depreciation.

Annex 5.3 An alternative way of deriving the AS curves

A different way of deriving the aggregate supply is to analyse how the general price level (GPL) affects the profitability of firms' production and hence, determines how much output is produced. In this approach, we distinguish between the short-run aggregate supply (SRAS) and long-run aggregate supply (LRAS) by changing the assumptions that underpin them.

In deriving the SRAS, we assume that wages are "sticky." This means to say that wages do not change very much. When the GPL increases, if wages are "sticky," firms find it profitable to increase production. This is because each unit of their output can be sold for a higher price while maintaining the same cost since wage rates remain unchanged. Hence, an increase in GPL would result in an increase in national output, giving rise to an upward sloping SRAS.

In deriving the LRAS, we assume that wages are perfectly flexible. As such, wage rates will always adjust such that full employment is reached. If there is unemployment (surplus of labour), wages will fall and employment would rise until full employment is reached. If the is a shortage of workers, wages will rise until equilibrium is established again when the shortage is eliminated and full employment is attained. By this reasoning, the national output would always be at the full-employment output regardless of what the GPL is. The LRAS is hence, a vertical line at Y_f.

The SRAS and LRAS are illustrated together in the following figure.

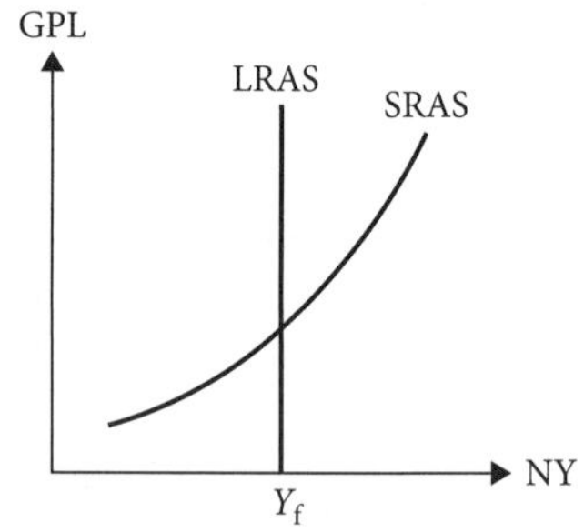

So, in the short run, when wages are sticky, we would use the SRAS for our AD–AS analysis but if the period of analysis is long (e.g., we want to know the effects of a change in AD 10 years later), we would use the LRAS.

In this derivation of the SRAS and LRAS, the reasons for the shifts in SRAS and LRAS are the same of the ones in the main text. Changes in average cost of production would shift the SRAS and changes in the full-employment output would shift the LRAS.

Annex 5.4 Why interest rate as the return to savings will be similar to interest rates as the cost of borrowing

Let us name the interest rate as the return to savings r_S and the interest rate as the cost of borrowing r_C.

r_C should be more than r_S as the difference between them is what the banks earn. If $r_C \leq r_S$, banks would not benefit from accepting deposits and making loans as their earnings from making loans would be less than their cost of giving interest payments to their depositors. Therefore, r_C must be more than r_S.

However, the gap between r_C and r_S should be very small as a result of competition between banks. Suppose Bank A offers $r_C = 5\%$ and $r_S = 1\%$. Bank A earns 4% (5% – 1%) on every dollar of savings that they loan out. Another bank, Bank B, could try to "steal" Bank A's depositors by offering $r_S = 1.5\%$ and "steal" Bank A's loans by offering a lower r_C of 4.5 %. Doing so is still in Bank B's interest as Bank B still earn 3% (4.5% – 1.5%) on every dollar of savings that they loan out. At this point, Bank C could come along and steal Bank B's business like what Bank B did to Bank A by offering $r_C = 4\%$ and $r_S = 2\%$. Doing so is also in Bank C's interest as Bank C earns of 2% (4% – 2%) on every dollar of savings that they loan out.

In this example, every new competitor drives down the r_C (r_C decreased from 5% to 4.5% to 4%) and drives up the r_S (r_S increased from 1% to 1.5% to 2%). In general, so long as there is a gap between r_C and r_S, a new bank can enter the picture and "steal" depositors and loans by offering a slightly higher r_S and a slightly lower r_C. Of course, there must be some minimum gap between r_C and r_S, such that any smaller gap would result in the earnings being less than the cost of running a bank. When this minimum gap is reached, no banks would try to further undercut the other banks, as doing so would result in a loss. The competition amongst banks will drive the gap between r_C and r_S towards this minimum possible gap. This explains why r_C and r_S are closely linked and will increase or decrease together.

Annex 5.5 The Mathematical Derivation of the Multiplier

This annex shows the mathematical derivation for $k = \frac{1}{1 - MPC_D}$

It will require knowledge of the sum to infinity of a convergent geometric series.

Let the initial increase in AD be *a*

The **first round of increase in income** would be *a*.

The first round of induced consumption would be $MPC_D.a$

The **second round of increase in income** would then be $MPC_D.a$

The second round of induced consumption would be $MPC_D(MPC_D.a) = MPC_D{}^2.a$

The **third round of increase in income** would then be $MPC_D{}^2.a$

And the cycle continues with continued rounds of increases in income.

The sum of all the increases in income $\Delta Y = a + MPC_D.a + MPC_D{}^2.a + MPC_D{}^3.a + ...$

We can rewrite this as $$\Delta Y = a(1 + MPC_D + MPC_D{}^2 + MPC_D{}^3 + ...)$$

The parts in the parenthesis at the right-hand side of the equation is actually the sum to infinity of a convergent geometric series with MPC_D as the common ratio.

So $$\Delta Y = a\left(\frac{1}{1 - MPC_D}\right)$$

Since *a* is the original increase in AD, $\left(\frac{1}{1 - MPC_D}\right)$ must be the multiplier.

Hence, $$k = \frac{1}{1 - MPC_D}$$

CHAPTER 6

MACROECONOMIC AIMS, PROBLEMS, AND POLICIES

The previous chapter introduced the aggregate demand–aggregate supply model as a tool for analysing the macroeconomy. In this chapter, we explore the standard of living in a country and the four aspects of a country's macroeconomic performance. The four aspects are economic growth, price stability, full employment, and a favourable balance of payments (BOP) position. For each aspect, we study the indicators to measure them, causes of strong/weak performance, and finally policies to correct them. We first start with understanding the standard of living.

6.1 The Standard of Living

The standard of living in a country refers to the average well-being of residents of a country. There are two aspects to well-being—material well-being and non-material well-being. Material well-being refers to the ability of the average resident to consume goods and services. Non-material well-being refers to the more qualitative aspects of life such as health, literacy, stress levels, and amount of greenery enjoyed by the individual.

6.1.1 Measuring the material standard of living

The material standard of living of a country can be measured by calculating the average income in that country. To do so, we need to take the total income of a country and divide it by the population. There are two ways to think about the total income of a country. One way is to define the total income of a country as the total income generated in a country. The other way is to define the total income earned by residents in a country. The two numbers may be different, as will be illustrated in subsequent paragraphs.

For the first way, since the total income generated in a country should be equal to the total output of a country (recall from Chapter 5 that national income equals national product), we can compute the total income generated in a country by adding up the value of all the output generated in that country. This number is also known as the Gross Domestic Product (GDP).

Definition(s):

Gross Domestic Product (GDP) is the total monetary value of all final goods and services produced within the geographical boundary of a country over a period of time, usually a year.

First, the GDP is a monetary value. So, if 100 chairs were produced in Singapore and each chair has a price of $25, these 100 chairs would add $2,500 (100 × $25) to Singapore's GDP.

Second, the GDP only includes the monetary value of the final goods and services. Intermediate goods and services are not included because there would be double counting if they were. Let us look at an example. Suppose an organic durian was harvested in Singapore and sold to a smoothie producer at a price of $50. Suppose this smoothie producer then used this durian to produce 10 durian smoothies and sold them at $12 each. The $120 worth of durian smoothies would already include the $50 value of the durian. So, in calculating Singapore's GDP, we would include the $120 worth of smoothies (since they are final goods) but not the $50 durian (since it was an intermediate good used to produce the smoothies). Including the $50 would be double counting since it is already a part of the $120.

Third, the GDP is bounded by geography. So, the output produced by Singaporean-owned factories overseas would not be counted.

Finally, the GDP is usually calculated for a year.

The other way to think about total income of a country is to think of it as the total income generated by the residents of a country. In this case, we would add up the incomes generated by all factors of production owned by residents of a country regardless of whether these factors of production were located in the country. This number is also known as the Gross National Income (GNI).

Definition(s):

Gross National Income (GNI) is the total monetary value of all final goods and services produced by factors of production owned by residents of a country over a period of time, usually a year.

The GNI can be derived from the GDP. Since the GDP is the total monetary value of all final goods and services produced within the geographical boundary of a country, to compute the GNI, we can remove the value of the final goods and services produced by foreign-owned factors of production, and include the value of final goods and services produced by locally owned factors of production overseas. An illustration to distinguish the two is provided in Fig. 6.1.

In mathematical notation

$$\text{GNI} = \text{GDP} + \text{Factor income from abroad} - \text{Factor income to abroad}$$
$$= \text{GDP} + \text{Net factor income from abroad}$$

Once we obtain the GDP or GNI, we can divide it by the population of a country to obtain the GDP per capita or GNI per capita. Both are measures of the average income in a country.

$$\text{GDP per capita} = \text{GDP}/\text{Population}$$
$$\text{GNI per capita} = \text{GNI}/\text{Population}$$

Figure 6.1: Illustrating the difference between GDP and GNI.

Now that we know how to compute GDP or GNI per capita, we should notice that it is not useful to just compute the GDP or GNI per capita for a country for a given year. For example, knowing that Singapore's GNI per capita was S$70,828 in 2017 is not meaningful. What is of interest is whether it has increased over time or whether it is higher than another country's. We call the former a comparison across time and the latter a comparison across space.

6.1.2 Comparing the standard of living over time using real GDP/GNI per capita

Recall that both GDP and GNI were total monetary values of final goods and services. In computing these monetary values, we have to use the prices of goods and services. However, prices could change over time. Hence, we could compute the GDP or GNI using "old" prices or "current" prices. This difference is known as "real" and "nominal".

Definition(s):

Real GDP refers to GDP calculated using base year prices. It removes the effect of price changes.

Nominal GDP refers to GDP calculated using current year prices. It does not remove the effect of price changes.

We illustrate the difference using an example. Suppose the following applied to Singapore.

Year	No. of chairs produced	Price of each chair	Nominal GDP (value of output at current year price)	Real GDP (value of output at base year price)
2010 (base year)	100	**$12**	$1,200 (100 × $12)	$1,200 (100 × **$12**)
2011	120	$15	$1,800 (120 × $15)	$1,440 (120 × **$12**)
2012	150	$18	$2,700 (150 × $18)	$1,800 (150 × **$12**)

The change in real GDP can also be approximated from the change in nominal GDP:

$$\% \text{ change in real GDP} = \% \text{ change in nominal GDP} - \% \text{ change in prices}$$

For comparisons across time, after we compute the real GDP, we divide it by the population to obtain the real GDP per capita[1]. We then observe the changes in the real GDP per capita. In the process, we hold the prices constant at the base year prices ($12 in the example above) so that changes in the real GDP per capita would be because the amount of goods and services actually produced on average changes as opposed to having the figure change simply due to changes in prices.

1 We could also use real GNI per capita but because it is troublesome to keep typing "GDP or GNI", we will stick to just typing "GDP". Nonetheless, the arguments also apply to GNI.

An increase in the real GDP per capita over time would mean that on average, real incomes (i.e., purchasing power) have increased. This means that material standard of living has improved over time as more goods and services can now be consumed by the average person. Conversely, a reduction in real GDP per capita over time means that material standard of living has worsened.

6.1.3 Limitations of comparing the standard of living over time using real GDP/GNI per capita

There are limitations to using real GDP or GNI per capita to compare whether the standard of living has improved over time. These include not taking into account

- Changes in income distribution
- Changes in non-material aspects of the standard of living
- Changes in the composition of the GDP
- Changes in the amount of unrecorded transactions

Changes in income distribution

An increase in the real GDP per capita over time may not mean an improvement in the standard of living for the average person if most of this increase in income is experienced only by a small group of rich people. In mathematical terms, the real GDP per capita is the mean income. This could increase without the median income increasing. Conversely, a reduction in the real GDP per capita might not imply a worsening of the standard of living for most people if it is only experienced by a small group of people.

Putting it concretely: Accounting for changes in income distribution: The Gini coefficient

To take into account changes in the income distribution, we first need a measure of the income distribution. One common measure is the Gini coefficient[2]. The Gini coefficient goes from 0 to 1, with 0 being a state of perfect equality (every single person having the same income) and 1 being a state of perfect inequality (one person in the country earning 100% of the country's income). Both 0 and 1 are very unlikely extremes. Most countries find themselves somewhere in between. The coefficient is sometimes scaled to 100. In such cases, a Gini coefficient of 0.42 would show up as 42. It is usually quite apparent whether one is working with scaled Gini coefficients since the Gini coefficient cannot exceed one without scaling.

The Gini coefficient can be used to supplement the real GDP per capita in analysing whether the standard of living has improved or worsened over time. Increases in the Gini coefficient would mean that incomes have become more unequal while decreases mean that they have become more equal. A constant Gini coefficient would mean that there is

2 The computation of the Gini coefficient can be found in Annex 6.1.

no change in the degree of inequality. Such information can help us determine whether changes in the real GDP per capita are due to increases in incomes for mainly the rich, the poor, or everyone. This can be summarised in the tables below.

If an increase in the real GDP per capita is accompanied by . . .

. . . an increase in the Gini coefficient:	The increase in incomes is mostly experienced by the rich since incomes have become more unequally distributed. Standard of living is unlikely to have improved for the median person.
. . . no change in the Gini coefficient:	The increase in incomes is experienced equally by everyone since there is no change in the income distribution. Standard of living is likely to have improved for the median person.
. . . a decrease in the Gini coefficient:	The increase in incomes is mostly experienced by the poor since incomes have become less unequally distributed. Standard of living is likely to have improved for the median person.

If a decrease in the real GDP per capita is accompanied by . . .

. . . an increase in the Gini coefficient:	The decrease in incomes is mostly experienced by the poor since incomes have become more unequally distributed. Standard of living is likely to have worsened for the median person.
. . . no change in the Gini coefficient:	The decrease in incomes is experienced equally by everyone since there is no change in the income distribution. Standard of living is likely to have worsened for the median person.
. . . a decrease in the Gini coefficient:	The decrease in incomes is mostly experienced by the rich since incomes have become less unequally distributed. Standard of living is unlikely to have worsened for the median person.

Note that the Gini coefficient supplements the real GDP per capita information. It is meant to be used together with information about the changes in the real GDP per capita. Changes in the Gini coefficient itself do not tell us whether the standard of living in the country has worsened or improved.

Changes in non-material aspects of the standard of living

An increase in the real GDP per capita over time may not mean an improvement in the standard of living if the non-material aspects worsen by a greater extent over the same period. For example, if average incomes increase but the living environment gets increasingly polluted and causes peoples' health to suffer, the overall standard of living may actually worsen. Conversely, a reduction in the real GDP per capita may not mean a worsening of the standard of living if the non-material aspects of the standard of living improve more.

Putting it concretely: Accounting for changes in non-material standard of living: The Human Development Index (HDI)

To also take into account, some non-material aspects of the standard of living, economists sometimes use the HDI[3] to measure changes in the standard of living instead. The HDI is a composite index made up of three dimensions—the (material) standard of living, health, and education. These are measured using real GNI per capita; life expectancy at birth; and the expected and mean years of schooling, respectively. Indices are calculated for each of the dimensions and then averaged to find give an overall index.

The HDI goes from 0 to 1, where a higher number reflects greater development (either because the real GNI per capita, health, or education indicators are better). Similar to the Gini coefficient, it is sometimes scaled to 100.

As the HDI is computed using both real GNI per capita and health and education indicators, it takes into account improvements in both material and some aspects of non-material standards of living. So, to account for changes in the non-material standard of living when deciding whether the standard of living in a country has improved, we could see if the HDI has increased over time. Unlike the Gini coefficient, we would not use the HDI to supplement the real GDP per capita information. We would replace it.

Changes in the composition of the GDP

An increase in the real GDP per capita over time may not show an improvement in the standard of living if the composition of the real GDP changes too. Recall that the real GDP measures the value of the output produced in a country at base year prices. The composition of the real GDP refers to percentage of each type of goods and services that are produced in a country. Referring back to the components of aggregate demand in the previous chapter, goods and services can be classified into consumption (consumer goods and services produced for households inclusive of imports), investment (capital goods and services produced for firms), government spending (goods and services produced for the government), and net exports (goods and services produced for foreigners minus imports). Of these components, only consumption and government spending (depending on what the government spends on) could have an impact on the current standard of living. This is because capital goods (investments) are clearly not consumed by households and will not have an impact on the current standard of living; exports are consumed by foreigners and will thus, also not have an impact on the standard of living in a country; and imports are already counted under consumption. An increase in real GDP per capita without an increase in consumption would mean that incomes increased but households have not spent more on consumer goods. They may have saved the increase in incomes. In that case, the standard of living would not have increased since households have not purchased more consumer goods. The future standard of living may improve since the current savings can be used to purchase consumer goods and

3 Please refer to http://hdr.undp.org/en/content/human-development-index-hdi for more details regarding the HDI.

services in the future. In general, to be sure that increases in the real GDP per capita reflect improvements in the standard of living, the percentage share of consumption in the GDP should be at least constant.

Putting it concretely: Composition of the real GDP affecting current and future standard of living

We have seen that only consumption and government spending affect the current standard of living. However, if we expand the analysis to include how the future standard of living may be affected by the composition of the real GDP, we find that the other components play a role too. This is summarised in the table below.

Component	Implication
Consumption ©	The higher the current level of consumption, the higher the current standard of living.
Investment (*I*)	The higher the current level of investments, the more capital goods are currently produced, the more capital goods there will be to produce consumer goods in the future, the higher the future standard of living.
Government spending (*G*)	This depends on what the government spends on. The higher the government spending on providing consumer goods to households, the higher the current standard of living. The higher the government spending on providing capital goods (e.g., building infrastructure), the higher the future standard of living.
Net Exports (*X* –*M*)	No effect on the standard of living. The level of import spending could affect current or future standard of living depending on whether consumer goods or capital goods are imported. However, that would already be captured under consumption and investment, respectively.

Changes in the amount of unrecorded transactions

An increase in the real GDP per capita over time may not mean an improvement in the standard of living as the real GDP does not take into account unrecorded transactions. In measuring the real GDP, only values of goods and services transacted in the market are included as only such goods and services have market prices that can be used to compute the value of the good (recall that the value of a good in the real GDP is its base year price). However, there could be goods and services produced and consumed in an economy that go unrecorded. For example, independent contractors may not declare their full activity (and hence, income) to avoid taxes. There could also be illegal activities (e.g., importing contraband cigarettes) that may be unrecorded. Such illegal activities belong to what is termed the "underground" or "shadow" economy. Apart from the shadow economy, non-market goods and services may also be unrecorded. Non-market goods and services refer to goods and services that are not transacted in the market (in contrast, in the underground economy, transactions do take place, just like in a black market). For example, cleaning one's own home is a service to oneself that is not recorded. Such unrecorded transactions cause the real GDP per capita to understate the standard of living as they are also goods and services consumed by households. And they make comparisons over time inaccurate as an increase in real GDP per capita could be offset by a reduction in the amount of unrecorded activities, causing a limited improvement in the standard of living. For example, if two neighbouring farmers stopped trading their produce directly with each other and sold them at the market to obtain income to buy the other's produce, the real GDP per capita would increase even though both farmers enjoy the same amount of goods and services as before.

6.1.4 Comparing the standard of living over space using GDP/GNI per capita converted using purchasing power parity exchange rates

Having looked at how the real GDP per capita can be used to compare changes in the standard of living over time and its limitations, we move to look at comparing the standard of living between countries (i.e., comparing the standard of living across space). In this case, we are interested in whether one country has a higher standard of living compared to another country at a particular point in time (e.g., whether Singapore has a higher standard of living than Malaysia in 2018).

We do so by converting the GDP or GNI per capita of each country into a common currency using the purchasing power parity (PPP) exchange rate. It is necessary to convert each country's GDP or GNI per capita into a common currency for comparison as each country's GDP or GNI per capita would be in its own domestic currency (e.g., Singapore's GDP per capita would be in Singapore dollars (SGD) while Malaysia's would be in Malaysian ringgit [MYR]). We cannot simply use the market exchange rate (i.e., the exchange rate that we see in the money exchange) to do the conversion as the market exchange rate may not reflect the relative cost of living in each country. For example, the market exchange rate between the SGD and MYR was about 1:3 in 2017. If we used this exchange rate, a Singapore resident earning 1000SGD a month in 2017 would appear to have a standard of living that is three times of a Malaysian resident earning 1000MYR a month in 2017. However, this could be inaccurate because the Singapore resident earning 1000SGD may not be able to purchase three times as much goods and services in Singapore compared to what the Malaysian resident can purchase in Malaysia. This is because the cost of goods and services in Malaysia (in MYR) may be less than three times the cost in Singapore (in SGD). For example, a bar of chocolate may cost 1SGD in Singapore and 2MYR in Malaysia. In that case, the Singapore resident earning 1000SGD would be able to buy 1000 bars of chocolate every month, whereas the Malaysian resident would be able to buy 500 chocolate bars a month. The standard of living of the Singapore resident is only twice that of the Malaysian resident (1000 chocolate bars a month compared to 500 chocolate bars a month) instead of three times, which is what the conversion using the market exchange rate would have implied. This is summarised in the table below.

	Singapore	Malaysia
GDP per capita (in domestic currency)	1000SGD	1000MYR
GDP per capita (in SGD) using market exchange rate of 1SGD = 3MYR	1000SGD	333.33SGD
Implication for standard of living	Standard of living in Singapore is three times that in Malaysia (1000SGD vs. 333.33SGD)	
No. of chocolate bars that the GDP per capita can buy in each country (assuming price in Singapore is 1SGD and price in Malaysia is 2MYR)	1000 (1000SGD/1SGD per chocolate)	500 (1000MYR/2MYR per chocolate)
Implication for standard of living	Standard of living in Singapore only two times that in Malaysia (1000 chocolates vs. 500 chocolates)	

The above problem happens because the market exchange rate 1SGD = 3MYR does not reflect the relative cost of living of 1SGD for one chocolate in Singapore and 2MYR for one chocolate in Malaysia.

So, to avoid the inaccuracy of using the market exchange rate to convert the GDP per capita into a common currency for comparison, economists use the PPP exchange rate instead. The PPP exchange rate is an exchange rate that reflects the relative cost of living. In the above example, the PPP exchange rate would be 1SGD = 2MYR since that is the cost of a bar of chocolate in each country. We call this the PPP exchange rate because by reflecting the cost of living, the purchasing power of the currencies is kept equal (i.e., 1SGD has the same purchasing power as 2MYR; both can purchase exactly one chocolate bar).

Definition(s):

The **purchasing power parity (PPP) exchange rate** is a conversion rate that reflects the cost of living in each country such that purchasing power is maintained after conversion.

After calculating the PPP exchange rate[3], economists can then use it to convert the GDP per capita of each country into a common currency to determine which country has a higher standard of living. This is summarised in Fig. 6.2 below.

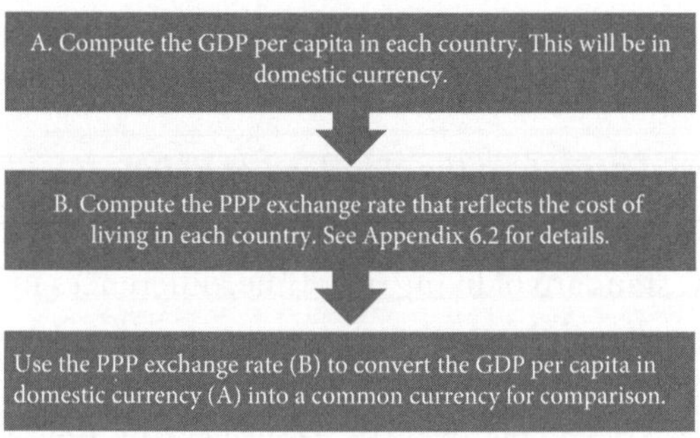

Figure 6.2: Steps to compare the standard of living across space.

4 Refer to Annex 6.2 for details of how to compute the PPP exchange rate

6.1.5 Limitations of comparing the standard of living over time using GDP/GNI per capita converted using PPP exchange rates

There are limitations to using GDP or GNI per capita converted using PPP exchange rates to compare whether one country has a higher standard of living than another. These include

- Differences in income distribution
- Differences in non-material aspects of the standard of living
- Differences in the composition of the GDP
- Differences in the amount of unrecorded transactions
- Difficulties in computing the PPP exchange rate

Differences in income distribution

Similar to how changes in the income distribution make it difficult to compare changes in the standard of living over time, differences in the income distribution between two countries make it difficult to determine whether one country has a higher standard of living than another. For example, the GNI per capita (at PPP) of Singapore was higher than Norway's in 2016. However, the Gini coefficient of Singapore was also higher than Norway's. This means that while the mean income in Singapore is higher than Norway's, the income in Singapore was more unevenly distributed. As such, it is hard to tell if the average (median) resident in Singapore earned a higher income than the average (median) resident in Norway. The Gini coefficient may help to give a better picture in some instances but not others. This is summarised in the table below.

If a GDP per capita (at PPP) of Country A > Country B, and . . .	
. . . Gini coefficient of A > B:	It is difficult to tell if the median income in Country A is higher than in Country B. It is difficult to determine which country has the higher standard of living.
. . . Gini coefficient of A = B	The median income in Country A is likely to be higher than in Country B. Standard of living in Country A is likely to be higher than in Country B.
. . . Gini coefficient of A < B	The median income in Country A is likely to be higher than in Country B. Standard of living in Country A is likely to be higher than in Country B.

Differences in non-material aspects of the standard of living

Similar to how changes in the non-material aspects of the standard of living make it difficult to compare changes in the standard of living over time, differences in the non-material aspects of the standard of living between two countries make it difficult to determine whether one country has a higher standard of living than another. For example, the GNI per capita (at PPP) of China was higher than Sri Lanka's in 2016. However, the pollution in China (especially Beijing) was also worse than Sri Lanka's (including the pollution in Colombo, its capital city). This makes it difficult to determine which country has the higher standard of living as one country has a higher material standard of living while the other has a better non-material standard of living. The HDI may be used instead to account for the education and health aspects of non-material standard of living (Sri Lanka's HDI was higher than China's). However, other aspects of non-material standard of living are still not reflected.

Differences in the composition of the GDP

Similar to how changes in the composition of the real GDP make it difficult to compare changes in the standard of living over time, differences in the composition of the GDP between two countries make it difficult to determine whether one country has a higher standard of living than another. For example, the GNI per capita (at PPP) of Singapore was higher than that of the United States in 2016. However, consumption's share of Singapore's GDP was only about 36% while it was about 69% for the United States. This makes it difficult to determine which country has the higher standard of living as one country has a higher average income (Singapore) but the other (United States) spends more of their income on consumer goods and services which causes it to enjoy a higher material standard of living.

Differences in the amount of unrecorded transactions

Similar to how changes in the amount of unrecorded transactions make it difficult to compare changes in the standard of living over time, differences in the amount of unrecorded transactions between two countries make it difficult to determine whether one country has a higher standard of living than another. This is especially so when we are trying to compare the standard of living between developed and developing countries. In developing countries, there is likely to be more subsistence farming where farm produce is consumed by the farmers' households instead of being sold in the markets. As such, the GDP per capita would understate the standard of living in developing countries more, compared to developed countries. This would cause the difference in the standard of living to appear larger than it actually is.

Difficulties in computing the PPP exchange rate

Finally, the comparisons across space could be inaccurate because of inaccuracies in the PPP exchange rate. This could happen because it is difficult to compute the PPP exchange rate in the first place. In the simple example we used in 6.1.4, the PPP exchange rate between SGD and MYR was simply based on the price of a bar of chocolate between two countries. In reality, to compute the PPP exchange rate, we would need a common basket of goods and services that are consumed in both countries to compare the cost of living. However, this could be difficult due to the different consumption pattern of each country. For example, households in temperate countries consume winter coats while households in tropical countries do not. So, winter coats would not be in the basket of common goods and services used to compute the PPP exchange rate. However, such an omission introduces an inaccuracy because the price of coats in temperate countries does affect its cost of living.

Putting it concretely: The Big Mac Index

In the simple example in the main text (Section 6.1.4), a chocolate bar was the good that was used to compute the PPP exchange rate between SGD and MYR (1SGD = 2MYR). In reality, *The Economist* newspaper did something similar in 1986 by using the Big Mac burger as the good to determine approximately what the PPP exchange rate ought to be. The Big Mac burger was chosen because it was a standardised product that was sold in many countries. They went a step further to use it to determine whether certain currencies were over or under valued. Go to http://www.economist.com/content/big-mac-index to read more about it.

6.1.6 Comparing the standard of living between countries over time

We have seen how the standard of living can be compared over time and over space separately. Having understood both, we can turn to comparing the standard of living between countries over time. The purpose of such as a comparison is to determine whether the gap in the standard of living between countries (over space comparison) has grown or shrunk with time (over time comparison). There are a few ways to do this and each way will be illustrated through the following scenario: We want to find out if the gap in the standard of living between Malaysia and Indonesia has shrunk between 2010 and 2015.

One way would be to compute the GDP per capita of both countries in 2010, convert them using a PPP exchange rate based on the cost of living in 2010, calculate the difference, and compare this difference with the same computations for 2015. If the difference has decreased, the gap in the standard of living has shrunk.

The second way would be to simply compute the percentage change in real GDP per capita for both countries from 2010 to 2015. This will allow us to see which country has growing faster. If the country that started with the lower standard of living grew faster, then the gap in the standard of living must be shrinking. However, if the country that started with the higher standard of living grew faster, then the gap in the standard of living must be growing.

Yet another way would be to compute the real GDP per capita for both countries, for both 2010 and 2015, and then convert them to the same currency using the PPP exchange rates, based on the 2010 cost of living (assuming the base year for computing the real GDP is 2010). We can then compare the difference in the real GDP per capita of both countries in 2010 against the difference in 2015 to see if the gap has increased. This method is similar to the first method. The only difference is that if we start with computing the real GDP per capita, then the PPP exchange rate used should be based on the base year prices instead of current year prices.

6.2 Economic Growth

Having studied how to compare the standard of living over time and space, and the limitations of doing so, we turn to study the first of four macroeconomic aims of a government—economic growth.

Definition(s):

Actual growth refers to an actual increase in the real national output (or real national income) of an economy.

Potential growth refers to an increase in the productive capacity (also known as the full-employment output) of an economy.

Sustainable growth refers to actual growth that can be sustained or maintained over a prolong period of time without environmental degradation and depletion of resources so that future generations can enjoy economic growth.

Inclusive growth refers to economic growth that can be enjoyed by the majority of the population, without worsening the income distribution and inequality.

6.2.1 Indicators for economic growth

Actual growth is measured by the percentage increase in real GDP over time. This is because real GDP is the measure of national output. The growth rate can be measured on an annual, quarterly, or even monthly basis.

Some economists do estimate potential growth by estimating the maximum that an economy can produce based on a production function but that is not in the A Level syllabus.

Sustainable growth is measured by a few indicators. First, there must be actual growth (increase in real GDP). To determine if this growth is sustainable, usually environmental indicators are used. For example, one indicator is the amount of carbon emitted per unit of output. For the growth to be sustainable, the increase in real GDP should be accompanied by a reduction in carbon per output.

Inclusive growth is also measured by multiple indicators. Apart from an increase in real GDP (actual growth), there should also be no change or a decrease in the Gini coefficient.

6.2.2 Causes of economic growth

The long-run economic growth rate is determined by how quickly the long-run aggregate supply (LRAS) increases while the short-run economic growth rate is determined by shifts in the aggregate demand (AD) and/or short-run aggregate supply (SRAS). This is illustrated by the business cycle in Fig. 6.3. The parts of the graph above the long-run trend are known as the peaks while the parts below are known as the troughs.

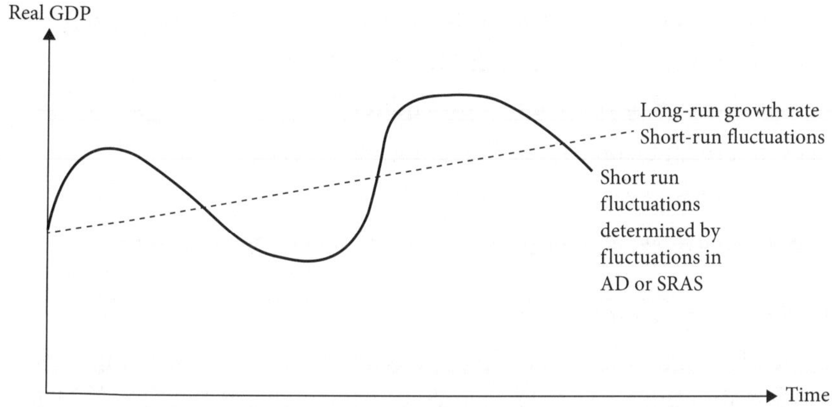

Figure 6.3: The business cycle.

The analyses of how changes in AD, SRAS, and LRAS affected national income (real GDP) were covered in Chapter 5. The following provides a recap.

Shifts in AD affecting economic growth

With reference to Fig. 6.4, an increase in AD (AD_0 to AD_1) would increase NY (Y_0 to Y_1) via the multiplier effect. This causes actual economic growth. Conversely, a fall in AD (AD_0 to AD_2) would decrease NY via the multiplier effect (sometimes referred to as the reverse multiplier effect) to (Y_0 to Y_2). This causes negative economic growth.

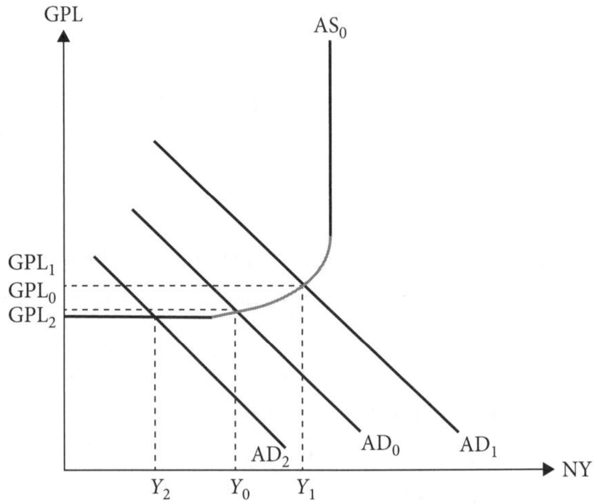

Figure 6.4: Changes in AD causing actual growth or negative growth.

The factors causing shifts in the AD were also covered in Chapter 5. They were

- Changes in disposable incomes, including taxes levied on personal income (affecting consumption)
- Changes in expected future price changes (affecting consumption)
- Changes in availability of credit (affecting consumption)
- Changes in interest rates (affecting consumption and investments)
- Changes in the level of technology (affecting investments)
- Changes in the business outlook/expectations of future profits (affecting investments)
- Changes in taxes levied on firms (affecting investments)
- Changes in the level of government expenditure
- Changes in foreign income levels (affecting net exports)
- Changes in exchange rates (affecting net exports)
- Changes in relative general price levels (GPLs) (affecting net exports)

Shifts in SRAS affecting economic growth

Changes in the SRAS can also affect actual growth. With reference to Fig. 6.5, increases in SRAS (downward shift from AS_0 to AS_1) would cause actual growth (Y_0 to Y_1) while decreases in SRAS (upward shift from AS_0 to AS_2) would cause negative growth (Y_0 to Y_2).

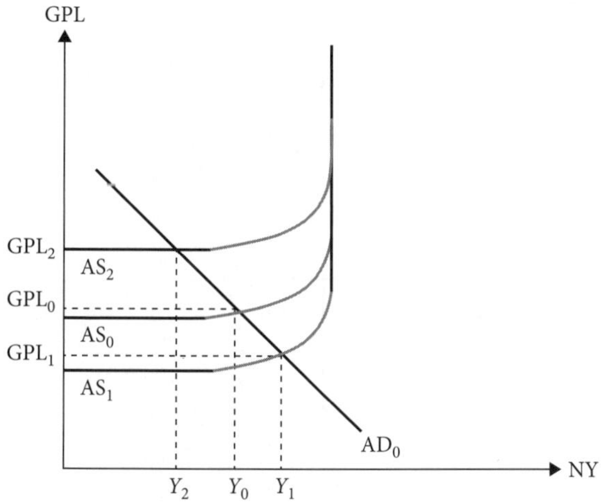

Figure 6.5: Changes in SRAS causing actual growth or negative growth.

The factors causing shifts in the SRAS were also covered in Chapter 5. They were:

- Changes in the prices of factor inputs
- Changes in productivity (due to changes in the quality of factor inputs or technology)

Shifts in LRAS affecting potential growth

Changes in the LRAS affect potential growth. With reference to Fig. 6.6, increases in LRAS (rightward shift from AS_0 to AS_1) would cause potential growth where the full-employment output (or productive capacity) increases from Y_{f_0} to Y_{f_1}. Conversely, decreases in the LRAS (leftward shift from AS_0 to AS_2) would cause negative potential growth (Y_{f_0} to Y_{f_2}).

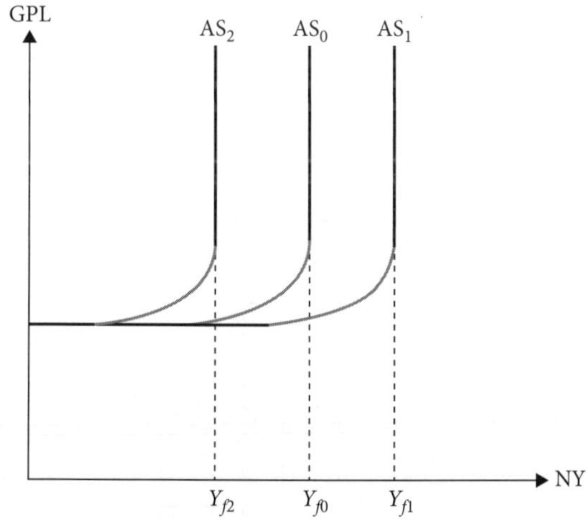

Figure 6.6: Changes in LRAS causing potential growth or negative potential growth.

Depending on the state of the economy (i.e., how close to full-employment the economy was operating), the shift in LRAS could also affect actual growth. Below are three scenarios showing how potential growth can happen (i) without actual growth, (ii) with some actual growth, and (iii) with an equal amount of actual growth.

If the economy was operating far from full-employment (i.e., horizontal portion of the aggregate supply (AS) curve)	If the economy was operating close to full-employment (i.e., upward-sloping portion of the AS curve)	If the economy was operating at full-employment (i.e., vertical portion of the AS curve)
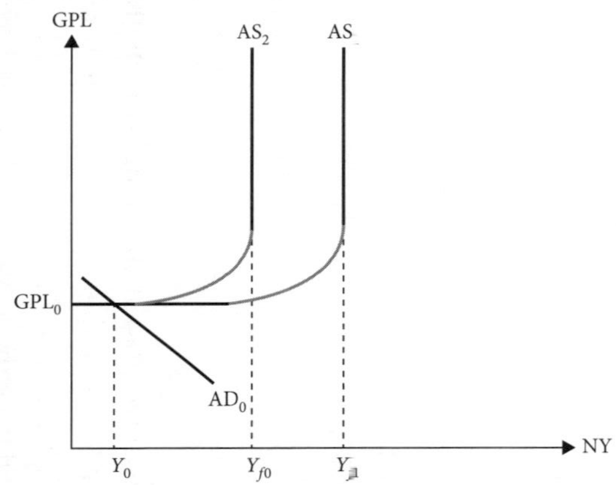	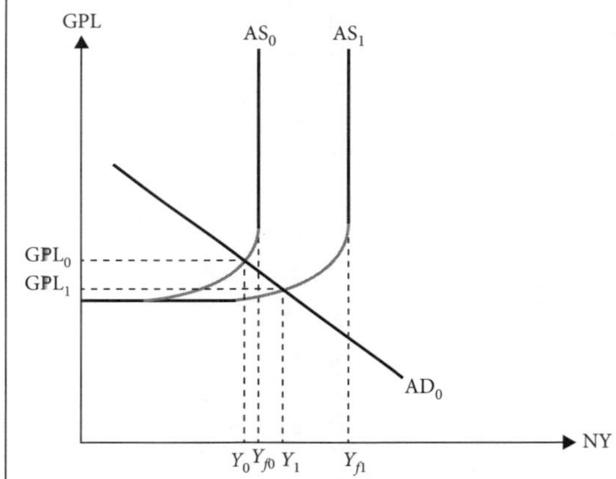	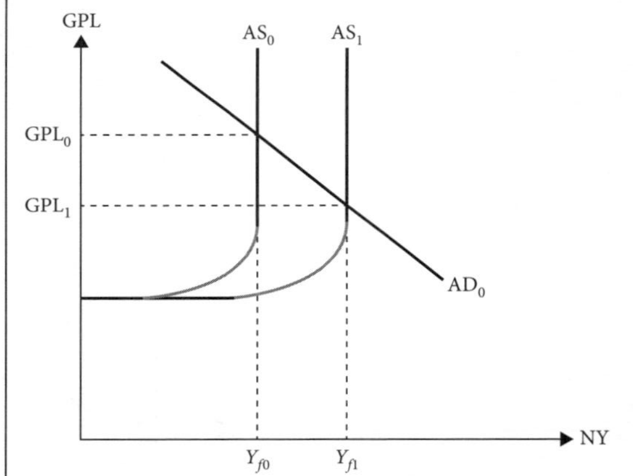
Increase in LRAS causes potential growth (Y_{f_0} to Y_{f_1}) without actual growth (no change in equilibrium Y).	Increase in LRAS causes potential growth (Y_{f_0} to Y_{f_1}) with some actual growth (Y_0 to Y_1).	Increase in LRAS causes potential growth (Y_{f_0} to Y_{f_1}) that is equal to actual growth (equilibrium Y also increases from Y_{f_0} to Y_{f_0}).

Conversely, a reduction in LRAS can also occur with no effect on actual growth, some negative growth, or the full extent of negative potential growth being translated into negative actual growth.

The factors causing shifts in thc LRAS were also covered in Chapter 5. They were

- Changes in the quantity of factor inputs
- Changes in productivity (due to changes in the quality of factor inputs or technology)

6.2.3 Consequences of poor economic growth

Most governments pursue economic growth. This is because economic growth creates benefits for households (consumers), firms, and the government. Poor economic growth refers to growth rates that are low or negative (i.e., a recession).

Definition(s):

A **recession** is a period of negative economic growth.

A **technical recession** refers to a situation where there has been two quarters of negative economic growth.

Effect of poor economic growth on consumers

The effect of poor economic growth on consumers can be analysed in terms of the effect on the standard of living, employment, and savings.

Standard of living—With economic growth, real GDP increases. Assuming no change in the size of the population (or that the population grows at a slower rate), the real GDP per capita increases. This means that average incomes of consumers will increase. This increases the purchasing power and hence, improves the material standard of living of consumers in the country. Additionally, with greater purchasing power, consumers can consume more and better healthcare services. The resultant better health outcomes improve the non-material standard of living. Conversely, when the economic growth rate is low, it may be outweighed by the increase in the size of the population, causing real GDP per capita to decrease, lowering both the material and non-material standard of living. The problem is worse when growth rates are negative.

Employment—Economic growth means that output has increased (i.e., increase in real GDP). To produce this increased output, more factors of production would need to be employed. This includes labour. Hence, growth creates employment. Conversely, when growth is low, employment is created at a slow rate. If this rate is lower than the rate at which the labour force[4] is growing, the number of people who are unable to find jobs will increase. This is detrimental to the welfare of households as employment is the means of providing incomes (similar to the previous point). The extent of the problem is heightened when the growth rate is negative.

5 A technical definition of the labour force will be provided in a later section. For now, just imagine the labour force as the number of labourers in the economy.

Savings—The previous two paragraphs showed how economic growth increased incomes through creating employment. Apart from allowing households to consume more goods and services which improve their current standard of living, the higher incomes also allow households to save more, which would improve their future standard of living. Conversely, when growth is low, there would be a negative effect on savings, and hence, a negative effect on the future standard of living.

Effect of poor economic growth on firms

The effect of poor economic growth on firms can be analysed in terms of the effect on profit. With economic growth, households enjoy an increase in income and hence, will consume more goods and services. From the firms' perspective, this is an increase in demand for their goods and services. The increase in demand allows firms to sell more of their output at higher prices, increasing their total revenue and hence, increasing profit. Conversely, low economic growth would mean slower increases in profit and negative economic growth (i.e., recessions) would cause decreases in profit.

Effect of poor economic growth on the government

The effect of poor economic growth on the government can be analysed in terms of how the government's aims and ability to achieve those aims is affected. The government's macroeconomic aims are to improve the standard of living for its citizens, and achieve economic growth, price stability, low unemployment, and a healthy BOP. The government's microeconomic aims are to achieve efficiency in markets and equity. The government's ability to use policies to achieve these aims depends on its budget position.

Standard of living—As explained in the Section 6.2.3.1, poor economic growth could worsen both material and non-material standard of living. This negatively impacts governments since improvements in the standard of living is one of the government's aims.

Economic growth—Poor economic growth could be self-perpetuating (i.e., poor economic growth now may cause poor economic growth in the future). This is because poor economic growth could affect businesses' and households' expectations of future profits and income, respectively. If poor economic growth causes firms to expect lower growth and hence, profits in the future, firms would reduce their investments (Marginal Efficiency of Investment [MEI] curve shifts left, causing a fall in investments at the current interest rate). This causes AD to decrease, which causes national income to fall further. Similarly, if poor economic growth now causes households to expect future income to be lower, households would reduce their consumption. This also causes AD and hence, national income to decrease. Hence, poor economic growth could cause continued poor economic growth. This negatively impacts governments since economic growth is one of the government's aims.

Price stability—The effect of poor economic growth on price stability is mixed. As explained in the previous paragraph, poor economic growth could lead to a fall in AD through causing business and consumer pessimism. This fall in AD could then cause a fall in the GPL, causing deflation. This negatively impacts governments since price stability is one of the government's aims, and price stability requires a low rate of inflation (more details in the later section on inflation). However, if the economy was facing high inflationary pressure, the reduction in AD would help to offset some of the inflationary pressure. This would lead to low inflation, which is desirable from the government's point of view.

Employment—As explained in Section 6.2.3.1, poor economic growth could cause more people to be unable to obtain jobs. This is also known as unemployment. This negatively impacts governments since low unemployment is one of the government's aims.

BOP—The BOP is a record of transactions between a country and the rest of the world. In general, countries prefer having more monetary inflow than outflow. The effect of poor economic growth on a country's BOP is mixed. On one hand, if poor economic growth causes foreign firms to pull out their operations from a country, there would be more outflow of money. This would worsen the BOP position. On the other hand, if poor economic growth causes domestic households to spend less on imports, there would be less outflow of money. This would improve the BOP position. More details regarding the BOP will be studied in a later section.

Efficiency—In microeconomics, there are a few aspects of efficiency—allocative efficiency, productive efficiency, and dynamic efficiency are some of the aspects studied in the A Level syllabus. Allocative efficiency and productive efficiency are static concepts. What this means is that these two concepts are about whether certain conditions are met at a particular point in time. Productive efficiency is about whether resources are fully maximised at a point in time and allocative efficiency is about whether the optimal combination of goods and services is produced at a point in time. To study the effect of economic growth on these two efficiencies, it is necessary to study the level of productive and allocative inefficiency before and after the increase in real GDP (growth). This would depend on how the economic growth came about. Details are provided in Annex 6.3.

In contrast to allocative and productive efficiency, dynamic efficiency is about whether there are positive changes over time. For a society as a whole, positive changes come about when new information is created and applied (i.e., when technology develops). This can only come about through R&D. Economic growth creates profits for firms and also raises the government's revenue from taxes. This increases the ability of firms and governments to engage in R&D, which improves dynamic efficiency. Conversely, poor economic growth lowers dynamic efficiency.

Equity—There is no clear causal relationship between economic growth and income inequality. Depending on the factor causing economic growth, income inequality could improve, stay constant, or worsen. The effect of economic growth on income inequality depends on the reasons for the growth. For example, growth due to foreign direct investments (FDIs), in the form of new factories that employ many low-skilled workers, would lift many out of poverty, reducing inequality (the growth comes from an increase in AD due to the increase in investments). However, growth from reductions in average cost, due to more widespread adoption of automation that replaces low-skilled labour, would worsen income inequality (the growth comes from the downward shift of the SRAS due to the lower average cost). Since income inequality is correlated with inequity, there is no clear relationship between growth and inequity.

Government's ability to achieve aims—The government's ability to achieve its aims depends on how much revenue it collects. For example, to reduce inequity, a government might provide income subsidies to the poor. The more revenue it collects, the more households it is able to help. Economic growth affects the government's tax revenue. With economic growth, incomes increase and governments collect more in income taxes. Conversely, poor economic growth reduces the government's tax revenue and ability to achieve its aims.

Putting it concretely: Is economic growth always a good thing?

While growth generates many benefits, it could create costs too. These include costs to the environment, worsened non-material standard of living, and worsened income inequality.

Economic growth involves the production of more goods and services. Such production tends to have a negative impact on the environment. For example, the production of clothes in the fashion industry has led to water pollution as dye run-offs enter water sources. Air pollution is another problem as more production requires more energy, which is usually produced by burning fossil fuels. A dramatic illustration of this is the rapid deterioration of China's environment as it has experienced high and sustained economic growth rates since its opening up.

Economic growth could also come at the expense of other aspects of non-material standard of living. For example, economic growth could be accompanied by longer working hours. This reduction in leisure worsens the non-material standard of living. A case in point is Singapore, where together with economic growth, workers now work one of the longest hours in the world. In countries where uneven economic growth has attracted workers in rural areas to move to the cities, families have had to live apart, which also contributes to a lower non-material standard of living.

Economic growth could also worsen income inequality. This is because most of the gains from economic growth in the modern era are experienced by asset owners. However, as the poor have no ability to accumulate assets while the rich do, economic growth has largely benefitted the rich more than the poor. This has worsened income inequality.

6.3 Inflation

We now turn to look at another macroeconomic aim—low inflation.

Definition(s):

Inflation refers to a sustained increase in the general price level (GPL).

Deflation refers to a sustained decrease in the GPL.

6.3.1 Indicator for inflation

The GPL is the average of the price of goods and services produced in an economy. In reality, economists use different indicators to measure this average price. The relevant one for the A Level syllabus is the consumer price index (CPI), although the GDP deflator is more accurate if the GPL is understood as the average of prices of all goods and services produced in the economy (i.e., the average price of all goods and services included in the real GDP). Refer to Annex 6.4 for details of the computation of the GDP deflator.

Definition(s):

The **Consumer Price Index (CPI)** refers to the price of a weighted basket of consumer goods and services expressed as a percentage of the price of the same basket at base year prices.

$$CPI = \frac{Current\ price\ of\ weighted\ basket\ of\ consumer\ goods\ and\ services}{Base\ price\ of\ weighted\ basket\ of\ consumer\ goods\ and\ services} \times 100\%$$

A CPI of 105 for a given year would mean that the price level in that year was 105% of the base year price level. For details of the computation of the CPI, please refer to Annex 6.4.

The inflation rate is the percentage change in the CPI.

$$Inflation\ rate = \frac{CPI_{current} - CPI_{previous}}{CPI_{previous}} \times 100\%$$

Inflation would mean that the inflation rate is positive while deflation would mean that the inflation rate is negative. Most countries have a positive inflation rate target. The targets are usually low inflation rates (e.g., the European Union's inflation target is about 2%).

6.3.2 Causes of inflation

Since inflation is the increase in the GPL, it can be caused by an increase in AD (when the economy is close to full employment) or an increase in the cost of production. The former is known as demand-pull inflation while the latter is known as cost-push inflation. They are illustrated by Figs. 6.7 and 6.8 respectively, where the increase in AD and decrease in SRAS cause the GPL to increase from GPL_0 to GPL_1 in each diagram.

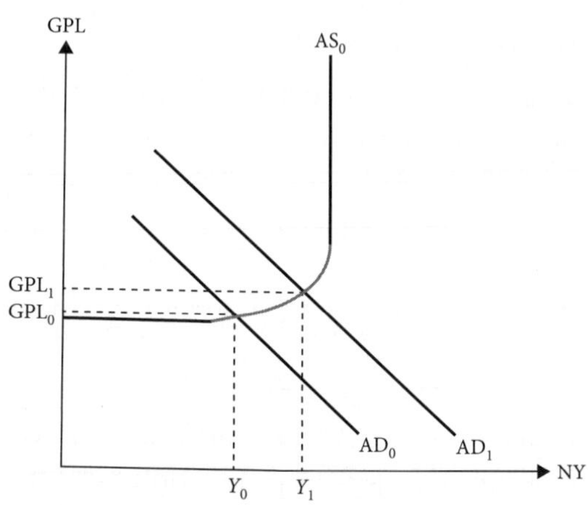

Figure 6.7: Demand-pull inflation.

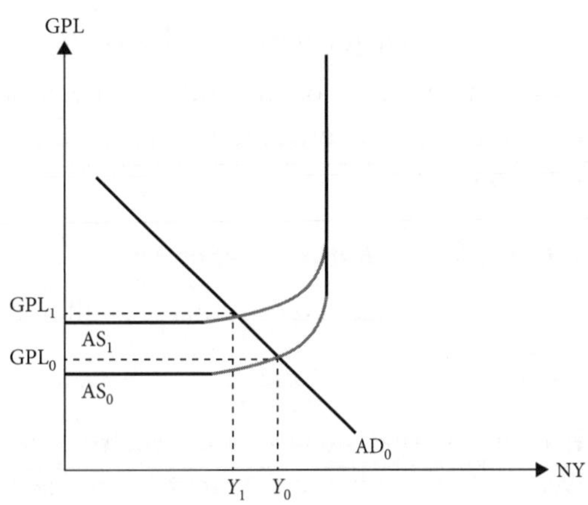

Figure 6.8: Cost-push inflation.

Conversely, deflation would be caused by a decrease in AD and/or an increase in SRAS.

The factors causing shifts in AD and SRAS were explained in Chapter 5. To recap, they were

Factors that shift AD

- Changes in disposable incomes, including taxes levied on personal income (affecting consumption)
- Changes in expected future price changes (affecting consumption)
- Changes in availability of credit (affecting consumption)
- Changes in interest rates (affecting consumption and investments)
- Changes in the level of technology (affecting investments)
- Changes in the business outlook/expectations of future profits (affecting investments)
- Changes in taxes levied on firms (affecting investments)
- Changes in the level of government expenditure
- Changes in foreign income levels (affecting net exports)
- Changes in exchange rates (affecting net exports)
- Changes in relative GPLs (affecting net exports)

Factors that shift SRAS

- Changes in the prices of factor inputs
- Changes in productivity (due to changes in the quality of factor inputs or technology)

Note that if the change in the price of factor inputs is due to a change in the price of imported factor inputs (e.g., increase in the price of imported oil causing the cost of production to increase), we term it imported inflation.

Theoretically, inflation can also occur due to leftward shifts of the LRAS. However, that rarely happens.

6.3.3 Consequences of undesirable inflation rates—high inflation

Governments aim for low inflation because both high inflation and deflation have negative consequences for consumers, firms, and governments. We will first look at the effects of high inflation.

Effect of high inflation on consumers

High inflation causes consumers to suffer an erosion of real income and real wealth and incur shoe leather cost.

Erosion of real income and wealth—Inflation reduces consumers' real income and real wealth. Income is the payment for households' provision of factors of production per time period (e.g., monthly wages) while wealth is the amount of money held by households at a point in time (e.g., the amount of money in a bank account). Income adds to wealth. Inflation reduces the real value of both. With inflation, the real value of households' income will decrease (i.e., the purchasing power of households' income will decrease), assuming no change in their nominal income. Similarly, inflation will erode the real wealth of households as the wealth can now be used to purchase fewer goods and services. Both the erosion of real income and real wealth worsen the material standard of living since the purchasing power of households is eroded. High inflation rates make the degree of erosion faster.

Shoe leather costs—Inflation also imposes inconvenience for consumers as prices increase. In a cash-based society, consumers would need to withdraw money more frequently or carry more cash in their wallets. In cashless societies, the inconvenience is reduced but is likely to still be existent (e.g., needing to top up e-wallets more often). All such inconvenience to consumers is known as shoe leather costs. High inflation imposes more shoe leather costs because prices rise faster.

Effect of high inflation on firms

High inflation causes firms to incur costs for gathering information for decision-making and menu cost.

Cost of information gathering—For firms, high inflation rates make business planning more difficult. High inflation rates also tend to be volatile (theoretically, it is possible to have high and stable inflation rates; practically, that is never observed). This volatility makes it difficult for firms to be sure of the estimated returns on investment and therefore, whether and how much to invest. The uncertainty imposes a cost in terms of needing to gather more information for decision making.

Menu cost—Inflation imposes an inconvenience cost on producers as they will need to update their price lists and costing estimates. Such inconveniences are known as menu costs. High inflation imposes more menu costs because prices rise faster.

Effect of high inflation on governments

High inflation affects governments through affecting the government's aim of achieving economic growth, efficiency, and equity.

Economic growth—High inflation makes it more difficult for businesses to estimate the return on investments. As such, risk-averse businesses (most businesses are risk averse) would reduce or delay their investments. The fall in investment then causes a fall in AD, causing a fall in national income (negative growth).

Efficiency—Inflation may result in allocative inefficiency. Markets achieve allocative efficiency through the price mechanism. In this mechanism, firms decide how much of their output to produce based on price signals. A firm will produce more output when the price of its good increases. However, this is assuming everything else remains constant, including the prices of other goods. Under this assumption, the increase in the price of the firm's good is an increase relative to the price of other goods too. This shows that society has increased its valuation of the firm's good relative to other goods. Thus, the firm producing more output results in allocative efficiency as more resources are channelled into producing a good which society values relatively more. With inflation, the prices of all (at least many) goods and services are increasing. As such, an increase in the price of a firm's good may not be an increase in price relative to the price of other goods. In this case, a firm increasing production may result in allocative inefficiency instead. The problem arises because inflation can confuse the price signals. High inflation worsens the extent of the problem.

Equity—Inflation could worsen inequity by causing a redistribution of income and wealth between the rich and the poor. The rich are better able to hold their wealth in financial assets like stocks (i.e., shares of companies) and bonds. This could give them a source of variable income (income that varies with the GPL). For example, inflation increases the nominal profits of firms as an increase in revenue and cost by a certain percentage and would also increase profits by that same percentage (e.g., if revenue of $100 and cost of $60 increase by 10% each, profit would also increase by 10% from $40 to $44). This causes the dividends to be paid out to shareholders to also increase in nominal terms. Hence, income from stocks (i.e., dividends) is variable. Variable income is not eroded by inflation since it rises and falls with the GPL. In contrast, the poor tend to be salaried workers earning only fixed incomes—income that does not vary with the GPL (e.g., salaries of $2000 a month). Hence, inflation will erode their real income since the fixed nominal income is able to buy fewer goods and services when prices increase. Since the rich have better access to variable sources of income than the poor, inflation erodes the real income of the rich less than the poor. This worsens the income distribution, causing inequity. The argument for wealth is similar. The rich are better able to hold their wealth in assets which have prices that vary with the GPL (e.g., housing). Thus, their wealth is less eroded by inflation than the poor who tend to hold their wealth in savings accounts in banks. High inflation worsens the problem by causing a greater degree of redistribution.

6.3.4 Consequences of undesirable inflation rates—deflation

High inflation imposes many costs but deflation is also undesirable. This is because deflation also imposes costs on consumers, firms, and governments.

Effect of deflation on consumers

Consumers may be negatively affected by deflation if they are debtors. This is because the real value of debt increases with deflation. For example, the purchasing power (real value) of a $1000-dollar debt increases when the price of goods and services decrease. When households repay their debts after a period of deflation, the amount of goods and services that they have to give up is more than when they borrowed the money.

Effect of deflation on firms

Deflation could reduce the profits of firms if it causes households to develop deflationary expectations. If deflation causes households to expect further deflation, they would postpone consumption since they expect prices to decrease in the future. The current reduction in consumption causes a fall in demand for firms. This would eventually translate into lower profits for firms.

Effect of deflation on governments

Deflation could cause the economy to enter a deflationary spiral where deflation causes economic contraction (fall in NY), which causes more deflation and so on and so forth. This has a negative effect on governments as economic growth is one of the government's macroeconomic aims. An economy can enter a deflationary spiral if deflation causes deflationary expectations. With deflationary expectations, households will postpone their consumption. This causes a fall in AD. The fall in AD then causes a reduction in NY and GPL. The reduction in GPL may then cause the deflationary expectations to continue, causing further postponement of consumption and reductions in AD. The loop then continues. It is important to note that the postponed consumption does not ever materialise as the subsequent reductions in income erode purchasing power. This was the case in Japan after the bursting of a property bubble in the early 1990s. The period of sluggish growth became known as "Japan's lost decade".

6.4 Unemployment

Definition(s):

Unemployment is the situation where a person who is willing and able to work is unable to find work.

6.4.1 Indicators for unemployment

The level of unemployment in an economy can be measured by the unemployment rate. The unemployment rate is the percentage of the labour force that is unemployed.

$$Unemployment\ rate = \frac{No.\ of\ unemployed\ people}{Labour\ force} \times 100\%$$

The labour force refers to the number of people in the economy who are willing and able to work. This would exclude retirees, students, and people not actively looking for work (e.g., housewives). Members of the labour force are either employed or unemployed.

The working age population is the number of people in a country above the working age. The percentage of the working age population that is in the labour force is known as the labour force participation rate.

$$Labour\ force\ participation\ rate = \frac{Labour\ force}{Working\ age\ population} \times 100\%$$

The relationship between the working age population, labour force, and number of unemployed people is summarised below.

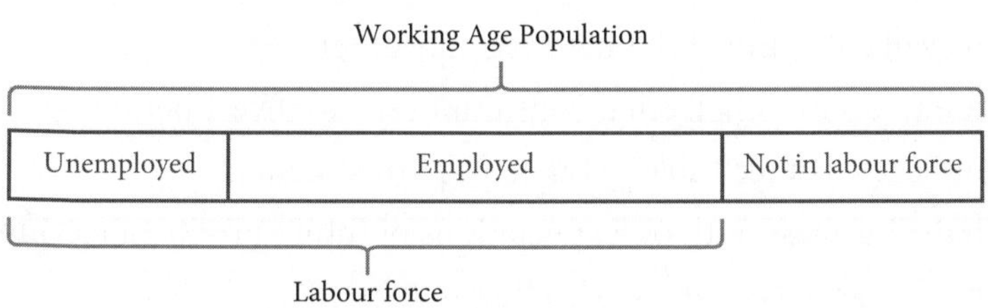

6.4.2 Causes of unemployment

There are three types of unemployment distinguished by their causes—demand-deficient unemployment (or cyclical unemployment), structural unemployment, and frictional unemployment.

Demand-deficient unemployment (or cyclical unemployment)

Demand-deficient unemployment is caused by a lack of aggregate demand. Reductions in AD increase demand-deficient unemployment. This is because reductions in aggregate demand cause fewer goods and services to be produced. As such, the demand for labour would also decrease. This causes fewer workers to be employed, giving rise to unemployment. Demand-deficient unemployment is also known as cyclical unemployment because reductions in AD cause the troughs in the business cycle (the term "cyclical" comes from the word "cycle"). The degree of demand-deficient unemployment can be illustrated by the gap between the full-employment output and the actual output. Figure 6.9 shows how a fall in AD increases the output gap which represents demand-deficient unemployment.

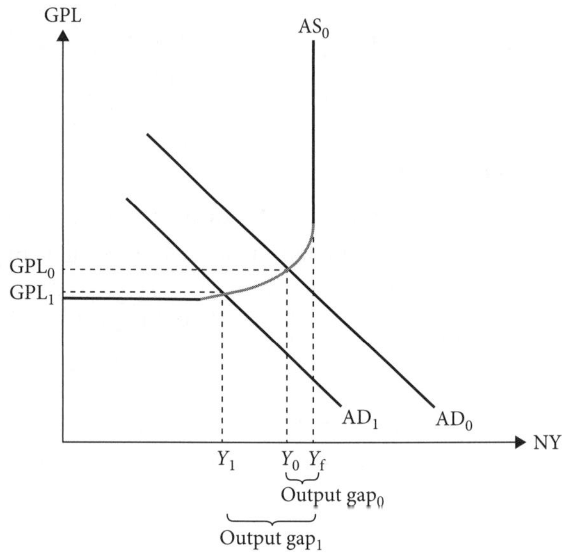

Figure 6.9: Illustrating an increase in demand-deficient unemployment.

Conversely, an increase in AD would reduce demand-deficient unemployment. The factors causing shifts in AD were explained in Chapter 5. They include

- Changes in disposable incomes, including taxes levied on personal income (affecting consumption)
- Changes in expected future price changes (affecting consumption)
- Changes in availability of credit (affecting consumption)
- Changes in interest rates (affecting consumption and investments)
- Changes in the level of technology (affecting investments)
- Changes in the business outlook/expectations of future profits (affecting investments)
- Changes in taxes levied on firms (affecting investments)

- Changes in the level of government expenditure
- Changes in foreign income levels (affecting net exports)
- Changes in exchange rates (affecting net exports)
- Changes in relative GPLs (affecting net exports)

Structural unemployment

Structural unemployment is unemployment due to a mismatch of skills. Unlike demand-deficient unemployment where there is a lack of jobs, in structural unemployment, jobs exist. However, the unemployed lack the necessary skills to fill in the vacancies.

Structural unemployment arises due to changes in the demand and supply conditions in specific labour markets, which is in turn due to changes in demand and supply of specific goods. For example, suppose a tax were imposed on all plastic products. This increases the cost of producing such goods and hence, reduces the supply. This in turn reduces the equilibrium output and increases the equilibrium price of plastic products. Since less plastic products would now be produced, plastic firms would reduce their demand for plastic workers. At the same time, since plastic products are now more expensive, consumers would switch to products made of other materials (e.g., wood). As such, the demand for wood products would increase. This would increase both the equilibrium price and output of wood products. To produce this higher output, wood firms would want to employ more wood workers. The demand for wood workers hence, increases. However, plastic workers who get laid off may not have the skills required to work with wood. As such, although there are vacancies for wood workers, plastic workers remain unemployed due to a lack of skills.

Factors causing changes in demand and supply were covered in Chapter 2.

The replacement of labour by technology is known as technological unemployment, which is also considered a type of structural unemployment.

Frictional unemployment

Frictional unemployment is unemployment due to the transition between school and work (i.e., a graduate being unemployed while he/she is in the process of applying for jobs and being interviewed), or the transition between jobs. It is primarily due to imperfect information. In all such transitions, there will be a period when the member of the labour force is unemployed because either the member or the firms looking to hire, need time to gather information. For example, when firms interview possible candidates, they are trying to gather information about which candidate is the best fit for the job. However, in this process of information gathering, the candidates remain frictionally unemployed.

6.4.3 Consequences of undesirable unemployment rates

Most governments pursue low unemployment rates or full employment. This is because unemployment imposes a cost on households (consumers), firms, and the government. In economics, full employment refers to the absence of demand-deficient unemployment. Full employment does not mean that the unemployment rate is zero since there would still be some degree of structural and frictional unemployment.

Governments pursue full employment because structural and frictional unemployment are part and parcel of an economy's workings, since a functioning economy will naturally experience changes in the demand and supply of specific goods and services and transitions between jobs. The assumption is that such forms of unemployment will not be permanent. For structural unemployment, the unemployed who lack the correct skillsets would naturally undergo training/re-training or accept a lower wage in the same industry. For frictional unemployment, after the job searching and interview processes, the unemployed would naturally be matched to jobs. However, if the structural and frictional unemployment is significant, governments would also aim to reduce them as all forms of unemployment imposes costs on households (consumers), firms, and the government.

Definition(s):

Full employment refers to the absence of demand-deficient unemployment.

Effect of unemployment on consumers

The effect of unemployment on consumers can be analysed in terms of the effect on the standard of living and savings.

Standard of living—Becoming unemployed represents a loss of income to households. This translates into a loss of purchasing power and hence a reduction in material standard of living. In terms of non-material standard of living, since unemployment imposes a psychic cost on the unemployed due to the stress of not being able to make ends meet and the shame of not being a productive member of society, it causes non-material standard of living of the unemployed to worsen too. Additionally, prolonged periods of unemployment may lead to anti-social behaviour such as rioting and petty crime, which reduces the non-material standard of living for everyone else too.

Savings—Since the unemployed have no source of income, they would have to run down their savings to fund their necessary expenses. Hence, higher unemployment would lead to lower household savings.

Effect of unemployment on firms

The effect of unemployment on firms can be analysed in terms of the effect on profit. Higher unemployment rates mean that the purchasing power of the population decreases. From the firms' perspective, this is a decrease in demand for their goods and services. The decrease in demand causes firms suffer a fall in profit.

Effect of unemployment on the government

Unemployment negatively affects the government through affecting its aims and its ability to achieve its aims.

Standard of living—As explained in the earlier section on effect of unemployment on consumers, unemployment could worsen both material and non-material standard of living. This negatively impacts governments since improvements in the standard of living is one of the government's aims.

Economic growth—Unemployment could affect economic growth negatively. This is because unemployment could reduce businesses' and households' expectations of future profits and income, respectively. If firms expect lower profits in the future due to the unemployment, they would reduce their investments (MEI curve shifts left, causing a fall in investments at the current interest rate). This causes AD to decrease, which causes national income to fall further. Similarly, unemployment causes households to expect future income to be lower, households would reduce their consumption. This also causes AD and hence,, national income to decrease. This negatively impacts governments since economic growth is one of the government's aims.

Government's ability to achieve aims—The government's ability to achieve its aims depends on how much revenue it collects. For example, to reduce inequity, a government might provide income subsidies to the poor. The more revenue it collects, the more households it is able to help. Unemployment affects the government's tax revenue. With more unemployment, governments collect less in income taxes. Additionally, with higher unemployment, there would be more government spending needed for unemployment benefits or its equivalents. This further reduces the amount of spending the government can devote to other areas.

6.5 Balance of Payments (H2 ONLY)

We now turn to study the last macroeconomic aim—a healthy Balance of Payments (BOP).

6.5.1 The BOP accounts

A country's BOP is a record of monetary flows between foreign economies and itself. The overall balance (known as the BOP position) shows the net overall position. A positive BOP position is known as a BOP surplus. This means that in total, more money has flowed into a country from foreign sources than out of it. Conversely, a negative BOP position (BOP deficit) means that more money has flowed out than flowed in from foreign countries.

Definition(s):

A **BOP surplus** refers to a positive BOP position. Total monetary inflows exceed monetary outflows.

A **BOP deficit** refers to a negative BOP position. Total monetary outflows exceed monetary inflows.

Money flows between countries for different reasons. For example, money could flow from Singapore to China when residents of Singapore purchase import items bought on Taobao from China. Money could also flow from Singapore to China when local firms decide to open new stores in China or when local residents decide to buy shares on the Chinese stock market. These different reasons for monetary flows across international borders make it necessary for the BOP to have subaccounts to classify them.

The two subaccounts in the BOP are the current account and the capital and financial account[5]. Each account captures monetary flows across international borders for different reasons.

The current account

The current account records monetary flows due to trade in goods and services, factor income payments (e.g., interest income from providing loans to foreign borrowers), and transfer payments. As such, the three accounts within the current account are the following:

- **Goods and services balance**—This is also known as the trade balance and is sometimes split further into the trade in goods balance and the trade in services balance. Export revenues are recorded as positive numbers and import expenditures are recorded as negative numbers. If export revenue exceeds import expenditure, the trade balance would be positive. We describe that as a trade surplus. It means that there is more monetary inflow from trade in goods and services than outflow. Conversely, if import expenditure exceeds export revenue, there is a trade deficit and there is more monetary outflow from trade in goods and services than inflow.

Definition(s):

A **trade surplus** refers to a positive balance of trade position. Export revenue exceeds import expenditure.

A **trade deficit** refers to a negative balance of trade position. Import expenditure exceeds export revenue.

- **Primary income balance**—This is the balance of factor incomes. Factor incomes from abroad such as profits repatriated from firms which have foreign operations are recorded as positive numbers (e.g., BreadTalk's repatriation of profits from China to Singapore is recorded as a positive figure in Singapore's primary income balance) while factor incomes to abroad, such as interest income paid to foreign banks that have made loans to local firms, are recorded as negative numbers. An overall positive figure means that there is more monetary income inflow than outflow and conversely, an overall negative figure means that there is more monetary outflow than inflow. The most common forms of income are income from loans (interest incomes) and investments (profits and/or dividends).
- **Secondary income balance**—This is the balance of transfer payments. Transfer payments are different from factor incomes. Factor incomes refer to payment in return for providing a factor of production (e.g., interest payments in return for obtaining a loan). In contrast, transfer payments are basically gifts of money. For example, when a worker remits money to his family overseas, he is not paying them in return for something. This remittance is a transfer payment. Transfers from abroad are recorded

6 Note that the naming of the subaccounts and items in each subaccount may differ slightly from country to country. Some countries just name the two accounts current account and financial account. This book is based on Singapore's norms.

as a positive figure in Singapore's secondary income balance, while transfers to abroad are recorded as negative numbers. An overall positive figure means that there is more transfer inflow than outflow and conversely, an overall negative figure means that there is more transfer outflow than inflow.

The capital and financial account

The current account records monetary flows due to the purchase of assets and incurrence of liabilities. Assets can be thought of as things that generate income while liabilities can be thought of things that cause one to incur payments. Assets could be in the form of physical assets (e.g., a factory or a shopfront or more broadly, a business) or financial assets, such as stocks and bonds. A stock is the shares of a company. For example, if there are 10,000 Apple shares available and you own one share, you own 0.01% of Apple. This share is an asset because as the owner of this 0.01% of Apple, you are entitled to 0.01% of its profits. A bond is essentially a loan. When you buy a bond from a company, you are lending it money in return for the interest the company has to pay you. The interest income earned from bonds make bonds assets. The different types of assets give rise to the different accounts within the capital and financial account. The overall capital and financial account position tells us the change in a country's net external asset position (termed Net international investment position [NIIP] in Singapore's BOP). It refers to the total external assets (foreign assets held by Singapore residents) minus total external liabilities (local assets held by foreign residents). For example, as of the end of 2016, Singapore had about $4.45 trillion worth of external assets and about $3.35 trillion worth of external liabilities. As such, our NIIP was about $0.92 trillion.

Direct investment—This account records the purchase of physical assets. Foreigners purchasing local assets (also known as an inflow of FDI or long-term capital inflow) are recorded as negative numbers. This is because when foreigners purchase local assets, locals have incurred liabilities as income from these assets that now have to be paid to the foreigners. This negative number represents a worsening of the locals' net asset position. Conversely, when locals purchase foreign assets, this is recorded as a positive number since the locals' net asset position has improved. Note that the convention here is different from the current account. In the capital and financial account, the inflow of money from foreigners purchasing local assets is recorded as a negative number while the outflow of money is recorded as a positive number.

Portfolio investment—This account records the purchase of financial assets (i.e., stocks and bonds). Foreigners purchasing local stocks and bonds (also known as an inflow of foreign portfolio investment (FPI) or short-term capital inflow or "hot money" inflow) are recorded as negative numbers as it represents a worsening of the locals' net asset position. Conversely, when locals purchase foreign stocks and bonds, this is recorded as a positive number since the locals' net asset position has improved. Similar to the direct investment account, the inflow of money from foreigners purchasing local assets is recorded as a negative number while the outflow of money is recorded as a positive number.

Financial derivatives and other investments—Financial derivatives are financial instruments that are derived from stocks and bonds (e.g., options and futures), while other investments are investments that do not fall into any of the previous categories. These two accounts are generally beyond the scope of the A Level syllabus.

Summary of the BOP

The table below summarises the BOP by using Singapore's BOP (in millions of dollars) for 2017.

Variables	2017	Interpretation
A. Current Account Balance (A1 + A2 + A3 + A4)	84,220.6	Total monetary inflow in the current account > total monetary outflow in the current account. Current account is in surplus.
A1. Goods Balance	116,966.3	Singapore exports more goods than it imports
A2. Services Balance	–8,445.1	Singapore exports less services than it imports
A3. Primary Income Balance	–15,907	Factor income inflow < factor income outflow
A4. Secondary Income Balance	–8,393.6	Transfer inflow < transfer outflow
B. Capital and Financial Account Balance (B1 + B2 + B3 + B4)	46,499.8	Singapore's net asset position has improved. More money is flowing out from locals purchasing foreign assets than money flowing in from foreigners purchasing local assets.
B1. Direct Investment	–53,789.6	Net asset position has worsened. Foreigners' purchase of local physical assets > locals' purchase of foreign physical assets.
B2. Portfolio Investment	47,356	Net asset position has improved. Foreigners' purchase of local financial assets < locals' purchase of foreign financial assets.
B3. Financial Derivatives	–18,692.8	Not relevant to the A Level syllabus
B4. Other Investment	71,626.2	Not relevant to the A Level syllabus
C Net Errors and Omissions	120.4	Not relevant to the A Level syllabus
D. Overall Balance (A – B + C)[a]	37,841.2	Total monetary inflow > total monetary outflow. BOP is in surplus.

A has a negative sign because in B, inflows of money are negative while outflows are positive. The negative sign transforms inflows into positive numbers and outflows into negative numbers to be consistent with A.

Source: http://www.tablebuilder.singstat.gov.sg/publicfacing/createDataTable.action?refId=1391

6.5.2 Causes of BOP surpluses and deficits

Since the BOP position is affected by the current account and the capital and financial account, the causes of a BOP surplus or deficit must be due to factors influencing the current account or the capital and financial account.

Factors influencing the current account

Factors can influence the current account through influencing the trade balance, primary income balance, or secondary income balance. These include the following:

- Foreign income level (affecting the trade balance)
- Other changes in global demand conditions (affecting the trade balance)
- Domestic income level (affecting the trade balance)
- Exchange rates (affecting the trade balance)
- Other changes in price of exports and imports (affecting the trade balance)
- The country's net asset position in the previous period (affecting the primary income balance)
- International commitments (affecting the secondary income balance)
- The size of the migrant population (affecting the secondary income balance)

Foreign income level (affecting the trade balance)—As explained in Chapter 5, under factors affecting net exports (X – M), if incomes in foreign countries increase, the rise in purchasing power would cause foreign consumers to increase their consumption. This could include the consumption of goods and services exported from the domestic country. When that happens, export revenue of the domestic country would increase, improving the trade balance and hence, the current account balance. Conversely, a fall in foreign incomes would worsen the current account balance.

Other changes in global demand conditions (affecting the trade balance)—Apart from changes in foreign income, other factors could affect the foreign demand for exports from the domestic country. For example, a change in taste and preferences towards the domestic country's exports would cause its demand to increase. The increase in exports of Korean dramas due to the "Korean wave" illustrates this. This would cause the domestic country's export revenue to increase, improving its trade balance, and current account position. Conversely, a shift of global demand away from the domestic country's exports would cause a worsening of the current account position.

Domestic income level (affecting the trade balance)—As explained in Chapter 5, under factors affecting net exports ($X - M$), if incomes in the domestic country increases, the rise in purchasing power would cause local consumers to increase their consumption. This could include the consumption of imports. When that happens, import expenditure of the domestic country would increase, worsening the trade balance and hence, the current account balance. Conversely, a fall in domestic incomes would improve the current account balance.

Exchange rates (affecting the trade balance)—Suppose the exchange rate appreciates (i.e., increases in value such that one domestic currency can be exchanged for more foreign currency), imports would become cheaper in the domestic currency while exports would become more expensive in the foreign currency. Since imports are now cheaper to locals, the quantity demanded of imports would rise. At the same time, since exports are more expensive to foreigners, the quantity of exports demanded by foreigners would decrease. For exports, since the price in domestic currency remains unchanged but the quantity of demand falls, export revenue in domestic currency must fall. For imports, assuming the demand for imports is price elastic, the increase in quantity demanded would be more than proportionate to the fall in price. This causes the import expenditure in domestic currency to increase. Taken together, the fall in export revenue and rise in import expenditure in domestic currency would cause a worsening of the trade balance and hence, the current account balance. Conversely, a depreciation would cause an improvement in the trade balance. However, a caveat to note is that in this explanation, we assumed that the demand for imports is price elastic. Annex 6.5 shows us what happens when we relax this assumption.

Other changes in price of exports and imports (affecting the trade balance)—Apart from changes in exchange rates, other reasons for changes in the price of exports and imports could also affect the trade balance. For example, subsidies given to domestic exporters could reduce the price of exports. Assuming the demand for exports is price elastic, the decrease in the price of exports would cause a more than proportionate increase in the quantity of exports in demand. This would increase the export revenue and hence, improve the trade balance. The current account position would then improve too.

The country's NIIP in the previous period (affecting the primary income balance)—A country's NIIP tells us whether a country holds more foreign assets or whether foreigners hold more of a country's local assets. Since assets generate income, the holding of foreign assets would generate factor income inflows in the next period while foreigners holding local assets would cause factor income outflows in the next period. Hence, changes in holdings of foreign and local assets would affect the primary income balance. For example, increased FDI inflows represent an increase in foreign holding of local assets. As such, in the next period, there would be an increase in primary income outflow as profits from these assets flow out to foreign countries. Conversely, reductions in foreign holdings of local assets would reduce the income outflow in the primary income balance. In a similar vein, increases and decreases in local holdings of foreign assets would improve and worsen the primary income balance, respectively.

International commitments (affecting the secondary income balance)—Aid given by one country to another is a form of transfer payment. The amount of such aid given or received is influenced by the international commitments a country makes. For example, if Singapore pledges to provide $1 billion in aid to other developing countries, this would be an outflow of transfer payments in the secondary income balance.

The size of the migrant population (affecting the secondary income balance)—The size of the migrant population can affect the level of remittance. A greater number of migrant workers in the country increases the outflow of remittances and hence, worsens the secondary income balance. Conversely, a larger number of locals working overseas would increase the amount of remittance inflows and hence, improve the secondary income balance.

Factors influencing the capital and financial account

Factors can influence the capital and financial account through influencing the direct investment and portfolio investment accounts. These include the following:

- International competitiveness (affecting direct investments)
- Global demand conditions (affecting direct investments)
- Exchange rates (affecting both direct and portfolio investments)
- Interest rates (affecting portfolio investments)
- Expected changes in exchange rates (affecting portfolio investments)

International competitiveness (affecting direct investments)—International competitiveness is a rather broad term. It can be thought of in terms of whether the goods and services in a country are competitive in the global market or whether a country is better able to attract FDI compared to other countries. In this section, it is the latter definition that matters. There are many aspects to international competitiveness such as how well developed the transport and energy infrastructure is, how skilled and cheap the labour force is, how high (or low) the corporate income taxes are, how politically stable the country is, how much corruption there is, etc. The World Economic Forum (WEF) uses the Global Competitiveness Index to formally measure the international competitiveness of countries. There are 110 indicators in their index that are organised into 12 pillars of competitiveness. Another commonly cited indicator for international competitiveness is the Ease of Doing Business Index compiled by the World Bank. For the A Level syllabus, it is sufficient to have a broad understanding of what international competitiveness means and how it affects the flow of direct investments. The more competitive a country, the more it attracts FDI inflows. For example, in the 2017–2018 global rankings for the Global Competitiveness Index, Singapore was the third most competitive country (the first was Switzerland followed by the United States). This is a factor behind our large FDI inflows.

Global demand conditions (affecting direct investments)—Global demand conditions can also affect FDI flows. To reduce transport cost and to become more responsive to the demands of their consumer markets, firms may wish to build their factories closer to their consumer markets (e.g., car manufacturers targeting European consumers building their car production plants in Europe). As such, when the global demand changes, the flow of FDI may change too. To illustrate this, note the expansion of Starbucks outlets in China. As the Chinese middle class expanded and became a sizeable consumer base, Starbucks opened more outlets in China. This opening of outlets is a form of FDI. The increase in demand for lifestyle goods and services in China led to an increase in FDI inflow into China from foreign lifestyle goods and services producers.

Exchange rates (affecting both direct and portfolio investments)—Exchange rates can affect both direct and portfolio investments. For direct investments, the exchange rate could affect the cost of production and expected return on investments. For example, from the point of view of manufacturers looking for a place to build a factory to produce goods to export to the United States, an appreciation of the Chinese Yuan makes it more expensive to build the factory and produce goods in China compared to doing so in Vietnam. This would reduce the FDI inflows into China[6]. Conversely, a depreciation of the Chinese Yuan would increase the FDI inflow into China. For portfolio investments, an appreciation may make the financial assets inaccessible to foreign buyers as it is now more expensive in their domestic currency. This would reduce portfolio investment inflows. Conversely, a depreciation would increase portfolio investment inflows.

Interest rates (affecting portfolio investments)—Portfolio investments flow to countries where the returns are the highest. For such investments, the returns are highly positively correlated with the interest rates. The higher the interest rate, the higher the returns on stocks and bonds. For bonds, this is obvious. Since the purchase of a bond is the giving of a loan, the interest rate would represent the rate of return on a bond since the interest rate is the return from loans. For shares, the reasoning is slightly more complex. A simplified explanation is as follows. Shares and bonds are alternative portfolio investments. If interest rates increase, the return on bonds increases. This would cause portfolio investors to switch from shares to bonds. This causes the demand for shares to decrease, which decreases the price of shares. With a lower price, if the dividends earned on the shares stay the same, the return on the shares effectively increase. This will happen until the return on the bonds and shares remains the same. This process is actually known as arbitrage. In any case, since interest rates represent the return on portfolio investments, the higher the interest rate, the greater the portfolio investment inflow. This was seen post the Great Recession in 2008 when the US government adopted quantitative easing. The reduction in interest rates in United States caused an increase in outflow of portfolio investments from United States to other countries.

Expected changes in exchange rates (affecting portfolio investments)—Expected changes in exchange rates also affect portfolio investments through affecting the expected returns. If the domestic currency is expected to appreciate, foreign portfolio investors would want to purchase more of the domestic financial assets. This is because if they purchase the domestic financial assets before the appreciation, after the currency appreciates, they would also earn a return from the appreciation of the domestic currency. This is intuitive. If a Singaporean expects the US dollar to appreciate, he would buy US currency. This is because after the appreciation, the US currency he holds would be exchangeable for more SGD.

6.5.3 Consequences of BOP deficits

Governments aim for healthy BOP positions. In reality, healthy BOP positions are more about the make-up of the BOP than about the overall BOP position per se (e.g., whether the current account deficit is too large as opposed to whether the BOP is in surplus or deficit). A healthy BOP is also context dependent (e.g., whether a current account deficit is too large depends on, amongst other things, the state of development; a developing country would naturally import more capital goods to build its infrastructure).

7 This effect could potentially be offset by foreign firms wanting to set up operations in China to sell to the Chinese as the returns in domestic currency would be higher if the Chinese Yuan appreciates. Nonetheless, for the A Levels, we usually relate an appreciation with a reduction in FDI inflows.

Nonetheless, where the overall BOP position is concerned, BOP surpluses are generally preferred to BOP deficits. This is because BOP deficits can impose costs on consumers, firms, and governments. The costs would differ depending on whether the country runs a floating exchange rate regime, a fixed exchange rate regime, or a managed float exchange rate regime. So, before we go into the consequences of a BOP deficit, we need to understand the exchange rate regimes.

Exchange rate determination

Exchange rates are determined in the foreign exchange market (Forex). The Forex is a market place where currencies are traded. For example, someone who wants to exchange SGD for US dollars is effectively selling SGD in the Forex and buying US dollars in the Forex.

The demand for a currency will come from foreigners who wish to buy the currency and will pay for it with foreign currency (e.g., the demand for SGD will come from US residents willing to pay US dollars to buy it). Foreigners want to buy SGD when they need to pay in SGD. For example, when they buy our exports, they will need to buy SGD to pay for them. Similarly, when foreigners wish to buy Singapore assets (i.e., carry out direct and portfolio investments), they will also need to buy SGD. In summary, the demand for SGD in the Forex comes from foreigners and is directly correlated with the monetary inflows into Singapore in the BOP (exports, direct, and portfolio investment inflows are all monetary inflows).

The supply of SGD, on the other hand, comes from locals who wish to sell SGD in exchange for foreign currencies (US dollars, in our example). Locals want to buy foreign currencies when they need to pay in foreign currency. For example, when we buy imports, we will need foreign currency to pay for them. In the same vein, when locals carry out outward direct and portfolio investments, we will also need to buy foreign currencies.

In summary, the supply of SGD in the Forex comes from locals and is directly correlated with the monetary outflows into Singapore in the BOP. In the Forex, the demand and supply of a currency determines its price. And, since the price of a currency in the Forex is in terms of another currency (e.g., price of SGD in the Forex would be the units of US dollars needed to be exchanged for one unit of SGD), the price of a currency in the Forex is also its exchange rate (Fig. 6.10).

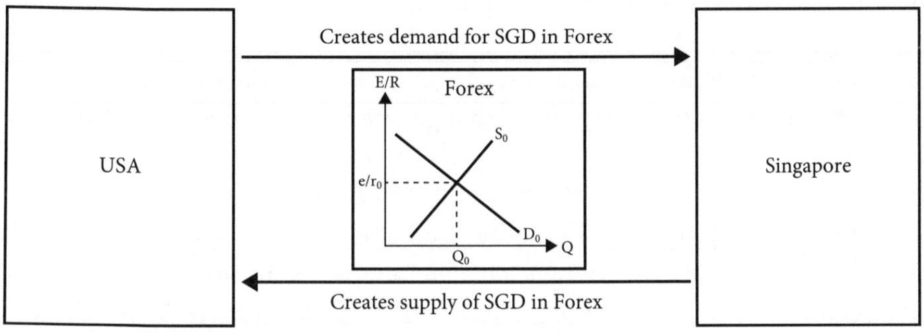

Figure 6.10: Illustration of the Forex.

Floating exchange rate system—A floating exchange rate system is one where the exchange rate is solely determined in the foreign exchange market (Forex) without any intervention from a country's Central Bank. A Central Bank is different from the commercial banks that households deposit their money with. A Central Bank is the national authority that oversees a country's monetary policy by influencing monetary instruments such as the exchange rate and interest rate. For Singapore, the Central Bank is the Monetary Authority of Singapore (MAS). For the United States, the Central Bank is the US Federal Reserve Board ("the Fed" for short).

Definition(s):

A **Central Bank** is the national authority that oversees a country's monetary policy by influencing monetary instruments such as the exchange rate and interest rate.

Figure 6.11 below illustrates the market for SGD in the Forex if Singapore adopted a floating exchange rate system.

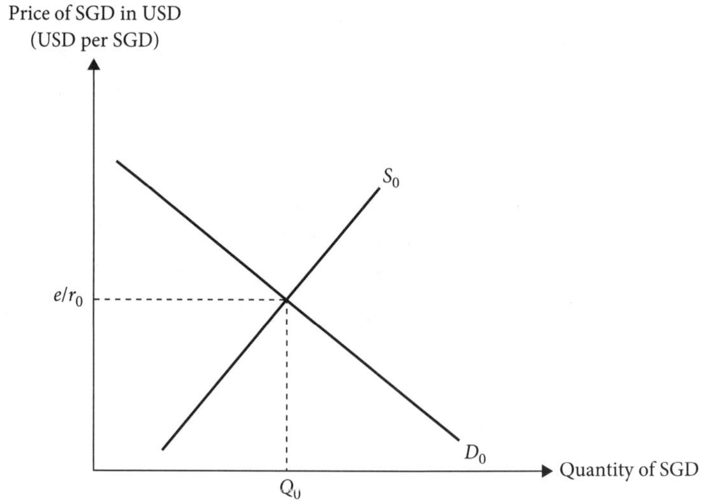

Figure 6.11: A floating exchange rate system.

The demand and supply of a currency in the Forex then determines the equilibrium exchange rate just like how the demand and supply of any good or service determines its equilibrium price. We note that there is no intervention from the Central Bank. This is better understood when contrasted against the fixed and managed float systems below.

Fixed exchange rate system—In a fixed exchange rate system, the Central Bank of a country would intervene in the Forex to keep the exchange rate at the desired level. This is illustrated in Fig. 6.12.

Suppose the exchange rate is supposed to be fixed at e/r_0. At demand D_0 and supply S_0, the equilibrium exchange rate is where the exchange rate peg is. In this case, the Central Bank would not need to intervene. However, suppose there were an increase in FDI flows from United States into Singapore. This would cause an increase in demand for SGD in the Forex as the US residents need to pay for the physical assets in SGD. Demand would rise from D_0

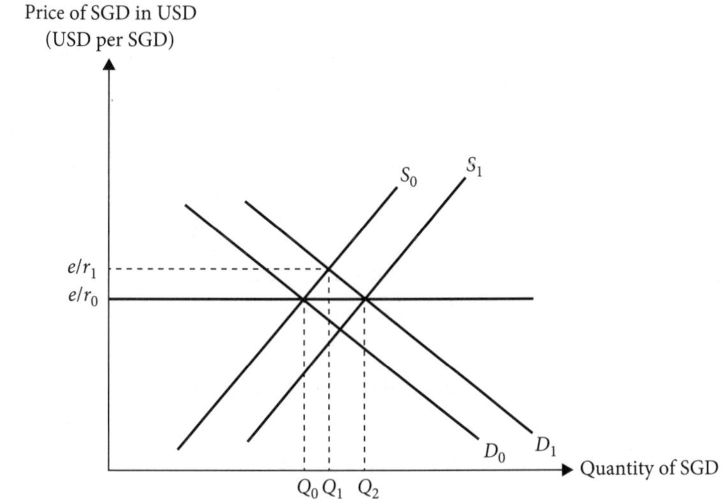

Figure 6.12: A fixed exchange rate system.

to D_1. If the Central Bank does not intervene, the SGD would appreciate from e/r_0 to e/r_1. However, if Singapore were running a fixed exchange rate system, the Central bank would not allow the currency to appreciate. As such, when the demand increases, to prevent the SGD from appreciating, the Central Bank would enter the Forex market to sell SGD in exchange for foreign currency. This would increase the supply of SGD from S_0 to S_1, and hence, keep the exchange rate at the fixed level. The opposite would also be true. If there is a fall in demand or increase in supply that exerts a downward pressure on the exchange rate, the Central Bank would step in by buying the Singapore currency in the Forex. This buying of SGD would increase the demand of SGD in the Forex and prevent it from depreciating.

Managed float exchange rate system—A managed float exchange rate system is also known as a dirty float. It is a combination of fixed and floating exchange rate systems. It is similar to a fixed system in that an upper and a lower band are fixed. They mark out the maximum and minimum value the Central Bank is prepared to let the currency reach. However, within these bands, the exchange rate is allowed to float. This is illustrated in Fig. 6.13.

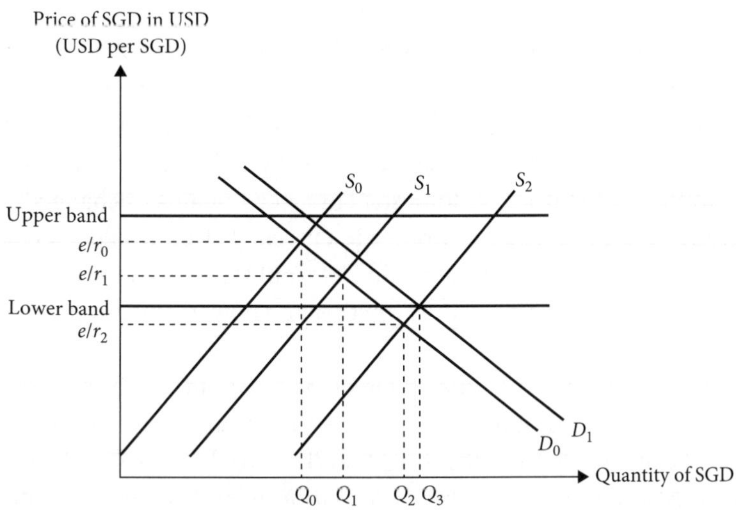

Figure 6.13: A managed float exchange rate system.

The upper and lower bands of the managed float are marked out by the horizontal lines labelled "Upper band" and "Lower band". Let us assume that the market demand and supply are currently D_0 and S_0. The equilibrium exchange rate is therefore e/r_0. Suppose the interest rates in United States increase. Singapore residents would then want to purchase more of United States' financial assets. This outflow of portfolio investments would cause an increase in supply of SGD in the Forex and Singapore residents would need to sell SGD in exchange for US dollars to pay for the US financial assets. If the supply increases from S_0 to S_1, the Central Bank would not intervene as the resultant exchange rate of e/r_1 is still within the upper and lower bands. However, if the increase is the supply of SGD is large (from S_0 to S_2), the Central Bank would need to intervene as the resultant exchange rate e/r_2 would be below the band. In that case, the Central Bank would step in by buying the Singapore currency in the Forex. This buying of SGD would increase the demand of SGD in the Forex from D_0 to D_1 and bring the exchange rate back within the band. The exchange rate would now be exactly at the lower band.

Consequences of a BOP deficit under a floating exchange rate

Having understood the different exchange rate systems, we can now study the consequences of a BOP deficit under a floating exchange rate system.

A BOP deficit means that the inflow of money is less than the outflow of money. Since inflows of money are directly correlated with the demand for the currency in the Forex and outflows of money are directly correlated with the supply of the currency in the Forex, a BOP deficit means that the demand for the currency in the Forex is less than the supply of currency in the Forex (or quantity demanded of the currency in the Forex being less than the quantity supplied of the currency in the Forex, to be more accurate). If the country runs a floating exchange rate system, the currency would depreciate. This imposes cost on consumers, firms, and governments.

Consumers—For consumers, the depreciation of the currency would erode the ability to purchase imports as depreciation causes imports to be more expensive. This causes a reduction in material standard of living as households are now able to consume fewer imported goods and services.

Producers—For producers, the depreciation could increase the cost of imported raw materials. This increase in cost would reduce their profits. However, the depreciation could benefit producers that export their products to other countries. This is because a depreciation would reduce the price of their goods in foreign currency; this would cause foreigners to buy more of their products. Given that the price in domestic currency remains unchanged, these exporters would enjoy an increase in revenue in domestic currency. This would increase their profits instead. So, the effect of a BOP deficit on producers would depend on whether and how much they rely on imported raw materials vis-a-vis whether and how much they export their products.

Government—For a government, the depreciation would have mixed effects on its macroeconomic and microeconomic goals. The depreciation would increase net exports and hence, the AD (see Chapter 5: Factors affecting AD). This would increase NY and hence, achieve economic growth. At the same time, the depreciation would increase the cost of imported raw materials and cause the SRAS to shift upwards (see Chapter 5.2.4 Factors affecting AS).

This would cause the NY to fall instead. Overall, the increase AD should outweigh the decrease in SRAS and cause NY to increase. This is a positive effect in terms of growth and should also reduce demand-deficient unemployment. However, there could be a negative effect where inflation is concerned. Since both the increase in AD and decrease in SRAS contribute to an increase in the GPL, the depreciation could lead to high inflation rates, which is not desirable from the government's point of view. In terms of the microeconomic effects, high inflation worsens inequity (see section 6.3.3 on Consequences of high inflation). Finally, in terms of the government budget, the depreciation of the currency would increase the foreign currency-denominated debt of governments if they had borrowed money from foreign banks or governments. This is because if the debt is denominated in foreign currency, the value of the debt in domestic currency would increase when the domestic currency depreciates. This has implications as interest payments on the debt would now require more local currency, which imposes an opportunity cost as these payments could have been used for other important areas of government spending such as education and health care.

Consequences of a BOP under a fixed exchange rate

Recall that a BOP deficit means that the inflow of money is less than the outflow of money and that since inflows of money are directly correlated with the demand of the currency in the Forex and outflows of money are directly correlated with the supply of the currency in the Forex, a BOP deficit means that the quantity demanded of the currency in the Forex is less than the quantity supplied in the Forex. If the country runs a fixed exchange rate, the Central Bank would need to prevent the currency from depreciating by buying the domestic currency in the Forex to prop up its demand. To do so, it would need to sell foreign currency from its foreign currency reserves. If it runs out of the foreign currency reserves, it would not be able to continue to buy its currency in the Forex to maintain the currency's value. This would then cause a large and sudden depreciation. Such was the experience of Thailand in the 1997 Asian Financial Crisis when the Thai Central Bank was forced to abandon its currency peg because it ran out of foreign reserves. In this case, the effects of the large and sudden currency depreciation would be similar to what is described in the previous three paragraphs.

Consequences of a BOP deficit under a managed float

If the country runs a managed float, the effect of a BOP deficit would depend on how large the deficit is. If the deficit is small enough such that the currency's depreciation would still be within the upper and lower exchange rate bands, then the effects would be the same as the effects under a floating exchange rate. If the BOP deficit is large enough to cause the currency to depreciate below the lower band, the Central Bank would have to step in and the effects would be the same as the effects under a fixed exchange rate.

6.6 Macroeconomic Policy—Fiscal Policy

The previous sections in the first half of this chapter dealt with the macroeconomic aims in terms of how they are measured, what causes them, and the consequences of not achieving the aim. The second half of this chapter deals with the macroeconomic policies that governments can employ to achieve their aims and the limitations faced in using these policies. Different governments will use different policies depending on the macroeconomic problem they are facing and the context of their country. This is because the context of the country determines the relative effectiveness of the policies.

The first macroeconomic policy we will study is fiscal policy.

Fiscal policy refers to the use of the government budget to influence macroeconomic outcomes. Just like how a personal budget records how much income one makes and how this income is to be spent, the government budget is made up of two parts—the sources of a government's revenue and the areas of government expenditure.

Definition(s):

Fiscal policy refers to the use of the government budget, tax revenue and government spending to influence macroeconomic outcomes.

For most part, a government's revenue is the taxes it collects. This would include taxes on households' income (personal income taxes), taxes collected from firms (corporate income taxes), taxes on consumption (consumption taxes such as the Goods and Services Tax [GST] in Singapore), industry-specific taxes (e.g., property taxes, alcohol taxes, cigarette taxes), and other taxes.

On the expenditure side, government expenditure can be split into operating and development expenditure. Operating expenditure is the expenditure on the day-to-day running of the government. It would include expenditure such as the salaries of civil servants. Development expenditure is expenditure on long-term projects. Spending on infrastructural renewal would come under this category. The operating and developmental expenditure is further split by the various ministries. Examples of the sources of the Singapore government's revenue and expenditure is provided in Figs. 6.14 and 6.15 below.

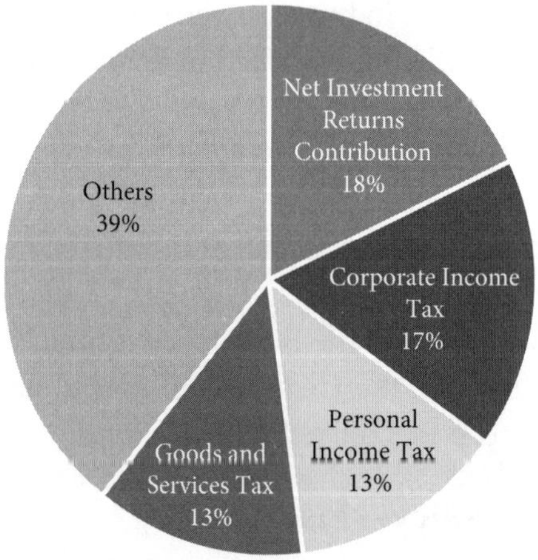

Figure 6.14: Sources of government revenue for Singapore (projected for 2018).

Source: http://www.singaporebudget.gov.sg/budget_2018/BudgetSpeech/RevenueExpenditure

Note: The four largest individual sources of revenue are net investment returns contribution (NIRC), corporate income tax, personal income tax, and GST. Others cover another 11 categories of revenue but each category is rather small. The NIRC is not a tax. It is from the returns to the government's investments. However, it has limited relevance to the A-Level syllabus.

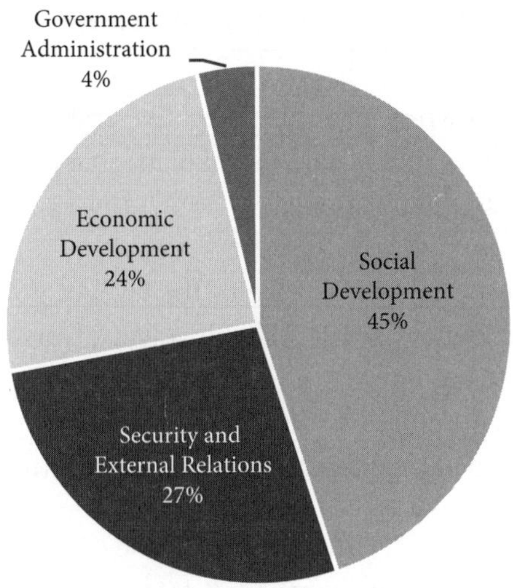

Figure 6.15: Areas of government expenditure for Singapore (projected for 2018).
Source: http://www.singaporebudget.gov.sg/budget_2018/BudgetSpeech/RevenueExpenditure
Note: Social development includes expenditure incurred by the Ministries of Education, National Development, Health, Environment and Water Resources, Culture, Community and Youth, Social and Family Development, Communications and Information, and Manpower (Financial Security). Security and external relations includes expenditure by the Ministries of Defence, Home Affairs, and Foreign Affairs. Economic development includes expenditure incurred by the Ministries of Transport, Trade and Industry, Manpower (excluding Financial Security), and Info-Communications and Media Development. Government administration includes expenditure incurred by the Ministries of Finance, Law, the Organs of State, and the Prime Minister's Office. Each of these ministries' expenditure can be further broken down into operating and development expenditure.

The budget position refers to the government revenue minus the government expenditure. If revenue exceeds expenditure, we say that the government budget is in a surplus. If revenue is less than expenditure, we say that the government budget is in a deficit. If the two are equal, we say that the budget is balanced.

Definition(s):

A **budget surplus** refers to a positive budget position where the government revenue exceeds its expenditure.

A **budget deficit** refers to a negative budget position where the government revenue is less than its expenditure.

A **balanced budget** refers to a budget position where the government revenue is equal to its expenditure.

By adjusting the level and type of revenue (e.g., adjusting the corporate income tax rates) and/or adjusting the level and type of expenditure (e.g., increasing expenditure on education), the government is able to influence the macroeconomy to achieve its aims.

6.6.1 Expansionary fiscal policy to correct weak growth, high unemployment, and/or deflation

If an economy is in a recession where growth is negative and unemployment is increasing, or suffering from deflation, a government may use expansionary fiscal policy to restore growth rates and bring the inflation rate back up.

Expansionary fiscal policy refers to the increase in the level of government spending and/or a reduction in the level of taxes to increase the AD. It involves a worsening of the budget position.

The increase in the level of government spending will increase AD since AD = $C + I + G + (X - M)$. This causes the AD to shift right and increases the national output via the multiplier process.

The reduction in taxes also affects the AD. A reduction in personal income taxes would increase households' disposable income. This increases their purchasing power and causes them to consume more. This causes an increase in consumption, which also increases AD and hence, national output via the multiplier process.

If the reduction is for corporate income taxes, the post-tax returns of investments increases. This increases the MEI and causes an increase in investments at the given interest rate. The increase in investment also increases AD and hence, national output via the multiplier process.

If the tax reduced is the consumption tax (e.g., reducing the GST), then consumption would increase. This also increases AD and hence, national output via the multiplier process.

Taken together, the increase in national output restores economic growth. Also, since national output increases, the demand for labour would also increase since it is derived from the production of goods and services. As such, demand-deficient unemployment would decrease.

The effect of expansionary fiscal policy on national output is illustrated below where the increase in AD from AD_0 to AD_1 causes an increase in national output from Y_0 to Y_1 (Fig. 6.16).

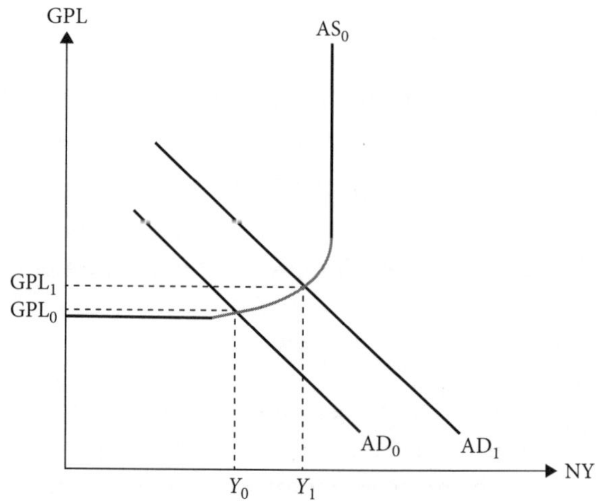

Figure 6.16: Expansionary fiscal policy causing economic growth.

Since the increase in AD also causes an increase in GPL, expansionary fiscal policy can also be used to achieve the aim of low inflation when the economy is experiencing deflation or too-low inflation.

Putting it concretely: Supply-side effect of expansionary fiscal policy

To achieve long-run growth, the type of tax and expenditure would matter. Reductions in corporate income taxes would stimulate investments which would lead to capital accumulation (recall that investment in aggregate demand [AD] is the purchase of capital goods). The increase in capital stock is an increase in the quantity of capital in the economy and will cause the productive capacity of the economy to increase. This causes the LRAS to increase, achieving potential growth too. In contrast, if the reduction in tax is for consumption taxes, the increase in consumption would not have the same effect of achieving potential growth. In the same vein, whether increases in government expenditure can affect potential growth depends on what the government spends on. If the increase in government expenditure is on infrastructure development, then the capital accumulation (note that infrastructure is considered a capital good) would also create potential growth. However, if the government's increased spending is not on productive assets (e.g., building more monuments of dubious cultural value), then there would be no increase in the LRAS.

In summary, the increased level of government spending and decreased level of taxes in expansionary fiscal policy would increase the AD. However, whether there would be an effect on aggregate supply (AS) depends on what exactly the increased government spending is on and exactly which type of taxes are reduced.

6.6.2 Limitations of expansionary fiscal policy to correct weak growth, high unemployment, and/or deflation

There are a number of possible limitations to expansionary fiscal policy to correct weak growth, high unemployment, and/or deflation. They include

- The size of the multiplier
- The crowding out effect from having to finance the measure
- Time lags
- Imperfect information in forecasting
- Policy conflicts
- Political acceptability

The size of the multiplier—In Chapter 5, we learnt that the extent to which national output increases in response to an increase in AD is dependent on the size of the multiplier. To recap, the size of the multiplier depends on the marginal propensity to withdraw (MPW) $(k = \frac{1}{\text{MPW}} = \frac{1}{\text{MPS} + \text{MPT} + \text{MPM}})$. As such, if a country has a high MPW, it would have a small multiplier. This would limit the effectiveness of expansionary fiscal policy to bolster economic growth. An example would be Singapore. Due to the Central Provident Fund (CPF) scheme, the marginal propensity to save (MPS) in Singapore is very high. An average CPF contribution rate of 20% would mean that the MPS is at least 0.2. Add to that the Asian culture of thrift and the MPS in Singapore would be even higher. Additionally, Singapore's import reliance causes the MPM to be high. Taken together, although Singapore's low income tax rates cause the MPT to be low, the MPW is still large due to the high MPS and MPM. As such, expansionary fiscal policy would have a limited effect in stimulating economic growth in Singapore. In fact, by one estimate, Singapore's multiplier is only about 1.1.

The crowding out effect from having to finance the measure—In adopting an expansionary fiscal policy, the government may end up running a budget deficit. For example, assuming that the budget was originally balanced, increase in government expenditure and reduction in taxes would cause the government expenditure to now exceed its revenue. When this happens, governments need to finance their spending, which means they need to find money to pay for their spending. To do so, governments will need to borrow money. This borrowing of money by the government represents an increase in demand for loans, which drives interest rates up. In response, firms would cut back investments as the higher cost of borrowing causes investments to no longer be profitable. As such, while the expansionary fiscal policy increases the AD, the fall in investments offsets some of this increase, causing the increase in national output and GPL to both be limited. This effect was experienced by many African nations in the early part of 2018. To highlight one specific example, Zambia's government's borrowing drove the interest rates up between 20% and 30%, crowding out many small local businesses who are unable to borrow at such high rates.

Time lags—Another limitation of expansionary fiscal policy is time lag. For most democracies, measures are passed as parliamentary bills. Hence, in order for governments to take action to increase government spending or lower taxes, bills must be drafted and then debated in parliament before they are approved. This process can introduce severe lags, especially if the politics in the country are such that there is no single overwhelming party that can push a bill through and politicians from different parties are unable or unwilling to compromise. To illustrate this, on average, 264 days[7] are needed to push a bill through the US Congress (although not all bills are about spending and taxes, and the days vary significantly). There is also an implementation lag after the bills are passed. Finally, because it takes time to work through the multiplier process, the full effect of the expansionary fiscal policy would be delayed.

Imperfect information in forecasting—Imperfect information in forecasting affects the appropriateness of both the timing and the extent of the expansionary fiscal policy. Governments may employ expansionary fiscal policy as a preventive tool if they forecast that the economy is going to slip into recession. However, if the timing is off, the expansionary fiscal policy may be introduced too early or too late. Too early could result in a bout of overheating where the increase in AD ends up fuelling demand-pull inflation while too late could result in

8 Source: https://www.congress.gov

a period of recession before the effects of the expansionary fiscal policy kicks in. Additionally, imperfect information about the extent of the recession could reduce the effectiveness of the expansionary fiscal policy. If the forecasted recession is a mild one, the government may employ only a mildly expansionary fiscal policy. However, if the actual recession turns out to be much deeper than forecasted, the effect of the expansionary fiscal policy would be too small.

Policy conflicts—Expansionary fiscal policy could cause conflicts in the macroeconomic aims. For example, if an economy was experiencing weak growth but high inflation (also known as stagflation, which many economies experienced during the oil crises from 1973 to 1974 and from 1979 to 1980), an expansionary fiscal policy might revive growth by increasing AD but also worsen the problem of high inflation by creating further demand-pull inflation. Apart from that, if an economy is experiencing low growth and a BOP deficit, an expansionary fiscal policy would also solve one problem at the expense of another. In this case, the growth created by the expansionary fiscal policy would increase the purchasing power of households. In turn, households would consume more goods and services, including imports. This increase in import expenditure would worsen the balance of trade and current account positions, thus, increasing the BOP deficit. The conflict may also be with the government's goals regarding fiscal sustainability. For example, after the European debt crisis in 2011, the UK government set goals to reduce their budget deficit. However, if they employ expansionary fiscal policy, the budget deficit would widen instead.

Political acceptability—Finally, expansionary fiscal policy may be limited by its political acceptability. This may seem counter intuitive as it is hard to imagine anyone opposing lower taxes and higher government spending. However, real life provides us with good examples. The tea party movement in America is one. Members of the tea party believe that a government should not spend beyond its means and are opposed to expansionary fiscal policy as it would widen the government's budget deficit. It is also possible that voters may reject cuts in corporate taxes on the grounds that such tax cuts benefit the rich more than the poor and result in higher income inequality.

6.6.3 Contractionary fiscal policy to correct high inflation and/or BOP deficit

If an economy is experiencing high inflation and/or a BOP deficit, the government could use a contractionary fiscal policy to bring down the inflation rate and/or reduce the BOP deficit.

Contractionary fiscal policy refers to the decrease in the level of government spending and/or an increase in the level of taxes. It involves an improvement of the budget position.

The decrease in the level of government spending will reduce AD since AD = $C + I + G + (X - M)$. This causes the AD to shift left. Increases in personal income taxes would reduce disposable incomes and consumption, causing a fall in AD. Similarly, increases in corporate income taxes reduces post-tax profits of investments and causes a fall in investments while increases in consumption taxes reduce consumption, causing further falls in AD. The decrease in AD then causes a fall in the GPL, offsetting some of the existing inflationary pressure to achieve a lower rate of inflation.

The effect of contractionary fiscal policy on GPL is illustrated below where the reduction in AD from AD_0 to AD_1 causes a fall in the GPL from GPL_0 to GPL_1 (Fig. 6.17).

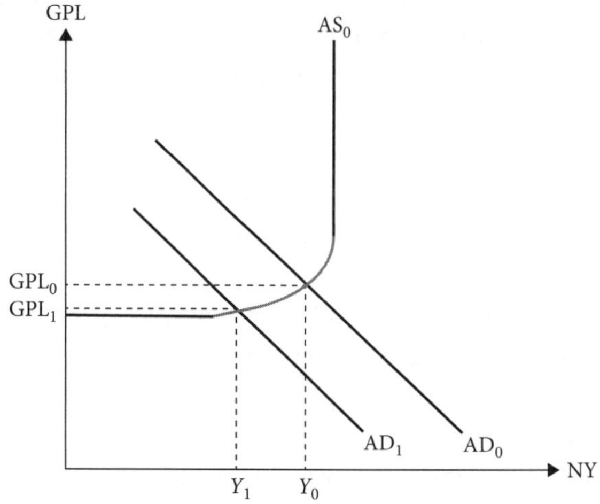

Figure 6.17: Contractionary fiscal policy causing a fall in GPL.

The contractionary fiscal policy causes an improvement in the BOP position through two effects—the expenditure-reducing and the expenditure-switching effect. For the expenditure-reducing effect, since the contractionary fiscal policy causes a fall in national income, households would also spend less on imports due to their reduced purchasing power. This reduction in import expenditure would cause an improvement in the balance of trade and current account positions and hence, a reduction in the BOP deficit.

The expenditure-switching effect comes about due to the fall in the GPL. Since the GPL is the price level of domestically produced goods and services, a reduction in GPL would cause local households to switch from consuming imports to consuming domestically produced goods. This would reduce the import expenditure. At the same time, since exports are domestically produced goods and services, a reduction in GPL also means that foreign consumers would switch towards consuming our exports since our exports are now relatively cheaper than their domestically produced goods and services. Assuming the demand for exports is price elastic, the quantity demanded for exports would increase more than proportionately, causing an increase in export revenue. Taken together, the increase in export revenue and fall in import expenditure would lead to an improvement in the balance of trade and hence, current account positions. This further reduces the BOP deficit.

6.6.4 Limitations of contractionary fiscal policy to correct high inflation and/or BOP deficit

The limitations of contractionary fiscal policy include

- Time lags
- Inflexibility in changing government expenditure
- Imperfect information in forecasting
- Policy conflicts
- Political acceptability

Time lags—The time lags that apply to expansionary fiscal policy would also apply to contractionary fiscal policy. In fact, the debate may take even longer as contractionary fiscal policy may involve cuts to cherished programmes.

Inflexibility in changing government expenditure—Contractionary fiscal policy may also be limited by the fact that sometimes, government expenditure cannot be reduced because of the nature of spending. For example, a multistage project to build a high-speed underground railway cannot be so easily terminated midway. If tunnelling has been completed, the government cannot leave the tunnels undeveloped as they may corrode over time.

Imperfect information in forecasting—The inaccuracies in forecasting that limit expansionary fiscal policy also apply to contractionary fiscal policy. For example, overestimating the extent of contraction needed to cool the economy and bring down the high inflation rate could result in the economy slipping into recession instead.

Policy conflicts—Similar to expansionary fiscal policy, contractionary fiscal policy could cause conflicts in the macroeconomic aims. For example, if the economy is experiencing stagflation, contractionary fiscal policy would result in the achievement of one aim (low inflation) at the expense of two others (worsened growth and higher unemployment).

Political acceptability—Contractionary fiscal policy may also be unacceptable to voters because the reduction in government spending could be in the form of withdrawal of subsidies or public services that citizens have becomes accustomed to. For example, in the UK, cuts to government spending on the National Health Service (NHS) often trigger protests and negative emotions as UK residents have come to see free healthcare as a right.

6.6.5 Fiscal policy to make growth inclusive and sustainable

Fiscal policy may also be used to make growth inclusive and sustainable. However, this is not done by simply changing the level of spending or taxes. Instead, it is done by making decisions about specific types of spending and taxes.

Achieving inclusive growth

Since inclusive growth refers to growth where the increase in incomes is spread out and enjoyed by many, the pursuit of inclusive growth can be thought of as the pursuit of two goals simultaneously – growth and equity. We have seen how growth can be achieved by lowering taxes and increasing government spending. To achieve equity/reduce inequity by adjusting government spending or taxes, the government can:

- Provide subsidies for necessities (studied in Chapter 4 where we saw that subsidies for necessities could reduce inequity by reducing the price of necessities, making them more affordable to the poor)
- Increase the progressiveness of the tax system to reduce income inequality

Implementing a progressive tax system – A progressive tax system is one where the higher one's income, the greater the proportion of income paid as taxes. For example, Singapore's income tax system is progressive because the first $20,000 of annual income is taxed at 0% (i.e., not taxed), whereas the next $10,000 is taxed at 2%, and each successive $10,000 is taxed at a higher percentage. Thus, the higher one's income, the higher the proportion of it as paid as taxes.

In comparison, a proportional tax system is one where the proportion of income paid as taxes remains constant even as income increases. Singapore's basic corporate tax rate of 17% is one such example. Both small and large firms generating different amounts of income pay the same proportion of their income as taxes.

Finally, a regressive tax system is one where the higher one's income, the lower the proportion of income paid as taxes. For example, Singapore's GST is regressive. The 7% tax on a $1000 TV would mean a tax amount of $70 for all consumers. However, this $70 is a larger proportion of a poor man's income than a rich man's income.

Definition(s):

A **progressive** tax system is one where the higher one's income, the greater the proportion of income paid as taxes.

A **proportional** tax system is one where no matter what one's income is, the proportion of income paid as taxes remains constant.

A **regressive** tax system is one where the higher one's income, the lower the proportion of income paid as taxes.

To achieve inclusive growth, countries can increase the progressiveness of their tax systems by increasing the top income tax rates (or lowering the bottom income tax rates) or reducing regressive taxes or both.

Achieving sustainable growth

Since sustainable growth refers actual growth that does not compromise the ability of future generations to achieve economic growth too, pursuing sustainable growth can be thought of in terms of pursuing two goals simultaneously – growth and environmental sustainability. We have seen how growth can be achieved by lowering taxes and increasing government spending. Achieving environmental sustainability can be interpreted as correcting negative externalities in the form of harm to the environment. To that end, governments can adopt taxes on negative externalities or providing subsidies for R&D to reduce the negative externality explained in Chapter 4.

6.6.6 Limitations of fiscal policy to make growth inclusive and sustainable

Limitations in achieving inclusive growth

- The limitations of price ceilings and subsidies for necessities were both studied in Chapter 4
- Increasing the progressiveness of the tax system faces a limitation in terms of trading off the incentive to work. A progressive income tax reduces the additional gain in income from working harder. An overly progressive one may cause workers to cut back on working since the returns to working decreases as income increases.

Limitations in achieving sustainable growth

The limitations of taxes on negative externalities or providing subsidies for R&D to reduce the negative externality were explained in Chapter 4.

6.6.7 Automatic stabilisers

Both expansionary and contractionary fiscal policy involve the government intentionally changing the level of taxes or government spending. As such, they are also known as discretionary fiscal policy as they are carried out at the discretion of the government. In contrast, the tax and benefits system that the government puts in place can have automatic effects on the economy.

Definition(s):

Discretionary fiscal policy refers to intentional changes to the level of taxes and government expenditure. It includes both expansionary and contractionary fiscal policies.

Automatic stabilisers refer to the effect that progressive tax and expenditure systems have in terms of smoothing the fluctuations in an economy.

A progressive tax and benefits system acts as an automatic stabiliser in the following manner. Suppose there is an increase in national income. As incomes rise, more people move into higher tax brackets. As such, they pay a greater proportion of their income as taxes. At the same time, as more people become employed, they lose their unemployment benefits. As such, the increase in household purchasing power is less than the increase in incomes. Thus, in the multiplier process, the next round of the increase in consumption (i.e., the induced consumption) is not as much. The subsequent effect of further increases in national income is thus, limited. This means that with a progressive tax and benefits system in place, during an economic boom, the system exerts an automatic drag on the economy such that the upswing is limited.

Conversely, during a recession, as incomes fall, people move into lower tax brackets with lower tax rates and the unemployed start receiving unemployment benefits. Hence, the fall in disposable incomes is limited. This also limits the extent of the fall in induced consumption and the resultant falls in national income. This means that with a progressive tax and benefits system in place, during an economic recession, the system exerts an automatic uplift on the economy such that the downswing is limited.

Taken together, the automatic stabilising effect of a progressive tax and benefits system would dampen the business cycles in an economy. This is illustrated in Fig. 6.18.

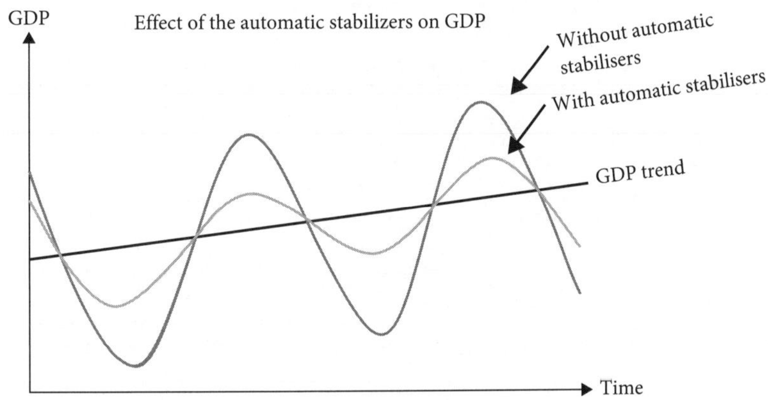

Figure 6.18: Effect of automatic stabilisers.

6.7 Macroeconomic Policy—Monetary Policy Centred on Interest Rates

Fiscal policy is carried out by governments using the government budget. In contrast, monetary policy is carried out by a country's Central Bank. Recall that a Central Bank is the national authority that oversees a country's monetary policy by influencing monetary instruments such as the exchange rate and interest rate.

Definition(s):

Monetary policy refers to the use monetary instruments such as the exchange rate and interest rate by the Central Bank to influence macroeconomic outcomes.

Most of the time, Central Banks need to choose between having control over the interest rate and having control over the exchange rate. This gives rise to two types of monetary policy—monetary policy centred on interest rates where the Central Bank chooses to control the interest rate, or monetary policy centred on exchange rates where the Central Bank chooses to control the exchange rate.

We have already learnt that the exchange rate is the price of a country's currency in terms of a foreign currency. To recap, the interest rate represents both the cost of borrowing and the return on savings in an economy.

Countries need to choose between the two instruments (interest rate vs. exchange rate) because of the monetary policy trilemma presented in the box below.

Putting it concretely: The monetary policy trilemma

The trilemma states that Central Banks can only choose two of the three following options:

- Free capital flows—This means that there are no or only limited barriers to monetary flows in the capital and financial account (i.e., direct and portfolio investments can flow into and out of a country easily)
- Control over interest rates—This means that the Central Bank can influence the interest rate in the country
- Control over exchange rates—This means that the Central Bank can influence the exchange rate of the country's currency in the Forex

This trilemma is represented in Fig. 6.19 below.

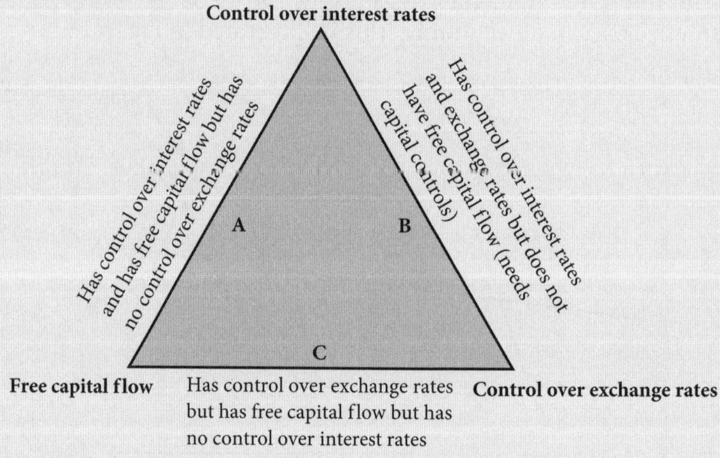

Figure 6.19: The monetary policy trilemma.

The Central Bank can either choose position A where it has control over interest rates and has free capital flow but has no control over exchange rates (e.g., United States, European Union), or position B where it has control over interest rates and exchange rates but does not have free capital flow (needs capital controls) (e.g., China), or position C where it has control over exchange rates but has free capital flow but has no control over interest rates (e.g., Hong Kong).

To understand why this is so, let us imagine that a Central Bank wants to have a high interest rate in its country. So it increases its interest rate. It does so by reducing the money supply in the country. Since money supply and interest rates have an inverse relationship[9], reducing the money supply drives up the interest rates. When that happens, if it has free capital flows, portfolio investments will flow into the country to earn the higher returns. This inflow of portfolio investments will cause the demand for the country's currency in the Forex to increase, causing its currency to appreciate. From this, we see that if a country wants to control the interest rate (have a high interest rate) and has free capital flow, it has to accept that its currency will appreciate. It cannot still insist on having a cheap currency (i.e., it loses control over the exchange rate).

Since most countries have largely free capital flow, it becomes necessary to choose between control over interest rates and exchange rates.

Economies that choose monetary policy centred on interest rates (interest rate policy for short) tend to be large and developed economies such as the United States, European Union, United Kingdom, and Japan.

6.7.1 Expansionary interest rate policy to correct weak growth, high unemployment, and/or deflation

If an economy is in a recession where growth is negative and unemployment is increasing, or suffering from deflation, a government may use expansionary interest rate policy to restore growth rates and bring the inflation rate back up.

Expansionary interest rate policy refers to the reduction in interest rates from an increase in money supply to increase the AD.

The reduction in interest rates lowers the cost of borrowing for both firms and households. For firms, this causes the number of profitable investments to increase (movement along the MEI) and hence, causes investments to rise. For households, the lower cost of borrowing stimulates spending on big ticket items such as cars that typically need to be financed through loans. Also, a lower interest rate is a lower return on savings, which reduces the opportunity cost of consumption. So, consumption will increase. The increase in investments and consumption will increase AD since AD = $C + I + G + (X - M)$. This causes the AD to shift right and increases the national output via the multiplier process.

Also, since national output increases, the demand for labour would also increase since it is derived from the production of goods and services. As such, demand-deficient unemployment would decrease.

9 The mechanism that links the money supply and the interest rates in not required at this level. Nonetheless, interested students can still look up the liquidity preference theory or the loanable funds theory.

The effect of expansionary interest rate policy on national output is illustrated below where the increase in AD from AD_0 to AD_1 causes an increase in national output from Y_0 to Y_1 (Fig. 6.20).

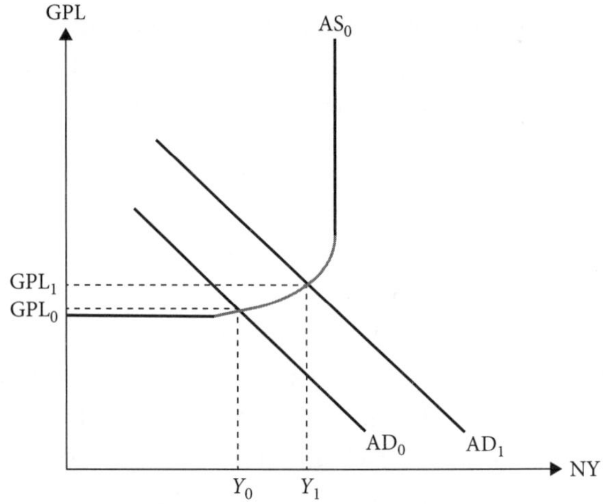

Figure 6.20: Expansionary interest rate policy causing economic growth.

Since the increase in AD also causes an increase in GPL, expansionary interest rate policy can also be used to achieve the aim of low inflation when the economy is experiencing deflation or too-low inflation.

Putting it concretely: Supply-side effect of expansionary interest rate policy

Since expansionary interest rate policy stimulates investments, it can also have a long-run effect on the LRAS. An increase in investments would lead to capital accumulation. The increase in capital stock is an increase in the quantity of capital in the economy and will cause the productive capacity of the economy to increase. This causes the LRAS to increase, achieving potential growth too.

6.7.2 Limitations of expansionary interest rate policy to correct weak growth, high unemployment, and/or deflation

There are a number of possible limitations to expansionary interest rate policy to correct weak growth, high unemployment, and/or deflation. They include:

- Interest rate inelasticity of consumption and investment due to animal spirits
- Time lags
- Imperfect information in forecasting
- Policy conflicts

Interest rate inelasticity of consumption and investment due to animal spirits—Animal spirits is a termed coined the economist John Maynard Keynes to describe human emotions. It can be interpreted as the level of consumer and business confidence. If animal spirits are low (i.e., if consumer and business confidence is low), then even with the reduction in interest rates, there would be limited increase in consumption and investments respectively. This lack of response to a change in interest rate is termed interest rate inelasticity. The limited effect on consumption and investment then causes a limited effect on the macroeconomic aims.

Time lags—Similar to fiscal policy, monetary policy could suffer from some implementation lag. However, this is seldom a real issue as Central Bankers are not elected members of the parliament and do not need to pass bills through parliament to make decisions. The lag could still exist because it takes time for the multiplier process to work. Nonetheless, monetary policy typically works faster than fiscal policy.

Imperfect information in forecasting—Similar to fiscal policy, if Central Bankers misestimate the timing and the extent of the reduction in interest rate that is needed, the policy may be too little and too late in preventing a recession.

Policy conflicts—Similar to expansionary fiscal policy, expansionary interest rate policy can cause a conflict in macroeconomic aims. In countries facing stagflation, the policy would restore economic growth at the expense of higher inflation due to the increase in AD. In countries facing weak growth and BOP deficits, the policy would restore economic growth at the expense of an even larger BOP deficit. This is because the reduction in interest rates would cause an outflow of portfolio investments, which affects the capital and financial account.

Putting it concretely: The liquidity trap and quantitative easing

In this section, the discussion on interest rate policy assumed that Central Banks are able to influence the interest rate through adjusting the money supply. In truth, however, Central Banks may be unable to reduce interest rates through increasing the money supply due to a liquidity trap. In a liquidity trap, the mechanism that translates an increase in the money supply to a reduction in interest rates stops working. However, this will require an understanding of interest rate determination which is beyond the A Level syllabus[1].

For this syllabus, it is sufficient to know that a liquidity trap is characterised by very low short-term interest rates and that when an economy is in one, the Central Bank is unable to push the short-term interest rate lower by increasing the money supply.

This was the case in a number of economies post the 2008 Global Financial Crises (also known as the "Great Recession"). In response, Central Banks of US and UK used an unconventional monetary policy termed Quantitative Easing.

Quantitative Easing involved the Central Bank buying bonds directly from financial institutions such as banks. With more cash in hand, banks would be more willing to make loans to households and firms since idle cash will not generate returns for them. To do so, these financial institutions would offer lower interest rates on loans. This stimulates consumption and investments, increasing AD and hence, national output.

In summary, Quantitative Easing still caused a reduction in interest rates. However, it did so through a method that is ordinarily not used by Central Banks.

[1]To understand the mechanism of a liquidity trap, please refer to look up the Liquidity Preference theory.

6.7.3 Contractionary interest rate policy to correct high inflation and/or BOP deficit

If an economy is experiencing high inflation and/or a BOP deficit, the government could use a contractionary interest rate policy to bring down the inflation rate and/or reduce the BOP deficit.

Contractionary interest rate policy refers to the increase in interest rates through reducing the money supply to reduce the AD.

The increase in interest rates increases the cost of borrowing for both firms and households. For firms, this causes the number of profitable investments to decrease (movement along the MEI) and hence, causes investments to fall. For households, the higher cost of borrowing reduces spending on big ticket items such as cars that typically need to be financed through loans. Also, a higher interest rate is a higher return on savings, which increases the opportunity cost of consumption. So, consumption will decrease. The decrease in investments and consumption will decrease AD since $AD = C + I + G + (X - M)$. This causes the AD to shift left. The decrease in AD then causes a fall in the GPL, offsetting some of the existing inflationary pressure to achieve a lower rate of inflation.

The effect of contractionary interest rate policy on GPL is illustrated below, where the decrease in AD from AD_0 to AD_1 causes a fall in GPL from GPL_0 to GPL_1 (Fig. 6.21).

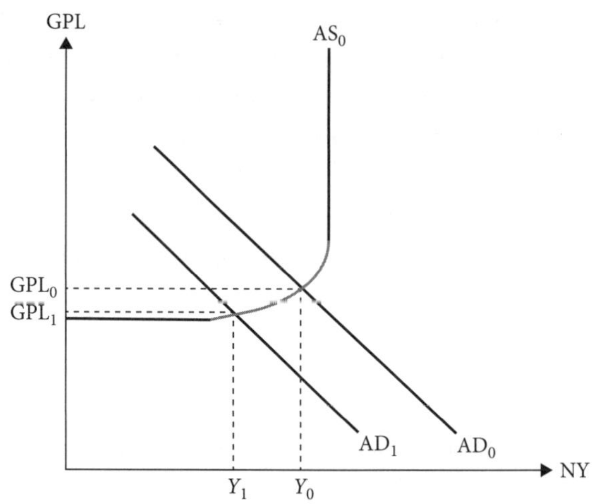

Figure 6.21: Contractionary interest rate policy causing a fall in GPL.

Just like contractionary fiscal policy, contractionary interest rate policy causes an improvement in the BOP position through two effects—the expenditure-reducing and the expenditure-switching effect. The expenditure-reducing effect is similar. Since the contractionary interest rate policy causes a fall in national income, households would also spend less on imports due to their reduced purchasing power. This reduction in import expenditure would cause an improvement in the balance of trade and current account positions and hence, a reduction in the BOP deficit.

The expenditure-switching effect is also similar. The fall in the GPL causes local households to switch from consuming imports to consuming domestically produced goods, reducing the import expenditure. At the same time, foreign consumers would switch towards consuming our exports since our exports are now relatively cheaper than their domestically produced goods and services. Assuming the demand for exports is price elastic, the quantity demanded for exports would increase more than proportionately, causing an increase in export revenue. Taken together, the increase in export revenue and fall in import expenditure would lead to an improvement in the balance of trade and hence, current account positions. This further reduces the BOP deficit.

Additionally, contractionary interest rate policy corrects the BOP deficit through attracting portfolio investments in the capital and financial account.

6.7.4 Limitations of contractionary interest rate policy to correct high inflation and/or BOP deficit

The limitations of contractionary interest rate policy include:

- Interest rate inelasticity of consumption and investment due to animal spirits
- Time lags
- Imperfect information in forecasting
- Policy conflicts
- Political acceptability

Interest rate inelasticity of consumption and investment due to animal spirits—High animal spirits (i.e., high levels of household and business confidence) would mean that households and firms may not reduce their consumption and investments in response to the increase in interest rates by much. As such, AD may only fall to a limited extent, causing a limited reduction in GPL.

Time lags—The time lags that apply to expansionary interest rate policy would apply to contractionary interest rate policy too.

Imperfect information in forecasting—The inaccuracies in forecasting that limit expansionary interest rate policy also apply to contractionary interest rate policy.

Policy conflicts—Similar to expansionary interest rate policy, contractionary interest policy could cause conflicts in the macroeconomic aims. For example, if the economy is experiencing stagflation, contractionary interest rate policy would result in the achievement of one aim (low inflation) at the expense of two others (worsened growth and higher unemployment).

Political acceptability—Finally, there may be some problems with political acceptability. While Central Banks are not elected and hence, do not have to answer to voters per se, they may face pressure from the government to adopt policies that do not cause unhappiness to voters. As such, it is possible that Central Banks may face pressure from governments to delay raising interest rates as such increases in the cost of borrowing may not be popular. In reality though, it is often the opposite. Since contractionary fiscal policies are unpopular, governments have a tendency to let the Central Banks take the full responsibility of cooling the economy (when necessary) using contractionary interest rate policy so that the government can avoid losing votes.

6.8 Macroeconomic Policy—Monetary Policy Centred on Exchange Rates

As explained in the previous section, most Central Banks have to choose between using interest rates or exchange rates as the instrument for monetary policy because of the monetary policy trilemma. In this section, we will study how monetary policy centred on exchange rates (exchange rate policy for short) works.

6.8.1 Depreciation/devaluation to correct weak growth, high unemployment, and/or deflation and/or BOP deficit

For Central Banks using an exchange rate policy, a depreciation or a devaluation (both refer to a lowering of a currency's value) can be used to correct the problems of poor economic growth (or a recession), high (demand-deficient) unemployment, deflation (or too-low inflation), and a BOP deficit.

To recap (from Chapter 5: Factors affecting AD), a depreciation causes the price of exports to decrease in a foreign currency and the price of imports to increase in the local currency. This causes foreigners to buy more exports and locals to buy fewer imports and switch to domestically produced goods instead. This increases (X-M) and causes the AD to increase. This in turn increases the national output via the multiplier process, restoring economic growth rates.

The effect of a depreciation on national output is illustrated below where the increase in AD from AD_0 to AD_1 causes an increase in national output from Y_0 to Y_1 (Fig. 6.22).

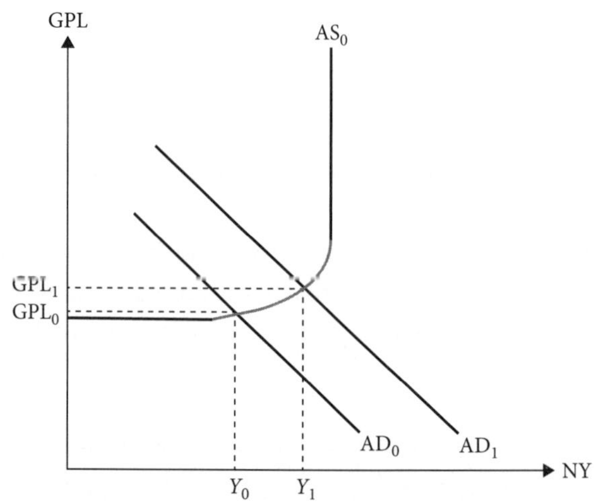

Figure 6.22: Depreciation causing economic growth.

Also, since national output increases, the demand for labour would also increase since it is derived from the production of goods and services. As such, demand-deficient unemployment would decrease.

Since the increase in AD also causes an increase in GPL, depreciation can also be used to achieve the aim of low inflation when the economy is experiencing deflation or too-low inflation. Additionally, with a depreciation, the cost of imported raw materials increase. This decreases the SRAS and causes it to shift up (Fig. 6.23 below), further adding to the increase in GPL.

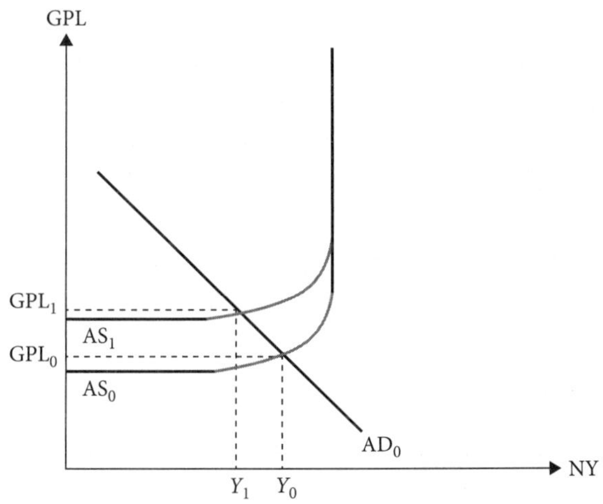

Figure 6.23: Depreciation increasing the GPL through decreasing SRAS.

A depreciation causes an improvement in the BOP position through the expenditure-switching effect, and through attracting direct and portfolio investment inflows.

To recap, with a depreciation, imports would become more expensive in the domestic currency while exports would become cheaper in a foreign currency. Since imports are now more expensive to locals, the quantity demanded of imports would fall. At the same time, since exports are cheaper to foreigners, the quantity of exports demanded by foreigners would increase. For exports, since the price in the domestic currency remains unchanged but the quantity demanded increases, export revenue in the domestic currency must increase. For imports, assuming the demand for imports is price elastic, the decrease in quantity demanded would be more than proportionate to the rise in price. This causes the import expenditure in the domestic currency to decrease. Taken together, the rise in export revenue and fall in import expenditure in the domestic currency would cause an improvement of the trade balance and hence, the current account balance.

Also, a depreciation attracts FDI inflows and portfolio investment inflows through lowering the cost of production and lowering the price of financial assets, respectively. These inflows in the capital and financial account also help to correct the BOP deficit.

6.8.2 Limitations of depreciation/devaluation to correct weak growth, high unemployment, and/or deflation and/or BOP deficit

A policy of depreciation has its limitations. They include

- Limited effect on growth due to import dependence
- Limited effect on AD due to small export component in AD
- Time lags
- Imperfect information in forecasting
- Policy conflicts

Limited effect on growth due to import dependence—Recall that a depreciation causes an increase in national output due to an increase in AD. However, the fact that it also decreases the SRAS offsets some of the increase in national output. This is because the higher cost of production from more expensive imported raw materials will cause producers to reduce their output. While the overall effect on national output should still be positive (see Figure 6.24), the more dependent on imported raw materials a country is, the larger the fall in SRAS, the lesser the overall increase in national output will be.

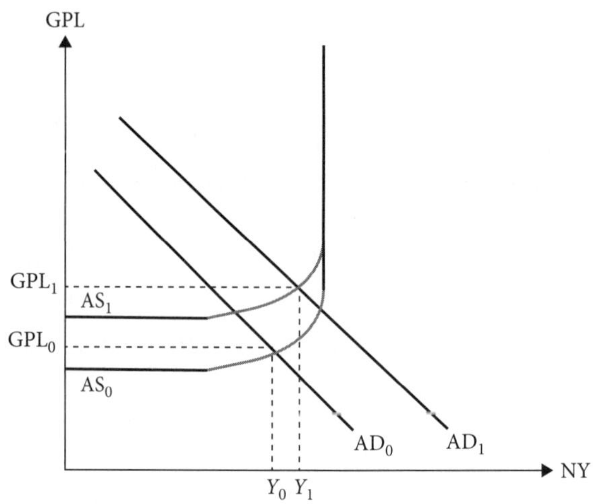

Figure 6.24: Overall effect of a depreciation.

Limited effect on AD due to small export component in AD—Since a depreciation increases the AD primarily through increasing the (X – M) component of AD, if (X – M) is a small component within the AD, the net effect on AD would also be limited. This is true for large consumption-driven economies like the United States (which also explains why the Fed chooses to use an interest rate rather than an exchange rate policy).

Time lags—This is similar to the time lag that can be experienced when Central Banks use an interest rate policy. Exchange rate policies require the same time lag.

Imperfect information in forecasting—This is similar to the possible misestimation of the timing and the extent of the interest rate policy that Central Banks adopt. The timing and extent of exchange rate policies can also be misestimated.

Policy conflicts—A depreciation can cause a conflict in macroeconomic aims. In countries facing stagflation, the policy would restore economic growth at the expense of higher inflation due to the increase in AD and the reduction in SRAS.

6.8.3 Appreciation/revaluation to correct high inflation

An appreciation or a revaluation (both refer to increasing a currency's value) can be used to correct the problems of high inflation.

To recap (from Chapter 5: Factors affecting AD), an appreciation causes the price of exports to increase in a foreign currency and the price of imports to decrease in the local currency. This causes foreigners to buy fewer exports and locals to buy more imports and switch away from domestically produced goods instead. This decreases $(X - M)$ and causes the AD to decrease. This decreases the GPL and hence, offsets the existing high inflation to achieve a low inflation rates.

Additionally, with an appreciation, the cost of imported raw materials decreases. This increases the SRAS and causes it to shift downwards, further reducing the GPL.

The effect of an appreciation on GPL is illustrated below, where the decrease in AD from AD_0 to AD_1 and the increase in SRAS from $SRAS_0$ to $SRAS_1$ causes a fall in GPL from GPL_0 to GPL_1. Both demand-pull and cost-push inflation have been offset to some degree (Fig. 6.25).

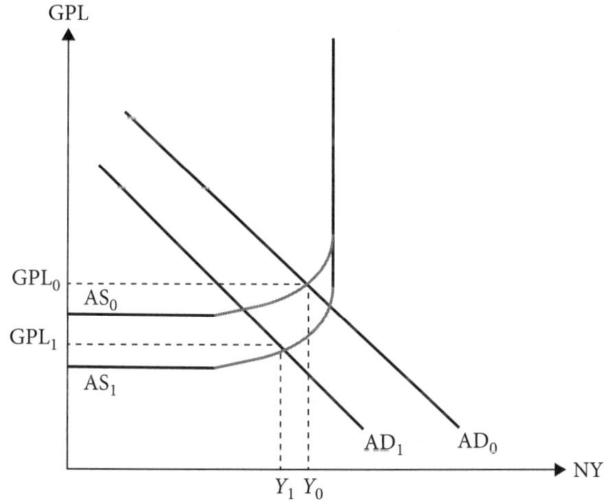

Figure 6.25: Appreciation reducing the GPL.

6.8.4 Limitations of appreciation/revaluation to correct high inflation

The use of appreciation to correct high inflation may face the following limitations:

- Limited effect on AD due to small export component in AD
- Limited effect on SRAS due to low reliance on imported raw materials
- Time lags
- Imperfect information in forecasting
- Policy conflicts

Limited effect on AD due to small export component in AD—Similar to how it limits a depreciation, a country with a low (*X* – *M*) component in AD will find that the extent of the fall in AD is limited when its currency appreciates. Thus, demand-pull inflation would be offset by a limited extent.

Limited effect on SRAS due to low reliance on imported raw materials—In a similar vein, if a country does not rely much on imported raw materials (i.e., resource-rich countries such as Australia which exports raw materials), the reduction in cost of production from the reduction in price of imported raw materials would be limited. As such, the rise in SRAS and resultant fall in GPL would be similarly limited.

Time lags—This is similar to the time lag that can be experienced when Central Banks use an interest rate policy. Exchange rate policies require the same time lag.

Imperfect information in forecasting—This is similar to the possible misestimation of the timing and the extent of the interest rate policy that Central Banks adopt. The timing and extent of exchange rate policies can also be misestimated.

Policy conflicts—An appreciation can cause a conflict in macroeconomic aims. In countries facing stagflation, the policy would bring down inflation at the expense of economic growth due to the decrease in AD and the increase in SRAS.

6.8.5 Why different Central Banks choose different tools

Having understood how interest rate and exchange rate policies work, we can develop a better understanding of why different Central Banks choose different instruments (interest rates vs. exchange rates). The main consideration is the relative effectiveness of each instrument. And, to consider the effectiveness, we need to first clarify what the Central Banks' primary aims are.

Since the global stagflation followed by hyper-inflation experienced in some economies in the 1970s, most Central Banks' aims are similar—to pursue low and stable inflation to create the conditions for economic growth. To this end, most Central Banks have inflation targets. As such, the primary aim of Central Banks is to achieve low and stable inflation.

So, the instrument of choice would depend on whether interest rates or exchange rates are more effective in achieving low inflation. This in turn depends on the context of the economy—whether the country is large or small and how open the country is.

Large economies versus small economies

The size of the economy is measured by its GDP—the higher its GDP, the larger the economy. Larger economies tend to have larger consumer bases and thus, tend to be more consumption driven. This means that consumption tends to be a very large part of the AD. For example, in the United States, consumption is between 65% and 70% of the GDP. As such, interest rate policy which targets consumption tends to be more effective.

In contrast, small economies tend to rely on exports to drive the economy as the domestic consumer base may be too small. As such, an exchange rate policy which targets exports tends to be more effective. This is one of the reasons why economies like Singapore adopt exchange rate policies.

Open economies versus less open economies

There are three aspects to economic openness—openness to trade, openness to capital flows, and openness to labour flows.

More open economies tend to trade more and become more reliant on trade. This makes them more reliant on exports as a source of demand for domestically produced goods and services and also more reliant on imports as a source of raw materials. This makes exchange rate policy more effective as it targets both exports and imported raw materials.

In contrast, less open economies would not be as reliant on exports and imported raw materials. This makes exchange rate policy less effective for these countries.

Additionally, greater openness to capital flows could increase the share of FDI within the total investments in a country. Since FDI tends to be funded externally, it is not responsive to changes in the domestic interest rate. Hence, the greater the share of FDI within a country's total investments, the less investments as a whole are responsive to changes in the interest rate (i.e., the greater the share of FDI in investments, the more interest rate-inelastic investments will be). Thus, more open economies would find that interest rate policies are less effective.

In contrast, in less open economies, the share of FDI within investments would be lower. This would make investments more interest rate-elastic and hence, increase the effectiveness of interest rate policy.

Hence, all else being equal, more open countries would be more likely to choose exchange rate policy while less open countries would be more likely to choose interest rate policies. This is again exemplified by the choice of policy instruments by the Fed and the MAS. The Fed chooses to use interest rate policy as the US economy is not as open while MAS chooses to use exchange rate policy as the Singapore economy is very open.

Putting it concretely: The special case of small, open economies like Singapore

Thus far, it seems like all Central Banks can choose whether to control interest rates or exchange rates. This is actually not true for all economies as the monetary policy trilemma actually makes some assumptions which may not hold in reality. The end result of this is that there are some economies that actually are interest rate takers and have to use exchange rate policy because they cannot control the interest rate in their country anyway.

To recap, in the monetary policy trilemma, when a country decides what interest rate it desires, it adjusts the money supply to achieve it. For example, if a Central Bank wishes to increase the interest rate in its country, it will reduce the money supply in the country. The increase in interest rate attracts portfolio investment inflows. However, such inflows also increase the money supply, which pushes the interest rate down again. To keep the interest rates at the desired level, the Central Bank would have to reduce the money supply by the same extent that the portfolio investment inflows increased it (i.e., if portfolio investment inflows increased the money supply by $1m, the Central Bank must reduce the money supply by $1m to offset it). This is how the Central Bank controls interest rates when there is free capital flow.

However, the assumption made here is that the Central Bank is able to adjust the money supply enough to offset the changes due to the portfolio investment flows. For small, open economies (SOEs), this assumption may not hold because the extent of the portfolio investment flows can be very large, relative to the size of the money supply in the first place.

So, if SOEs tried to set an interest rate above the global interest rate, portfolio investments would flow in, increasing the money supply and causing a fall in the interest rate until it is equal to the global interest rate. The Central Bank would be unable to do anything about it. Conversely, if the interest rate was below the global interest rate, portfolio investments would flow out, decreasing the money supply, and causing a rise in the interest rate until it is equal to the global interest rate. As such, SOEs cannot even set their own interest rates in the first place. Their interest rates would naturally follow the global interest rate. We say that SOEs are interest-rate takers.

Thus, for SOEs like Singapore, the MAS uses exchange rates as the monetary policy instrument because:

1. Singapore is an interest rate taker and has no control over the interest rate to begin with
2. Exchange rates have a larger effect on our economy than interest rates, in any case

6.9 Supply-side policies

Fiscal policy, interest rate policy, and exchange rate policy are called demand-management policies as they primarily target the AD, although they could also have supply-side effects. They are also classified according to the instrument used (fiscal policy through the government budget, interest rate policy through the interest rate, and exchange rate policy through the exchange rate). In contrast, supply-side policies cover a broad range of policies and do not have specific instruments. Any policy that affects the aggregate supply (AS) (whether LRAS or SRAS or both) is a supply-side policy.

Supply-side policies can be broadly classified into interventionist policies (where governments intervene in markets) and market-based policies (where governments use market forces instead). The following is a non-exhaustive list of examples of various types of supply-side policies and how they work.

6.9.1 Interventionist supply-side policies

Interventionist supply-side policies are policies where the government intervenes in the market. To recap (from Chapter 2) government intervention could refer to taxes, subsidies, direct provision, provision of information, quotas and the like. These could be used to improve the quality of factors of production, to increase the quantity of factors of production, and to encourage both the development and use of technology.

To improve quality of factors of production

To improve the quality of factors of production, governments could adopt targeted subsidies. For example, governments could implement or increase subsidies on education and re-training to encourage more people to receive more education and be re-trained. This improves the quality of the labour force, which causes an increase in labour productivity. An increase in labour productivity then increases LRAS by increasing the productive capacity and increases SRAS by reducing the unit labour cost of output. This shifts the entire AS curve outwards. Singapore's education subsidies and the SkillsFuture programme are examples of such policies.

A compulsory education policy such as the one in Singapore is another example of a supply-side policy that improves the quality of labour.

To increase quantity of factors of production

To increase the quantity of land, governments may carry out land reclamation. For example, parts of the east coast in Singapore as well as Jurong Island are actually reclaimed. The increase in quantity of land increases the productive capacity and causes the LRAS to shift rightwards.

Schemes to encourage enterprise such grants for start-ups and provision of incubator spaces for would-be entrepreneurs to test out their ideas are a form of supply-side policy that aims to increase the quantity of enterprise in an economy. Since enterprise is also a factor of production, a greater quantity of it increases the productive capacity and causes the LRAS to shift rightwards.

Immigration policies can also be classified as supply-side policies as they can affect the quantity of labour in an economy. For example, an expansion of work visas granted to foreigners (effectively increasing the quota of foreign labour allowed into a country) allows more foreign labourers to work in a country. This increases the size of the labour force in the country (increase in quantity of labour) and hence, increases the productive capacity. The LRAS shifts rightwards.

Supply-side tax cuts are tax cuts on firms to encourage investments (similar to expansionary fiscal policy) and tax cuts on households to encourage more people to enter the labour force as the returns to working are now higher. Such tax cuts were conceived under the US President Ronald Reagan who mistakenly believed that a reduction in tax rates could increase the government's tax revenue, through encouraging more people to work (i.e., the increase in the tax base would more than offset the reduction in tax rates). While the effect of tax cuts on tax revenue turned out to be incorrect, it is undeniable that tax cuts on firms and households do encourage more investment and increase the labour force participation rate.

Investments increase the capital stock in a country (increase in quantity of capital), and greater labour force participation rates increase the size of the labour force (increase in quantity of labour). These cause the productive capacity to increase and the LRAS to shift rightwards in the long run.

Government expenditure on developing infrastructure also counts as a supply-side policy as infrastructure is a form of capital. Development of infrastructure adds to the capital stock and increases the productive capacity too.

To improve technology (development or use)

Finally, there could be interventionist supply-side policies aimed at encouraging the development and/or use of technology.

The development of technology could be encouraged by policies such as grants for R&D or through direct provision where the government employs researchers to carry out research. For example, the Agency for Science, Technology, and Research (A*STAR) in Singapore is a publicly funded statutory board under the Ministry of Trade and Industry (MTI) that carries out R&D.

The use of technology can be encouraged through subsidies too. Governments can subsidise firms' purchase of existing productivity-enhancing technology. For example, the Singapore government introduced the Productivity and Innovation Credit (PIC) scheme in 2010 which allowed businesses to enjoy tax deductions when they incurred expenditure on automation expenditure (amongst other activities). Such tax deductions are effectively subsidies.

The development and adoption of technology increases the level of productivity in the economy. Since productivity is a measure of output per unit of factor input, an increase in productivity would mean that the existing quantity of factors of production can produce more (increase in productive capacity) and that the factor cost of producing each unit of input would decrease (fall in unit cost of production). As such, both LRAS and SRAS would increase, shifting the AS outwards.

6.9.2 Market-based supply-side policies

In contrast to interventionist supply-side policies where the governments intervene in markets, market-based supply-side policies rely on increasing competition in markets to drive efficiency. Market-based supply-side policies can be classified into policies that try to increase the level of competition in product (goods and services) markets and policies that try to increase the level of competition in factor markets.

To increase efficiency in product markets

To increase competition in product markets, governments can reduce the barriers to entry (especially artificial ones) that prevent firms from entering a market. Such policies can be generic (reduces barriers to entry across a broad spectrum of markets) or industry-specific (reduces barriers to entry in a specific market).

A generic market-based supply-side policy would be the reduction in red tape faced when firms apply for business licences. These reductions in red tape is termed deregulation. Suppose a government reduces the number of documents that need to be filed to apply for a business licence by half. This would make it easier for new firms to enter all industries. The lowered barriers to entry increase the number of firms in all industries and hence, the level of competition faced in all industries. The increased competition spurs firms to become more efficient by adopting more productive methods of production. This increased productivity then increases both LRAS and SRAS, shifting the LRAS outwards. To illustrate the difference that red tape can make, we can contrast the number of days it takes to obtain a business licence in Switzerland (top of the Global Competitiveness Index ranking in 2017) and India (ranked 40th). In Switzerland, it only takes 10 days to start a business while it takes 29.5 days in India. We can see that the ease of starting a business is directly correlated with how productive an economy is.

Governments could also introduce more competition into specific industries by adjusting industry-specific licencing requirements. For example, the Singapore government has been progressively introducing more competition into the telecommunication industry by granting additional licences to allow more telecommunication firms to enter the market. These include the licence granted to M1 in 1995, to Starhub in 1998, and to TPG Telecom in 2016. Increasing the level of competition in the industry increases the productivity in the industry. This can then have wider effects on the rest of the economy as the greater competition amongst the telecommunication firms could lead to a reduction in the price of telecommunication services. This lowers the cost of production across many other sectors of the economy (most firms require telecommunication services), increasing the SRAS. A similar idea was at work when the Singapore government privatised the energy generation market, to increase the level of competition amongst energy generators to lower the price of electricity. In this case, the handing over of ownership from the public to the private sector is known as privatisation. Privatisation was what the Thatcher administration in the UK adopted when they wanted to increase productivity in the UK economy.

Barriers to entry can also be lowered by removing specific bottlenecks. One example could be the availability of credit (loans). New firms may be deterred from entering a market because they are unable to obtain loans. To correct this, a government could set up its own loan scheme or act as a guarantor for loans taken out by start-ups.

Another example of introducing more competition into product markets is to reduce trade barriers such that imported products can compete with domestically produced products, and reducing barriers to direct investments such that foreign firms can establish a local presence and compete with local firms.

To increase efficiency in factor markets

Instead of increasing competition in the product markets, governments can increase the competition in factor markets instead. For example, governments can increase the competition for jobs in the labour market by weakening trade unions.

Trade unions are organised groups of workers in the same profession (the same trade) who band together to further the rights of benefits of these workers. For example, the Air Line Pilots Association—Singapore (ALPAS) protects and fights for the rights of air line pilots in Singapore.

Definition(s):
Trade unions are organised groups of workers in the same profession (the same trade) who band together to further the rights of benefits of these workers.

Trade unions reduce the competition amongst workers for jobs as they operate by collectively bargaining with employers for the welfare of all union members. So, instead of workers competing amongst themselves for limited jobs and benefits, workers band together through the union to demand better pay and benefits from employers.

While unions help prevent exploitation of workers by employers, it could reduce productivity by inducing complacency amongst members as the risk of getting fired or pay cuts decreases. This is especially so if unions turn militant and unreasonably demand more from employers by threatening strikes.

Governments can reduce the power of trade unions by making collective bargaining illegal or making strikes illegal. When trade unions become weaker, workers will have to work harder as they enjoy less protection from the trade unions. This increases productivity and shifts the AS curve outwards.

Putting it concretely: Trade unions in Singapore: the tripartite model

The standard model of trade unions is one where trade unions are pitted against employers, since employers typically are against pay increments and better benefits as these represent costs and a reduction in profit. As such, to get their way, trade unions may have to resort to strikes as a bargaining chip.

However, from a larger perspective, such strikes are bad for everyone as they result in a loss of income for workers, a loss of profit for businesses, and also cause foreign firms to not want to invest in a country due to the political instability that strikes cause.

As such, Singapore adopts a unique tripartite model of bargaining. The three parties in the tripartite are the trade unions (represented by the National Trade Union Congress [NTUC]), employers (represented by the Singapore National Employers Federation [SNEF]) and the government (represented by the Ministry of Manpower). The NTUC is not permitted to act independently as strikes that have not been sanctioned are illegal. Instead, all requests and disputes are discussed between NTUC and SNEF with the government acting as the arbiter (judge) of what is fair.

Under this framework, the current agreement is that, to keep business costs under control while protecting the interest of workers, wage increments should keep in line with increases in productivity. This will allow firms to remain competitive while still allowing workers to earn higher wages from becoming more productive.

Apart from tackling trade unions, governments can also increase competition in the labour market by amending labour laws to give companies more say over hiring and firing or adjusting the maximum working hours. For example, France's President Emmanuel Macron aims to increase productivity in France by making it easier for French firms to fire and hire workers.

6.9.3 Macroeconomic effects of supply-side policy

Having understood a range of different examples of supply-side policies, we turn to analyse their effects on the economy. These effects can be analysed in terms of the effect on economic growth, inflation, unemployment, and the BOP position

Effect of supply-side policies on economic growth

When supply-side policies increase the productive capacity of an economy, the LRAS shifts rightwards and potential growth is attained. Whether this potential growth also translates into actual growth depends on the state of the economy. If the economy is close to full employment, the potential growth would also translate into actual growth as there is sufficient demand. If the economy is not close to full employment, there would be potential growth but no actual growth. Refer to "Shifts in LRAS affecting potential growth" in Section 6.2.2 for details.

When the supply-side policies reduce the cost of production in an economy, the SRAS shifts downwards and actual growth is attained.

When the policies cause both a rightward and downward sift of the AS (i.e., an outward shift of the AS), both potential and actual growth will be achieved.

Effect of supply-side policies on inflation

When supply-side policies increase the productive capacity of an economy, the LRAS shifts rightwards. If the economy is close to full employment, this rightward shift will also bring down the GPL, offsetting any existing inflationary pressures. If the economy is not close to full employment, this rightward shift would have no effect on the GPL. The relevant diagrams to illustrate these can be found under "Shifts in LRAS affecting potential growth" in Section 6.2.2.

When the supply-side policies reduce the cost of production in an economy, the SRAS shifts downwards, causing the GPL to decrease. This offsets any existing inflationary pressure to cause a lower rate of inflation (or possibly deflation).

When the policies cause both a rightward and downward sift of the AS (i.e., an outward shift of the AS), the GPL would also decrease.

Effect of supply-side policies on unemployment

Depending on the exact supply-side policy adopted, there could be effects on cyclical, structural, and frictional unemployment.

Cyclical unemployment—If the supply-side policy results in an increase in national output without any change in productivity, there would be an increase in the demand for labour which is derived from the need to produce output. Productivity matters because if the national output increased because of an increase in productivity, there might be no job creation, since the increased output can be produced by the existing labourers who have become more productive. This has been experienced in the United States where the economic recovery post the 2008 crisis created fewer jobs than expected because it was paired with an increase in productivity.

Structural unemployment—If the supply-side policy involves subsidising skills-retraining for displaced workers, there would be a reduction in structural unemployment as the unemployed pick up relevant skills to enter new industries. However, if the supply-side policy encourages automation, there could be technological unemployment (a subset of structural unemployment) as productivity is increased by replacing workers with machines. In that case, supply-side policies could worsen structural unemployment instead.

Frictional unemployment—If the supply-side policy creates more churn in the economy, frictional unemployment would increase. Churn can be thought of as changes or movements in an economy. For example, if the supply-side policy involves dismantling trade unions, workers and employers would need more time to be matched as trade unions can no longer act as middle man. To illustrate this, we can imagine a situation where a bakery wishes to hire a baker. If a trade union exists, the bakery could approach the trade union to request a baker. Similarly, bakers can approach the trade union to help them get placed. Without a trade union, matching the baker to vacancy would be harder. However, if the supply-side policy involves making the labour market more efficient but creating platforms to match workers and jobs better (e.g., through developing a job-matching site), then frictional unemployment would decrease instead.

Effect of supply-side policies on the BOP position

If the supply-side policy results in a fall in the cost of production and hence the GPL, it could have an expenditure-switching effect. Domestically-produced goods would become cheaper to foreign consumers and imports would become relatively more expensive to domestic consumers. Foreign consumers would switch towards the domestic country's exports while domestic consumers would switch away from imports to domestically produced goods and services. Assuming the demand for exports is price elastic, the rise in the quantity demanded of exports would be more than proportionate to the fall in its price, causing export revenue to increase. At the same time, the fall in the demand for imports would cause a fall in import expenditure. The rise in export revenue and fall in import expenditure would improve the balance of trade position and hence, the current account position. This would improve the BOP position.

At the same time, if the supply-side policies make the country more attractive to FDI (e.g., supply-side policy of developing infrastructure), the FDI inflows would also improve the BOP position.

6.9.4 Limitations of supply-side policies

Just as how the effect of supply-side policies depend on the specific supply-side policy employed, the limitations of supply-side policies are policy-specific. Nonetheless, below are some common ones:

- Impact on government budget
- Time period
- Conflict of aims
- No guarantee of success
- Political acceptability

Impact on government budget—Most supply-side policies require government spending (e.g., building new infrastructure, various subsidies). This could be a problem for governments that are already running budget deficits, as further borrowing could lead to the crowding out effect.

Time period—Some supply-side policies only show their effects in the long run (e.g., construction of infrastructure like new airports can take years). As such, they may be limited in solving pressing short-run problems (e.g., limited usefulness in bringing down short-run inflation).

Conflict of aims—Supply-side policies may create new problems when solving existing ones. For example, increasing productivity through encouraging automation could be at the expense of higher structural unemployment. Also, increasing competition in the product market to encourage higher productivity may also entail a trade-off in terms of the economies of scale that firms can reap. This is because with higher competition, the size of each firm would decrease. This shrinkage in the scale of production would make firms less able to reap internal economies of scale.

No guarantee of success—Some supply-side policies may have no guarantee of success. For example, R&D grants do not guarantee successful R&D outcomes. Also, subsidies for re-training may not be successful if there are other factors preventing labourers from attending the courses. There is also the possibility of vendors coming up with poorly designed courses meant to fleece the government. Such courses would not improve the productivity of those who attend it.

Political acceptability—Some supply-side policies may face resistance from voters. For example, attempts by French presidents to lengthen the cherished 35-hour work week in France have sparked protests. Similarly, movements to reduce the power of trade unions often incite protests from voters.

A summary table for how the four macroeconomic policies can be used to correct macroeconomic problems is presented below. This table excludes trade policies as those would be covered in more detail in Chapter 7.

Summary table for the macroeconomic policies that can be used for different macroeconomic problems

Macroeconomic problem(s)	Fiscal policy	Interest rate policy	Exchange rate policy	Supply-side policy
Recession/low growth	Expansionary—increase *G* and/or decrease *T*	Expansionary—increase money supply to reduce i/r	Depreciation/ devaluation	Policies to increase LRAS and/or SRAS
High unemployment	Expansionary—increase *G* and/or decrease *T*	Expansionary—increase money supply to reduce i/r	Depreciation/ devaluation	Policies to reduce structural unemployment
Deflation/too-low inflation	Expansionary—increase *G* and/or decrease *T*	Expansionary—increase money supply to reduce i/r	Depreciation/ devaluation	Do nothing. Trying to increase GPL through supply-side policies to reduce AS is unwise
High inflation	Contractionary—decrease *G* and/ or increase *T*	Contractionary—decrease money supply to increase i/r	Appreciation/ revaluation	Policies to increase LRAS and/or SRAS. The latter is more important as inflation is a short-run phenomenon
BOP deficit	Expenditure-switching and reducing decrease *G* and/ or increase *T*	Expenditure-switching and reducing decrease money supply to increase i/r	Depreciation/ devaluation	Expenditure-switching—policies to increase SRAS

Summary for Chapter 6

1. The standard of living has two aspects—material and non-material.
2. Material standard of living can be measured by GDP per capita or GNI per capita.
3. Comparisons of standard of living over time are done using the change in real GDP per capita.
4. Comparisons of standard of living over space are done using the GDP per capita converted into a common currency using the PPP exchange rate.
5. Both comparisons over time and space face limitations. These include not taking into account the non-material standard of living and the income distribution.
6. The HDI is a composite index that takes into account the GNI per capita, health, and education. The latter two help reflect non-material aspects of the standard of living.
7. Income distribution is measured by the Gini coefficient. 0 means perfect equality while 1 means perfect inequality. The Gini coefficient supplements the GDP or GNI per capita data to give us a better picture of a country.
8. The four macroeconomic aims are economic growth, low inflation, full employment, and a healthy BOP position (avoidance of a BOP deficit).
9. Economic growth is measured by the percentage change in real GDP.
10. Actual growth is caused by factors that increase the AD, SRAS, and/or LRAS.
11. Potential growth is caused by factors that increase the LRAS.
12. Economic growth is sustainable when it can be sustained over the long run. This assumes not exhausting the natural resources in a country.
13. Economic growth is inclusive when it occurs without a worsening of the Gini coefficient.
14. Economic growth is desirable as it creates benefits for households, firms, and the government.
15. Nonetheless, there are some costs of economic growth.
16. Unemployment is measured by the unemployment rate, which is the percentage of the labour force that is unemployed.
17. Unemployment could be demand-deficient in nature (caused by decreases in the AD), structural in nature (caused by changes in the demand and supply of specific labour markets), or frictional in nature (caused by imperfect information as people transit between jobs).
18. Full employment is the state in which there is no structural or frictional unemployment.
19. Low unemployment or full employment is desirable because unemployment imposes costs on consumers, firms, and governments.
20. Inflation is measured by the percentage change in the CPI.
21. Inflation is caused by increases in the AD (demand-pull inflation) and/or decreases in the SRAS (cost-push inflation).
22. Low inflation is desirable because both high inflation and deflation imposes costs on consumers, firms, and governments.

23. The BOP is a record of monetary flows between a country and the rest of the world. It is made up of the current account, and the capital and financial account.
24. The current account is made up of the balance of trade, the primary income balance, and the secondary income balance.
25. The capital and financial account is made up of direct investment flows and portfolio investment flows.
26. A BOP surplus means that in total, more money is flowing into the country than out of it. A BOP deficit means that in total, more money is flowing out of a country than into it.
27. The BOP position is determined by factors that affect the current account and capital and financial account.
28. Avoidance of a BOP deficit is desirable because BOP deficits impose costs on consumers, firms, and governments.
29. To correct macroeconomic problems, governments can use macroeconomic policies such as fiscal policy, monetary policy based on interest rates, monetary policy based on exchange rates, and supply-side policies.
30. Fiscal policy is the use of the government budget to affect the macroeconomy.
31. A budget surplus is a state where the government revenue exceeds its expenditure. A budget deficit is a state whether the government expenditure exceeds its revenue.
32. An expansionary fiscal policy refers to an increase in government expenditure and/or a fall in taxes. A contractionary fiscal policy refers to a decrease in government expenditure and/or a rise in taxes.
33. Fiscal policy has limitations. These include the size of the multiplier and the crowding out effect.
34. Interest rate policy is the use of interest rates to affect the macroeconomy. It is carried out by the Central Bank.
35. An expansionary interest rate policy refers to a decrease in interest rates. A contractionary interest rate policy refers to an increase in interest rates.
36. Interest rate policy has limitations. These include animal spirits causing consumption and investments to be interest-rate inelastic.
37. Exchange rate policy is the use of exchange rates to affect the macroeconomy. It is carried out by the Central Bank.
38. Depreciations/devaluations are expansionary while appreciations/revaluations are contractionary.
39. Exchange rate policy has limitations. These include (*X*(*M*) being a small component of AD and the degree of import dependence.
40. Supply side policies are any policies that affect the AS. They can be classified into interventionist or market-oriented policies.
41. Supply-side policies have limitations. These include the impact on the government budget, the time period needed for them to be effective, and the possible conflicts in aims.

Annex 6.1 Computing the Gini coefficient

To compute the Gini coefficient, we must first derive the Lorentz curve. The Lorentz curve plots the cumulative share of national income on the vertical axis against the cumulative share of the population (from the poorest to the richest) on the horizontal axis. To illustrate, suppose the poorest 10% of the population earned only 2% of a country's national income, and the next poorest 10% of the population earned 5% of the country's national income. Cumulatively, the poorest 10% earned 2% of the country's national income and the poorest 20% earned 7% (2% + 5%) of the country's national income. Assuming we have data on the income shares of the other segments of the population, we could then plot the Lorentz curve below (Fig. A6.1).

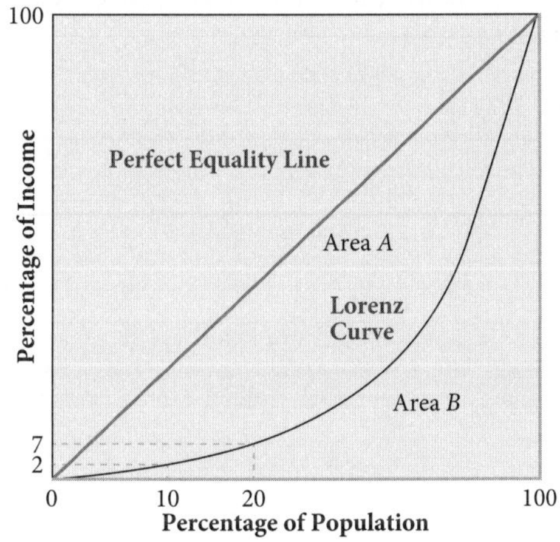

Figure A6.1: The Lorentz curve.

The Gini coefficient is then simply area A divided by area $(A + B)$.

If there was perfect equality, the Lorentz curve would be a straight diagonal line running from the bottom left corner to the top right corner **(in red)**. Area A would be zero. Hence, the Gini coefficient would be zero.

If there was perfect inequality, the Lorentz curve would be an inverse L-shaped curve **(in blue)**. Area A would be equal to area $(A + B)$. Hence, the Gini coefficient would be 1.

Annex 6.2 Computing the PPP exchange rate

To compute the PPP exchange rate, we need to first find a common basket of goods and services that are consumed in the two countries. This basket should have a number of different items and different quantities of each item based on how much consumers in the two countries consume them. For example, a simplified basket might contain 3 kg of carrots, 2 tubes of toothpaste, 10 tee-shirts and so on.

Once we have determined a common basket, the price of this basket of goods and services is computed in both countries (e.g., price of this basket may be SGD100 in Singapore and MYR240 in Malaysia).

The ratio of the prices of the basket would be the PPP exchange rate (i.e., SGD100 = MYR240. Therefore, the PPP exchange rate is SGD1 = MYR2.4).

Annex 6.3 Effect of economic growth on productive and allocative efficiency

The only model that allows us to study both economic growth and productive and allocative efficiency on the same diagram is the PPC.

Illustrating economic growth on the PPC

Actual growth is illustrated by the economy producing more goods and services (e.g., point *A* to point *B*) in Fig. C6.1.

Potential growth is illustrated by the economy's PPC shifting outwards (e.g., PPC_0 to PPC_1) in Fig. C6.2.

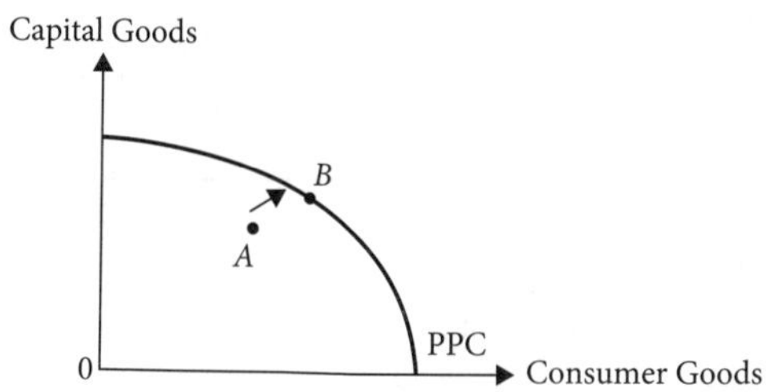

Figure C6.1: Actual growth on a PPC.

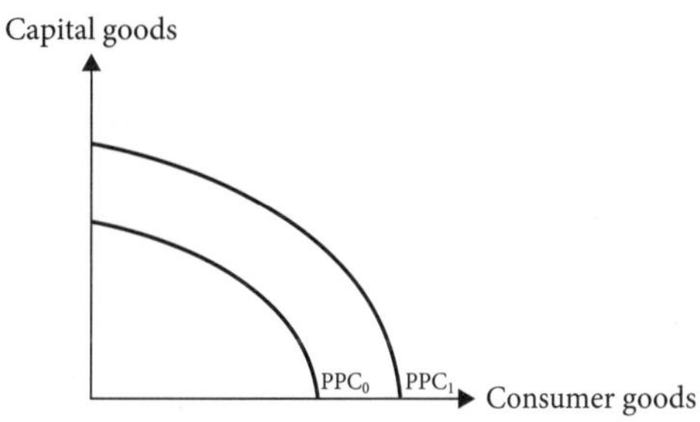

Figure C6.2: Potential growth on PPC diagram.

Illustrating productive efficiency on the PPC

For a given PPC, points within the PPC (e.g. point *A* in the Fig. C6.3 below) are productively inefficient but points on the PPC (e.g., point *B*) are productively efficient.

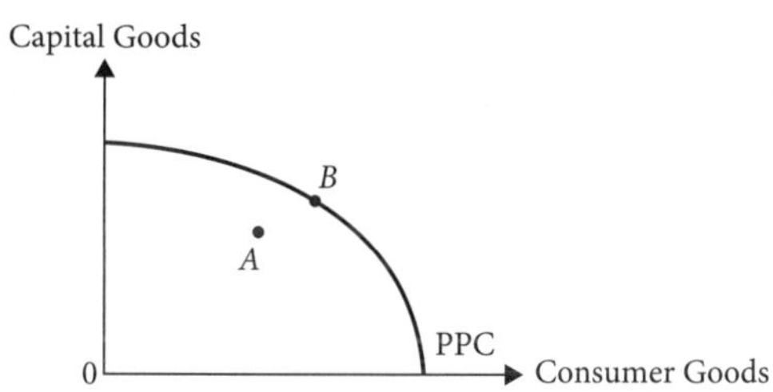

Figure C6.3: Productive efficiency and inefficiency on a PPC

Economic growth and productive efficiency

The effect of economic growth on productive efficiency depends on the reason for growth. Below are a few possible cases.

As should be apparent by this stage, while it is possible to analyse the effect of economic growth on productive efficiency, it is not very meaningful to do so since increases in productive inefficiency are not necessarily negative (e.g., Scenario 2 on the next page).

Scenario 1: Actual growth and no potential growth (i.e., growth due to increase in AD or SRAS)	Scenario 2: Potential growth and no actual growth (i.e., increase in LRAS when AD cuts AS at the horizontal portion)	Scenario 3: Potential growth and actual growth (i.e., increase in LRAS when AD cuts AS at the vertical portion)
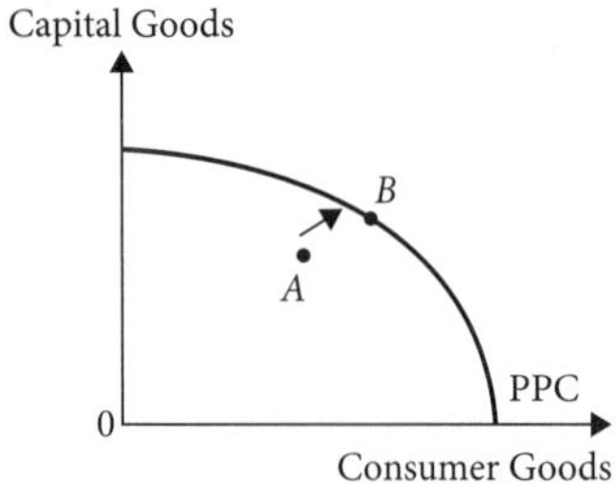	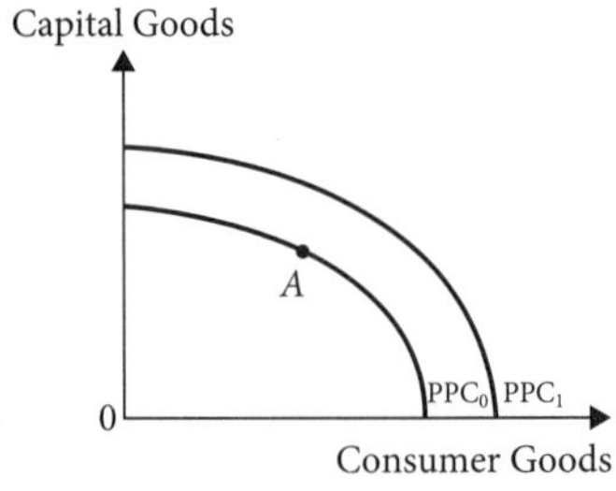	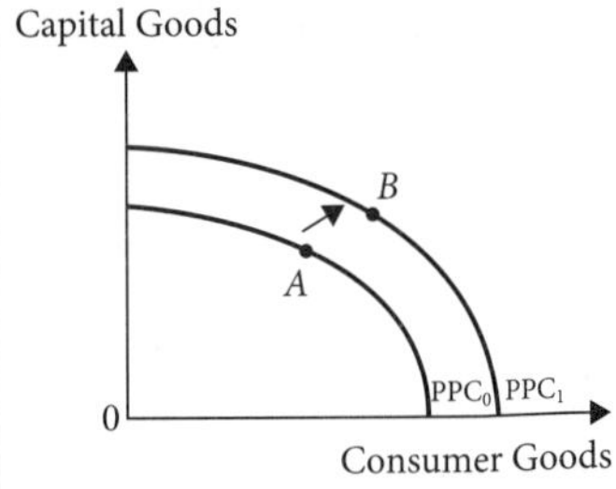
Productive inefficient before growth Productive efficient after growth Growth reduced productive inefficiency	Productive efficient before growth (based on point A and PPC_0) Productive inefficient after growth (based on point A and PPC_1) Growth increased productive inefficiency	Productive efficient before growth (based on point A and PPC_0) Productive efficient after growth (based on point B and PPC_1) Growth had no effect on productive efficiency

The situation is similar for allocative efficiency. Allocative efficiency is about whether resources are allocated to produce the optimal combination of goods and services (i.e., whether the economy is at the optimal point on a given PPC). Economic growth means more goods and services are produced overall. Depending on what the increased output is (i.e., whether the increase in output is capital or consumer goods), allocative inefficiency could be reduced or increased. Nonetheless, like productive efficiency, such analyses are not meaningful, since an increase in allocative inefficiency is not necessarily bad.

Annex 6.4 Computing the GDP deflator and the CPI

To compute the CPI, we need to first find the basket of goods and services that is representative of what consumers actually consume. This basket should have a number of different items and different quantities of each item based on how much consumers typically consume them. For example, a simplified basket might contain 3 kg of carrots, 2 tubes of toothpaste, 10 tee-shirts, a car, rental, and so on.

We then calculate the price of this basket every year. The price of the basket in the base year is known as the base year price. It is set to 100. The price of the basket in every other year is then calculated as a percentage of the base year price. For example, if the price of the basket were $200 in the base year, $205 the next year, and $240 the year after, the CPI for the base year would be 100, that in the next year would be 102.5 ($205 is 102.5% of $200), and it would be 120 in the year after ($240 is 120% of $200).

The GDP deflator is similar, except that instead of starting with a basket of consumer goods, the "basket" includes all goods and services produced in the economy. Effectively, it then becomes the nominal GDP (current price of all goods and services multiplied by their quantities) divided by the real GDP (base year price of all goods and services multiplied by their quantities).

Annex 6.5 The Marshall–Lerner condition

In the main text, we considered the case of what happens to the trade balance when the value of the currency changes, assuming the demand for imports is elastic. This Annex looks at what happens more generally.

To recap, the trade balance refers to the export revenue minus the import expenditure. It is important to note that export revenue and import expenditure should both be in the domestic currency as the BOP is recorded in the domestic currency.

The effects of an appreciation on export revenue and import expenditure in the domestic currency are captured in the table below. Note that all prices are in the domestic currency. So, while an appreciation would increase the price of our exports to foreigners (because they would need more units of their currency to exchange for each unit of our currency), the price in the domestic currency remains the same. For imports, while the price in the foreign currency remains unchanged, the price in the domestic currency decreases.

<table>
<tr><th></th><th colspan="3">Appreciation</th></tr>
<tr><td>1. Export revenue
$(X = P_X \times Q_X)$</td><td colspan="3">• P_X stays constant
• Q_X decreases
• Export revenue decreases</td></tr>
<tr><td rowspan="3">2. Import expenditure
$(M = P_M \times Q_M)$</td><td colspan="3">• P_M decreases
• Q_M increases
• Change in import expenditure depends on PED_M</td></tr>
<tr><td>If $|PED_M| > 1$</td><td colspan="2">If $|PED_M| < 1$</td></tr>
<tr><td>Rise in Q_M > Fall in P_M
→ Import expenditure increases</td><td colspan="2">Rise in Q_M < Fall in P_M
→ Import expenditure decreases</td></tr>
<tr><td rowspan="3">Net exports
$= X - M$
$= (P_X \times Q_X) - (P_M \times Q_M)$</td><td rowspan="3">Since X decreases (fr row 1) and M increases (fr row 2)
→ $X - M$ must decrease</td><td colspan="2">Since X decreases (fr row 1) and M also decreases (fr row 2)
→ Change in $X - M$ depends on extent of fall in X and extent of fall in M</td></tr>
<tr><td>Fall in X > Fall in M</td><td>Fall in X < Fall in M</td></tr>
<tr><td>$X - M$ decreases</td><td>$X - M$ increases</td></tr>
</table>

From the above, we can see that appreciation's effect on net exports would depend on the changes in export revenue compared to the changes in import expenditure. If $|PED_M| > 1$, since *X* falls and *M* rises, $X - M$ will definitely decrease. However, if $|PED_M| < 1$, since *X* and *M* both fall, we will need to compare the extent of the fall in X against the extent of the fall in *M* to determine if $X - M$ rises or falls overall.

Fortunately, an economist and a mathematician (named Alfred Marshall and Abba P. Lerner, respectively) worked out the mathematics[8] and showed that so long as $|PED_X + PED_M| > 1$, an appreciation would lead to a fall in $(X - M)$, assuming $X - M$ was originally 0. The condition of $|PED_x + PED_M| > 1$ is named the Marshall–Lerner condition.

The Marshall–Lerner condition can also be applied to a depreciation. If there is a depreciation, net exports will increase assuming the Marshall–Lerner condition holds.

10 The mathematical proof is not within the scope of this book but can be looked up quite easily. One source is https://en.wikipedia.org/wiki/Marshall%E2%80%93Lerner_condition.

CHAPTER 7

INTERNATIONAL ECONOMICS (H2 ONLY)

7.1 Globalisation

Globalisation is the phenomenon in which countries become more interconnected economically, socially, and politically.

Economically, globalisation is the phenomenon in which economies become increasingly interconnected and integrated due to the increase in the international trade of goods and services, the increase in labour flow, and the increase in capital flow.

Globalisation is neither a contemporary nor a modern term, it is a continuous process linked to the development and evolution of mankind. While the early stages of globalisation required decades or even centuries before obvious signs of progress could be seen, in the recent century, globalisation can be observed in a much faster and a more accelerated pace than before.

One of the main forces promoting globalisation is the improvement in technology in the areas of transportation and communication.

There has been improvement in transport technology across all modes of transportation, intra- and inter-country. Be it over land, sea, or air, almost all the modes of transportation are able to carry a larger load and move at a faster speed between countries. It is now easier, faster, and cheaper to transport humans and goods around the world.

Improvements in communication technology promote a faster, more accurate, and cheaper flow of information. This in return promotes the flow of humans and goods around the world. From the era of land lines to fax machines to the Internet today, people are more connected and informed than before. Firms are also able to interact with their consumers more to promote consumption. The rise of online shopping resulted in an increase in the sales of goods and services and the trade between nations.

Another force promoting globalisation is the change in societal and cultural norms. Long distance travels today are less daunting than before and becoming more of a social norm. This change is partially caused by the improvement in technology as transport safety has improved significantly over time, not to mention the ease of communicating across long distances.

Also, as more governments are seeing the potential positive impacts of globalisation, they are becoming more willing to open their economies by reducing trade barriers with foreign countries, in terms of trade and human flow.

7.1.1 Effects of globalisation

The effects of globalisation can be examined through one of these three phenomena:

- Increase in international trade of goods and services
- Increase in labour flow between countries
- Increase in capital flow between countries

The increase in international trade of goods and services can be further divided into the increase in imports and the increase in exports.

The increase in labour flow can be seen as an increase in labour inflow and outflow.

The increase in capital flow can be further divided into the increase in the flow of foreign direct investment (FDI) and the increase in the flow of hot money as well as inflow and outflow.

Definition(s):

Foreign direct investment (FDI) refers to the transfer of funds across borders with the intention to purchase and acquire physical capital to produce goods and services.

Hot money refers to the transfer of funds across borders with the intention to earn from the higher interest rates or changes in the exchange rate.

These three phenomena could be examined from the perspective of changes in net value as well as absolute change. It is also important to look at the impact of these economic phenomena on the various economic agents such as households, firms, and governments of both the source country and the destination country of the flow as shown in Table 7.1. The source country is where labour, capital, goods, and services originate from. The destination country is where labour, capital, goods, and services flow into.

Table 7.1: Impact of globalisation.

Increase in international trade of goods and services		**Increase in labour flow**		**Increase in capital flow**			
Increase in exports	Increase in imports	Increase in labour inflow	Increase in labour outflow	Increase in FDI inflow	Increase in FDI outflow	Increase in hot money inflow	Increase in hot money outflow
Impact on source country/impact on recipient country							
Impact on household firms and governments							

7.1.2 Benefits of globalisation

Macroeconomic benefits of globalisation

PROMOTION OF ACTUAL ECONOMIC GROWTH

The increase in international trade of goods and services could lead to an increase in exports or net exports for an economy. As an economy exports more goods and services abroad or when net exports increase, the economy's aggregate demand (AD) will increase, resulting in an increase in real output and actual economic growth via the multiplier effect as shown in Fig. 7.1.

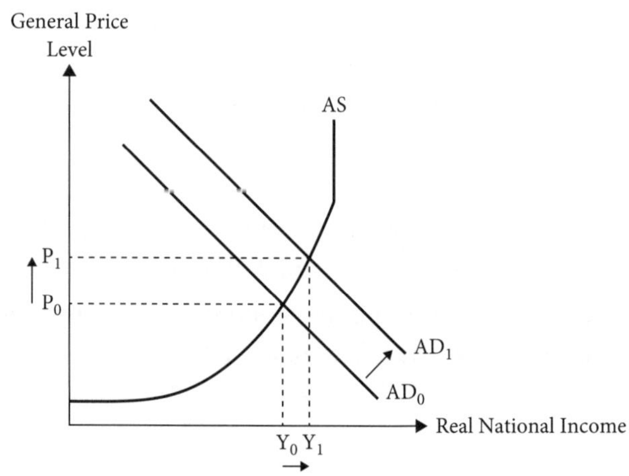

Figure 7.1: Increase in AD.

The increase in capital flow could lead to a net inflow of capital from abroad in terms of either FDI or hot money and this could also contribute to the increase in AD. Inflow of FDI could directly increase the level of investment for the recipient country and this increases the economy's AD. The flow of hot money will increase the money supply and the liquidity in the financial institutions which will then promote lending and borrowing. Increase in borrowing for consumption and investment will increase the economy's AD.

PROMOTION OF POTENTIAL ECONOMIC GROWTH

The increase in the flow of capital goods and labour allows economies to import more factors of production. The increase in the amount or quantity of labour and capital goods that an economy possesses, as well as the importation of better quality labour and capital goods would contribute to an increase in the productive capacity of an economy, resulting in potential economic growth.

The inflow of FDI from abroad could also lead to the transfer of skills and technology that the economy did not previously possess. The domestic workforce could learn technical know-how or management skills from foreign firms and this improves the quality of labour force. Foreign firms might also bring along with them higher level of technology and knowledge and this would lead to technology transfer. The increase in the technology level would contribute to an increase in the productive capacity for an economy, resulting in potential economic growth.

The increase in trade, especially in terms of imports, would increase the degree of competition domestic firms face from abroad. Domestic firms are more likely to embark on research and development to innovate or improve their production of goods and services in order to remain competitive. The investment into research and development could lead to improvement in technology and this would contribute to the increase in productive capacity of the economy, resulting in potential economic growth.

As the economy's productive capacity increases, it experiences potential economic growth and its long-run aggregate supply (LRAS) also increases. This would also promote actual economic growth and lower the general price level as shown in Fig. 7.2.

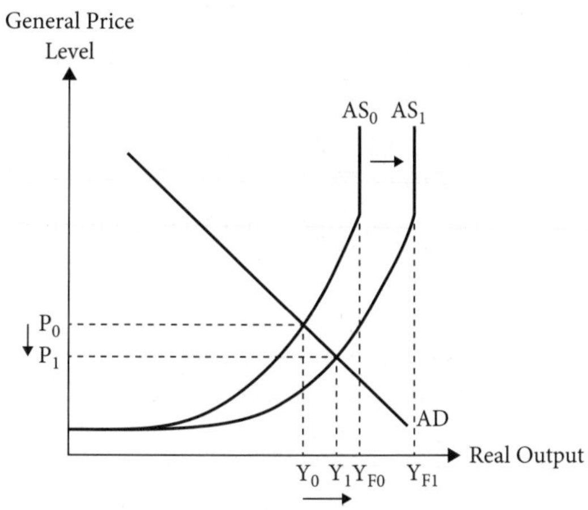

Figure 7.2: Increase in LRAS.

REDUCTION IN UNEMPLOYMENT AND HIGHER WAGES

Economies that experience actual economic growth due to globalisation would likely see a decrease in unemployment. The increase in real output during actual economic growth would increase the demand for factors of production, including labour. The increase in demand for labour would result in an increase in wages, which is the price of labour, and the increase in the number of employed lowers the economy's unemployment rate.

IMPROVEMENT IN BALANCE OF PAYMENTS POSITION

An economy might experience an increase in net exports or net inflow of capital, which would improve the economy's balance of payments position.

An increase in net exports occurs when the increase in exports is more than the increase in imports; this would positively affect the current account. This usually occurs for economies whose goods and services are competitive in terms of price and quality when compared to foreign goods and services.

An improvement in the current account could also occur for economies when a significant number of its citizens work abroad, as these migrant workers remit their income back to their home country.

Economies that provide FDI may also experience an improvement in its current account when the FDI generates profits in the future, and these profits are then transferred back to the source country of the FDI.

A net inflow of capital occurs when the inflow of FDI and hot money is more than the outflow of FDI and hot money; this would positively affect the capital and financial account. As the current account and the capital and financial account are the two main accounts of balance of payments, improvements in either or both accounts could lead to improvement in balance of payments positions of an economy.

REDUCTION IN INFLATIONARY PRESSURE

Globalisation allows economies to have access to more sources of goods and services. The increase in the supply of goods and services from abroad leads to lower prices in imported goods and services, thus, increasing the short-run aggregate supply (SRAS) of the economy. Lower prices for imported final goods and services could lead to lower imported price push inflation while lower prices for imported factors of production could lead to lower imported cost push inflation, assuming that the economy is experiencing imported inflation.

The increase in SRAS due to cheaper imports also leads to actual economic growth and a lower general price level, assuming ceteris paribus as seen in Fig. 7.3.

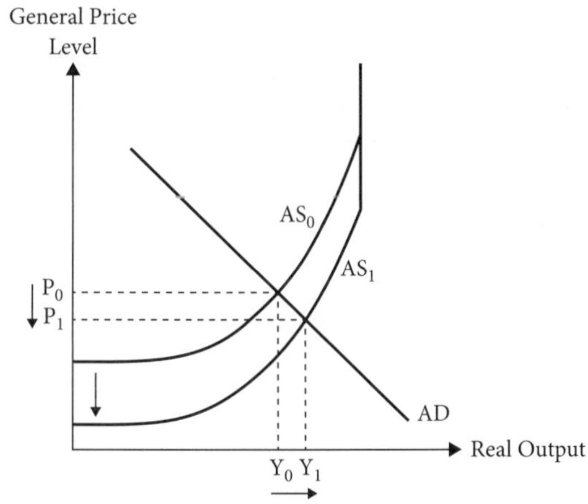

Figure 7.3: Increase in SRAS.

Microeconomic benefits of globalisation

LARGER VARIETY OF GOODS AND SERVICES AND LOWER PRICES FOR CONSUMERS

Globalisation allows economies to have access to more sources of goods and services, and exposes consumers to a larger variety of goods and services. As the supply of goods and services from abroad increases, this would lead to lower prices of imported goods and services.

As globalisation exposes domestic producers to more foreign competition, domestic firms often attempt to compete using lower prices or non-price competition such as research and development, (R&D) which might increase the variety of goods and services. R&D could also improve the quality of goods and services enjoyed by consumers.

HIGHER PROFITS FOR FIRMS

With increased access to more markets abroad, firms might experience an increase in the demand for their goods and services from abroad. The increase in demand would likely lead to an increase in the firms' output, total revenue, and profits.

As the firms' output increases, firms might be able to enjoy cost savings and a decrease in average cost as they experience internal economies of scale. The decrease in average cost might lead to higher profits for firms. The cost savings could also be transferred to consumers in terms of lower prices as firms embark on price competition with foreign firms.

HIGHER LEVEL OF EFFICIENCIES FOR SOCIETY

Globalisation would increase the number of substitutes and competition from abroad, causing domestic firms to be less complacent and instead aim to produce at the lowest possible average cost, in order to maximise profits or to remain price competitive. Thus, the market will be more productive efficient.

With the increase in the number of firms, each firm will have less market share and market power. As each firm's demand will become more price elastic, the firm's ability to exploit consumers is reduced and the market will be more allocative efficient.

Globalisation would decrease the prices of imports and increase the degree of competition from abroad. Firms would be more willing to conduct R&D in order to remain competitive, increase demand, or make their goods and services less substitutable. These investments in R&D would promote a higher degree of dynamic efficiency in the market.

7.1.3 Costs of globalisation

Macroeconomic costs of globalisation

WORSENING OF BALANCE OF PAYMENTS POSITION

Economies might experience a decrease in net exports and net capital outflow, worsening their balance of payments position.

A decrease in net exports occurs when the increase in imports is more than the increase in exports, which would negatively affect the current account. This usually occurs for economies whose goods and services are not competitive in terms of price and quality when compared to foreign goods and services, as globalisation increases the degree of competition from abroad. Households might import more goods and services and might substitute domestically produced goods with imports.

A worsened current account could also occur for economies with a significant number of working foreign nationals as these migrant workers remit their income back to the economies they originate from.

Economies with a significant amount of FDI from abroad could also experience a worsening of the current account when profits generated by FDI are transferred back to their source countries.

A net capital outflow occurs when the inflow of FDI and hot money is less than the outflow of FDI and hot money, which would negatively affect the capital and financial account. Net capital outflow due to net outflow of FDI usually occurs for economies that are less competitive in terms infrastructure, stability, technology, quality of labour force, and corporate tax rate when compared to other economies, as these factors would reduce firm's expected returns of investment and lower business sentiments. Net capital outflow due to net outflow of hot money could be due to the worsening of business sentiments, interest rate, and exchange rate.

As a current account and a capital and financial account are the two main accounts of balance of payments, worsening in either or both accounts could worsen the balance of payments position.

FALL IN REAL NATIONAL INCOME AND REAL OUTPUT

Economies might experience a decrease in net exports and net capital outflow, worsening their balance of payments position and causing a fall in AD.

As the economy imports more goods and services from abroad or when net exports decrease, the economy's AD will decrease, resulting in a fall in real national output via the multiplier effect. If households substitute domestically produced goods with imports, the increase in imports would be accompanied with a decrease in domestic consumption, also reducing AD.

Net outflow of capital in terms of either FDI or hot money would also lead to a fall in AD as a fall in FDI could directly decrease the level of investment for the recipient country, which will decrease that economy's AD. A decrease in hot money inflow will also decrease the money supply in the financial institutions, which will discourage lending and decrease AD.

When the AD falls, the economy will experience a fall in real output and real national income via the multiplier effect as shown in Fig. 7.4.

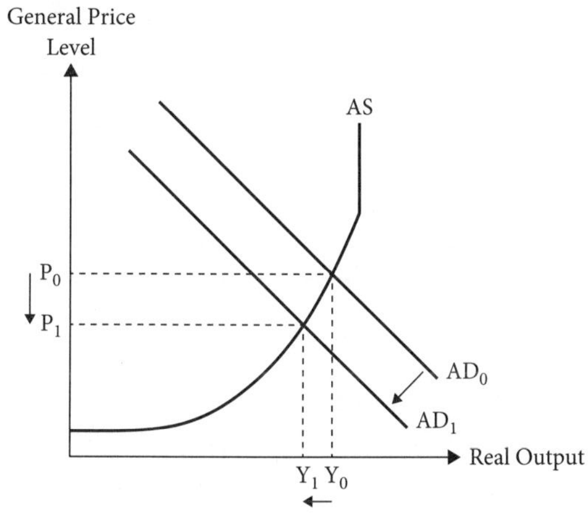

Figure 7.4: Decrease in AD.

INCREASE IN UNEMPLOYMENT AND LOWER WAGES

Economies that experience a fall in real output due to globalisation are likely see an increase in unemployment as the decrease in real output would lead to a decrease in demand for factors of production, including labour. The decrease in demand would result in a decrease in wages and the number of people employed, thus, causing a higher unemployment rate.

DEMAND-PULL INFLATION

Economies that experience actual economic growth due to the increase in AD are also likely to experience demand-pull inflation as seen in Fig. 7.1. Even though the real national income increases when AD increases, the negative impact of inflation will still be experienced by the population, especially for fixed income earners and workers whose incomes increase at a slower rate than the inflation rate.

HUMAN CAPITAL FLIGHT

Human capital flight occurs when an economy loses highly skilled and educated labour to other economies. This is also known as "brain drain". As globalisation promotes labour mobility across borders, economies might lose their highly skilled and educated workers as these workers might be attracted to other economies that provide better remuneration, wages, and working and living conditions.

The negative impact of human capital flight is that these economies would experience negative potential growth and a fall in LRAS as the full employment output decreases due to lesser quantity and lower quality of labour available in the economy. A fall in LRAS would lead to inflation and a fall in real output for the economy as shown in Fig. 7.5.

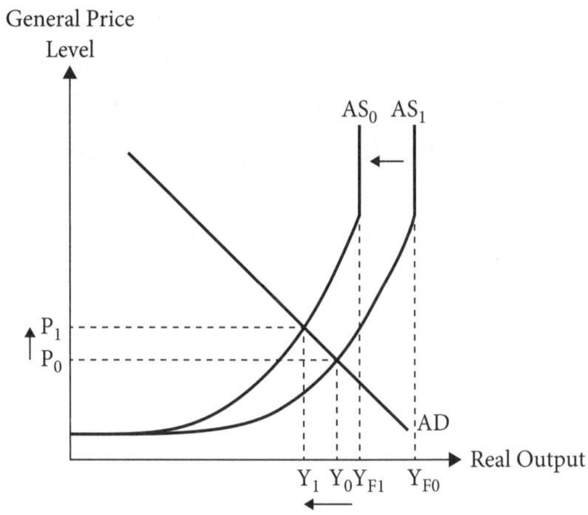

Figure 7.5: Fall in LRAS.

CROWDING OUT OF DOMESTIC INVESTMENT

Significant inflow of FDI might lead to the crowding out of domestic investment as these foreign firms utilise resources that domestic firms could have utilised instead, which might result in fewer resources being available for domestic firms and domestic firms becoming less willing and able to invest. Economies with a significant amount of investment owned by foreign firms instead of domestic firms could have a negative long-term impact on balance of payments as profits from FDI might transfer back to their source economies. An economy's dependence on foreign firms for growth could also make it more susceptible to external forces and events.

OVER DEPENDENCY ON CERTAIN INDUSTRIES

Economies that possess a significant endowment of raw materials such as oil, gas, and coal could be overly dependent on these industries for actual economic growth. Economies whose actual economic growth or increase in real national income is derived from exporting raw materials could face unsustainable economic growth and make it difficult for other non-resource-related industries to develop and grow.

While exports of raw materials could, in the short term, positively affect an economy's balance of payments, national income, and employment, this type of growth is not sustainable as raw materials are usually non-renewable and will eventually run out. Once these resources run out, the economy is negatively affected. Balance of payments is likely to worsen due to a fall in exports earnings, government expenditure is likely to be reduced due to a fall in tax revenue from raw materials, and there will be higher unemployment and lower income in industries related to raw materials. Economies could experience a balance of payments deficit and budget deficit.

Also, overdependency on the exports of raw materials would increase the economy's susceptibility to external forces such as the fluctuation of prices of these raw materials in the international market. When prices of these raw materials decrease, exports earnings and tax revenue will also decrease.

Exports of raw materials would lead to an increase in demand for the economy's currency and result in appreciation. Appreciation would lead to other non-resource-related industries such as manufacturing and services to become less price competitive compared to other economies. This would reduce the ability of these industries to grow and develop in terms of price, quality, and comparative advantage.

Microeconomic costs of globalisation

WORSENING OF INCOME INEQUALITIES

Globalisation might result in the worsening of income inequality within an economy if the economic growth is not inclusive. Non-inclusive growth could be due to the creation of a dual economy, where one side of the economy consists of industries that benefited from globalisation, while the other side consists either of industries not affected by globalisation or those negatively affected by globalisation. Economic agents related to industries benefitting from globalisation would experience an increase in income, while those related to industries not affected by globalisation or negatively affected by globalisation would not see an increase in income or even a decrease in income. This would result in the worsening of income inequality or the widening of the income gap.

Another cause of worsening income inequality within economies is an increase in labour mobility. As labour is now more mobile and able to flow from one country to another, the demand for skilled labour will increase as their skills are required by many economies. The increase in demand for skilled labour would cause the wages of skilled labour to increase. On the other hand, supply of unskilled labour is likely to increase as unskilled labour flows from foreign countries, usually from developing economies. An increase in the supply of unskilled labour would cause the wages of unskilled labour to decrease. The continuous movement in labour will eventually lead to a worsening of the income gap between the skilled and unskilled labour.

As seen in Fig. 7.6, as the demand for skilled labour increases from D_{Skilled} to D'_{Skilled}, the wages of skilled labour increases from WS to WS'. On the other hand, as the supply of unskilled labour increases from $S_{\text{Unskilled}}$ to $S'_{\text{Unskilled}}$, the wages of unskilled labour decreases from WU to WU'. This would worsen the income gap from the original WSWU to WS'WU'.

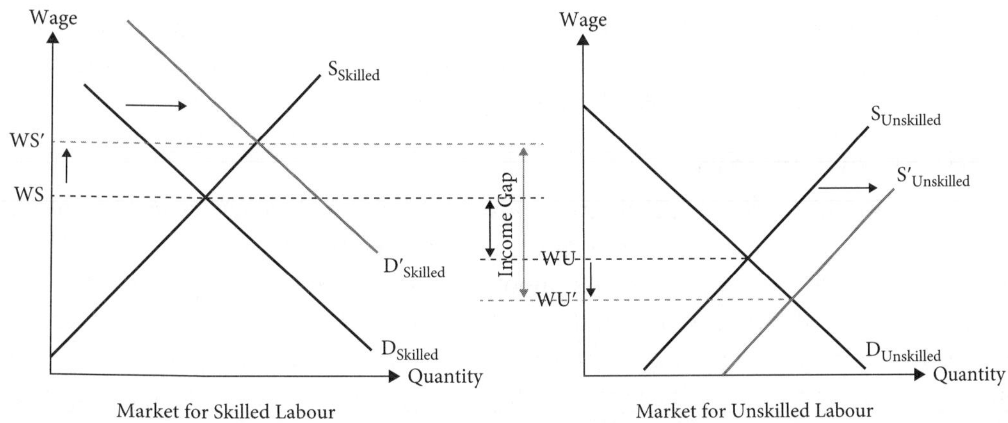

Figure 7.6: Worsening of income gap between the skilled and unskilled labour.

POLLUTION AND ENVIRONMENTAL DEGRADATION

Actual economic growth and the increase in real national output brought about by globalisation might result in pollution and environmental degradation. The production of goods and services might cause market failure due to negative externalities in production. As real output increases during actual economic growth, the amount of pollution produced is likely to increase as well. For example, air and water pollution are the common result of an increase in the production of goods and services, and this pollution would lead to an external cost or health care cost incurred by third parties. Other negative externalities include environmental destruction and congestion.

SURVIVAL OF DOMESTIC FIRMS AND INDUSTRY

Globalisation would expose households to cheaper goods and services imported from abroad, and these imports could be substitutes to domestically produced goods and services. As households switch to relatively cheaper imports, domestic firms would experience a fall in demand for their goods and services.

Domestic firms that are not competitive in terms of cost, price, and/or quality when compared to foreign firms would experience a fall in total revenue and profits; they might even have to shut down and leave the industry.

Industries that are new and in the early stages of development, also known as infant industries, are likely to be less competitive when compared to foreign competition in terms of cost, price, and/or quality. Given time to develop and grow, these industries might become competitive; but with free trade, it is likely that these firms will not survive and will be forced to shut down.

MARKET DOMINANCE BY FOREIGN FIRMS

Globalisation could lead to a reduction in competition. If domestic firms are unable to compete with foreign firms, market power will be consolidated by such large foreign multinational companies. Large foreign multinational companies are likely to be more competitive in terms of both price and non-price competition compared to smaller domestic firms. Large foreign firms, with their internal economies of scale and financial reserves, are able to drive out smaller firms with lower prices and better quality goods and services, thereby establishing their market dominance. With domestic competitors driven out, large foreign firms now possess more market power. Their market dominance can lead to more exploitation of consumers in terms of higher prices. Thus, instead of increasing the number of firms and competition in the economy, free trade might lead to market dominance by foreign firms.

DUMPING BY FOREIGN FIRMS

Globalisation would increase an economy's exposure to unfair trade practices such as dumping. Dumping occurs when a foreign firm exports goods to another economy and sells them at a price below the cost of production. As imports become relatively cheaper, the demand of domestic firms will decrease, reducing the total revenue and profits of domestic firms. This could lead to domestic firms shutting down, and leaving an industry dominated by foreign firms. While lower prices are beneficial for consumers, prices are likely to increase to an even higher level once the foreign firms dominate the industry. Shutting down domestic firms would also increase unemployment in the economy.

Summary for Chapter 7

Globalisation is the phenomenon in which countries become more interconnected economically, socially, and politically.

The effects of globalisation can be examined through the increase in international trade of goods and services, labour flow and capital flow between countries

Benefits and costs of globalisation can be viewed in terms of Macroeconomic and Microeconomic impact.

Macroeconomic benefits of globalisation include:

- actual and potential economic growth
- reduction in unemployment and higher wages
- improvement in balance of payments position
- reduction in inflationary pressure

Microeconomic benefits of globalisation include:

- larger variety of goods and services and lower prices for consumers
- higher profits for firms
- higher level of efficiencies for society

Macroeconomic costs of globalisation include:

- worsening of balance of payments position
- fall in real national income and real output
- increase in unemployment and lower wages
- demand-pull inflation
- human capital flight
- crowding out of domestic investment
- over dependency on certain industries

Macroeconomic costs of globalisation include:

- worsening of income inequalities
- pollution and environmental degradation
- survival of domestic firms and industry
- market dominance by foreign firms
- dumping by foreign firms

Benefits of globalisation can be used as the case for free trade and economic integration and arguments against protectionism

Costs of globalisation can be used as a case for protectionism and as an argument against free trade and economic integration.

Annex 7.1 Equalisation of wages of similar jobs between countries

One of the effects of globalisation is the equalisation of wages of labour doing similar jobs in different countries. Due to the increase in labour mobility, labour can now move or flow from one country to another. When labour moves from one country with lower wages to another country with higher wages, supply of labour in both countries will change.

For example, assuming country A has lower wages compared to country B, labour in country A will move to country B to seek higher wages. The supply of labour in country A, the originally lower wage country, will decrease from SA to SA' as labour moves away to Country B, resulting in a shortage of labour and causing wages to increase from WA to W'. On the other hand, the supply of labour in Country B, the originally higher wage country, will increase from SB to SB' as labour moves into it from Country A, resulting in a surplus of labour and causing wages to decrease from WB to W'. The continuous movement in labour will eventually lead to both countries having the same wage W,' as shown in Fig. 7.7.

Labour originally located in countries with lower wages will benefit from the equalisation of wages due to globalisation at the expense of labour originally located in countries with higher wages.

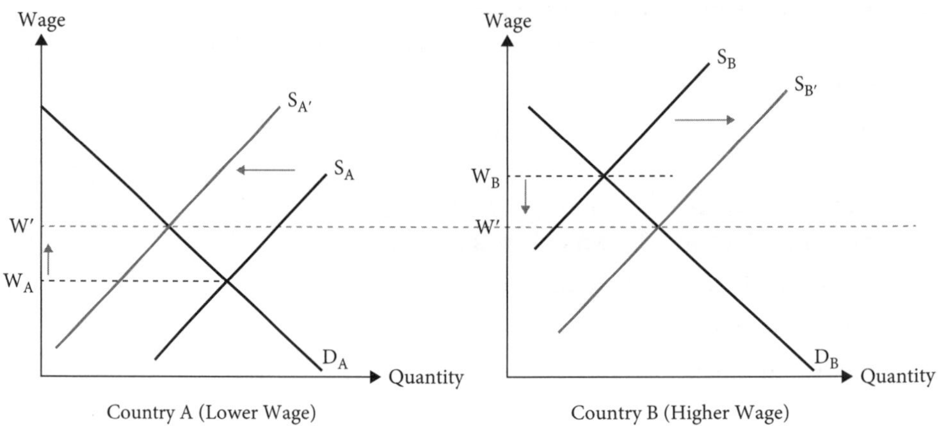

Figure 7.7: Equalisation of wages between countries.

7.2 International Trade and Free Trade

7.2.1 International trade

Why do countries trade?

International trade takes place when an individual or a firm in one country purchases goods and services from another country. Households import final goods and services while firms import factors of production from abroad. The basis of international trade can be attributed to either demand or supply factors, except that the consumers' demand and producers' supply are located in two different countries.

Demand factors

The demand of imports is affected by how much consumers are willing and able to buy goods and services from another country. The key factors affecting imports are taste and preferences, income level, and relative price level between economies.

Taste and preferences: Individuals or firms import goods and services that domestic firms do not produce, or prefer goods and services produced by another country which might be of better quality or have greater consumer appeal, compared to domestically produced goods and services.

Income level: Demand for imports is affected by the population income level. As the population becomes richer and wealthier, their demand for normal and luxurious goods and services from abroad will also increase.

Price level: Imports could be cheaper than domestically produced goods and services, making it more appealing to import instead of buying from domestic firms. Imports could also be relatively cheaper when compared to domestically produced goods and services, either when domestic goods and services become more expensive or imports become cheaper. When domestically produced goods and services become relatively more expensive compared to imports, the demand for imports will increase.

Supply factors

The supply of exports is affected by how much producers are willing and able to produce and sell goods and services to another country. The key factors affecting export are factor endowments and level of technology.

Factor endowments: Different countries are endowed with different amounts and different types of factor endowments in terms of land, labour, capital, and entrepreneurship. Some countries are endowed with large populations which translate to a large labour force; others are endowed with large amounts of natural resources such as oil or arable land. Other than quantity, factor endowments can be seen in terms of quality of factors of production, like the skill of labour, arability of land, and geographical location of the country. Some countries are also endowed with climate suited to produce certain goods and services such as farms and fisheries. Although globalisation has led to the increased mobility of factors of production, differences in factor endowments continue to exist as some resources remain, to some extent, immobile.

Level of technology: Different countries possess different levels and types of technology. Different countries also conduct different types and degrees of R&D in their technology. This results in some countries being able to produce certain goods and services that require a higher level of technology capability, better than other countries. Although technology can be transferred from one country to another across the world, technology is continuously being invented and improved, which will still create differences in the technology that each country possesses.

Due to differences in supply factors in terms of factor endowments and level of technology, international trade can be justified using the concepts of opportunity cost through the theory of comparative advantage.

The theory of comparative advantage

Due to differences in the level of the factors of production that each country is endowed with as well as the technology that each country currently possesses, different countries will have different opportunity costs when producing various goods and services. The opportunity cost of producing one good is measured by the amount of another good that could have been produced instead, if the same factors of production were diverted to the production of the other good.

> *Definition(s):*
>
> A country is deemed to have **comparative advantage** in the production of a good or service when they can produce that good or service at a lower opportunity cost compared to another country.

The theory of comparative advantage states that due to differences in opportunity cost when producing goods and services between countries, countries should specialise in the production of goods and services they have a comparative advantage in and trade it in exchange for goods and services that they do not have a comparative advantage in, assuming a beneficial term of trade.

> *Definition(s):*
>
> **Terms of trade,** also known as the exchange ratio, is the amount of one good in exchange for the other good.

Countries can benefit from specialising and exporting products in which they have a comparative advantage and importing products in which they do not have a comparative advantage.

The theory of comparative advantage has the following assumptions:

- There are two countries, each producing two goods.
- For each country, the opportunity costs of producing the two goods are constant.
- For both countries, all factors of production are fully and efficiently employed.
- Factors of production are perfectly mobile within each country but perfectly immobile between countries.

- There is free trade or no trade barriers between the two countries.
- There is no transport cost.

The two countries will each specialise in the production of a good or service they have a lower opportunity cost in and export it to the other country. For specialisation and trade to be mutually beneficial for both countries, the terms of trade must be between the two countries' opportunity cost to produce each good. If a beneficial term of trade is fulfilled, both countries can consume both goods beyond their original production possibility curve. As free trade is one of the assumptions for the theory of comparative advantage, the theory is also used to justify why economies should embark on free trade and remove existing trade barriers.

The theory of comparative advantage will be explained using the following two explanations:

- Explanation no. 1 can be used to justify the validity of the theory of comparative advantage in the case where a country is able to produce more of both goods than the other country, usually the case of large countries versus small countries. It can be used to justify why small countries like Singapore are able to trade with large countries like China who can produce more goods and services than Singapore.
- Explanation no. 2 can be used to justify the validity of the theory of comparative advantage in the case where each country is able to produce more of one good than the other country, usually the case of large countries versus large countries. It can be used to justify why large countries like the United States are able to trade with large countries like China.

Explanation no. 1 of the theory of comparative advantage

The theory of comparative advantage can be explained in the case where a country has an absolute advantage in the production of both goods compared to the other country. Absolute advantage refers to the ability of one country to produce more of a good using the same amount of resources. Using the example of Germany and India, assuming a scenario prior to specialisation and trade, both countries can produce cars and textiles. The maximum amount of either good both countries can produce when they fully devote all their factors of production to the production of either of the two goods can be seen in Table 7.2a. It can also be represented in the form of the production possibility curves as seen in Fig. 7.8.

Table 7.2a: Production possibilities of Germany and India before specialisation and trade.

	Cars		Textiles
Germany	1000 units	**OR**	500 units
India	200 units		400 units

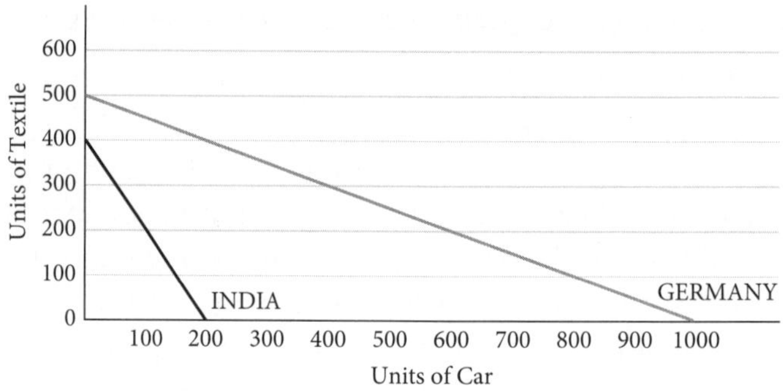

Figure 7.8: Production possibility curves of Germany and India before specialisation and trade.

Even though Germany can produce more of both goods than India, both countries can still benefit from specialisation and trade as India still has a comparative advantage in one of the two goods, which can be determined when comparing the opportunity cost of producing each good shown in Table 7.2b.

The opportunity cost of producing cars is measured in terms of the amount of textiles that could have been produced instead, and vice versa. The opportunity cost of producing 1 unit of car can be calculated by dividing both original number of cars and textiles by the number of cars that each country can originally produce. Similarly, the opportunity cost of producing 1 unit of textile can be calculated by dividing both original number of cars and textiles by the amount of clothing that each country can originally produce.

Table 7.2b: Opportunity cost of producing car and textile for Germany and India.

	Opportunity cost of producing	
	1 unit of car	**1 unit of textile**
Germany	0.5 unit of textile	2 units of car
India	2 units of textile	0.5 unit of car

From Table 7.2b, Germany's opportunity cost of producing 1 unit of car is 0.5 unit of textile and India's opportunity cost of producing 1 unit of car is 2 units of textile. As Germany's opportunity cost in producing cars is lower than India's, Germany has the comparative advantage in the production of cars and therefore, should specialise in the production of cars.

On the other hand, Germany's opportunity cost of producing 1 unit of textile is 2 units of car and India's opportunity cost of producing 1 unit of textile is 0.5 unit of car. As India's opportunity cost in producing textiles is lower than Germany's, India has the comparative advantage in the production of textiles and therefore, should specialise in the production of textiles.

When Germany chooses to specialise in the production of cars by devoting all its resources to the production of cars, assuming perfect factor mobility, the output of cars by Germany will now be 1000 units while output of textile becomes zero.

On the other hand, when India chooses specialisation in the production of textile by devoting all its resources to the production of textile, assuming perfect factor mobility, the output of textile by India will now be 400 units while output of cars becomes zero.

Tables 7.2c: Consumption level after specialisation and trade.

	Cars	Textiles
Germany	1000 – 100 = 900 units	0 + 100 =100 units
India	0 + 100 = 100 units	400 – 100 = 300 units

For specialisation and trade to be mutually beneficial for both countries, the terms of trade must be between the two countries' opportunity cost to produce each good as seen in Table 7.2b. Based on Table 7.2b, a beneficial term of trade for 1 unit of car must be between 0.5 and 2 units of textile. On the other hand, a beneficial or suitable term of trade for 1 unit of textile must be between 0.5 unit of car and 2.5 units of car.

Assuming a beneficial term of trade, such as 1 unit of car for 1 unit of textile, both Germany and India could now consume beyond their original production possibility curve, if Germany trades 100 units of cars for 100 units of textile with India. The new combination of cars and textiles both countries can now consume will be shown in Table 7.2c.

Due to specialisation and trade based on the theory of comparative advantage, assuming a beneficial term of trade, both countries can enjoy a larger amount of both goods beyond their original production possibility curve as shown in Figs. 7.9a and b. Therefore, due to differences in their opportunity costs, countries could benefit by specialisation and free trade.

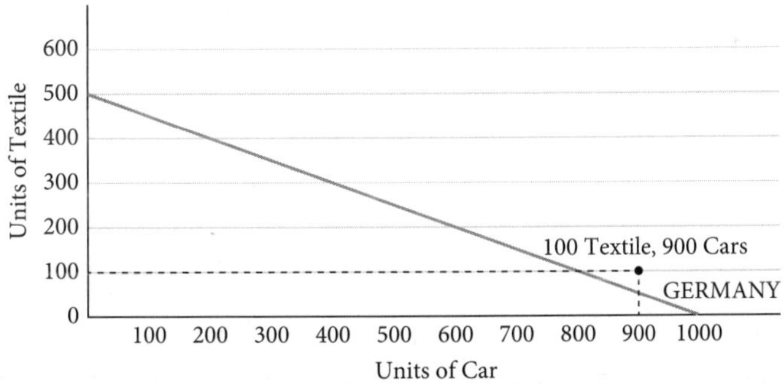

Figure 7.9a: Germany's PPC after specialisation and trade.

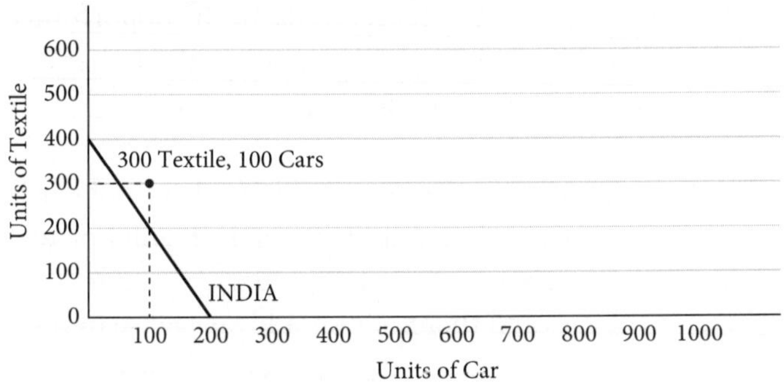

Figure 7.9b: India's PPC after specialisation and trade.

Explanation no. 2 of the theory of comparative advantage

The theory of comparative advantage can also be explained in the case where each country is able to produce more of one good than the other country. Using the example of Germany and India, assuming a scenario prior to specialisation and trade, both countries devote half of their factors of production to the production of two goods, cars and textiles. The maximum combination of both goods both countries can produce can be seen in Table 7.3a. It can also be represented in the form of production possibility curves as seen in Fig. 7.10.

Table 7.3a: Production possibilities of Germany and India before specialisation and trade.

	Cars	Textiles
Germany	500 units	200 units
India	200 units	400 units
Total Output	700 units	600 units

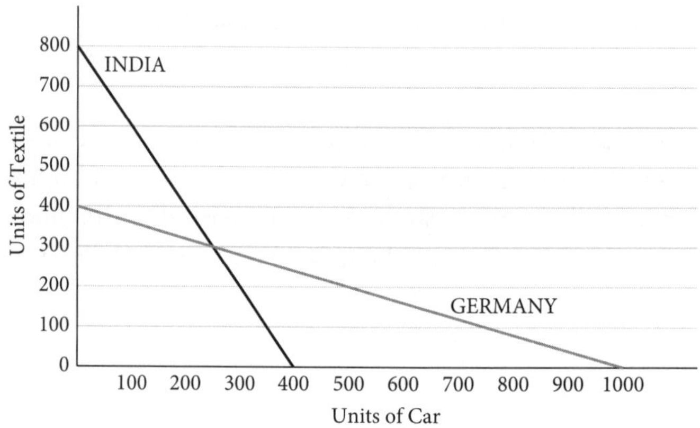

Figure 7.10: Production possibility curves of Germany and India before specialisation and trade.

The opportunity cost of producing cars is measured in terms of the amount of textiles that could have been produced instead, and vice versa. The opportunity cost of producing 1 unit of car can be calculated by dividing both the original number of cars and textiles by the number of cars that each country can originally produce. Similarly, the opportunity cost of producing 1 unit of textile can be calculated by dividing both the original number of cars and textiles by the amount of clothing that each country can originally produce.

From Table 7.3b, Germany's opportunity cost of producing 1 unit of car is 0.4 unit of textile and India's opportunity cost of producing 1 unit of car is 2 units of textile. As Germany's opportunity cost in producing cars is lower than India's, Germany has the comparative advantage in the production of cars and therefore, should specialise in the production of cars.

Table 7.3b: Opportunity cost of producing car and textile for Germany and India.

	Opportunity cost of producing	
	1 unit of car	**1 unit of textile**
Germany	0.4 units of textile	2.5 units of car
India	2 units of textile	0.5 units of car

On the other hand, Germany's opportunity cost of producing 1 unit of textile is 2.5 units of car and India's opportunity cost of producing 1 unit of textile is 0.5 unit of car. As India's opportunity cost in producing textile is lower than Germany's, India has the comparative advantage in the production of textile and therefore, should specialise in the production of textile.

If Germany chooses to specialise in the production of cars by devoting all its resources to the production of cars, assuming perfect factor mobility, the output of cars by Germany will be 1000 units while the output of textiles becomes zero.

On the other hand, if India chooses to specialise in the production of textiles by devoting all its resources to the production of textiles, assuming perfect factor mobility, the output of textiles by India will be 800 units while the output of cars becomes zero.

Table 7.3c: Gains from specialisation.

	Cars	**Textiles**
Germany	1000 units	0 units
India	0 units	800 units
Total Output	1000 units	800 units

The gains from trade when each country specialises in the production of the good they have a comparative advantage in will be the increase in total output of both goods as shown in Table 7.3c, which is now higher than before specialisation as shown in Table 7.3a. The total output of car will increase from 700 to 1000 units while the total output of textiles will increase from 600 to 800 units.

For specialisation and trade to be mutually beneficial for both countries, the terms of trade must be between the two countries' opportunity cost to produce each good, as seen in Table 7.3b. Based on Table 7.3b, a beneficial term of trade for 1 unit of car must be between 0.4 unit of textile and 2 units of textile. On the other hand, a beneficial or suitable term of trade for 1 unit of textile must be between 0.5 unit of car and 2.5 units of car.

Tables 7.3d: Consumption level after specialisation and trade.

	Cars	**Textiles**
Germany	1000 – 250 = 750 units	0 + 250 = 250 units
India	0 + 250 = 250 units	800 – 250 = 550 units

Assuming a beneficial term of trade, for example, 1 unit of car for 1 unit of textile, both Germany and India could now consume beyond their original production possibility curve, if Germany trades 250 units of car for 250 units of textile with India. The new combination of cars and textiles both countries can now consume is shown in Table 7.3d. Comparing Tables 7.3a and 7.3d, both countries now enjoy a larger amount of both goods.

Due to specialisation and trade based on theory of comparative advantage, assuming a beneficial term of trade, both countries can enjoy a larger amount of both goods beyond their original production possibility curve as shown in Figs. 7.11a and b. Therefore, due to differences in their opportunity costs, countries could benefit by specialisation and free trade.

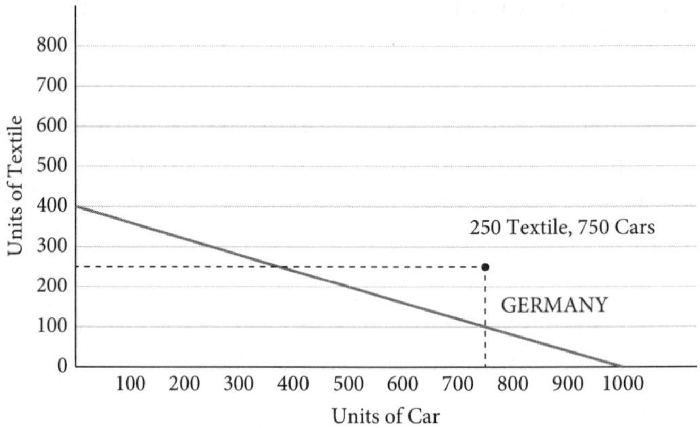

Figure 7.11a: Germany's PPC after specialisation and trade.

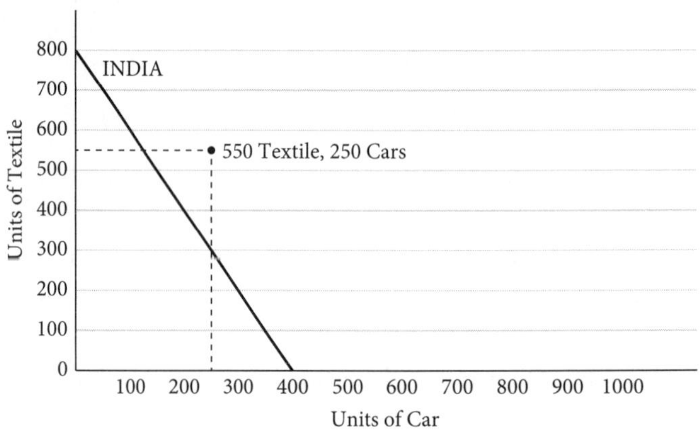

Figure 7.11b: India's PPC after specialisation and trade.

Non-beneficial terms of trade

In order for specialisation and trade to be beneficial for both countries, the terms of trade have to between the two countries' opportunity cost of producing each good. If the terms of trade are not beneficial, or not between the two countries' opportunity cost of producing, only one of the two countries will benefit.

Using the same example from the section *Explanation no. 2 of the theory of comparative advantage* (p.351), a beneficial term of trade for 1 unit of car must be between 0.4 unit of textile and 2 units of textile. On the other hand, a beneficial or suitable term of trade for 1 unit of textile must be between 0.5 unit of car and 2.5 units of car as shown in Table 7.3b.

An example of a non-beneficial term of trade would be 1 unit of car for 5 units of textile. Germany can now trade 100 units of car for 500 units of textile with India. The new total amount of cars and textiles both countries can now consume can be seen in Table 7.4.

Table 7.4: Non-beneficial terms of trade for India.

	Cars	Textiles
Germany	1000 – 100 = 900 units	0 + 500 = 500 units
India	0 + 100 = 100 units	800 – 500 = 300 units

Comparing Table 7.3a with Table 7.4, Germany will benefit from a higher amount of both goods whereas India will be worse off, with a lesser amount of both goods. India will be better off not specialising and not trading with Germany.

An example of a non-beneficial term of trade will be 1 unit of car for 0.1 unit of textile. Germany can now trade 600 units of cars for 60 units of textile with India. The new total amount of cars and textiles both countries can now consume can be seen in Table 7.5.

Table 7.5: Non-beneficial terms of trade for Germany.

	Cars	Textiles
Germany	1000 600 = 400 units	0 + 60 − 60 units
India	0 + 600 = 600 units	800 – 60 = 740 units
Total Output	1000 units	800 units

Comparing Table 7.3a with Table 7.5, India will benefit from a higher amount of both goods whereas Germany will be worse off with a lesser amount of both goods. Germany will be better off not specialising and not trading with India.

As can be seen again, for specialisation and trade to be beneficial for both countries, the terms of trade must be between the two countries' opportunity cost to produce each good.

Dynamic comparative advantage

A country's comparative advantages are primarily determined by factor endowments and level of technology. As these two factors are not constant and likely to change over time, changes in opportunity cost and possible changes in comparative advantage can occur. Therefore, a country's comparative advantage is dynamic and can be gained or lost over time.

The gain in comparative advantage happens when the opportunity cost of producing the good decreases. On the other hand, the loss in comparative advantage, also known as erosion of comparative advantage, happens when the opportunity cost of producing the good increases.

CHANGES IN THE LEVEL OF FACTOR ENDOWMENTS

One possible cause of the loss or erosion of comparative advantage is due to the depletion of factor endowments. The depletion of a country's resources changes how many goods and services it can produce and therefore, changes its opportunity cost. Using the same example from *Explanation no. 2 of the theory of comparative advantage* (p.353), before India's depletion of resources, Germany and India's production possibility and opportunity cost can be seen in Table 7.6.

Table 7.6: Before India's depletion of resources.

	Cars	**Textiles**
Germany	500 units	200 units
India	200 units	400 units
	Opportunity cost of producing	
	1 unit of car	**1 unit of textile**
Germany	0.4 units of textile	2.5 units of car
India	2 units of textile	0.5 units of car

For example, in the event that India's arable land for cotton growing are depleted, India will now produce lesser amount of textiles. If the amount of textiles that India can produce decreases from 400 to 50, assuming ceteris paribus, India's opportunity cost in producing 1 unit of car will now be 0.25 unit of textile and opportunity cost in producing 1 unit of textile will now be 4 units of car as shown in Table 7.7. Though Germany's opportunity cost of producing cars and textiles remains constant, due to changes in India's opportunity cost, Germany now has gained a comparative advantage in the production of textiles. India will no longer has a comparative advantage in the production of textiles and should no longer specialise in its production.

Table 7.7: After India's depletion of resources.

	Cars	**Textiles**
Germany	500 units	200 units
India	200 units	50 units
	Opportunity cost of producing	
	1 unit of car	**1 unit of Textile**
Germany	0.4 unit of textile	2.5 units of car
India	0.25 unit of textile	4 units of car

CHANGES IN TECHNOLOGICAL LEVEL

Another possible cause of the loss or erosion of comparative advantage is due to the changes in technological level. As a country's level of technology improves, it changes how much goods and services it can produces and therefore, changes the opportunity cost. Using the same example from the *Explanation no. 2 of the theory of comparative advantage* (p.351), before Germany's technological progress, Germany and India's production possibilities and opportunity costs can be seen in Table 7.8.

Table 7.8: Before Germany's technological progress.

	Cars	Textile
Germany	500 units	200 units
India	200 units	400 units
	Opportunity cost of producing	
	1 unit of car	**1 unit of Textile**
Germany	0.4 units of textile	2.5 units of car
India	2 units of textile	0.5 units of car

For example, in the event that Germany's technological level in producing textiles increases, Germany will now produce a larger amount of textiles. If the amount of textiles that Germany produces increases from 200 to 1500, assuming ceteris paribus, Germany's opportunity cost for producing 1 unit of car will now be 3 units of textile and its opportunity cost in producing 1 unit of textile will now be 0.33 unit of car as shown in Table 7.9. Though India's opportunity cost of producing cars and textiles remains constant, due to changes in Germany's opportunity cost, Germany has gained a comparative advantage in the production of textiles. India will no longer have a comparative advantage in the production of textiles and should no longer specialise in the production of textiles.

Table 7.9: After Germany's technological progress.

	Cars	Textiles
Germany	500 units	1500 units
India	200 units	400 units
	Opportunity cost of producing	
	1 unit of car	**1 unit of Textile**
Germany	3 units of textile	0.33 unit of car
India	2 units of textile	0.5 unit of car

7.2.2 Trade patterns

A country's trade patterns consist of key trade-related information such as trading partners, types, and the amount of goods and services traded. A country's trade patterns can be used to determine its type of economy, current economic performance, as well as expected future economic performance. Trade patterns can also be examined over space and time.

Trade patterns usually divide the information into two categories: information related to the country's exports and information related to the country's imports.

Information on trading partners consists of the origins of imports and the destinations of exports. Types of goods and services traded consist of those that are imported and exported. The amount of goods and services traded consists of information about the quantity of goods and services imported and exported. This information can be shown in terms of the quantity of imports from different trading partners and the quantity of exports to different trading partners.

A basic breakdown of trade patterns would consist of the country's key types of exports and imports, amount exported and imported, destinations of exports, and origins of imports as shown in Table 7.10. A more detailed breakdown of trade patterns provides more details for each of the components as shown in Table 7.11

Table 7.10: Basic trade pattern.

Types of Exports		Types of Imports
Amount Exported	**Trade Pattern**	Amount Imported
Destinations of Exports		Origins of Imports

Table 7.11: Detailed trade pattern.

Trade Patterns			
Merchandise (Goods)		Services	
Top merchandise exported	Top merchandise imported	Top services exported	Top services imported
Top destinations for merchandise exports	Top origins for merchandise imported	Top destinations for services exports	Top origins for services imported
Total merchandise exports	Total merchandise imports	Total services exports	Total services imports
Total merchandise trade (Exports + Imports)		Total services trade (Exports + Imports)	
Total trade volume			

Developed countries tend to import low-value or low value-added goods such as agriculture or simple manufactured goods while exporting high-value or high value-added goods such as electronics and automobiles. Developing countries, on the other hand, tend to import high-value or high value-added goods such as electronics and automobile while exporting low-value or low value-added goods such as agriculture or simple manufactured goods. Singapore's trade patterns can be analysed using Singapore's non-oil merchandise trade pattern (Table 7.12) and Singapore's services trade pattern (Table 7.13).

It is important to note that global trade patterns are constantly changing depending on changing economic conditions and landscapes around the world.

Singapore's trade patterns

Table 7.12: Singapore Merchandise Trade Pattern 2018 (At Current Prices)

Top 3 non-oil merchandise exported	1. Machinery and transport equipment: S$ 263.6 billion, 58.3% 2. Chemicals and chemical products: S$ 79.6 billion, 17.6% 3. Miscellaneous Manufactured Articles: S$ 47.9 billion, 10.6%	1. Machinery and transport equipment: S$ 231.0 billion, 60.5% 2. Chemicals and chemical products: S$ 40.7 billion, 10.7% 3. Miscellaneous manufactured articles: S$ 39.7 billion, 10.4%	Top 3 non-oil merchandise imported
Top 5 destinations for non-oil merchandise exports	1. China 2. Hong Kong 3. Malaysia 4. European Union 5. Indonesia	1. China 2. European Union 3. Malaysia 4. United States 5. Taiwan	Top 5 origins for merchandise imported
Total merchandise exports	S$555.7 billion	S$500.2 billion	Total merchandise imports
Total non-oil merchandise trade (Exports + Imports)	S$1,055.9 billion		

Source: https://www.singstat.gov.sg/modules/infographics/singapore-international-trade

Table 7.13: Singapore Service Trade Pattern 2018 (At Current Prices)

Top 3 services exported	1. Transport: S$ 69.4 billion, 28.0% 2. Financial: S$ 36.6 billion, 14.8% 3. Travel: S$ 27.7 billion, 11.2%	1. Transport: S$ 72.9 billion, 28.9% 2. Travel: S$ 34.2 billion, 13.6% 3. Business Management: S$ 21.5 billion, 8.5%	Top 3 services imported

(*Continued*)

Table 7.13: Singapore's services trade pattern. (*Continued*)

Top 5 destinations for services exports (2017 Data)	1. United States 2. Japan 3. Australia 4. China 5. Ireland	1. United States 2. Netherlands 3. China 4. Hong Kong 5. Japan	Top 5 origins for services imported (2017 Data)
Total exports of services	S$ 248.2 billion	S$ 252.2 billion	Total imports of services
Total services trade (Exports + Imports)	S$ 500.4 billion		

Source: https://www.singstat.gov.sg/modules/infographics/singapore-international-trade

7.2.3 Free trade

Free trade is a situation in which countries exchange goods and services without any form of trade barriers. This usually occurs after the countries sign Free Trade Agreements (FTAs) or similar trade agreements. The removal of trade barriers increases the flow of goods and services between countries as countries will export and import more. One of the international organisations that promotes trade and free trade between countries is the World Trade Organisation (WTO).

The WTO is the only international organisation dealing with the global rules of trade between nations. Its main function is to ensure that trade flows as smoothly, predictably, and freely as possible. It provides the platform for trade negotiations, the implementation and monitoring trade agreements and the settling of trade-related disputes among members.

Source: https://www.wto.org/english/thewto_e/whatis_e/what_we_do_e.htm

Key arguments for free trade

Free trade is one of the contributing factors towards a more globalised world as it promotes trade between economies. Therefore, the benefits of free trade consist of the benefits of globalisation relevant to an increase in trade. These benefits form the basis for the arguments for free trade and economic integration, as well as the arguments against protectionism.

PROMOTION OF ACTUAL ECONOMIC GROWTH

Free trade and the removal of trade barriers would reduce the prices of a country's exports in foreign countries, making the exports more price competitive, leading to an increase in exports or net exports for the economy. As an economy exports more goods and services abroad or when net exports increase, the economy's AD will increase, resulting in an increase in real output and actual economic growth via the multiplier effect as shown in Fig. 7.12.

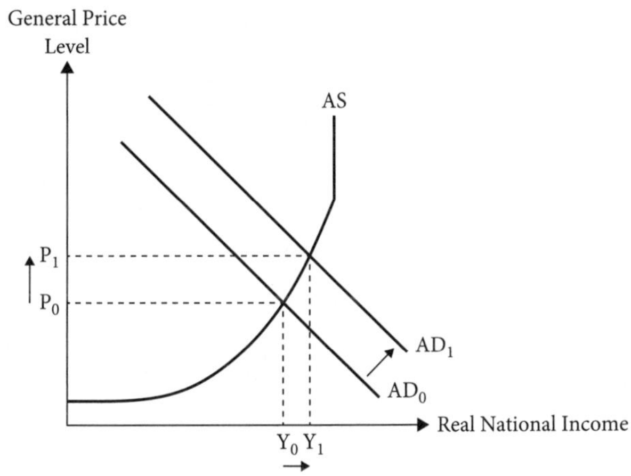

Figure 7.12: Increase in AD.

IMPROVEMENT IN BALANCE OF PAYMENTS POSITION

An economy that experiences an increase in exports or net exports could also see an improvement in the economy's balance of payments position. An increase in net exports occurs when the increase in exports is more than the increase in imports, which would positively affect the current account. This usually occurs for economies whose goods and services are competitive in terms of price and quality when compared to foreign goods and services. As the current account is one of the two main accounts of balance of payments, improvements in the current account could lead to improvement in the balance of payments position of an economy.

REDUCTION IN INFLATIONARY PRESSURE

Free trade and the removal of trade barriers would reduce the prices of imports from foreign countries, making imports cheaper and increasing the SRAS of the economy. Lower prices of imported final goods and services could lead to lower imported price push inflation, whereas lower prices of imported factors of production could lead to lower imported cost push inflation, assuming that the economy is experiencing imported inflation.

As an economy experiences an increase in SRAS due to cheaper imports, it would also lead to actual economic growth and a lower general price level, assuming ceteris paribus, as seen in Fig. 7.13.

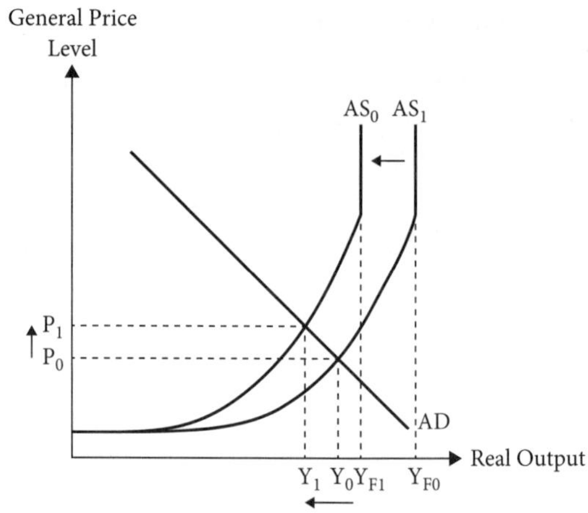

Figure 7.13: Increase in SRAS.

LARGER VARIETY OF GOODS AND SERVICES AND LOWER PRICES FOR CONSUMERS

Free trade and the removal of trade barriers would allow a country to have access to more sources of goods and services, exposing consumers to a larger variety of goods and services. The increase in the supply of goods and services from abroad leads to lower prices of imported goods and services.

Free trade also exposes domestic producers to more foreign competition, encouraging domestic firms to compete using lower price or non-price competition such as R&D which might increase the variety of goods and services. Such R&D could also improve the quality or lower the prices of goods and services enjoyed by consumers.

Assuming country A originally does not embark on international trade, the market price (P_D) and market quantity (Q_D) of a good or service, such as corn, in country A is determined through the interaction between domestic demand ($D_{Domestic}$) and domestic supply ($S_{Domestic}$) of corn as shown in Fig. 7.14. If the world price of corn is lower than country A's domestic price P_D, country A will be an importer of corn. Assuming that country A is unable to influence global demand and supply of rice, country A can import an unlimited amount of rice at the prevailing world price P_W; therefore, the supply of corn from the world market for country A will be perfectly price elastic, a horizontal supply curve at P_W as shown in Fig. 7.14. With free trade, the market price of rice in country A will now decrease from P_D to P_W, while the market quantity of rice will increase from $0Q_D$ to $0Q_W$. Of the new market quantity of $0Q_W$, $0Q_1$is produced domestically while Q_1Q_W is imported from abroad. Consumers will be better off as they enjoy a larger quantity of corn at a lower price, and consumer surpluses will increase from a situation without trade (area A) to a situation with free trade (area A + B + C + D). Consumer surplus increases by area B + C + D. However, domestic production will decrease from $0Q_D$ to $0Q_1$ and imports will increase from zero to Q_1Q_W.

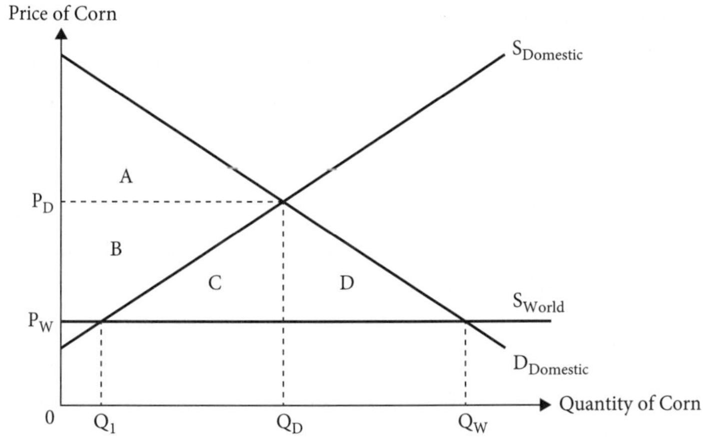

Figure 7.14: Market of corn from no trade to free trade.

Assuming country A originally already embarked on international trade but imposed tariffs on the imported corn, the world supply curve would be $S_{World + Tariff}$ instead, as country A can still import an unlimited amount of corn from the rest of the world but at a higher price. With free trade and the removal of trade barriers, the world supply curve will increase from $S_{World + Tariff}$ to S_{World}. The market price of corn in country A will now decrease from P_{WT} to P_W as shown in Fig. 7.15. Of the new market quantity of $0Q_W$, $0Q_1$ is produced domestically whereas Q_1Q_W is imported from abroad. Consumers will be better off as they enjoy a larger quantity of corn at a lower price, and consumer surplus will increase from a situation of trade with tariff (area A + B) to a situation with free trade (area A + B + C + D + E + F). Consumer surplus increases by area C + D + E + F. However, domestic production will decrease from $0Q_2$ to $0Q_1$ and imports will increase from Q_2Q_{WT} to Q_1Q_W.

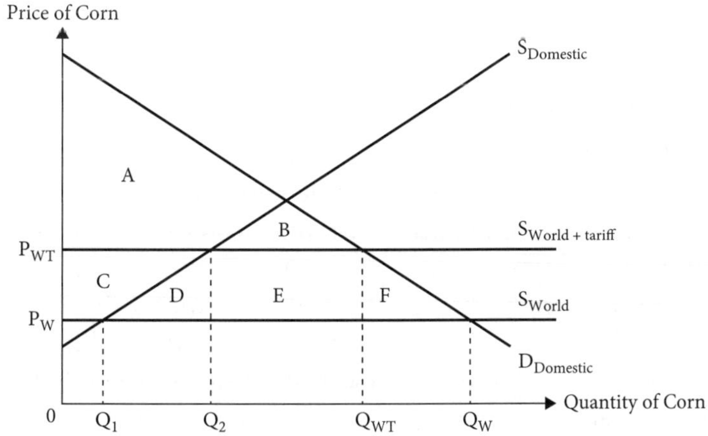

Figure 7.15: Market of corn from trade with tariff to free trade.

HIGHER PROFITS FOR FIRMS

Free trade would reduce the prices of firms' exports in foreign countries, making exports more price competitive which in turn could lead to an increase in exports, likely increasing the firms' output, total revenue, and profits.

With increased access to more markets abroad, firms might experience an increase in the demand for their goods and services from abroad. The increase in demand would likely lead to an increase in the firms' output, total revenue, and profits.

As the firms' output increases, firms might be able to enjoy cost savings and a decrease in average cost as they experience internal economies of scale. The decrease in average cost might lead to higher profits for firms. The cost savings could also be transferred to consumers in terms of lower prices as firms embark on price competition with foreign firms.

Free trade would also increase firms' access to cheaper factors of production from abroad, likely decreasing the cost of production and increasing firms' profits.

HIGHER LEVEL OF EFFICIENCIES FOR SOCIETY

Free trade would increase the number of substitutes and competition from abroad, causing domestic firms to be less complacent and instead aim to produce at the lowest possible average cost in order to maximise profits or to remain price competitive. Thus, the market will be more productive efficient.

With the increase in the number of firms, each firm will have less market share and market power. As each firm's demand will become more price elastic, the firm's ability to exploit consumers is reduced and the market will be more allocative efficient.

Free trade would decrease the prices of imports and increase the degree of competition from abroad. Firms would be more willing to conduct R&D in order to remain competitive, increase demand, or make their goods and services less substitutable. These investments in research and development would promote a higher degree of dynamic efficiency in the market.

Key arguments against free trade

FALL IN REAL NATIONAL OUTPUT

Free trade and the removal of trade barriers would reduce the prices of a country's imports from foreign countries, making imports more price competitive. This could lead to an increase in imports or a decrease in net exports for the economy. As an economy imports more goods and services from abroad or when net exports decrease, the economy's AD will decrease, resulting in a decrease in real output via the multiplier effect, as shown in Fig. 7.16. If households substitute domestically produced goods with imports, the increase in imports would be accompanied by a decrease in domestic consumption, thus, also reducing AD.

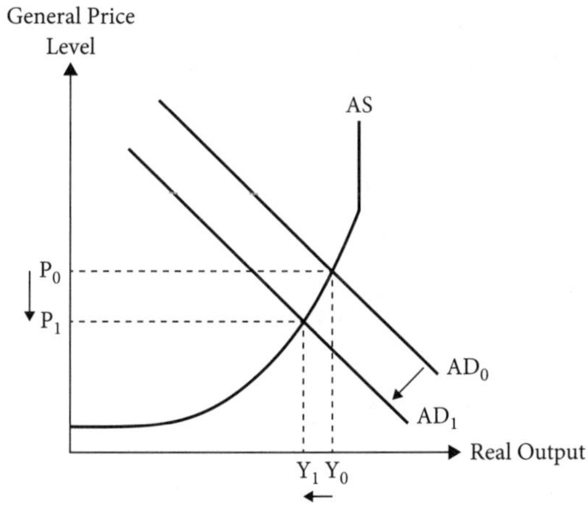

Figure 7.16: Decrease in AD.

WORSENING OF BALANCE OF PAYMENTS POSITION

An economy that experiences an increase in imports or a decrease in net exports could also see a worsening of the economy's balance of payments position. A decrease in net exports occurs when the increase in imports is more than the increase in exports, which would negatively affect the current account. This usually occurs for economies whose goods and services are uncompetitive in terms of price and quality when compared to foreign goods and services. As the current account is one of the two main accounts of balance of payments, a worsening of the current account could lead to a worsening in the balance of payments position of an economy.

INCREASE IN UNEMPLOYMENT AND LOWER WAGES

Economies that experience a fall in real output due to free trade are likely see an increase in unemployment as the decrease in real output would lead to a decrease in demand for factors of production, including labour. The decrease in demand for labour would result in a decrease in the number of people employed as well as the wages for those employed.

POLLUTION AND ENVIRONMENTAL DEGRADATION

Actual economic growth and the increase in real national output brought about by free trade might result in pollution and environmental degradation. The production of goods and services might cause market failure due to negative externalities in production. As real national output increases during actual economic growth, the amount of pollution produced is likely to increase as well. For example, air and water pollution are the common results of an increase in the production of goods and services, and this pollution would lead to an external cost or health care cost incurred by third parties. Other negative externalities include environmental destruction and congestion.

SURVIVAL OF DOMESTIC FIRMS AND INDUSTRY

Free trade would expose households to cheaper goods and services imported from abroad, and these imports could be substitutes to domestically produced goods and services. As households switch to relatively cheaper imports, domestic firms experience a fall in demand for their goods and services.

Domestic firms that are not competitive in terms of cost, price, and/or quality when compared to foreign firms would experience a fall in total revenue and profits; they might even have to shut down and leave the industry.

Industries that are new and in their early stages of development, also known as infant industries, are likely to be less competitive when compared to foreign competition in terms of cost, price, and/or quality. Given time to develop and grow, these industries might become competitive; but with free trade, it is likely that these firms will not survive and will be forced to shut down.

MARKET DOMINANCE BY FOREIGN FIRMS

Free trade could lead to reduction in competition. If domestic firms are unable to compete with foreign firms, market power will be consolidated by such large foreign multinational companies. Large foreign multinational companies are likely to be more competitive in terms of both price and non-price competition compared to smaller domestic firms. Large foreign firms, with their internal economies of scale and financial reserves, are able to drive out smaller firms with lower prices and better-quality goods and services, thereby establishing their market dominance. With domestic competitors driven out, large foreign firms now possess more market power. Their market dominance can lead to more exploitation of consumers in terms of higher prices. Thus, instead of increasing the number of firms and competition in the economy, free trade might lead to market dominance by foreign firms.

DUMPING BY FOREIGN FIRMS

Free trade would increase an economy's exposure to unfair trade practices such as dumping. Dumping occurs when a foreign firm exports goods to another economy and sells them at a price below the cost of production. As imports become relatively cheaper, the demand of domestic firms will decrease, reducing the total revenue and profits of domestic firms. This could lead to domestic firms shutting down, leaving the industry dominated by foreign firms. While lower prices are beneficial for consumers, prices are likely to increase to an even higher level once the foreign firms dominate the industry. Shutting down domestic firms would also increase unemployment in the economy.

7.3 Protectionism

Protectionism measures can be introduced by the government to pursue economic objectives and resolve economic problems in the economy. These measures are usually imposed to reduce or mitigate the negative impact of globalisation and free trade. In some cases, protectionism can also be implemented as a politically motivated tool to influence another country through its economy. The arguments against free trade are also the arguments for protectionism.

Protectionist measures refer to the imposition of government policy aiming to protect or shield domestic firms from foreign competition. Protectionist measures are trade barriers that would reduce trade between two countries, and are generally classified into tariffs and non-tariff measures. Non-tariffs consist of quotas, import licences, subsidies, and foreign exchange controls.

Tariffs and quotas are two of the most common forms of trade barriers set up by government.

7.3.1 Tariffs

A tariff is a tax or charge imposed or levied by the government on either imports or exports of goods and services. In the context of protectionism, tariffs are usually imposed on imports. A custom duty, on the other hand, is a tax imposed or levied by the government only on the imports of goods and services.

An imposed tariff can be either a specific tariff or an ad-valorem tariff. A specific tariff is a fixed amount of tax based on per unit of the imported good, regardless of the price of the good. An ad valorem tariff is a tax based on a percentage of the price of the imported good. Both the specific and ad-valorem tariffs will cause in an increase in the prices of the imported goods.

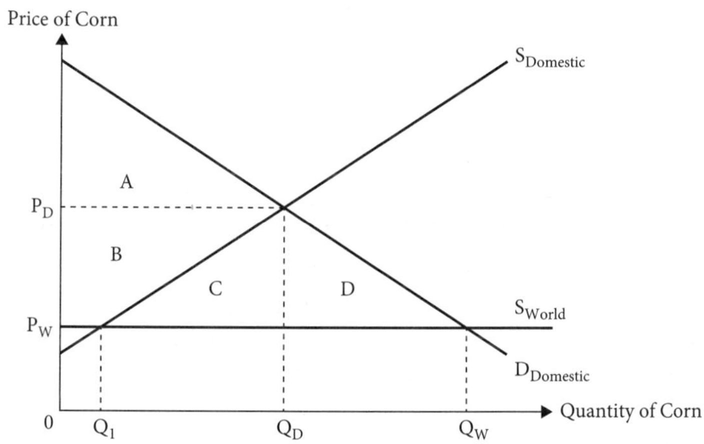

Figure 7.17: Market of corn from no trade to free trade.

Assuming country A originally does not embark on international trade, the market price (P_D) and market quantity (Q_D) of a good or service, such as corn, in country A is determined through the interaction between the domestic demand ($D_{Domestic}$) and domestic supply ($S_{Domestic}$) of corn as shown in Fig. 7.17.

If the world price of corn is lower than country A's domestic price P_D, country A will be an importer of corn. Assuming that country A is unable to influence the global demand and supply of rice, country A can import an unlimited amount of rice at the prevailing world price P_W. Thus, the supply of corn from the world market for country A will be perfectly price elastic, a horizontal supply curve at P_W, as shown in Fig. 7.17 and Fig. 7.18.

With free trade, the market price of corn in country A will now decrease from P_D to P_W, while the market quantity of corn will increase from $0Q_D$ to $0Q_W$. Of the new market quantity of $0Q_W$, $0Q_1$is produced domestically while Q_1Q_W is imported from abroad. Consumers will be better off as they enjoy a larger quantity of corn at a lower price, consumer surplus will increase from a situation without trade (area A) to a situation with free trade (area A + B + C + D). Consumer surplus is increased by area B + C + D. However, domestic production will decrease from $0Q_D$ to $0Q_1$ and imports will increase from zero to Q_1Q_W.

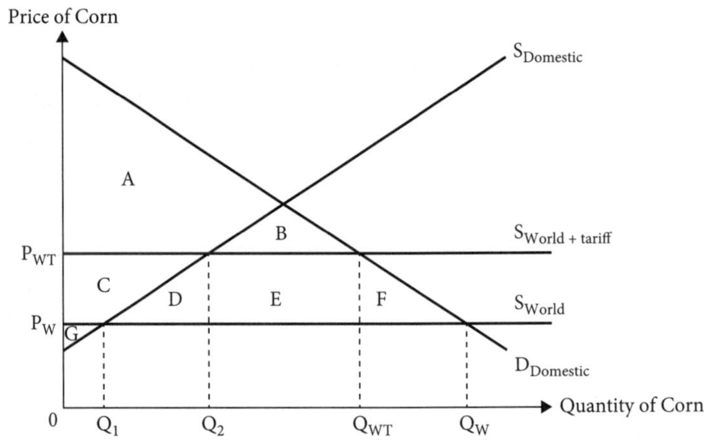

Figure 7.18: Market of corn from free trade to trade with tariff.

From Fig. 7.18, when country A imposes a tariff on corn, the amount of tariff being $P_W P_{WT}$, the world supply curve decreases from S_{World} to $S_{World + Tariff}$. The supply curve is still horizontal as country A can still import an unlimited amount of corn from the rest of the world but at a higher price that includes the tariff. The market price of corn in country A will now increase from P_W to P_{WT}. Of the new market quantity $0Q_{WT}$, $0Q_2$ is produced domestically while Q_2Q_{WT} is imported from abroad. Domestic production will increase from $0Q_1$ to $0Q_2$ and imports will decrease from Q_1Q_W to Q_2Q_{WT}.

Effects of a tariff on the consumers

Compared to a time of free trade, consumers will be worse off now as they now consume a smaller quantity of corn from Q_W to Q_{WT} at a higher price from P_W to P_{WT}. Consumer surplus will decrease from area A + B + C + D + E + F to area A + B, a loss of area C + D + E + F.

Effects of a tariff on the domestic producers

Compared to a time of free trade, domestic producers now produce at a higher price of P_{WT} instead of P_W and a larger amount of rice at $0Q_2$ instead of $0Q_1$. Domestic producers' total revenue will also increase from $0P_W \times 0Q_1$ to $0P_{WT} \times 0Q_2$. Domestic producers' surplus will increase from area G to area G + C.

Effects of a tariff on the government

Compared to a time of free trade, the government of country A will now gain additional tariff revenue of area E, which is the tariff imposed ($P_W P_{WT}$) multiplied by the quantity imported (Q_2Q_{WT}).

Due to a decrease in imports, assuming ceteris paribus, country A can see an improvement in the balance of trade and balance of payment, as well as an increase in AD, which might lead to positive impacts on government's macroeconomic objectives.

Effects of a tariff on the society as a whole

A tariff will lead to market failure as the loss in consumer surplus (area C + D + E + F) is more than the gain in producer surplus (area C) and government tariff revenue (area E). Society as a whole will incur a net welfare loss or deadweight loss of areas D + F.

7.3.2 Quotas

In the context of international trade, a quota is a government-imposed trade restriction that limits the amount of goods that can be imported or exported. Import quotas determine the maximum amount of goods that can be imported into the country.

With free trade, the market price of corn in country A will be P_W, while the market quantity of rice will be $0Q_W$. Of the new market quantity of $0Q_W$, $0Q_1$ is produced domestically while Q_1Q_W is imported from abroad (Fig. 7.19).

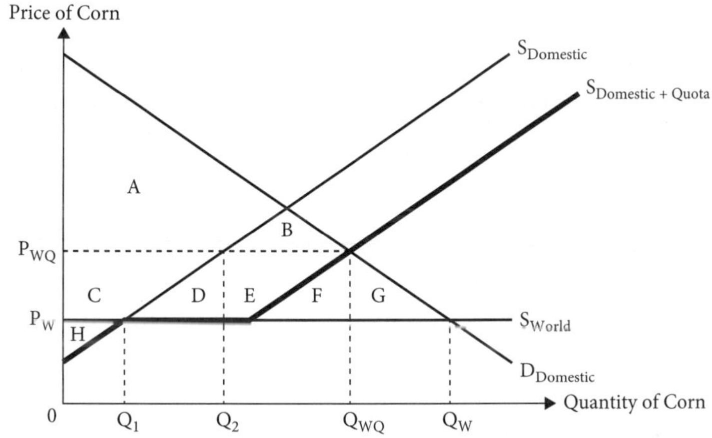

Figure 7.19: Market of corn from free trade to trade with quota.

When country A imposes an import quota of Q_2Q_{WQ} on corn, the world supply curve will no longer be valid and a new supply curve, $S_{\text{Domestic + Quota}}$, consisting of domestic supply plus the imported amount determined by the quota, is created.

The market price of corn in country A will now increase from P_W to P_{WQ}. Of the new market quantity of $0Q_{WQ}$, $0Q_2$ is produced domestically while Q_2Q_{WQ} is imported from abroad. Domestic production will increase from $0Q_1$ to $0Q_2$ and imports will decrease from Q_1Q_W to Q_2Q_{WQ}.

Effects of a quota on the consumers

Compared to a time of free trade, consumers will be worse off as they now consume a smaller quantity of corn from Q_W to Q_{WQ} at a higher price from P_W to P_{WQ}. Consumer surplus will decrease from area A + B + C + D + E + F + G to area A + B, a loss of area C + D + E + F + G.

Effects of a quota on the domestic producers

Compared to a time of free trade, domestic producers now produce at a higher price of P_{WQ} instead of P_W and a larger amount of rice at $0Q_2$ instead of $0Q_1$. Domestic producers' total revenue will also increase from $0P_W \times 0Q_1$ to $0P_{WQ} \times 0Q_2$. Domestic producers' surplus will increase from area H to area H + C.

Effects of a quota on the government

The government of country A will not gain any additional revenue when a quota is imposed. However, due to a decrease in imports, assuming ceteris paribus, country A can see an improvement in the balance of trade and balance of payments as well as an increase in AD, which might lead to positive impacts on government's macroeconomic objectives.

Effects of a quota on the society as a whole

A quota will lead to market failure as the loss in consumer surplus of area C + D + E + F + G is more than the gain in producer surplus of area C. Society as a whole will incur a net welfare loss or deadweight loss of areas D + E + F + G.

7.3.3 Other protectionism measures

Import licences

Import licences are permits granted by the government to allow firms to import goods from abroad. While this works similarly to a quota, this can be used to control the quality, quantity, and type of goods imported.

Subsidies

Subsidies can be given to domestic firms as a protectionism measure, aiming to reduce domestic producers' cost of production and price, thereby making domestically produced goods relatively cheaper and more price competitive against foreign imports in both the domestic and foreign markets.

Foreign exchange controls

Foreign exchange controls involve government control over the purchase and sale of foreign currencies. As foreign currencies are required for international trade, effective control over the amount of foreign currencies that can be exchanged would effectively influence the amount of goods and services that can be imported.

7.3.4 Arguments for protectionism

Promote actual economic growth

Protectionism would increase the prices of a country's imports from foreign countries, making the imports less price competitive. This could lead to a decrease in imports or an increase in net exports for the economy. As an economy imports fewer goods and services from abroad or when net exports increase, the economy's AD will increase. If households substitute imports with domestically produced goods, the decrease in imports would be accompanied by an increase in domestic consumption, also increasing AD. When AD increases, the economy will experience an increase in the real output and real national income via the multiplier effect and result in actual economic growth (Fig. 7.20).

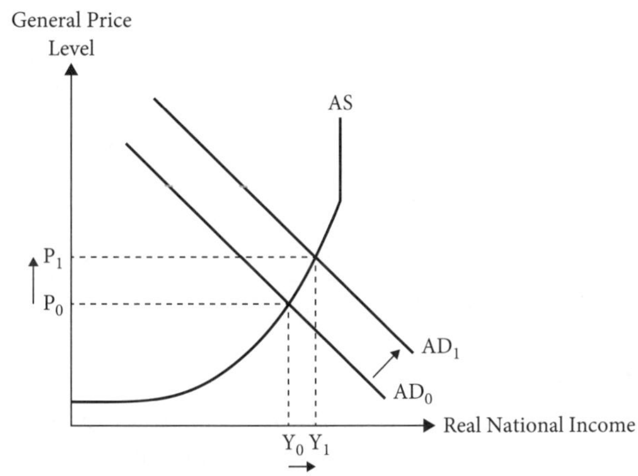

Figure 7.20: Increase in AD.

Improvement of balance of payments position

Protectionism would increase the prices of imports and decrease the degree of competition from abroad by making imports relatively more expensive. Households would import lesser goods and services and might instead substitute imports with domestically produced goods. A decrease in imports expenditure would improve the balance of trade and current account. As the current account is one of the two main accounts of balance of payments, improvement of the current account would lead to an improvement of the balance of payments position of an economy, ceteris paribus.

Promote employment and higher wages

Economies that experience actual economic growth or an increase in real output due to protectionism are likely see a decrease in unemployment, as the increase in real output would lead to an increase in demand for factors of production, including labour. The increase in demand would result in an increase in the wages and an increase in the number of employed, leading to a lower unemployment rate.

This could be specifically used to reduce or resolve unemployment caused by immobility of labour, when protectionism measures are imposed in industries where domestic firms employ a significant amount of potentially occupational immobile labours.

Protecting domestic producers

The main beneficiaries of protectionism are the domestic producers. As most protectionist measures would reduce the competitiveness of imported goods and services, domestic producers producing substitutes or similar goods would experience an increase in demand, resulting in greater revenue, profits, as well as producer surpluses.

Prevention of market dominance by foreign firms

Protectionism would reduce the amount of competition faced by domestic firms and it can prevent market power from being consolidated by large multinational companies. Protectionist measures such as tariffs would reduce the price competitiveness of large multinational companies by making their goods relatively more expensive. Households would consume fewer imports and the demand for goods produced by domestic firms will increase, thus, increasing the total revenue and profits of domestic firms. This would prevent domestic firms from shutting down and leaving the industry, and prevent the industry from being dominated by foreign firms. While higher prices might not be beneficial for consumers, protectionism prevents the possibility of an even higher price level once foreign firms dominate the industry. Also, the survival of domestic firms would also lead to a decrease in unemployment in the economy.

Prevention of dumping by foreign firms

Protectionism decreases an economy's exposure to unfair trade practices such as dumping. While foreign firms dump their goods by exporting goods to another economy and selling them at a price below the cost of production, protectionist measures such as tariffs would increase the price of these "dumped" goods, reducing the effectiveness and negative impact of dumping. As imports become relatively more expensive, the demand for goods produced by domestic firms will increase, increasing the total revenue and profits of domestic firms. This would prevent domestic firms from shutting down and leaving the industry, and prevent the industry from being dominated by foreign firms. While higher prices might not beneficial for consumers, protectionism prevents the possibility of an even higher price level once foreign firms dominate the industry. Also, the survival of domestic firms would also lead to a decrease in unemployment in the economy.

7.3.5 Arguments against protectionism

Retaliation by trading partners

Most of the benefits of protectionism assume that trading partners will not retaliate with similar protectionist measures. When trading partners retaliate with similar protectionist measures on domestic firms, it will cancel out the potential benefits of protectionism.

Protectionist measures, when imposed by a trading partner, would similarly increase the prices of a domestic producer's exports in foreign economies, making exports less price competitive and this could lead to a decrease in exports. Firms would also have lesser access to more markets abroad and experience a decrease in the demand for their goods and services from abroad, likely leading to a decrease in the firms' output, total revenue, and profits.

The decrease in demand for exports would also likely lead to a decrease in AD. When AD decreases, the economy will experience a decrease in real output and real national income via the multiplier effect and result in negative actual economic growth, as seen in Fig. 7.21.

A decrease in export earnings would decrease the balance of trade and negatively affects current account. As the current account is one of the two main accounts of balance of payments, improvement of the current account would lead to an improvement of the balance of payments position of an economy, ceteris paribus.

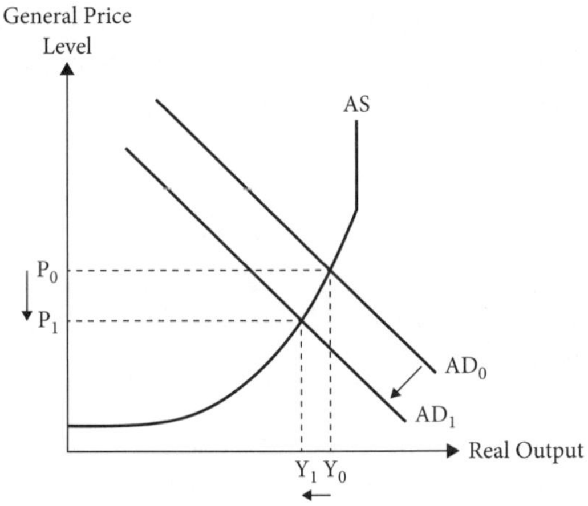

Figure 7.21: Decrease in AD.

Cost push inflation

Protectionism would increase the prices of imports from foreign countries, making imports more expensive and decreasing the SRAS of the economy. Higher prices of imported final goods and services could lead to higher imported price push inflation, whereas higher prices of imported factors of production could lead to higher imported cost push inflation, assuming that the economy is experiencing imported inflation.

A decrease in SRAS due to more expensive imports would also lead to negative actual economic growth and a higher general price level, assuming ceteris paribus, as seen in Fig. 7.22.

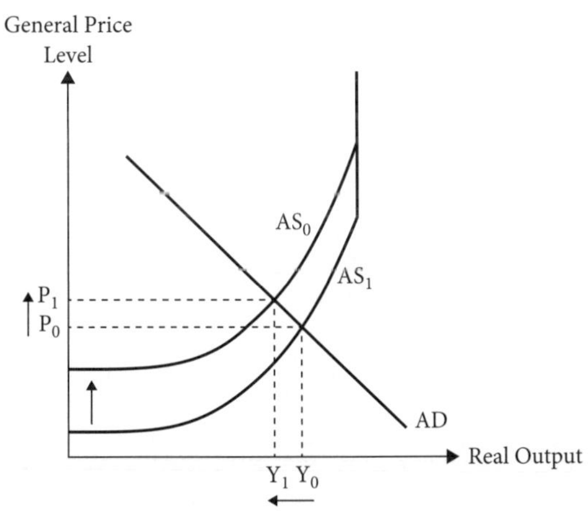

Figure 7.22: Decrease in SRAS.

Lesser variety of goods and services and higher prices for consumers

Protectionism decreases a country's access to sources of goods and services, and consumers are exposed to a narrower variety of goods and services. A decrease in the supply of goods and services from abroad would lead to higher prices of imported goods and services.

Protectionism also decreases domestic producers' exposure to foreign competition. This would discourage domestic firms from competing using lower price or non-price competition, such as R&D which might decrease the variety of goods and services.

Lower level of efficiencies for society

Protectionism would decrease the number of substitutes and competition from abroad, causing domestic firms to be more complacent, so they might not aim to produce at the lowest possible average cost in order to maximise profits or remain price competitive. Thus, the market will be less productive efficient.

Protectionism would decrease the number of firms and substitutes from abroad, so each firm will have a larger amount of market share and market power. As each firm's demand becomes more price inelastic, the firm's ability to exploit consumers is increased and the market will be less allocative efficient.

Protectionism would increase the prices of imports and decrease the degree of competition from abroad. Firms would be less willing to conduct R&D in order to remain competitive, increase demand, or make their goods and services less substitutable. The reduction of investments in R&D would promote a lower degree of dynamic efficiency in the market.

Annex 7.2 Impact of tariffs in an economy's balance of payments position

A tariff, a protectionist measure, would increase the prices of imports and reduce the quantity imported. However, the impact on import spending would depend on the price elasticity of demand for imports (PED_M). If PED_M is elastic, an increase in the price of imports would lead to a more than proportionate decrease in quantity imported, thereby decreasing total import spending while improving the balance of trade and balance of payments position, ceteris paribus. On the other hand, if PED_M is inelastic, an increase in price of imports would lead to a less than proportionate decrease in quantity imported, thereby increasing total import spending while worsening the balance of trade and balance of payments position, ceteris paribus.

Also, it is important to note that the above also assumes that all else remains constant. In the event that the trading partners retaliate with protectionist measures on the country, any improvement in the balance of payments position will most likely be offset.

7.4 Trade Agreements and Economic Integration

By signing trade agreements such as free trade agreements between two or more economies, member economies become more interconnected and integrated. In the context of economics, the purpose of trade agreements and economic integration is usually to help countries achieve their respective economic goals. Most countries are part of one or more trade agreements with other countries, some regional with their neighbours while others international with their trading partners.

7.4.1 Various forms of trade agreements

The four key types or stages of trade agreements and economic integrations are free-trade area, customs union, common market, and monetary union. Among the four stages, free-trade area has the least amount of economic integration whereas monetary union has the most. The various trade agreements and their extent of economic integration can be seen in Fig. 7.23.

Free-trade area

A free-trade area is one of the most common types of economic integration where two or more countries agree to eliminate trade barriers by signing free trade agreements with each other. However, each country continues to have autonomy in their trade policies with other countries not in the free trade area.

Examples of FTAs	Members
Association of South East Asian Nations (ASEAN)	Brunei, Cambodia, Indonesia, Laos, Malaysia, Myanmar, Philippines, Singapore, Thailand, and Vietnam
European Free Trade Association (EFTA)	Iceland, Liechtenstein, Norway, and Switzerland
North American Free Trade Agreement (NAFTA)	Canada, Mexico, and the United States

Examples of FTAs	Members
South Asian Association for Regional Cooperation (SAARC)	Afghanistan, Bangladesh, Bhutan, India, Nepal, the Maldives, Pakistan, and Sri Lanka.

Source: http://asean.org/asean/asean-member-states/
Source: http://www.efta.int/about-efta/the-efta-states
Source: http://www.naftanow.org/faq_en.asp#faq-1
Source: http://saarc-sec.org/about-saarc

Customs union

A customs union has a higher degree of economic integration compared to a free trade area, with the characteristics of a free-trade area; however, each individual country no longer has autonomy in its trade policies with other countries outside the custom union. All countries in

Examples of customs unions	Members
Central European Free Trade Agreement (CEFTA)	Albania, Bosnia and Herzegovina, Macedonia, Moldova, Montenegro, Serbia, and Kosovo

(*Continued*)

(Continued)

Examples of customs unions	Members
South African Customs Union (SACU)	Botswana, Lesotho, Namibia, South Africa, and Swaziland.

Source: http://cefta.int/cefta-parties/

Source: http://www.sacu.int/index.php

the custom union adopt a common policy towards other non-member countries, such as the same tariffs and quotas with non-member countries. A customs union also acts as an entity in trade negotiations and agreements with non-members.

Common market

A common market has a higher degree of economic integration compared to a customs union, with the characteristics of a customs union. Member countries also operate as a single market with the removal of all restrictions on the movement of factors of production such as labour and capital within the common markets. Labour is able to cross all borders and move to find employment within all member countries without any restrictions. Other features of common market include the following:

- A common system of taxation
- A common system of laws and regulations for production, employment, and trade
- Free movement of labour, capital, materials, and goods and services
- The absence of special treatment by member governments of their own domestic industries

Example of common market	Members
Caribbean Community (CARICOM) Single Market and Economy (CSME).	Antigua and Barbuda, Barbados, Belize, Dominica, Grenada, Guyana, Jamaica, Saint Kitts and Nevis, Saint Lucia, Saint Vincent and the Grenadines, Suriname, and Trinidad and Tobago

Source: https://caricom.org/our-work/the-caricom-single-market-and-economy-csme

Monetary union

A monetary union has a higher degree of economic integration compared to a common market. Member countries adopt a common currency and a single central bank that will be responsible for monetary policies for all the member countries.

Example of monetary union	Members
European Monetary Union 	Austria, Belgium, Bulgaria, Croatia, Cyprus, Czech Republic, Denmark, Estonia, Finland, France, Germany, Greece, Hungary, Ireland, Italy, Latvia, Lithuania, Luxembourg, Malta, the Netherlands, Poland, Portugal, Romania, Slovakia, Slovenia, Spain, Sweden, United Kingdom

Source: https://ec.europa.eu/info/business-economy-euro/economic-and-fiscal-policy-coordination/economic-and-monetary-union_en

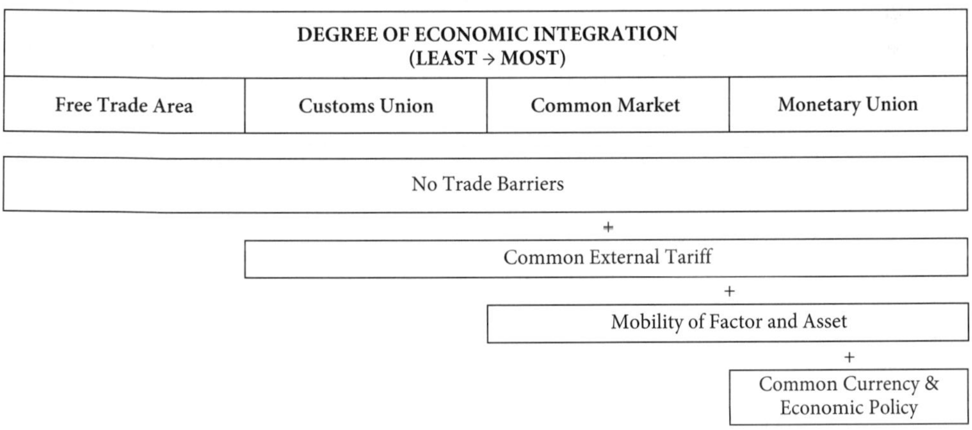

Figure 7.23: Various trade agreements and their extent of economic integration.

7.4.2 Impact of trade agreements and economic integration for member countries

As trade agreements and economic integration promotes free trade and globalisation, the impact of trade agreements would consist of the benefits and costs of globalisation.

The benefits and arguments for trade agreements and economic integration summarised in Table 7.14 would include both:

- The arguments for free trade
- The arguments against protectionism

Table 7.14: Benefits and arguments for trade agreements and economic integration.

Benefits of globalisation	Key arguments for free trade	Arguments against protectionism
Macroeconomic Benefits of Globalisation	• Promotion of actual economic growth • Improvement in balance of payments position • Reduction in inflationary pressure • Larger variety of goods and services and lower prices for consumers • Higher profits for firms • Higher level of efficiencies for society	• Retaliation by trading partners • Cost-push inflation • Lesser variety of goods and services and higher prices for consumers • Lower level of efficiencies for society
• Promotion of actual economic growth • Promotion of potential economic growth • Reduction in unemployment and higher wages • Improvement in balance of payments position • Reduction in inflationary pressure		
Microeconomic Benefits of Globalisation		
• Larger variety of goods and services and lower prices for consumers • Higher profits for firms • Higher level of efficiencies for society		

The costs of and arguments against trade agreements and economic integration summarised in Table 7.15 would include both:

- The arguments against free trade
- The arguments for protectionism

Table 7.15: Costs of and arguments against trade agreements and economic integration.

<table>
<tr><th>Costs of globalisation</th><th>Key arguments against free trade</th><th>Arguments for protectionism</th></tr>
<tr><td>Macroeconomic Costs of Globalisation</td><td rowspan="4">• Fall in real national output
• Worsening of balance of payments position
• Increase in unemployment and lower wages
• Pollution and environmental degradation
• Survival of domestic firms and industries
• Market dominance by foreign firms
• Dumping by foreign firms</td><td rowspan="4">• Promote actual economic growth
• Improvement of balance of payments position
• Promote employment and higher wages
• Protecting domestic producers
• Prevention of market dominance by foreign firms
• Prevention of dumping by foreign firms</td></tr>
<tr><td>• Worsening of balance of payments position
• Fall in real national income and real output
• Increase in unemployment and lower wages
• Demand-pull inflation
• Human capital flight
• Crowding out of domestic investment
• Over dependency on the certain industries</td></tr>
<tr><td>Microeconomic Costs of Globalisation</td></tr>
<tr><td>• Worsening of income inequalities
• Pollution and environmental degradation
• Survival of domestic firms and industry
• Market dominance by foreign firms
• Dumping by foreign firms</td></tr>
</table>

Annex 7.3 Trade creation

Trade creation is one of the phenomena that can occur when a country signs a free trade agreement or joins a trading bloc. Trade creation could happen during economic integration when the production of goods shifts from domestic producers to foreign producers, thereby creating trade.

One scenario is that the goods could be produced domestically due to the existence of tariffs causing imports to be more expensive than domestically produced goods. With the removal of tariffs during economic integration, imports will now be cheaper than domestically produced goods as shown in Table 7.16. This would result in the goods being imported, thus, creating more trade between the two economies.

Table 7.16: Trade creation.

	Before Economic Integration	After Economic Integration
Domestic producers	\$1.50	\$1.50
Foreign producers	\$1.70 (assuming \$0.50 tariff)	\$1.20

Another scenario is that goods are already being imported, even with the existence of tariffs, as domestic goods are more expensive than imports with tariffs. With the removal of trade barriers during economic integration, imports will become even cheaper, resulting in consumers importing more goods and therefore, creating more trade between the two economies.

For example, even with the existence of a tariff at P_{WT}, the economy is currently importing Q_2Q_{WT} of good A from abroad. With economic integration, the price of imported good A will decrease from P_{WT} to P_W and the economy will now import Q_1Q_W which is higher than before economic integration, thereby creating more trade between the two economies, as shown in Fig. 7.24.

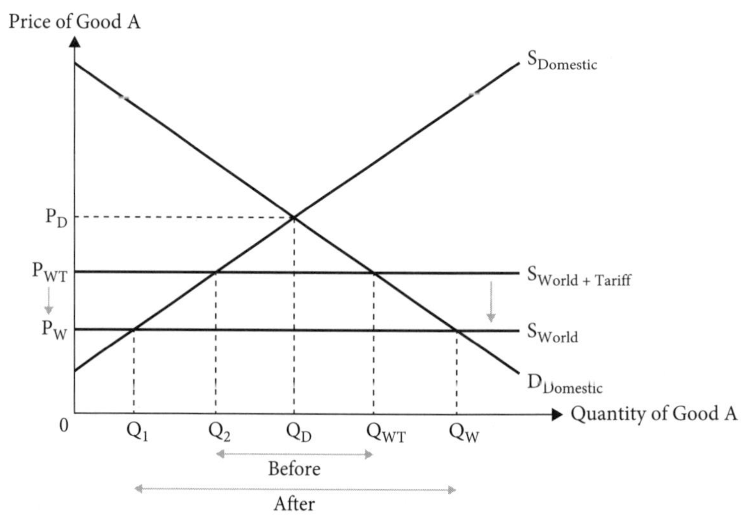

Figure 7.24: Trade creation.

Annex 7.4 Trade diversion

Another phenomenon that can occur when a country signs a free trade agreement or joins a trading bloc is trade diversion. Trade diversion could happen during economic integration when imports shift from a lower cost producer from a non-member country to a higher cost producer from a member country. The reason for this diversion is that imports from the lower cost country subjected to tariffs could have higher prices than imports from a higher cost country not subjected to tariffs.

For example, assume country A can import the good from either country B or country C. Country B produces the good at $1.20, which is a lower price compared to country C's price of $1.50. When both countries B and C are imposed with the same amount of tax $0.50, country A will import from country B as it is cheaper than country C.

However, when country C signs a free trade agreement with country A or joins the trading bloc that country A is part of, the $0.50 tariff no longer applies – the tariff of $0.50 is imposed on country B and not on country C, so the price of good sold by country B will remain $1.70, which is now more expensive than country B's $1.50. Therefore, due to the tariff, trade is diverted from country B, who is a non-member country, to country C, who is a member country of the trade agreement as shown in Table 7.17.

Table 7.17: Trade diversion.

	Original Price of imports from	**Price + $0.50 tariff on both countries**	**Prices after country C joins a trading bloc where country A is in**
Country B (non-member)	$1.20	$1.70	$1.70
Country C (member)	$1.50	$2.00	$1.50

The above scenario shows the possibility of trade being diverted away from non-member countries and this could be a source of motivation for governments to join free trade areas, or similar agreements, even if they do not gain any other benefits. A fall in exports would lead to many negative impacts on any economy, which governments will try to avoid.